Zimbabwe

the Bradt Travel Guide

Paul Murray

edition
2

www.bradtguides.com

Bradt Travel Guides Ltd, UK
The Globe Pequot Press Inc, USA

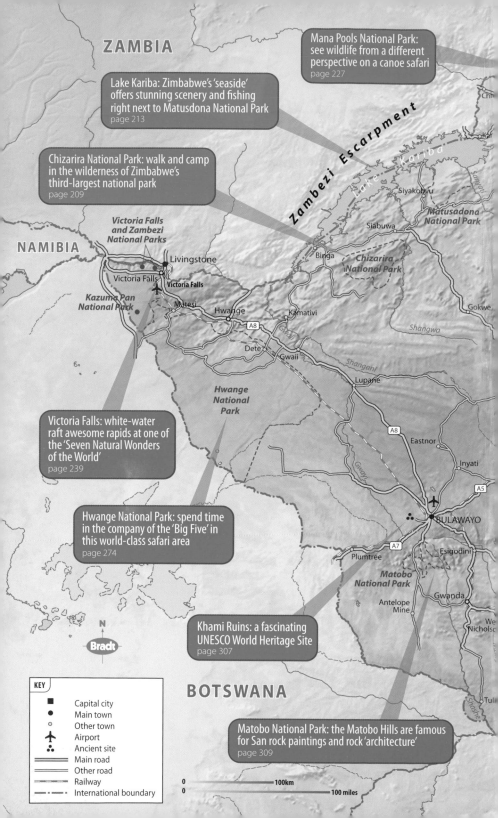

ZAMBIA

Mana Pools National Park: see wildlife from a different perspective on a canoe safari
page 227

Lake Kariba: Zimbabwe's 'seaside' offers stunning scenery and fishing right next to Matusdona National Park
page 213

Zambezi Escarpment

Chizarira National Park: walk and camp in the wilderness of Zimbabwe's third-largest national park
page 209

Lake Kariba

Siyakobyu

Matusadona National Park

NAMIBIA

Victoria Falls and Zambezi National Parks

Livingstone

Victoria Falls

Binga

Siabuwa

Chizarira National Park

Victoria Falls

Kazuma Pan National Park

Matesi

Hwange

Kamativi

Gokwe

A8

Shangwa

Dete

Gwaii

Shangani

Victoria Falls: white-water raft awesome rapids at one of the 'Seven Natural Wonders of the World'
page 239

Hwange National Park

Lupane

A8

Eastnor

Inyati

A5

BULAWAYO

Hwange National Park: spend time in the company of the 'Big Five' in this world-class safari area
page 274

Esigodini

A7

Plumtree

Matobo National Park

Khami Ruins: a fascinating UNESCO World Heritage Site
page 307

Antelope Mine

Gwanda

We Nicholso

BOTSWANA

Tuli

Shashe

Matobo National Park: the Matobo Hills are famous for San rock paintings and rock 'architecture'
page 309

KEY

- ■ Capital city
- ● Main town
- ○ Other town
- ✈ Airport
- ⁙ Ancient site
- ═══ Main road
- ─── Other road
- ╫╫╫ Railway
- ─·─·─ International boundary

Bradt

0 ——— 100km
0 ——— 100 miles

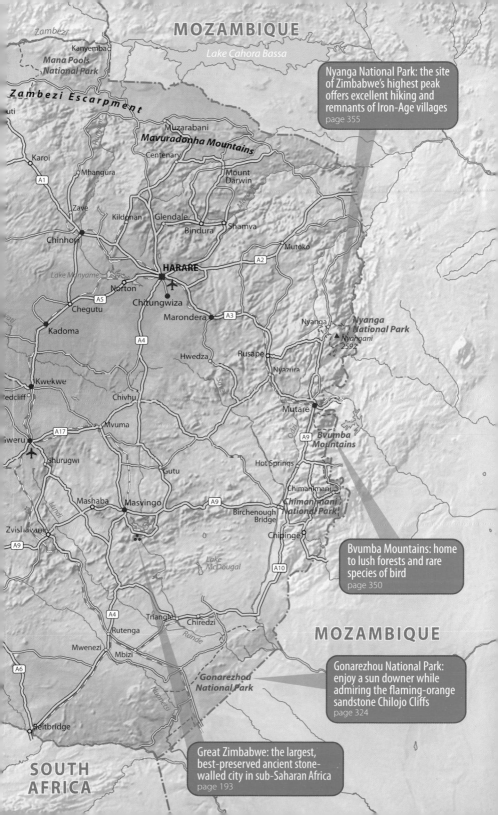

MOZAMBIQUE

Zambezi   Kanyemba   Lake Cahora Bassa

Mana Pools National Park

Nyanga National Park: the site of Zimbabwe's highest peak offers excellent hiking and remnants of Iron-Age villages
page 355

Zambezi Escarpment

Muzarabani

Mavuradonha Mountains

Karoi   Centenary

Mhangura   Mount Darwin

A1

Zave   Kildonan   Glendale

Chinhoyi   Bindura   Shamva

Mutoko

Lake Manyame   **HARARE**   A2

Norton   Chitungwiza

Chegutu   Marondera   A3

A5   Nyanga

Kadoma   A4   **Nyanga National Park**
Nyahgani 2592

Hwedza   Rusape

Kwekwe   Nyazura

dcliff   Chivhu   Mutare

A17   Mvuma   **Bvumba Mountains**   A9

Gweru

Shurugwi   Gutu

Hot Springs

Mashaba   Masvingo   Chimanimani
Chimanimani National Park

Zvishavane   Birchenough Bridge

A9   Chipinge

A9

Bvumba Mountains: home to lush forests and rare species of bird
page 350

Lake McDougal

A10

MOZAMBIQUE

Triangle   Chiredzi

A4   Rutenga   *Runde*

Mwenezi   Mbizi

Gonarezhou National Park: enjoy a sun downer while admiring the flaming-orange sandstone Chilojo Cliffs
page 324

A6

Gonarezhou National Park

Beitbridge

SOUTH AFRICA

Great Zimbabwe: the largest, best-preserved ancient stone-walled city in sub-Saharan Africa
page 193

Zimbabwe
Don't miss...

Victoria Falls
Rising mist and the steady roar of the Zambezi River signal your arrival at this magnificent World Heritage Site. Test your nerve at the end of a bungee rope or take to the skies above the falls for a different perspective of this justifiably famous natural wonder of the world
(MM/I/FLPA) page 239

Hwange National Park
One of the finest national parks in Africa, Hwange contains a remarkable diversity of wildlife, including the 'Big Five' and both black and white rhino
(SS) page 274

Mana Pools National Park

Drift along the banks of the Zambezi River and come face to face with elephants, hippo and crocodile on an unforgettable canoe safari
(SS) page 227

Matobo National Park

This spectacular national park contains hundreds of rock paintings and unusual rock formations such as the balancing rocks (pictured), as well as one of the highest concentrations of leopard in Zimbabwe
(MPF/MP/FLPA) page 311

Great Zimbabwe

As the largest and best-preserved ancient stone-walled city in sub-Saharan Africa, the ruins of Great Zimbabwe lie at the heart of the country's enigmatic, historical past
(SS) page 193

Zimbabwe in colour

above left Renowned for its extreme sports, Victoria Falls offers adventurous visitors the opportunity to bungee-jump from dizzying heights (AVZ) page 264

above right Walking safaris are well developed in Zimbabwe and trekking through the bush creates an intimate wildlife-viewing experience (SS) page 79

below Take your safari to new heights from the back of an African elephant near Victoria Falls (AVZ) page 265

above   Enjoy spectacular sunsets on the shores of Lake Kariba (SS) page 213

above right   Hike among ancient trees in the 'Valley of Giants', Chirinda Forest Reserve — the southernmost rainforest in Africa (AVZ) page 337

right   White-water rafting on the Zambezi River is a must for adrenaline junkies (SS) page 261

below   Traditional game drives provide spectacular viewing opportunities from the safety and comfort of a vehicle (AVZ) page 76 & 8

AUTHOR

Paul Murray spent all of his working life in the travel industry. He first fell in love with Zimbabwe and its people more than 25 years ago while driving his ageing father around the country in a battered old hire car. Since then, Paul has filled the equivalent of three complete passports with Zimbabwe stamps.

Twelve years ago, Paul took an early retirement; he and his wife bought a 4x4 and a house near Durban, allowing them to go touring and camping around the whole of southern Africa. Paul spends a considerable part of each year in Zimbabwe and, as well as writing this book, he's involved in a number of other initiatives promoting tourism to the country.

AUTHOR'S STORY

My introduction to southern Africa began with a journalistic 'jolly' to Zimbabwe in 1988 to cover an air rally, during which I was transported in a scary little light aircraft around just a few of the many delights the country had to offer. Countless visits later, and despite long forays into all the neighbouring countries, Zimbabwe and its people became my firm favourite.

Having left the world of work and indulged in several years of extensive African travel, I felt the urge to start using my brain again. Then, during a trip to northern Mozambique, my friends and I found ourselves in places that weren't mentioned in the guidebooks so I seized the chance, made copious notes and sent them off to Hilary Bradt. An invitation to write this book followed, so the next three years were spent in almost constant touring of the country and having my eyes opened to yet more fascinating and wonderful aspects of Zimbabwe and its people. The logistics at that time were challenging to say the least and I was humbled to benefit from the Zimbabwean people's great generosity and their ability to 'make a plan' when times get tough.

The country still has its problems although much has changed for the better since the first edition was published. From the visitor's point of view, the biggest problem is that there's way too much to see and do in one short visit. By all means see the main tourist spots, but do try and explore off the beaten track too. Your efforts will be rewarded tenfold.

Reprinted October 2014
Second edition published September 2013
First published 2010

Bradt Travel Guides Ltd, IDC House, The Vale, Chalfont St Peter, Bucks SL9 9RZ, England
www.bradtguides.com
Print edition published in the USA by The Globe Pequot Press Inc, PO Box 480, Guilford, Connecticut 06437-0480

Text copyright © 2013 Paul Murray
Maps copyright © 2013 Bradt Travel Guides Ltd
Photographs copyright © 2013 Individual photographers (see below)
Project Managers: Greg Dickinson & Kelly Randell
Cover image research: Pepi Bluck, Perfect Picture

British Library Cataloguing in Publication Data
A catalogue record for this book is available from the British Library

ISBN-13: 978 1 84162 460 0
e-ISBN: 978 1 84162 771 7 (epub)
e-ISBN: 978 1 84162 673 4 (mobi)

Photographs Ariadne Van Zandbergen (AVZ); Corbis: David Snyder (DS/C); Dreamstime: Rfurtado (R/D); Ed Oelofse (EO); FLPA: Frans Lanting (FL/FLPA), Gerard Lacz (GL/FLPA), Gerry Ellis/Minden Pictures (GE/MP/FLPA), Ignacio Yufera (IY/FLPA), Imagebroker (I/FLPA), Konrad Wothe/Minden Pictures (KW/MP/FLPA), Michael and Patricia Fogden/Minden Pictures (MPF/MP/FLPA), Michael Müller/Imagebroker (MM/I/FLPA), Richard Du Toit/Minden Pictures (RDT/MP/FLPA), Terry Whittaker (TW/FLPA), Winfried Wisniewski (WW/FLPA); Mike Unwin (MU); Paul Murray (PM); Shutterstock: Debbie Aird Photography (DAP/S), EcoPrint (E/S), Neal Cooper (NC/S), Pal Teravagimov (PT/S), PHOTOCREO Michal Bednarek (PMB/S); SuperStock (SS); Tony Heald/Nature PL/SuperStock (TH/NPL/SS)
Front cover African elephant drinking, Mana Pools National Park (TH/NPL/SS)
Back cover Girl in traditional dress (SS); Bungee-jumping is a popular activity at Victoria Falls (AVZ)
Title page Frescoes at Cyrene Mission Chapel (PM); A magnificent greater kudu (WW/FLPA); Sunset at Lake Kariba (SS)

Maps David McCutcheon FBCart.S; colour base relief map by Nick Rowland FRGS

Typeset from the author's disc by Wakewing, High Wycombe
Production managed by Jellyfish Print Solutions; printed and bound in India
Digital conversion by the Firsty Group

Foreword

My first experience of Zimbabwe came in 2005 when my wife, Louise, and I were invited to join a re-enactment of Livingstone's first journey down the Zambezi to Victoria Falls as part of the 150th anniversary celebrations. We travelled in traditional dugout canoes and camped on the Zambia side of the river at night. By the end of the trip my appetite for Africa was truly whetted and I resolved to return.

The chance finally came in 2007, and despite people telling me I was mad, I decided to bring the whole family – Louise, my stepson Alexander and our baby daughter Elizabeth – with me. It was mainly my interest in conservation that led me back to Zimbabwe. The country has some of the best game viewing in Africa – with the 'Big Five' found in three of its national parks and rare opportunities for walking safaris – but its conservationists, guides, rangers and safari tourism operators need all the help they can get.

From reading the UK media, I was braced for aggressive police roadblocks and angry crowds, but there was absolutely none of that. Obviously the economy is a mess, and I'm not a Mugabe fan, but the people were extremely nice, extremely patient and resilient, and very glad to see us. From what I've seen of Zimbabwe, it's perfectly safe for tourists.

Paul Murray has shown real dedication to the country and its people by carrying out research for this guide whilst the political situation was still fragile, and I praise Bradt's continuing commitment to covering destinations that have suffered, and for which tourist revenue is a vital means of recovery. It is my sincere wish that this book will assist in Zimbabwe's regeneration.

Finally, I'd like to add that there's this idea in the UK that by coming to Zimbabwe, you're supporting the regime and putting yourself in danger, but this is simply not true. By staying away from Zimbabwe, all you're doing is making things even harder for all the people involved in tourism and conservation here, and depriving yourself of a fantastic time.

Sir Ranulph Fiennes OBE
Explorer

Acknowledgements

In my travels I have met countless people, too many to mention, who contributed information or much needed assistance. To all of them I owe sincere thanks. Individuals to whom I am indebted include (in alphabetical order) Brian Latham – grateful thanks for your valuable comments and input; Bryony Acutt of African Albida and GoToVictoriaFalls; Caroline Perkins of Armadillo Travel who has been wonderfully helpful; Choice Mushunje of Parks and Wildlife Management Authority of Zimbabwe; Christopher Scott of Scottyphotography; Dale-lyn Russell of Utopia Inn, Mutare; Dick Pitman for his brilliant ZIM4x4 website and newsletter as well as a lot of excellent advice; Gavin and Shaylene Best at Elephant Camp – dear departed friends, I say no more; Glynis Vaughan of ZNSPCA; Fredi and Rita Ruf for providing a wonderful home from home in Bulawayo and a base for my various forays; Jane High of Chimanimani Tourist Association; Johnny Rodrigues of Conservation Taskforce, for his regular wildlife updates; Jono Hudson of Safari Lodge Victoria Falls; Judith Mkahanana of Utc Harare – thanks for facilitating my visit; Louise of Inn on the Vumba; Mags Varley and staff (especially the brilliant and enthusiastic Joy) of Backpackers Bazaar – a mine of information in the Falls; Mike Unwin, Bradt wildlife author – thanks for checking the natural history copy and providing much needed improvements; big thanks to Monika Korn of Safari Source who made my information gathering so much easier; Ndai Mukwena at ZTA in Jo'burg; Paul and Gail Dewhurst previously of Inn on Ruparara (where are you now?) – wonderful hosts, and thanks for the comp, the only one I accepted during the whole of my research; Paul Hubbard – grateful thanks for writing the cave painting material and for your fantastic input in taking the time to correct the historical sections in this edition – all without my even asking you!; Pete Baxter of Chimanimani Bushwalking Company; Ron and Tish White at Imbabala – thanks Codgers for your wonderful friendship and hospitality; Russell Gammon for the loan of his books; Sally Wynn from www.wildzambezi.com who proved to be a mine of information and allowed me to use some of her excellent copy as well as answering so many of my questions; Sandy Ramsay of Travel World Masvingo; Tina Pigors of Top of the Range; Val Bell of Bulawayo Publicity Association – the best in the country and a great help to me; Wellington Jana for cultural input and being an all-round good guy, but it's time for you to return to Zim now; Wildlife and Environment Zimbabwe for my game-count participation and wildlife updates; Wilma Griffiths of Wild Horizons newsletter and valuable Falls advice; and Yvonne Jangles of Abercrombie & Kent.

I'd like to round up by saying thanks to Trish Berry, Chris Worden and staff of Zambezi Safari and Travel who provided so much copy and advice. Thanks guys! A number of readers of the first edition have contributed invaluable information, notably Alison Parsons, Paul Sively, Sally Kent and Thomas Viger.

A very special mention for my old mate, Chris Mosley, who navigated, cooked, kept me company and stuck with me for a month while we drove round doing my research – he thought he was joining me for a holiday!

Huge thanks to the Bradt editorial staff, especially Adrian Phillips, for getting me involved in the first place and to Greg Dickinson, who held my hand throughout the updating process. Finally and overwhelmingly, I offer mega thanks to my wife, Frances, who accompanied me throughout virtually all of this research – often when she would probably have preferred to be somewhere else. While I was thoroughly enjoying myself, she spent hours alone in the car as I dashed in and out of places and then she had countless lonely days adding up to many months at home, as I bashed away on my laptop, engrossed and refusing to speak. Not only is she a patient and understanding author's wife but also a brilliant route planner and navigator, absolutely vital when so many miles have to be covered in such a short time. Who needs a GPS when you've got Frances! So although it's an old cliché, it's absolutely true to say that without her wonderful support, it wouldn't have been possible.

DEDICATION

This book is dedicated to the memory of my late dear friends, Gavin and Shaylene Best. They were two of the first Zimbabweans I met more than 25 years ago and were largely responsible for helping me fall in love with their country.

Together, over many years and with a small group of friends, we drove the whole region and during those trips Gavin taught me everything I now know about travelling through Africa with a 4x4 and a tent. Shay kept us all laughing throughout those journeys. My involvement with this book was a direct result of one of those trips, so I owe this whole fascinating experience to them.

In December 2008, Gav was killed by an elephant as he was protecting the life of one of his beloved orphaned baby elephants, and as a result my best mate never got the chance to read 'his' book and I never got the chance to thank him for his inspiration. Shay shocked us all when she died suddenly in 2011, leaving another huge gulf in our lives.

Contents

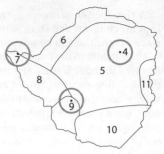

NOTE ABOUT MAPS

Several maps use grid lines to allow easy location of sites. Map grid references
are listed in square brackets after listings in the text, with page number
followed by grid number, eg: [156 C3].

LIST OF MAPS

USING THIS BOOK AND FEEDBACK REQUEST

Research for the first edition of this book took place against a background of political and economic turmoil at a time when Zimbabwe was struggling to cope with record hyperinflation (with figures rapidly approaching, and possibly exceeding, the all-time world record set by Hungary in 1946). Since then the country has stabilised almost beyond belief due to the introduction of the US dollar and the Government of National Unity. This has resulted in rapid and impressive improvements in the most popular tourism areas, while in the less frequented places change is perhaps less evident but there, nonetheless.

Zimbabwe is at a crossroad tourism-wise and it's still a case of almost constantly changing standards. I have made every effort to update the listings sections but please bear with me if some of them, especially in the less well-travelled areas, don't entirely chime with what you have experienced.

It is for this reason that I write regular updates on the Bradt updates website (*www.bradtupdates.com/zimbabwe*) and for these I rely heavily on readers' contributions. Naturally, any information regarding such changes or relating to your experiences in Zimbabwe – good or bad – is very gratefully received. Send your comments to Bradt Travel Guides, IDC House, The Vale, Chalfont St Peter, Bucks SL9 9RZ, England; e info@bradtguides.com.

Introduction

It's hard to believe – given the newspaper headlines and television images of the last decade or so – that throughout the 1980s and 1990s, Zimbabwe was southern Africa's most vibrant and developed destination, outstripping all the neighbouring countries in both tourism facilities and visitor numbers, with the possible exception of much larger South Africa. The economy was buoyant and the country was aptly labelled 'the breadbasket of southern Africa'. The situation changed dramatically in 2000 with the enforced implementation of the Land Reform programme, which stipulated the transfer of white-owned farming land to black residents. This project caused a dramatic decline in agricultural exports (one of the country's largest sectors), followed quickly by hyperinflation, soaring unemployment, and fuel and consumer goods shortages. These problems – accompanied by worldwide negative media coverage – brought tourism to a sudden halt.

However, since 2009 a new power-sharing government – the ruling Zanu-PF party and the two factions of the MDC – is being heralded as a sign of positive change. Inflation has been halted by the replacement of the Zimbabwe dollar with the US dollar, and this has allowed companies to trade with a degree of normality. Goods have returned to the supermarket shelves, there's fuel in the petrol pumps, many properties that were mothballed have been renovated, and brand-new tourist facilities have been built while existing ones are being extended. The public transport and communications infrastructure is still poor in less travelled areas but the country is definitely working now, rather than simply trying to survive. Water shortages and power cuts are still crippling some industries and making domestic life very difficult in many areas but there has been a mind-shift in attitudes. People are more positive about the future, more encouraged, and there is an exciting, if cautious, air of optimism pervading the country. People have been able to catch a breath and start working towards the future. During the bad years, towns and villages were quiet, almost deserted and you seldom saw young men walking around – most having sought a better life in neighbouring countries. Today, towns have returned to their former bustling state with traffic clogging the roads and people of all walks of life filling the pavements and markets, going about their everyday business.

So it's time to rediscover Zimbabwe's stunning attractions and World Heritage Sites; from the magnificent Victoria Falls and Zambezi River to Matobo National Park's ancient cave paintings; the game-rich national parks and Bulawayo's local craft markets and, above all, to meet or reacquaint yourself with the country's delightful people. This guide is a tribute to the Zimbabweans who stayed in their country, often because they had little other choice but generally because they had faith in and wanted to contribute to Zimbabwe's future. All have had to endure varying degrees of hardship and they have done so with an amazing stoicism and unfailing sense of humour. Their long-deserved change in fortune appears to have started and it is my sincere hope that this guidebook will play a small part in the rebuilding process by encouraging travellers to visit/return to this unforgettable country. Travelling in Zimbabwe is safe (it always was), so beat the crowds, go now and be an important part of the country's rebirth.

SHOULD YOU GO TO ZIMBABWE?

It's safe to say that tourism in Zimbabwe, at the time of writing, is a shadow of its former self – with the exception of Victoria Falls, Hwange National Park and the Lower Zambezi area. People were either frightened to visit, believing it to be dangerous or they, particularly Britons and South Africans, were voting with their feet and deciding not to support the current regime by boycotting the country. The following text provides answers to travellers' two most pertinent questions. They are very much my own views but they're born out of many years and countless miles of driving all around the country – through good times and bad.

IS IT SAFE? Emphatically, 'Yes'. My wife and I have driven the length and breadth of the country, most of the time on our own, for the last 20 years, including during the last two elections. During all those miles we have not encountered even a hint of trouble. We adopted nothing more than the standard, sensible and obvious safety measures recommended for independent travel anywhere in the world. Far from feeling intimidated or nervous, I have been met everywhere by incredibly friendly, welcoming and helpful people. That includes the authorities and the police. Police roadblocks are a common phenomenon and, in particular, seem to strike fear and apprehension into the hearts of many independent travellers. Don't worry, though. The officers at roadblocks are perfectly capable of recognising a genuine tourist from a political activist or a local resident and invariably treat the encounter as an opportunity to break their boredom and chat to somebody from overseas. They'll check your documents and occasionally poke around the car looking for faulty lights or your warning triangles and fire extinguishers. Yes, you'll get a small fine for any transgressions but I've never once encountered anything other than politeness and respect. If you approach the road checks in a relaxed manner, invariably, these encounters involve a few laughs and jokes and end with your being wished a safe journey.

It's generally recognised by experienced travellers that ordinary Zimbabweans are probably the most friendly and welcoming citizens of all the countries in the region. They used to enjoy having us in their country; then we stopped visiting and now they desperately want us back.

Furthermore, as a personal example of our faith in the safety of this country, my stepson got married a few years ago (in the 'bad old days' of 2007) and we encouraged the couple to spend their honeymoon in Zimbabwe. If my wife had thought there was even a whiff of danger she wouldn't have let her son and new daughter-in-law within 1,000 miles of the country. The only harassment they received was from mosquitoes.

Despite the above, it would be naive not to recognise that crime has increased as a result of the economic implosion and its legacy of unemployment, but I still regard Zimbabwe as one of the safest countries I've ever visited (I travelled extensively as an airline employee) and certainly many times more secure than South Africa. Any violence you read about is invariably and exclusively politically motivated and does not involve tourists or tourism areas.

IS IT MORAL? At the time of writing, Robert Mugabe (aged 89) is in his 25th year as president. Sadly, the post-independence era has been dogged by continual reports of human rights abuses. The government has been charged by the international community with rigging elections and using violence against political opponents and their supporters.

Following the economic collapse, probably four million people, nearly a third of Zimbabwe's population, left the country as either economic or political refugees. A large proportion of those that stayed faced potentially fatal conditions such as malnutrition, AIDS, malaria and other various illnesses, made all the more risky due to an almost complete lack of publicly accessible medical facilities. It's estimated that the life expectancy of the average Zimbabwean dropped to half of what it was before this government came to power. Thankfully, that figure is now rising dramatically.

As a direct result, many potential tourists have decided to boycott this country, believing that by visiting Zimbabwe they are helping the current regime not only financially but also by giving it a measure of legitimacy. Should you therefore boycott Zimbabwe in the hope that it might in some small way make a difference?

Throughout the decade following the events of 2000, the mass tourism boycott hasn't made a jot of difference. At least, no positive difference.

It seems that in Zimbabwe's case the boycott has only had a negative effect on ordinary citizens. Tourism used to provide employment for thousands of people and supported many, many others, but these jobs were lost when tourists and travel agents crossed Zimbabwe off their lists. So many people who used to rely on tourism became desperate and joined hordes of other unemployed, migrating, usually illegally, to nearby countries where most found abject misery and violence rather than the streets paved with gold that they were hoping for.

And while admittedly a proportion of your tourism spend will end up in government coffers, it's only a very small percentage.

It is now 2013 and much has changed for the better. The government has now recognised the vast benefits that tourism can bring to the country and is putting its money where its mouth is by encouraging investment in tourism infrastructure and services. Not only is this starting to provide a much needed boost in employment but increasing visitor numbers can only encourage exchange of ideas and exposure to the outside democratic world. Since 2010 tourism hot spots have seen a surge in visitor numbers from around the world (except the UK, which largely continues with its boycott) and these numbers are growing year on year. Wildlife is also benefiting. Without financial support from tourism, many waterholes go unpumped, anti-poaching patrols only operate at a fraction of their potential, and subsistence hunting goes virtually unchecked. Finally, it should be stressed that the international organisation Tourism Concern currently offers no advice against travel to Zimbabwe. In short you will do much more to help the country and its wonderful people recover by visiting it, rather than boycotting it.

I am of course aware of all the counter-arguments, many of which deserve serious consideration, but at the end of the day, I take advice from all the many Zimbabweans I meet – ordinary citizens, black and white – all of whom, without exception, earnestly want tourists to return to their country.

Part One

GENERAL INFORMATION

ZIMBABWE AT A GLANCE

Location Landlocked and immediately north of South Africa
Bordering countries South Africa, Botswana, Namibia, Zambia and Mozambique
Area 390,580km^2
Climate November–March hot and wet, April–August moderate and dry, September–October dry and increasingly hot
Independence 18 April 1980 (from Britain)
Capital Harare
Other major towns Bulawayo, Masvingo, Mutare, Gweru and Victoria Falls
Type of government Democratic Presidential Republic
Head of state President Robert Mugabe
Main political parties ZANU-PF (Zimbabwe African National Union – Patriotic Front) and MDC (Movement for Democratic Change of which there are two factions: the MDC(T) and smaller MDC(N). The main parties are in a tentative power-sharing agreement – the Government of National Unity.
Main national parks Hwange, Victoria Falls, Zambezi, Matobo, Chizarira, Matusadona, Mana Pools, Nyanga, Bvumba, Chimanimani and Gonarezhou
Currency In 2009 the Zimbabwe dollar (ZIM$) was withdrawn; various hard currencies are now allowed but the US dollar is now the universally accepted official currency and the country uses US dollar notes (no US coins).
Economy Agriculture, tourism, mining and forestry
Population 10–12 million (estimate), with mass migration and AIDS causing great uncertainty in numbers since the last census in 2002.
Main ethnic groups Shona 80%, Ndebele 14%, white 0.5%, others 3%
Languages Shona and Ndebele (or Sindebele) are first languages for most, although English is the official language.
Religion Syncretic (mixture of Christian and traditional) 50%, Christian 25%, traditional 24%, Muslim and others 1%
Time GMT+2
Electricity supply 220/240V AC; sockets are frequently UK-style 3 square pin, but increasingly changing to South Africa-style 3 round pin and 2 pin. Newer and upmarket tourism outlets use South African-style sockets.
Newspapers Media restrictions have been significantly lifted by the Unity government so most papers are now independent with the *Daily News* and *Newsday* recent additions. The *Herald* and *Chronicle* are state controlled. There are a growing number of independent online papers.
International dialling code +263. When calling from outside Zimbabwe, drop the initial zero from the local area code or from the cell number.
Phone numbers in this book The area code for landline numbers is stated at the beginning of each town/area section. Numbers starting 07 are mobile.
Flag Seven horizontal bands with central black, then red, yellow and green top and bottom. White triangle inset on left containing stylised yellow Zimbabwe bird national symbol on a red five-pointed star in the centre of the triangle.
National holidays 1 January (New Year's Day), variable (Easter), 18 April (Independence Day), 1 May (Workers' Day), 25 May (Africa Day), 11 August or nearest Monday (Heroes Day), 12 August or nearest Tuesday (Defence Forces Day), 22 December (National Unity Day), 25 December (Christmas Day), 26 December (Boxing Day)

1

Background Information

GEOGRAPHY

Zimbabwe is a landlocked country bordered by five countries: Mozambique to the east, South Africa to the south, Botswana to the southwest, Zambia to the northwest, and Namibia at the western tip – where, interestingly, the borders of Zimbabwe, Zambia, Botswana and Namibia meet at Kazungula. The great Zambezi River flows along its northwestern border with Zambia, and the Limpopo along the southern border with South Africa.

It is generally regarded as the northernmost country in 'southern Africa', lies between 15°S and 22°S latitude, and 25°E and 33°E longitude on the southern African great plateau, and covers an area of 390,580km² – approximately three times the size of England or half the size of Texas.

Topographically, the country has a broadly central *highveld* area (veld, pronounced *felt*, is a grassland region that when combined with 'high', 'middle' and 'low' describes plateau elevations), which is frequently described as the Zimbabwe Plateau and has an average elevation of around 1,500m. Running roughly northeast–southwest across this central area is the Great Dyke, a central ridge notable for its wealth of valuable minerals, including gold and diamonds, which continue to be mined along its length.

This *highveld* ridge is fringed on both sides by extensive and gradually sloping *middleveld* areas averaging just over 1,000m, and culminates in two very separate *lowveld* areas where the lowest elevation is around 150m. These two areas are in the far southern corner, from Gonarezhou National Park to Beitbridge, and in a northeasterly direction all along the Zambezi Valley and around to the northern border with Mozambique.

In the north and northwest, the *highveld* drops dramatically towards the river valley, forming the Zambezi Escarpment, while in the south, the slope towards the Limpopo is more gradual. The Matobo Hills, at the southern end of the Great Dyke near Bulawayo, form another significant topographical feature notable for the profusion of huge granite *dwalas* or whalebacks set alongside formations of giant 'balancing' rocks.

The other defining highland feature of the country is the Eastern Highlands, a narrow, 250km-long, north–south mountain range in the east of Zimbabwe, occupying the central section of the border with Mozambique and rising to 2,592m at Mount Nyangani in the north of the range.

The world-famous, 1.7km-wide Victoria Falls are at the northwestern tip of the country while further downstream the Zambezi is dammed at the town of Kariba, forming the massive 200km-long Lake Kariba, one of the world's largest manmade lakes and the second largest in Africa. Apart from the Zambezi, a number of smaller rivers rise in the *highveld* and radiate outwards to irrigate the south and north.

CLIMATE

Zimbabwe enjoys a pleasantly temperate-to-tropical climate year-round, though with significant variations influenced by the country's topography as well as the seasons.

There are three distinct climatic regions: the central *highveld* plateau, covering most of the country, is generally temperate, while the Eastern Highlands have a significantly cooler climate with much higher year-round rainfall. Low-lying regions such as Hwange, the upper Zambezi, and Gonarezhou in the southeast are significantly warmer year-round and hot in the summer.

The summer and winter seasons are generally defined in terms of rainfall, the latter being virtually rain free. Spring and autumn are simply transitional periods but not generally evident as distinct seasons.

Summer (November–April) is eagerly awaited by humans and wildlife alike, as it usually marks the onset of rains after several months of drought. Rainfall frequently occurs in brief, heavy afternoon downpours, often accompanied by dramatic electrical storms, only to be followed moments later by long periods of sunshine; alternatively a wet weather system may set in, bringing prolonged steady rain and distinctly cool temperatures for a number of days.

Rainfall peaks in December, January and February with monthly falls of 150–190mm, significantly higher in the Eastern Highlands, sometimes reaching 2,000mm per annum. Maximum summer temperatures generally range from 25°C to the high 30s although it can feel much hotter as the moisture in the ground and on vegetation quickly evaporates after rain, creating periods of high humidity. Low-lying areas such as the Zambezi Valley, Kariba, Hwange, Gonarezhou and the Limpopo Valley experience hotter conditions, with temperatures frequently climbing well into the 40s. Night-time summer temperatures drop to 15–20°C.

Winter (May–October) offers maximum temperatures on average 5–10° cooler than summer depending on location, with an abundance of blue skies and sunshine and virtually no rain. The early months are cool, warming up significantly to a hot, dry period through September and October. October is often referred to as 'suicide month' with its high temperatures and increasingly moisture-laden air building up to the first rains. Clear skies over the Kalahari sands in the west can bring distinctly chilly nights, so it is not unusual to wake up for your early morning game drive to find a ground frost, especially in Hwange National Park. The Bulawayo area, too, can experience low night-time temperatures so accommodations with heating will be welcome. The Eastern Highlands are considerably cooler and wetter, with year-round rainfall, and the area provides a perfect respite from the sometimes unpleasant heat and humidity in the rest of the country.

This is the theory at least. In reality, traditional climates and seasons seem to be getting much less predictable and it is possible to be distinctly chilly in midsummer and uncomfortably hot in winter when it should be cool. The onset of rains seems to be getting later in the year and recent years have seen devastating droughts.

HISTORY

LATE STONE AGE Central and eastern Africa are generally viewed as the birthplace of the human species, so today's Zimbabwe is of great significance to archaeologists. The earliest period for which it is possible to build a reliable picture of human life in the Zimbabwe region is the Late Stone Age, generally said to have begun only around 13,000 years ago. Prior to that, the period between 40,000 and 13,000 years ago is called the Late Middle Stone Age, during which time there is a huge shift in human behaviour with the first evidence of family life, organised hunting and the controlled use of fire.

Stone Age development proceeded in a southerly direction in the region. Early microlith (small stone tool) finds, indicating the onset of the Late Stone Age, in areas north of the Zambezi in what is now Zambia, pre-date those found further south in Zimbabwe by as much as 20,000 years. An explanation for this apparently slow rate of development over a relatively small area may be found in climate change. A wetter climate, gradually moving down from the north, would have begun shifting the balance to woodland over open grassland, attracting different game species and requiring different hunting techniques. Spears were effective in open country but not in woodland, which demanded weapons deployed with great stealth at relatively close range. Thus the bow and arrow, with its small and intricate microlith arrowhead, was gradually developed. Only as the climate changed in the more southerly regions thousands of years later did such refined hunting tools appear there.

EARLY PEOPLES The inhabitants of Late Stone Age southern Africa are generally called *Khoisan*, a term that actually refers to a language group still in use in the region. There were in fact two closely related peoples, the San and the Khoi, each with their own variations of a language identified by distinctive 'click consonants'. The difference between the two groups was essentially one of lifestyle: the larger of the two groups, the San, were hunter-gatherers and the Khoi largely pastoral. Both peoples occupied Zimbabwe during the Late Stone Age and are believed to have enjoyed a degree of coexistence when conditions allowed.

The Khoisan have commonly been referred to as 'bushmen', a term that went through a spell of political incorrectness but has now regained acceptance. The Khoisan were widely dispersed throughout Zimbabwe and further north in central and east Africa. Even today small groups of them cling to something approaching a traditional lifestyle in isolated parts of Namibia and Botswana. They have been televised, eulogised and studied like a species of threatened animal, and patronisingly viewed as a quaint surviving relic of primitive man.

As a result we have been given a rather romantic view which is by no means totally accurate. Rather than 'migrating' throughout the subcontinent, each group operated in a large but defined territory, and when food and water sources dried up in one place they picked up their minimalist possessions and moved to another camp, though always within their own territory. Group size was determined by the availability of food and water, in arid areas perhaps no more than 20 people. Although our televisions show us 'bushmen' skilfully tracking game in the barren desert, in truth meat formed a relatively small proportion of their diet. Most of their diet was made up of roots, nuts and fruits, grubs, honey and small animals.

The Khoisan – who inhabited coastal areas or regions with plentiful rainfall and vegetation – formed larger groupings and put down more permanent roots. While still basically a hunting and foraging people, there is evidence that they learned alternative food production methods from people of other cultures. Some Khoisan began keeping sheep, goats or cattle, generally as a supplement to their foraging lifestyle, but some groups adopted a largely pastoral way of life. This progress to a herding lifestyle also corresponds roughly to the time they started making pottery. The fact that their distinctive click consonants are found in some other Bantu languages reveals a degree of integration with neighbouring peoples. (The term 'Bantu' defines a family of several hundred languages, all with common roots, originating in central/west Africa.) Cave paintings and other rock art (see *Rock paintings*, pages 312–15) confirm the long occupation by Khoisan of large areas of present-day Zimbabwe.

IRON AGE The southerly spread of Iron Age culture in Africa began in west Africa around 2,500 and can be charted from the styles of pottery found in any given area. The earliest Iron Age pottery found in the Zimbabwe area (Bambata Cave in Matopos) dates from around 2,200 years ago. The particular style of pottery found here shows that the new culture was introduced by Bantu-speaking peoples arriving from further north via eastern Africa. These immigrants spoke a Bantu variant called *chiShona*.

Major lifestyle changes included the spread of livestock keeping and the introduction of farming to produce millet and later sorghum and *ropoko* as staple starches, as well as other crops. More robust thatched houses were built from *daga* (clay or mud), forming villages of a size depending on the productivity of the soil and climate. Mining, smelting and metalworking appeared, for the production of crafts, weapons and tools. This period also gives us the first evidence of trade, with seashells and overseas crafts from the Mozambique coast found at Zimbabwean sites from as early as the 2nd century AD.

The taller, darker-skinned Bantu immigrants intermarried with the Khoisan, and their languages mixed, but ultimately the Bantu were dominant and their language and lifestyle took over in the region. The hunter-gatherer Khoisan continued to live their Stone Age existence in many places, predominantly areas that would not support farming communities, but this was effectively the beginning of their marginalisation, pushed further south and west or into more remote and inhospitable areas.

The term 'Iron Age' conjures up images of rather primitive cultures, yet the Late Iron Age – generally accepted as starting in Zimbabwe around the 9th and 10th centuries – actually reveals a sophisticated political and cultural environment, with rapid advances in technology. Following on the heels of iron processing, copper was discovered and worked in the region and then, crucially for its future wealth, gold. Trade flourished between the gold-bearing Zimbabwe Plateau and the ports of the Mozambique coast, with exports of ironware, gold and ivory being traded for glass, porcelain, woven fabrics and trinkets from Europe, Egypt and the Far East. There was also a thriving trade in African slaves.

11TH–15TH CENTURIES The new-found gold brought unparalleled wealth to the region and the ruins of the city-state of Great Zimbabwe – just south of today's Masvingo – epitomise the growth of the economy. While it's not possible to be specific due to the widespread looting and destruction of artefacts, building of the city-state commenced in the 11th century and continued for about 300 years. Originally a hilltop village, it quickly developed into an impressive walled citadel housing the Shona rulers who commanded not only the gold route to the coast but a community of many thousands in the surrounding hills who farmed and provided the labour for the metal industries. While certainly the most impressive ancient gold-based site in the country, Great Zimbabwe was by no means the only gold production and trading centre; hundreds of lesser ruins have been found throughout the plateau area. Despite its rapid economic growth, it suffered an equally rapid decline in fortunes, and the city appears to have become deserted within the space of around 400 years.

15TH CENTURY In the aftermath of Great Zimbabwe, the next phase of Zimbabwean history brings us much more detailed information about the autonomous Shona kingdoms and dynasties that ruled large swathes of the country. It also features a prolonged and complex period of political turmoil and violence.

Great Zimbabwe splintered into a variety of smaller dynasties. The most powerful of these was created around 1420 by Mutota, a *mambo* (king) who became known as Mwene Mutapa (the Great Plunderer), a title subsequently bestowed on all future rulers of this dynasty of Munhumutapa (Monomotapa in its anglicised spelling). Mutapa ruled a kingdom encompassing most of northern and eastern Zimbabwe and well into Mozambique until his death in 1450. His son and successor, Mutope, shifted the base of the empire to Fura Mountain near Mazowe, just north of today's Harare. He continued trading successfully with the Arabs (who already had thriving trade connections in Mozambique and subsequently sought gold further inland), building on the massive empire that effectively controlled the whole of eastern Zimbabwe. By 1494, a series of coups and overthrows following Mutope's death had split the empire north and south. Changamire, Mutope's son, went on to form the Changamire dynasty.

Another Great Zimbabwe breakaway group were the Torwa (meaning 'strangers'), who moved west and, around 1480, based their kingdom, Butua, near what is now Bulawayo, at Khami (Kame on some maps). The Torwa continued their predecessors' trade in gold and cattle and their influence was considerable across southern and western regions, well into today's Botswana. Excavations at the ruins of Khami have revealed local pottery, ivory, metal weapons and crafts as well as artefacts traded from overseas as evidence of an extremely prosperous culture.

16TH–17TH CENTURIES By the early years of the 16th century the Portuguese, who had begun to establish a trading presence on the coast of Mozambique, had seen gold artefacts being traded by the Swahili (Bantu people from the east African coast) and Arabs and heard stories of vast empires in the interior. This was interpreted by some as the fabled land of Ophir, home of King Solomon's mines, and the Portuguese wanted a piece of the action. They embarked on nearly two centuries of exploitation and double dealing, pitting *mambos* against each other in an attempt to gain influence and, ultimately, gold. They replaced the Arab and Swahili traders of old and gained a stranglehold on the gold trade. Various attempts were made to remove them but it was not until the early 1690s that the Changamire drove the Portuguese back into Mozambique, where they were to remain.

By now the Changamire, led by their greatest *mambo*, Dombo, were the dominant force, having in 1684 overcome the southwestern Torwa to form the Rozwi ('destroyers') Empire that covered more than half of present-day Zimbabwe and was to remain in power into the 1830s.

18TH–19TH CENTURIES Throughout most of the 18th century, the area south of Zimbabwe was in a state of turmoil, rocked by violent skirmishes between competing, highly militarised Nguni chiefdoms. (Nguni is a collective name for a large and varied grouping of peoples who occupied much of eastern and southern Africa.) The resulting strife gave rise to a series of mass migrations, as defeated clans were forced off their land. Many of these clans in turn carried out their own attacks as they searched for new territory.

A new element in this process of migration and realignment was the arrival of the Boers – the South African farming settlers spreading northwards from their original Cape area. This whole process has become known as the *mfecane*, a Zulu word meaning 'the crushing' or 'the scattering', and it's estimated that up to two million people were slaughtered in the process. The *mfecane* is hugely significant for Zimbabwe, as it was during this period that the Zulu nation was born; and from the Zulus arose the Ndebele (see box below).

COLONIAL ERA While his predecessors had, for several centuries, busied themselves with conquering and being conquered by indigenous forces, Lobengula's (see below) reign coincided with an altogether different threat: the white man. White hunters and traders had already been allowed onto Ndebele territory in return for supplying

BIRTH OF THE NDEBELE

DINGISWAYO (1780–1817) Little is known about the early years of Dingiswayo, born the son of the powerful Mthethwa clan chief, but as a young man he was exiled, allegedly for plotting to kill his own father. He returned to the fold on the death of his father, sometime around 1800, and promptly seized the chieftainship from his elder brother. It is said that during his exile he encountered, and was greatly impressed by, European army organisation and discipline, and he subsequently revolutionised regional warfare tactics by successfully introducing these ideas to his own regiments and bringing together a number of disparate, autonomous groups into one cohesive force.

SHAKA (1787–1828) One of Dingiswayo's trusted soldiers was an impressive young man called Shaka, son of the chief of the Zulus, at that time still a minor clan. As Shaka was promoted through the ranks he built on Dingiswayo's military ideas and developed his own innovative battle tactics revolving around harsh discipline and hand-to-hand fighting, with the replacement of the throwing spear by the short stabbing spear. He also perfected the battle tactic known as 'horns of the buffalo', in which the enemy were encouraged forward while concealed troops on either side moved round and encircled them.

After his father's death around 1816, Shaka became chief of the Zulu clan and it is very likely that he engineered Dingiswayo's eventual death, allowing him to take full control of the Mthethwe in 1817, subsequently renaming them Zulus. Shaka's rule over the next decade was harsh and violent and as a result of his overwhelming military successes, Shaka eventually created the vast kingdom seen on today's maps of South Africa as KwaZulu Natal. It was perhaps inevitable that after a relatively short reign, characterised by extreme violence towards any potential rival, Shaka would amass so many enemies that he would meet his own treacherous and bloody death. This was carried out by his two half-brothers, Dingane and Mhlangane, in 1828.

MZILIKAZI (1790–1868) In 1818 the two most powerful kingdoms in the region, the Zulus under Shaka and the Ndandwe commanded by Zwide, embarked on a bitter war with each other, setting off the chain reaction of *mfecane* wars.

It's around this time that the name Mzilikazi appears on the scene. He was a Khumalo clan chief, grandson of Zwide, but who chose to ally his fighting force with Zwide's great rival, Shaka, quickly becoming one of his trusted generals. Their relationship, however, was short-lived, souring in 1821 when Shaka turned on Mzilikazi after a disagreement over cattle ownership. Mzilikazi's army was routed but he and the other survivors took flight, heading on their own rampage, firearms, and it was only a matter of time before they found evidence of the area's gold-bearing potential. The British hunter Henry Hartley made the first gold discovery (at the old Rozwi mines) in 1865 and two years later a German-American called Adam Renders was the first white man to see Great Zimbabwe, believing it to be the fabled King Solomon's mines. These two discoveries initiated a gold rush; the search for 'the second rand' (rand is the South African term for a major gold-bearing area, 'the first rand' being the vast mine of Witwatersrand near Johannesburg) began in earnest, apparently in a bid to confirm the long-held belief of British, German, Afrikaner and Portuguese speculators that Lobengula's large territory was rich in mineral deposits,

roaming far and wide into Botswana and north to Zambia before eventually settling in what is now Zimbabwe.

By the year 1800 the Rozwi Empire, centred on the Zimbabwean plateau, was well into its decline, weakened by continuous internal strife amongst what had become little more than a loose confederation of regional chiefdoms. The leadership was subsequently poorly prepared to withstand the next onslaught, first from Nguni invaders from the northeast led by Zwangandaba, one of whose generals, a formidable woman called Nyamazuma, has been credited with killing the last of the Rozwi *mambos* in 1836.

Mzilikazi's Khumalo forces had in the meantime been expanding in numbers and strength. He had renamed them the Ndebele (people of the long shields) to differentiate them from the Zulus, and they were slowly making their way northwards from their base not far from today's Pretoria. Mzilikazi himself split off from the main contingent with a small detachment to follow the Kololo army towards the northwest while the bulk of his force headed for the region of the Matobo hills. Mzilikazi pursued his own mission for two years, but then learnt that in his absence his son Nkulumane had been installed as king. Upon hearing this news in 1840 he rushed southwards, reasserted his position, dispatched those responsible, and his son was never heard of again – no doubt he was assassinated.

Having re-established himself, he found the area was still ruled by the Nguni invaders with Nyamazuma being prominent amongst their hierarchy. In what may be considered an unusual decision in these violent times, Mzilikazi cleverly opted for marriage to the powerful Nyamazuma as an alternative to warfare, combining their personal lives and, more importantly, their armies. The Ndebele became the dominant force in southern Zimbabwe through the oppression or annexation of resident or neighbouring Shona peoples.

Mzilikazi established his base at Inyati near today's Bulawayo, and it was here that he rekindled his friendship with the missionary Robert Moffat, allowing Moffat to set up a mission station – not so much because he saw any value in his people being converted to Christianity, but because he recognised the potential benefits of having an influential white man as his friend.

LOBENGULA (1845–94) Mzilikazi died in 1868 after a long period of ill health, giving rise to a rather messy succession struggle. His son Lobengula was appointed king but objections were made on the basis that the title rightfully belonged to the elder son, Nkulumane, who had not been seen for nearly 30 years. A search for him revealed nothing other than an impostor, so Lobengula was eventually installed in 1870 after a brief civil war, and moved the Ndebele base to Bulawayo.

primarily gold. Meanwhile, the young British businessman Cecil John Rhodes – who had already made a fortune from the diamond mines in Kimberley, South Africa, already had his eyes on this land. But not only for its untapped mineral wealth. He was desperate to gain control of Lobengula's Matabeleland in the south and southeast and the northeasterly Mashonaland territories in order to advance his dream of a trade route from the Cape to Cairo.

By the late 1880s Lobengula was becoming increasingly irritated and suspicious of the continuous parade of concession seekers eager to participate in the development of a 'second gold rand'. Lobengula was intelligent and politically aware, extremely wary of signing away his territory to 'white devils', and had so far kept them at bay except for one Piet Grobler, an emissary of Paul Kruger. Kruger was state president of the South African Republic (Transvaal) and would later become leader of the resistance against the British in the second Boer War. In 1887, Grobler claimed a treaty of alliance with Lobengula, giving the right of abode for Boer settlers.

Rhodes needed to neutralise this Grobler Treaty and prevent further threats to his grand plan, so his team brought in John Moffat, son of Robert the famous missionary, who lived locally and was one of Lobengula's friends. Moffat drew up a document declaring peace and amity between Queen Victoria and the Ndebele, and Lobengula agreed to this Moffat Treaty, which prevented him from granting land concessions without prior British permission. This had the effect of excluding non-British concession hunters, but Rhodes was already in a desperate race with other British concerns, notably the Bechuanaland Exploration Company and figured he would have to use more subtle means. He assembled a small negotiating team, Rudd, Maguire and Thompson – a business partner, an old friend, and an agent – and charged them with securing a further treaty with Lobengula to give him, Rhodes, sole rights to mine the territory.

Rudd's team drew up a carefully worded document in formal legal language and a missionary, the Revd C D Helm, was tasked with translating it for the illiterate Lobengula. The king was in no hurry, and sought much counsel from his advisors or *indunas* who were unconvinced. A Bechuanaland Exploration Company delegate also involved himself, obviously trying to employ spoiling tactics.

Nevertheless, in late 1888, after many a week's delay, the king eventually signed the so-called Rudd Concession. In return for 1,000 Martini-Henry rifles and a supply of ammunition, a steam-powered gunboat on the Zambezi River (or a cash alternative) plus £100 per month, Lobengula granted Rudd, Maguire and Thompson exclusive rights over all minerals in his territories between the Zambezi and Limpopo, the right to exclude any other concession seekers and, amazingly, full power to do all things they deemed necessary to further the mining operation. Helm's translation appears to have been accurate and honest, and it is thought that Lobengula would have understood the treaty's literal meaning, so how could he have so willingly signed a document apparently giving away his state's land for such a pittance?

Throughout the negotiations Rudd had spoken of nothing more than the right to dig mines and had carefully avoided giving Lobengula any inkling of Rhodes's actual ambition, which was to gain 'sovereignty' over the land, something that was justifiably anathema to the king. It later transpired that Rudd had given verbal assurances via Helm to Lobengula that no more than ten white men would prospect or mine for minerals and that they would be under Lobengula's direct control. But this crucial proviso was omitted from the written document, and what Lobengula clearly failed to understand were the hidden implications of 'full power to do all things they deem necessary'.

Lobengula was by all accounts an astute man but he was being feted, patronised and lied to by Rhodes's men, who hugely played down the economic significance and implications of this agreement. Against Rhodes, one of the richest, most ruthless and single-minded businessmen of his time, Lobengula, once described by Rhodes as 'one naked old savage', stood no chance in these negotiations. The king soon realised he had been duped and immediately sent two envoys to petition Queen Victoria and her government, but their complaints were ignored.

After the signing of the Rudd Concession, which granted only mining rights, Rhodes hastened back to England to gain the Queen's seal of approval for his chartered British South Africa Company (BSAC). This was duly accomplished and on 29 October 1889 the BSAC was given sweeping powers to build on the Rudd Concession and administer the country and undefined regions to the north.

Now it was time to populate these areas with white settlers, so Rhodes assembled the Pioneer Column, comprising some 200 civilians who had been promised land and mining rights, many of them Afrikaner Boers whom Rhodes was courting for political reasons, together with 500 police to protect them. In April 1890, guided by the renowned hunter Frederick Courtney Selous, they began a trek northwards from the Cape towards Mashonaland. Although Lobengula had a good deal of influence in Mashonaland, he was understandably happier for the prospectors to start digging up Shona soil than the Matabeleland of his Ndebele people. Aware of this, the column carefully skirted Matabeleland. In September of that year they eventually halted, built a fort which they named Salisbury after the prime minister (and which later became the capital of Rhodesia) and began looking for gold.

It soon became apparent that gold was not being found in sufficient quantity to support the settlers, thereby providing no tax income for the financially struggling BSAC. This area was never going to be the sought-after 'second rand', so increasingly farming became the only alternative for the settlers. This latter activity was of course illegal, as the Rudd Concession granted only mining, not land-owning rights.

Lobengula, by now thoroughly dismayed by his betrayal by Rhodes and suspicious of all the white activities around him, would never voluntarily concede land sovereignty. Well, not quite. The king in fact signed what is known as the Lippert Concession. In return for a relatively small amount of cash this granted Edward Lippert, an agent of one of Rhodes's land-claiming rivals, the sole rights for 100 years to use Lobengula's land as he saw fit, ie: for farming, building, grazing, whatever. In this way it seems that Lobengula, in the belief that Lippert was a rival of Rhodes, hoped to pit the opposing land and mining interests against each other. It was not one of Lobengula's wisest moves, however, misfiring spectacularly when Lippert subsequently sold these rights to Rhodes for £1,000,000. Nobody should be too surprised at the suggestion that Rhodes shrewdly engineered this whole deception by himself. Whatever the truth, Rhodes now had paper proof that all of Lobengula's territory had become BSAC property.

Things were, however, not going well financially for the BSAC. Gold was not forthcoming and Rhodes knew that the long and arduous ox-wagon trek from the south to bring provisions to the settlers at Salisbury would be prohibitively expensive. So, in Rhodes's typically arrogant and increasingly reckless style, he directed his friend and colleague, Dr Leander Starr Jameson, to attempt to force a route through from Salisbury to the Mozambique coast and claim the port of Beira. In other words, amazingly, a private British company was planning to invade and seize Portuguese territory.

The failure of this venture after much international political intrigue involving Britain, Portugal and the powerful king of Gaza, Gungunhana, together with the by now disappointing gold finds, led Rhodes to bring matters to a head and make a move into Lobengula's Matabele territory.

Whatever the dubious legalities of Rhodes's concessions and agreements, Lobengula still considered himself sovereign. Rhodes knew this would always be the case and had long realised that to gain Lobengula's territory, force would be necessary. A pre-emptive strike would be totally unacceptable both to his political masters in England and amongst his very vocal liberal peers in the Cape government, so he had only one alternative: to provoke an attack in order that he could then retaliate with full force. Lobengula had long honoured a pledge not to harm whites and to keep well clear of them on his frequent raiding forays on the Shona, but it was on one of these punitive expeditions around Fort Victoria in July 1893 that Rhodes's plan came to fruition. While the Ndebele were busy fighting the Shona and asking for the return of refugees who had gained access to the fort, they were chased off by the BSAC officer in charge and his men, who subsequently killed or wounded many of them. Although the Ndebele kept to their bargain and offered no resistance, Jameson reported back that the Ndebele had in fact attacked the company's men and that he was preparing for war. Using this lie as a pretext to attack the Ndebele and take over their land, Jameson was able to put Lobengula's men to flight. The BSAC had fewer men but they were disciplined and their arms included the Maxim gun, so it was a very unequal fight and the various skirmishes resulted in major Ndebele casualties.

In early November BSAC troops found that Lobengula had already deserted and burnt his Bulawayo city and fled northwest. Anxious to capture the king alive, a small detachment of troops led by Captain Alan Wilson gave chase in early December, but were completely outmanoeuvred by the king's men, who after a full day's fighting took every one of their lives at the Shangani River. This militarily small and uncharacteristic defeat was extremely significant to both sides and Rhodes erected what some people consider to be a somewhat oversized memorial, near to the place he had earmarked as the site of his own grave, to commemorate the death of these 34 'heroes'.

Lobengula was never heard of again, though various stories suggest either that he died of smallpox shortly thereafter or that he took poison when he heard the last of his warriors had surrendered. His exact fate has never been confirmed, and this is still a matter of great concern to the Ndebele as his spirit is in an unknown place and presumably in limbo, without the benefit of due ceremony.

With Lobengula chased out of the country and the Ndebele supposedly defeated, there was now no obstacle to Rhodes gaining complete control over both Mashonaland and Matabeleland. While it is true that there was considerable disquiet amongst certain liberal and senior elements of the British House of Commons, the government stuck to its principle of 'not wanting to get too involved in the affairs of the colonies lest it cost us a lot of money' and in 1894 reluctantly handed over full administration of all Lobengula's territories to Rhodes and his British South Africa Company.

The First Chimurenga (1896–97)

From 1894, with the Ndebele defeated and ruled by the fledgling BSAC, Bulawayo flourished. But all was not plain sailing for the company and the settlers. In the aftermath of the recent conflict, Rhodes treated the conquered territory as property of the company. Vast acreages of prime farmland and virtually all the cattle were confiscated and handed over to the white settlers. The population, stripped of its traditional way of life, was marginalised and treated as nothing more than a source of cheap labour. A hut tax of ten shillings a year was introduced both as a source of revenue and as an 'encouragement' for people to work in order to pay it. Life for both the Shona to the north and east and the Ndebele in the south was becoming intolerable but – not for the first time and certainly not for the last – the white ruling class appeared to have no idea of the resentment that was brewing up. To make matters worse, everybody was suffering the effects of locust plagues, prolonged drought and a devastating outbreak of rinderpest, a deadly and contagious cattle disease. These three natural disasters were seen as a consequence of the white man's conquests and in late March, spurred by the disastrous defeat of BSAC troops in the infamous Jameson Raid against the Boers in Transvaal, the Ndebele rose up. From hidden bases in the Matobo hills, they terrorised, raided and killed hundreds of settlers in farms and towns, and in April 1896 laid siege to Bulawayo. Although the Ndebele took their oppressors by surprise, they were again no match for superior BSAC troops, and their resistance was relatively short-lived. By the end of May sufficient troops had arrived to retake Bulawayo.

Meanwhile, further north and for all the same reasons, the Shona also took matters into their own hands, though considerably less effectively. Their revolt was swiftly stamped on, but not before more than 100 settlers had perished.

Back in Matabeleland the Ndebele, who had retreated to the hills, continued their resistance, using guerrilla tactics against which the BSAC force was ill-prepared and creating something of a stalemate. In what many biographers refer to as Rhodes's finest hour, he and five others 'fearlessly' rode unarmed into the Matobo hills to meet with the Ndebele *indunas* and negotiate peace. While they certainly did ride in unarmed, the meetings had been prepared well in advance and took place over several months before a relatively peaceful settlement was reached at the end of October. Rhodes was forced to listen to the demands of 'the natives' and make significant concessions, a situation he must have found profoundly unsettling.

So although the war, the *chimurenga* (Shona for 'struggle'), failed to end white rule, it acted as a very rude wake-up call for Rhodes and the British government, and did result in at least some restoration of dignity for the population.

The name 'Rhodesia' was increasingly accepted in common parlance and the icing on Cecil Rhodes's cake came in 1897 when the British government made it official. Rhodes was jubilant. Not only did he have the distinction of ruling his own, huge private empire, but it had been officially named after him.

After Rhodes In 1902, Rhodesia lost its founder. Cecil Rhodes, 48 years old and never blessed with robust health, caught a severe chest cold on a sea voyage back to Cape Town and died a few weeks later on 26 March.

The first decade of the new century saw a burgeoning European population in the region, with a massive influx of immigrants following the formation of an all-white legislative council in 1899. The country was renamed Southern Rhodesia, as distinct from Northern Rhodesia (now Zambia) on the other side of the Zambezi, and remained under the administration of the BSAC, but by the early 1920s the company was losing its grip. In 1922, settlers led by Sir Charles Coughlan won a referendum for self-government by a healthy majority. These were predominantly new European immigrants, concerned about Afrikaner domination in the likely event that Rhodesia joined the Union of South Africa, and not the early 'Pioneers' with their greater ties to the south.

The following year, bedevilled by falling profits, the BSAC cut its losses and handed over Rhodes's country to the imperial government. The new British colony, under the premiership of Coughlan, was notionally non-racial in that suffrage was extended to blacks, but there was a slight catch. To qualify they had to have British citizenship, as well as earning an annual income above a certain (high) threshold. Unsurprisingly, few blacks got the vote. Equally unsurprising is that this period saw the first stirrings of black nationalism. Although 'apartheid' is a word generally associated with South Africa and seldom used in relation to Zimbabwe's colonial past, Southern Rhodesia's 'separate development' system pre-dates South Africa's own policies by several decades.

The Southern Rhodesia Native Association, the Rhodesian Bantu Voters Association and later the Rhodesia African National Congress were all dedicated to improving the lot of the majority population, although these fledgling human rights organisations achieved little against the might of British rule.

The Land Apportionment Act of 1930 further entrenched white domination by confiscating vast areas of the most fertile farmland, allocating 11,300,000ha to one million blacks and 19,500,000ha to 50,000 whites. This was followed by further legislation over the years that excluded blacks from skilled jobs and prevented them from living in white areas. So-called Tribal Trust Lands, large rural areas suitable only for subsistence farming, were created for black occupation, so just as Rhodes had done several decades earlier, these laws condemned Rhodesia's blacks to a life of subservience and cheap labour. As conditions worsened with even more punitive legislation, resistance became more organised, and by the 1950s the first general strike was held. The City Youth League, formed in Salisbury, merged in 1952 with the Rhodesia African National Congress (ANC) to form the Southern Rhodesia ANC, led by Joshua Nkomo. The ANC was banned in 1959 but re-emerged as the National Democratic Party (NDP).

Meanwhile, in 1953 the long-discussed and controversial political linking of Southern Rhodesia, Northern Rhodesia and Nyasaland to form the Federation of Rhodesia and Nyasaland eventually came to fruition under the premiership of Sir Garfield Todd. The Federation, a semi-independent state also known as the Central African Federation, was intended as a 'halfway house' between the old white-dominated states of southern Africa and newly independent ones with black majority rule. Its parliament was based in Salisbury (Harare), with 36 seats, six of them allocated to the black majority.

Todd was listening to the British government's desire for more equality for Africans and was, by the norms of the time, considered a liberal – but this was to be his downfall. More conservative voices representing most of the white minority became increasingly worried by the trend of concessions to the blacks, and before Todd could erode the privileged way of life any further, he was removed from office in 1958. His successor, Edgar Whitehead, was also considered too ready to accommodate the majority, so in 1962 he in turn was kicked out of office and replaced by Winston Field, leader of the right-wing Rhodesian Front.

By now the electorate (white), stunned by the trend in neighbouring states towards independence and majority rule and increasingly unsettled by the growth of unrest in their own country, certainly felt the need for a right-wing government. The NDP had led a series of strikes and protests resulting in violence from both sides, leading the government to announce a state of emergency. South Africa's apartheid system appeared to many to be the way forward, and the NDP was banned, along with all black political rallies and meetings.

THE STRUGGLE FOR INDEPENDENCE In 1964, with Southern Rhodesia doggedly pursuing its path towards becoming an independent white-ruled state, the Federation collapsed, with Northern Rhodesia and Nyasaland gaining independence as Zambia and Malawi, respectively.

Winston Field was the next political casualty. In 1964, after failing to secure independence following the Federation's dissolution, he was forced to resign in favour of the even more right-wing Ian Smith.

Smith wasted no time, knocking on British prime minister Harold Wilson's door and seeking independence, but the latter made it clear this would only be a possibility if several important conditions were met, all based around Britain's insistence that Rhodesia make significant progress towards racial equality in preparation for black majority rule. This was anathema to Smith, who was later quoted as saying, 'I don't believe in black majority rule ever in Rhodesia, not in a thousand years'. Clearly there would be no meeting of minds on this issue, so following the overwhelming mandate he received in the 1965 election, Smith in November defiantly issued his Unilateral Declaration of Independence (UDI).

The National Democratic Party, banned after the labour unrest of 1959–60, resurfaced as the Zimbabwe Africa People's Union (ZAPU), again led by the former ANC leader, Joshua Nkomo. Internal party strife led a faction to break away as the Zimbabwe African National Union (ZANU), and for the first time, its leader, Robert Gabriel Mugabe, stepped onto the world stage. ZAPU, it should be noted, was largely Ndebele in membership, while ZANU was predominantly Shona. This tribal split was later to have a massive influence on the shaping of Zimbabwe's politics. One of Smith's first acts as prime minister in 1964 was to ban both ZAPU and ZANU and imprison most of their leaders, an action that would have serious implications for the country's future. The immediate result was to push both movements outside the country, where they began to set up guerrilla forces.

Diplomatic measures to persuade Smith to back down included two rounds of talks with Wilson in 1966 and 1968 aboard British warships, but Wilson was not up to the match and failed to dent Smith's intransigence. Smith's UDI was condemned throughout the international community and, led by Britain, the UN imposed economic sanctions on Rhodesia. Far from bringing the country to its knees, however, the sanctions only made Rhodesia more self-reliant, and what it couldn't manufacture it merely imported from South Africa or Portuguese-run Mozambique (both unofficially supportive of Smith's regime), or from many other 'sanction busting' countries. Some very prominent British companies also defied the sanctions and continued to do business with Rhodesia.

In 1970 Smith declared Rhodesia a republic and issued a new constitution that contained significant concessions to electoral equality – or so he and his parliament thought. Their offer of 'equal partnership between black and white' as an alternative to majority rule was at best disingenuous, and did not go nearly far enough to satisfy Britain. More importantly, ZANU and ZAPU dismissed the new constitution out of hand. A further round of talks in 1971 was scuppered at the last minute by the surprise intervention of Bishop Abel Muzorewa's newly formed United African National Council – set up together with a cleric, the Revd Canaan Banana, to oppose Smith's new constitution.

By now, although for Ian Smith the writing was on the wall in capital letters, he appeared blind to the obvious. Throughout Africa, colonial powers had been voluntarily conceding territories or having them forcibly reclaimed. Rhodesia's own neighbours were gaining their independence and adopting majority rule (with the notable exceptions of Mozambique and South Africa) and the trend appeared unstoppable. Indeed, frustrated nationalists in his own country had already mounted isolated attacks, so the future, one would have thought, was there for all to see. It was only a matter of time before Rhodesia began its freedom struggle and descended into civil war, yet Smith refused to budge an inch, determined to cling to power.

War and negotiations (1966–79) Although ZAPU had already launched a couple of attacks on Rhodesian forces, the liberation war, also known as the Rhodesian Bush War, is generally accepted as starting in April 1966 with a ZANU attack in Chinhoyi. The next few years saw a series of guerrilla attacks that were ill-planned, unco-ordinated and largely ineffective, but during this time both party's armies had been busily recruiting and setting up camps in neighbouring countries – the Russian-trained ZANLA (ZANU) in Mozambique and the Chinese-trained ZIPRA (ZAPU) in Zambia and Tanzania. By 1973, the entire population had been politicised (frequently by force and against their will) into providing support and shelter for one or the other of the guerrilla factions, and both armies were ready to notch up the fighting. A bloody guerrilla war was well under way, forcing many whites to flee. One of Rhodesia's military responses was the formation of the extremely effective Selous Scouts, a highly unconventional force that developed a range of clandestine tactics to counter those used by the 'terrorists' (or 'terrs' as they were locally known).

Portuguese rule in Mozambique ended in 1974 and the new black, Marxist government was fully on side with Rhodesia's freedom fighters, leaving South Africa as the only country in the region supportive of the Smith regime. But that support was soon to end. South Africa realised that its policies towards its neighbour's embarrassingly illegal regime were totally out of kilter with the rest of the world so Prime Minister Vorster, together with Zambia's president Kenneth Kaunda, began pushing Rhodesia to bring the war to an end. Smith was shocked by South Africa's change of heart, especially Vorster's withdrawal of the police contingent guarding their common border. He was eventually persuaded to release various nationalist leaders from jail as a prelude to peace talks. The talks were, however, a dismal failure and only resulted in further acrimony. Fighting continued into 1975, and the next year or so saw a series of splits and realignments within the nationalist parties.

It was now America's turn to get involved. Secretary of State Henry Kissinger pressed for majority rule at a conference in Geneva at the end of 1976. Reluctantly, Smith accepted the concept of majority rule as laid down in the Kissinger plan. ZANU and ZAPU had meanwhile been persuaded to merge as the Patriotic Front (PF), but this distinctly uneasy alliance could agree on nothing other than rejection of the Kissinger plan. Neither side would agree on amendments, and talks collapsed in a stalemate.

Smith, who by now had accepted the need for change, felt that he had bent over backwards in negotiations brokered by the British and Americans, only to have each attempt fail. Now it was time for his own initiative, an 'internal settlement'. Further talks with the hard-line PF were not an option for him, and he sought agreement with the smaller, more moderate factions led by Bishop Abel Muzorewa and Ndabaningi Sithole, ZANU's founder. They agreed a proposal for a mixed black and white transitional government. An election called in April 1979 made Muzorewa the first black prime minister of Rhodesia, now to be called Zimbabwe-Rhodesia.

But it was doomed to fail. Policies were heavily weighted towards white aspirations, giving them more than a quarter of the seats in parliament and control of the police, army, civil service and judiciary. The PF was vehemently against the arrangement. Predictably, given the bias of the new government, it failed to gain international recognition. Not only had Smith's political initiative fallen at the first fence but his country was still embroiled in an increasingly bitter and bloody guerrilla war that was proving impossible for him to win.

The Lancaster House Agreement Ian Smith's situation was now desperately weak, with Rhodesia a pariah state in the international community. The British government, under newly elected prime minister Margaret Thatcher, persuaded all parties to attend talks in September 1979 at Lancaster House in London, under the guidance of Lord Carrington, Secretary of State for Foreign and Commonwealth Affairs. Also in attendance were Zambia's president Kenneth Kaunda and Tanzania's president Julius Nyerere.

Given the entrenched views of all parties, it was clear that any successful compromise would only be the result of strenuous negotiation. Mugabe dug his heels in, especially regarding land reform, but after heavy pressure from Thatcher and Carrington and a US promise of funding for land reform, an uneasy agreement was finally reached in December after more than 40 meetings.

While the Lancaster House Agreement was a major political breakthrough, many observers saw it as still too heavily skewed towards white interests. Less than 3% of the population would retain 20% of the seats in the new parliament, and there was to be no compulsory land redistribution for at least ten years. Instead land reform was to proceed on a 'willing seller, willing buyer' basis, whereby farmers prepared to sell up would be bought out by funds funnelled through the British government. Proponents held that it was a pragmatic solution offering a generous transition period, in particular for white farmers who, despite their monopoly on productive farmland, were after all feeding the whole nation and providing nearly half the country's foreign-exchange earnings.

Following the agreement a ceasefire and amnesty were declared, the UDI structure was dismantled and, with a promise of free elections within six months, international sanctions were lifted.

INDEPENDENT ZIMBABWE Under an interim constitution which gave the country its first general election, Robert Mugabe's ZANU-PF swept to power in March 1980 (4 March was election day, 18 April saw the first president of Zimbabwe sworn in), winning nearly three times as many seats as Joshua Nkomo's ZAPU-PF. The election was monitored by international observers who accepted it as fair (with a few qualifications) and Zimbabwe became the latest African state to gain recognised independence, with the Revd Canaan Banana as its first president. Mugabe served as prime minister until 1987 when he declared himself Executive President.

The first few years of independence were a honeymoon period. Mugabe became the darling of the international community, especially Britain, by appearing magnanimous in his treatment of whites. Despite having been incarcerated by Smith for ten years, his speeches stressed that there would be a place for everyone in the new Zimbabwe, with no recriminations; indeed he even appointed white ministers in his cabinet. Britain breathed a sigh of relief and embarked on a programme of aid and investment, and the economy took off.

But while Mugabe conducted his love affair with the outside world, pressing matters were occupying his mind at home. Despite having trounced Nkomo in the polls, Mugabe continued to view ZAPU as a threat, especially after allegations of a ZIPRA plot to overthrow him. He ordered the arrest of prominent ZAPU supporters, dismissed Nkomo from his cabinet and removed ex-ZIPRA commanders from the army.

When in 1983 factional guerrilla fighting resumed in Matabeleland (ZAPU's Ndebele homeland) Mugabe sent in his North Korean-trained Fifth Brigade on a programme of what would today be termed 'ethnic cleansing'. Nkomo fled to England and for two years Operation Gukurahundi ('spring rain' or 'blowing the chaff from the wheat') saw the murderous Fifth Brigade commit widespread human rights abuses, including torture, rape and the purging of whole villages. Casualties were estimated in the hundreds of thousands, with up to 20,000 dead, yet the world, including the British government which was well aware of the situation, averted its gaze. What is now being described as an act of genocide went largely unreported. After Gukurahundi, Nkomo was allowed to return, and ZANU paid lip service to a reconciliation with ZAPU, a process that culminated in the merging of both parties.

Apart from Gukurahundi's devastating effects on the Ndbele, and the introduction of universal suffrage, the first decade of independence offered little change for the majority of the people in Zimbabwe, black or white, because the Lancaster House Agreement's ten-year transition period virtually ensured that the status quo was maintained. That said, it did result in the growth of an economy previously in decline and the emergence of a substantial black middle class.

Land 'reform' (1980–2000) The Lancaster House Agreement aimed to assist land reform by redistributing productive land to impoverished blacks, using the system of 'willing buyer, willing seller'. This was to be funded largely by and through Great Britain.

While some white farmers were not exactly 'willing sellers', others appreciated the situation and went to the first stage in selling their properties. The law stated that any farm to be sold first had to be offered to the government, which would then issue an 'intention to purchase' or 'decline to purchase' notice. In the latter case the farm could then be sold on the open market. Overwhelmingly the government issued 'decline to purchase' notices. It goes without saying that the impoverished masses meant to be the beneficiaries couldn't even begin to think about purchasing a farm on the open market. By the end of the 1980s less than half the targeted 162,000 families had been resettled, but not because farmers were refusing to sell their farms.

After ten years of independence, the government could at last cast off the shackles of the Lancaster House Agreement, and swiftly passed a constitutional amendment allowing for the confiscation of land, with 'fair' compensation but no right of appeal. This was followed by the 1992 Land Acquisition Act, which effectively did away with fair compensation and resulted in the confiscation of nearly 1,500 productive farms. The concept of voluntary land redistribution had failed through a combination of government unwillingness to spend the money allocated for the purpose – and to a certain extent by landowners' intransigence.

The land grabs started and with them the spectre of this agricultural nation losing a large proportion of its foreign earnings as well as its reputation as the breadbasket of southern Africa. International alarm bells started ringing, but Britain was already concerned, having given Zimbabwe £44 million to help fund land reform, not to mention tens of millions more in other aid, with only a dismal number of resettled families to show for it. (ZANU-PF claimed it had only received £17 million.)

Far worse, it is alleged that instead of benefiting the landless poor, many of these farms were being given to Mugabe's supporters. In his book *Cry Zimbabwe*, Peter Stiff (South African author specialising in southern African political and military subjects) cites a report drawn up by Margaret Dongo, President of the Zimbabwe Union of Democrats, in which she lists 413 farms and their new owners – MPs, cabinet ministers, lawyers, police officials, military officers, senior civil servants, influential businessmen and others whose new farms had effectively been paid for by the British taxpayer. In view of this, Britain pulled the plug on further funding and in doing so became Mugabe's number one enemy.

The relatively few poor people who did benefit from resettlement received no financial assistance or agricultural training, so without the wherewithal to purchase equipment, seed and fertiliser, they were condemned to a future of subsistence farming on formerly productive land. They were not given title to their new land so were unable to use it as collateral to raise loans.

By 1998 dispossessed farmers had stopped paying back the bonds on their properties in sufficient numbers and Zimbabwe's banks were suffering vast losses. The World Bank and the EU had frozen aid and loans. The loss of productive farming (made worse by a disastrous drought) was turning Zimbabwe into a food-importing country for the first time, and eventually government realised that something had to be done. Attempts to court popularity by confiscating white-owned land were backfiring spectacularly in terms of the country's economy. A Land Conference was convened in Harare, attended by Britain, international donors and investors. Together with the Zimbabwean government they drew up a list of principles acceptable to all parties and promised more aid to get land reform back on track. But by 2000 the plan had ground to a halt.

Politics and the economy (1980–2000) Operation Gukurahundi had battered the Ndebele and left a brooding resentment towards the president and ZANU-PF. In the first general election since independence, in June 1985, ZANU is alleged to have used the widespread violent tactics that were to become an electoral hallmark. Mugabe increased his majority with blacks, although voters in Matabeleland retained all of their 15 seats.

Drawn-out, difficult negotiations over the following two years resulted in December 1987 in the merger of ZANU-PF and ZAPU-PF, with the disappearance of the ZAPU name altogether. That same month a constitutional amendment was passed abolishing the position of prime minister, and Mugabe assumed power as Zimbabwe's first Executive President. Canaan Banana, who had been instrumental in the merger talks, stepped down as president, not to appear again until the late 1990s, mired in scandal and convicted of sodomy, a crime in Zimbabwe to this day. The constitutional change also removed the Lancaster House guarantee of 20 seats for white parties.

These years saw a continuing spiral of economic decline. Staple commodities were hit, with the dwindling of the asbestos market, fluctuations in world tobacco prices and a drop in the value of gold all taking a heavy toll. Zimbabwe's government had become a byword for corruption in world media, with many major players allegedly squirrelling away vast sums from the national coffers. In an attempt to recoup some losses government introduced ever more punitive business taxes that actually reduced revenues even further, as companies were forced into tax evasion in order to stay afloat. The 1990s were years of growing unrest as the deteriorating economy began having a direct effect on the population. Late in the decade a series of events would eventually rock the country and turn it into an economic basket case.

War veterans The Zimbabwe National Liberation War Veterans Association was notionally an organisation of ex-combatants from the recent war, numbering some 50,000. After being demobilised in 1980 they received a two-year gratuity package that was quickly eroded by inflation. Fuelled by what they saw as politicians and others growing rich around them, they began a series of violent demonstrations in a demand for more cash for themselves. Their leader, Chenjerai Hunzvi (who preferred to be known as 'Hitler' Hunzvi), was ironically no more an actual war veteran than were many of his membership: he had spent the entire liberation war studying medicine in Poland, while the very young age of many of the cash claimants suggests that they would have been mere embryos or toddlers at the time of the conflict. For this reason, the movement is commonly referred to as 'so-called' War Vets.

Although the treasury could ill afford it, rather than alienate this large and potentially dangerous association, Mugabe took the opposite course and got them on his side with an amazingly generous handout. From December 1997 each was awarded a further gratuity of ZIM$50,000 and a tax-free monthly pension of ZIM$2,000 – at a time when the average black wage was about ZIM$1,000 per month.

Stay-aways To help pay for this crippling new drain on the country's finances, personal income tax, fuel tax and other taxes were raised, but for the first time the financially beleaguered population rebelled, obeying the trade union movement's call for a one-day 'stay-away' or national strike in December 1997. Parliament promptly dropped most of the new tax hikes. Spurred on by ever-inflating prices and the success of the strike, the Zimbabwe Congress of Trade Unions again challenged the government to address the high taxes and spiralling inflation situation. The government did nothing so once again the nation took the day off work – in fact two days – on 3–4 March 1998.

Interests in the Congo Despite its economic woes, Zimbabwe was an oasis of tranquillity compared with other parts of the continent. The fallout from the Hutu–Tutsi genocide in Rwanda left the region in turmoil, during which rebel leader Laurent Kabila assumed power in the Congo in 1988, sparking further conflict within and outside that country. Neighbouring countries took sides according to their own interests, but President Mugabe decided to enter the fray by providing military assistance to Kabila. There appeared to be no political or strategic advantage to be gained by this but Mugabe's enthusiasm for the venture soon became clear. Put simply, he was committing his country's troops and equipment to keeping Kabila in power in return for a raft of lucrative business deals. These involved the wholesale extraction of diamonds, gold, copper, cobalt and even timber. The government admitted to pouring ZIM$1 million per day into the Congo, a massive drain on rapidly dwindling resources.

ZIMBABWE AFTER 2000 Zimbabwe's constitution, based on the amended Lancaster House Agreement, was generally being seen as outdated. Accordingly, the government drafted a new constitution that included a proposal to limit the presidency to two successive five-year terms – but this was not to be retroactive, potentially allowing Mugabe to stay in power until 2010. This increase in presidential tenancy was to be tempered by creation of the post of prime minister, who would assume day-to-day control of the country. Another crucial aspect of the proposed constitution was the power of government to repossess white-owned land without any obligation to pay compensation. If compensation were to be paid, it would have to come from the UK, Mugabe stated. He believed this proposal would be popular in the rural areas where he enjoyed most of his support, so, despite a parliamentary majority sufficiently large to pass the new constitution, he decided to hold a referendum in 2000. This proved a disastrous misjudgement when the count revealed a 55% to 45% vote against him, albeit with a turnout of just over 20%. Mugabe had suffered the first major blow of his rule, and the repercussions as he took revenge were to set this troubled country on another round of turmoil.

The Movement for Democratic Change Countrywide public consultation meetings were conducted in the run-up to the new constitution, with many groups voicing concern over the increasing powers to be granted to the executive presidency.

One result of this process was the formation of a new political party, the Movement for Democratic Change (MDC), under the leadership of Morgan Tsvangirai, a prominent trade union leader. Having gobbled up the main opposition party, ZAPU, Mugabe was on track for his oft-stated goal of a one-party state, so the emergence of this new opposition was, to say the least, inconvenient. Tsvangirai's moderate approach appealed to the educated and urban population, while most of ZANU-PF's support came from rural areas where the impoverished people were more easily manipulated.

Land invasions The referendum was seen by all as a personal defeat for Mugabe and led to widespread celebration at home and abroad as the beginning of the end of his reign. The embattled president had to do something quickly. He remained convinced that the confiscation of white-owned land would regain support, despite popular rejection of a referendum that would have permitted just that.

His earlier generosity to the war veterans put them firmly on his side, and they were now unleashed in a countrywide rampage of violence aimed at the country's 4,000 commercial farmers. Many were given just hours to leave their properties and, at any sign of resistance, were beaten or hacked with *pangas* (machetes). Over several years around a dozen farmers and as many as 100 farm workers were killed. Animals were slaughtered or left to starve, pets and horses killed and homes ransacked or torched. Police stood by, having been ordered not to intervene. About 300,000 farm workers lost their jobs and over a million people were displaced, according to the UN.

Unlike Gukurahundi, with whites among the victims this hit the world's media. Less noted was the fact that many times more blacks – farm workers and their families – were suffering as badly as or worse than their employers (many of whom were able to leave the country and set up again with money they had previously exported). Over the four years following the referendum, all but about 300 farmers were forced off their land. Asset stripping was the name of the game, with few if any of the land recipients experienced or even interested in farming. The resulting dramatic fall-off in agricultural production was the single most important factor in the catastrophic economic decline that was about to unfold.

The presidential election of 2002 The increasing strength of the MDC posed a real threat to Mugabe, and his 2000 poll failure drove him to employ a range of methods to ensure that he won the presidential election to be held in 2002. Among the allegations were widespread intimidation and violence targeted at opposition officials and potential voters alike. War veterans and youth militia roamed the country, seeking out anyone who could not produce a ZANU-PF membership card and, using beatings, rape, torture or murder, 'persuading' villagers to vote for Mugabe. Suspected MDC supporters were rounded up and sent to militia camps for enforced 're-education'. Less violent allegations included tampering with voter rolls, banning opposition rallies, muzzling independent media and simply rigging the results as necessary. It was not uncommon for the total of votes for Mugabe in a constituency to greatly exceed the actual number of voters. Drought and reduced agricultural production meant that the population was becoming increasingly hungry, with government-controlled grain stocks reportedly being routinely allocated to card-holding ZANU-PF members only.

Not surprisingly, Mugabe gained a sizeable majority. Nearly all of Tsvangirai's votes came from urban areas, less susceptible to ZANU-PF's tactics. Although Mugabe's hand-picked election observers, mostly from sympathetic African countries (including South Africa) and Russia, declared the polls 'free and fair', independent Western observers said they were flawed, and there was widespread international condemnation. The UK, EU, Australia and the US refused to recognise the result and applied personal sanctions on Mugabe and key officials, focusing on travel bans and the freezing of bank accounts. The Southern African Development Community's Parliamentary Forum also declared that the election was not an expression of the people's will. The Commonwealth was poised to suspend Zimbabwe's membership when Mugabe pulled out voluntarily.

Murambatsvina and a split MDC In what is widely regarded as a government sting just before the 2002 presidential election, Morgan Tsvangirai was shown on video talking of plans to overthrow Mugabe, whereupon he was arrested and tried for treason. Although he was acquitted the following year, this harmed him politically and led to the first split within his party, with an opposition faction led by Welshman Ncube.

By employing tactics similar to those of 2002, ZANU-PF gained a two-thirds majority in the March 2005 parliamentary elections. Again international observers declared them flawed.

In May 2005 Mugabe embarked on Operation Murambatsvina. Roughly translated as 'clearing away the filth', Murambatsvina was ostensibly an attempt to rid urban streets of unsightly shacks, illegal trading stalls and the criminality that had blossomed as the poor migrated from rural areas into towns. But it served to punish urban people who had voted for the opposition and to drive them into the rural areas where their votes could be more easily manipulated. Police (usually drafted in from other areas) forced people to destroy their own properties before evicting them from town with only the possessions they could carry. Many were not economic refugees but long-term residents with established businesses, albeit mostly in the informal sector. Swathes of the country's townships were destroyed. Many of the homes were solid, brick structures, hardly the targeted 'shacks'.

Estimates vary, but the UN has suggested that 700,000 people were rendered jobless and a further 2.4 million countrywide were affected. The government hindered NGOs' emergency aid operations, and responded to criticism by setting up isolated 'transit camps' that were often little more than fenced-off areas with no shelter or facilities. All this happened during Zimbabwe's cold winter months.

Yet more elections loomed for late September 2005, this time for the newly reinstated upper house, the Senate. The now-split MDC was unable to decide whether to field candidates. Ncube said 'yes' while Tsvangirai argued that the MDC should not endorse another corrupt election. Ncube narrowly won a vote amongst party leaders but Tsvangirai, as party president, stood firm, and the MDC all but boycotted the election. With no meaningful opposition, ZANU-PF romped home. The MDC, seen by many to have scored an own goal, was in disarray.

Economic and political crisis By March 2006, annual inflation exceeded 900%, and Zimbabwe dollars were becoming useless. By early 2009, on average prices were doubling every 1.3 days under an almost unfathomable inflation rate and the final issue of Zimbabwe dollars saw banknotes with a denomination of 100 trillion dollars. Shop shelves were routinely empty and people had resorted to barter. The situation of simply printing ever-increasing amounts of money was unsustainable so in February of that year the Zimbabwe dollar collapsed completely and trading in a range of foreign currencies was permitted, with the US dollar effectively becoming the official currency.

While Western governments became increasingly vocal in condemnation of the Mugabe regime, he continued to enjoy regional support, with the exception of close neighbours Botswana and Zambia. Throughout this period South Africa's president, Thabo Mbeki, despite being in a position to exert strong pressure on Mugabe, steadfastly stood by his policy of 'quiet diplomacy'. Increasingly the media accused him of doing nothing, and latterly of actively supporting Mugabe.

The year 2007 saw an increasing number of measures interpreted by many as signs of desperation. There was a major crackdown on opposition rallies, including those of WOZA, the leading women's rights organisation. The government admitted jamming hostile foreign radio stations, then passed a bill to allow state monitoring of private phone calls, faxes and emails. In an effort to weed out international charities and humanitarian agencies deemed hostile, all were deregistered and forced to re-apply to operate in the country. Tough new security and media laws were introduced to stifle opposition. A bill was mooted allowing Zimbabwe to take majority ownership of foreign companies, including mines and banks, although in 2009 it had yet to be signed into law.

Elections of 2008 February 2008 saw Simba Makoni, a senior member of ZANU-PF, announce his intention to stand against Mugabe in the first internal presidential challenge in two decades. Although Makoni stood no chance in the polls, his open stand was seen as a breakthrough. The two MDC factions – Tsvangirai's MDC T and the breakaway MDC M, led by its newly elected president, Arthur Mutambara, polled separately but agreed to combine their results for the parliamentary vote. (Welshman Ncube retook leadership of the MDC Mutambara faction in January 2011.)

After suspicions of widespread irregularities in both the presidential and the parliamentary polls, the results were painfully slow to be declared. Preliminary results suggested that MDC had won 60% of parliamentary seats and that Tsvangirai had beaten Mugabe with just over 50% in the presidential vote. On 26 April election officials announced that the combined MDC had won a historic parliamentary victory. On 2 May officials said Tsvangirai had won 47.9%, more than Mugabe, but as this was below the required 50% threshold, a run-off was required. This was fixed for 27 June. Tsvangirai was detained yet again and Mugabe, threatening that war vets would take up arms if he lost, vowed that MDC would never rule.

During this time the international media reported hundreds of opposition supporters and officials being detained and frequently beaten, some to death. Mounting violence led Tsvangirai to announce that he was pulling out of the run-off in order to put an end to the violence. The UN Security Council unanimously condemned Zimbabwe's 'campaign of violence'.

Mugabe held the run-off anyway. Voters had their fingers dyed red and those found without the stain were either forced to vote or faced recrimination. Despite this there was believed to be wholesale spoiling of votes, but yet again Mugabe emerged victorious.

Britain and the US spearheaded a campaign to persuade Mugabe to step down, but a proposed UN resolution to impose new sanctions was vetoed by Russia and China as well as by Mbeki's South Africa.

The Unity Government 2009 onwards In July 2008, talks led by Mbeki to negotiate a power-sharing agreement raised hopes. On 15 September Mugabe and Tsvangirai signed a draft deal known as the Global Political Agreement (GPA): Mugabe would remain as president and Tsvangirai was offered the post of prime minister, although they failed to reach agreement on the allocation of cabinet posts.

Wrangling continued into the new year, with Tsvangirai coming under pressure from Mbeki and fellow SADC (Southern African Development Community) leaders to accept Mugabe's cabinet proposals, which included his retention of army, police, CIO and finance posts. In January 2009, Tsvangirai announced his party's readiness to join a power-sharing government (Government of National Unity) and on 11 February he was sworn in as prime minister. The following month Tsvangirai suffered a personal tragedy when his wife was killed in a car collision while he was driving.

Political and economic progress since the introduction of the unity government has been a mixed bag. On the one hand, the introduction of the US dollar has brought a large measure of stability to the country with sections of the population benefiting in terms of food security, increased employment, prosperity and a general sense of calm and normality in the country. (Although, as always in these situations, those in poverty are the last to see improvements and many are still patiently waiting, as formal employment remains an unattainable goal.)

On the political front, however, while there was an outward semblance of peace, the two parties were simply co-existing in an extremely uneasy truce. While ZANU and the president retained power over the police, security services and the armed forces, leaving Tsvangirai's MDC apparently relatively powerless, in reality every measure that was to be passed by parliament required the agreement of both sides, giving the prime minister an effective power of veto. In practical terms this resulted in a stalemate. The overarching issue was future elections. Both parties wanted elections to achieve a decisive result for themselves but while MDC insisted (with SADC backing) that they could only be conducted after agreed reforms that guaranteed free and fair elections had been incorporated in a new constitution, ZANU and the president wanted to push ahead with elections without the constitutional reforms. One of the major issues at the time of writing was the controversial Indigenisation Bill requiring foreign businesses to grant 51% of their shareholding to local investors. Despite the fact that MDC steadfastly refused to agree to this, foreign investment in the country dropped off dramatically, the Stock Exchange fell to dramatic lows and local investment drained out of the country resulting in an almost completely stagnated economy. In November 2012 though, the world's number one platinum mining company signed a deal handing over the majority of its shares to indigenous Zimbabweans, an act that became a precursor to many further deals, a major boost to the president's policies.

It's interesting at this stage to note how regional politics altered after South Africa's change of presidency from Mbeki to Zuma, both of whom acted as mediators in SADC negotiations with Zimbabwe. While the former is now being described as a Mugabe supporter and apologist and carried SADC with him, Zuma is apparently taking a harder line and as his country is by far the most important member of SADC (and the most affected by the Zimbabwe situation) the majority view in SADC has now become that constitutional change must be implemented before elections. In early 2013, both parties agreed the draft constitution which was then due for a public referendum in March. A higher than expected turnout resulted in an overwhelmingly positive vote, paving the way for elections to take place, with the timeframe of June to September being widely mooted.

GOVERNMENT AND POLITICS

Zimbabwe is a presidential republic with a bicameral parliament consisting of an upper house (the Senate) and a lower house (the House of Assembly). Parliament and the executive president are elected by universal franchise every five years.

If no presidential candidate gains an absolute majority (over 50% of the vote), a further run-off election is required.

The Senate has 93 members. Of these, 60 are elected by popular vote to represent the provinces; ten are provincial governors nominated by the president; 16 seats are occupied by traditional chiefs elected by the Council of Chiefs; two are held by the president and deputy president of the Council of Chiefs; and five are appointed by the president.

The House of Assembly has 210 members with 200 elected for five-year terms by their constituencies and ten appointed by the president.

The current president, Robert Mugabe of ZANU-PF, has held the post since 1987 and was re-elected in 2008. The opposition MDC, comprising two factions, now holds the majority of seats in the House of Assembly and its leader, Morgan Tsvangirai, occupies the post of prime minister, in a power-sharing agreement brokered in early 2009.

ECONOMY

Although the introduction of the land-reform programme in 2000 is often quoted as the trigger for the collapse of Zimbabwe's once-vibrant economy, the country's decline was already well under way prior to that (see pages 19 and 22–3). Zimbabwe's exceptionally fertile land traditionally provided the basis for the country's wealth. Subsistence farming kept the rural population well fed, while commercial farms provided export income from a wide spectrum of agricultural products, including principally tobacco, coffee, tea, sugar, cut flowers, cotton, fruit and vegetables. Maize was produced in sufficiently high volumes for Zimbabwe to be called 'the breadbasket of southern Africa'. Beef and animal farming in general were all major foreign currency earners. Mineral resources were abundant along the central Great Dyke region, with gold, nickel, diamonds, chromite, asbestos, coal, iron and tin fuelling a mining industry that thrived for decades. Forestry in the Eastern Highlands produced timber for both pulp and the building industry. Tourism was a major foreign currency earner contributing close to 10% of the GDP.

Today, the picture is very different. Commercial agriculture has suffered a steep decline and Zimbabwe is now a net importer of foodstuffs with rural populations dependent on foreign aid. Tobacco farming has, however, started to revive and with such vast mineral wealth the mining industry offers great potential if the revenues are allowed to benefit the country. With the notable exception of Victoria Falls and a few other hot spots foreign tourism has yet to recover in the rest of the country, from a peak of 1.4 million visitors in 1999 to a low of just over 200,000 ten years later. Formal unemployment is close to 90%, domestic manufacturing output is negligible but imports from China, from textiles and clothing to cars, are soaring. Recent finds of alluvial diamonds near Mutare, one of the world's richest deposits and easily mined, could still make a considerable contribution towards rebuilding Zimbabwe's economy. Although there is still wholesale profiteering and smuggling out of the country there are signs that an element of official control is beginning to exert itself (see box, page 344).

Life for urban Zimbabweans has begun to improve dramatically but there was great concern about the rural population, many of whom initially had little or no access to US dollars. Today though, although poverty is rife in rural areas, the US dollar has at least given people much needed financial stability.

In towns, almost as soon as the US dollar was introduced by the Government of National Unity, shop shelves filled, fuel stations across the country had stocks

What did hyperinflation mean to the ordinary people? As inflation spiralled out of control the Reserve Bank began printing banknotes of ever-higher denominations – millions, billions and then trillions – and when it all got completely out of hand the bank would simply knock a dozen or so zeros off the currency and issue a new set of notes. A direct result of this was that people's savings were rendered useless, plunging them further into poverty.

By early 2009, no fewer than 22 zeros had been cancelled. The largest note to be issued just before its collapse was 100 trillion Zimbabwe dollars (14 zeroes). It became impossible to get a meaningful inflation rate, but in February 2009 one financial website quoted the inflation rate at 516 quintillion % (516 followed by 18 zeros) annually. Government attempted to blame shopkeepers for inflation and in 2007 decreed that prices of every commodity and service be slashed by 50%, forcing retailers to sell goods below cost. If they closed up shop, they were jailed. By mid-2007, over 7,600 shopkeepers and business leaders had been detained under suspicion of inflating prices. Economic refugees (some legal, most illegal) flooded across the border to South Africa in their thousands and those that were lucky enough to find work in that increasingly hostile country sent money and goods back across the border to their families. Were it not for this massive influx of informal cash into the country, the plight of Zimbabwe's population, bad enough as it already was, would doubtless have reached far greater proportions.

The Zimbabwe dollar had become virtually useless, yet it was illegal to hold or deal in foreign currencies. Nevertheless, trading in US dollars had quietly become the norm for many, so in 2008 the government finally relented and made it legal for businesses to use foreign currencies. By February 2009, the Zimbabwe dollar had completely collapsed and the US dollar, and to a lesser extent the South African rand, had been accepted as the official hard currency. Now, with a meaningful currency officially in use the runaway inflation rate immediately came to a dramatic halt. (Amazingly, this author noted in a news report in late 2012 that Zimbabwe's official annual inflation rate was lower than UK's!)

of petrol and diesel and the country slowly returned to a semblance of normality. As this book goes to print in 2013 there is no obvious evidence of the amazing financial collapse of the previous decade although it will be some time before industry catches up to its previous healthy state.

PEOPLE

Zimbabwe's population saw exceptional growth during the 20th century, rising from around 500,000–600,000 at the start of the century to just under 13 million in 2000, with a growth rate of around 3%. Following the economic meltdown that started around 2000, resulting in a steady out-migration of up to four million, perhaps a third of the black population is believed to have sought a better life outside Zimbabwe. A high proportion of whites also left.

AIDS has taken a huge toll with an estimated adult HIV infection rate of over 14.3% in 2010. The last (very unreliable) census was in 2002, so only rough estimates can be made of the current population. A national census was due to be conducted in mid-2012 but this was suspended amidst controversy that the results might be manipulated for political ends. One 2011 estimate put the population figure at just over 12 million but this is generally thought to be an overestimate based on the expectation of large numbers of returning refugees. Life expectancy reached an all-time low of 37 and 34 years for men and women, respectively, during the 2000s, the lowest in the world for a country not at war but given the recent economic upturn this has already risen to 49 years. Some 38% of the population is urbanised.

ETHNIC GROUPS Black ethnic groups constitute some 98.5% of the population. Whites, mainly of British origin, have left the country in significant numbers and now probably form only 0.5%. Most of the remainder are of Chinese or Indian origin. About 70% of the population lives in rural areas.

All of Zimbabwe's indigenous people are of Bantu origin. The Shona, who form nearly 80% of the population, have a strong regional clan structure, with six main groupings: Zezuru, based in the *highveld* around Harare; Manyika and Ndau, in the east of the country; Korekore, in the north and northeast; Karanga, in the Midlands; and smaller Rozwi groupings. The majority of Shona live in Mashonaland – the north, central and eastern two-thirds of the country.

The Ndebele, descendants of South Africa's Zulus, occupy Matabeleland in two tribal groups, the Ndebele and the Kalanga, in the southern and western parts of the country, centred on Bulawayo. They comprise around 14% of the population.

Smaller ethnic groups include the Batonga, south of the Zambezi around Binga (isolated from the majority of their people in Zambia by the flooding of the river to form Lake Kariba); the Venda, a predominantly South African people centred in the south around Beitbridge; and the Shangaan of Gonarezhou, whose traditional land extends into Mozambique and South Africa.

LANGUAGE

While English is Zimbabwe's official language, it is only used as a first language by white Zimbabweans and in government, legal and business environments. Shona, given that people's numerical dominance of the population, is the most widely spoken language, with separate dialects in use by the subgroups mentioned above.

Sindebele (or Ndebele), the language of the Ndebele people, is a 'click' language introduced by the migrating Nguni people from Zulu-speaking areas further south, and is completely different from Shona (see pages 367–8).

RELIGION

Zimbabwe's religious split is broadly 50% syncretic (a blend of Christianity and traditional religion), 25% Christian and 24% traditional, with Islam and others making up the remaining 1%. Recent years have seen a rapid escalation of evangelical worship with Apostolic and Pentecostal groups gaining increased popularity. Two very large religious groups that stand out to the visitor are the Vapostori and the Zion Christian Church. The former mix traditional religion with Christianity and can be seen in groups worshipping outdoors, often in very isolated locations wearing white robes, while the latter is a very popular messianic religion and its devotees can be recognised by the metal star badge worn medal-style on a dark green cloth background on their everyday clothes.

TRADITIONAL RELIGION Religion in its widest sense impacts on simply every aspect of daily life. Shona and Ndebele traditional religions recognise a supreme being that created the universe and is ever-present, overseeing the everyday lives of the people. The Shona god is called Mwari, the Ndebele's uMlimu. There is no clear equivalent of what we know as prayer, but rather a complex process involving a chain of intermediaries.

People believe the spirits of deceased ancestors return to the community and have a powerful influence on all aspects of family and community life. These ancestors are often from only two or three generations back and it is via these benevolent guardian spirits that communication with Mwari is made. Health, harvest and drought are common reasons to involve Mwari or uMlimu. In addition there are malevolent spirits whose influence is manifest in bad luck, illness or death. These spirits may occasionally be invoked through diviners perhaps to punish a perceived wrongdoer or to avenge a death. But here too, communication with ancestral spirits is accomplished through spirit mediums, people of considerable power and influence in the community.

The dead are usually buried close to the traditional home, with the grave being both sacred and feared for its association with its occupying spirit. Mourning lasts about a year, during which time ceremonies are held to appease the spirit in preparation for it to become a family guardian.

MISSIONARY INFLUENCE The Revd Robert Moffat opened Zimbabwe's first mission station close to Bulawayo in 1859, under the auspices of the London Missionary Society, and in subsequent decades they attempted to introduce not only a new religion but an alien culture that included commerce, education and Christian morality. Various Protestant groups continue to send missionaries to Zimbabwe, although none are today as numerous as the Catholics. As elsewhere in Africa, people associated missionaries and their religion with wealth, envying their fancy clothes and guns, but have been reluctant to give up their centuries-old beliefs. Many have taken a pragmatic course and assimilated elements of Christianity into their traditional beliefs. This complex, syncretic religion serves half of Zimbabwe's population today.

EDUCATION

Over 90% of Zimbabwe's population is literate in English, and the once-excellent education system has undoubtedly given its people the best command of the English language in the whole of Africa. This is a legacy of the pre-independence emphasis on educating the black majority and was continued for some years by Robert Mugabe, who was a teacher in his earlier years and gave English teaching a high priority. In practical terms, English-speaking visitors to Zimbabwe will have no problem making themselves understood in towns and tourist areas, although they may struggle in more remote rural areas.

Recent economic circumstances have led to a drastic reduction in education as rural schools close and children are sent to work, so the impressive literacy statistics are expected to be temporarily hit. Mozambique aside, Zimbabwe is surrounded by similarly English-speaking countries, so other European languages are hardly spoken except in some larger hotels and lodges.

Some people, generally older men in rural areas, speak Chilapalapa – or Silolo as it is sometimes known – a Creole language mixing Bantu, English and Afrikaans, developed to enable employers to communicate with their staff (Bantu languages are difficult for most Westerners to learn). Its use tends to cause offence among educated people (most of the population), who associate it with the old colonial master–servant relationship. See the box in *Chapter 3*, page 144, for more about Chilapalapa.

CULTURE

Zimbabwe's culture has a long oral tradition of folklore and storytelling which, far from being mere entertainment, maintained a sense of cultural identity by keeping each generation in touch with its historical and ancestral past. Storytelling 'performances' were often augmented with music, song and dance. Around the middle of the 20th century, aided by outside influence as well as encouragement from within the country, the various elements of oral tradition began to separate out to form what we now see as all the individual genres of modern performing arts, yet they continue to draw heavily on traditional themes often producing a fascinating blend of old and new.

Zimbabwe's key traditional musical instruments – drums, *mbira* and the marimba – are still very evident in some modern musical forms but are frequently augmented by electric guitars to produce a fusion style of old and new.

Sunguru music emerged as Zimbabwe's home-grown, modern musical style in the early 1980s with notable recent performers like Alick Macheso and Tongai Moyo, while *chimurenga* (socially aware), *jit* (electric pop) and *rumba* (Zimbabwe style) all emerged towards the end of the last century bringing fame to Thomas Mapfumo, The Bhundu Boys and Leonard Zhakata respectively, among of course, many others. Gospel remains extremely popular while more recently the music scene has drawn heavily on Western influences producing a rap, R&B and hip hop-based variation called urban grooves.

Musical lyrics (in common with Zimbabwean poetry) frequently carry heavy political themes. Older songs reflect the trials of the independence struggle with an almost seamless follow through to today, picking up the social issues that have dominated the last 30 years. Interestingly for 'protest' lyrics, both sides of the political divide are represented.

Music and poetry are frequently combined: look out for a performance by Albert Nyathi, Zimbabwe's foremost dub poet who combines social angst with humour and controversy, using blues and jazz music as backing, to scintillating effect.

As with the other art forms, dance is extremely popular in Zimbabwe but until very recently was almost invariably associated with ceremony and religion rather than entertainment. That is still the case though it's a vibrant scene and change is constantly being incorporated. So while modern influences are gradually being introduced, altering the appearance and occasion for the dance, the traditional significance of the movements and the dances tends to remain as of old. So in many of today's performances you will see modern sets and costumes utilised to stunning effect to bring ancient and traditional dances into the 21st century.

Zimbabwe's literature post independence has seen an explosion of black writers, too prolific to detail. Many chronicle the immediate pre- and post-independence periods and bring a fascinating, hitherto unseen black insight into both rural and urban conditions during these periods of political turmoil. In typical Zimbabwe style, many writers use comedy to bring to life what would otherwise be a harrowing narrative. There's a burgeoning selection of short-story anthologies (see *Appendix 3*, page 372) but it can be frustrating trying to find examples as the country's bookshops are woefully understocked (at the time of writing). Craft and curio shops in Harare, Bulawayo and Victoria Falls are often good sources for these books. Check the websites of Weaver Press (*www.weaverpresszimbabwe.com*) and 'amaBooks (*www.amabooks.net*) for titles and availability.

SAFARI DRIVE

The ultimate way to explore Zimbabwe

Safari Drive has been organising tailor-made, self drive safaris in Zimbabwe since 1993.

With expert knowledge of the roads, driving conditions and routes, Safari Drive gives you the freedom and security to embark on an adventure of a lifetime. Self drive safaris offer versatile, independent travel with the freedom to explore at your own pace.

Personal itineraries are tailored to your time frame, level of 4x4 driving experience and budget.

Choose from a range of accommodation from luxury lodges to camping

Safari Drive trips include:

- Expedition equipped Land Rovers for up to four people
- In-country briefing & backup
- Satellite phone
- Handbook

- Roof tent
- Water tanks
- Satellite navigation with Tracks 4 Africa
- All camping equipment

+44 (0)1488 71140 | info@safaridrive.com
www.safaridrive.com AITO assured

2

Natural History and Conservation

For more on wildlife in Zimbabwe, check out Bradt's Southern African Wildlife. *See page v for a special discount offer.*

FLORA

Although a country's vegetation can be a fascinating subject in its own right, its importance for most visitors to Zimbabwe is its role in the types of animals and birds to be found in any given place. Navigating around the subject can be a semantic minefield, as it is common to find English, Afrikaans and Latin names all in the same sentence. Moreover there is much duplication, with the same subject frequently described with several different names.

LANTANA: A VERY UNDESIRABLE ALIEN

Originating in South America and exported as an ornamental plant, *Lantana camara* has become one of the most invasive plants in the tropical world. Despite its pretty pink, white and blue flowers, this rampantly spreading plant, having escaped from early gardens, has become a real monster bush across southern Africa.

It forms dense, thorny thickets and monopolises the space around it by releasing chemicals that prevent the germination and growth of most other plants, either natural or cultivated. The leaves are highly toxic to herbivores and although some goats will eat the berries, no other land animals will touch it. Birds, on the other hand, love the berries, and therefore spread the seeds far and wide. Lantana also reproduces by sending out suckers and prickly creepers, quickly smothering the surrounding vegetation, to the extent that it's become an extremely serious ecological problem. Not only are indigenous plants being wiped out but so too are the insects and birds that rely on them.

Control is difficult, expensive and labour-intensive. Slash-and-burn only stimulates the growth of suckers while chemical methods are generally too costly. Dedicated teams work tirelessly to eradicate lantana on a local basis, but so widespread is the problem that it's like trying to hold back the tide. Currently, biological methods are being trialled – flies, moths, beetles and bugs are being imported and tested against the menace – although this is controversial as no-one can be sure that these foreign critters won't develop into undesirable aliens themselves.

Recent commercial developments may provide the answer. Lantana is now being given a value: it can be turned into charcoal products to form *braai* briquettes or, more importantly, affordable cooking fuel for rural communities. Not only does this new initiative offer a commercial reason for harvesting the weed, but its use may also slow the destruction of fuel hardwoods.

THE BIOMES OF ZIMBABWE The word 'biome' is used to describe a specific ecosystem and is generally defined by its most prominent vegetation type, be it trees, grassland, shrubs or a combination. This in turn determines the types of animals that live there. The type of biome depends on factors including climate, elevation, topography and soil.

Zimbabwe includes three types of biome: arid savanna (*lowveld*), moist savanna (*highveld*) and forest. If you overlay a map of these biomes on a contour map of the country you will find a high degree of correlation. Arid savanna is found on the low-lying southern, western and northern fringes of the country; moist savanna covers the central region; while forest is limited to the mountainous Eastern Highlands.

Savanna is sometimes referred to as *bushveld* or tropical grassland, but the latter term is misleading in a southern African context because it ignores the presence of large numbers of trees, forming sometimes dense woodland. In fact many first-time visitors to Zimbabwe are surprised to see so many trees in these wildlife areas, being accustomed to television images of east African game parks where there's often barely a tree to be seen. Kazuma Pan National Park (see *Chapter 8*, pages 286–8) is about the only Zimbabwean example of such a treeless environment. Grassland can also be surprisingly lush and dense and, when unchecked by animals or fire, can grow to a height of well over 2m.

The difference between arid and moist savanna is related to rainfall levels.

Arid savanna These lowland areas typically receive up to 500mm of annual rainfall but support a wide variety of vegetation and consequently a huge and diverse population of game and birdlife. Visitors frequently comment on the apparent paradox of large numbers of animals surviving in such a hot, parched landscape, but anyone visiting outside of the traditional late-winter safari season will see a completely different picture, of the verdant vegetation that flourishes on these relatively fertile soils. Zimbabwe's arid savanna lands carry a rich variety of trees, although *mopane* and several varieties of acacia dominate. Indeed the high incidence of acacia gives this biome its alternative name, *thornveld*. A high percentage of the country's many antelope species thrive here, as well as elephants, giraffe and buffalo, so of course predators are never far away. It is therefore no surprise that the main game-viewing national parks all lie in these areas.

Moist savanna With higher annual rainfall, up to 1,100mm, different plant species flourish on Zimbabwe's central plateau, and its woodland is noticeably more dense. *Bushveld* is a commonly used alternative name, but two other words also creep into descriptions of this biome's vegetation. *Brachystegia* is a genus of broadleaved deciduous trees which dominate the Zimbabwe *highveld*, and *miombo* is the Shona word for these trees. *Msasa* is the local name for the very common *Brachystegia spiciformis*, with African teak, *Pterocarpus angolensis*, also found in abundance. The soil is less fertile up here, and the grasses less nutritious with a sour taste, so only the less demanding grazers and browsers do well here.

Forest The forest biome is associated with high annual rainfall, and in Zimbabwe that occurs only in the Eastern Highlands. Before man's intervention and the introduction of commercial forestry, Afromontane (ie: African mountain) forest covered most of the lower slopes of the Eastern Highlands. Only a few isolated patches remain today, restricted to the Chipinge–Chimanimani area and further north in the Bvumba Mountains.

BUSH FIRES

NATURAL Natural fires are caused by lightning hitting tinder-dry grassland, with flames fanned by the wind. While these appear damaging to both plant and animal life in the short term, they are part of the natural scheme of things, clearing the ground for fresh new growth and returning nutrients to the soil. Under normal circumstances, and provided these fires occur on a reasonably regular basis, little long-term damage is done to established trees and bushes, as their normally thick bark is simply scorched. These are termed 'cool' fires. Within days of the first rains the blackened landscape quickly turns green with a carpet of healthy new shoots. Some plants actually require fire before their seeds will germinate.

The problem comes if there has been a long period since the previous fire, allowing a build-up of thick, tall, dry grass and vegetation. Now there is so much fuel on the ground that a 'hot' fire develops and rampages along, consuming all in its path.

MANMADE Fires may be deliberately set by agriculturalists, and even in national parks, essentially to mimic what happens in nature. They can be used to clear and rejuvenate land, allowing new growth for cattle or wildlife, or to prevent dangerous accumulations of flammable material. Landowners aim for cool fires, avoiding windy days and using firebreaks and beaters to prevent the fires from getting out of control.

Accidental fires are caused by any number of circumstances, often simply carelessness, but they are also frequently the result of deliberately lit fires getting out of control.

Once a 'hot' fire takes hold, the results can be devastating. In Zimbabwe there are no mechanical or aerial bombardment facilities available to fight bushfires, so dangerous, on-the-ground tactics must be employed. One of these is backburning, which involves estimating the direction of the fire and then lighting another, much smaller line of fire some distance ahead of it, to clear the ground of fuel, creating a firebreak. The art is to prevent this new fire from itself getting out of control, an all-too-frequent occurrence if the wind changes.

These true rainforests have a rich variety of large evergreen trees, and their defining feature is a totally closed overhead canopy. They can be magical, ancient places, dark and dank at the same time, but they support little mammal life other than small antelope and monkeys. They are, on the other hand, a Mecca for birders, home to many highly sought-after 'specials'.

FAUNA *with Mike Unwin*

Viewing wildlife is top of the list of activities for most first-time visitors to Zimbabwe and this country certainly offers excellent opportunities. Many will already be familiar with the larger game species and able to identify them without expert help. That may not be the case with some antelopes, however, as well as the many smaller creatures and the 660-odd species of birds here. This guidebook is not the place to describe and identify them all, so the following section aims rather to highlight some of the better-known species and to describe the more interesting aspects of their life in the bush. It concentrates on the larger mammals but also includes a brief overview of the common reptiles and birds. The 'Big Five', incidentally, are not necessarily the largest but acquired their name from hunters who considered them to be the most challenging of the trophy species. Each is highlighted here.

For a more detailed and comprehensive account I strongly recommend the very readable *Southern African Wildlife* by Mike Unwin. In compiling the following pages I have drawn extensively on Mike's book. See box, page 61, for a list of other recommended field guides.

CATS

Lion (*Panthera leo*) (one of the 'Big Five') The lion, Africa's apex predator, seems to be something of a contradictory creature. Massively powerful – a large male weighs up to 230kg and is capable of killing a buffalo – it nonetheless spends much of its time asleep and appears to be fundamentally lazy. The truth is that, like many large carnivores, lions' high-protein diet means they can satisfy their metabolic requirements with short bursts of hunting and thus spend the rest of their time conserving energy.

Lions have a highly developed social system. A typical pride of 12 to 15 individuals will comprise a group of closely related females with their cubs, plus one or two unrelated males. The males are on constant guard for incoming 'foreign' males who, if they can take control of the pride, will often kill any cubs in order to bring the lionesses back into oestrus and thus quickly spread their own genes. A mating pair will copulate an amazing 40–50 times a day over a period of perhaps four days. After a gestation period of 110 days an average of three or four cubs are born. Life is far from idyllic for these youngsters, with only around 10% surviving until their second birthday. Starvation and injury – the latter both from predators and conflict with other lions, adult males especially – both take a heavy toll. Of those that make it, the females stay in the pride while the males are pushed out from around 15 months to fend for themselves.

A lion pride will hunt effectively as a group but, despite appearances, does not work to a planned strategy. In fact, several lionesses will each select their own target, but when the first animal is taken down the rest of the hunt tends to be abandoned and everyone piles in for the meal. It's usually only at this stage that the male arrives to dominate the scene, having left the actual hunting to the more agile and faster females. It's a myth that lions always dispatch their prey quickly: once a large prey animal has been incapacitated, the pride may start feasting without bothering to kill it first. No quarter is given at meal times, when it's strictly a case of survival of the fittest, leaving younger or subordinate members of the pride at the back of the queue.

Lions are found in all Zimbabwe's main conservation areas, with good populations in Hwange National Park, Mana Pools, Matusadona, Gonarezhou and Chizarira. They are not always easy to see, being primarily nocturnal, but when in lion country you should, at least, hear their distinctive 'roar' at night (in reality, a series of moaning grunts). You should never turn and run if you come face to face with a lion on a walking safari, as this may trigger its chase response. In general, however, lions shun contact with people and in any such encounter your guide will advise what to do.

Leopard (*Panthera pardus*) (one of the 'Big Five') This is the second largest of Africa's cats: half the size of a lion, with males weighing up to 90kg and the much smaller females up to 60kg. It is an elegant and impressive animal, whose shy,

Leopard

solitary and largely nocturnal nature makes it difficult to find. Nevertheless, the leopard's broad diet and adaptability to different types of habitat make it by far the most successful of Africa's big cats. Although lions may sometimes scramble up to a low branch, the leopard is the only big cat that feels truly at home in a tree; indeed it is even agile enough to catch monkeys in the branches.

Leopards are sometimes mistaken for cheetahs but may be distinguished by their more powerful build and the characteristic rosette pattern of their spots. Unlike the cheetah, which is built for speed, a leopard relies on stealth, stalking its prey to within pouncing distance. Having killed, however, it cannot relax and must often abandon its meal to marauding lions or hyenas. To guard against this hazard, the leopard will either drag its kill into dense undergrowth to eat or haul it up a convenient tree out of reach of other predators – the latter feat revealing the cat's amazing strength, as it will sometimes hoist up an animal almost twice its own weight. Prey varies from larger mammals such as warthog and impala to smaller creatures such as rodents, dassies, birds, fish and even insects. The leopard's elusive nature allows it to live close to human habitation, where its raids on goats, sheep and even domestic pets make it a very unpopular neighbour.

Leopards breed at any time of year and, after a gestation of 100 days, give birth to, usually, two or three cubs that the mother looks after until they are about 18 months old. If you are out in the bush and wonder why somebody is sawing wood so far from a village, you are probably hearing the rasping call of the leopard. These beautiful creatures are resident in all Zimbabwe's national parks, with an especially dense population in the Matobo Hills.

Cheetah (*Acinonyx jubatus*) Although around the same height, even a little taller than the leopard, the cheetah has a much slimmer, more elongated body and an appreciably smaller head. Its spots are small and solid black, not forming rosette patterns like a leopard's, and its face displays unmistakeable black 'teardrop' lines below each eye.

Cheetahs favour open spaces and seek out raised vantage points from which to spot prey. This is a hunter whose success depends on speed rather than strength. Its strong hind legs and extremely supple spine win it the accolade of the fastest animal on land, capable of reaching 100km/h in just three seconds – on a par with the acceleration of the fastest sports cars. But if it hasn't brought down its prey within a few hundred metres – usually by means of a sharp swipe from behind – the cheetah gives up exhausted and must recoup its strength before the next attempt. The long tail acts as a balancing 'rudder' as the cat performs amazingly agile, high-speed direction changes. Its non-retractable claws, unique among cats, function like the spikes on running shoes.

Cheetahs start to feed as soon as they have made a kill, as they lack the strength to fight off larger predators and scavengers. Favourite prey includes impala, as well as other small antelope, hares and large birds – even ostriches. They do not form prides but patrol their territories either singly or in small groups. By contrast with lions, a small group of cheetah will comprise young

Cheetah

males; females are solitary, unless accompanied by their cubs. Males will scent-mark their home range and fight, sometimes to the death, when they meet rivals.

Once widespread, cheetahs are now under threat and your only realistic chance of seeing a truly wild one is in Hwange National Park. They are, however, being bred on some ranches and conservancies for reintroduction into the wild.

Serval (*Felis serval*) With a shoulder height of 60cm, the serval falls somewhere in size between a domestic cat and a cheetah. It has a similar slim body and long legs, but a proportionately shorter tail than the cheetah, with larger spots that merge into stripes on the neck and shoulders. Its conspicuously large ears are an adaptation for detecting the slightest noise of its rodent prey in the long grass. Servals are nocturnal, and hunt small mammals, birds, reptiles and insects. They frequent long grass or reeds, often near water, and are widespread in Zimbabwe – though hard to see.

Serval

Zimbabwe's other two cats are the **Caracal** (*Felis caracal*) and **African wildcat** (*Felis sylvestrys*), both of which are rarely seen. The former is the size of a serval, but with a plain tawny-brown coat, lynx-like tufts on its ears, and a more powerful build that allows it to take prey up to the size of small antelope. The latter is the ancestor of the domestic cat and looks – not surprisingly – like a slim tabby, with distinctive rufous ears. It is widespread but very shy.

Caracal

DOGS
Wild dog (*Lycaon pictus*) (also known as Cape hunting dog and African painted wolf) This is probably the most threatened large carnivore in Africa, having in the past suffered wholesale persecution as vermin and been brought close to extinction as a result. Today there are thought to be fewer than 4,000 individuals left and the species is the subject of intensive conservation programmes throughout its range. If you are lucky enough to see one, however, this highly sociable animal is unmistakable, with its slim body – about the height of a German shepherd – large rounded ears and muddled pattern of black and brown blotches on a tan background.

Wild dogs have the highest hunting success rate of any large predator. Hunting is a co-operative endeavour in which a combination of speed and stamina allows the pack to pursue prey for several kilometres before finally overhauling it. They will hunt a wide range of species, preferring impala-sized antelope but being quite prepared to tackle the young of larger animals, even buffalo. The kill is a messy affair, with the victim quickly succumbing to shock or loss of blood.

African wild dog

Social life for wild dogs revolves around a mature breeding pair, and all subordinate pack females share duties in raising the pups, which are born in litters of around ten. This species is best seen in Hwange National Park and is rare elsewhere – although its nomadic habits mean it may turn up unexpectedly: I've seen a pack within a stone's throw of the Kazangula border post and they patrol nearly all the way to Victoria Falls in the Zambezi National Park.

Black-backed jackal (*Canis mesomelas*) This
attractive canine has a pointed, fox-like head and a broad black and silver saddle along the back that tapers towards a bushy tail. It stands up to 40cm at the shoulder and weighs 6–10kg. Though largely nocturnal, this jackal is often seen trotting around at dawn and dusk, usually alone but sometimes in pairs. Even if you don't get to see one you'll probably hear its drawn-out quavering howl, one of Zimbabwe's classic wildlife sounds. Black-backed jackals thrive on a wide range of foods, including berries and other fruits, carrion and live prey, the last ranging from rodents and birds to small antelope. Farms and smallholdings are happy hunting grounds, and this cunning, wary predator is notoriously difficult to trap. It is widespread throughout Zimbabwe, though most common in low-lying, arid areas.

Black-backed jackal

Side-striped jackal (*Canis adustus*) Similar in size to the black backed jackal,
this species appears uniformly grey, apart from a rather faint pale stripe along each flank. It is found across much of Zimbabwe, generally favouring wetter and more wooded conditions than its cousin. Its call is also different, being more reminiscent of an owl's hoot.

Bat-eared fox (*Otocyon megalotis*) This charming, cat-sized little fox lives almost

exclusively on termites, although other insects, rodents and reptiles supplement its diet. Its apparently oversized ears are used to detect minute underground sounds. Bat-eared foxes pair for life and are often seen in small family groups. After a gestation of 60 days they produce four to six cubs in an underground den, which they may either dig themselves or adapt from one dug by another species. Bat-eared foxes are not widespread in Zimbabwe but can be seen in the Kalahari sand areas of Hwange and Zambezi national parks.

Bat-eared fox

HYENAS
Spotted hyena (*Crocuta crocuta*) The poor old hyena has probably the worst
reputation of any African animal. Its popular image is of a mangy, cowardly scavenger, and its furtive manner and ungainly appearance – with sloping back and long neck – hardly help matters. Yet hyenas deserve respect: these intelligent and versatile carnivores are feared by almost every animal in the bush, sometimes forcing even lions to abandon a kill. Not only are they expert scavengers – performing a vital ecological service in the process – but they are also highly efficient hunters, capable of bringing down animals as large as kudu. Their formidable jaws are powerful enough to crush almost any bone and they are not too fussy about what they sink their teeth into: pilots on bush airstrips will often protect the tyres of their aircraft with thorny acacia branches to prevent them being shredded by an inquisitive hyena.

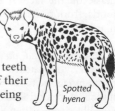
Spotted hyena

Hyena society is both heavily hierarchical and matriarchal, with the only reliable way to distinguish the two sexes being the female's slightly greater size. An exceptionally high level of male hormones in females raises their aggression level. It also gives rise to a bizarre physiological oddity: a grossly enlarged, penis-like clitoris. The female's narrow birth canal is responsible for a very high mortality rate, both among cubs and injured mothers.

The nocturnal whoops, shrieks, giggles and cackles of hyenas may entertain the camper, but beware: these are dangerous creatures. You never see hyena on a trophy-hunter's wish list, so – although persecuted in farming areas – they have never had cause to fear man in traditional wildlife areas. Consequently these canny predators have become pretty well habituated to humans, especially around campsites. This is particularly so at Nyamepi in Mana Pools National Park, where hyenas patrol the camp at night looking for anything resembling food and can make your nocturnal visit to the toilet block more than a little unnerving. Never sleep outside your tent in hyena country: there are numerous tales of those who have been seriously disfigured – or worse – as a result.

Brown hyena

Brown hyena (*Parahyena brunnea*) If you are very lucky you may catch sight of this smaller and shaggier relative of the spotted hyena, but only in Hwange and the arid Kalahari sand areas bordering Botswana. It is a much more solitary animal and tends to avoid competition with its larger cousin.

Aardwolf (*Proteles cristatus*) This is the smallest of the hyenas and, although its sloping back gives it a similar appearance, is

Aardwolf

actually a very different animal from the other two. It is largely nocturnal, sleeps in burrows and hunts little more than termites. Although widespread, aardwolves are shy and seldom seen. While it must not be confused with the aardvark, a totally unrelated animal, the aardwolf does tend to use the aardvark's burrows. (*Aard* means 'earth' in Afrikaans.)

GENETS AND CIVETS These nocturnal animals are frequently referred to as cats but actually belong to the Viverridae family of carnivores. You may come across one around camp, where they hang around hoping to pick up a snack or two.

African civet (*Civettictis civetta*) This rather hunchbacked animal, the size of a small dog, has a grey, coarse coat patterned with black blotches and stripes, and a dark 'bandit's mask' on the face. It enjoys a wide range of foods, from fruits and insects to reptiles and small mammals.

African civet

Tree civet (*Nandinia binotata*) This elusive and rare animal is found only in the few surviving patches of montane forest of the Eastern Highlands. It forages for fruit among the taller trees but may also descend to feed on carrion, rodents and insects at ground level. With its lithe form and long banded tail it more closely resembles genets than its larger cousin.

Small-spotted genet (*Genetta genetta*) and **large-spotted genet** (*Genetta tigrina*) Both species are common in Zimbabwe, with the large-spotted generally preferring higher-rainfall habitats. Where their ranges overlap, in the southwest of the country, the two are best told apart by the size and pattern of their spots (larger and blotchier in the large-spotted) and the colour of their tail tip (white in the small-spotted; black in the large-spotted). Both are about a metre long, nocturnal and largely solitary, feeding mainly on insects, birds and small mammals. They are equally at home on the ground or in the trees. Your best chance of seeing one is on a night drive or around camp in the evenings.

MONGOOSES Zimbabwe is blessed with no fewer than nine species of mongoose. This can present something of an identification problem, especially as they tend to dash around at lightning speed, but there are clear differences in behaviour, appearance and habitat that make life easier.

Social mongooses A troop of up to 30 mongooses scampering around by day will be one of two species. The **banded mongoose** (*Mungos mungo*) is 50–65cm long (including tail) and identified by a dozen dark bands across the back of its grey-brown coat. This highly sociable species feeds on a variety of items, from insects and other invertebrates to reptiles, birds, eggs, amphibians and carrion. It prefers habitats with plenty of cover and proximity to permanent

Banded
mongoose

water, with the Victoria Falls area and neighbouring Zambezi National Park being good spots. The much smaller **dwarf mongoose** (*Helogale parvula*) measures only 35–40cm, half of that being tail, and is the smallest carnivore in southern Africa. It is uniformly dark brown and commonly forages in troops of 12 or more, never straying far from the safety of its burrow system – often in a termite mound. The troop's strict hierarchy revolves around a dominant pair. Note that the other well-known and endearing social mongoose, the meerkat (or suricate), does not occur in Zimbabwe.

Solitary mongooses The **slender mongoose** (*Galerella sanguinea*) is a small, diurnal species, readily identified from its habit of curling its long black-tipped tail over its body when running for cover. About the same size as the banded mongoose, but slimmer, its diet of birds, rodents and reptiles even includes the occasional small snake. The **white-tailed mongoose** (*Ichneumia albicauda*) is the largest of the family, weighing up to 5kg and measuring nose to tail 125cm or more, and can be identified by its brownish-grey coat and a long white hairy tail. This nocturnal species eats largely insects and carries its head characteristically low when foraging. The metre-long **large grey mongoose** (*Herpestes ichneumon*) is generally nocturnal but may also be seen by day patrolling its riverine habitat, especially in the Zambezi Valley. Its diet is similar to that of most of the others and also includes fairly large snakes. The **water mongoose** (*Atilax paludinosis*) is a shaggy-haired, dark brown species found alongside permanent water towards the east of the country. It feeds mostly on amphibians and crabs, and takes readily to water – often being mistaken for an otter.

OTHER SMALL CARNIVORES
Honey badger (*Mellivora capensis*) Yes, it's a badger and it does eat honey, but don't for a moment think this is a cuddly little creature. Although it measures only

1m, including its short tail, and weighs no more than 14kg, the honey badger has a reputation for ferocity second to none. Even lions steer clear – and campfire storytellers claim that if one sinks its teeth into you, only a bullet will make it let go. Honey badgers have

Honey badger

a slinky appearance, with a silver-grey upper body and black underparts, and a characteristic jogging gait. You may well spot one by night around busy safari camps, where it has learnt to scavenge. Its diet includes almost any small creature it can find, as well as carrion and fruit, but its name comes from its habit of breaking into beehives, both wild and manmade. It enjoys a unique symbiotic relationship with a bird, the **greater honeyguide** (*Indicator indicator*), which directs the badger to a bees' nest and shares in the resulting feast.

Striped polecat (*Ictonyx striatus*) This widespread, nocturnal carnivore is rarely seen, despite its striking black-and-white striped coat. Its main claim to fame lies beneath its tail: like the skunk, it is able to squirt a foul-smelling liquid from its anal gland when threatened.

Cape clawless otter (*Aonyx capensis*) This is a large animal, measuring up to 160cm and weighing up to 18kg. It eats mainly crabs and molluscs, plus some fish and frogs, and uses its long, dextrous 'fingers' to delve in mud and murky waters, finding most of its food by touch. Droppings consisting largely of crushed crab shell indicate an otter's presence; the similar water mongoose tends to discard larger pieces of shell. Although largely aquatic, this otter may stray sometimes several kilometres from water in

Cape clawless otter

the search for alternative food sources such as small mammals, birds and insects.

ANT AND TERMITE EATERS

Aardvark (*Orycteropus afer*) (also known as antbear) This weird-looking mammal is not related to South America's anteaters, as many assume, but is the sole member of the primitive order Tubulidendata, so named for its unique tubed teeth. Although

Aardvark

it may appear to have been cobbled together with parts left over from the Creation, these all make perfect sense for a specialist feeder on ants and termites. Its huge donkey-like ears and long, extremely sensitive snout are adapted to locate underground activity. And, when it finds a nest, its immensely powerful front legs and strong claws are able to rip into even the most compacted soil, the muscular, almost kangaroo-like tail providing a sturdy anchor while the digging continues. When the termite colony is eventually opened, the aardvark's long sticky tongue darts in and out, collecting insects, larvae and eggs. This food is seasonal, with termites on the menu in the wet season and ants in the dry. It's been estimated that aardvarks can get through more than six litres of termites in a night – perhaps not surprising for what is actually quite a large animal, weighing up to 70kg and not far short of 2m in length. Despite abundant evidence of its presence in the form of burrows and three-toed tracks, you'll be very lucky ever to see the animal itself.

Pangolin (*Manis teminckii*) This is another enigmatic creature that you are, unfortunately, unlikely to see. Like the aardvark, it feeds on termites, but it is

Pangolin

very different in design: whereas the aardvark's body focuses on strength (and it is, in fact, a formidable fighter), the pangolin opts for defence in the form of an encasement of strong, sharp-edged, overlapping scales that cover the upper parts of its body. When threatened or attacked it simply rolls itself up into a virtually impenetrable armoured ball. A pangolin searches for termites on all fours, but if it needs a burst of speed it will move on just its hind legs, using its tail for balance. Its sticky, mucus-covered tongue can extend 40cm, nearly half its entire body length. Pangolins are not related to the superficially similar-looking South American armadillos.

PRIMATES There are only five members of this order to be found in Zimbabwe (not counting ourselves), of which three are monkeys and two bushbabies.

Chacma baboon (*Papio hamadryas ursinus*)
Baboons are widespread in Zimbabwe, often loitering around camps and tourist areas. They are by far the largest monkey – a big male weighs up to 40kg and females about half that – and are easily identified by their dog-like muzzle and the inverted U shape in which they hold their tail – almost as though broken.

Common baboon

Baboon troops can number in excess of 100 individuals and comprise complex hierarchies. A dominant male leads the whole troop. He is often supported by a number of older males and they, in turn, are followed by all the other adult males, who organise themselves by rank. There are frequent squabbles and fights as rank and order are established and challenged. All females are subservient to all adult males, but they too have their hierarchy, which appears to be determined by birth and seldom changes. Only the older, senior males are allowed to mate with the receptive females, although young males carry on a degree of 'monkey business' with females not in oestrus. After a six-month gestation period, the single born infant is initially carried slung under the mother's chest but then moves up to ride on her back as it gets older.

Baboons are omnivorous. While plant matter such as bulbs, roots, fruit and seeds makes up the bulk of their diet, they will also kill birds, mice, hares and even small antelope. A big male, with its canine teeth longer than those of a lion, is a formidable opponent and it is only lion and leopard that will take baboons on. While a leopard may occasionally snatch an unwary baboon from its night-time tree roost, it is careful to avoid the wrath of the troop by day.

From a distance baboons can appear quite appealing, especially the young ones. But visitors must never be tempted to feed them. Once these intelligent primates associate humans with food they lose their fear and can become extremely dangerous (remember those teeth). Some, consequently, are destroyed.

Vervet monkey (*Cercopithecus aethiops*)
These small monkeys seem to be everywhere, from deep in the bush to bouncing precociously around the suburbs. They weigh up to 6kg, and have a thick pepper-and-salt grey coat, a black face and a prominent white brow that tends to give them rather a surprised expression. Sexually active males sport a splendidly vivid pale blue scrotum.

Vervet monkey

Vervets form troops of 20 or more and are highly social and hierarchical. They are active during the day, equally at home in trees or on the ground as they forage for their mainly vegetarian diet of fruit, seeds and leaves. They will also take insects, invertebrates and even nestling birds.

You should never feed vervets, even accidentally, as they can become a problem around camp and will dash off with your lunch as soon as your back is turned. But neither, on the other hand, should you shoot at them with catapults or pellet guns, as some tourists have been known to do.

Samango monkey (*Cercopithecus mitis*) At up to 8kg this monkey, also known as the blue monkey, is somewhat larger than the vervet. Its darker grey coat is tinged with brown, and its face has long cheek hair and no white brow. As a forest dweller its habitat is fast shrinking, and in Zimbabwe samangos are found only in the remaining patches of indigenous forest in the east. Despite this restricted range, however, they are not hard to see in the right habitat – especially the Vumba region. They live in troops of up to 35 individuals and, as they are largely arboreal, you'll need to look up into the trees to spot them. The best clue to their presence is the crashing of foliage as they rampage through the canopy and their loud barking 'Jack!' alarm call. These monkeys eat fruit, flowers, leaves and gum, and will also take the occasional insect. Their habit of debarking young trees while searching for gum makes them unpopular with plantation farmers.

Thick-tailed (greater) bushbaby (*Otolemur crassicauditus*) Of the two bushbabies in the region, this small cat-sized one is much the larger, weighing up to 1.5kg. It is grey-brown in colour, with a long bushy tail the same length as its body. Both nocturnal and arboreal, these animals would be difficult to locate were it not for the bright red reflections of their large eyes when caught in a spotlight. You are most unlikely to see one roosting by day. Bushbabies are extremely agile as they leap among the branches, foraging for fruit and the tree gum that constitutes a major part of their diet. They also eat meat in the form of insects, reptiles and small birds. Females mark their territories by urinating on their hands before leaping, thereby spreading their scent wherever they land. The alarm call of this species sounds not unlike the cry of a distressed baby, hence the name.

Lesser bushbaby (*Galago moholi*) Often referred to as a night ape, this little creature is even more endearing than its larger cousin. Not only does it have proportionately larger eyes and ears, but its hindlegs seem spring-loaded, enabling it to leap huge distances from branch to branch. It's only the size of a small squirrel yet it can cover 5m in one bound – always using its hindlegs on landing. Lesser bushbabies can become quite habituated to humans: one family group I've come across always starts its nightly forage with a visit to the fruit-laden bird table, less than 3m from the glowing barbecue.

Lesser bushbaby

HERBIVORES
African elephant (*Loxodonta africana*) (one of the 'Big Five') Almost everything about this animal – which may reach 4m at the shoulder and weigh six tonnes – is extraordinary. Mature elephants require 150kg of food each day (large ones even more) to fuel that bulk and can drink 200 litres in one sitting. The trunk is much more than just an elongated nose: it is an amazingly strong multi-purpose tool that

can pick up anything from a peanut to a fallen log. It is used for feeding, drinking (holding up to 20 litres of water), smelling, breathing (even as a snorkel in deep water) and fighting. The huge earflaps are extremely thin, criss-crossed with a dense network of blood vessels on the underside, and act like a car radiator to cool the animal's blood by as much as 5°C. The ivory tusks are enlarged incisor teeth that serve for fighting, digging for roots and stripping bark, and are frequently used in conjunction with the trunk to rip off branches.

An elephant's acute senses of hearing and smell combine to warn of danger several kilometres away. One night I watched a series of elephants passing along their regular trail and was amazed to see each stop to sniff the ground at precisely the spot where I had briefly stood chatting to two people a full two days previously. It is believed they can communicate over great distances using very low-frequency ultrasound, and research is currently being conducted to establish whether their feet act as long-distance vibration receptors.

Small family groups of females and youngsters are led by an older, experienced matriarch, while the adult and sub-adult males form their own bachelor groups or roam singly. Elephants are extremely sociable animals, and one of the finest sights in Africa is to watch many of these groups coming together, greeting each other, and displaying what appears to be affection. Temporary herds sometimes several hundred strong may gather during the dry season in areas where food or water is concentrated.

A female elephant may mate with several males at any time of the year and, after a gestation period of 22 months, gives birth to a single calf, usually at night, weighing around 120kg. The youngster suckles for several years from teats that, unusually in mammals other than primates, are situated between the front legs.

Large populations of elephant occur in several of Zimbabwe's national parks, notably Hwange (where huge herds cross the border from Botswana), Mana Pools and Gonarezhou – although the last once suffered from horrific poaching and its elephants are consequently wary of man and reputedly bad-tempered.

An elephant cannot run, technically speaking, because only one of its feet can leave the ground at a time, so it just has varying speeds of walking. But don't be fooled: these huge animals can accelerate remarkably quickly and reach an impressive, not to say alarming, pace.

See box, pages 268–9 for more about population control and elephant-back riding.

Hippopotamus (*Hippopotamus amphibious*) The most common view you get of this enormous, two-tonne, amphibious animal is a small pair of ears and nostrils protruding just above the water's surface, and that's because it spends most of the daylight hours semi-submerged. A hippo's skin is very sensitive to sunlight and it thus needs the cooling effect of water to regulate its body temperature. Totally submerged, hippos can hold their breath for about six minutes. They are remarkably agile underwater, with their huge bulk being supported by the buoyancy of the water. From dusk to dawn, however, they emerge and wander the land in search of grazing, covering up to 30km in one night.

One of the many impressive things about hippos is their 'yawn': a gaping of the massive mouth that is, in fact, a display of aggression and features an awe-inspiring set of teeth. The longer you spend in the company of these lumbering animals, the more you realise how bad-tempered they can be. Why else, after all, would a huge vegetarian be bestowed with such formidable weapons? Territorial fights are frequent and lengthy, not to say dramatic for the human onlooker, as the leviathans do battle amidst much roaring, grunting and watery turmoil. It's not unusual to come across hippos with horrific wounds; some even die from their injuries.

Mating, on a happier note, takes place in the water – which is not surprising, given hippos' bulk. After a rather variable gestation period of 225–7 days, a single 30–40kg calf is born, on land, amongst dense cover. In its early days, the youngster suckles underwater, where its mother takes care to guard it from crocodiles. On land lion and hyena are a threat to youngsters, although a healthy adult hippo has no predators.

Experts are divided over the hippo's widespread reputation as the most lethal animal in Africa, not least because of the lack of reliable statistics. Nevertheless, these bulky vegetarians can be extremely zealous guardians of their territory and are potentially dangerous both on land and water. There are three basic rules when in hippo territory: never get between a hippo and the water, as they will invariably dash directly for the safety of deep water when frightened and you do not want to be in their way; never take them by surprise if you are on the river – let them know you are coming by periodically tapping your canoe with the paddle; and finally, if you are on a riverside walking safari, learn from my experience and check continually for trees that you could quickly scramble up. Never underestimate this massive animal: despite its great bulk and stumpy legs a charging hippo can easily outrun a man.

Rhinos (one of the 'Big Five')

Once widespread throughout southern Africa, both species of rhino have suffered heavy persecution. The white rhino was virtually wiped out at the end of the 19th century, disappearing from Zimbabwe entirely, but has since recovered through intense conservation programmes in South Africa and translocation elsewhere. The black rhino fared rather better until a poaching onslaught in the second half of the 20th century brought it to the verge of extinction across Africa, including in Zimbabwe, and its status today remains precarious. Rhinos have been hunted solely for their two horns, which comprise a compacted hair-like material. These are ground to powder and used as traditional medicine and aphrodisiac in the Far East. Poaching for this lucrative market remains an enormous ongoing problem, but a number of conservation programmes have succeeded in breeding and reintroducing rhinos to parts of their former ranges, and increasingly effective anti-poaching measures have been adopted in many regions.

The two species are similar in appearance but there are distinct differences that, with a little practice, make identification easy. Just don't expect them to be either black or white: both are the same shade of grey – or whatever the colour of the mud in which they have been wallowing. So why do we call them black and white? Noticing an obvious difference in their mouthparts, early German hunters are said to have described the larger, more common grazing variety as *weit* (wide) mouthed. English hunters incorrectly translated this as 'white', and decided therefore to call the other 'black'. And here's another way to tell your rhinos apart: when on the run, the white rhino 'shepherds' her calf in front of her; the black rhino calf, by contrast, follows mum. To see rhinos you must visit areas where managed populations have been reintroduced. The principal ones are Hwange and Matobo national parks, and possibly Matusadona.

White (square-lipped) rhinoceros (*Ceratotherium simum*)

This is by far the larger of the two species and, with a big bull weighing in at a massive 2,300kg, enjoys the distinction of being the world's largest land mammal after the two elephants. Apart from size, its feeding technique and the consequent shape of its mouthparts provide the key

White
rhino

diagnostic feature. The white rhino has a wide, square-ended muzzle adapted for grazing, so you tend to see it with its head to the ground. This is the more even-tempered and sociable of the two species and it's not uncommon to see a group of half a dozen or more. The male is very territorial, marking the boundaries of his 'manor' with urine sprays and depositing his droppings in a series of strategically placed middens, into which he scrapes deep furrows with his three-toed back feet. A diet of grass gives this rhino fine, quite dark-coloured dung.

Fights between competing males can be drawn-out affairs, sometimes resulting in serious injury or worse. They are usually associated with mating, which can take place at any time of year. Single calves are born after a 16-month gestation period,

RHINO HORN

Male and female rhinos of both species carry two horns made of keratin, a hard, continually growing protein found in hair, hoofs, human fingernails and most animal horns. Powdered rhino horn has been used in Far Eastern traditional medicine for centuries, notably to reduce fever and as an aphrodisiac. Although it may have a very minor influence on fever it is nowhere near as effective as aspirin, and any aphrodisiac qualities are purely psychosomatic – though possibly no less potent for that.

In recent decades, rhinos have been mercilessly poached to satisfy these markets, leaving the black rhino an endangered species that relies totally on interventionist conservation tactics to ensure its survival. Their legal guardian in Zimbabwe, the Parks and Wildlife Management Authority, has historically been woefully under-resourced and, despite good intentions, has over the years faced a losing battle against a particularly well-armed and experienced enemy. In Zimbabwe then, as well as in neighbouring countries, rhino survival has fallen almost entirely into the hands of private enterprise with the welcome growth of conservancies, an amalgamation of landowners who have changed their land use from cattle to wildlife.

De-horning has today become the prime anti-poaching strategy used by conservancies – practically the only areas where rhinos are still found. Some oppose this practice, believing it wrong to deprive the animal of its prime weapon, but experience seems to show that the animals' behaviour is largely unaffected. De-horned rhinos are sometimes still targets: poachers who have tracked one for days only to find it has no horns will probably kill it anyway, to prevent wasting any more time on it in future. Nonetheless, conservancies can use funding from tourism and trophy hunting to mount expensive conservation operations backed up by effective anti-poaching patrols, with the result that de-horning is turning out to be very effective. Another method is to embed a satellite-tracking transmitter into the horn, allowing the poachers to be located – although this method can only be effective once the animal has been killed.

Although Zimbabwe has a 'shoot to kill' policy for poachers, education and alternative employment are increasingly being seen as more effective strategies and captured poachers are now frequently 'turned' to utilise their considerable tracking skills in the battle against their former occupation. As ever though, the poacher is at the bottom of a long chain and there is recognition that until the 'Mr Bigs' of this gruesome trade are apprehended, the slaughter will continue.

and stay with their mother for two to three years. Both species have poor eyesight, relying on scent and hearing to sense danger. Although a healthy adult rhino has no natural enemies, the young are vulnerable to attack by lion and hyena.

Black (hook-lipped) rhinoceros (*Diceros bicornis*) At around half the weight of its cousin, this much rarer species has an altogether different disposition, being both more solitary and more aggressive. Its feeding style is also different and diagnostic: the prehensile, pointed upper lip is adapted for grasping twigs and stripping leaves, so the animal invariably holds its head up when feeding. This diet also means that the black rhino's preferred habitat is wooded rather than grassy savanna, which makes it far more difficult to spot than the white. But if you are happy to accept evidence of its presence in the absence of a sighting, the coarse, woody, light-coloured dung at their latrines tells you this is black rhino territory. The breeding habits and gestation period are similar to the white rhino's.

Black rhinoceros

Giraffe (*Giraffa camelopardalis*) This unmistakable, graceful animal is the tallest in the world, with mature males reaching a lofty 5m or more and weighing in at over 1,200kg. When fleeing danger the loping, slow-motion-like stride can carry them at speeds up to 60km/h. A powerful pump is required to get the blood up to a brain that high, and indeed the giraffe has the largest heart of any animal: 20 times the size of a human's. The animal's great height is, of course, an adaptation for feeding from treetops, where no other browser can reach and the choicest young leaves are often to be found. Giraffes' favourite food comprises various species of acacia, and their amazingly tough, prehensile, 45cm tongue enables them both to strip the leaves and deal with the tree's horribly thorny defence system.

Being tall has significant feeding advantages as well as providing the very best viewpoint for spotting danger, but it poses an obvious challenge when it comes to drinking. The only way a giraffe can get its mouth down to water level is by adopting an ungainly position with front legs splayed, which leaves it vulnerable to lion attack. As a result you will often see a lone giraffe at a waterhole making repeated attempts to get its head down, only to snatch it upright again at the last minute in order to scan the surroundings. This can go on for ages before it actually plucks up courage to drink. Giraffes in a small group fare better, as individuals can act as lookout for each other. Fortunately, much of the giraffe's water requirement is satisfied by the moisture contained in the leaves it eats.

When it's time to mate, competing males engage in a power struggle known as 'necking', in which they swing their long necks and heavy heads at one another. Although this ritual may look charming from a distance, the animals are in fact delivering formidable and destructive blows. The gestation period is a lengthy 450 days. It results in a gangly calf that is extremely vulnerable to predators and, as a result, has to be up and running within an hour of birth.

You'll see plenty of giraffe in Hwange and Zambezi national parks and another good-sized population in Gonarezhou. Interestingly, there is no evidence of giraffes ever having populated Mana Pools and the Lower Zambezi region, where it is thought the precipitous escarpment may always have posed an insurmountable barrier.

Burchell's zebra (*Equus burchellii*) There are two species of zebra in southern Africa but only Burchell's is found in Zimbabwe. It is of course a type of horse and in those terms it stands at about 13 hands, or 1.3m. And you never see a skinny one; zebras' body shape (especially their charmingly plump hindquarters) suggests that they cope very well, even in conditions when other animals are obviously struggling. With a reputation of being almost impossible to tame, zebras' feisty and confident nature gives them a distinct advantage over more timid species around the waterhole. Their characteristic black-on-white stripes provide excellent camouflage in wooded or bushy surroundings, but as they spend much of their time in open grassland it is thought that these stripes may also act to confuse predators as they try to select a victim from the running herd. Zebras generally form small family groups of four or five, and the unattached males join up in bachelor herds. Elsewhere, larger aggregations may occur during seasonal migrations.

African buffalo (*Syncerus caffer*) (one of the 'Big Five') These hefty cattle have a fearsome reputation that is largely undeserved. They form huge mixed herds and your walking guide will have no hesitation in approaching as close as he can to them, safe in the knowledge that as soon as they catch your scent they will all thunder off to a safe distance. That said, old bulls tend to wander off from the herd to live a largely solitary existence and it is true that they really don't appreciate being disturbed. It's these bad tempered old '*daga* boys' (so called because of the mud they love to wallow in) that are responsible for giving the rest a bad name and they are indeed fearsome creatures. Their long 'W'-shaped horns meet in the middle to form a massive bony 'boss', a worrying weapon indeed when powered by 800kg of raw muscle.

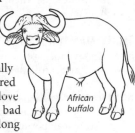
African buffalo

Otherwise buffalo are gregarious grazers, feeding mainly at night and seeking water at the beginning and end of the day. If you do see them beside water, please don't refer to them – as one of the people on your game vehicle invariably will – as 'water buffalo'. That is the name of a totally different Asian species often seen yoked to a plough – something not too many people would attempt with an African buffalo.

Pigs

Warthog (*Phacochoerus africanus*) Everybody rather unkindly remarks on how ugly these pigs are, yet they can be rather endearing characters around camp. Warthogs are intelligent enough to have quickly worked out that humans in safari camps don't fit into the predator category. This allows them to graze relatively unbothered. To do this they shuffle around on their front knees, gorging on the lush, watered lawns. In the bush they graze and dig up roots by day and at nightfall make their homes in disused aardvark burrows – although they are perfectly capable of digging their own. Lion and leopard are their principal predators, though the tusks of an adult male can inflict serious wounds and the outcome of such a fight is by no means guaranteed. Unusually, the warthog reverses into its burrow so that, if required, it can use its tusks in self-defence.

Warthog

The rather unfortunate appearance of this, one of my favourite bush creatures, at least helps to distinguish it from the next animal in the list. A warthog's large head has two pairs (one pair in females) of prominent wart-like protrusions, for which scientists have yet to find a purpose. Its piggy little eyes are set high on the head and the snout boasts a bushy moustache. Both sexes have tusks that are actually highly developed canine teeth; those of the male are particularly impressive weapons. Short legs give warthogs a dumpy appearance and the hair on their bodies is sparse and whiskery, except for a long straggly mane. Their thin hairless tail ends in a ragged tuft; when running, they hold this tail up vertically, presumably enabling the group to stick together in tall grass.

Bushpig (*Potamochoerus larvatus*) Nowhere near as much fun as the warthog, bushpigs are shy, reclusive and nocturnal and, as such, you are unlikely to see them, despite their being relatively common throughout Zimbabwe. This species is the same size as the warthog but has a thicker, longer, red-brown coat and lacks the facial warts. It favours forests and woodland, as the name suggests, but has also taken to raiding crops and is never far from water. Although basically herbivorous, bushpigs occasionally take small mammals. If you are compiling a quiz for friends, ask them the collective name for a group of bushpigs. Answer: 'a sounder'.

SMALL MAMMALS Zimbabwe is home to a wide variety of rodents, bats and insectivores. Most are small and elusive, and thus not covered here. Visitors may, however, come across the following more easily identified species.

Rock dassie (*Procavia capensis*) and **yellow-spotted dassie** (*Heterohyrax brucei*) Also known as hyraxes, these two animals are very similar in appearance and can be seen scampering around or simply sunning themselves in rocky habitats such as the Matopos. Growing up to 4.5kg they look just like large rodents, but in fact they are no such thing; it's believed their closest relatives are elephants and dugongs. The biggest danger to dassies comes from the air, as they are preyed upon by a number of raptors, especially the black eagle. For this reason one animal in the group is always on sentry duty while the others feed, either by grazing or browsing. Their gestation period of nearly eight months is long for such a small animal. At birth the two to four young are extremely well developed, and they are able to feed independently within days.

Rock hyrax

Cape porcupine (*Hystrix africanaeaustralis*) You are much more likely to pick up one of the discarded quills than see this nocturnal rodent itself. If you do spot one, however, it is both unmistakable and impressive. Growing up to a metre in length and weighing nearly 20kg, it makes itself look even bigger when alarmed by raising its long, erectile mane. The banded quills are used in defence, with the porcupine turning its back on any threat. Although it is a myth that these quills can be fired at an enemy, they are nevertheless easily detached and any animal foolish enough to attack will usually be left with a number of them deeply embedded in its flesh, with painful and sometimes fatal results. The tail quills are shorter, hollow and open-ended, and can be shaken together as a warning rattle. Porcupines feed mainly on roots, tubers and bark, but they may also scavenge the occasional animal carcass. You can often identify a porcupine's burrow by the presence of gnawed bones, which it uses to supplement its mineral intake as well as sharpen its teeth.

Springhare (*Pedetes capensis*) These rodents (not hares) are often spotted during a night drive, as they hop along on curious kangaroo-style legs foraging for their diet of grass, roots and other low-level vegetation. They weigh up to 3.5kg and grow to 85cm, half of that being tail. During the day they sleep in their burrows, frequently blocking the entrance with soil for safety.

LARGE ANTELOPE These cloven-hoofed grazers and browsers belong to the same family (Bovidae) as buffalo. They range in size from the massive eland to the tiny blue duiker. All males have horns, but in more than half of species these are absent from the female. Unlike deer, which shed their horns annually, antelope keep theirs for life.

Eland (*Taurotragus oryx*) This is by far the biggest antelope, with bulls standing up to 1.7m at the shoulder and weighing nearly one tonne, and females weighing about half as much. They are tawny-grey in colour and have a distinctly square profile. Males sport a huge dewlap, and both sexes have medium-length, straight horns. Eland are browsers and able to gain most of their moisture from their food, although they will drink if water is available. Despite their size, they are shy animals, the usual sighting being a rear view as the animals trot away into the bush. Although rather cow-like in appearance, eland are excellent jumpers and perfectly capable of clearing a 2m fence. If you are staking out a waterhole at night you'll recognise them approaching by the odd clicking noise made by their hooves as they walk. In Zimbabwe eland occur naturally only in the western lowlands, including Hwange National Park, the Eastern Highlands and parts of the Lower Zambezi Valley. Note that the Eland Sanctuary in Chimanimani is now devoid of these animals. However, they have been widely reintroduced to smaller reserves and game farms, where they are much more easily seen.

Eland

Kudu (*Tragelaphus strepsiceros*) Kudu are large antelopes, with males standing up to 155cm. Although similar to eland in their height and general grey-brown colour, they are much lighter and leggier in build and thus unlikely to be confused. Only males have horns – as with all members of the 'spiral-horned antelope' tribe – and these wonderful spiralling appendages grow to become the largest of any antelope, with record measurements of over 180cm. Kudus are adorned with six to ten thin white body stripes, which provide excellent camouflage in the dense thickets they favour, and conspicuously large, round ears. They are widespread throughout most of the country, including outside protected areas, but will quickly leap off into dense bush when disturbed.

Greater kudu

Nyala (*Tragelaphus angasii*) The mature male of this medium-sized, 115cm-tall antelope is unmistakable, with his odd, shaggy appearance. The body is sooty grey, with a series of white vertical stripes similar to a kudu's and a white, erectile mane that runs from head to bushy tail. Long dark hair hangs from the throat and underbelly, but the lower legs are short-haired, yellowish and spindly looking. The horns are lyre shaped. Females are smaller and lack the long hair, their rich chestnut coat being prominently emblazoned with white stripes. Nyala prefer well-watered riverine habitats. They are rare in Zimbabwe, but may be seen in Gonarezhou and Mana Pools.

Bushbuck (*Tragelaphus scriptus*) These are the smallest of the spiral-horned antelope, growing to 80cm at the shoulder. Their attractive chestnut coat is dappled and streaked with white spots and stripes, which provide excellent camouflage in the woody and riverine thickets that they prefer, especially when the ewe gives birth, hiding her calf in the undergrowth for several weeks. Bushbuck are widespread in Zimbabwe and adapt to a variety of habitats, though always requiring some cover. They are easily seen at Victoria Falls.

Bushbuck

Sitatunga (*Tragelaphus spekii*) Common further north, the sitatunga is rare in southern Africa and only found in one tiny area of Zimbabwe. Unique amongst antelope, it is semi-aquatic and conceals itself deep amongst papyrus swamps; your only (very slim) chance of spotting one is along the Zambezi at Kazungula. Males stand at nearly 1m, with a longish brown coat and horns of up to 60cm. If you saw one on dry ground (which you won't), you would notice its very long and splayed hooves, which are an adaptation to life on marshy ground.

Sitatunga

Roan (*Hippotragus equius*) The roan, measuring over 140cm at the shoulder, is second in size to the eland and one of the three so-called 'horse-like' antelopes. It has a sturdy grey-brown body, a black-and-white marked face, and heavily ridged, swept-back horns. Roan are rare, but you might come across them in Hwange, the Zambezi Valley or Gonarezhou. The cow gives birth away from the herd in dense bush. After a few days of constant care she returns to the herd alone, leaving the calf hidden in the bush and only visiting it to suckle at the beginning and end of the day. The calf joins the herd, generally a small grouping of up to a dozen animals, after about two weeks.

Roan antelope

Sable (*Hippotragus niger*) This is many people's favourite antelope, with the male's coal-black body, white underbelly, black-and-white masked face and long, gracefully back-curved horns. The horns are formidable weapons in self-defence, with the animal dropping to its knees in order to stab its attacker, but they are seldom used against rival males. Females are smaller, reddish brown and have shorter, straighter horns; they adopt a similar child-care policy to the roan. Zimbabwe has the largest population of sable in southern Africa, and herds of up to 30 individuals can readily be found in Hwange, Zambezi National Park and the Matopos.

Sable antelope

Gemsbok (*Oryx gazelle*) The gemsbok or oryx has similar facial markings to the sable but there the resemblance ends. It has a thickset, mainly grey body about 1.2m in height but the horns are its most outstanding feature: nearly the same length as the height of the animal, they are slim, straight and form a beautiful 'V' shape when viewed head on. This animal's favoured habitat is arid Kalahari savanna to the west of Zimbabwe, but small numbers stray into Hwange from Botswana at the easternmost extreme of their range. Perfectly adapted to a hot, arid biome, the gemsbok can do without water for much of the year. Its complex nasal blood system cools brain blood like a radiator, allowing it to sustain a body temperature of an amazing 45°C and thus minimise fluid loss through perspiration.

Oryx

Waterbuck (*Kobus ellipsiprymnus*) Perhaps not the most visually impressive of the antelopes, this large, stocky species can become endearingly trusting of humans around camps, often treating our environment as a refuge from predators. It is grey-brown in colour and grows to 1.3m in height, with the males carrying curved, ringed horns that may measure nearly 1m. Both sexes have a prominent white-hoop marking around the rump that makes them unmistakable from the rear, and their long, coarse coats look inappropriate in such a hot climate. As their name suggests, waterbuck frequent riverine habitats. They are found in good numbers along the Zambezi Valley, grazing and occasionally browsing amongst the reeds and grassland from Kazungula to the Zambezi Escarpment. Good populations also occur in Gonarezhou and the Lowveld. Some say their flesh is unpalatable to lions, but tell that to the herd I got to know on the floodplain of Kazangula. All of them quickly disappeared after lion moved into the area.

Waterbuck

Reedbuck (*Redunca arundinum*) This medium-sized (just less than 1m tall) antelope enjoys tall grass and a permanent water source, and is found over much of Zimbabwe – including in higher, better-watered regions. It is sandy-fawn in colour, with paler underparts, and has a prominent dark spot – a scent gland – below the ear. The horns, found in the male only, average 40cm in length, and curve outwards and forwards. Reedbuck are monogamous and give birth mainly in the summer. The ewe hides her single lamb in reeds for several months before introducing it to the ram and other family members.

Reedbuck

Blue wildebeest

Blue wildebeest (*Connochaetes taurinus*) This is arguably the least attractive antelope, with an ungainly front-heavy appearance and a backline that slopes down, hyena-like, towards its rump. Its large head sports a long nose, shaggy beard and cow-like horns, and a long mane runs along its back towards a horse-like tail. The grey-brown coat appears dark from a distance but can hardly be described as 'blue'. Wildebeest usually form herds of up to 30 and are often seen in the company of zebra. In Zimbabwe you won't find the familiar television scenes of vast herds on migration: here wildebeest are restricted to the western and southerly fringes, notably in Hwange. The largest southern African population is in neighbouring Botswana, where numbers have crashed since the 1980s following the erection of veterinary fences across key migration routes. (A distressing account of this catastrophe, which resulted in the death of tens of thousands of animals, can be read in *Cry of the Kalahari* by Mark and Delia Owens.) In the mating season of March to May, a male wildebeest will attempt to gather a harem of cows into his territory, although these cows are difficult to control and will frequently mate with several neighbouring bulls. Wildebeests' grassland habitat offers no hiding places, so wildebeest calves – unlike those of many antelope that rely on concealment – have to be up and running within minutes of birth to keep up with the herd.

Red hartebeest (*Alcelaphus buselaphus*) and **Lichtenstein's hartebeest** (*Sigmoceros lichtensteinii*) Either of these would be a very lucky sighting in Zimbabwe; the red is much the more common but Hwange is at the extreme east of its range, while Lichtenstein's is simply a rare animal in southern Africa, being found only in Mozambique and southeastern Zimbabwe – ie: Gonarezhou. The two are similar in appearance, both standing at 1.25m and having the same distinctive sloping profiles, although Lichtenstein's is a shade or two lighter than the more chestnut-coloured red. Their heads are long and narrow, with double twisted horns set high. If you think you have spotted either of these, check first to make sure it's not the more common tsessebe.

Hartebeest

Tsessebe (*Damaliscus lunatus*) Very similar in size and appearance to the hartebeest, this animal is slightly smaller and darker and can be distinguished by horns that are lyre-shaped rather than twisted. Tsessebe are found in central and western areas of Zimbabwe, and are grazers that require a constant water source. A territorial bull will defend a specific area in which his small herd of around half a dozen cows and young live permanently. Calves can run with the herd very soon after birth.

Impala (*Aepyceros melampus*) It would be hard to design a more graceful animal than the impala; Bambi could have been modelled on a youngster. With a shoulder height of 90cm, a slender body and long legs, the male also boasts a magnificent set of lyrate horns that reach some 60cm in length. Impalas have a number of delicate black markings on their reddish-fawn bodies, including stripes on the rear and a little tuft of hair above each hind hoof that covers a scent gland. The slender legs are immensely powerful and enable a fleeing impala to take off in a series of catapulting leaps that are believed to demonstrate their fitness to any would-be pursuer.

Impala are extremely common in Zimbabwe's *lowveld*, including in all the national parks, although absent from the higher central and eastern areas. You will sometimes see them in herds of several hundred. The rutting season is a period of noisy aggression as rams compete for territory, the dominant

Impala

ones separating out a dozen or so ewes from the herd to form their own little harem. Impalas' healthy population can be largely attributed to two advantageous breeding tactics: they have a degree of control over their fertility, with the ability to hold back in times of drought; and the females tend to drop their lambs almost in unison in early summer, in effect flooding the market with a glut of young and thus ensuring a high survival rate.

SMALL ANTELOPE Many of the smaller antelope are hard to see, being timid and – in some cases – nocturnal. You should, however, come across at least one or two, including the klipspringer, steenbok and common duiker.

Klipspringer (*Oreotragus oreotragus*) One of the world's most agile hoofed mammals, the klipspringer spends its life browsing amongst rocky outcrops, cliffs and gorges. You are virtually guaranteed to see them in the Matobo Hills if you continually check the skyline, where they often stand silhouetted as they survey the world below. Klipspringers grow to 60cm and weigh up to 13kg (the ewe is 2–3kg heavier than the ram). They owe their stocky appearance to their thick coat, in which the hairs stand out from the body rather than lying flat. This coat may serve to cushion them from falls or, more likely, act as an insulator. The tiny, downward-pointing hooves are specially adapted to grip, enabling the klipspringer to tiptoe with great speed and agility over seemingly impossibly steep rocks. Only the male has the short, straight horns, but both sexes have prominent facial scent glands, with which they mark twigs as they pass by.

Klipspringer

Suni (*Neotragus moschatus*) This tiny, pretty antelope is largely nocturnal and secretive. Although common in neighbouring Mozambique, it is rare in Zimbabwe, being restricted to small patches in the northeast and southeast. One of the smallest antelopes, it measures only 35cm at the shoulder and weighs no more than 5kg. Finding a suni is made even more difficult by the dense riverine undergrowth that it frequents. If you are keen to see one, however, start your quest in the Mahenye area of northern Gonarezhou, where the guides claim to find them regularly.

Steenbok (*Paphicerus campestris*) Common in open grassland throughout central and southwestern Zimbabwe, this 50cm-tall animal is notable for its large ears and the thin, sharp, vertical horns of the male. Generally seen singly or in pairs, the steenbok is unusual among antelopes in its habit of digging a shallow scrape in which to cover up its urine and droppings – possibly to avoid detection by predators.

Steenbok

Oribi (*Ourebia ourebi*) Superficially similar to a steenbok, this antelope is slightly larger, with smaller ears, a more yellowish coat and distinct black-tipped tail. The two can also generally be told apart by their range and habitat, as oribi prefer higher-rainfall grassland and do not occur in the southwest of the country. In Gonarezhou, however, the ranges overlap.

Sharpe's grysbok (*Raphicerus sharpie*) Although common across much of Zimbabwe, little is known about this secretive, nocturnal, 50cm-tall antelope. It is similar to a steenbok in appearance, though its coat is longer, more reddish in colour and flecked with white, while its profile is noticeably more hunched. Males sport a pair of short, straight horns. Grysbok like good bush cover, with a preference for rocky vegetation at the base of hills.

Common duiker *(Cephalophus natalensis)* The duiker – pronounced as in 'biker' – is found all over southern Africa, except for desert regions, and is common across Zimbabwe both in and out of parks. When disturbed it lies low, but it may panic and break cover, bounding away on a characteristic zigzag course. At 50cm the common duiker is the same height as several other small antelopes, but is stockier and at 20kg weighs somewhat more; again, the female is bigger than the male. The ram's horns reach an average of 11cm; what may look at first sight like a third small horn between them is, in fact, a tuft of hair.

Blue duiker *(Philantomba monticola)* At 35cm tall and no more than 4kg, this is southern Africa's smallest antelope. A timid denizen of forest undergrowth, it is largely nocturnal and very seldom seen. It occurs only in the forests of the Eastern Highlands where it forages for berries and other fruits, also taking the occasional insect. Other populations live along the southeastern coastal strip of South Africa, where they are commonly snared for bushmeat. This diminutive antelope's main natural enemy is the crowned eagle.

REPTILES
Nile crocodile *(Crocodylus niloticus)* This huge beast, which may top 5m in length and weigh 1,000kg or more, has an ancestry going back more than 150 million years. Its fearsome reputation is well earned, and it is probably responsible for more human fatalities than any other large animal in Africa. Adult crocs snatch prey such as impala from the bank, with big individuals even capable of tackling a buffalo. They also steal kills from other animals and will happily tuck into decaying carrion.

Like that of all cold-blooded reptiles, a crocodile's metabolism slows down during winter and it can go for months without feeding. Breeding takes place during summer. The female excavates a shallow nest in a sandbank before depositing about 80 hard-shelled eggs. These take three months to hatch, with the gender of the hatchlings determined by the temperature inside the nest during the middle month (if it's below 31.7°C or above 34.5°C they will be female). The youngsters hatch underground, whereupon the female digs them out and gently carries them in her mouth to the shallows. She guards her brood until they are old enough to make their own way in life.

Crocodiles are found in rivers, dams and waterholes throughout low-lying areas of Zimbabwe. Heavy persecution in the past, however, means they are uncommon outside national parks.

Lizards Zimbabwe is home to dozens of species of lizard. The following are among the more conspicuous and well known.

Water monitor or Nile monitor *(Varanus niloticus)* This is the largest lizard in the region, reaching up to 2m in length, and is frequently seen basking on a riverside branch or by the water's edge. Its broad diet embraces anything from crustaceans and mussels to the eggs of both birds and crocodiles. In turn it often finds itself the prey of crocs and eagles, especially the large martial eagle. A clutch of up to 60 eggs is laid in an inhabited termite mound, which provides conditions of perfect temperature and humidity for incubation. The eggs hatch a year later when spring rains soften the mound allowing the hatchlings to emerge. It's frequently referred to by its Afrikaans name – *leguaan*.

Agamas (Agamidae) The best known of these chunky, long-legged lizards is the **tree agama** (*Acanthocerus atricollis*), and you will often encounter males dashing around tree trunks as they chase rivals, nodding their bright blue head in display. Females are well camouflaged and less easily seen. The similar, but smaller **Kirk's rock agama** (*Agama kirkii*) dashes around granite outcrops, flaunting its bright purple body and orange head.

Flat lizard (*Platysaurus intermedius*) The males of these beautiful little lizards display most of the colours of the rainbow and are named from their ability to squeeze into the smallest of cracks, especially in exfoliating granite outcrops. The best place to find them is at Rhodes's Grave in Matobo National Park, where they have become habituated to humans, dashing around your feet as they scrounge titbits from your picnic.

Flap-necked chameleon (*Chamaeleo dilepis*) Like all chameleons, this species is best known for its ability to change colour to suit its surroundings, rendering it almost invisible amongst foliage. Fortunately it generally fails to mimic tarmac, so be alert for a green leaf on long legs lurching across the road as you drive by. Indeed, this may be the only time you see a chameleon, as its bad reputation in African folklore may mean your guide is reluctant to point one out. Chameleons have a prehensile tail and tong-like toes to help grasp foliage. They use their independently rotating, conical eyes to spot prey, then capture it by shooting out a long, sticky, telescopic tongue. You might encounter a chameleon anywhere in Zimbabwe's *bushveld* areas, most commonly during the rainy season.

Tropical house gecko (*Hemidactylus mabouia*) This is the most widespread and conspicuous of many species of gecko. It tends to inhabit buildings, as the name suggests, preying on insects drawn to electric lights. Geckos' ability to dash around walls, ceilings and windows is thanks to their amazing toes. These are not sticky, as you might imagine, but are tipped with pads of hair-covered scales called scansors, which provide adhesion through molecular attraction. You'll doubtless find these endearing creatures in your lodge at some time in your stay, but treat them with respect because they are helping to keep your room insect free.

Snakes Snakes are never far away in Africa. You will seldom see them, however, as most sense your arrival from the vibration of your footsteps and generally slither out of your way. They also have other unusual sensory organs, primarily developed for catching prey. Their tongue flicks out to 'taste' the air and they can interpret the result using the Jacobson's organ in the roof of the mouth; some species even have heat-sensitive pits along their lips so they can detect the infrared radiation of prey.

African rock python (*Python sebae*) At up to 5m in length, this is Africa's largest snake. It is widespread throughout Zimbabwe, preferring savanna and scrub – often near water, where it can remain submerged for long periods. Pythons hunt mostly at night, taking anything from dassies and game birds to monkeys, small antelopes and even crocodiles. They seize their prey in sharp teeth, then immediately wrap their coils around its body. Death comes by asphyxiation rather than crushing. Depending on the size of the meal, digestion can take weeks and pythons may often be found basking in the sun while this process continues.

Boomslang (*Dispholidus typus*) This snake grows up to 1.5m and has a potentially fatal, haemotoxic venom. The good news is that it's quite a shy tree snake that preys on lizards, birds, frogs and chameleons, and the position of its fangs – at the back of the mouth – means it cannot easily bite large animals (such as man). While its very variable colouration of dull brown to bright green makes it potentially difficult to identify, it has proportionally the largest eyes of any African snake. The boomslang is widespread in Zimbabwe across a variety of habitats.

Black mamba (*Dendroaspis polylepis*) The black mamba is Africa's largest and most feared venomous snake, occasionally exceeding 4m in length. It occurs throughout the country in savanna and *bushveld*, where it inhabits termite mounds, hollow logs and rock crevices. Grey in colour, its name comes from the black mouth lining, a sight you'd rather not be faced with. The black mamba, like most snakes, prefers to avoid people, but if cornered it will raise its gaping head, even to chest height, in an impressive threat display. Sudden movement may provoke a strike, so the best advice in this situation is to freeze then back off very slowly. The venom is a potent neurotoxin, causing death by respiratory failure, but human fatalities are rare.

Green mamba (*Dendroaspis angusticeps*) Slightly less venomous (though still potentially fatal to humans) than its black cousin and just over half its length, this bright green snake is very shy and is found only in isolated forest areas of the Eastern Highlands. You are thus unlikely to see it.

Mozambique spitting cobra (*Naja mossambica*) Despite its name, this common snake is found all over Zimbabwe and in very similar habitats to the black mamba. Again, it prefers to retire from a threat, but if cornered it may rise up, spread its hood and spit its venom. It aims for the eyes and, over a range up to 3m, is frighteningly accurate. A bite is used to subdue prey and can occasionally prove fatal in humans. This species is one of the smaller cobras, reaching 1–1.2m in length, and is distinguished by the black banding on its throat.

Puff adder (*Bitis arietans*) This large and extremely common snake grows to an average of 1m. Its head is flat and triangular and its plump body marked with a chevron pattern. You should learn to recognise this species, as it is responsible for most serious snakebites in the region. Invariably described as lazy and aggressive, puff adders prefer camouflage to flight, so most human victims tend to get bitten when they inadvertently tread on one.

Tortoises
Leopard tortoise (*Geochelone pardalis*) This is by far the largest and most common of Zimbabwe's tortoises, growing up to around 10kg – and occasionally much larger if allowed to reach its full lifespan of 50 years or more. The spotted pattern of its carapace (shell) and plastron (belly shield) provide an effective armour against predators, so probably the biggest threat to a slow-moving adult tortoise is fire. Eggs and the hatchlings, however, are extremely vulnerable to a variety of predators.

BIRDS With Zimbabwe's tally of over 650 recorded species the following account can only offer a brief overview. It concentrates on the most prominent groups, with short descriptions of some of the more interesting and conspicuous species.

Herons and egrets These are long-legged, long-necked, long-billed birds generally found near water. The large **grey heron** (*Ardea cinere*) is very common and the same species as found in Europe, while the slate grey and rufous **goliath heron** (*Ardea goliath*) is the largest heron in the world, standing at 140cm. Smaller species include the **squacco heron** (*Ardeola ralloides*), well camouflaged among aquatic vegetation, and the **cattle egret** (*Bubulcus ibis*), which has all-white plumage and feeds on insects disturbed around the feet of grazing animals.

Storks Superficially similar to herons, storks have longer, heavier bills and fly with their necks extended (herons' have theirs retracted). The **saddle-billed stork** (*Ephippiorhynchus senegalensis*), with its brilliant yellow, black and red bill, is one of Zimbabwe's most elegant birds and often seen fishing on large rivers, floodplains, dams and marshes. At the opposite end of the beauty spectrum is the huge 150cm-tall **marabou stork** (*Leptoptilos crumeniferus*). This scavenger is commonly seen in game parks squabbling with vultures over a carcass, its huge bill and featherless head and neck caked in blood.

Other waterbirds The **hamerkop** (*Scopus umbretto*) is a rather odd-looking bird, similar to but neither stork nor heron. It's the size of a large crow, with brown plumage and a strange backward-facing crest that gives its head the shape of a hammer. Usually seen singly beside fresh water, it builds a gigantic domed nest that is often hijacked by other creatures. Among a profusion of smaller waterbirds, including ducks, geese, grebes and coots, is the handsome **African jacana** (*Actophilorsis africanus*), sometimes referred to as the lilytrotter for its ability to skip across floating water vegetation on very long toes. Two plovers of note are the very common **blacksmith plover (lapwing)** (*Vanellus armatus*), named for its metallic 'clinking' call, and the **white-crowned plover (lapwing)** (*Vanellus albiceps*), with distinctive yellow wattles dangling from the base of its bill. The latter is found only in the north along the Zambezi.

HOW TO UPSET YOUR BIRDING GUIDE

You need to be aware that a few years ago, ornithological authorities in Africa embarked on a name-standardisation programme aimed at eliminating the often different names used in different countries for the same bird. This process makes a lot of sense but change is often not welcomed and it has upset many Zimbabwean birders and I suspect those of every country, as they see their familiar names being changed. New guidebooks reflect these changes and you'll often see your guide stiffen and narrow his eyes when you refer to what used to be called a dikkop as a 'thicknee', a grey lourie as a 'go-away bird' (where's the sense in that?) or the lovely Heuglin's robin as a 'white-browed robin chat'. Younger guides are much more receptive to these revolutionary developments but beware the older ones with beards and bellies. My advice is to use the old names while out in the bush but to liven up the discussion around the campfire by casually raising the matter after a few beers.

Large ground birds No bird comes larger than the **ostrich** (*Struthio camelus*), standing over 2m tall and weighing 80kg or more. Flightless, it gets around on long, strong legs at speeds of up to 60km/h. The **kori bustard** (*Ardeotis kori*) is arguably the world's heaviest flying bird, weighing up to 17kg and standing 120cm tall, and is reasonably common in open areas of Zimbabwe's game parks – often near herds of grazers. The **crowned crane** (*Balearica regularum*) is found in open grassland, farmland and marshy areas and has a golden crest ornamenting its black and white face. The largest of several hornbills in Zimbabwe, the **southern ground hornbill** (*Bucorvus leadbeateri*) is a heavy turkey-sized bird, up to 90cm, with black plumage and a crimson, naked face and throat pouch. Unfortunately this bird is hunted for the pot and is becoming quite uncommon, though small groups are to be found in protected wooded areas and are often seen foraging along the roadside in Hwange

BIRDING

Zimbabwe's varied geography and vegetation create a wide variety of habitats supporting an astonishing roll call of over 650 recorded species. That's nearly three-quarters of southern Africa's total of over 900 birds, and equates to truly exciting birding, especially when you factor in the chance of spotting one of the continent's rarest prizes, the African pitta. With such a wealth of species it's impossible for a destinational guidebook to describe even the most common birds; for this you need a specialist guide. Instead, the following notes are meant to encourage those not yet smitten to take up the hobby of birding. It's natural for first-time visitors to concentrate on large mammals, but birding opens up a whole new world of observation and it's all too easy to get hooked.

It's simple and cheap to get started, and you're never far from a bird, even in cities. All you need is a reasonable pair of binoculars, a field guidebook and preferably a knowledgeable guide to explain the basics. Finding your way round a guidebook is relatively simple because the main families are generally very distinct from one another and readily identifiable. The most popular books cover the whole of southern Africa so, having decided which family your bird belongs to, it's a matter of checking which species occur in your area. This usually leaves you with relatively few to choose from.

Birds, however, tend to enjoy their privacy and have a habit of flying off just as you raise your binoculars for a closer look. Raptors are difficult to identify in flight as there's seldom anything to relate their size to, and plumage colours and patterns can change considerably as the bird matures. Some birds, such as nightjars, can be identified by their call (which is just as well because you'll seldom see one and even if you did, the six species in Zimbabwe all look virtually the same). And then we have the 'LBJs' (little brown jobs), the drab little birds of a wide variety of species that are pretty well indistinguishable from one another.

The rest, however, come in a dazzling array of colours, shapes and sizes, exotic and often bizarre, so your first forays into the bush will have you struggling to keep up as you frantically juggle binos and book. Before too long, you'll find yourself in that growing fraternity of enthusiasts who have their binoculars trained on a distant treetop while everyone else in the vehicle is taking photographs of the elephant.

For recommended guidebooks, see *Appendix 3*. For advice on binoculars, see the box, *Choosing binoculars*, page 117 in *Chapter 3*.

and Zambezi national parks. It roosts in trees, from where it delivers its distinctive – and most unbirdlike – booming call just before dawn.

The **secretary bird** (*Sagittarius serpentarius*) is a large ground-dwelling raptor that is usually seen striding through open grassland on the lookout for reptiles, birds, rodents and other small prey. Death is delivered by powerful blows from the feet. It stands up to 120cm tall and has a raptor's hooked bill, a drooping crest, a long tail, and predominantly grey plumage set off by black 'trousers'.

Game birds Francolins are squat, partridge-like birds that dash in and out of the undergrowth. Many are similar in appearance, but can be distinguished by face or leg colour. **Swainson's francolin** (*Francolinus swainsonii*), for instance, has a red face, with black bill and legs. More easily identified is the **helmeted guineafowl** (*Numeda meleagris*), with its dark grey body covered in white spots, and naked red head. It runs around in noisy flocks that rely on the goodwill of drivers as they dash in front of the vehicles. Guineafowl are widely farmed for their meat and eggs.

Raptors Birds of prey include eagles and vultures as well as many smaller hawks, kites, buzzards and harriers. They can be difficult to identify in flight as there's usually no size reference in the sky and the plumage of some species changes significantly as the bird grows from juvenile to adult. Of the seven species of vulture found in Zimbabwe, often three or four of them around one carcass, the **lappet-faced vulture** (*Torgos tracheliolus*) is the largest, with a massive bill that can rip open all but the toughest hide. You'll often hear the distinctive high-pitched cry before you see the **African fish eagle** (*Haliaeetus vocifer*), with its dark brown body and white head. This distinctive raptor perches in trees high above the water before swooping down for a fish weighing anything up to 2.5kg. The **bateleur** (*Terathopius ecaudatus*), with its short tail and wide wings, has a characteristic flight action: occasional flaps and a sideways rocking glide reminiscent of a tightrope walker – hence the French name. The massive **black** or **Verreaux's eagle** (*Aquila verreauxii*) favours rocky hillsides, and there's a healthy and much studied population in the Matobo Hills. A smaller and, in summer, extremely common raptor is the **yellow-billed kite** (*Milvus migrans*), which has a distinctive forked tail that is constantly twisting like a rudder while in flight.

Doves, cuckoos and coucals Among many species of pigeon and dove, the ubiquitous **Cape turtle dove** (*Streptopelia capicola*) announces its presence with its cooing 'work harder, work harder' call, while the small **emerald-spotted dove** (*Turtur chalcospilos*) is fond of woodland, and has a brilliant metallic green patch on its wing covers. Cuckoos are brood parasites, laying their eggs in the nests of others. All are summer visitors, including the **red-chested cuckoo** (*Cuculus solitarius*), with its distinctive descending three-note call. Coucals are related, but are larger birds that make their own nests. The **Senegal coucal** (*Centropus senegalensis*) is Zimbabwe's most common species, while the very similar **Burchell's coucal** (*Centropus burchellii*) avoids the central and western parts of the country. Both are quite secretive, enjoying dense undergrowth and reeds, so you'll probably hear their repetitious, bubbling call before you see them.

Parrots, turacos and trogon The only parrot you're likely to see in Zimbabwe is **Meyer's parrot** (*Poicephalus meyeri*). Its small size and predominantly brown-green plumage means it's difficult to spot in trees, but you'll hear parties coming as they dash around in flight screeching loudly. Turacos (formerly known as louries) are beautiful, crested woodland birds generally favouring riverine habitats. The

purple-crested turaco (*Musophaga porphereolapha*) has striking blue and green plumage with crimson primary feathers, and is only absent from the west of the country. **Schalow's turaco** (*Tauraco schalowi*) will be a lucky find around Victoria Falls, while the very similar **Livingstone's turaco** (*Tauraco livingstonii*) is found only in the far northeast. The **Go-away bird** (grey lourie) (*Corythhaixoides concolor*), is the only plain member of this group, and takes its name from its plaintive 'g-waaay, g-waaay' call. It is found everywhere but the Eastern Highlands. The **Narina trogon** (*Apaloderma narina*) is richly coloured, with its vivid green and red plumage. This elusive forest bird spends the summer months in the Eastern Highlands and Gonarezhou, and moves to the Zambezi Valley in winter.

Owls and nightjars

All of southern Africa's 12 species of owl inhabit Zimbabwe. They range from the diminutive **pearl-spotted owlet** (*Glaucidium pearlatum*), at only 18cm, to the **giant** or **Verreaux's eagle owl** (*Bubo lacteus*), at a huge 65cm. The uncommon **Pel's fishing owl** (*Scotopelia peli*) is a prized sighting, for which Gonarezhou offers the best chances. Nightjars, like owls, are nocturnal, but these insectivorous birds are more closely related to swifts. Six species inhabit Zimbabwe and all but one are remarkably similar in appearance. The male of the **pennant-winged nightjar** (*Macrodipteryx vexillarius*) is the odd one out – at least in its summer breeding plumage, when it trails extremely long streamers from its wings. Otherwise you'll be certain to hear the distinctive quavering 'Good Lord deliver us' call of the **fiery-necked nightjar** (*Caprimulgus pectoralis*), a year-round resident.

Bee-eaters

These extremely colourful birds have long tails, long curved beaks and are extremely agile in flight as they chase bees and other insect prey, making repeated sallies from a favourite perch. All nest in holes, and on a summer canoeing trip on the Zambezi you'll see large numbers of the **southern carmine bee-eater** (*Merops nubicoides*), dashing around their colonies in the riverbank. Zimbabwe's three permanent and common residents are the **little bee-eater** (*Merops pusillus*), **swallow-tailed bee-eater** (*Merops hirundineus*) and **white-fronted bee-eater** (*Merops bullockoides*) – all widely distributed, and nesting in holes in sandy riverbanks.

Rollers

These birds are named for their acrobatic, tumbling flight as they perform their aerial courtship display. You'll probably first see the chunky, dove-sized **lilac-breasted roller** (*Coracias caudate*) perched on roadside power lines and be unimpressed with its apparently drab plumage. But in flight it becomes one of the most dazzlingly colourful birds in the region, flaunting brilliant blue wings. This species is widely distributed across savanna woodland regions. The **racket-tailed roller** (*Coracias spatulata*) is a much more elusive bird, favouring *mopane* woodland and notable for its two spatula-shaped tail extensions.

Hoopoes

A hysterical cackling sound in the trees will alert you to a group of **green (red-billed) woodhoopoes** (*Phoeniculus purpureus*) as they clamber around the branches probing for insects with their long curved beaks. Their cousin the **African hoopoe** (*Upupa africana*) looks very different: it also has a long thin beak, but its plumage is cinnamon with bold black and white markings, and it sports an erectile crest that creates a rather comical appearance as it pecks around bush and grassland, frequently in suburban gardens.

Kingfishers

Kingfishers are rather squat birds with short tails and long, heavy beaks. Although commonly associated with water, several species live far from

Once you've spotted your animal, bird or tree you will want to identify it and there is a wide range of very good field guides available. Internet shopping is fine if you know exactly what you want, but for this sort of book there is nothing quite like leafing through several in the shop. In practical terms you will want to be able to find the relevant page as quickly as possible, so pay particular attention to the book's indexing system and layout.

For just one book to cover all the creatures you are likely to see (plus many more), I would strongly recommend Mike Unwin's comprehensive and extremely readable *Southern African Wildlife*, published by Bradt. It is richly illustrated with photographs, and covers mammals, birds, reptiles and invertebrates. A more compact alternative is *The Wildlife of Southern Africa* by Vincent Carruthers, which has illustrations and brief descriptions of all the common fauna and flora. More specifically, *A Field Guide to the Larger Mammals of Southern Africa* by Chris and Tilde Stuart, is an excellent book with over 500 photographs and very good descriptive text to help in identification.

Birdwatching is a more specialist hobby and there is a variety of books that cater to the market, especially in South African bookshops. You have first to choose between photographic guides and those with illustrations. Perhaps surprisingly, it is much easier to identify birds from illustrations as they are carefully drawn to exhibit the often minuscule differences between species. Photographs, on the other hand, are subject to such factors as lighting, background, angle of shot and condition of bird, so the photo in the book can appear quite different from what you see in real life.

Beginners should check out *What's That Bird: A Starter's Guide to the Birds of Southern Africa* by Kenneth Newman. Otherwise, the two most popular field guides are *Newman's Birds of Southern Africa* and the *SASOL Guide to the Birds of Southern Africa* by Sinclair, Hockey and Tarboton, both of which have excellent illustrations and are easy to use. For photographs, try Ian Sinclair's *Birds of Southern Africa* – I use this as a backup to my *Newman's*. If you plan to travel further north than Zimbabwe, you will need Ian Sinclair and Peter Ryan's *Birds of Africa: South of the Sahara*. It is a lovely book, but there are well over twice the number of birds covered and identification can therefore take much longer than with one restricted to southern Africa.

As well as mammals and birds, there are specific guides to all aspects of the region's natural history, from reptiles and butterflies to trees and plants. Apart from Mike Unwin's book, all of the above field guides are published by Struik, which is the most comprehensive southern African wildlife publisher. South African bookshops, including the one at Johannesburg Airport, generally have a good range on their shelves.

Those who prefer a more high-tech format may want to consider a CD-ROM or MP3 format. *Roberts' Multimedia Birds of Southern Africa* was the first to be published in CD form. As well as the usual illustrations and photographs it includes identification aids such as video clips, bird sounds, nest and egg information, a listing facility and an excellent section pointing out top birding spots all around the region. iPod and other tablet users will find excellent apps from both SASOL and especially Roberts. These are basically digital versions of their guidebooks but complete with audio birdcalls and other features that make identification much simpler.

Natural History and Conservation   FAUNA

2

any water source and feed predominantly on insects. Two fish eaters to look out for, as they hover then plunge into the water, are the 45cm, brown and mottled **giant kingfisher** (*Megaceryle maxima*), and the much smaller, dazzlingly coloured **malachite kingfisher** (*Alcedo cristata*). Both can be found throughout the country, especially along the Zambezi and at wooded dam sites. Most common, perhaps, is the **pied kingfisher** (*Ceryle rudis*), which falls between the two in size and has black and white plumage.

Hornbills
The very large southern ground hornbill, mentioned on pages 58–9, has a number of much smaller relatives. These ungainly looking birds have heavy bills and are all hole nesters. The female seals herself into the nest with mud and droppings, leaving only a small aperture through which the male feeds her. The common and widely distributed **yellow-billed hornbill** (*Tokus leucomelus*) will be ever-present on your game drives and around your campsite. Look out also for the larger and less common **trumpeter hornbill** (*Bycanistes bucinator*), which has a huge casque on its upper bill and long feathery trousers. It is found from Victoria Falls all along the Zambezi to the north, and sometimes in riverine forest in the east.

Woodpeckers and barbets
Woodpeckers clamber around branches with a specially adapted toe arrangement (two pointing forwards, two backwards), as they probe crevices for insects and grubs. This and their habit of excavating nest holes give rise to the telltale tapping sound by which they are often located. Four species occur in Zimbabwe, of which the widespread **cardinal woodpecker** (*Dendropicos fuscescens*) is the smallest, but you'll need patience and a good pair of binoculars to tell them apart. Barbets are closely related but chunkier, thick-billed birds of woodland and garden. The **crested barbet** (*Trachyphonus vaillantii*) is the largest, and its mottled plumage gives it a scruffy appearance. You will probably hear the **black-collared barbet** (*Lybius torquatus*) (no mention in the name of its vivid scarlet face and breast) before you see it: male and female perform a rapid, head-bobbing duet that has been described as 'too-puddly, too-puddly', repeated a number of times.

Honeyguides
These smallish birds are brood parasites, like cuckoos. Six species occur in Zimbabwe, but only the **greater honeyguide** (*Indicator indicator*) lives up to its name. When this bird locates a bees' nest it will lead a honey badger – or even a person – to the nest using much frantic twittering and flapping. Once the larger animal has broken in and taken its fill, the bird can then feed on the wax and larvae left behind.

African pitta
(*Pitta angolensis*) This thrush-sized bird, one of the most sought-after species on the continent, deserves a mention, as Zimbabwe is one of the few places it can be seen. Although very brightly coloured, it is extremely inconspicuous as it forages in thick undergrowth. Chizarira National Park and the remote interior of the Zambezi Valley near Masoka village are the best places to find it, although you'll need expert guidance to gain access.

Passerines (perching birds)
Well over half of Zimbabwe's bird species fall under this heading. The following are among those you are most likely to encounter.

Drongos, crows and orioles The cheeky, all-black **fork-tailed drongo** (*Dicrurus adsimilis*) is seen everywhere in the bush, generally flying down from a perch to hawk insects but also mobbing much larger birds and robbing others of their catch. The

pied crow (*Corvus albus*) is a large, opportunistic bird often seen around human settlements. Orioles are starling-sized, predominantly yellow birds notable for their beautiful, liquid call. Most common is the **black-headed oriole** (*Oriolus larvatus*), found throughout the country in woodland and riverine habitats.

Bulbuls and babblers The **black-eyed bulbul** (*Picnonotus barbatus*) is the most common of several bulbul species, often frequenting settlements and gardens, where it entertains with a variety of calls. The **terrestrial bulbul** (*Phyllastrphus terrestris*) is, as its name suggests, most commonly found foraging close to the ground. **Arrow-marked babblers** (*Turdoides jardineii*) are aptly named, not only for their white-streaked plumage but also for the excited rasping 'scrrr scrrr' these thrush-sized birds make when foraging as a group; not dissimilar to the sound of green woodhoopoes.

Robins Two robins are worthy of note here. The **white-browed robin chat**, previously known and probably for decades to come as **Heuglin's robin** (*Cossipha heuglini*) is a handsome, orange-bellied bird, with a black head and white browstripe, commonly seen in gardens and around camp. It has a rich, ventriloquial song. The smaller **Swynnerton's robin** (*Swinnertonia swinnertoni*) is restricted to the forests of the Eastern Highlands, where it is much sought after by birders.

Shrikes and flycatchers Some shrikes are known as 'butcher birds' for their habit of impaling prey – from insects to small lizards – on a handy thorn spike to be eaten later. The common **fiscal shrike** (*Lanius collaris*) is often seen in *highveld* gardens terrorising its neighbours. The **crimson-breasted boubou** (*Laniarius atrococcineus*), found in the southwest *thornveld* and Hwange, and the secretive **gorgeous bush shrike** (*Telophorus sulfureopectus*), best seen in Gonarezhou, are much more colourful. Flycatchers are small insectivorous birds, of which the most striking is the **paradise flycatcher** (*Terpsiphone viridis*). Breeding males of this summer migrant sport extremely long and elegant red-brown tail feathers and in urban areas they often choose nest sites very close to buildings, presumably as protection from more wary predator birds. Their nests are barely eggcup size.

Starlings and oxpeckers You won't go far before you see one of the beautifully iridescent, blue-green glossy starlings. Four species look remarkably similar, with only subtle differences in their shimmering plumage, but the **long-tailed glossy starling** (*Lamprotornis mevesii*), mainly found in low-lying areas, is easily identified by its much longer tail. The **plum-coloured starling** (*Cinnyricinclus leucogaster*) is a widespread summer visitor whose stunning purple head and topcoat contrasts with a clean white underbelly. **Oxpeckers** are closely related to starlings, but feed by picking off ticks and other bloodsucking insects from the hides of large animals, including cattle, giraffe and rhinoceros. Two species live in Zimbabwe, and are best distinguished by their bill colour and choice of host.

Sunbirds Sunbirds are small, insect- and nectar-eating birds, whose thin, curved beaks are adapted for probing flowers. They are notable for the iridescent, colourful plumage of the males, although to tell one species from another you need to get them to sit still! Among the most common and striking is the **scarlet-chested sunbird** (*Nectarinia senegalensis*).

Weavers and queleas Weavers are seed-eating birds named for the intricate suspended nests woven by males from grasses and stripped vegetation. This is often a thankless task, as the nest is a lure to a mate and, if the female rejects her suitor's handiwork, the male must strip it down and build a better one. Each species of weaver builds a different-shaped nest. Most weavers are yellow with black heads and speckled wings and can be difficult to differentiate, but the **red-headed weaver** (*Anaplectes rubriceps*) lives up to its name, with the breeding male sporting a crimson head and shoulders. The **red-billed quelea** (*Quelea quelea*) is a small, sparrow-like bird of the same family that congregates in flocks hundreds of thousands strong. These are the scourge of arable farmers, capable of stripping fields bare of grain if their natural grass-seed diet runs out. Flocks change direction abruptly in mid-air, like shoals of fish, their innumerable tiny wingbeats combining in a startling roar at take-off.

Finches and waxbills These tiny seed-eating birds are often multi-coloured and intricately patterned. Three favourites are the dazzling **melba finch** (*Pytilia melba*), the common **blue waxbill** (*Uraeginthus angolensis*) and the long-tailed **violet-eared waxbill** (*Granatina granatina*). All species are usually seen feeding on the ground.

Widows, bishops and whydahs Widows are generally noted for the long tails of breeding males, although Zimbabwe only has one such, the **red-collared widow** (*Euplectes ardens*) of the east and north. The **red bishop** (*Euplectes oryx*) is a stocky little bird with a black body and face and a scarlet collar and crown. Whydahs, like cuckoos, are brood parasites, each species with its own waxbill host. Unlike cuckoos, however, the much more sociable fledglings grow up alongside the host's nestlings rather than turfing them out of the nest. Breeding males sport very long tails but for the rest of the year look like their more boring females. Two to look out for are the **pin-tailed wydah** (*Vidua macroura*), a feisty little devil around the bird table capable of seeing off much larger rivals, and the **paradise wydah** (*Vidua paradisaea*), which is more colourful and has a heavier tail.

NATIONAL PARKS

The full title of Zimbabwe's national parks authority is Zimbabwe Parks and Wildlife Management Authority (ZPWMA) but in this book I shall refer to it either by its acronym, or more regularly as 'Parks', the term most frequently used by Zimbabweans.

Most people associate Zimbabwe's national parks with the principal wildlife reserves – Chizarira, Gonarezhou, Hwange, Kazuma Pan, Mana Pools, Matobo, Matusadona and Zambezi – but the parks authority administers a much wider network of properties including botanical reserves and recreational parks including Ewanrigg, Chimanimani, Bvumba, Nyanga and Victoria Falls among others.

Three national parks – Victoria Falls, Matobo and Mana Pools – are UNESCO Natural World Heritage Sites (the other two World Heritage Sites – Great Zimbabwe and Khami Ruins – are manmade).

The national park system was set up in the early to mid-20th century with the aim of making use of unproductive land, but this philosophy changed with the creation of the Department of National Parks and Wildlife Management in 1964 and the passing of the Parks and Wildlife Act in 1975. As well as consolidating the status of the national parks this act transferred ownership of any wildlife on private land from the state to the landowner. Private owners were thereby encouraged to see 'their' wildlife as an asset worth protecting.

The national parks were designated wildlife protection areas, and their establishment caused widespread disruption to human populations, who were simply removed from their traditional lands and relocated. In later, more enlightened, years the CAMPFIRE (Communal Areas Management Programme for Indigenous Resources) project was established to convert neighbouring indigenous people into stakeholders so they could benefit from elements of the wildlife industry and contribute to wildlife conservation.

Despite, or perhaps because of, the originally heavy-handed approach to wildlife conservation, Zimbabwe created what is arguably the most varied and best-stocked system of accessible parks in southern Africa. Not only are they relatively affordable, but the general lack of retaining fences gives Zimbabwe's parks a genuine sense of wilderness and a very natural feel.

The recent political and economic situation has, however, taken a heavy toll on the wildlife. The ZPWMA, once the finest scientific and conservation body in the region, is a shadow of its former self in terms of financial viability. Visitor numbers and revenue have plummeted. Starved of income, anti-poaching patrols are hamstrung through lack of vehicles, fuel and equipment, visitor facilities are poorly maintained and wildlife suffers when waterholes run dry because of broken pumps and fuel shortages. Poaching – for subsistence, the massive regional bushmeat and the international ivory and rhino-horn markets – has escalated, sometimes unchecked.

Despite this bad news there is great hope for the future. Tourism is one of Zimbabwe's main revenue earners, and wildlife viewing is a key attraction for visitors. Wildlife has a remarkable ability to recover, and all it needs here is a return to political normality, bringing visitors back to the parks, the reinstatement of good governance and wildlife management, and cash to resume policing to reduce poaching to manageable levels. The great expertise and dedication to conservation, shown by so many people in Parks, the conservancies and the tourism sector generally, means that every effort is being be made to return the national parks to their former glory. It has been extremely encouraging during the updating process of this book for me to see how Parks have resurrected their previously moribund website, bringing it once again to a useful and up-to-date resource.

Despite their current problems, Zimbabwe's national parks are a pleasure to visit. There are fantastic concentrations of game in Hwange, rhino thrive in Matobo and are doing well in Matusadona, elephant abound in Mana Pools and massive herds of them come to drink in the river in Zambezi National Park as they make their regular treks between Hwange and neighbouring Chobe. Wild dog are making a comeback in Hwange and many other areas after decades of persecution by farmers, with lion and especially leopard represented in very healthy numbers, testament to the prolific populations of prey species.

Chizarira and Gonarezhou national parks are vast, true wilderness areas offering intrepid visitors a spectacular and way-off-the-beaten-track African experience that few other countries can offer. And their wildlife is returning after years of persecution. And if mountain scenery is your priority, the Eastern Highlands have no fewer than three Parks-administered areas to keep you occupied.

Not only this but Zimbabwe is actively co-operating with several neighbouring countries to establish 'transfrontier parks' – parks linked across country borders allowing game to roam and migrate much more freely.

ZIMBABWE PARKS AND WILDLIFE MANAGEMENT AUTHORITY (*Head office & main booking office, cnr Sandringham Dr & Borrowdale Rd, Botanical Gdns, Harare;* 04 706077/8; e *bookings@zimparks.co.zw; www.zimparks.org*) Other offices are in Bulawayo, Mutare, Gweru, Victoria Falls, Hwange and Masvingo. ZPWMA has recently made great improvements to its website.

Entry fees The entry fee for each park depends effectively on its popularity (Victoria Falls National Park, for example, though the smallest, is the most expensive), with parks graded National Park Category 1, 2 or 3. Entry fees (and Parks accommodation; see *Accommodation* in *Chapter 3*) depend further on your nationality: international visitors pay the most; those from the 15 SADC (Southern African Development Community) member states pay approximately 75% of international rates (upon presentation of passport or ID), while Zimbabweans pay even less. While the parks are pricey for overseas tourists, they are nowhere near as expensive as their equivalents in Botswana.

You should pay in US dollars; although other currencies are, in theory, acceptable, attendants may not have rand, euro and sterling rates to hand and certainly won't have change in those currencies.

Entry fees per person The rating category of each park is indicated at the beginning of each national park section that follows.

NP Category 1 – (Victoria Falls Rainforest) International US$30; SADC US$20
NP Category 1 – (Hwange) International US$20; SADC US$15
NP Category 2 – International US$15; SADC US$12
NP Category 3 & 4 – International US$10; SADC US$7
Children aged 6–12 pay 50%; children under 6 are admitted free.

Note: As of early 2013 expensive pricing variations were announced for Mana Pools and Gonarezhou. Previously, visitors to these parks were charged a single entry fee for stays of up to seven days. Now, a daily charge has been introduced. Mana Pools will charge US$20 (international), US$15 (SADC) *per day*. And at Gonarezhou you will be charged US$15, US$12 per day respectively.

There are also per-vehicle charges: US$5 for each private vehicle with up to five seats; additionally, US$5 for a trailer or caravan. Try to arrive with small banknotes, as small change is frequently not available.

TRANSFRONTIER CONSERVATION AREAS
Transfrontier national park initiatives involve neighbouring countries, all recognising that no single country 'owns' its wildlife. Where several countries have adjacent but separated game parks, fences are being taken down and borders opened to allow animals to extend their range and to encourage seasonal migration. Once open, tourists will be able to pass across these international borders within the boundaries of the parks.

The largest of these Transfrontier Conservation Areas (TFCA), also known as 'peace parks', is currently the Great Limpopo TFCA, linking Mozambique's Limpopo, South Africa's Kruger and Zimbabwe's Gonarezhou national parks together with smaller sanctuaries and safari areas to form a massive protected area of some 35,000km². More than 500 bird and nearly 150 mammal species will make this one of the finest accessible wildlife-viewing areas in the whole of Africa. This is just the first phase in creating an even bigger conservation area to measure 100,000km².

However, the Kavango-Zambezi TFCA will be even larger, encompassing the Okavango and Zambezi river basins where the borders of Zimbabwe, Botswana, Namibia, Zambia and Angola converge. It will become the world's biggest conservation area and will eventually span an area of nearly 300,000km², taking in no fewer than 36 national parks, and game-rich areas.

3

Practical Information

WHEN TO VISIT

Zimbabwe offers a very pleasant year-round climate, but the best time to visit depends on which activities you wish to pursue and which regions you want to visit.

FOR WILDLIFE To maximise wildlife viewing, the dry, winter months of July–October are the best. In the dry season, natural water sources become scarce in the bush, encouraging game to congregate around a relatively small number of artificially pumped *pans* or waterholes near lodges and specific game-viewing areas.

In the summer rains, surface water is generally abundant so animals get all they need in more natural circumstances, but as the game becomes dispersed you will tend to see far fewer. At this time of year, vegetation becomes much more luxuriant, acting as an effective screen severely restricting your view into the bush. For more detail see *Wildlife viewing*, under *Activities* in this chapter, page 75.

If your interest is in birdlife, Zimbabwe offers excellent all-year viewing but the summer months are outstanding as the count swells considerably with the arrival of migrants. Think in terms of 650 species countrywide. Some safari camps and national parks close down altogether in the wet period immediately after New Year.

FOR WATERFALLS Victoria Falls will no doubt feature in your first visit. During and after the rains in the Zambezi catchment area in March–June, the falls are full and totally awesome. But your experience consists of massive amounts of thundering spray and little else. It can be virtually impossible to see anything of the actual waterfalls. In the dry season (the time most visitors arrive for wildlife viewing) the water volume is reduced to a relative trickle over some of the cataracts, but you are rewarded with awesome views of the gorges and their fascinating geological structure. For the best of both worlds, visit in June to August.

FOR WATERSPORTS For Zambezi river-based adrenalin activities such as white-water rafting and kayaking, the low water levels during winter (August–January) are best. At high water (May–July, January–March), rafting is restricted to the lower run of rapids, numbers 11–23, as the river is too full and fast for the complete series. After very heavy rains (March–April), these activities are prohibited altogether until water levels subside. Please note that the above dates are totally dependent on rainfall levels in the catchment area so can vary considerably.

Kariba and the Zambezi Valley offer water-based activities, boating and canoeing year-round, but these are best enjoyed outside the hot, humid summer months.

FOR OTHER ACTIVITIES Walking, fishing and horseriding are year-round activities to be found in the Eastern Highlands, although summer rainfall can be high and blanketing mists frequently block out the mountain views. The cool, dry winter and spring offer the best conditions, but bring warm clothes for evenings and make sure your accommodation has a cosy log fire. Winter brings forest fires to this region, with the smoke causing a haze that can spoil views.

HIGHLIGHTS

VICTORIA FALLS A World Heritage Site and one of the 'Seven Natural Wonders of the World', this awesome waterfall is a compulsory stop at any time of year, although different seasons offer completely different viewing opportunities. There are also plenty of adrenalin sports on offer, from white-water rafting and body-boarding to bungee-jumping and gorge-swinging. Elephant-back safaris and river cruises are also available. See pages 255–60 for more information.

ZAMBEZI NATIONAL PARK Right on the doorstep of Victoria Falls, this small and beautifully riverine park has seen a dramatic resurgence of game after years of poaching. As well as the usual plains game, wild dog are regularly seen together with other predators – lion and leopard.

HWANGE NATIONAL PARK Hwange is one of the finest national parks in Africa, with an incredible diversity and abundance of wildlife with the 'Big Five' including both black and white rhino. It is especially noted for its large elephant population. See pages 274–86.

GREAT ZIMBABWE This fascinating ancient stone-walled city is by far the largest and best preserved in sub-Saharan Africa, and is a World Heritage Site. Masvingo is the nearest town. See pages 193–200.

LAKE KARIBA AND MATUSADONA NATIONAL PARK Lake Kariba is Zimbabwe's own 'seaside' resort offering luxurious houseboats and lodges, fishing and wildlife viewing. The southern lakeshore features an excellent selection of exclusive lodges and camps from which you can explore Matusadona's rugged and beautiful wilderness areas before chilling out with a sundowner watching the sunset over the lake. Matusadona is a 'Big Five' national park. See pages 213–25 and 221–5.

EASTERN HIGHLANDS The Eastern Highlands offer some of the most beautiful mountain views in southern Africa, with fishing, hiking, golf, horseriding and unrivalled birding. Cool off up here in the 'Cotswolds of Africa' during the summer months. There are three very different centres: Chimanimani in the south, Nyanga in the north and the beautiful Bvumba Mountains in between. See pages 335–65.

MANA POOLS NATIONAL PARK The tranquil riverine habitat attracts abundant wildlife that can be viewed from foot, vehicle or canoe, while further inland Chitake Springs presents unrivalled, close-up wildlife viewing. Book early, as many Zimbabweans (and visitors) consider this to be their favourite park and accommodation is limited. See pages 227–33.

GONAREZHOU AND CHIZARIRA NATIONAL PARKS These are both wilderness parks in the truest sense of the word, where you can camp in undeveloped, unfenced sites right in amongst the wildlife. Lodges are available for non-campers just outside both parks. Gonarezhou (see pages 324–33) has the awesome sandstone Chilojo Cliffs overlooking the Runde River; rugged Chizarira (see pages 209–13) features the cliffs and gorges of the Zambezi Escarpment.

BULAWAYO Zimbabwe's second-largest town, Bulawayo is friendly, laid-back and oozing colonial history. It is home to the National Art Gallery and Natural History Museum. Within an hour's drive there are sites of great historic interest including possibly the most beautiful example of drystone walling at Nalatale. See pages 291–309.

MATOBO NATIONAL PARK This small national park just south of Bulawayo boasts some of the most dramatic and photogenic rock 'architecture' in southern Africa, and is the best place in Africa to see accessible examples of San rock paintings. Rhino, leopard and ten species of eagle live here. See pages 311–18.

KHAMI RUINS Khami, just outside Bulawayo, has the second most impressive ancient ruins in Zimbabwe, with intricate, drystone walling. This is another of Zimbabwe's World Heritage Sites. See pages 307–9.

HARARE Zimbabwe's cosmopolitan capital has a multitude of shops, hotels and restaurants, as well as a thriving arts scene. A few years ago not many visitors came here – now it should definitely be considered for your itinerary. See pages 153–71.

PLANNING YOUR TRIP

Zimbabwe's attractions, natural and manmade, are spread across a country as large as Great Britain and Ireland combined. You will need to be selective unless you have unlimited time on your hands. There are several ways to arrange your visit, each with its benefits and limitations.

OFF-THE-SHELF ITINERARIES
High street agencies The easiest, cheapest but most restrictive option is a ready-made tour from a brochure or travel agent. Don't expect expert advice, though – I've met people desperate to see big game who were booked into the wrong places at entirely the wrong time of year. But this is an option for first-time visitors on a tight budget and short of time. These trips will include nothing more than the most popular tourist hot spots, giving you only a brief introduction to limited parts of the country.

Specialist agencies These agencies also offer ready-made packages but with a more diverse and interesting range of destinations and activities, with accommodations tending to be more exclusive and personal. Many specialist safari agencies haven't sent clients to Zimbabwe for years, however, and could well be out of touch with current conditions. There's a growing number of small Zimbabwean agencies who know their country inside out and offer bespoke packages to suit your individual requirements. See pages 84–7 for a list of operators.

Overland trips This is a variation on the above, in which you join a group and are guided around in an adapted vehicle – part bus, part truck. These trips tend to include several countries to give a broader African experience, but they're very much whistle-stop tours. Accommodation is usually camping. You should only consider these trips if you are gregarious and easy-going. They appeal to younger people, although some cater for older visitors. A vast range of pan-African itineraries is on offer, but at the time of writing most limit their Zimbabwe exposure to Victoria Falls and Hwange, although several are now expanding their range to include Matopos and Great Zimbabwe. See pages 84–7 for a list of operators.

DESIGNING YOUR OWN ITINERARY Many people are attracted by the romance and flexibility of truly independent travel and relish the opportunity to research, book and conduct their very own trip. You can either plan to get around under your own steam (see *Getting around*, pages 120–2), or ask a specialist agency to put together a bespoke package for you. The first option involves a self-driving trip and a lot of time spent making reservations, while an agent can take care of all the logistics, including transport. In either case, try to build in as much flexibility as possible, so you can extend or shorten your stay as you go along. The following sections provide further details – *Suggested itineraries* (see below), *Activities* (see pages 73–83) and *Tour operators* (see pages 84–7).

SUGGESTED ITINERARIES

The following section indicates key highlights and the *minimum* time to see them without rushing. You can link them and – allowing for travel and transfers – build an itinerary to fit the time you have. In a country like Zimbabwe, with its wealth of attractions, there's an understandable temptation to try to see as much as possible. But driving distances can be long and tiring, museums and galleries should not be hurried, and wildlife, the prime objective for most people's visits, can be lamentably unreliable in turning up at the right place at the right time. Then like buses they all arrive together but by then you may find you've run out of time.

So as you enthusiastically link these modules together, have a map and a calendar to hand and, when in doubt, cut something out! Also try to build in some real relaxation time, preferably by the Zambezi or close to a busy waterhole.

The following timings make no allowance for travelling between different areas and, I repeat, are what I consider to be absolute minimums. As a very rough guide to driving times, although the open road speed limit is 120km/h you should probably base your trip on an average speed of about 80km/h.

VICTORIA FALLS AND HWANGE NATIONAL PARK These are within a couple of hours' drive of one another and should both feature in a first-time visit. Three days in Victoria Falls gives you time to see the falls, check out the shops, spend a day and night in the Zambezi National Park and have a full day of activities. Four days in Hwange lets you get around the two main areas of the park, Main Camp and Sinamatella. For variety, stay at the Parks lodge at Sinamatella and at a private lodge in the Main Camp area. Self-drivers should book at least one guided early morning and dusk game drive.

BULAWAYO AND AROUND The focus is on historic sites, Matobo National Park and Bulawayo's museum and art gallery. The Natural History Museum is Zimbabwe's best museum, and this together with the National Art Gallery will take the best part of one day. Allow two days for Matobo, including rock paintings, Rhodes's grave at World's View and the Whovi game reserve with its rhino, black and white. Make time to visit the Cyrene Mission and the Khami Ruins (one day). For Danangombe and Nalatale Ruins and Old Bulawayo add one day.

ITINERARY COMBINATIONS

There's an almost infinite variety of combinations of the above but the following itineraries may be considered. I have assumed that for most people this is their first trip to Zimbabwe, so all these itineraries include Victoria Falls and Hwange National Park. If you are using an agent you should discuss these with them and consider variations if appropriate.

ONE WEEK Spend your time in Victoria Falls and Hwange National Park.

TEN DAYS Victoria Falls – Hwange National Park – Bulawayo area and Matobo National Park. Return via Victoria Falls or Bulawayo.

TWO WEEKS Either extend the ten-day itinerary (listed above) to include Masvingo and Great Zimbabwe, returning via Bulawayo, or extend the ten-day trip to take in Harare via Gweru. Return from Harare.

THREE WEEKS You can either extend the two-week Masvingo/Great Zimbabwe trip to take in the Eastern Highlands (south to north) from Chimanimani to Nyanga, returning via Harare, or extend the ten-day or two-week trip via Harare and visit either Matusadona lakeside or Mana Pools National Park. Return via Harare.

ONE MONTH Victoria Falls – Hwange National Park – Bulawayo/Matobo National Park – Masvingo/Great Zimbabwe – Eastern Highlands – Harare – Mana Pools and/or Matusadona. Return via Harare.

SELF-DRIVE This second set of itineraries caters for self-drivers arriving from South Africa and looking for an element of camping. They may have previously visited Zimbabwe, so I have not included Victoria Falls and Hwange National Park in all of these itineraries.

NB: circular routes entering from South Africa (Musina/Beitbridge) require a fully equipped 4x4.

Two weeks
Beitbridge – Gonarezhou National Park – Eastern Highlands – Harare – Masvingo – Beitbridge.
Beitbridge – Masvingo – Bulawayo – Hwange – Victoria Falls.

Three weeks
Beitbridge – Gonarezhou National Park – Masvingo – Bulawayo – Hwange National Park – Victoria Falls. Return via Botswana.
Beitbridge – Bulawayo – Hwange National Park – Binga – Chizarira National Park – Victoria Falls. Return via Botswana.

One month
Beitbridge – Masvingo – Eastern Highlands – Harare – Mana Pools or Matusadona national parks – Bulawayo. Return via Plumtree and Botswana.
Beitbridge – Bulawayo – Hwange – Binga – Chizarira – Matusadona – Mana Pools – Harare – Beitbridge.

GONAREZHOU NATIONAL PARK Gonarezhou offers scenic African wilderness rather than intensive wildlife viewing. For great wildlife viewing you are recommended to use a professional guide. The southwestern area of the park, around Mabalauta, is relatively small and its loop roads and viewpoints can be covered in one day. The northern section has more to offer, and I recommend at least three days to follow the Runde River, camping at Chipinda Pools and Chilojo Cliffs and staying at Chilo or Mahenye lodge (assuming it has been rebuilt). Seeing both areas of the park requires a lengthy road detour outside the park.

GREAT ZIMBABWE AND LAKE MUTIRIKWE To do justice to Great Zimbabwe, the country's enigmatic, historical heart, most people will want to spend half a day here. Lake Mutirikwe is a popular recreational park with a small game reserve off one shore, home to several rhinos. Consider building in one day here for rest and relaxation in this beautifully scenic area.

EASTERN HIGHLANDS This is a difficult area on which to put a timescale because most visitors want to take part in an activity – walking, fishing, golf, horseriding or birdwatching – and only they know how long they want to spend. The suggested timings are purely for sightseeing purposes, so you can add on as much as you like for your activities. You should also build in one day for driving between south and north.

Chimanimani
The village, Bridal Veil Falls and a drive round the very scenic area will occupy one day. Allow as much time as you want for walking in the mountains, but three days will let you cover the main routes.

Mutare and the Bvumba Mountains
You could occupy one day in Mutare, visiting the museum and Cecil Kop Nature Reserve, but most people head straight for the Bvumba. It's a compact area and one to two days will allow you to slowly drive all around it. Horseriding, hiking and golf are possible extras, while birdwatchers will be keen to spend several days here.

Juliasdale, Nyanga and Troutbeck
You can easily spend one day checking out the spectacular Honde and Pungwe viewpoints before moving up to Nyanga National Park. You'll need three days here to visit the Ziwa ruins, Nyangwe and Chawomera forts, the reconstructed pit structure village, the reservoirs and Nyangombe Falls. Allow a half-day for the hike to the summit of Mount Nyangani.

LAKE KARIBA, MATUSADONA AND MANA POOLS These three venues together form the perfect water- and land-based safari area. If you've come all the way to see any one of them it makes sense to visit all three.

Lake Kariba
Almost everybody visiting the region finds themselves at Kariba town because it's the meeting point for most activities – houseboats, canoe trips, transfers to Matusadona and Mana Pools. The dam wall is worth a visit (one day). Few overseas tourists stay on the houseboats, although they're brilliant if you're with a group of friends. The best way to enjoy the lake is at one of the small camps along the shore.

Matusadona National Park
The north shore of the park has excellent camps, all offering drives and walks into the game-rich interior, as well as boat trips featuring

game, waterbirds and some of the best sunsets you'll ever see. Try to spend five days, perhaps split between two camps for variety.

Mana Pools National Park This is many people's favourite park in Zimbabwe, remote, unspoilt, game-rich and relatively empty of people. Canoe trips are magical, and you'll experience Africa in a way few others do. Book three days canoeing, maybe from Chirundu to Mana Pools. The area is home to some of the finest guides in Africa, so game drives and walks are as good as they get. Stay at one of the luxury camps near the pools themselves for an additional three days' wildlife viewing.

CHIZARIRA NATIONAL PARK Chizarira, like Gonarezhou, is a Mecca for wilderness seekers and keen campers though relative inaccessibility means it's very lightly visited. Two nights in the northern area will find you camping on the gorge rim followed by a night in the bush. You may want to add one night in the comfort of a lodge in the north. Then head off to camp further south. Most visitors will find Chizarira a little too inaccessible on their own so will come here on a guided walking safari.

HARARE Harare offers good shopping, great accommodation and restaurants (see pages 165, 159–62 and 162–4), and Lake Chivero Recreational Park (see pages 169–70) just outside town.

WILDLIFE ACTIVITIES

WILDLIFE VIEWING Wildlife viewing – and of the 'Big Five' in particular – is the main reason most people take their first trip to Africa. Zimbabwe offers some of the best wildlife viewing on the continent, and you have a high probability of spotting most of the big species in plentiful numbers and delightful settings. Zimbabwe has also long been credited with having the best professional guides in Africa – their training regime is extremely rigorous and only the very best make it through to get the qualification. Nevertheless even with this great combination, don't expect your experience to match those of television producers who spend months or even years waiting to shoot a single stunning film sequence. If you go expecting to see an elephant giving birth, a pride of lions tackling a crocodile or a leopard hauling an impala up a tree, you may be disappointed. But if you want to visit one of the last areas in the world where game is free to roam, follow your guide for a close-up view of a group of giraffe, sit quietly in your vehicle surrounded by a herd of snuffling, rumbling elephants, with a good chance of spotting a pack of wild dogs, then your visit to Zimbabwe will stay with you for the rest of your life. You are free to self-drive around most of Zimbabwe's parks, which gives you a large degree of independence, but be sure you have a good 4x4 and check the relevant section of the guide regarding driving conditions in the parks you will be visiting. Also, even if you are self-driving, don't exclude the idea of booking a guided safari; your experience can be enhanced immeasurably by employing a professional guide.

Booking Broadly speaking there are two ways of booking your game drives, either directly with the camp or lodge you are staying at, or using an agent (see page 75 in this chapter). Each offers a rather different experience.

Lodges and camps All the lodges and camps near national parks offer game-viewing activities. Most run their own independent game drives using their own vehicles and professional guides and offer fully inclusive rates that usually include two activities per day. They operate for the sole benefit of their own guests, so group size will be determined by the number of clients in camp. Check the number of rooms or beds to get an idea of maximum numbers, if you are not keen on joining a large group. These companies normally use converted Toyotas and Land Rovers, ideal for open-sided, high-seated viewing, but it's still a good idea to check that they don't use enclosed minibuses which have far more restrictive viewing and very little feeling of being 'out in the bush'. That said, if you are very nervous of being exposed to wildlife in an open vehicle, the minibus offers a great introduction. After your drive the guiding staff will be around camp so you have the chance to talk to them

ZIMBABWE'S PROFESSIONAL GUIDES

It's generally accepted that Zimbabwe has Africa's most rigorous training programme for its guides with the result that this country has produced some of the very best guides on the continent, and continues to do so.

It's a lengthy process, taking far longer to complete than a university degree course – as a vocational training programme, it doesn't get much tougher.

First, the trainee has to prepare for the Learner's theory examination requiring detailed knowledge of the living world – ecology and conservation, together with comprehensive knowledge of birdlife and all animal life in the region including insects and vegetation. It's not enough to know the common names either; they're also expected to know the Latin names of all the common species. But guiding is so much more than being able to point out and identify flora and fauna. They must also be well versed in tourism and environmental laws as well as having a working knowledge of first aid and vehicle maintenance, firearms and ballistics. That's the basics, which should take in the region of two years to complete and a successful Learner's exam will allow the guide to drive an open game vehicle with clients.

Then follows an apprenticeship to a qualified guide lasting at least another two years, often longer. Here the 'appy' immerses him/herself in the life of guiding by shadowing their mentor and learning people skills, camp management, animal behaviour and dealing with everyday problems. It's during this period that the mentor guide will give the apprentice a number of testing tasks out in the bush to ensure that he or she can deal with the most difficult living conditions and dangerous situations. Before completing the licence the apprentice must shoot large predators in threatening situations – they must demonstrate their ability to do this as their clients' lives will be their responsibility. During this apprenticeship a number of written exams need to be completed.

Finally, before a full licence is granted, there's a two-day written exam, a two-hour oral test followed by a week in the bush where the prospective guide must look after a board of six to ten expert examiners as clients for whom he/she must set up camp, cook, guide and answer their questions throughout the ordeal. Their well-being is his/her responsibility and you can guarantee they won't be the easiest of clients!

After all this theory and practical work, with the danger and the stress of proving they can ensure the safety of your clients, it's no surprise to learn the first-time pass rate is way less than 10%.

further about what you've seen. If a lodge or camp quotes game-viewing activities separately, that often means they use an outside operator, so again it's wise to ask about group size and vehicles.

Safari agents or consolidators If you are staying in a town hotel, touring or booking from home, it is often necessary to use one of the wealth of agencies who will book your wildlife viewing with their preferred operators. Of course, they'll also be offering this service to as many other clients as they can, so you may end up as part of a large group, sometimes several vehicles driving around the park in convoy. While it's great to have your first sighting of a pride of lions snoozing in the afternoon sun, the thrill is somewhat lessened if the bored animals are surrounded by half a dozen camera-clicking minibuses.

This is not to say there aren't excellent agencies offering more intimate experiences – but you need to ask questions about group size, whether yours might be amalgamated with others, and vehicle type.

Where and when to go
If this will be your first experience of big game and you want to see as many different animals as possible, quickly, head first for the deservedly popular Hwange National Park, where there is a huge diversity of game in prolific numbers, followed by Mana Pools and Matusadona. Other parks, while scenic and often much less visited, generally have lower concentrations of animals and tend to cater for people who have been wildlife viewing before and want to experience some of the last, accessible, true wilderness destinations in Africa.

Wildlife viewing is very seasonal so be sure to book in the dry season; otherwise you may well be disappointed. The winter months of June/July to October are the best throughout Zimbabwe.

Most animals need to drink at least once a day, but in the winter natural water sources dry up and game rely on a small number of artificially pumped pans and waterholes. These provide excellent wildlife-viewing opportunities. A note of caution here. If the preceding wet season has had poor rains, drought will be a major problem in the long dry winter months and although you are likely to see very large concentrations around the waterholes, all of the wildlife will be under severe stress as elephants totally dominate these scarce water sources. These scenes which often include dead and dying animals can be quite harrowing to witness. Once the rains come, water becomes freely available throughout the bush and the animals disperse, making them more difficult to find. Furthermore, in the wet season, grasses and other vegetation grow prolifically, forming a screen through which you will see little.

Although I have watched herds of hundreds of elephant coming down to drink in the Zambezi in the middle of a summer wet spell, you should play safe and aim for dry season viewing.

If on the other hand birds are your priority, the wet summer season brings in a host of migratory species, providing an experience not to be missed.

Children
Quite a few safari camps and lodges have a 'no children' policy or adopt a minimum age limit sometimes as high as 16 years old. There are genuine practical reasons for this. Be sure to check with your agent or directly with the accommodation to see if there is an age limit imposed. See *Travelling with children* on page 113 for more information.

THE GAME DRIVE
The majority of visitors will book their game drives through an agent or by using the facilities offered by their accommodation (see page 73). You

may, however, wish to drive yourself around Zimbabwe – being independent has huge attractions and I thoroughly recommend it – but make sure you book some guided game drives as well, or you will miss out on the full wildlife experience. A good guide has an intimate knowledge of their area and can take you to specific locations to find certain animals. They will amaze you with their ability to spot things that you would have driven straight past, and can talk you through what you

THE GREAT HUNTING DEBATE

There are few subjects more likely to inflame passionate discussion around the campfire than trophy hunting. The practice of killing animals for trophies rather than food originated in the colonial days and is now widespread throughout southern Africa. It forms an extremely lucrative sector of Zimbabwe's tourism industry, yet its followers sit uneasily alongside the majority of tourists who are there simply to observe and photograph the wildlife. Take a look at the map and wherever you see the words 'conservancy', 'safari area' or 'forestry' land, you are mostly looking at hunting areas. In Zimbabwe's wildlife tourism sector there is no shortage of people involved in this industry, and there's a good chance that one or more of your hosts or guides will have served their time as a professional hunter.

SAFARI AREAS These are large tracts of wilderness land frequently adjoining national parks and administered by the ZPWMA, hence to all intents and purposes national parks but closed to the general public and leased to hunting concessionaires. 'Parks' allocates the concessions for a fee, determines quotas, and takes a percentage of the revenue. In safari areas, strict quotas should be applied and monitored by park rangers with only specific animals allowed to be taken, giving regard to species, sex, age and overall health of the population involved. A professional hunter (PH) and Parks ranger must accompany each hunt to ensure that only appropriate animals are selected. Wherever possible the PH must despatch any wounded animals, but those that escape have to be paid for by the client to encourage hunters to follow and kill them rather than let them wander off to die slowly in the bush. In this way, suffering is kept to a minimum. This is all termed 'ethical' hunting. Unethical hunting occurs when the all-powerful dollar allows the rules and quotas to be ignored. The following is but a brief précis of the opposing arguments.

PRO-HUNTING ARGUMENTS The hunting industry will argue that, far from being destructive to wildlife, ethical hunting ensures its survival, protecting the large tracts of natural environment required to support game from human encroachment. Having paid these large fees, hunting operations wish to protect their interests by funding or organising anti-poaching patrols and pumping waterholes for the benefit of all wildlife. This lobby argues that the 'offtake' of hunted animals is extremely small compared to the overall benefits to wildlife in general.

Local communities also benefit directly from hunting by receiving the resultant meat and programmes have been introduced whereby some local communities also receive monetary grants from hunting operations which helps engender a more 'wildlife friendly' approach to wildlife and reduces poaching. Many overseas hunting organisations raise large sums of money for conservation initiatives.

ANTI-HUNTING ARGUMENTS Putting aside the issues surrounding the ethics of killing wild animals for pleasure, opponents of hunting claim that virtually all are seeing and answer any questions. Another major plus of a guided drive is the specially designed open-sided vehicles that have you seated much higher up than even the tallest 4x4 can offer (try to avoid the enclosed minibuses for this reason). A further important reason for using commercial game drives is that some of the best viewing is at dusk and dawn, the very times when private vehicles are banned from driving in the national parks.

the benefits to wildlife, the environment and local communities claimed by the hunting industry can be achieved in a much more sustainable manner by photographic safari operators. They are sceptical about the benefits actually being received by local communities and say that local employment benefits far more from photographic tourists who tend to stay in expensive lodges requiring far more staff, than hunters who usually lead quite spartan lives out in the bush.

They claim that a target animal can generate much more income through its photographic potential than as a one-off hunting target; and that hunting takes out the largest, strongest and most healthy animals changing the gene pool in total contradiction of natural selection. Hunting also disrupts natural family/herd dynamics which can be extremely detrimental.

Animal suffering is another major issue for opponents, on the grounds that by no means all clients are accomplished shots, leaving many wounded animals to die slowly in the bush, especially where bow hunting is concerned. And it's always a body shot rather than a much more efficient head shot to ensure the trophy is unmarked.

HUNTING IN ZIMBABWE TODAY Up until the late 1990s this country's hunting industry was arguably the best regulated and most ethically conducted in the world, certainly in this region. But the politics and land-reform programme of recent years has left many of the most lucrative hunting concessions and conservancies in the control of individuals who are reported to have thrown the rule book and any concept of ethics out of the window.

That is not to say there are no 'ethical' hunting operators left in Zimbabwe, because there most definitely are, but it is beyond the scope of this author to find a path through this minefield, so this sector of the tourism industry is not represented in this book.

CONCLUSION? Both sides present convincing arguments and few find it easy to change their entrenched views. Many hunting professionals leave the industry because of the direction it is taking in Zimbabwe, while on the other hand a growing number of 'anti-hunting' people arrive at what they feel is a distinctly unpalatable conclusion: although they deplore the practice of killing animals for pleasure, they can't ignore the fact that if it wasn't for the industry, vast tracts of virgin land that support wildlife today would have been destroyed many years ago and given over to subsistence farming and cattle ranching.

As a footnote, neighbouring Botswana and Zambia have surprised many by banning trophy hunting, to come into effect during 2013/14. It will be very interesting to see what effect, positive or negative, this has on wildlife and conservation efforts. One thing is virtually certain – as a result, Zimbabwe will 'benefit' from an even greater influx of hunters.

Game drive protocol The rules are few but are based not only on consideration for the animals and the environment, but for your fellow travellers and those who will follow after you. Your guide will brief you about keeping quiet and still when close to animals, and when it's OK to take photographs. If you are in an open vehicle, stay seated, still and quiet; this way wildlife is unable to recognise you as a human, whereas the moment you stand up or wave your arms around they recognise their old foe and take to the bush (or some will attack depending on how close you are).

For self-drivers it is essential that you keep to established roads and tracks and on no account set off into the bush on your own little 4x4 adventure. Your tyre tracks may last for years and you will cause untold damage, environmentally and aesthetically. Always drive within the prescribed speed limit and never try to drive right up to any animal as you will either scare it off or provoke an attack.

If there is game on the road, do not hassle them out of the way, stop at a distance and let them move off in their own time. Never feed any animal; and, needless to say, take all litter back to camp with you, leaving no trace of your visit.

Safety This is generally not an issue so long as you are accompanied by a professional guide, as they are extremely well trained, are obliged to carry a weapon, and take no chances when with clients. On the other hand this is not a Disney theme park and accidents do happen! So a few words of caution are necessary if you are travelling independently, especially so if you are in one of the national parks where you are free to walk or camp without a guide.

In some Zimbabwe national parks (not all), visitors are allowed considerably more freedom than in those of neighbouring countries, on the basis that your safety is your own responsibility and that you will use your common sense. In this way you are often allowed to camp in unfenced sites. Unfortunately, there is a common mindset amongst cosseted Westerners that 'they wouldn't let us do this if it wasn't safe'. Nothing could be further from the truth. That's why guides are required to carry weapons. Virtually all larger species of game and many smaller ones are capable of inflicting serious injury or death.

If you do decide to leave your vehicle in the quest for, say, a better camera angle or a toilet break, you can do so in safety provided you are aware of the surroundings and risks. You may not have seen a lion yet today, but are you quite sure there isn't one under that bush behind which you intend to relieve yourself? And it is not just the obvious candidates – elephant, lion, leopard, buffalo, rhino, hyena, crocodile, hippo, snakes and baboons – even antelopes can be dangerous in the wrong circumstances. Get out only in areas of open or sparse vegetation, always stay close to your vehicle and never be tempted to walk into thick bush. Elephants may look gentle and lumbering, but can be notoriously moody and fleet-footed. If you are too close, they may attack you and even your vehicle, before you can get it into gear. Be especially wary of female elephants with calves, and of bulls in *musth* (a state of sexual arousal which can make a normally placid animal irritable and grumpy; you can easily recognise this state by weeping temporal glands on the side of their face, and a huge dripping penis).

Some books offer advice on what to do when faced with a charging elephant (stand your ground and hope it's a mock charge), buffalo (lie flat on the ground) or lion (shout loudly and look big and threatening), but my advice is not to get in that situation in the first place. Guides go through years of training and practical experience of understanding and anticipating animal reactions, and no book will make you an instant expert. The very best advice is to stay in or close to your vehicle, camp only at designated sites and be ever vigilant, especially at night.

One final issue you may want to consider when camping and thinking of going off for a midnight stroll – Zimbabwe's parks staff have a 'shoot to kill' policy for poachers so it's quite a good idea to stay at your campsite.

Savour the experience There is a temptation to commit everything you see to your memory card, but this means you see everything through the camera lens. When the trip is over you have hundreds of very nice shots (which few of your friends will be genuinely interested in) and then you realise you haven't really *seen* very much. Unless you are a keen photographer, rather than photographing absolutely everything, take time to quietly observe and perhaps only raise the camera for that really special shot or to quickly snap scenes that will jog your memory later.

WALKING OR MOBILE SAFARIS There is nothing better than a long walk in the bush with an experienced professional guide to give you a real appreciation of the African environment. All your senses will be on the alert, and as you walk your guide will be describing intimate details of the insects, birds and plants and how they interact in this complex ecosystem. Watch dung beetles rolling their huge and perfectly rounded burdens with their back legs; see how ant-lions hunt; let a honeyguide bird lead you to a bees' nest. All the time your heart is in your mouth because you don't know what's behind the next bush. Your guide will encourage you to use your senses of hearing and smell, as well as sight. With a little experience you will be able to identify certain birds by their calls and if you are downwind from elephant or buffalo you may pick up their strong scent before you see them. Never be afraid to ask your guide even the most basic of questions because if he can see you are really interested he will be encouraged to offer even more information.

Walking safaris are well developed in Zimbabwe, with some of Africa's most experienced guides operating in the major national parks. There are a number of types of walk depending on your time, the standard of luxury you are looking for and, yes, your level of fitness.

One major selling point for these walking/camping trips is often left out of the brochures. The guides who run these trips are invariably 'larger than life', tend to have a brilliant sense of humour and are excellent raconteurs. With just a little prompting and encouragement, the evenings you spend around the campfire listening to their outrageous and hilarious stories of life in the bush will stay with you forever.

Wilderness trails Wilderness trails are walking safaris suited to active and more adventurous people. They are **'full participation'** camping safaris over a number of days during which participants and camp staff carry all gear and provisions in backpacks. These are small groups, usually with a maximum of around six clients. Water availability (springs and rivers), weather conditions, game activity, fitness and the interests of members on safari generally determine the route and pace of these trails. Traditional tracking methods are used and bush skills are put to a fine test on these safaris – the objective is often to find specific game species including lion, leopard or black rhino. These safaris are not military-style 'route marches' but a fair degree of fitness is required. Camps are generally basic, often consisting of little more than two-man dome tents.

Back-up walking trails The backed-up walking trails, also over a number of days, generally provide more creature comforts than the wilderness trails. They trace a specific walking route through a wilderness area to rendezvous points *en route*,

3

where overnight camps have been established by a support team. Accommodation standards vary from relatively basic fly camps to deluxe, tented camps.

Fixed-base walking trails Walking safaris from fixed bases are the relatively short walks you do from your place of accommodation, often offered as an alternative activity to a game drive or river cruise. These bases have more resources and additional staff on hand; creature comforts and extra activities are usually more readily available. Generally speaking, the smaller tented and seasonal bush camps are located within the boundaries of national parks and game reserves, while permanent lodges are usually found bordering outside these areas. Lodges are generally larger, with accommodation in individual chalets and bungalows, and in many cases they offer standards comparable to those found at some of the best hotels in southern Africa's capital cities. The tented camps usually centre around a communal lounging/dining area with accommodation in large walk-in tents, often with en-suite facilities. Standards range from traditional to luxurious. Seasonal bush camps tend to incorporate some tented accommodation but are largely made from local materials including reeds, thatch and timber. They close in the wet season and are often rebuilt from scratch at the beginning of the dry season. As with the tented camps, bush camps tend to be small, often accommodating a maximum of around six guests.

Walking activities from these fixed bases usually take place in the early morning and evening when game is more active. Vehicles are often used to get within closer reach of areas where game is more prolific. Professional guides are resident at all of these camps, often supported by learner guides and scouts.

RULES WHEN WALKING IN THE BUSH

with thanks to the Zambezi Society
- Caution and common sense will help, paranoia will not.
- If you are likely to be nervous, take an armed guide with you.
- Respect the fact that the animals are wild and may behave unpredictably, especially if they are frightened, wounded or have young.
- Don't walk alone or at night; walk at times of day when predators are less active, ie: mid-morning to mid-afternoon.
- Walk quietly so that all your senses can be fully alert, and be aware of what's around you at all times.
- Avoid long grass or thick bush – if you can't see out, climb a tree or an anthill.
- Avoid the temptation to get too close to animals for that ultimate photo opportunity. Instead use binoculars or a telephoto lens.
- If you are taking photographs, make sure that somebody else keeps an eye on the surroundings and can warn you if anything approaches.
- Walk downwind of any animals that you see or hear and take time and effort to divert if you have to; this is especially important if there are females with young.
- If you come unexpectedly close to an animal, including a snake, stop, try to remain calm and then back off very slowly, or stay still until it moves off. Do not run or shout.
- Never swim in rivers or pools, and stay back from the water where banks are shallow. Crocodiles are the Earth's longest surviving and most successful predators!

CANOE SAFARIS Many people would challenge my earlier comment that there is nothing better than a walking safari to give you an appreciation of the African environment. Cruising on the Zambezi in a canoe is possibly an even more appealing way to be at one with nature, and like bush walking there is a similar range of comfort options. Words like 'tranquil' and 'serene' leap to mind as you gently paddle downstream, wending your way round pods of hippo and marvelling at how close you can get to that elephant quenching his thirst from the bank. Binoculars and cameras will be used to the full with the dazzling array of riverine birds and wildlife on offer, but don't put your paddle down for too long or you'll find yourselves drifting a little too close for comfort towards hippo territory.

You'll generally be in a large, Canadian-style, two-man fibreglass canoe that is very stable and requires no previous skill to manoeuvre. Within the first few paddle strokes you'll learn that the steering all happens from the back while the front person mainly provides motive power. (Couples need to work out in advance who takes up which role, and if you've come on this holiday to mend a fraught relationship, perhaps stick to game drives.)

In exactly the same way as with the walking safaris, you can choose from 'full participation', 'backed up' or 'fixed-base' trips. There are shorter morning or afternoon canoe safaris on the Upper Zambezi using inflatable canoes, taking you alongside the magical Zambezi National Park and down some minor rapids, ideal if you are staying in Victoria Falls. For the more adventurous, longer-distance canoeing takes place along the Lower Zambezi in the Chirundu/Mana Pools stretch of river.

Nights are spent on the bank or camping on sandbars, often with only a mosquito net between you and the stars (if you're on a backed-up trip you'll have a tent to sleep in and staff to look after you). One of the enduring sights on my own honeymoon canoe trip, indeed in my whole life, was the twin reflections on an almost mirror-like river of the setting sun in one direction as the full moon rose in the other. You may also experience a 'legover'. This entails bringing the canoes alongside one another with everyone hooking one leg over the side of the next to form a raft and then simply drifting downriver with the current. An essential ingredient of this manoeuvre is breaking open the coolbox for a couple of beers.

On a more serious note and at risk of stating the obvious, these trips are not without safety issues. You are sharing the river with some very dangerous creatures and they will attack if you unwittingly take them by surprise or enter their territory. But these trips are all hosted by an armed professional guide and they will give you a full safety briefing prior to setting out each day, as well as guiding you through the safe channels of the river. River guides must pass stringent proficiency tests and gain extensive experience before qualifying to run trips.

October and November are uncomfortably hot and humid in the Zambezi Valley so you'll need plenty of sun protection. The wet season starts in November and ends early in April, with most rain in January and February. Don't be put off by the rains: it's warm, the rain pattern is mostly thunderstorms followed by sunshine, the birding is excellent and a violent African thunderstorm is an experience in itself. (You just don't want to be in the middle of the river when lightning strikes!) Just pack a poncho for canoeing and keep some dry clothes for camp. May and June offer the best weather in the valley and the game starts improving on the Zambezi shoreline.

Things can get busy during the safari season from July to late September; high season rates apply and advance booking is essential. Low season is generally December–June.

If you are making your own way to join a canoe trip, most of which base themselves in Kariba, pay particular attention to your transport arrangements. Your pick-up for the start of the trip will probably be early morning and the flights from Victoria Falls, Hwange and Harare, assuming they are operating again, all arrive in Kariba too late in the day, as does the ferry from Mlibizi so plan to arrive the day before the trip starts. Private charter flights operate from Harare and Victoria Falls or you can easily drive from Harare.

Needless to say, canoes don't come with a lot of baggage-carrying capacity so travel light, with a pack weighing no more than 10kg. If you have more luggage you can leave the remainder at your operator's office for collection on return. Your canoe operator will give you a full briefing on all these matters. See pages 229–30 for a list of operators.

HORSEBACK SAFARIS If you are an experienced horserider this is an excellent way to indulge in your hobby as well as getting close to big game. The great benefit is that wildlife does not associate horses with danger and can't recognise the lump on the horse's back as a human being. The horse's scent also goes a long way to overpowering that of its rider so it's possible to get much closer to game than would otherwise be possible.

It goes without saying that you do need to be a competent rider as there may be occasions when you need to beat a hasty retreat. Ask plenty of questions about the sort of horse you will be riding, be honest about the level of experience you have and make sure your travel insurance covers you for this activity. As well as a long-standing operation in the Zambezi National Park, based in Victoria Falls, which also caters for novice riders, there is an excellent horseriding company run by the folks who pioneered these safaris in Mavuradonha. These safaris take seven days and involve six or seven hours in the saddle every day, so are only appropriate for fit and experienced riders. Other riding opportunities with the focus on scenery rather than game can be found in the Matopas and Eastern Highlands. Most operators have a weight limit for riders, generally around the 95kg mark although often less. See pages 226 and 265 for a list of operators.

HIDES Several national parks have hides positioned overlooking a waterhole where you can sit and observe game arriving to drink without disturbing them. Hides come in different sizes and varying grades of comfort, although most are best described as rudimentary. One of my favourites is at Camp Hwange and comprises nothing more than a 'jumble' of tree branches and logs arranged in a totally natural-looking fashion around the base of a large acacia tree. You may wish just to have a quiet hour or so watching animals at sunset, but far better, if you have time, to spend the night in one. You must first check with the National Parks office about which hides you are allowed to sleep in and book them accordingly.

Not only will you get all the best animal action at dusk and dawn but you'll be amazed at the level of night-time activity as well. Don't expect a peaceful night, though; the last time my wife and I 'slept' at Guvalala Platform in Hwange we were treated to a gaggle of hyenas serenading us just a few metres away with their full-on vocal range of howls, giggles and snarls that were variously hilarious or terrifying depending on whether we were already awake, or they woke us up. We had elephants below us with loudly rumbling stomachs and occasional wild trumpeting as squabbles were sorted out while they splashed around in the water. As well as the lovely calls of jackals and nightjars, we heard lions quite close, calling to one another. Zimbabwe!

You'll need to take sleeping kit and minimal camping gear including chairs and of course food and water, but importantly on arrival at the hide, check you are happy with the toilet facilities, as a busy waterhole is hardly the best place to wander around in search of a convenient bush in the middle of the night.

If you can schedule it over a full moon period you'll be in for a magical experience and surprised by what you can see with your binoculars at night, but check with National Parks or Wildlife and Environment Zimbabwe (*www.wezmat. co.zw*) for the dates of the annual Hwange game count. It is generally over full moon in September, and over this period all the hides (as well as much of the Parks accommodation) are blocked off for the census takers, and many of them take the opportunity to stay for the whole week.

Advance bookings should be made with the National Parks office in Harare or Bulawayo, or you can simply take your chance on arrival, as in recent years there has been no telephonic connection between towns and parks. This does sometimes result in double bookings, especially at the popular hides in Hwange such as Masuma, Mondavu Dam and Deteema.

PHOTOGRAPHIC SAFARIS Harare-based professional photographer Christopher Scott (\ *0772 440052;* e *enquiries@scottyphotography.net; www.scottyphotography. net*) offers photographic tuition safaris throughout Zimbabwe (and neighbouring countries), catering for all levels of expertise. These are especially valuable to people who want to step up from the 'point-and-shoot' stage and of course you'll be able to test your new-found skills on the animals and scenery of one of the most photogenic countries in the world. Chris can offer tailor-made trips for groups that want to go to specific places and he also does organised trips on specific dates for a minimum of four people. Also check his other website (*www. funphotographywild.com*).

HIKING The Eastern Highlands – which range from Chimanimani northwards via Bvumba to Nyanga – offer scenic beauty in abundance and any number of places to base yourself for a walk into the hills. You can venture into the hills for a couple of hours or design a route that is hiking on a grand scale, although the elevations are not daunting and the terrain is not challenging to a reasonably fit person.

You should nevertheless be an experienced hiker and equip yourself properly, as weather conditions can quickly change. That is standard advice around the world, but Zimbabwe hills do present their own specific issues.

Many established trails, such as can be found in the Chimanimani National Park mountains, have become indistinct and overgrown from light or non-existent footfall in recent years. Severe weather since 2000 has also eroded many of them. Add to this the fact that there are few if any detailed hiking maps available, and you have a recipe for getting lost. Along with the usual necessities of food, water, map (if available), compass, good boots, waterproofs and warm clothing, you may want to consider a handheld GPS. The great benefit of these instruments is that if you do get hopelessly lost you can always backtrack or return to your starting point.

The Mozambican border runs down the spine of the Eastern Highlands, so ensure that you stick to paths, consult your paper or GPS map and don't get carried away with the scenic beauty and stray across the border. Older guidebooks warn of landmines left over from earlier conflicts in this area, though Parks staff do not consider this an issue any more.

The other important requirement when you head for the hills is to tell someone your route and estimated arrival time, and check in with them when you return. This is less easy if you are camping overnight, or planning a multi-day route that doesn't return to your origin.

TOUR OPERATORS AND AGENTS

For the purposes of this section a travel agent is loosely defined as a company offering a broad range of 'general' holidays worldwide while a tour operator tends to be much more of a specialist focussing on specific countries or interests. Many companies advertise trips to Africa, but few include Zimbabwe. Most pulled out because of the political situation, but this continues to improve dramatically and I expect options from tour operators and travel agents to follow suit.

Before you present an agent or operator with your fledgling plans, try to ensure they can be fitted into your available time, bearing in mind the potentially long distances involved – especially if you plan to visit other countries as well – and the fact that many activities are seasonal and weather-dependent. This will not be a budget holiday so do everything possible to ensure your agent is offering you value for money. Shop around, armed with lots of questions to see how knowledgeable they are about the destinations you want. Make sure there is ample opportunity to discuss your trip – face to face, by phone or email – before firming up your plans. Don't let them persuade you with their own 'standard' packages instead of the places you really want to visit unless they can demonstrate good practical reasons for doing so. Steer clear of companies that will only take you to a very small range of specific destinations – a good operator should offer a range of destinations around the country and be able to assemble the whole package, including transfers, accommodation, safari operators and activities. You may want to organise your own long-distance flights.

In addition to companies in your own country, there are many excellent Zimbabwean 'destination management companies' who can handle all elements of your stay (although possibly not flights to and from the country). These local agencies have the great advantage of being on the spot and aware of local conditions. They are experienced in creating individual packages based around your specific needs and budget with the ability to advise on practical itineraries and recommended accommodations. With them you stand much more chance of arranging a genuinely bespoke and tailormade holiday. While those listed may say they will book any accommodation you find in this book, most will protect their reputation if they feel individual places are unsuitable or below the standard they set.

UK

Abercrombie & Kent ☎0845 4851558; www.abercrombiekent.co.uk. One of the oldest operators to the region. Upmarket.

Bailey Robinson ☎01488 689777; www.baileyrobinson.com. Tailor-made luxury safari itineraries.

Cazenove & Loyd Safaris ☎020 7384 2332; www.cazloyd.com. Bespoke upmarket itinerary planners.

Expert Africa ☎020 8232 9777; e info@expertafrica.com; www.expertafrica.com. Africa specialists who've supported Zimbabwe throughout recent years. Very experienced in Zim. See ad, inside back cover.

Hartley's Safaris ☎01673 861 600; e info@hartleys-safaris.co.uk; www.hartleys-safaris.co.uk. Tailor-made safaris throughout the region.

Imagine Africa ☎020 7622 5114; (USA) +1 888 882 7121; e info@imagineafrica.co.uk; www.imagineafrica.co.uk. Award-winning tour operator specialising in luxury holidays in Africa.

Natural World Safaris ☎01273 691642; e sales@naturalworldsafaris.com; www.naturalworldsafaris.com; see also advert on page 150. Specialists in tailor-made journeys to Zimbabwe.

Ngoko Safaris ☎01582 766864; e fiona@ngoko.com; www.ngoko.com. A range of safaris to suit individual needs.

Oasis Overland ☎01963 363400; e info@oasisoverland.co.uk; www.oasisoverland.co.uk; see also advert on page 238. Experienced adventure travel company specialising in overland tours.

Okavango Tours & Safaris ☎020 8347 4030; e info@okavango.com; www.okavango.com

Rainbow Tours ☎020 7666 1250; e info@ rainbowtours.co.uk; www.rainbowtours.co.uk; see also advert on page 289. Africa & Latin America specialists, recently bought by worldwide travel group.

Safari Consultants ☎01787 888590; e info@ safariconsultantuk.com; www.safari-consultants. co.uk; see also advert in colour section, page 16. Long-established, knowledgeable tailor-made specialists to East & southern Africa, & the Indian Ocean islands. See ad, colour page 16.

Safari Drive ☎01488 71440; e info@safaridrive. com; www.safaridrive.com. See ad, page 30.

Steppes Travel ☎01285 880980; www. steppestravel.co.uk. Worldwide itinerary designers including Zimbabwe.

Tim Best Travel ☎0207 5910300; www. timbesttravel.com. Individually planned holidays.

Zambezi Safari & Travel Co ☎01548 830059; e info@zambezi.co.uk; www.zambezi.co.uk. Personal service run by Zimbabweans completely up to date with today's Zimbabwe. Specialists in Lower Zambezi Valley.

US

Adventure Travel Desk ☎1 508 653 4600; e info@african-safari.com; www.african-safari.com

Africa Adventure Company ☎1 800 882 9453, 954 491 8877; www.africa-adventure.com

African Safari Consultants ☎1 928 717 8275, 866 733 4263 (TF); www.safariconsultants.com

Expert Africa ☎1 800 242 2434 (TF); e zimbabwe@expertafrica.com; www. expertafrica.com

Eyes on Africa ☎1 800 457 9575, 773 549 0169; www.eyesonafrica.net

Travel Beyond ☎1 952 475 2565; www. travelbeyond.com

AUSTRALIA

Adventure World ☎freephone 1 300 295049; www.adventureworld.com.au

African Wildlife Safaris ☎03 9249 3777; www. africanwildlifesafaris.com.au

The Africa Safari Co ☎02 9541 4199; e enquiries@africasafarico.com.au; www. africasafarico.com.au

SOUTH AFRICA

African Adrenalin ☎011 888 4037; www. africanadrenalin.com

Afrizim ☎031 762 2424; www.afrizim.com

Air Holidays ☎011 803 8223/4; www. airholidays.co.za

Flame of Africa ☎031 762 2424; e foaweb@ flameofafrica.co.za; www.flameofafrica.co.za

Jenman African Safaris ☎021 683 7826; e info@jenmansafaris.com; www.jenmansafaris. com. One of South Africa's biggest & most experienced safari operators to Zimbabwe. See ad, page 272.

Livingstone Safaris ☎021 686 3788; e info@ livsat.com; www.livsaf.com

Rhino Africa ☎21 469 2600; UK 0808 238 0044 (TF); www.rhinoafrica.com

KENYA

Run Wild Safaris ☎+254 20 2013757; e info@ runwildsafaris.com; www.runwildsafaris.com

Overland trips Zimbabwe used to feature in all southern African overland itineraries but virtually all of the companies ceased operations in the country with the exception of a few tentative forays into Victoria Falls. Now that they can rely on getting fuel and catering supplies, many are reinstating their old itineraries and including such destinations as Hwange and Matobo national parks, Great Zimbabwe and Harare. Absolute Africa even features a houseboat on Lake Kariba in its brochure. Itineraries are changeable and various so below is a list of companies that venture further into Zimbabwe than just Victoria Falls.

Absolute Africa www.absoluteafrica.com
Acacia Zimbabwe www.acacia-africa.com
Drifters www.drifters.co.za
Dragoman www.dragoman.com
Exodus Travels www.exodus.co.uk. Includes Great Zimbabwe, Matobo & Hwange national parks.

Explore www.explore.co.uk. Includes Great Zimbabwe, Matobo & Hwange national parks.
Nomad www.nomadtours.co.za
Oasis www.oasisoverland.co.uk

IN ZIMBABWE The following locally based companies (known as destination management companies) offer trip-planning advice for independent travellers and can arrange all facets of your trip (except international flights), including accommodation, transfers and activities. Most use or at least recommend preferred operators and have set itineraries, but may be willing to accommodate your requests if your choices meet their standards.

Defu Travel & Tours ☎04 778803/6; e reservations@defutravel.co.zw; www.defutravel.co.zw

Msuna Safaris and Travel ☎04 705703/16; www.msuna.co.zw

Nyati Travel ☎04 495804; e info@nyati.co.zw; www.nyati-travel.com. See ad, page 152.

Silver Tours ☎013 41060, 43313; e silvert@mweb.co.zw; www.silvertours.co.zw

Sunset Tours ☎04 2900604; e sunsetspecials@sunset.co.zw; wwwnsunset-tours.com

The Travel Shop ☎09 74768; m 0772 372730; enquiries@travelshop.co.zw

Tourism Services Zimbabwe ☎04 251551/8, 013 43368; e info@tourservzim.co.zw; www.tsz.co.zw

Southern Africa Touring Services ☎04 776840; e sats@sats.co.zw; www.southern-africa-touring.com

Vimbiso Safaris m 0712 447160; e reservations@vimbisosafaris.com; www.vimbisosafaris.com

The agencies below are small specialist companies run by local people with a wealth of experience and offering a very personal, bespoke itinerary planning service. The great thing about these agents is that they have up-to-date, hands-on knowledge of conditions in the country, invaluable at a time when the tourism industry is changing so quickly.

Africa Spectacular ☎09 244990; m 0772 231819; e afspec@yoafrica.com; www.africaspectacular.com. Countrywide, but specialists on Kariba.

Agents Africa ☎013 43105; e john@agentsafrica.co.zw; www.agents-africa.co.zw

Armadillo Travel ☎04 334538, 303958; m 0772 283823; e reservations@armadillotvl.com; www.armadillotvl.com

Coordinating Zimbabwe ☎09 245051; e cozim@coz.co.zw; www.cozimafrica.com

Eco Logical Africa ☎09 888790; e colin@ecologicalafrica.com; www.ecologicalafrica.com. Privately piloted & guided safaris.

Exclusive Touch Africa ☎013 43444; e enquiries@exclusivetouchafrica.net; www.exclusivetouchafrica.net

The Safari Source ☎0773 089958; e monika@thesafarisource.com; www.thesafarisource.com. See ad, colour page 8.

Travel Wild Zimbabwe ☎013 45122; e office@zimbabwe-holidays.com; www.zimbabwe-holidays.com. See ad, page 272.

Zimbabwean safari operators (see also specialists listed in specific safari destinations)

Backpackers Africa Backpackers Bazaar, Victoria Falls; ☎013 44611, 45828, 42208; m 0712 404968; e backpack@africaonline.co.zw; www.walkafrica.com. Leon Varley is one of Zimbabwe's most respected guides & specialises in walking safaris in Hwange & Chizarira national parks.

Cameron Harvey Safaris m 0712 201733; e relax@warthogs.co.zw; www.warthogs.co.zw. This owner-operated company based at Warthogs organises safaris around Zimbabwe for individuals

& small groups. They'll work around your own budget, time frame & interests.

Forever African Safaris ☎09 246968; m 0712 648 328, 216 654; www.foreverafricansafaris.com. Terry & Sheona Anders offer very personalised, luxury mobile tented & walking safaris in Hwange, Victoria Falls, Gonarezhou, Mana Pools & Mlibizi (fishing safaris).

John Stevens Guided Safaris Africa ☎04 490612; e info@johnstevenssafaris.com; www.

johnstevenssafaris.com. This company provides bespoke safaris, anything from backpacking wilderness walks to lodges on the Zambezi River. Prior to setting up his safari business, John was warden of Matusadona & Mana Pools national parks so he has a vast knowledge of the Zambezi Valley.
Khangela Safaris m 0772 234676; e khangelasafaris@hotmail.com; www. khangela.com. Mike Scott has been guiding for more than 20 years & runs safaris throughout the country. He specialises in walking & camping safaris in Mana Pools & with Zimbabwe's other parks on request.
Kazuma Trails \013 40857; m 0712 213 840, 214 399; e info@mobile-safaris.com; www. mobile.safaris.com. David Carson offers a range of backed-up walking & camping safaris in Hwange & Kazuma Pan, catering for different levels of client fitness, luxury & duration. He's an accomplished

wildlife photographer able to offer his experience & advice to guests. He also runs Camp Hwange.
Off2Africa \04 338894; m 0772 309271; e beck@off2africa.travel; www.off2africa.travel. Safaris in all of Zimbabwe's national parks.
Private Guided Safaris Kenya m 0773 819834/5; e ant@privateguidedsafaris.com; www. privateguidedsafaris.com; Skype: antkaschula. This small, family-run company offers a non-luxury though very professional safari experience giving you a genuine back-to-basics nature experience. Trips are ideally suited to active people who enjoy a combination of activities such as walking, canoeing, hiking & fishing. Specialists in Gonarezhou National Park.
Tailormade Safaris \09 232376; e info@ tailormade-safaris.com; www.tailormade-safaris. com. Tented adventures to Hwange, Mana Pools, Matopos, Matusadona & Vic Falls.

RED TAPE

Visas and entry requirements are subject to change and you should always contact the Zimbabwean embassy or consulate in your country for the latest information. Zimbabwe government websites may not be up to date and should not be relied upon.

DOCUMENTS Passports must be valid for at least six months from date of entry. Zimbabwe requires a completely blank page in your passport for its full-page visa (check the countries below that are exempt from visas). Therefore, on arrival you should have at least three blank pages – for Zimbabwe and for possible onward countries.

You must also carry tickets or documentation for onward or return travel and possess sufficient funds for your stay.

The immigration form requires minimal information on destination and length of stay, as well as an indication of how much foreign currency you are taking in. In the 'destination' box, enter the first or main point on your itinerary, rather than a whole list or the word 'touring'. Zimbabwe is particularly sensitive about international journalists and writers visiting the country, and those intending to work in Zimbabwe must apply for official accreditation. Journalists arriving on holiday should carefully consider how they describe their occupation in the form's 'occupation' box, as using the 'j' word may cause a lengthy delay at the very least.

For safety, make copies of all your important documents – relevant pages of passport, flight ticket, driving licence, credit cards, etc – and keep these separate from the originals.

VISAS Residents of the following countries do not require visas: Antigua, Bahamas, Barbados, Belize, Bermuda, Botswana, Cayman Islands, Cyprus, Democratic Republic of Congo, Fiji, Grenada, Guyana, Hong Kong, Jamaica, Kenya, Lesotho, Malawi, Malaysia, Maldives, Malta, Mauritius, Montserrat, Namibia, New Zealand, Singapore, St Lucia, St Vincent and the Grenadines, Swaziland, Tanzania, Trinidad and Tobago, Turks and Caicos Island, Uganda, Zambia.

Residents of South Africa are granted a gratis visa on entry.

Residents of the following countries may buy a visa on arrival (but check before you go as rules change): Argentina, Australia, Austria, Belgium, Brazil, Canada, China, Denmark, Egypt, Finland, France, Germany, Ghana, Greece, Iceland, Indonesia, Ireland, Israel, Italy, Japan, Kuwait, Liechtenstein, Luxembourg, Monaco, Netherlands, New Zealand, Norway, Poland, Portugal, Puerto Rico, Seychelles, South Korea, Spain, State of Palestine, Sweden, Switzerland, United Arab Emirates, UK, USA.

TRAVEL ADVISORIES

Most governments issue advisory notices to their citizens regarding travel to other countries (see your own government website). These warn of potential dangers, usually safety- or health-related. Under certain circumstances they may advise against all or all but essential travel, to the whole country or to specified areas.

In Zimbabwe's case there have been negative advisories from a variety of countries in recent years, frequently recommending against travel around election dates or to certain parts of the country. These advisories are there to protect you but they tend to be extremely conservative and geographically imprecise, often warning against travel to areas far removed from any conceivable threat (political violence and war-veteran activity are currently the most common ones cited). For example, in late 2008 a UK advisory warned against all but essential travel to Harare, Manicaland and rural Mashonaland. There were indeed hot spots, but this blanket ban ruled out the whole of east and northern Zimbabwe, including many towns, several national parks and vast tracts of land that had seen no trouble since the independence war. Indeed it is my firm view that any genuine tourist would have to be amazingly unlucky, or more likely, amazingly unwise to find themselves caught up in any problems as these are invariably related to internal politics.

The Zimbabwe hospitality industry, and many regular travellers, feel these recommendations are often unnecessarily cautious, overly general and inconsistently applied. Remember they are only recommendations and it is your choice whether to ignore a travel advisory but if you do, be aware of the following serious consequences.

Once a government travel advisory is issued, most insurance companies will pull the plug on your cover, even if the reason for a claim is completely unrelated to the reason for the travel warning. If you drop your camera in the Zambezi on a peaceful canoe safari after quite reasonably ignoring a 'rural Mashonaland' warning, you would find yourself having to replace it with your own money. More importantly, if you have a medical issue you could find yourself paying for very expensive private health care and possibly even your emergency repatriation.

Look for an insurer who will cover you for everything except incidents specified in the travel advisory, rather than adopting a blanket ban on cover. You should also ask where you would stand if a travel warning were issued after your booking was confirmed but before travel. Would they refuse to cover you if you travelled? Or if you heed the advice and decide not to travel, will they compensate you for cancellation?

One further point: if you ignore a travel advisory you will find your country's consular officials less sympathetic than usual if you have to turn to them for assistance.

Residents of other countries must pre-purchase their visa. Single-, double- and multiple-entry visas are available but only the first two can be obtained in advance or on entry. For a multiple-entry visa you must apply in writing to the Chief Immigration Officer (*Dept of Immigration Control, Private bag 7717, Causeway, Harare*).

Holiday visas are normally valid for six months with a maximum stay of 90 days, but this may vary. Around election times, for instance, you may be granted a much shorter stay (although this can generally be extended once in the country). It is also quite usual for border officials to grant you an initial 30 days, with the advice that you can extend your visa by visiting any immigration office in the country. This will mean you'll have to carefully plan your itinerary in order to be close to an immigration facility at the due date. Check the validity of your visa before you leave the immigration desk as I've experienced several instances where mistakes have been made. The second entry of a double-entry visa must occur within six months of issue. Some border officials may incorrectly insist that both trips must be *completed* within six months of purchasing this visa, and demand that you purchase a second visa.

Visa fees Single/double-entry visas for most countries are US$30/45 (US$55/70 for the UK and US$65/130 for Canada). Pre-purchasing the visa at a Zimbabwe embassy or consulate in your country saves you time on arrival, but it can be cheaper to purchase it on arrival. You can pay for it in a variety of hard currencies, some better value than others depending on exchange rates. All main border points accept US dollars, sterling, euros, South African rand (ZAR) and the currency of the nearest neighbouring country. If you intend paying in anything other than US dollars be sure to have the exact money or be prepared to have change delivered in US dollars at whatever exchange rate they happen to be using. Smaller borders tend to only recognise US dollars, rand and the neighbouring currency. Have plenty of small notes so you can pay the exact fee, as change is frequently not available.

Make sure you receive a visa payment receipt and retain it for the duration of your trip. You may quite reasonably assume the visa stamp itself is sufficient proof that you have purchased it but there have been recent incidents where immigration officials have been involved in scams, so a receipt is your security.

DUTY-FREE ALLOWANCE Each visitor may bring in 400 cigarettes and five litres of liquor, up to two litres of which may be spirits. Currency must be declared on arrival. Any extra fuel carried in cans is dutiable up to a maximum of 200 litres. You are allowed to bring in up to US$300 worth of goods per calendar month. However, the situation regarding gifts for Zimbabwe residents changes on a regular basis so check the latest allowances with the recipient as near as possible to the date of arrival. For instance, at the time of writing, domestic refrigerators are dutiable if they are gifts (but you are allowed a vehicle fridge/freezer if it is obviously a camping or leisure model). Permits are issued on arrival for firearms and ammunition. The import of drugs, honey, pornographic or obscene material, toy firearms, flick knives and lockable knives is prohibited (although your multi-tool will present no problem). Fresh meat and agricultural products including seeds and bulbs require an import licence.

EMBASSIES

IN ZIMBABWE You can obtain a complete list of embassies on http://zw.embassyinformation.com. The following embassies and consulates are situated in Harare.

❸ **Australia** 1 Green Close, Borrowdale; ✆04 853 23555; www.zimbabwe.embassy.gov.au
❸ **Canada** 45 Baines Av; ✆04 252181/5; www.zimbabwe.gc.ca
❸ **Botswana** 22 Phillips Av; ✆04 729551
❸ **Denmark** UDC Centre, 59 Union Av; ✆04 758185
❸ **France** 11th Floor, Old Mutual Centre, cnr 3rd St & Jason Moyo Av; ✆04 705738; www.ambafrance-zw.org
❸ **Germany** 30 Ceres Rd, Avondale; ✆04 705231
❸ **Israel** 6th Floor, Three Anchor Hse, 54 Jason Moyo Av; ✆04 756808
❸ **Italy** 7 Bartholomew Cl, Greendale; ✆04 497200; www.ambitalia.co.zw
❸ **Japan** 18th Floor, Karigamombe Centre, 53 Samora Machel Av; ✆04 757861
❸ **Netherlands** 2 Arden Rd, Highlands; ✆04 776701

❸ **New Zealand** Eastgate Centre, 8th Floor, Green Bridge, cnr 2nd St & Robert Mugabe Rd; ✆04 759221; www.nzembassy.com/southafrica
❸ **Norway** Chancery, 5 Lanark Rd, Belgravia; ✆04 252426
❸ **Portugal** 12 Harvey Brown Av, Milton Pk; ✆04 253218
❸ **Russia** 70 Fife St; ✆04 701957
❸ **South Africa** 7 Elcombe St; ✆04 753147/9
❸ **Spain** 16 Phillips Av; ✆04 738681
❸ **Sweden** 7th Floor, Pegasus Hse, 52 Samora Machel Av; ✆04 790651
❸ **Switzerland** 9 Lanark Rd, Belgravia; ✆04 703997
❸ **UK** 7th Floor, Corner Hse, cnr Samora Machel & Leopold Takawira Av; ✆04 772990; www.britainzw.org
❸ **USA** 172 Herbert Chitepo Av; ✆04 250594

ZIMBABWE EMBASSIES AND HIGH COMMISSIONS OVERSEAS

❸ **Australia** High Commission, 11 Culgoa Circuit, O'Malley, Canberra ACT 2606; ✆02 6286 2700
❸ **Belgium** Embassy, Josephine Charlotte Sq 11, 1200 Brussels; ✆02 7625808
❸ **Botswana** High Commission, Plot 8895, PO Box 1232, Gaberone; ✆039 14495
❸ **Canada** High Commission, 332 Somerset St W, Ottawa, Ontario K2P 0J9; ✆237 4388/9
❸ **France** Embassy, 5 Rue Lord Byron, 75008 Paris; ✆01 5688 1600
❸ **Germany** Embassy, Kommandantenstr 80, 10117 Berlin; ✆030 2062263
❸ **India** High Commission, E12/7 Vasant Vihar, New Delhi 110021; ✆261 40430/1
❸ **Italy** Embassy, Via Virgilio 8, 2nd Floor 193, Rome; ✆06 6830 8265
❸ **Japan** Embassy, 5-9-10 Shironganedari, Minato-ku 108, Tokyo; ✆03 32800331/2

❸ **Malawi** High Commission, 7th Floor, Gemini Hse, PO Box 30187, Lilongwe; ✆01 774413
❸ **Mozambique** High Commission, Av Kenneth Kaunda 816/820, Caixa Postal 743, Maputo; ✆021 490699
❸ **Namibia** High Commission, Gamsberg Bldg, PO Box 23056, Windhoek; ✆061 227738
❸ **Russia** Embassy, Serpov per 6, Moscow; ✆095 2484364/7
❸ **South Africa** High Commission, 798 Merton Hse, Arcadia, Pretoria; ✆012 3425125
❸ **Sweden** Embassy, Herserudsvagen 5A, 7th Floor Lidingo, Stockholm; ✆08 246695
❸ **Switzerland** Embassy, 27 Chemin William Barbey, 1292 Geneva; ✆22 7583011/3
❸ **UK** High Commission, 429 The Strand, London WC2R 0SA; ✆020 7379 1167
❸ **US** Embassy, 1608 New Hampshire Av NW, Washington, DC 20009; ✆202 332 7100

TOURIST INFORMATION

The Zimbabwe Tourist Authority (ZTA) has offices, or at least a representative, at most overseas embassies and consulates (see list above). Their contact details in Zimbabwe are ✆ +263 4 758730/34, 61 2656, 773 384844 or 775 169117; e info@ztazim.co.zw; www.zimbabwetourism.net. Their website contains basic information but is unreliable and at the time of writing was not responding. Their offices generally contain a range of leaflets and brochures and the staff always try to be helpful, but some people have reported that the information on offer is not particularly comprehensive. If that's the case when you enquire, an alternative is to contact one or more of the specialist agencies listed on pages 84–7, many of whom have excellent and very comprehensive websites.

MAPS AND GPS

MAPS Pre-purchase should be your goal: lack of demand means few shops stock Zimbabwe maps, even in neighbouring South Africa. In Zimbabwe, stocks are likely to be unreliable at least for the life of this book.

A good basic map to start with is the AA's *Motoring in Zimbabwe*, with country, large town and some national park maps, and general motoring information. While useful for initial planning, its small scale (1:2,500,000) lacks many smaller but useful dirt roads.

The Zimbabwe Tourism Authority (*Kopje Plaza, 105 Jason Moyo Av;* ✎ *04 758730/4;* e *marketing@ztazim.co.za; www.zimbabwetourism.co.zw*) publishes a 1:1,900,000 sheet map that is easy to read and ideal for general planning although again without smaller roads. The reverse has general information in English, French and German.

I have relied on two excellent maps produced by Zimbabwe's Department of the Surveyor General: the 1:1,000,000 ZIMAP *General Map of Zimbabwe* sheet map and the *Atlas of Zimbabwe*. The former features most roads, tar and dirt, that you are likely to require, although geographical and contour markings can make it difficult to read especially in poor light, the latter is a road atlas based on the above sheet map, in book form and without the contour markings, making it easier to read. At the back are 23 pages of detailed maps of all major towns and most national parks. Both of these maps should be available from the Surveyor General offices in Harare (*49 Samora Machel Av, PO Box CY 540, Causeway*) and Bulawayo (*Tredgold Bldg, Leopold Takawira Av, PO Box CY 1580*), or in Stanfords in London (*www.stanfords.co.uk*).

Two other good sheet maps are published by International Travel Maps and Books (*www.itmb.com*) and Map Studio (*www.mapstudio.co.za*). They are both of similar scale – 1:1,100,000 and 1:200,000 – and very easy to read, although neither gives much detail for remote driving destinations. The latter has some key GPS marks and very clear town maps on the reverse.

In Zimbabwe the Surveyor General offices in Harare and Bulawayo (see above for addresses) offer a range of regional and town maps including some national parks. AA offices in larger towns usually stock a map of the town, and several local publicity associations produce tourist maps of their area. Strangely, while there is a National Parks information leaflet for each of the parks, none of them contains a map.

If you are having trouble locating maps in your own country, check Exclusive Books in South Africa at OR Tambo Johannesburg airport but don't rely on it. Note that while it is easy to navigate the major roads, the names of villages and small towns often differ from map to map depending on whether they were published before or after the indigenisation of many place names. For example, Chituripase in southern Zimbabwe is sometimes shown as Chipise.

GPS Although they can be lifesavers in many African countries, it is perfectly possible to traverse the length and breadth of Zimbabwe without one (this book was researched without a single GPS co-ordinate to follow). That said, I have often found my GPS useful and keep it switched on in the car as a backup to my maps

Many road junctions have had their signposts stolen so a GPS can be useful here, and many roads and tracks in less well-visited national parks have become indistinct, even non-existent. Rather than risk getting lost in the bush, most visitors will not take a chance when in doubt but will return to camp the way they came, but a GPS can give you the confidence to take a chance. Even without pre-programmed co-ordinates the GPS's map will tell you the direction you should be heading. The same goes for hiking. Having said that, *never* set the GPS to 'offroad' in a national park and simply crash through the bush following the arrow. In addition the various data shown on a GPS – speed, distance, elevation, rate of climb, etc – can add a whole new element of interest to your walk or drive.

But once you have spent your money on the clever little thing and marvelled at its capabilities, it's all too easy to fall in love with it and put all your trust in it. You should still equip yourself with a map and, if you are hiking, a compass. Carry spare batteries and don't forget that rechargeables, while commendably green, are nowhere near as durable as standard batteries. If you have a handheld device, purchase a lead so you can draw power from your vehicle's 12V supply, and an external aerial if necessary.

An excellent book by Lawrence Letham, *GPS Made Easy* (published by Cordee), explains the basics of navigation and the intricacies of the GPS system, and takes you through practical examples.

GPS software If you are using Garmap's *Street Maps of Southern Africa*, be sure that you have the latest version; earlier versions have far less information on Zimbabwe, some of which is quite inaccurate.

Tracks4Africa (*www.tracks4africa.co.za*) is a dynamic online mapping and information system continually being expanded by direct input from a community of enthusiastic GPS users. You can download maps and destinational information for around ZAR100/US$8. Zimbabwe information is being rapidly expanded.

GPS co-ordinates in this guide I have occasionally included GPS co-ordinates in this book, but have avoided plastering it with them for the simple reason that they are largely unnecessary, adding them only for locations that are difficult to find or where fairly crucial signposts are missing. The datum used is the worldwide WGS84 with co-ordinates displayed as degrees/minutes/seconds.

GETTING THERE AND AWAY

BY AIR The main long-haul carriers all made the commercial decision to stop operating direct flights to Zimbabwe in 2007–08. The only exception was Air Zimbabwe, which operated a twice-weekly service from London Gatwick. However in 2012, after years of financial instability and industrial unrest, the airline ceased operating.

As I write this, there are only two major longhaul carriers operating from Europe direct into Zimbabwe, but the situation is very likely to change with the improving economic and political situation and the excellent news that Victoria Falls airport is due to be extended to facilitate longhaul aircraft. KLM route their daily flights to Harare via Lusaka and Emirates with a five times per week service from Dubai also routed via Lusaka in Zambia.

That is the good news, but with the demise of Air Zimbabwe's domestic flight network, passengers who fly into Harare must then find other means than air to get to their onward destination in Zimbabwe. So for now virtually every overseas passenger flies to Johannesburg and can usually connect the same day to Harare, Victoria Falls or Bulawayo. Naturally, your choice of Zimbabwean airport depends on your itinerary, but both Victoria Falls and Bulawayo are considerably smaller and offer friendlier and more hassle-free formalities than Harare. Bulawayo is currently (late 2012) undergoing refurbishment and extension. Harare will in due course return to its position as principal entry point, as it's so far the only airport with the capacity to handle larger aircraft.

From the UK to Johannesburg British Airways (BA), South African Airways (SA) and Virgin Atlantic (VG) each operate two or three daily non-stop flights from London Heathrow to Johannesburg with a flight time of approximately 11 hours. The internet provides a number of other airlines offering flights to Johannesburg from London routed via European and Middle Eastern airports, but while these can be considerably cheaper than direct flights they of course involve a time and inconvenience penalty.

From Europe to Johannesburg Lufthansa and South African Airways fly to Johannesburg from Munich and Frankfurt, and United Airlines from Frankfurt. Air France operates from Paris CDG and Iberia from Madrid.

From USA and other destinations If individual countries do not operate direct flights to Johannesburg, passengers must route there via Europe.

From Johannesburg to Zimbabwe South African Airways operates daily direct to Harare, Victoria Falls and Bulawayo with a flight time of around 2 hours. British Airways (Comair) flies daily direct to Harare and Victoria Falls, and to Bulawayo via Harare.

From Johannesburg to Livingstone, Zambia For several years the route of choice for budget-minded travellers was on 1time to Livingstone and then road transfer across the bridge into Victoria Falls – a much cheaper option than SAA or BA direct to the Falls. At the time of writing 1time had just suspended all its services and appeared to be going into liquidation leaving this route vacant.

From Durban to Zimbabwe In late 2012 SA Express started operating to Harare three times weekly with a 2 hour flight time.

Regional flights are operated between Harare, Gaberone, Windhoek, Maputo, Lilongwe, Lusaka, Dar es Salaam and Nairobi on those country's national carriers. Unfortunately, at the time of writing, fares and timetables were too variable to make quoting them worthwhile; refer to individual airline websites.

Airlines Flights, schedules and booking details can be found on all of the following websites: Air France (*www.airfrance.com*);); British Airways (Comair) (*www.britishairways.com*); Lufthansa (*www.lufthansa.com*); South African Airways (*www.flysaa.com*); United Airlines (*www.united.com*); Virgin Atlantic: (*www. virgin-atlantic.com*).

BY BUS Several luxury, air-conditioned coach services regularly ply the route between Johannesburg and Bulawayo and Harare, with a driving time of approximately 13 and 17 hours, respectively. Most operate mainly during daylight hours, but a couple are overnighters. Given the hazards and the standards of Africa's roads, my inclination would be to choose a daylight service whenever possible.

Greyhound ☎+27 83 915 9000; www. greyhound.co.za. This is the most comfortable & reliable, operating services from Johannesburg to Harare & Bulawayo (different services). Their website is efficient & you can book online.

Intercape ☎+27 021 380 4400; www. intercape.co.za. Operates from Johannesburg to Harare via Masvingo & Victoria Falls via Bulawayo.

Pioneer Coaches ☎+263 4 663780/2, +27 11 0429198; e solutions@pioneerafrica.com; www.pioneerafrica.com. Zimbabwean company with booking offices in Zimbabwe & South Africa They operate from Johannesburg to Harare,

Bulawayo, Gweru & Mutare using 'luxury' & 'semi luxury' coaches.

Senatar Express Desk in Getaway Safaris in Victoria Falls in the Landela Centre on Livingstone Way; ☎+263 13 41480; e vicfalls@senatar.co.zw. Operates a daily express bus (not coach – their word) between Johannesburg & Bulawayo & on to Victoria Falls. The total journey takes 24hrs (17hrs to Bulawayo). There is no website but three years ago I was told it would be up & running 'soon'! Coaches from Jo'burg depart from Park City Station in the city centre & drop off at the Road Port terminus on 5th St & Robert Mugabe Rd in Harare.

Zimbabwe is not well served by direct bus services from other neighbouring countries with only Francistown (Botswana) operating to Harare on ZUPCO buses – maybe not everybody's first choice of bus service.

BY RAIL The only scheduled rail service to Zimbabwe from any neighbouring country is a three times a week service between Francistown, Botswana, and Bulawayo.

BY ROAD

Border crossings When driving from South Africa, most people feel (usually wrongly) they are committed to entering at Musina/Beitbridge. Although the border is open 24 hours, allow a lot of time for formalities at this very busy border so that, once through, you still have at least an hour's daylight to reach the first possible overnight accommodation on the way to Masvingo or Bulawayo. The Zimbabwe side of the border has an appalling record for confusing signage, horrendous queues and notorious 'helpers', 'facilitation agents' or more accurately unofficial touts, who offer to speed you through the process at an exceptionally high price of several hundred dollars. The more you use these rip-off artists, the more you encourage them. You can usually dramatically cut your delays here by arriving at the border before 10.00, preferably avoiding weekends. If you do have a problem here and feel you've been ripped off, had bribes demanded etc, there is a Zimbabwe Tourism representative based at the Petroport service station as you leave town. It's unlikely she will be able to achieve much for you but it's important that you report these occurrences – the more of us who do, the more chance there is that the authorities will clean the place up.

If you are heading from South Africa to Victoria Falls or Bulawayo, you can avoid the hassle and frequent delays of Beitbridge by crossing into Botswana at Groblers Bridge/Martins Drift and entering Zimbabwe at Plumtree, Pandamatenga or Kazungula. Plumtree, although busy, brings you in close to Bulawayo; Pandamatenga is convenient for the northern part of Hwange and Victoria Falls (4x4s only); and from Kazungula you have a pleasant 50-minute drive to Victoria Falls.

South Africa
Beitbridge 24hrs; nearest town Musina.
Extremely busy with commercial & local traffic; long, slow queues, confusing disorganised 'system'. Arrive early & midweek if possible & don't use touts.

Botswana
Plumtree ⏰ 06.00–20.00; nearest town Francistown. Very busy, long queues possible.
Pandamatenga ⏰ 08.00–16.00 (closes unofficially at lunchtime); nearest towns Chobe

& Kasane. Sleepy & laid-back. Quick entry direct to Hwange National Park; 4x4 required to reach Victoria Falls road & Hwange

Kazungula ⊕ 06.00–20.00; nearest town Kasane. Small, relatively easy-going, but getting busier.

Zambia

Victoria Falls ⊕ 06.00–20.00; nearest town Livingstone. Busy with tourists but not commercial traffic.

Kariba ⊕ 06.00–18.00. Quiet tourist post.

Chirundu ⊕ 06.00–18.00. Very busy with traffic from Lusaka to Harare. This became the region's first 1-stop border post in Dec 2009, significantly speeding up the formalities in theory but reports of long delays on the Zim side.

Mozambique

Espungabera ⊕ 06.00–18.00. 8km from Chirinda Forest. Nearest town Chimoio. Small, relaxed & friendly.

Mukumbura ⊕ 06.00–18.00. Little known & little used.

Nyamapanda ⊕ 06.00–18.00; nearest town Tete. Busy with commercial traffic to Harare from the Tete Corridor.

Forbes-Mutare ⊕ 06.00–18.00; nearest town Chimoio. Busy with traffic to/from the Mozambican port of Beira.

Sango/Chicualacuala ⊕ 06.00–18.00; no close towns of note. Useful entry into Gonarezhou from Kruger via Pafuri Gate.

Documents There's a degree of misinformation and confusion over whether you need a carnet de passage (think of it as a passport for your car) to enter Zimbabwe. Guidebooks and magazine articles frequently state it as a requirement. Check the websites and some say yes, others say no. The AA recommends it on one web page and then says it isn't required on another! From my own personal experience gained from countless visits to Zimbabwe over more than a decade driving a South African-registered vehicle, I have never yet used or been asked for a carnet, simply relying on my registration document. If you're planning to tour a number of countries, especially including those in central/northern Africa, then it's a different story but in recent years I have taken vehicles into Zimbabwe, Namibia, Botswana, Zambia and Mozambique without ever being asked for a carnet.

If the vehicle is yours but you haven't completed payments on it, or if it's a hired car, you will need a letter of authorisation from the bank or hire company giving you permission to take it out of the country, as well as the vehicle licence papers, both of which need to be signed by a commissioner of oaths.

If you are the fully paid-up owner you will need the original registration document, or a copy certified by a commissioner of oaths.

Before you exit the previous country make sure you have received the necessary paperwork from that country's border officials. Your vehicle will need a Temporary Export Permit (TEP) from the country in which it is registered, to allow you to return with it. South Africa has now dispensed with the TEP but has replaced it with another document – a Traveller Declaration form number DA331– on which you must list items of value that you will be taking back into RSA, cameras, binos, laptops, etc. The form also requires your vehicle details. This form is not always automatically offered so you must ask for it.

International Driving Permits and all driving licences issued by the Southern African Development Community (SADC) (an organisation of 15 member states set up to foster political and socio-economic co-operation) countries are valid in Zimbabwe. Citizens from other countries can use their national licence for up to 90 days. Licences must bear the driver's photograph and if it's not printed in English you must carry a translation of the text, also with a photograph attached.

Insurance Regardless of what sort of comprehensive vehicle insurance you already have, Zimbabwe requires you to buy their own third party insurance on entry to the country. It is now collected by the customs official – US$30 – along with your road access fee and carbon tax payment (except at Beitbridge where it's collected separately) so at least you don't have to visit a scruffy little Portakabin or shed as you used to in the past.

If you are driving a hired vehicle there is an additional 'insurance' fee payable, the Commercial Vehicle Guarantee costing another US$30.

Formalities All Zimbabwe's road border posts have similar entry and departure procedures. Smaller ones are relatively relaxed, with friendly and polite officials.

On entry to Zimbabwe you complete a simple immigration form and if necessary purchase a visa. At this stage you receive a gate pass – a slip of paper to be stamped at each stage in the process and presented at the exit barrier to prove you have been through all the necessary formalities.

From immigration you move to customs, where you fill in a Temporary Import Permit (TIP) for your vehicle (valid for 30 days). For this you need chassis number and engine number (both numbers are shown on the vehicle's registration document) and an indication of the vehicle's value. Trailer and caravan details are also required. You must detail brands, serial numbers and value of goods such as radios, laptops, cameras etc that you are taking into the country; I have never encountered any problems offering only minimal details. There is usually a register by the customs counter to be completed with basic vehicle details including the serial number of your TIP.

After that you pay the Road Access Fee (currently US$10 and Carbon Tax, levied according to engine capacity (ranges from US$6 for under 1,500cc to US$30 for over 3,000cc) and valid for 30 days. If you will be in the country for longer than 30 days you will have to buy further Carbon Tax certificates as well as extending your TIP along your route as these are frequently checked at police roadblocks. As this can only be done at major towns and border posts you'll need to factor this into your itinerary. If you enter at Beitbridge you also pay (US$7) to cross the Limpopo bridge. Drivers of hired vehicles must ensure they have all necessary documentation from the hirer to avoid lengthy delays at the border.

At some stage between completing the formalities and the exit barrier, your documents will be checked and you may be questioned on what goods you are taking in. Finally, hand your fully stamped gate pass to the barrier official and enter the country.

HEALTH *with Dr Felicity Nicholson*

The economic meltdown in the decade of 2000 onwards had a dramatic effect on Zimbabwe's health-care system, resulting in chronic shortages of manpower, medical supplies and equipment, even in the capital, Harare. Since 2009 the situation has improved greatly but the country is still playing catch-up in an effort to rebuild its medical infrastructure. Public hospitals are still extremely understaffed and generally very poorly equipped. Well-run private clinics and hospitals can be found in Harare and Bulawayo and are capable of dealing with common emergencies but facilities in the rest of the country are sketchy and changeable. For serious conditions, evacuation to South Africa is invariably the best option unless the patient can't be moved. Comprehensive **medical insurance** should therefore be a priority. Outside of towns and on safari, your lodge or camp will be well versed in first aid but will probably only stock basic medications. Most if not all of the upmarket lodges as well as many of the smaller camps, subscribe to MARS, a countrywide medical **air evacuation service** so you should be well catered for in an emergency if you're staying at one of these establishments. Independent travellers can subscribe to MARS, but conditions apply (see page 98).

Emergencies aside, Zimbabwe is a generally low risk in medical terms but of course with the proviso of malaria, which is endemic in large areas of the country that tourists are likely to visit. The country's tourism sector has a long and enviable history of catering for 'high end' visitors, so hygiene requirements are well understood and standards in camps, lodges and hotels are generally on a par with first world countries. That said, municipal water supplies have suffered greatly from under-investment and poor maintenance in recent years so be very wary about drinking tap water in town accommodations. Safari accommodations obtain water from boreholes, which provide some of the nicest water you are likely to drink. Pharmacies can be found in towns around the country but stocks may not be very comprehensive.

The incidence of HIV/AIDS is hard to gauge accurately, but in 2010 the estimated adult infection rate was 14.3%, with 1.3 million people living with AIDS.

The guidelines below relate to tropical Africa in general, since travellers may well want to spend time in more than one country.

BEFORE YOU GO

Immunisations Preparations to ensure a healthy trip to Zimbabwe require checks on your immunisation status: it is wise to be up to date with tetanus, polio and diphtheria (now given as an all-in-one vaccine, Revaxis, that lasts for ten years), and hepatitis A. Immunisations against meningococcus, typhoid and rabies may also be recommended. Yellow fever vaccination is not needed for health as there is no yellow fever in Zimbabwe. However, if you are entering the country from a yellow fever endemic area then you will be asked to show proof of vaccination against yellow fever. The decision to take yellow fever vaccine should be made on an individual basis so ask a health care professional well before your intended trip. Note that the South African health authority has classified Zambia as a yellow fever risk country and is very strict on allowing people arriving from Zambia into the country if they haven't been immunised. Regardless, if the vaccine is not suitable you should arrive with an exemption certificate and an additional doctor's letter explaining the reasons why you could not be vaccinated. Immunisation against cholera may be recommended for Zimbabwe but is not a requirement.

Hepatitis A vaccine (Havrix Monodose or Avaxim) comprises two injections given about a year apart. The course costs around £100, but in the UK may be available on the NHS; it protects for 25 years and can be administered even close to the time of departure. Hepatitis B vaccination should be considered for longer trips (two months or more) or for those working with children or in situations where contact with blood is likely. Three injections are needed for the best protection and can be given over a three-week period for those aged 16 or older if time is short. Longer schedules give more sustained protection and are therefore preferred if time allows and must be used for those under 16. Hepatitis A vaccine can also be given as a combination with hepatitis B as 'Twinrix', though two doses are needed at least seven days apart to be effective for the hepatitis A component, and three doses are needed for the hepatitis B. Again this schedule can be used only for those aged 16 or over.

The injectable typhoid vaccines (eg: Typhim Vi) last for three years and are about 75–80% effective. Oral capsules (Vivotif) may also be available for those aged six and over. A dose of three capsules over five days lasts for approximately three years but may be less effective than the injectable forms, especially if they are not taken correctly. They should be encouraged unless the traveller is leaving within a few days for a trip of a week or less, when the vaccine would not be effective in time. Meningitis vaccine containing strains A, C, W and Y may be recommended, especially for trips of more than four weeks (see *Meningitis*, page 108). Vaccinations for rabies are ideally advised for everyone, but are especially important for travellers visiting more remote areas, especially if you are more than 24 hours from medical help and definitely if you will be working with animals (see *Rabies*, pages 108–9). Rabies is endemic in Zimbabwe so unless they are domestic pets that you know, treat all dogs, especially strays, with great caution.

Experts differ over whether a BCG vaccination against tuberculosis (TB) is useful in adults: discuss this with your travel clinic.

In addition to the various vaccinations recommended above, it is important that travellers should be properly protected against malaria. For detailed advice, see below.

Ideally you should visit your own doctor or a specialist travel clinic to discuss your requirements, if possible at least eight weeks before you plan to travel.

Travel clinics and health information A full list of current travel clinic websites worldwide is available on www.istm.org. For other journey preparation information, consult www.nathnac.org/ds/map_world.aspx. Information about various medications may be found on www.netdoctor.co.uk/travel.

Travel insurance Before you travel, make sure that you have adequate medical insurance – it will take a long time for the country's public medical infrastructure to fully recover from its virtual collapse in the early 2000s, so any treatment you require will have to be in a private facility and may well involve evacuation to another country. All good policies will cover for repatriation costs but most only pay for the flight home and not the costs that may be incurred by getting you from the place of the incident to the airport. This could involve you in considerable cost if you fall ill or have an accident in one of the more remote areas of the country. Nowadays the range of cover available is very wide – choose whatever suits your method of travel. Be aware that if you plan to use cycles or scooters in Zimbabwe, not all policies cover you for this form of transport. Remember to take all the details with you, particularly your policy number and the telephone number that you have to use in the event of a claim. You must also have access to sufficient cash or a credit card as most medical facilities will require you to pay before treatment. Your insurance policy will only reimburse you after you have put in a claim.

Many fully inclusive lodges and tourism facilities subscribe to MARS (*Medical Air Rescue Service;* \ +263 4 753677, 740848, 75044; f +263 4 790594; e nigel@ marshre.co.zw; www.mars.co.zw), a private Zimbabwe-based medical service provider offering emergency road or air evacuation to the nearest medical facility. Control centres and medical teams around the country are on call 24 hours a day. If your lodge doesn't subscribe, or you are travelling independently, you can take out your own cover with a MARS Tourism subscription. It is, however, important to understand that the small daily tourism subscription does not fund MARS evacuation costs and they have to claim costs back from your insurance company. MARS therefore needs an authorisation letter from your insurer guaranteeing reimbursement before they issue you with the evacuation cover.

Prescription drugs If you have important prescription drugs, *never* put them in your checked baggage in case it goes missing – this is especially important if you are transiting via OR Tambo Airport at Johannesburg, which has a dreadful reputation for losing baggage. Airline security is very stringent these days so you must carry a copy of your prescription and have a letter from your GP authorising your possession of any injectable drugs. Contact your airline(s) well in advance to make arrangements for any drugs that need to be kept refrigerated or administered by injection in flight. You will probably have to hand over all of these drugs and sharp equipment to airline staff at security so your first job once you board must be to contact the senior crew member on the aircraft to ensure that everything has been safely loaded. Check that the crew are aware of your drugs whenever there is an aircraft or crew change.

Malaria prevention Malaria is probably the greatest health risk to travellers in Zimbabwe because it is prevalent in many areas visited by tourists. There is no vaccine against malaria, but using prophylactic drugs and preventing mosquito bites will considerably reduce the risk of contracting it. Seek professional advice to ascertain the preferred anti-malarial drugs for Zimbabwe at the time you travel. If mefloquine (Lariam) is suggested, start this 2½ weeks (three doses) before departure to check that it suits you; stop it immediately if it seems to cause depression or anxiety, visual or hearing disturbances, severe headaches, fits or changes in heart rhythm. Side effects such as nightmares or dizziness are not medical reasons for stopping unless they are sufficiently debilitating or annoying. Anyone who has been treated for depression or psychiatric problems, who has diabetes controlled by oral therapy or who is epileptic (or has suffered fits in the past) or has a close blood relative who is epileptic, should probably avoid mefloquine. Lariam, whilst very effective, has a particularly poor reputation amongst safari operators who are at 'the receiving end' with clients suffering side effects and who see the results, first hand, far more frequently than those who prescribe it.

In the past doctors were nervous about prescribing mefloquine to pregnant women, but experience has shown that it is relatively safe and certainly safer than

PERSONAL FIRST-AID KIT

This is highly recommended in Zimbabwe given the often poor availability of medical supplies in some pharmacies. A minimal kit contains:

- A good drying antiseptic, eg: iodine or potassium permanganate (don't take antiseptic cream)
- A few small dressings (Band-Aids)
- Suncream
- Rehydration salts
- Insect repellent; anti-malarial tablets including treatment for those going to remote places; impregnated bed-net or permethrin spray
- Aspirin and paracetamol
- Antifungal cream (eg: Canesten)
- Ciprofloxacin or norfloxacin, for travellers' diarrhoea
- Tinidazole for giardia or amoebic dysentery (see below for regime)
- Antibiotic eye drops, for sore, 'gritty', stuck-together eyes (conjunctivitis)
- A pair of fine-pointed tweezers (to remove hairy caterpillar hairs, thorns, splinters, coral, etc)
- Alcohol-based hand rub or bar of soap in plastic box
- Condoms or femidoms
- A digital thermometer

the risk of malaria. That said, there are other issues, so if you are travelling to Zimbabwe whilst pregnant, seek expert advice before departure.

Malarone (proguanil and atovaquone) is as effective as mefloquine. It has the advantage of having few side effects and need only be continued for one week after returning. However, it is expensive and because of this tends to be reserved for shorter trips. Malarone may not be suitable for everybody, so advice should be taken from a doctor. It can safely be used for up to a year though the cost may be prohibitive, and a paediatric form of tablet for children weighing 11kg or more is also available, prescribed on a weight basis.

Another alternative is the antibiotic doxycycline (100mg daily). Like Malarone it can be started one day before arrival. Unlike mefloquine, it may also be used by travellers with epilepsy, although certain anti-epileptic medication may make it less effective. In perhaps 1–3% of people there is the possibility of allergic skin

LONG-HAUL FLIGHTS, CLOTS AND DVT

Any prolonged immobility including travel by land or air can result in deep vein thrombosis (DVT) with the risk of embolus to the lungs. Certain factors can increase the risk and these include:

* Previous clot or close relative with a history
* Being over 40 but increased risk over 80 years
* Recent major operation or varicose veins surgery
* Cancer
* Stroke
* Heart disease
* Obesity
• Pregnancy
* Hormone therapy
* Heavy smoking
* Severe varicose veins
* Being very tall (over 6ft/1.8m) or short (under 5ft/1.5m)

A deep vein thrombosis (DVT) causes painful swelling and redness of the calf or sometimes the thigh. It is only dangerous if a clot travels to the lungs (pulmonary embolus). Symptoms of a pulmonary embolus (PE) include chest pain, shortness of breath, and sometimes coughing up small amounts of blood and commonly start three to ten days after a long flight. Anyone who thinks that they might have a DVT needs to see a doctor immediately.

PREVENTION OF DVT
* Keep mobile before and during the flight; move around every couple of hours
* Drink plenty of fluids during the flight
* Avoid taking sleeping pills and excessive tea, coffee and alcohol
* Consider wearing flight socks or support stockings (see *www.legshealth. com*)

If you think you are at increased risk of a clot, ask your doctor if it is safe to travel.

reactions developing in sunlight; the drug should be stopped if this happens. It is also unsuitable in pregnancy or for children under 12 years.

Chloroquine and proguanil are no longer thought to be effective enough for Zimbabwe but may be considered as a last resort if nothing else is deemed suitable.

All tablets should be taken with or after the evening meal, washed down with plenty of fluid and, with the exception of Malarone (see above), continued for four weeks after leaving.

TRAVELLING/IN ZIMBABWE

Malaria Some travellers like to take a treatment for malaria, as well as prophylaxis, if they are travelling for more than the standard two- or three-week holiday. Given the necessity to start treatment immediately after the onset of symptoms and the potentially extensive journey time from a safari destination in Zimbabwe to a properly equipped medical facility, self-diagnosis and treatment should be given consideration. Whatever you decide, you should seek up-to-date advice to find out the most appropriate medication. Coartem has been the treatment drug of choice by Zimbabweans for a number of years and has recently been approved by drug authorities in many Western countries. It is available in large Zimbabwe towns but there have been media reports of counterfeit drugs in some developing countries so it is better to purchase it before you travel.

There is no malaria transmission above 3,000m; at intermediate altitudes (1,800–3,000m) the risk exists but is low. In Zimbabwe, all relatively low-lying areas including Victoria Falls, all of the Zambezi Valley, Kariba, Matusadona, Mana Pools and southern areas like Hwange and Gonarezhou National Park are high risk malarial areas. The wet summer months have the highest infection rates but you should take precautions year round.

In addition to taking anti-malarial medicines, it is important to avoid mosquito bites between dusk and dawn, which is when the anopheles (malaria-carrying) mosquito is most active. Use a three-pronged approach employing prophylactics, repellents and barrier methods – clothing and bed-nets. Pack a DEET-based insect repellent (ideally containing 50–55% DEET), such as one of the Repel range or in South Africa, Tabard and Peaceful Sleep – they come in a variety of applications: spray, lotion, wipes and soaps. And take either a permethrin-impregnated bed-net or a permethrin spray so that you can treat bed-nets in hotels. Permethrin treatment makes even very tatty nets protective and mosquitoes are also unable to bite through the impregnated net when you roll against it. Putting on long clothes (including long-sleeved shirts or blouses) at dusk means you can reduce the amount of repellent needed; but be aware that malaria mosquitoes hunt at ankle level and will penetrate through socks as well as other, even quite heavy materials, so apply repellent to your feet and ankles too. Safari activities often set out in the afternoon but return after dusk so you should carry a small pack containing your long clothes and repellents. Travel clinics usually sell a good range of nets, treatment kits and repellents. Do not assume your accommodation will provide repellents – you must bring your own.

There is a range of effective plug-in electrical appliances that release vapourised repellents into your room but bear in mind that most of the lodges and camps in Zimbabwe have no mains electricity and switch their generators off during the night, rendering these methods useless.

Small electronic gadgets that emit a very high-pitched sound don't seem very effective either and shouldn't be relied upon. Mosquito coils burn with a toxic smoke and help if you are sitting round a table outdoors but indoors they can smell rather unpleasant and some brands are not recommended for indoor use at all, especially in tents – always check the label.

☞ **Important** While you are away, assume that any high fever lasting more than a few hours is malaria, regardless of any other symptoms. Always seek medical help but if none is immediately available due to the remoteness of your location, tell your lodge or camp host as they will be able to advise an appropriate course of action. And remember that malaria may occur anything from seven days into your trip to up to one year after leaving Africa. If symptoms appear after you have returned home, visit your doctor immediately, and stress that you have been travelling in a malarial area. Some types of malaria have a dormancy capability and can recur later so if you have suffered from the illness be very wary if the symptoms recur even though you may not have been in a malaria area recently.

Travellers' diarrhoea At least half of those travelling to the tropics/developing world will experience a bout of travellers' diarrhoea during their trip; the newer you are to exotic travel, the more likely you will be to suffer. By taking precautions against travellers' diarrhoea you will also avoid typhoid, cholera, hepatitis, dysentery, worms, etc. Travellers' diarrhoea and the other faecal-oral diseases come from getting other peoples' faeces in your mouth. This most often happens from cooks not washing their hands after a trip to the toilet.

However, hygiene standards in the catering establishments most visitors frequent in Zimbabwe are generally on a par with similar places in the developed world so don't allow paranoia to take over at mealtimes. But if you are eating from rural (as opposed to 'on safari') food sources or in cheap accommodations anywhere in Zimbabwe, the maxim to remind you what you can safely eat is:

PEEL IT, BOIL IT, COOK IT OR FORGET IT.

This means that fruit you have washed and peeled yourself, and hot foods, should be safe, but raw foods, cold cooked foods, salads, fruit salads prepared by others, ice cream and ice are all risky, as are foods kept lukewarm in restaurant or hotel buffets. Self-service or buffet meals are popular, so try to eat these when the food is hot and freshly cooked – for example a late buffet lunch eaten in the mid-afternoon will have been sitting around a long while.

While on safari though, from my experience you have very little to worry about. The kitchen will invariably be catering for a small number of clients, which means there will be a set menu, but it will be freshly and hygienically prepared for each meal. (Don't expect to see too many antibacterial wipes in use though!) If you do get travellers' diarrhoea, see box for treatment.

From water It is also possible to get sick from drinking contaminated water, so try to drink from safe sources. Many rural establishments in Zimbabwe, including most safari camps have their own boreholes providing very pure water so drinking ice and salads seldom present any problems. Always check whether the water is potable in town accommodations, especially the cheaper ones, and use your good sense when questioning hotel staff on this subject. This is especially important in today's Zimbabwe where municipal water suppliers frequently struggle to maintain supplies due to infrastructure problems. Never trust tapped water in national parks or other campsites. To make risky water safe it should be brought to the boil, passed through a good bacteriological filter or purified with chlorine dioxide tablets.

Micropur tablets are tasteless but take at least two hours to become effective. If you buy bottled water make sure the seal is intact. Iodine is no longer recommended for sterilising water.

Insect bites and consequences It is crucial to avoid mosquito bites between dusk and dawn; as the sun is going down, don long clothes and apply repellent on any exposed flesh. This will protect you from malaria and a range of nasty insect-borne viruses. Malaria mosquitoes are voracious and hunt at all body levels, and can penetrate through socks and quite thick clothing. Sleep under a permethrin-treated bednet or in an air-conditioned room. During the day it is wise to wear long, loose (preferably 100% cotton) clothes if you are walking through scrubby country; this will deter ticks as well as tsetse flies and day-biting Aedes mosquitoes that may spread dengue and yellow fever. **Tsetse flies** hurt when they bite and are attracted to the colour blue; locals will advise on where they are a problem and where they transmit sleeping sickness.

Minute pestilential biting **blackflies** spread river blindness in some parts of Africa between 19°N and 17°S although the disease is extremely rare in Zimbabwe; it is caught close to fast-flowing rivers since flies breed there and the larvae live in rapids. The flies bite during the day but long trousers tucked into socks will help keep them off. Citronella-based natural repellents do not work against them. Do not confuse blackflies with the very common mopane flies, which are actually very small bees that don't bite and although annoying, are harmless.

Ticks are ever present in Zimbabwe and they frequently spread disease. They are associated with cattle, wildlife, horses and domestic pets so there's a reasonably good chance of picking them up especially if you go on game walks through high

TREATING TRAVELLERS' DIARRHOEA

It is dehydration that makes you feel awful during a bout of diarrhoea and the most important part of treatment is drinking lots of clear fluids. Sachets of oral rehydration salts give the perfect biochemical mix to replace all that is pouring out of your bottom but they do not taste nice. Any dilute mixture of sugar and salt in water will do you good, so if you like Coke or orange squash, drink that with a three-finger pinch of salt added to each glass. Otherwise make a solution of a four-finger scoop of sugar with a three-finger pinch of salt in a glass of water. Or add eight level teaspoons of sugar (18g) and one level teaspoon of salt (3g) to one litre (five cups) of safe water. A squeeze of lemon or orange juice improves the taste and adds potassium, which is also lost during a bout of diarrhoea. Drink two large glasses after every bowel action, and more if you are thirsty. If you are not eating, then you need to drink three litres a day plus the equivalent of whatever is pouring into the toilet. If you feel like eating, take a bland, high-carbohydrate diet. Heavy, greasy foods will probably give you cramps.

If the diarrhoea is bad, or you are passing blood or slime, or you have a fever, you will probably need antibiotics in addition to fluid replacement. A three-day course of Ciprofloxacin 500mg twice daily (or Norfloxacin) is appropriate treatment for dysentery and bad diarrhoea. If the diarrhoea is greasy and bulky and is accompanied by 'eggy' burps, the likely cause is giardia. This is best treated with Tinidazole (2g in one dose repeated seven days later if symptoms persist).

undergrowth or go horseriding. Lyme disease, which can have unpleasant after-effects, has now been recorded in Africa, but tickbite fever is much more common. The latter is an unpleasant, flu-like illness, but still worth avoiding. If you get the tick off whole and promptly the chances of disease transmission are reduced to a minimum.

Tickbite fever Tick bite fever symptoms can be very similar to malaria with intense headaches, nausea, aching limbs and neck stiffness and fever, but the treatment is totally different so you need to be able to tell the difference. The key to diagnosis is at the source of infection – the bite. Whereas the mosquito usually leaves a pale itching bump, the tick produces a sore, inflamed raised lump with a small black mark at the bite site. In some cases a rash appears. The antibiotic doxycycline is an effective treatment for this debilitating but seldom serious condition.

Dengue fever This mosquito-borne disease resembles malaria but there is no prophylactic available to deal with it. The mosquitoes that carry this virus bite during the daytime, so it is worth applying repellent if you see them around. Symptoms include strong headaches, rashes and excruciating joint and muscle pains with high fever. Dengue fever lasts for only a week or so and is not usually fatal if you have not previously been infected. Complete rest and paracetamol are the usual treatment. Plenty of fluids also help. Some patients are given an intravenous drip to keep them from dehydrating. Dengue may be a serious illness particularly with repeated infections so it is best to avoid it in the first place.

Sleeping sickness African trypanosomiasis, or sleeping sickness, is a parasitic infection caused by *Trypanosoma brucei*, transmitted by the tsetse fly. There are two sub-species: one predominates in east and southern Africa and usually causes an acute infection, whereas the other predominates in central and west Africa and causes a slower progressive, chronic infection. In the UK, travel-associated cases are rare, but those that have been reported have usually been associated with travel to the game parks of East Africa.

QUICK TICK REMOVAL   *Dr Jane Wilson-Howarth*

You're likely to find two types of ticks – grey, leathery, blood-engorged insects or very small crab-like creatures, often difficult to spot. The big ones are unpleasant but easy to remove, the small ones more difficult. Manoeuvre your finger and thumb such that you can pinch the tick's mouthparts, as close to your skin as possible, and slowly and steadily pull away at right angles to your skin. This often hurts. Try to surprise the tick, as once disturbed they quickly dig in and hang on tenaciously. Jerking or twisting will increase the chances of damaging the tick, which in turn increases the chances of disease transmission, as well as leaving the mouthparts behind. Burning the tick with a cigarette end is often recommended but is not advised as it causes the insect to regurgitate into the bite wound, causing infection.

Once the tick is off, dowse the little wound with alcohol (local spirit, whisky or similar is excellent) or iodine. An area of spreading redness around the bite site, or a rash or fever coming on a few days or more after the bite, should stimulate a trip to a doctor.

Where does sleeping sickness occur? Sleeping sickness occurs in 36 African countries where the tsetse fly vector occurs. In the UK, cases are occasionally reported in travellers returning from game parks in east Africa. Most recently a case was reported in a UK traveller who had returned from Zambia and Zimbabwe and in 2012 a small number of cases were contracted in the Kariba/ Zambezi Valley area.

How do you catch sleeping sickness? The parasite is transmitted by the bite of an infected tsetse fly. Tsetse flies are around the size of a honeybee. In east and southern Africa, the main reservoirs for the parasites are domestic and wild animals such as antelope and cattle. The tsetse flies here tend to inhabit savanna and woodland areas. One bite from an infected tsetse fly is enough for a human to become infected. Trypanosomiasis cannot be spread directly from person to person.

How long can you have the infection before developing symptoms? For east and southern African trypanosomiasis, first symptoms (skin lesion around the bite with lymphadenopathy) will occur one to15 days after the bite, with fever occurring after one to three weeks. For west African trypanosomiasis, symptoms may not present for some weeks after the infective bite. East African trypanosomiasis is a much faster-progressing disease than the west African form, which can progress over a number of years.

How can you avoid getting sleeping sickness? There is no vaccine or drug to prevent sleeping sickness. The only way to prevent it is to avoid tsetse fly bites and be aware of the risk. Tsetse flies love shade and are attracted by movement and dark colours, particularly blue. They have been known to follow moving vehicles, therefore windows should remain closed when driving through endemic areas. Your guide will alert you when in these areas or if you are self-driving just be on the lookout for the first one to enter your vehicle – you can't mistake them. Travellers are advised to wear insecticide treated close-weave and loose-fitting clothing and use a good repellent containing N, N-diethylmetatoluamide (DEET) on exposed skin. If sunscreen is also being used, repellent must be applied after sunscreen. More information about the disease is available from the NaTHNaC website (*www. nathnac.org/travel/index.htm*).

***Putsi* or tumbu flies** These are a problem in areas of eastern, western and southern Africa where the climate is hot and humid. The adult fly lays her eggs on the soil or on drying laundry and when the eggs come in contact with human flesh (when you put on clothes or lie on a bed) they hatch and bury themselves under the skin. Here they form a crop of 'boils', each of which hatches a grub after about eight days, when the inflammation will settle down. In *putsi* areas either dry your clothes and sheets within a screened house, or dry them in direct, hot sunshine until they are crisp, or iron them. Laundries at safari camps will always iron all your clothes and bed linen.

Jiggers or sandfleas These are another kind of flesh feaster. They latch on if you walk barefoot in contaminated places, and set up home under the skin of the foot, usually at the side of a toenail where they cause a painful, boil-like swelling. These need picking out by a local expert; if the distended flea bursts during eviction the wound should be dowsed in spirit, alcohol or kerosene, otherwise more jiggers will infest you. You are very unlikely to suffer from these unless you walk barefoot in local villages.

Bilharzia or schistosomiasis *with thanks to Dr Vaughan Southgate of the Natural History Museum, London, and Dr Dick Stockley, The Surgery, Kampala*
Bilharzia or schistosomiasis is a disease that commonly afflicts the rural poor of the tropics. Two types of the disease exist in sub-Saharan Africa – *Schistosoma mansoni* and *Schistosoma haematobium*. It is an unpleasant problem that is worth avoiding, though can be treated if you do get it. This parasite is common in slow-moving water sources such as Lake Kariba and tranquil stretches of the Zambezi. The most risky shores will be close to places where infected people use water, wash clothes, etc.

It is easier to understand how to diagnose it, treat it and prevent it if you know a little about the life cycle. Contaminated faeces are washed into the lake, the eggs hatch and the larva infects certain species of snail. The snails then produce about 10,000 *cercariae* (larvae) a day for the rest of their lives. The parasites can digest their way through your skin when you wade or bathe in infested fresh water.

Winds disperse the snails and cercariae. The snails in particular can drift a long way, especially on windblown weed, so nowhere is really safe. However, deep water and running water are safer, while shallow water presents the greatest risk. The cercariae penetrate intact skin, and find their way to the liver. There, male and female meet and spend the rest of their lives in permanent copulation. No wonder you feel tired! Most finish up in the wall of the lower bowel, but others can get lost and can cause damage to many different organs. *Schistosoma haematobium* goes mostly to the bladder.

Although the adults do not cause any harm in themselves, after about four to six weeks they start to lay eggs, which cause an intense but usually ineffective immune reaction, including fever, cough, abdominal pain, and a fleeting, itching rash called 'safari itch'. The absence of early symptoms does not necessarily mean there is no infection. Later symptoms can be more localised and more severe, but the general symptoms settle down fairly quickly and eventually you are just tired. 'Tired all the time' is one of the most common symptoms among expats in Africa, and bilharzia, giardia, amoeba and intestinal yeast are the most common culprits.

HAIRY CATERPILLARS

These are easy to spot when indoors, as they are up to 10cm long and covered in long grey-brown hairs. If their hairs come into contact with your skin you will suffer several days of intense prickly stings followed by itching. While not a risk to your health they are painful and very irritating.

Their normal habitat is in vegetation, but populations can explode in periods following heavy rains, when they have an annoying habit of finding their way into your bush camp. Although it's a simple matter to physically remove them, the damage has already been done. When they are disturbed they wriggle violently for a second or two and this has the effect of releasing thousands of invisible hairs into the air and onto whatever surface they were sitting on. This is a good reason to keep your suitcase or clothing bag zipped up at all times. If you find them in your room, especially on your bed or on towels, talk to the camp manager and ask to have bedclothes, towels and so on changed for fresh ones. If they do get you, you can try all the usual remedies – antihistamine cream, calamine lotion, vinegar, bicarbonate of soda paste – but in my own painful experience, the only remedy is the slow passage of time. I have been told these are caterpillars of the pearl spotted moth, a beautifully marked, palm sized creature.

Although bilharzia is difficult to diagnose, it can be tested at specialist travel clinics. Ideally tests need to be done at least six weeks after likely exposure and will determine whether you need treatment. Fortunately it is easy to treat at present.

Avoiding bilharzia If you are bathing, swimming, paddling or wading in fresh water that you think may carry a bilharzia risk, try to get out of the water within ten minutes.

- Avoid bathing or paddling on shores within 200m of villages or places where people use the water a great deal, especially reedy shores or where there is lots of water weed.
- Dry off thoroughly with a towel; rub vigorously.
- If your bathing water comes from a risky source try to ensure that the water is taken from the lake in the early morning and stored snail-free; otherwise it should be filtered or Dettol or Cresol should be added.
- Bathing early in the morning is safer than bathing in the last half of the day.
- Cover yourself with DEET insect repellent before swimming: it may offer some protection.

Skin infections Any mosquito bite or small nick in the skin provides an opportunity for bacteria to foil the body's usually excellent defences; it will surprise many travellers how quickly skin infections start in warm humid climates and it is essential to clean and cover even the slightest wound. Creams are not as effective as a good drying antiseptic such as dilute iodine, potassium permanganate (a few crystals in half a cup of water), or crystal (or gentian) violet. One of these should be available in most towns. If the wound starts to throb, or becomes red and the redness starts to spread, or the wound oozes, and especially if you develop a fever, antibiotics will probably be needed: flucloxacillin (250mg four times a day) or cloxacillin (500mg four times a day). For those allergic to penicillin, erythromycin (500mg twice a day) for five days should help. See a doctor if the symptoms do not start to improve in 48 hours.

Fungal infections also get a hold easily in hot moist climates, so wear 100% cotton socks and underwear and shower frequently. An itchy rash in the groin or flaking between the toes is likely to be a fungal infection. This needs treatment with an antifungal cream such as Canesten (clotrimazole); if this is not available try Whitfield's ointment (compound enzoic acid ointment) or crystal violet (although this will turn you purple!).

Prickly heat A fine pimply rash on the torso is likely to be heat rash; cool showers, dabbing (not rubbing) dry, and talc will help; if it's bad you may need to check into an air-conditioned hotel room for a while. If you are on safari, slowing down to a relaxed schedule, wearing only loose, baggy 100% cotton clothes and sleeping naked under a fan reduce the problem.

Sun damage Give some thought to packing suncream. The incidence of skin cancer is rocketing as Caucasians are travelling more and spending more time exposing themselves to the sun. Keep out of the sun during the middle of the day and, if you must expose yourself to the sun, build up gradually from 20 minutes per day. Be especially careful of exposure in the middle of the day and of sun reflected off water, and wear a T-shirt and lots of waterproof suncream (at least SPF30) when swimming. Sun exposure ages the skin, makes people prematurely wrinkly and increases the risk of skin cancer. Cover up with long, loose clothes and wear a hat when you can. The glare and the dust can be hard on the eyes, too, so bring UV-protecting sunglasses and, perhaps, a soothing eyebath.

Heat exhaustion, heatstroke In many parts of Zimbabwe summer temperatures can soar into the 40s and even shade offers little relief at these temperatures. The keys to avoiding these heat-related conditions (heatstroke is a medical emergency when the body becomes unable to regulate its temperature) is to keep out of direct sun as much as possible, wear suitable protective clothing – especially hats – avoid strenuous activity and above all drink copious amounts of water throughout the day. One relatively easy way to monitor your hydration level is by the frequency with which you urinate. If you are passing only small amounts of urine infrequently (less than three or four times a day) and the urine is dark yellow, then you need to increase the amount you are drinking whether you feel thirsty or not. If you do begin to suffer from heat exhaustion – fatigue, dizziness, nausea, heavy sweating and confusion are all symptoms – then it's time to take oral rehydration salts. If commercial powders are unavailable, see box, page 103, *Treating travellers' diarrhoea*, for an easy rehydration recipe.

Meningitis This is a particularly nasty disease as it can kill within hours of the first symptoms appearing. The telltale symptoms are a combination of a blinding headache (light sensitivity), a blotchy rash and a high fever. Immunisation with the newer tetravalent vaccine ACWY protects against the most serious bacterial form of meningitis and is sometimes recommended for longer-stay trips to Zimbabwe or if you are working closely with the local population – in particular with children. A single injection gives good protection for three years. Other forms of meningitis exist (usually viral) but there are no vaccines for these. Local papers normally report outbreaks. If you show symptoms go to a doctor immediately.

Sexual risks Travel is a time when we may enjoy sexual adventures, especially when alcohol reduces inhibitions. Remember the risks of sexually transmitted infection are high, whether you sleep with locals or fellow travellers (who may already have slept with locals). More than half of HIV infections in British heterosexuals are acquired abroad and AIDS is a serious problem in Zimbabwe, with an estimated 14% of adults living with AIDS. Use condoms or femidoms, preferably bearing the British kite mark and ideally bought before travel. If you notice any genital ulcers or discharge get treatment promptly.

Ebola So far this has only occurred once in Zimbabwe, in 2003, brought in by a patient from outside the country. It is a rare, but deadly, highly contagious, virally induced disease which causes haemorrhagic fever. In the unlikely event of an outbreak, protective measures will be taken and you should follow whatever local advice is given.

Animals
Rabies Rabies can be carried by all mammals and is relatively common in Zimbabwe so beware the village dogs and any strays. It is passed on to man through a bite, scratch or a lick of an open wound. You must always assume any animal has rabies, and seek medical help as soon as possible after contact. This means, however much of an animal lover you are, resist all temptations to befriend or

pet stray animals. If you do get bitten, immediately scrub the wound with soap under a running tap or while pouring water from a jug. Find a reasonably clear-looking source of water (but at this stage the quality of the water is not important), then pour on a strong iodine or alcohol solution of gin, whisky or rum. This helps stop the rabies virus entering the body and will guard against wound infections, including tetanus.

Pre-exposure vaccinations for rabies are ideally advised for everyone, but are particularly important if you intend to have contact with animals and/or are likely to be more than 24 hours away from medical help. Ideally three doses should be taken over a minimum of 21 days as this will change and simplify the treatment course. Contrary to popular belief these vaccinations are now relatively painless.

If you are bitten, scratched or licked over an open wound by a sick animal, then post-exposure prophylaxis should be given as soon as possible, though it is never too late to seek help, as the incubation period for rabies can be very long. Those who have not been immunised will need a full course of injections and in most cases the first dose of vaccine is given with a weight-determined injection of rabies immunoglobulin (RIG). This is expensive (around US$800) and may be very hard to come by, but if you have had the full course of pre-exposure vaccination then it is not needed. This is a good reason to vaccinate travellers before they go if they have time.

And remember that, if you do contract rabies, mortality is 100% and death from rabies is probably one of the worst ways to go.

Snakebite Snakes rarely attack unless provoked and bites to travellers are unusual. You are less likely to get bitten if you wear stout shoes and long trousers when in the bush. Most snakes are harmless and even venomous species will only dispense venom in about half of their bites. If bitten, then, you are unlikely to have received venom; keeping this fact in mind may help you to stay calm. Many so-called first-aid techniques do more harm than good: cutting into the wound is harmful; tourniquets are dangerous; suction and electrical inactivation devices do not work. The only treatment is antivenom. In case of a bite, which you fear may have been from a venomous snake:

- Try to keep calm – it is likely that no venom has been dispensed.
- Prevent movement of the bitten limb by applying a splint.
- Keep the bitten limb BELOW heart height to slow the spread of any venom.
- If you have a crepe bandage, bind up as much of the bitten limb as you can, but release the bandage every half-hour.
- Evacuate to a hospital that has antivenom. You must rely on local knowledge for this information.

And remember:

- NEVER give aspirin; you may offer paracetamol, which is safe.
- NEVER cut or suck the wound.
- DO NOT apply ice packs.
- DO NOT apply potassium permanganate.

If the offending snake can be captured without risk of someone else being bitten, take it to show to the doctor – but beware, since even a severed head is able to dispense venom in a reflex bite.

Nobody involved with Zimbabwe tourism can be in any doubt about the power of the international media, which effectively put the industry into a ten-year hibernation. We have been told in graphic detail that there is widespread violence, with murder, beatings, police brutality and torture. Zimbabwe *must* be a very dangerous place because even South Africans, who are quite prepared to live in one of the most violently criminal countries on the planet, are frightened to come here. Of course Zimbabwe has obligingly provided all the gory news fodder necessary to sell papers and have us glued to our television screens, and certain sections of the population have indeed had a horrid time for many years.

But, and it's a big but, every scrap of that violence has been tied up one way or another with politics. This means that tourists are not – and never were – under any threat of violence, provided they keep clear of political activities.

By what authority can I write this? My wife and I have spent many months driving all round Zimbabwe for many years including throughout the early 2000s during periods of heightened political tension. Not once have we encountered anything other than friendly, courteous, welcoming people including the police. Dare I say it, even the justifiably reviled Green Bombers (see *Glossary*, page 370) (or were they war vets?) shook hands and wished us well as we drove off after one of their unofficial roadblocks. We were obviously tourists and therefore of no interest to them.

So what about normal crime? First, it's almost inevitable that as soon as one starts to compile a list of anti-crime precautions, even though most of them are simple and very obvious, one is in danger of implying that the destination has significant crime problems. Zimbabwe, along with several neighbouring countries, has traditionally been virtually crime-free, to the extent that many rural tourist accommodations don't even have locks on their doors. Crime against tourists always used to be absolutely minimal, but with so few people visiting the country in recent years there are no statistics, and although one suspects the situation may be slightly worse today, you should still look on Zimbabwe as an extremely safe country for visitors.

With such a large proportion of the population being reduced to poverty and with a situation of extremely low (formal) unemployment, it's no wonder that a very small minority have resorted to crime. This is nearly all property-related, with a significant increase in Harare's residential burglary rate but, unlike in South Africa, virtually none of it involves gratuitous violence.

THEFT Residential burglary, of course, doesn't affect tourists, but personal theft occasionally does. As with nearly everywhere else in the world, in Zimbabwe you are now advised to take sensible precautions that were hardly necessary a few years ago.

Theft from lodges and camps is almost unheard of. The local culture is strongly against crime, and staff (who are invariably the prime suspects) tend to live in close communities so anyone displaying a sudden increase in wealth would be quickly flushed out. A further deterrent is the tactics police tend to use in this part of the world. It's common for all potential suspects to be taken in for questioning and roughed up until one confesses or points the finger at the villain. For this reason, if you should lose something in camp, please make absolutely sure you haven't simply mislaid it before you report it to the management and set off a chain of events that can be very unpleasant for all involved. Needless to say, don't put temptation in staff's way by leaving valuable objects on show in your room; items of even modest value to you can be immensely tempting to low-paid Zimbabweans.

Urban hotels carry a slightly higher risk of theft from rooms but, again, I believe this to be insignificant. Nevertheless if you are carrying a large amount of cash always try to use the hotel or lodge safe rather than walking around with it on your person.

MUGGING As ever, it's when walking around town that you're potentially most at risk, and it has to be said that Harare has the worst reputation of all Zimbabwean towns. (Note that Victoria Falls has its own contingent of tourist police.) It's important to realise that local inhabitants seldom get mugged or have their pockets picked; it's tourists who offer the richest pickings. In your own culture you may not consider yourself particularly wealthy but to poor Zimbabweans the very fact that you can afford to fly halfway round the world to get to their country is clear evidence that you are (backpackers included), in their terms, rich beyond belief.

Tourists are usually very easy to spot so you may want to consider the following in order to blend in a little more. Local people seldom wear shorts in town so wear long trousers – jeans are fine – and perhaps a regular shirt. Safari clothing is ideal for the game drive but in town it looks out of place. 'Bumbags' ('fanny packs' to Americans) simply cry out 'tourist' and of course they are there for one reason only, to carry your valuables and as such are an excellent target. Instead, buy a concealed body belt and be sure to have sufficient cash for the day in your pockets so you don't have to publicly delve around beneath your clothing to access your belt. Spread any cash you have over various pockets so you only need to pull out small amounts when paying for anything. One reader has recommended taking a selection of ziplock plastic bags, which are ideal for dispersing around your pockets and clothing.

If you stand on a street corner consulting a map or even this guidebook it's obvious you're unsure of your whereabouts, and you could well attract unwelcome attention. (On the other hand, as it's Zimbabwe, a local person is much more likely to introduce himself and offer help.) Try to walk around with an air of confidence as if you know exactly where you're going. Cameras are also a sure sign you're on holiday. Keep your jewellery to an absolute minimum: it may be only dress jewellery and a cheap watch but a mugger won't know that. Mobile phones are much sought after in Africa and it's wise not to use them in the street, as they are so easy to snatch. Why not carry all these things around in a cheap plastic shopping bag – totally insecure, but nobody would expect you to have anything of value in it.

PRECAUTIONS Without getting paranoid about it, be aware of your surroundings as you walk about. The central shopping areas are safe but try not to stray into the obviously poorer parts of town, and keep your pockets and bags guarded when you're in crowded places like markets or bus stations. All towns have dodgy areas so ask at your hotel or guesthouse which places should be avoided. If you want to get to a slightly distant location it's best to take a taxi even though it may be within walking distance; and my advice would be to always use a taxi at night, except for very short distances in well-lit areas. If you can walk in a group, so much the better.

If you're on your own in a bar it would be good to keep your wits about you and be wary of accepting ready-poured drinks from friendly strangers. Even though I haven't heard of the problem in Zimbabwe, neighbouring countries, especially Mozambique, have a problem with doped drinks, and there's no reason to believe that this scam won't or hasn't already spread across the border. And of course, don't make yourself an easy target by rolling out of a bar or nightclub having had too much to drink, and then wandering around looking for a taxi.

The above dos and don'ts may seem lengthy but in reality they are exactly the same level of precautions I would suggest to visitors to my nearest big town in the UK, and only a fraction of those necessary where I live in South Africa. And for what it's worth I probably feel safer walking around in Zimbabwe than any other country I've ever visited, with the possible exception of Singapore.

WOMEN TRAVELLERS Women travelling in Zimbabwe, either on their own or in pairs, are certainly safer here than in most other countries of the world. Provided you take normal, reasonable precautions you'll find the place remarkably hassle free to travel through. Don't forget that not too many years ago Zimbabwe was a major tourist destination, so most people are well used to travellers of all sorts. Around town in the day, the usual dress sense applies: don't wear provocative clothing, which generally means covering your shoulders and taking care not to bare midriffs or show too much leg – knee-length skirts, jeans and trousers are fine. If you do get a bit skimpy clothing-wise, while you won't be at risk you will probably attract attention and be regarded in a negative light. Additionally, there have been recent reports of police lecturing women who they consider inappropriately dressed in some of the larger towns. Dress more conservatively in the evening and in bars or your intentions may be misconstrued. Where possible, team up with friends before you get to a bar, rather than waiting alone to meet them there. As always, laid-back Victoria Falls is something of an exception, where single women are extremely common (numerically speaking) and taken for granted.

As a lone, female traveller any attention you may attract will almost certainly be purely inquisitive. The way you are travelling (ie: without a man) tells people that you are clearly a very capable person and the very opposite of vulnerable. Basically if you can fend off an unwelcome advance in London, New York or Paris you will have no problem in Zimbabwe.

That is not to say that you will not be an object of great interest to both men and women. Africa is generally very conservative and male dominated, with women having definite roles in life, none of which involve swanning off around the world without a man. Two of the first questions you will invariably be asked are 'Where is your husband?' and 'How many children have you got?' This is all very important information and tells them a lot about you. Big families are good news in Africa; everybody has them so where are your children? You shouldn't get too defensive about this because men too are expected to father children and I frequently get asked about the number of kids I have.

Depending on their age, childless women travellers may want to invent a husband and a child or two because women of marriageable age who decide not to have children are generally regarded in African cultures as lazy or even worthless. Similarly, men without children are usually considered inadequate.

Finally, a word of advice: sanitary products have been notoriously absent from Zimbabwe's shop shelves in the last few years and although conversion to the US dollar has greatly improved the shelf-stocking situation, it would still be wise to take sufficient stocks with you for your whole trip.

GAY AND LESBIAN TRAVELLERS *(with advice from Gays and Lesbians of Zimbabwe)*
Zimbabwe, in common with most African countries, has an extremely conservative attitude towards homosexuality, and its president has hardly been reticent in voicing his views on the subject, regularly using the word 'homosexual' as a term of abuse. So what are the implications for gays and lesbians visiting the country?

In Zimbabwe, sex between men is a criminal offence as is any show of affection in public that may be construed as sexual. Sex between women is not illegal but lesbians excite revulsion in many younger Zimbabwean men and there is strong disapproval of women who refuse to marry and have children. Cross-dressing for men is illegal. Nevertheless, if you are discreet, you are very likely to be safe although, for men, there is a good possibility of being blackmailed if you have sex with a local person with fewer resources than yourself.

Zimbabwe is not uniformly homophobic and an urban generation is now growing up with the knowledge that gay and lesbian people exist in their midst, but it is still best to be very discreet about your sexuality unless you are sure you're in safe company.

Anti-gay sentiment is not usually expressed in terms of physical violence but can result in verbal abuse. However, most people will keep their opinions to themselves and then 'bitch' about you later. White males tend to have a very macho outlook on life and few will have had any contact (knowingly) with gays, and it's not uncommon to hear anti-gay jokes and comments voiced in public.

There are no gay clubs or bars and there are very few, if any, that can be described as gay-friendly. If you want to be in a club with other gay or lesbian people, it is best to make arrangements beforehand. The best advice is to contact GALZ on arrival (*www.galz.co.zw*). GALZ puts on a programme of entertainment for its members at the GALZ Centre in Harare (*35 Colenbrander Rd, Milton Park;* \ *04 741736*), a safe haven for gay and lesbian people. They have a good relationship with their local police station so there is little possibility of a raid although recent reports suggest this may be changing. The Bulawayo centre does the same thing for people in Matabeleland.

It is not known what the HIV prevalence rate is amongst the local gay community but you are advised to use protection at all times, since the prevalence is likely to be higher than in the general population, which itself has much higher rates than in the West.

TRAVELLING WITH CHILDREN Zimbabweans love children and are generally extremely accommodating and helpful to families; and the country is without doubt an exciting place for children to see wildlife up close, bringing those television nature programmes dramatically to life. However, if you are planning a holiday to include a significant amount of wildlife viewing there are a number of issues to take into consideration. First, you'll need to check whether there is a minimum age at the places you want to stay. Before the economic turmoil, the minimum age limit was sometimes as high as 16 years old; operators relaxed this rule when tourist numbers dropped off, but it's likely to be reinstated once tourism takes off again. The age limit was set in place for good reasons: in wildlife-rich areas, animals frequently enter the unfenced grounds of safari camps/lodges, so children will need constant supervision; and when out on safari, close encounters with lions and elephants are naturally very exciting for children – however, noisy and impulsive reactions are likely to startle wildlife and thereby jeopardise the enjoyment, or even the safety, of everyone. Children need to be able to remain calm and quiet.

Second, a typical wildlife-viewing day has several hours of 'down time' between morning and evening activities and since safari camps tend by their very nature to be in remote areas, some children may get bored. Few camps have facilities to keep children occupied.

DISABLED TRAVELLERS People with physical disabilities may find it rather difficult to enjoy many of the popular attractions of Zimbabwe. Towns are usually fairly navigable by wheelchair, although pavements can be uneven and frequently non-existent, with only the alternative of travelling on the side of the road itself, which may very well be pot-holed. Many people will feel distinctly uneasy at this prospect, given traffic volumes and the fact that drivers feel they have an absolute right of way. Crossing roads can be an issue as there are frequently deep storm gullies requiring a detour to the next 'bridge'. Dropped curbs exist in a few of the larger towns but even here they seem to be completely unplanned so you never know where the next one will be. Although most upmarket town-centre accommodations and facilities are wheelchair-friendly and becoming increasingly so, many of the wildlife-related venues are in remote areas and specifically designed to blend in with natural surroundings that do not readily lend themselves to wheelchair access. In practical terms this means there can be long distances between chalets and the central guest area and paths can be steep, often involving flights of steps, areas of sandy ground, rock-strewn paths and all manner of obstacles.

NOTES FOR DISABLED TRAVELLERS

Gordon Rattray (www.able-travel.com)
With Zimbabwe's recent troubles, improving access for people with disabilities will not have been a priority. However, before this the country was one of the most developed in the region so will be quite possible for many disabled visitors. Don't anticipate level-entry public buildings and curb-cuts everywhere, but do expect able and willing help from a local population who will be delighted to welcome visitors back. If you are a confident traveller and are prepared to compromise slightly then this might just be the perfect time to go!

ACCOMMODATION In general, it is not easy to find disabled-friendly accommodation. Only top-of-the-range hotels and lodges have adapted rooms while budget guesthouses and campsites are more basic. Occasionally (more by accident than through design) bathrooms are step-free and spacious, but they usually contain standard fittings only.

TRANSPORT
By road Most tour companies use 4x4s and minibuses, which are higher than normal cars, usually making entry more difficult. Similarly, buses and minibuses have no facilities for wheelchairs, and getting off and on can be a hectic affair. But that does not necessarily mean these options are to be discounted; drivers, guides and fellow passengers are usually prepared to assist. Do remember, however, that they are not trained in these skills so you must thoroughly explain your needs and stay in control of the situation.

By air If you need assistance then let the airline know in advance and arrive early for your departure. During the flight, anyone who uses a pressure-relieving wheelchair cushion should consider using it instead of or on top of the fitted seat cushion. There is no guarantee that aisle chairs will be present at airports in Zimbabwe, so expect to be manhandled if you cannot transfer unaided. As with vehicle transfers, explain your preferred method of transfer carefully beforehand.

HEALTH AND INSURANCE Zimbabwean hospitals and pharmacies can be basic, so if possible take all essential medication and equipment with you. It is advisable to pack this in your hand luggage during flights in case your main bags don't

The point that was made to me over and over is that virtually everyone comes for the wildlife viewing but people with physical disabilities cannot be catered for as the vehicles used are completely inaccessible to them. Therefore there is – they reason – no necessity to make adaptations to their buildings or grounds. The problem with this approach is that it assumes that everyone with a disability is completely physically incapable. Access to these high, open wildlife-viewing vehicles can indeed be difficult, requiring a degree of agility to climb in, but with assistance a lot of folk can manage it.

WHAT TO TAKE

CLOTHING Comfort rather than fashion is the key word here and climatic conditions are the biggest consideration when you are packing. Depending on the

arrive immediately. Doctors will know about 'everyday' illnesses, but you must understand and be able to explain your own particular medical requirements. Depending on the season it can also be hot; if this is a problem for you then try to book accommodation and vehicles with fans or air conditioning, and a useful cooling aid is a plant-spray bottle.

Travel insurance can be purchased in the UK from Age Concern (\ *0800 169 2700; www.ageconcern.org.uk*), who have no upper age limit, and Free Spirit (\ *0845 230 5000; www.free-spirit.com*), who cater for people with pre-existing medical conditions. Most insurance companies will insure disabled travellers, but it is essential that they are made aware of your disability.

SAFETY For anyone following the usual security precautions (see pages 111–12) the chances of robbery are greatly reduced. In fact, as a disabled person I often feel more 'noticed', and therefore a less attractive target for thieves. But the opposite may also apply, so do stay aware of where your bags are and who is around you, especially during car transfers and similar activities.

SPECIALIST OPERATORS There are currently no disability-specialised operators running trips to Zimbabwe, but several operate in neighbouring countries so I expect this will change. Most mainstream travel companies will listen to your needs and try to create an itinerary that suits.

FURTHER INFORMATION

Books Bradt Travel Guides' *Access Africa: Safaris for People with Limited Mobility* is packed with useful advice and resources for disabled adventure travellers.

Online
www.able-travel.com A regularly updated website with both worldwide and country-specific information.
www.globalaccessnews.com A searchable database of disability travel information.
www.rollingrains.com A searchable website advocating disability travel.
www.youreable.com A UK-based general resource for disability information, with an active forum.
www.apparelyzed.com A site dedicated to spinal injury, but containing information that other disabilities will also find useful. It also hosts a hugely popular forum.

time of your trip you may find yourself sweltering in the sun and humidity, or literally freezing in an open game-viewing vehicle before sunrise. It is not unusual to experience both extremes in the same day – even on the same game drive. You can also get quite cold in summer and very hot in winter. Nevertheless packing for Zimbabwe is relatively easy as you simply design a basic lightweight travel wardrobe and then adjust it according to the season and your destinations.

In town Zimbabwe is casual but conservative when it comes to town. T-shirts are fine for both sexes during the day (but a regular shirt would be better), as are 'formal' shorts, although shorts on men in winter months will instantly shout out 'tourist'. Skimpy extremes including singlets or anything that would be construed as beachwear are not appropriate in town and may invite unwanted attention from both public and police, and if you do wear a T-shirt avoid any with provocative or inappropriate slogans. Shirtless men are not appreciated even in the very touristy setting of Victoria Falls. In the evening, hotels and restaurants tend to welcome smart/casual wear and frequently ban T-shirts, shorts and sandals.

Rainwear It's a good idea to pack a light rainproof jacket for summer downpours; buy one that packs down to nearly nothing so it doesn't take up any space. For stays in the Eastern Highlands at any time of year some lightweight rainproof gear is necessary, especially if you are planning walking or fishing, and in the winter take plenty of warm clothing for the evenings.

On safari

Sun protection Many wildlife-viewing vehicles are open, with just a canvas roof offering minimal protection from the sun, so your safari wardrobe should be based around a selection of lightweight, loose-fitting garments with a mixture of long- and short-sleeved shirts or blouses together with both shorts and long trousers. Skirts are not really compatible with climbing in and out of these vehicles and denim never really feels comfortable in the heat. Longs are necessary not only for sun protection and warmth but also as a mosquito barrier in the evening. Aim for fabrics with a high natural fibre content.

Warmth You'll need to wrap up for night and early morning drives in winter, especially in Hwange National Park, and even summer drives can be surprisingly chilly at dawn and after sunset. So pack a warm sweater or fleece and a light tracksuit. A light windproof jacket can be a welcome addition on a game drive in an open vehicle at any time of year. Your drive may start off chilly just after dawn and end up hot when the sun has risen, and vice versa, so use layers to take off or put on as the temperature rises or falls.

Colours The colour of your clothing is also a factor. As the whole object is to see as much wildlife as possible it is important to blend in with the surroundings as much as you can, even when you are in a vehicle. It is therefore no surprise that all safari clothing comes in varying shades of brown, khaki and green – definitely no bright colours or white. Incidentally, tsetse flies home in on dark blue-coloured clothes. You may be tempted to blend into the surroundings completely and make a fashion statement at the same time by packing your trendy camouflage gear. Don't: it's actually illegal for civilians to wear camouflage clothing in Zimbabwe and you really don't want to risk being marched off for questioning, having been mistaken for a member of some armed force or militia.

Head cover A wide-brimmed hat or at least a cap is essential to keep the sun out of your eyes and off your head and neck to prevent sunstroke.

Footwear Sandals are cool and comfortable around camp but I would wear light shoes on a game drive. Unlike in South Africa where it is practically a cardinal sin

CHOOSING BINOCULARS

Binoculars are an essential piece of equipment for wildlife viewing and you will find a bewildering array of models on the market. Generally speaking, if you think you will get plenty of long-term use out of them, invest in as good a pair as you can afford. On the other hand, if you don't already own a pair you are unlikely to use them much after this trip, in which case you would be wise to buy one of the excellent-value cheaper instruments now on the market.

Unless you have very specific requirements your decision will be a compromise between quality, price, size and weight. Binoculars are a very personal piece of equipment and you can only make a good choice after actually looking through a few to see how well suited each is to your own eyes. For this reason I would avoid the temptation to buy straight off the internet. Check wildlife and birding magazines to see what's on offer, then go to a good camera shop and take their advice. Unfortunately you can never successfully trial wildlife-viewing binoculars in a shop situation but ask to take them out into the street and compare as many as you can as it is surprising how some will suit your eyes better than others. This is especially so if you wear spectacles. Good optics come into their own in low-light situations so try to avoid sampling them in bright sunshine.

Several factors need to be considered but the main question is how much magnification you should have. This is indicated by the first of the two figures quoted on every binocular specification, eg: 8 x 42. For general use go for either 8 or 10 times magnification. Some birders choose 12 but remember the higher the magnification, the heavier the instrument and the harder it is to hold steady.

The second figure on the specification indicates the instrument's field of view. In practical terms this defines the light-gathering capability. The higher the figure, the better they perform in low-light conditions, dawn and dusk, which can often be the best game-viewing times. Anything over 30 will do the job well, 40+ even better.

Good-quality optics tend to come with a weight penalty and you should give this careful consideration. What may seem to be a perfectly acceptable weight in the shop can turn into a horribly uncomfortable lump hanging round your neck in hot and humid conditions, especially if you also tote a chunky SLR camera. If you can afford top-of-the-range binoculars, then you can combine superb optics with the lighter weight of metals such as titanium.

Go for waterproof ones if possible as these will also be dustproof, a major consideration in Africa. If you want to get a good few years out of them, buy a really robust pair (which will invariably be heavy) with a rubber outer covering, as they tend to be much abused pieces of kit. Always carry a good lens-cleaning cloth and use it with great care or you will soon scratch the delicate lens coating.

to step outside the vehicle in national parks, in some places in Zimbabwe you can do so on your own or your guide may lead you a short distance away on foot to point out something of significance. If you have ever stepped on a devil thorn or seen what an acacia thorn can do to a car tyre, you will know why I recommend shoes rather than sandals. If you are planning to go on walking safaris, a good pair of well-broken-in walking shoes is essential. Long socks offer protection from small, unwanted guests lurking in the undergrowth and you may want to invest in elasticated gaiters to keep sharp seeds out of your socks.

Evening wear Your choice of evening clothing depends on climate and the style of your accommodation, but while there are no formal dress codes, reasonably smart casual wear is appreciated in most lodges and upmarket camps. Given the mosquito issue, your long safari gear is appropriate and practical.

OTHER ITEMS A small backpack is invaluable for carrying water and stowing your spare clothing etc. Be sure to pack a good torch or headlight – with sufficient batteries of course. They're essential for camping but you'll also need them at night in your camp or lodge after the generator's been turned off. A multi-tool of the Leatherman variety is extremely useful around camp, but if you wear one as a matter of course, don't forget to pack it in your luggage rather than absent-mindedly wearing it to the airport! Pack a portable mosquito net if you plan to camp or stay in budget accommodation. Ziplock plastic bags are extremely useful for all those small loose items that invariably end up scattered all around your luggage.

ELECTRICITY

Zimbabwe's electricity supply is 220/240 volts AC and *most* sockets in the country are still of the UK three-square-pin type. During the lean years these were often replaced with the more easily obtainable South African three-round-pin and small two-round-pin sockets, so be sure to take the appropriate adaptors for your appliances; an international multi-adaptor is best. Newer buildings are all being equipped with South African-style round-pin sockets and gradually this type is taking over as accommodations are being renovated. Zimbabwe relies largely on imported electricity but the power supply has become horribly erratic in recent years, with outages and long hours of load-shedding still a frequently daily occurrence. Most properties have backup generators but there can still be fuel-supply problems in outlying areas. Take a good surge protector if you intend using your laptop or similar digital devices.

Try not to let your camera and phone batteries get too low on power before you recharge, and take advantage whenever the power is on because there may not be any electricity when you need to charge up. Bear in mind that very few safari and bush camps are connected to mains electricity, relying on generators that they only run for certain hours. Most places can arrange recharges for you. For the above reasons it's advisable to take standard AAAs and AAs rather than rechargeables.

If your trip involves significant amounts of camping, don't expect to find mains hook-ups at campsites as very few are wired up; your only source of power for recharging batteries will be your vehicle's 12V system. Alternatively an appropriately sized inverter in your vehicle will supply 240 volts if you have a lot of charging to do or need to use a laptop.

MONEY

Although officially all major hard currencies are acceptable, the US dollar reigns supreme throughout the country. If you do use other currencies – the rand is generally acceptable in many parts of the country – you will tend to get a poor exchange rate. The availability of small change is an ever-present problem so take plenty of low-denomination notes. Additionally, the smallest unit of US currency in Zimbabwe is the US$1 note, no coins, so you'll frequently be given change in rand coins, sweets or other small items sold by the shop.

The other great news brought by US dollarisation is the instant disappearance of that eternal pest, the money-changing tout.

CREDIT CARDS Throughout most of the decade from 2000, ATMs were non-existent and credit and debit cards were completely unacceptable in shops and fuel stations although some upmarket hotels and restaurants accepted them. The situation today is greatly improved although most retail purchases including fuel must still be made in cash. The great news now though is that ATMs are up and running in all reasonable-sized towns. It must be noted though that Visa cards are almost invariably the only ones acceptable in Zimbabwe. MasterCard, American Express and all the others can seldom be used here (or in several neighbouring countries) although as this book goes to press, MasterCard is quickly rolling out ATM facilities in Zimbabwe. Nevertheless, if you only take one card, make sure it's Visa. Be sure to advise your bank that you'll be using your card overseas, otherwise they may block it when you first try to use it.

TRAVELLERS' CHEQUES Zimbabwe is one of the countries where travellers' cheques were commonly accepted in payment for tourism facilities and in many shops, and of course they benefit from being far more secure than carrying quantities of cash. Their downside is the time it can take cashing them at the bank. You will also need prior assurance that the exchange rates applied are realistic. Nowadays, with the resurgence of ATMs and payment by plastic, travellers' cheques are falling into disuse so you are advised to check in advance whether they are acceptable where you are hoping to use them.

BANK OPENING HOURS Banks are normally open 08.00–15.00 Monday, Tuesday, Thursday and Friday, 08.00–13.00 Wednesday and 0800–11.30 Saturday.

TIPPING Tipping for good service is the norm in Zimbabwe. Aim for 5–10% in restaurants (but always check that a service charge isn't already added to the bill) and about US$1–2 for hotel porters. If your taxi has a meter then feel free to tip the driver, but if he simply quotes you a fare, don't tip, as he will almost certainly have built this into his price. Around US$1 or US$2 per day is fine for cleaners and maids in hotels and town lodges.

Safari camps and lodges present more of a dilemma. Check with the management about what system they operate. There's often a staff tip box to be shared amongst the 'backroom' staff: there are no hard and fast rules here and too many variables to recommend a fair across-the-board amount, but bear in mind that most staff receive relatively low salaries so your US dollars in the box will certainly be gratefully received. Senior guiding staff often tend to be tipped individually, maybe between US$5–10 per person per day depending on their service, but only give them the money at the end of your stay rather than after each occasion.

BUDGETING

Zimbabwe has what is generally known as a 'high value, low impact' tourism policy in common with some neighbouring countries. Speaking plainly this means that travellers on a tight budget will find it quite difficult to get around and experience anything like the best the country has to offer. This situation is exacerbated by the current lack of decent public transport, which means travellers have to incur the added expense of a self-drive or the services of an agent. Self-drivers will find petrol at around US$1.50 per litre and diesel a few cents cheaper (2013 prices).

Allow an average of US$12–20 for a main course in a town restaurant and beers are around US$3 although up to US$5 at large hotels. In the shops, a 200ml can of tonic or soda water can set you back a full US$1; a cheap bottle of South African wine will cost US$6–9 and a bottle of imported whisky is in the region of US$25–35. Bread tends to be sweet, crumbly and goes stale quickly so at around US$1 a loaf, pretty poor value. A 330ml bottle of still water is about US$1. People on a self-catering holiday will find groceries, especially canned and packet foods, very expensive. Much of the fruit and veg in supermarkets is quite low quality and very pricey and tends to be much better value in local markets, although it's completely seasonal so the range can be rather limited. Given the problems with small change, most vegetable stallholders arrange their goods in piles each costing US$1. If possible, try to stock up in Harare or Bulawayo rather than Victoria Falls which is universally extremely expensive.

There is very little 'shoestring' accommodation other than camping and what there is, is nearly all in town centres far removed from the national parks and other attractions most people want to visit. Victoria Falls, Bulawayo and Harare cater reasonably well for this end of the market. National Parks entrance fees reach a maximum of US$30 per person, (see page 66 for the parks that charge entry per day) with cars and trailers costing extra, but their rates for lodge and chalet accommodation are now coming in line with many private lodge prices with rates averaging around US$50–75 per person per night. However, parks charge per unit of accommodation rather than per person so a couple in a two-bedroom lodge will not find it good value. Most private safari-lodge accommodation sits in the upmarket to luxury bracket, with prices commonly in excess of US$500 per person per night. Safari lodges with these sorts of rates are all fully inclusive of meals and game-viewing activities.

A typical two-week holiday booked through a specialist agent with three nights' luxury accommodation at a selection of the key destinations such as Victoria Falls, Hwange, Mana Pools and Matusadona might set you back something like US$5,000–6,000 per person sharing. This would include all transfers, including charter flights and scheduled flights to/from Johannesburg, full board and all activities at safari camps. There are of course a huge number of variations that can affect the final price so this is only a rough indication.

GETTING AROUND

Zimbabwe, recently emerging from a decade of near-terminal economic decline, still suffers from chronically dilapidated and underfunded public transport. The national **airline** has now ceased operation (although they occasionally announce an ad hoc domestic route or two); apart from two routes the railways are to be avoided; and the domestic bus system is in a constant state of change, although improving. Local **buses** (known as 'chicken buses') are usually packed to the roof and unreliable with no schedules and frequent breakdowns.

Things are rapidly improving, though, with the emerging number of newly painted and apparently modern private **coaches** spotted rushing along the main highways, especially those linking Harare, Bulawayo, Victoria Falls and Beitbridge. It's encouraging to see new or newish names like City Link, Senator Express, Pioneer, PCG Motorways, Eagle Liner, KK Cheetah and the evocatively named Tombs Travel among others but keeping track of which companies ply which routes is difficult and which ones to recommend is even more difficult in this ever-changing market. It's a feature of virtually all of these services that they very seldom display their phone numbers on the buses, making it almost impossible to contact them, and even if you could get hold of them it's pointless to print schedules and fares in a book that will have a currency of several years. There are, however, four companies that seem to be consistent and have been operating for some years – City Link, Pathfinder, Pioneer and Senatar Express (which isn't to say that others shouldn't be investigated). My experience and other feedback suggest that phone and internet enquiries can be enormously frustrating (only Pathfinder currently has a website with useful details such as routes, timetables and fares) so there's no beating making a personal enquiry at a bus station, major hotel or local tourism information service once you have arrived in Zimbabwe. See individual *Getting there* sections for Harare, Bulawayo and Victoria Falls in the relevant chapters.

Hitchhiking can be very frustrating, because of the relatively low volumes of traffic on Zimbabwe's roads, plus the fact that it is prohibited in the national parks. If you do hitch you will probably find that local drivers will expect you to pay.

In view of the above, self-drive is currently the only viable option for fully independent travellers, although it's sometimes possible to combine the currently limited coach or charter air services with the services of a transfer agent or destination management company (see *Tour operators*, pages 84–7).

BY AIR With the virtual closure of Air Zimbabwe there is as yet no scheduled substitute for the internal network they used to operate although a number of private, light-aircraft operators are rapidly filling some of the gaps. However, these have been set up mainly to service the 'high end' remote camps and their fares are pitched accordingly – a far cry from the low-cost fares we have become accustomed to elsewhere. As this is such an ever-changing market and in view of the fact that your camp, lodge or tour operator will arrange all necessary transfers, I have not attempted to list those operating at the time of going to press.

SELF-DRIVE Self-driving is really the only way for independent travellers to get around. It gives you the freedom to plan your own route, itinerary and accommodation, and eat wherever you like, and you can visit areas that few tourists have even heard of. Zimbabwe is an easy, friendly and pleasant country to drive in. Its network of tarred roads is in very good condition, due largely to light traffic volumes during a decade of fuel shortages, and in 2013 all the main intercity routes embarked on a process of road resurfacing. Petrol and diesel have again become readily (though by no means universally) available although if you're travelling long distances, filling stations can be very distant from each other so it's wise to fill up when the opportunity arises.

Maps, GPS and planning On your trip, good maps are essential, and a GPS unit can be invaluable especially in the national parks. For advice and information see *Maps and GPS*, pages 91–2 above.

Have a good road map to hand when you are route planning, and where possible seek advice on roads, for all is not necessarily as it appears on the map.

Anyone who wants to visit remote regions along the Zambezi Valley in their own vehicle but hesitates to do it all by themselves can contact **ZIM4x4** (m *0772 324224;* e *info@zim4x4.co.zw; www.zim4x4.co.zw*). Dick Pitman, an experienced 4x4 driver, vice-chair of the Zambezi Society, author, conservationist and wilderness photographer, offers a range of services to responsible, conservation-minded 4x4 owners who wish to visit the Kariba and Zambezi Valley region. He and his wife Sally know parts of these areas that few others visit and they lead their accompanied self-drive tours in their own vehicle, arranging qualified wildlife guides, canoe guides and other specialist tour leaders as required. If you don't have your own 4x4 you can hire one of his. Unaccompanied 4x4 drivers can subscribe to the ZIM4x4 backup service, which provides advice on accommodation, routes, fuel availability, vehicle requirements and other relevant topics, as well as being a contact point in case of problems.

Driving licence Drivers from SADC countries can use their licences in Zimbabwe. Drivers from other countries can use licences issued in their own country for up to 90 days. Those with non-English-language licences should obtain an International Driving Permit. Anyone with an older paper licence (as in the UK) should update it with a plastic one with a photograph on it, or get an International Driving Permit. And see *Getting there and away, By road*, page 95.

Before you set out Vehicle reliability is an absolute necessity. If you have a breakdown or run out of fuel, you will almost certainly be reliant on someone stopping to help, as rural mobile phone coverage is scant; even in towns, phone connections can be hit or miss. Even if you find a garage or workshop, the chances of finding spare parts are slim, although spares and competent facilities for most popular makes are available in Harare.

Spares and accessories A basic spares kit should include fuses, light bulbs, vehicle oils, brake and hydraulic fluids as well as radiator hoses, belts and a spare thermostat. For overheating problems, make room for a five-litre bottle of water for radiator top-ups. Take spare spark plugs (glow plug for diesel engines). I also carry air and fuel filters, the latter particularly useful against contaminated fuel.

You should also assemble a box of miscellaneous useful items such as Jubilee (hose) clips, cable ties, electrical wire, insulating tape, metal putty, silicone sealant and an aerosol can of light oil. Don't underestimate the value of a box of miscellaneous nuts, bolts, washers, steel wire, webbing straps, cord and duct tape. Also pack a circuit tester.

Take a strong torch or lamp, but you'll also find a head-mounted light invaluable when you need to use both hands.

Your recovery kit should include a good set of battery jump leads (buy expensive ones and know how to use them correctly), a strong tow rope and a comprehensive selection of tools rather than the minimalist kit that comes with the car. A spade or shovel is essential; those little collapsible ones sold in camping shops are not man enough for serious mud-shifting. You can also invest in one of the several varieties of sand tracks although with careful driving you'll seldom need them.

Wheels and tyres Carry two full-size spare wheels if you possibly can, especially if you're planning lengthy off road excursions.

Assuming your tyres are tubeless, there are plug kits available to fix most small punctures. I also carry a spare tube for my tubeless tyres in the event of a large gash or hole. You will also need a good pump. I recommend an old-fashioned foot or hand pump as a backup to your battery-operated one. There are many types of jack available – just ensure that yours will fit under the vehicle when a tyre is deflated!

Legalities You are required by law to carry a fire extinguisher (1kg for light vehicles, 1.5kg for heavy vehicles) with up-to-date service history and the relevant standard certification stamp from the country of manufacture*; spare wheel with the means to change it; and two red warning triangles to be used in the event of a breakdown – two more if you're pulling a trailer or caravan. Go for the more robust ones as the lightweight plastic ones need to be weighted down to stop them blowing over. **Reflectors**, as follows, must be of 'honeycomb' or 'diamond' grade**:

- Two white (60mm x 50mm) either side at front (or 60mm diameter if circular).
- Two red (60mm x 50mm) at either side of rear (or 60mm diameter if circular).
- Continuous red reflector strip (50mm wide) to within not less than 400mm of the outer edges at rear for pick-ups and twin/double cabs and light trailers/caravans.**
- Continuous yellow reflector strip down sides of both vehicle and trailer if combined length is more than 8m.
- GVM (gross vehicle mass) and NMV (non motorised vehicle, ie: trailer/caravan) weight figures to be shown on left side of pick-ups and twin/double cabs and trailers/caravans in front of rear wheel arch.
- Trailers to have a reflective white 'T' and a reflective red 'T' (honeycomb type) on a black background facing to the front and rear of the trailer respectively.'
- Reflectors are not required inside vehicle doors and nor is there any requirement to carry reflective jackets in private vehicles – although it's sensible to carry one in case of an emergency, especially at night.

* In theory it should carry certification from the Standards Authority of Zimbabwe but it seems to be recognised that nobody outside of Zimbabwe can source items with the relevant Zimbabwe certification, so neighbouring countries' certification stamps are currently being accepted. Have the service history adequately displayed and make sure the meter needle is in the green sector.
** I have never seen this tape in red or white in any shop in South Africa so recommend you use standard reflective tape and explain that 'diamond' tape is unavailable. Every driver will have the same story so hopefully sense will prevail.

It is a legal requirement to wear **seatbelts**. It is also illegal to use a **mobile phone** when driving.

You **drive on the left**, and intersections in and around towns tend to have roundabouts (traffic circles). South Africans and Americans should note the different priority system from their 'first come, first served' four-way stop system. As you approach a roundabout you must give way to the driver on your right who is already on the roundabout.

Road-sign distances are metric. Speed limits are generally 60km/h in town, and 80km/h and 120km/h as you get out onto the open road. There's a speed limit sign with which many drivers will be unfamiliar. It's the UK-style white circle with a black diagonal stripe. This is a 'derestricted speed' sign that effectively means a 120km/h maximum. If drivers in the opposite direction flash their lights at you it's a sure sign of either a speed trap ahead or animals on the road.

Fines for relatively minor infringements are usually US$10 and for exceeding the speed limit by 1–50km/h expect a fine on a sliding scale between US$5–20. More serious offences will incur a court appearance or arrest. If the police officer demands the maximum US$20 fine for exceeding the speed limit by only a small amount, it's well worth politely querying this and pointing out that a small excess speed should only attract a small fine.

A recent and not altogether welcome innovation is the introduction of toll roads. In a nutshell, all main roads have become toll roads and there are usually two toll barriers between major towns. The fee is currently US$1, so again, be sure to have plenty of small notes handy (and these are good places to offload those really shabby ones).

In common with other African countries, Zimbabwe's president and ministers, when on the move, do so at top speed in a large convoy of expensive black cars, complete with sirens, flashing blue lights and full-beam headlights. If you see such a cavalcade, in front or behind, immediately pull right off the road (not just to the side), as it's illegal to occupy the same stretch of tarmac when these officials are in your vicinity. If you don't respond quickly enough you will, at the very least, get arrested.

Police roadblocks These are one of the frustrations of driving around Zimbabwe. Generally speaking they are few and far between and if you're driving a foreign-registered vehicle you'll tend to be waved through with no more than a smile and a friendly 'Have a nice day'. But on certain unannounced occasions, they will literally flood the roads with roadblocks giving the police the instruction to check thoroughly for any vehicle or paperwork infringements, however minor, and to fine accordingly. The key is to make sure your vehicle is in tip-top condition and conforms to the regulations outlined above. I have always found that the police are unfailingly polite and friendly at these roadblocks; that said, in the unlikely event that you are stopped and feel you are being treated irregularly or unfairly there's help at hand specifically for this purpose in the Zimbabwe Police Public Relations Department: call Superintendent Ncube on ☏ 04 748836; m 0772 719730, 0712 769768; or Inspector Chigombe on m 0772 965030. There's also a 24-hour service number: ☏ 04 703631.

Directions When you are given verbal directions that include 'robots', don't worry: this is the regional term for traffic lights. You may also be told to look out for a turning 'just after the 35km peg'. Pegs are white-painted kilometre markers and can be very helpful, although many are now broken or overgrown. That's why I haven't referred to many in this book.

Fuel As I write this in early 2013, fuel is generally but not always available at every station so play safe and try to fill up long before your gauge reaches empty. Note you can only pay for fuel with cash, not debit or credit cards.

Even if fuel is freely available at the time of your visit, bring in some jerrycans, as there are some very long distances between filling stations and rural ones aren't always fully stocked. It's quite common to find a fuel station that has plenty of petrol and diesel but is suffering from a power cut so has no means of pumping it. You can bring in the fuel you can carry in the vehicle's tank tax-free; anything more in spare cans is dutiable, with a maximum of 200 litres.

The latest generation of diesel vehicles do not take kindly to dirty or contaminated fuel so my advice is to always carry a can containing fuel you know you can trust.

Out-of-town breakdowns Even a well-maintained vehicle can break down so always take sufficient food and water to see you through a lengthy roadside wait. It's a legal requirement to deploy your red warning triangles behind and in front of your broken-down vehicle, but not everybody has these. If you come across a series of broken branches laid in the road, slow down: these are the local, organic substitute for warning triangles. Though hot by day, it can get very cold at night, so have sufficient warm clothes and blankets. Unless you know you are close to a town or village, everyone in your party should stay with the vehicle and wait for assistance rather than dispersing into the countryside looking for help.

This advice becomes a never-to-be-broken golden rule in the event of a breakdown in a national park or wilderness area. Your vehicle will be easy to spot during a search and the chances of one of your party wandering off and actually finding help are remote. It's more likely that you will get totally lost and unable to relocate your vehicle; very possibly a wild animal will find you first. If you do decide to defy the rules and feel your only option is to set out walking in a wildlife area, your handheld GPS will be invaluable. Mark your vehicle's position so that you can find it again, and give anyone you leave with the vehicle precise details of the track and direction you are heading in. If you are on your own, write this information on a dated, timed note visible to anyone who finds your empty car. Take water! The very worst thing to do is to send everybody in your party off in different directions. As you walk, make sure you whistle, sing or talk to yourself all the way; this will hopefully warn animals of your presence and they'll obligingly run away. Try to stick to open areas, but if you have to plunge into dense thickets, stop first and *listen*. Then shout and clap your hands and generally make as much noise and fuss as you can. This is the precise opposite of good bush practice, of course. Good luck, you'll certainly need it!

Two-way radios Some experienced overland drivers fit two-way radios to their vehicles to communicate with others in their convoy or party. It is, in fact, illegal to possess or use these radios without holding the appropriate licences from the Zimbabwean authorities. Such licences are area- and frequency-specific and there is currently no clear-cut and effective means by which temporary licences can be acquired by visitors. ZIM4x4's communications adviser, Dick Pitman, who has extensive experience in this field, suggests that owners of vehicle-mounted sets should declare them at the border on entry and retain the paperwork. This still doesn't allow you to use it, but may at least offer some protection if your vehicle is inspected at a roadblock by someone who knows the law.

Pot-holes Pot-holes are car wreckers and can be lethal. Avoid driving at night at all costs and be especially careful during rain when that innocuous-looking puddle could easily be a deep, water-filled pot-hole.

Night driving Most guidebooks advise against driving at night in Africa. My advice is stronger: don't even consider it unless it's an absolute necessity. By nightfall many pedestrians, cyclists (with no lights) and drivers have too many beers in their belly to worry about road safety. Be especially careful of 'month-end' syndrome: drivers and pedestrians who have just received their pay and enjoyed a lengthy session at the local *shebeen*.

Zimbabwe is heavily used by Zambian and Mozambican truckers driving massive vehicles, and many prefer to drive at night when there are no traffic police about. Their headlamps are frequently poorly adjusted, they hammer along at high

3

speed and you frequently come across major crashes where a driver has presumably fallen asleep at the wheel.

Animals Donkeys and cows have no road sense at all. Donkeys will stand by the road with a sad little expression and then try to commit suicide by stepping out in front of you at the last moment. Cows are a little more predictable: if you see one crossing in the distance you can be fairly sure that others will follow. Goats are reasonably intelligent in this regard, but can dash out at a moment's notice. The rule is to be vigilant and slow right down whenever you see animals on or by the roadside. Warn oncoming drivers with your hazard lights if you have just passed animals in the road.

As well as road signs warning of wildlife a telltale sign of game presence is piles of elephant or buffalo dung in the road or the obvious stains these leave on the tarmac. If elephants have crossed or walked there you can be sure other game is in the area too. The still-warm tarmac in early evening also entices birds to settle dozily in the road, and next morning as the sun comes up, they are there again so hoot to warn them of your approach.

Accidents If you are unlucky enough to hit an animal or person, you could be in for big trouble because, however drunk or careless the person may have been, as a stranger in a car it will always be your fault. You must stop and try to sort out the situation on the spot, offering to take the casualty to hospital or to pay for the dead or injured animal. According to most people, the going rate is about US$500–600 for a cow, US$120–150 for a donkey and about US$25 for a goat. Dogs are free. Of course this doesn't mean you should necessarily pay those sums without discussion. You may well have sustained significant damage to your vehicle and might wish to argue, with some justification, that the accident wouldn't have happened if the owner had controlled his animals properly rather than let them wander around unsupervised. But if you do find yourself in a negotiating position, do so from a position of authority and strength, or the locals will exploit your weakness. If the police are required you must drive to the nearest town or village with a police station and report the matter as soon as possible. You will then be required to take the policeman back to the incident location, as he will almost certainly have no vehicle or fuel. Far better to drive slowly and carefully in the first place.

Crime Zimbabwe is way behind some of its neighbouring countries in car crime, but rampant poverty is forcing some people to take desperate measures. You should keep doors locked and windows closed when driving slowly through towns, and remove all items of value from sight. Be vigilant at filling stations, and never leave the car unlocked or unattended while paying for fuel or buying from the shop. If you are hit by another vehicle in town, drive to an area that you consider safe (preferably outside a police station) before getting out of your car. If someone 'helpfully' points out a flat tyre – or anything else that requires you to get out of your car – ignore them, drive off and check it out later.

Two-wheel drive or 4x4? A 2x4 sedan will severely restrict your driving limits. Tar roads and many dirt roads are in relatively good condition and some people argue that 4x4 is unnecessary in Zimbabwe. That is indeed the case if you are only driving to and within towns. Elsewhere (and you'll be surprised how much non-tar driving you find yourself doing) a 4x4 is necessary – and it's essential if you're driving on dirt roads in the rains.

In practical terms you seldom require all four wheels to be driven (except on sand, and off-road in the wet season) but the rugged nature of many tracks often demands high ground clearance and tough suspension, and that generally only comes with a 4x4 vehicle. Most 2x4 pick-ups will do the job in all but the most difficult conditions.

National park roads are a challenge for a sedan and a high percentage of these are currently inaccessible to anything other than a high-clearance vehicle. High ground clearance also has the benefit of affording better wildlife-viewing potential.

Dirt roads The terms 'dirt' and 'gravel' refer to untarred roads, which can be either excellent or uncomfortable and dangerous, depending on how they are maintained. Paradoxically, a smooth dirt road is potentially very dangerous, as drivers are tempted to speed up. However smooth the ride may be, a gravel surface offers far less traction than tar. Four-wheel drive gives you more traction and thus more controllability when braking and cornering. Always engage it, however smooth the surface appears, and stick to a maximum of 80km/h. In the rains, dirt roads can suffer from flooding and become treacherously slippery, after which they can dry up into rock-strewn, deeply rutted nightmares.

One of the inevitabilities of dirt roads is the horrible phenomenon of corrugations – close, regularly spaced transverse ruts that threaten to shake the fillings out of your teeth and loosen every nut and bolt in your car. At 80km/h even a 4x4 cannot negotiate a sudden obstacle or tight corner on rough dirt roads, so stick to a maximum of 50–60km/h on corrugations; it may be slow and uncomfortable but you will be in control of your vehicle, and do less damage to its suspension.

Overtaking on dirt roads requires more consideration and courtesy than on tar roads. Whether it is dry or wet, your tyres throw up considerable dust, mud and even stones, so if you decide to pass someone you must consider what you will be throwing into their windscreen. If you do give in to the urge to pass, check the road well ahead, pass relatively slowly and stay on the overtaking side of the road as long as it is safe to do so, to avoid spraying debris into his windscreen.

Sand roads Zimbabwe is blessed with a number of deep sand roads, generally in national parks, that can frequently become deeply rutted. Depending on the vehicle and your driving experience, these can bring you to a standstill. Here are a few tips.

Lower your tyre pressures to about 1.2 bar for greater contact surface area; much lower pressures than that risk scrubbing the tyres off the rim. (This precaution is recommended in all the 4x4 driving books and magazines but I know plenty of experienced safari drivers who never bother to deflate their tyres.) Drive in as high a gear as you can without risking stalling. If the track is deeply rutted don't fight the wheel, let the car steer itself. Be very careful approaching blind bends as there may be a vehicle coming in the other direction, travelling in the same ruts as you. If you get stuck, try first to move off in a low-range gear. Always carry a spade or shovel and make sure you've got some sand tracks for really tricky situations. Come off the throttle the moment your wheel(s) start to spin or you'll quickly dig yourself in.

Grass seeds These can be quite dangerous. If you are driving through tall grass, which often grows in the central rut between tyre tracks, you should periodically stop and check there are no clumps of seeds and grass trapped in tight spaces underneath the vehicle. Many a car fire has been started by the heat from the exhaust or engine igniting such build-ups. Seeds will also clog up your radiator, causing overheating, unless you fit a protective seed net, available from 4x4 accessory shops.

Car hire You can either hire a car in Zimbabwe or bring one in from a neighbouring country. That decision may well be based on whether you want a car for your entire holiday or for just a few days here and there. Either way, car rental in Zimbabwe is extremely expensive, especially for a 4x4 – think in terms of over US$1200 per week. If you go for two-wheel drive, check the small print, as there will almost certainly be a prohibition against driving on dirt roads – which means that much of the country and all of the national parks will be off-limits to you.

Bringing a hire car in from another country is problematic: most big-name companies refuse to let their vehicles into Zimbabwe. That should be your first question to any rental company. The best option is one of several specialist companies in South Africa that provide 4x4s completely equipped with camping gear; some will also assist with route planning etc. When you enter the country with a hire car you will now be hit with another tax on top of all the others – the Commercial Vehicle Warranty costing you US$30.

If you are hiring within Zimbabwe there are only two international companies, Avis and Europcar, both operating on a franchise basis, with collection facilities at Harare, Bulawayo and Victoria Falls airports as well as in town. Their depots in Mutare and Masvingo were closed at the time of research. This is an extremely expensive option, especially if you want a 4x4 and the choice of vehicles is limited. Note that in common with many airlines, car hire companies require you to pay for the car using the same credit card that you booked with so if you're a multi-card carrier make sure you bring the correct one.

See *Legalities*, pages 123–4, for the regulations regarding reflective strips and make sure the hirer is happy for them to be applied; and note that if you are hiring a pick-up, even a double cab, the vehicle must have the GVM (gross vehicle mass) displayed.

Vehicle smuggling is a big problem, especially out of South Africa, so it is essential that you have the correct documentation, including a declaration from the hire company that you have their permission to take their vehicle out of the country. Ensure that you are issued with a Temporary Export Permit at the border before you leave the country in which the car is registered.

Specialist car hire companies
South Africa
🚗 **Britz Car Hire** www.britz.co.za
🚗 **Bushlore Africa** www.bushlore.com
🚗 **Just Done It** ☎+27 (0)21 791 3904; www.4x4hire.co.za
🚗 **Ivory 4x4 Hire** www.ivory4x4hire.co.za
🚗 **Southern Offroad Car Rental** www.4x4hire.co.za. Land Rovers & Land Cruisers.
🚗 **Jenman Safaris** ☎+27 (0)21 683 7826; 0861JENMAN; e info@jenmansafaris.com. www.jenmansafaris.com

Namibia
African Tracks www.sa-venues.com

Local car hire companies
🚗 **Avis** e enquiry@avis.cozw; www.avis.co.zw
🚗 **Europcar** www.europcar.co.zw
🚗 **Excellence Car Hire** e excelinc@africaonline.co.zw
🚗 **Diesel Car Hire** www.dieselcarhire.co.za
🚗 **LED** e info@ledcarrental.co.zw
🚗 **Msuna Safaris and Travel** e christina@msuna.co.zw
🚗 **RockShade** www.rockshade.co.za
🚗 **Showman Tours** www.showmantours.co.zw
🚗 **Silver Tours** Victoria Falls; www.silvertours.co.zw
🚗 **UTC** www.utc.co.zw

Internet agencies A number of internet search agencies will check the market and get you the best deal. If you use these agencies, make sure you are happy with the company they have chosen for you, in terms not only of the vehicle and rates but also of conditions and small print.

🚗 **AfricaPoint** www.africapoint.com
🚗 **Argus Car Hire** www.arguscarhire.com
🚗 **Car Hire Centre** www.car-hire-centre.co.uk
🚗 **Cardboardbox Travel Shop** www.carhirezimbabwe.org

🚗 **Zimbabwe Car Rental** http://zimbabwe.rentalcargroup.com

Advice and support

Automobile Association of Zimbabwe 24hr emergency roadside helpline ☎04 776760/4; head office: Fanum Hse, 2 Kenilworth Rd, Newlands, Harare; ☎04 788173/6; Fanum Hse, Leopold Takawira Av, Bulawayo; ☎09 70063; Fanum Hse, cnr Lobengula Av & 6th St, Gweru; ☎054 24251; Fanum Hse, cnr Robert Mugabe Av & 4th St, Mutare; ☎020 64422.

4x4 essentials The following is for the benefit of people who plan to hire and drive a 4x4 for the first time.

There is a bewildering variety of transmission and drive-train systems, with manufacturers offering ever-more complex variants with every upgrade. It would be beyond the scope of this guidebook to offer anything other than the barest introduction to this subject. So, after reading this it is suggested that you (1) thoroughly read your vehicle's instruction manual; (2) buy and read an off-road driving manual; and then (3) book yourself on an off-road training course, if possible using the same type of vehicle you'll be taking to Zimbabwe. Apart from allowing you to see in controlled conditions what you and your vehicle are capable of, they are also great fun.

Bear in mind that a 4x4 by itself won't get you out of, or indeed prevent you getting into, a sticky situation. There are three parts to the equation – the terrain, the vehicle and the driver, and only one of those has a brain. So weigh up the hazard or obstacle first, and if it looks iffy, don't try it unless there's someone on hand to pull you out!

ACCOMMODATION

Zimbabwe offers a wide range of accommodation styles, from top-class luxury in some of Africa's best hotels and safari lodges to small, intimate, often family-run bush camps. Away from the main tourist centres, keep an open and relaxed frame of mind. The tourism industry is picking itself up off its knees after a decade of near-terminal decline. Once you get chatting to owners and staff you'll appreciate why the decoration in your room is perhaps a little tired or why the vehicles on your game drive are a little shabby. You'll come away full of admiration for the way Zimbabweans manage to turn adversity into a success.

HOTELS While Harare and Bulawayo have a few luxury hotels, virtually all Zimbabwe's best hotels are in Victoria Falls. Although there's great accommodation in all key tourist areas, town-centre hotels in other than these three towns tend to cater for the business market, attracting adjectives such as 'plain' and 'uninspiring'.

LODGES Don't read too much into the word 'lodge', as various owners apply it to virtually every type of accommodation. Probably the largest lodge in the country is the beautiful and massive Safari Lodge in Victoria Falls, yet in the residential area of the same town there are several small guesthouses and bed and breakfasts also using the name 'lodge'. Many safari lodges in or adjacent to national parks are in the top price bracket, but their rates are invariably fully inclusive, covering all meals, some if not all drinks, plus safari activities. Some also include transfers.

SAFARI CAMPS These can be similar to lodges, often smaller and more rustic, but also located in and around national parks to cater for game-viewing activities. They range from A-frame thatched chalets to large tents under a thatch roof, or sometimes just canvas. But don't assume this is downmarket accommodation. Many of these camps are truly luxurious, beautifully furnished and often with brick-built en-suite facilities attached to the tents. They are frequently raised off the ground with wooden decks and walkways connecting the accommodation tents to the central 'boma'. Canvas is used with great effect to provide a wonderful 'African safari' atmosphere. As with the best lodges, catering can be to an amazingly high standard, and the same rate structure applies.

Most people on wildlife-viewing safaris choose to move from camp to camp in different areas, typically spending a maximum of three or four nights in any one place.

GUESTHOUSES AND BED AND BREAKFASTS The largest concentrations of these are in the residential areas of Victoria Falls, Harare and Bulawayo, where many people have converted their houses into commercial premises, although others are purpose-built. Unlike in the UK, for instance, where guests may share the house with the owners, most in Zimbabwe offer self-contained accommodation. Most serve only breakfast but many are full board or will provide an evening meal on request.

BACKPACKERS As most of the popular activities in Zimbabwe (wildlife viewing, for instance) are priced on the high side as well as being inaccessible by public transport, Zimbabwe has never really catered for the budget traveller, preferring to aim at the 'high end' visitors. Consequently, outside of Victoria Falls and in the centres of main towns there is little, decent backpacker accommodation and what there is may not be considered cheap by international standards. Note that you will often find really cheap accommodation in towns but unless it is specifically marketed to backpackers there's every chance it will be used for purposes other than sleeping.

NATIONAL PARKS ACCOMMODATION Most national parks offer lodge, cottage and/or chalet accommodation. Note that you pay per unit of accommodation, not per person. These used to be considerably cheaper than privately run establishments and were best described as utilitarian, with most being very run-down. Many international visitors felt they were not particularly good value for money. All are furnished, with bed linen and towels, basic kitchen equipment, crockery and cutlery for self-catering. They conform to a similar design throughout the Parks system and generally offer a choice of one to three twin and double bedrooms. Cottages and lodges have their own kitchens and bathrooms, while chalets tend to have external cooking and communal washing facilities.

A few years ago there was a plan to upgrade the facilities in all of the parks – a great start was made at the Zambezi National Park but thereafter the programme faltered and slowed down considerably with only Sinamatella so far receiving attention. During the research for this guidebook, only Hwange Main Camp offered a restaurant service (elsewhere in the Parks system restaurants and bars remain unstocked and unmanned), so with one exception, a national parks visit is, for now, a fully self-catering affair.

Some parks, including Gonarezhou and Chizarira, only have rustic accommodation just a notch up from camping, and because shelter is often minimal it's prudent to have a tent as a standby for inclement weather.

CAMPING Zimbabwe offers the enthusiastic camper an almost unique African experience. In many of the national parks, including Mana Pools, Gonarezhou, Chizarira and Zambezi, you are allowed to camp in specified but unfenced wildlife areas. While there are some obvious potential dangers, with care and good sense you can reduce these almost to zero and enjoy real wilderness camping you are likely to find in few other places. Only by sitting around a campfire under vast starry skies, listening to the nightly symphony of grunting hippos, the full vocal repertoire of hyenas, hissing cicadas, the occasional owl and nightjar, and perhaps a lion grunting in the distance, can you claim to have experienced the real African bush.

All national parks have designated camping spots (though you can free-camp in Chimanimani) and you must always use these and never drive off into the bush to find somewhere more isolated. The official sites are always near wildlife gathering places such as rivers or waterholes, or near scenic viewpoints, and as such are excellent places to overnight. Some parks, such as Hwange and Mana Pools, operate an 'exclusive' system whereby only one group may occupy a campsite at a time and they charge the same rate regardless of how many people are staying. This makes it extremely expensive if there are only two of you. Other parks cater for several groups at a time but the individual sites are usually isolated from one another. The 'undeveloped' sites offer only the most basic facilities – a long-drop toilet and a *braai* (barbecue) stand while the 'developed' sites have running water and an ablution block, though no electricity. Facilities tend to be run-down and in need of refurbishment, but all of the numerous parks' sites where I have stayed have been clean and well tended.

ACCOMMODATION PRICE CODES AND STYLE CATEGORIES

There is a great deal of price inconsistency across Zimbabwe with Victoria Falls and Harare accommodation generally priced much higher than other parts of the country. As this makes it difficult to compare the style of hotels countrywide on a purely price basis, this book lists accommodation under four broad style categories to indicate levels of comfort and facilities. Each entry is then given a price bracket. Prices are based on a single international visitor staying one night in a double room during high season.

Many of the private lodges in national parks are in the top price bracket. This is because they tend to be fully inclusive and their rates include all meals and activities, and often drinks and transfers.

STYLE CATEGORIES
Luxury Outstanding quality in every respect
Upmarket Good sized, well appointed rooms, comprehensive facilities with above average catering
Standard Comfortable with efficient service and good facilities. Reasonably varied menu, if offered
Basic Simple, minimal facilities but clean (eg backpackers)

PRICING BRACKETS
$$$$$	US$300+
$$$$	US$200–299
$$$	US$100–199
$$	US$50–99
$	up to US$49

Most towns have a municipal campsite but apart from Victoria Falls and Bulawayo (and perhaps Masvingo) many have fallen into disrepair and are not recommended.

National Parks camping rates
Camping is now generally charged per person unless otherwise specified. Exclusive campsites, however, tend to charge per site and can work out extremely expensive if there are only a couple of you. Per person rates are generally US$10, rising to US$15 in Hwange, Zambezi, Matusadona, with Chizarira at US$20. Mana Pools (no regional rate here) ranges from $20 at Nyamepi up to US$150 and US$200 for the exclusive sites. Up-to-date rates can be found on the National Parks website (*www.zimparks.com*). You can also check www.wildzambezi.com for latest rates at all the parks and campsites along the Zambezi Valley including Matusadona and Chizarira.

Tents
As an alternative to conventional tents you might consider a rooftop tent. Several 4x4-hire companies in South Africa have these available. They can be mounted either on your vehicle roof or on a trailer, and are remarkably quick to set up. One advantage is that they are off the ground, offering an added sense of security. A disadvantage is that access is by ladder, which can be an impediment when answering the call of nature in the middle of the night. Vehicle-mounted ones must be packed up each time you go for a drive, so many people prefer to mount one on a trailer.

If you are using a conventional tent, bear in mind that many camping spots are situated on ground that has a virtually impenetrable crust, so standard wire tent pegs and a rubber mallet don't stand a chance. The pegs (long nails) I use are about 8mm in diameter and driven in by a hefty club hammer (admittedly not ideal equipment for backpackers).

Make sure your tent has a good anti-insect mesh to keep the mosquitoes out. You can burn a mosquito coil inside the tent with the entrance closed for 30 minutes before you go to bed, but never sleep in a tent with one burning all night.

Fires and firewood
Many people feel there is no better way to end a day in the bush than to sit round a campfire and *braai* over wood coals. It just seems a very natural way to do things, but there are environmental issues to complicate matters. Southern Africa is rapidly being denuded of trees, especially the slow-growing hardwoods that provide the best firewood. By buying firewood on the roadside, you may be supporting a needy person's livelihood but you are also contributing to habitat destruction. Even collecting fallen wood around the campsite (national parks generally prohibit this) has a downside: as fallen wood rots it becomes home for a host of bugs and beetles, all essential parts of the food chain.

On a safety level it's also a rather bad idea to send your friends and family out into the bush to gather wood, especially as previous campers will already have taken everything from nearby. As well as predators, think snakes and scorpions, who often lie up under useful-looking firewood.

It's easy to cook without wood using gas, and you can now buy bags of charcoal and *braai* briquettes made from invasive alien brushwood (see box, *Lantana: a very undesirable alien*, page 31, *Chapter 2*). You can take up the offer of Parks staff to bring you wood (for a small fee), but they are just collecting fallen wood themselves! Many of the cooking grids in National Parks *braai* stands are missing or unusable, so bring your own and be prepared to improvise.

Be extra careful when lighting fires in the dry season, as one gust of wind could start a bushfire. If there's anything more than a gentle breeze, don't make a fire.

Only light one on bare ground, preferably on the site of previous fires, and keep a plentiful supply of water to hand. If the camping site is overgrown, try to build a ring of stones around the fire area to stop any fire creep, dispersing the stones when you leave. Don't build under low overhanging branches and always keep the fire small and controllable. Never leave it unattended. When you turn in for the night, don't build it up in the mistaken belief that it will deter nocturnal visitors; douse it. When you leave, bury or widely scatter the ashes.

Toilets While most parks provide either flush or long-drop toilets, you may occasionally find you need to dig your own, which is why a small shovel should be an essential part of your kit. Your toilet should be well away from where anybody else is likely to camp but not so far into the bush that animals could be a danger; at all costs try to avoid using it after dark. Keep well away from any watercourse to avoid pollution. Hyenas have a charming habit of digging up human waste, so make a hole around 30cm (1ft) deep. (Faeces take a long time to decay in dry sandy soils.) Few things are more guaranteed to spoil an otherwise pristine camping spot than scraps of toilet paper, so take matches or a lighter to burn the paper afterwards, before filling the hole back in. Make absolutely sure there is no chance for the flames to spread.

For more on this delicate subject, try Kathleen Meyer's environmentally authoritative, brilliantly written and splendidly titled book, *How to Shit in the Woods* (Ten Speed Press).

Safety If you pitch in a designated site all the animals will know you are there and give you a wide berth, at least while you are active around camp (Nyamepi in Mana Pools, where the hyenas are habituated to humans and regularly patrol the tents at night looking for scraps, is an exception). In the morning, check the surrounding ground for spoor to see who has been inquisitive during the night. Treat these finds as a thrill rather than a threat as no animal will spontaneously attack a human within a zipped-up tent. Take note of that word, *zipped*. There have been a couple of cases of people being dragged from unzipped tents by sick or wounded lions, animals that had been unable to catch their natural prey. There was indeed a hyena attack during my last visit to Hwange but the victim had unwisely opted to sleep under the stars and had her face badly bitten. Whatever the temperature, the golden rule is to always use your tent, securely zip it before retiring and check the surrounding area with a strong torch before venturing out for a toilet visit.

Hyenas, jackals, honey badgers, monkeys, baboons and other scavengers will be attracted to any food waste you leave out, so bag it up and keep it in your vehicle. Elephants are extremely fond of citrus fruits, so also keep your oranges and lemons in the car.

Think very hard before taking small children on a camping trip into these unfenced areas. Unless you are prepared and able to keep them under 24-hour surveillance, leave them at home with Grandma.

Environment In March 2012 Mana Pools was the first of Zimbabwe's parks to introduce an excellent 'carry in – carry out' policy. Now, visitors are given a plastic rubbish bag at Nyamepi and are requested to use this for all non-combustible, non-biogradeable trash and to hand this in to park rangers on exit. This system is being rolled out to all national parks and has also been implemented at Zambezi National Park. Expect it to be in operation in all parks by the time you read this.

Pots, dishes, clothes (and even ourselves) occasionally need to be washed and we stock our home kitchens with some very strong detergents to make the job easier.

Leave these at home and buy the mildest and most environmentally acceptable soap and washing liquids you can find. If there's a river or lake by your campsite, collect washing water in a bowl but don't throw your dirty water back in the river. Depending on the source, it may be wise to boil the water before washing up. Environmentally aware campers find that river sand alone makes a pretty good job of cleaning dishes (but don't use it on your non-stick pans).

The whole attraction of this sort of camping is the sense of being in a place that belongs to nature, divorced from all signs of human habitation, so it is vital that we remove all traces of our presence when we leave the site, in order that later visitors can enjoy it as we have. Collecting all litter and waste should be an obvious action, but it's surprising how many people ignore their cigarette butts and beer-bottle tops. After you have packed up, have a last walk around looking for any traces of your presence; and don't be too proud to pick up other people's rubbish. Dump your bagged rubbish in the bins at the national park entrance. Any biodegradeable waste you leave behind should be buried.

Pollution is more than just litter: noise, music, as well as your high-power camping lights, can ruin someone else's stay. You can now buy small camping generators that are marketed as 'silent'. Well, they are no such thing, as anyone who's had the misfortune to camp near one will tell you. Please leave these at home when you come to Zimbabwe.

RATES AND BOOKING Prices vary widely but it must be said that international travellers on a tight budget will struggle with accommodation in Zimbabwe. Despite the economic turmoil and hyperinflation of the old Zimbabwe dollar, accommodation prices for international guests have remained reasonably stable, as they always had to be quoted in US dollars and paid for in hard currencies. So, with US dollarisation, not much has changed. But the strange economic times have thrown up some anomalies. Quite a few excellent establishments have dropped their prices in an attempt to attract scarce visitors, while other modest, even poor-standard places have kept their rates inordinately high.

THREE-TIER PRICING

Zimbabwe, along with most of its neighbours, adopts a discriminatory charging system throughout much of the accommodation sector and the national parks. Zimbabweans pay a very small amount, residents of neighbouring countries pay a reasonable 'regional' rate, and international visitors are charged a top rate.

Parks officials suggest that locals pay taxes that support the parks so are already subsidising them. This is at best simplistic as taxes go to central government, with little filtering out to the National Parks system.

If the policy were to allow poor Africans to enjoy their heritage, the scheme would be thoroughly laudable, except that the fees are still way too high for the average citizen. Its purpose is simply to maximise revenue based on visitors' nationality on the premise that all overseas visitors are wealthy and can afford higher prices.

I have seen disappointed European backpackers at the Victoria Falls entrance unable to go in because of the high fee while much wealthier people who happen to live in the region park their top-of-the-range 4x4s and get in paying much less.

Many establishments including National Parks apply a three-tier system, charging different rates for domestic, regional and international visitors. The rate brackets shown in this guide are those for internationals, the highest rate, so regional visitors will often get a pleasant surprise.

Booking Pre-booking the main elements of your trip, notably safari accommodation and activities, is an absolute necessity. Many safari camps are extremely remote and only cater for a small number of guests, so if you turn up unannounced you will invariably be disappointed and faced with an extremely long drive to find an alternative. In and around towns, you'll find hotels, lodges and guesthouses freely available to walk-in guests – at least until tourism takes off again, at which time pre-booking will again become a necessity. You must always pre-book National Parks accommodation directly through their Harare reservations centre (04 706077/8; e bookings@zimparks.co.zw).

Booking from overseas with Zimbabwe-based operators or lodges was a major challenge for years as the country's telecommunications network had seen little upkeep or investment. Landline-based communication – including fax and email – was subject to periodic collapse. Since early 2010, though, email communication has made huge strides although one is still frustrated with regular internet signal drop-outs. If you still have difficulty getting through, the motto is 'try, try and try again'. Don't assume that a non-reply to your email is down to lack of interest; on the contrary, everybody is desperate for your business but they may simply not have received your enquiry.

Booking in the national parks The National Parks accommodation reservation process for independent travellers is a bit hit and miss to say the least. You have to book through the central Harare office (see page 158). Without a requirement to pre-pay, many visitors and commercial concerns book ahead but fail to turn up, without having cancelled their bookings. With low visitor numbers this isn't a problem, but those who remember the good old busy days complain that you could never get a confirmed booking anywhere near peak game-viewing season; the mantra from parks was, 'fully booked', and in the most popular parks, especially Hwange, this is still often the case especially at weekends and during the popular late winter months. Some people take a chance and arrive unbooked, hoping that a no-show will throw up a vacancy late in the afternoon. Even if Harare does grant you a booking, dodgy communications means the park may not hear about it, so someone without a booking could arrive before you and get the lodge or campsite you think you booked.

The lesson is: always try to make a booking through Harare, keep any paperwork and try to turn up early. If you prefer to take every day as it comes and not book in advance, be prepared to wait at reception until late afternoon until staff are confident their bookings won't show up, and to vacate on day two if they show up late. (Note that you cannot do this at Mana Pools, where you are *obliged* to book in advance.)

Peak season for National Parks accommodation is July to September and December.

If you are not prepared to partake in this 'lottery' the only alternative is to book your visit with a local tour operator.

EATING AND DRINKING

WESTERN FOOD Eating out in Zimbabwe was always excellent value, by which I mean very good quality yet inexpensive in international terms. More recently though, the virtual collapse of the agricultural industry means that good-quality raw materials generally have to be imported and in the process drive up prices. Expect around US$12–20 for a main course in a good restaurant. Virtually all restaurants and accommodations serve international menus with a heavy emphasis on steak, which is excellent in this country, and you'll also find a variety of game meats on many menus. Vegetarians, generally speaking, have more difficulty finding an imaginative menu in what is essentially a nation of carnivores. Restaurant prices in the main towns are remarkably consistent so this book does not categorise them into price brackets. Any restaurants that differ from this norm are highlighted in their relevant entries. Safari lodges and camps serve set meals so if you have any special dietary requirements be sure to advise them at the time of booking so they can accommodate you accordingly. Given the often remote locations of these camps, don't wait until you arrive before stating your dietary needs, as it will then be too late for them to cater according to your needs.

LOCAL/RURAL FOOD Until recently the country was not only self-sufficient in food, but also farmed in such abundance that it earned the sobriquet 'the breadbasket of southern Africa'. Since 2000, economic and political instability, farm invasions and droughts have combined to turn the country into not only a net importer of maize but dependent on international food aid.

The staple starch for Zimbabweans is maize (*meallie*), although millet and sorghum are alternative grains grown mainly in the *lowveld* areas. *Sadza*, a heavy mash made from ground maize and water, forms the basis of every meal, supplemented with a relish – essentially anything that is available to impart a different flavour. Generally the sadza is rolled by hand into a small ball, moulded into a slight cup shape and dipped into the relish. Common relishes are vegetable-based, frequently green leaves like rape, either cultivated or collected wild, with tomato or onion if available. Groundnuts are grown and pounded to make a sauce with onions, something of a delicacy. Commercially produced fermented milk, known as *lacto*, is another popular relish. Chicken eggs are seldom eaten as they are needed to produce more hens. Maize cobs are commonly eaten roasted as a snack.

Rural Zimbabweans make great use of nature's free resources, so wild mushrooms, fruits, seeds and wild plants are harvested. Their diet also includes a surprising number of insect species as protein sources – crickets and locusts, flying ants and a variety of caterpillars, not forgetting, of course, the plump and fried *mopane* worms. Cattle tend to be kept as an expression of wealth, and used as beasts of burden rather than a food source, although they are eaten following a ritual or ceremonial sacrifice. Other meat such as goat, mutton and chicken is commonly eaten depending on the wealth of the family. *Nyama* is the Shona word for meat, so you won't go far in Zimbabwe before hearing the words *sadza ne nyama*, ie: *sadza* and meat stew, the standard meal for most Zimbabweans (including many whites). Needless to say, nothing is wasted, so stewed chicken heads and feet, bony offcuts and offal that would be considered unpalatable by many Westerners are all consumed. Fish from rivers and lakes include chessa, barbel or squeaker, fighting tigerfish, Kariba *kapenta* and, rarely, the huge vundu, the largest freshwater fish in the Zambezi, growing to over 50kg.

Urban Zimbabweans are more Western-orientated. Bread is popular, as are fast foods, especially fried chicken. Yet even in towns only a fool would try to separate a Zimbabwean, black or white, from their *sadza*.

DRINKS There's a wide range of Zimbabwean-brewed lager-type beers available and they come in either brown or green bottles. Brown beers such as Castle are 'ordinary' beers while green bottles such as Zambezi or Bollingers denote premium beers carrying a slightly higher price. Imported beers command the highest prices. However, most local people purchase their Zimbabwean beer in cans these days rather than bottles. It's quite common to have to pay a refundable deposit on glass bottles. *Chibuku* is the name given to local, mainly rurally consumed 'beer', a thick fermented concoction that is either brewed at home or commercially produced.

Bottle stores in large towns sell a range of imported South African wines. Zimbabwean wines, previously shunned by all but the desperate, have improved greatly in recent years and you should be sure to sample the Mukuyu and Private Cellar ranges. These will often be the wines served at safari camps.

All types of spirits are widely available with imported brands obviously commanding far higher prices. But with alcohol freely available in shops, supplies of mixers such as tonic water, ginger and soda can be erratic and you wouldn't expect to find them in smaller towns.

The bars in the big Victoria Falls and Harare hotels are understandably expensive but generally speaking prices are reasonable and far cheaper than most European countries, although usually higher than South Africa.

PUBLIC HOLIDAYS

1 January	New Year's Day
March/April (variable)	Easter
18 April	Independence Day
1 May	Workers' Day
25 May	Africa Day
11 August (or nearest Monday)	Heroes Day
12 August (or nearest Tuesday)	Defence Forces Day
22/23 December	National Unity Day
25 December	Christmas Day
26 December	Boxing Day

SHOPPING

CONSUMABLES Major towns have shopping facilities for all the goods you are likely to need for a self-catering trip. If you want to make it easy, head for a supermarket, as most people do: Zimbabwe high streets don't tend to have specialist shops such as greengrocers, butchers and hardware stores. You'll always find a pharmacy on the main shopping street, and plenty of clothing stores, although outside Harare, Bulawayo and Victoria Falls don't expect to find any designer gear. Smart and expensive safari clothing can be found in specialist outfitters in these three towns. Local markets invariably offer better value than shops but tend to have less choice of goods.

SOUVENIRS Here we're mainly talking about curios, fabrics and works of art, all of which Zimbabwe has in glorious abundance. Many crafts are made in the local community, with the artist directly receiving a proportion of the sale proceeds.

Curios such as wood and stone carvings can be found all over the country in specialist shops, as well as in market stalls in tourist areas. Although most of this stuff is churned out in mass quantities and can hardly be called art, a lot of it is actually quite appealing. Many animals depicted in the carvings bear little relation to the real thing but they are clearly the result of the carver's sense of humour, and if they bring a smile to your face, why not buy one?

Bear in mind the environmental issues surrounding **woodcarvings**. Not only are Zimbabwe's hardwood forests and woodlands being denuded for firewood, but the carvings industry also exacts a very heavy toll. When you look at some of the larger carvings lining the roadside, it's clear that whole trees have been destroyed to form just one figure. Vendors are becoming aware of these concerns, and many say the timber is from naturally fallen trees, but it's likely that only a tiny minority are sourced this way. Generally speaking a fallen tree will have done so because of

BARGAINING

This is a subject guaranteed to get after-dinner conversation hopping. It is not the Western way of buying things, and without a fixed price many people are concerned about paying more than an item is actually worth. Many tourists loathe the idea of haggling the price of a minor curio with someone whose annual income is infinitely smaller than their own, and would gladly pay the full asking price. Others treat it almost as a gladiatorial sport, spending hours screwing the very lowest price out of a hapless salesperson. Good sense and fair practice lie somewhere in between. It is worth remembering that bargaining is the norm in informal situations (except in Zimbabwe's shops) and you are not expected to pay the first price offered. Unfortunately there's no magic formula for what percentage you should haggle down to – different vendors have different pricing policies.

Bargaining for fruit and veg in the market is not generally necessary, although if you're buying a lot from one stallholder it's OK to ask for a small discount. Check out several sellers; if prices seem similar, nobody is trying to rip you off. Most tourists don't buy raw food goods so there is no culture of inflating prices.

Curio sellers are a different matter, as they deal only with tourists and are often slick operators (although outside the main tourist areas, most are anything but slick – just honest artists or traders trying to scratch a living). As town shops don't bargain, they can give you an idea of going prices, so you may want to visit a few of these before going into the market or to a roadside stall. In the end it should simply be a matter of how much an item is worth to you. When you have decided roughly the price you are prepared to pay, let the bargaining begin. Remember that this is normal commerce, not a sport; the idea is to quickly agree a price that is fair to both of you.

Curio sellers have had a hard time of it in recent years with the huge drop in visitor numbers, and plenty of Zimbabweans are desperate enough to sell goods at much less than their real value just to be able to buy the next meal for their family. So play fair and don't raise expectations of a sale by getting into a bargaining situation over an item you have little intention of buying. It's all too easy to do this by casually asking the price as you stroll by.

Bartering is a variation on bargaining. Someone may offer craftwork in exchange for your shoes or T-shirt. Some visitors take old clothing along specifically for this purpose, though I would like to think 'rich' Westerners would donate such garments to needy causes rather than using them as currency.

Finally, Zimbabweans have a great sense of humour and are delightful people, so please try to leave them with the same impression of you.

disease and will be of little use for carving. A forestry accreditation scheme was set up in late 2009 to endorse carvings made from sustainable sources, but it will be some time before it becomes implemented nationwide.

There is some delightful **jewellery** on offer in a range of materials, incorporating semi-precious stones, amber, silverware or intricately carved wood and stone, including rich green malachite bracelets, earrings and necklaces. Hopefully you'll want to help reduce poaching and won't be tempted to buy ivory, but if you do you'll need plenty of documentation to take it out of the country, and more to import it into your own. Note that some street sellers will offer you 'ivory' that is nothing of the sort. When you tell them firmly that you don't agree with buying ivory, they will actually admit that it's really only bone and the price will plummet accordingly.

Other craftware reflects Zimbabweans' great creativity and the ability to 'make a plan' when conventional raw materials are unavailable. If bottle tops, drinks cans, telephone cable and elephant dung sound like unlikely materials for decorating your living room, walk into a curio shop in Victoria Falls and prepare to be amazed. You'll find the most charming **sculptures** fashioned out of discarded metal, and elephant droppings, bleached and processed, make a rough paper ideal for photo albums, visitors books, etc. Natural materials such as guineafowl and peacock feathers, porcupine quills and seedpods are combined with delicately coiled wire to embellish these handmade creations so that each one is truly unique. On a larger scale, recycled metal is used to make lifelike, life-size warthogs, guineafowl and storks intended as garden ornaments (weld art) – although there's no reason they can't live indoors (I have a whole menagerie, including a full-sized ostrich, in my lounge).

There's a dazzling array of **fabrics** available for both clothing and furnishing, many of them incorporating traditional designs. You can buy bolts of fabric or ready-made curtains, tablecloths and cushion covers. Certainly anyone looking to furnish or dress in bold, rich earth colours and patterns should start their fabric sourcing in Zimbabwe.

Traditional **basket** makers produced utilitarian items but even these carried attractive patterns. Now skills have been honed to produce a wealth of intricate woven patterns, often with coloured inserts, again drawing on symmetrical, cultural designs. (If you are buying basketware and planning to travel through Botswana check first because at the time of writing Botswana was banning their importation.)

Shona **stone carvings** are a relatively modern art form, but have achieved international acclaim in recent decades and are much sought after by galleries and collectors. Some are finely crafted animals and human faces, while the majority are beautifully smoothed and rounded, stylised forms drawing on ancestral spirits, gods, humans and animals for inspiration. You'll see many in the shops of Harare, Bulawayo and Victoria Falls, but look for genuine art rather than mass-produced tourist items. Don't be concerned about getting these heavy items home, as every retail outlet has a connection with a packing and shipping agent.

Probably the largest item you will be tempted to buy is teak furniture. You may be lucky enough to find something manufactured from recycled railway sleepers although the supply of these has pretty well dried up and they are now on the expensive side of expensive. Alternative woods are now being used, so quiz your supplier to make sure they are coming from renewable sources.

ARTS AND ENTERTAINMENT

Zimbabwe has an amazingly rich and vibrant arts scene covering all genres from stone and scrap-metal sculptures (weld art) to the full range of performing arts. This art scene was well established in relation to most other countries in the region, thanks to a long tradition of encouragement and sponsorship both from within and outside the country. However, like everything else in recent Zimbabwe, art in general has suffered from the politico-economic situation. Interestingly, though, some genres, such as song, poetry and theatre, have grown by espousing protest themes.

Zimbabwe's contemporary art scene can trace its origins back to the late 1950s when the then curator of the National Gallery, Frank McEwan, possibly following the example set in the 1940s by Canon Paterson of Cyrene Mission and Father Groeber of Serima Mission, recognised the innate artistic talent of the Shona people and established workshops in which they were encouraged to develop their creativity, not by instruction but by learning from each other. From this process emerged the outstandingly successful new genre of Shona stone sculpture. It was so successful worldwide that it quickly came to overshadow the other emergent art forms. In 1975 in an effort to establish some balance, two very influential people in the local art world, Derek Huggins and Helen Lieros, opened **Gallery Delta** in Harare as a showcase for established and emerging contemporary artists working in graphics, textiles, ceramics and of course paintings. Talented artists were few and far between in the early days but things really took off in the 1980s and Gallery Delta thrives today mounting exhibitions throughout the year. Their intimate courtyard provides space for theatre and jazz performances (see page 164).

Another very important and influential venue in Harare, mainly for performing arts, is the **Book Café** (see page 164). It is heavily oriented towards up-and-coming artistes and on their website you'll see no end of initiatives (including workshops and discussion groups) under way to encourage this talent. Here you'll find a packed programme of alternative music and poetry performances and there's really no better place than here to get in touch with Zimbabwe's current music and poetry scene. Visitors from earlier years will note that the venue has changed since 2012.

Not to be missed if you are here at the right time is the week-long **Harare International Festival of Arts** (*www.hifa.co.zw*). The festival takes place around April/May. Billing itself as a celebration of the best of Zimbabwean arts and culture, it's actually the annual culmination of the work of a charitable trust involving countrywide training programmes for young people including street youths. It runs outreach and training programmes to develop not just latent artistic talent but also leadership and management skills. The extra component gained from collaborating with regional and international performers is seen as vital to increasing Zimbabwe's artistic depth. The festival itself takes place in Harare and while it features the complete range of performing arts, only a look at their website can give you an idea of the very impressive range of performances on offer. Also in Harare during March/April the Pambeni Trust, in conjunction with the Book Café, present a five day Youth Festival with a wide variety of musical genres from throughout the continent. The **Bulawayo Music Festival** is held every two years at the Acadamy of Music though it is much smaller than HIFA. The next festival is scheduled for 2014; contact Michael Bullivant (e *music@gatorzw*) for more details. Also in Bulawayo is the annual **Intwasa Arts Festival** (*www.intwasa.org*) with a fun, eclectic mix of performances and events.

For several years now Victoria Falls has hosted the Falls Fest over the New Year period and this has an excellent combination of ethnic and western rock music.

On a smaller scale, the **Chimanimani Arts Festival** also offers a brilliant array of performances but for now it is necessary to do an internet search for details of the next three-day festival.

A great website to check what's going on is www.zimbabwearts.org.

MEDIA

Zimbabwe's own broadcast media are state-controlled by the Zimbabwe Broadcasting Corporation (ZBC) with no independent radio or TV stations allowed. (This state of affairs has a long tradition in the country and directly follows the example set by pre-independence premier Ian Smith.) One of the first goals of the Government of National Unity was to relax or repeal many of the media restrictions, but perhaps unsurprisingly there has been slow progress on this front.

Radio is the most accessible news medium and is used to good effect in rural areas by government, especially during the run-up to elections, although satellite stations from foreign countries occasionally provide a counter view. Newspapers have a reasonably good measure of independence and several are openly critical of the regime but the situation here is fluid, resulting in the periodic firing of journalists and editors by the Ministry of Information and the banning of those titles deemed to be too critical. Needless to say, as the internet becomes more and more available urbanised Zimbabweans have access to a range of news programming undreamt of just a few years ago. Many accommodations boast DSTV satellite programming in their rooms. Television addicts may be thrilled at the prospect but subsequently disappointed when they discover the very thin range of programming generally on offer.

If you would like to keep up to date with the very latest Zimbabwe news, log onto www.zimonline.co.za; www.zimbabwesituation.com; www.zimdiaspora.com; www.thezimbabwean.co.uk or www.zim2day.com.

Major state-run newspapers are the *Chronicle*, the *Standard*, *Herald*, *Sunday Mail*, and independents include the *Independent*, *Daily News*, *Telegraph*, *The Zimbabwean* and *Financial Gazette* (although this is now considered by many to be effectively state run).

COMMUNICATIONS

With chronic power shortages, blackouts are common and telephonic communication has been hard hit. While landlines have suffered from years of non-maintenance mobile phone networks are picking up the slack.

LANDLINES The once well-developed landline system now provides a rather shaky service, with frequent network collapses, the result of lack of maintenance (plus cable theft). Nevertheless it is rapidly getting more reliable.

Zimbabwe's country code is 263. Area codes are shown in listings or at the start of sections on larger towns in *Part Two: The Guide*.

MOBILE TELEPHONES Coverage by mobile telephone ('cellphone' in southern Africa) has been very patchy in Zimbabwe, and generally available only in the vicinity of towns. However, 2011 saw the erection of a large number of signal masts around the country and the mobile phone situation has greatly improved. Local SIM cards are now readily available and the networks are not as oversubscribed as previously. Nevertheless, persistence is frequently required when dialling and be prepared for the signal to drop mid-conversation. If you happen to be close to an international border, you may be able to pick up a good roaming signal from the neighbouring country's network. Mobile phone numbers begin 07.

SATELLITE TELEPHONES Self-drivers to remote areas may consider it prudent to purchase or hire a satellite telephone for emergency use, especially if you are in a

3

convoy of one. Many roads and tracks in the national parks and rural Zimbabwe are so remote that in the event of an accident or breakdown it could be days before another vehicle passes by. Used in conjunction with a GPS, a satellite phone allows you to describe your precise location.

The prevailing political situation demands great discretion when using a satellite phone. These have been considered by the authorities as evidence that you are a foreign journalist, and you may have a lot of explaining to do and may face arrest. Don't use it anywhere in public, and keep it hidden in your car, well out of the way of roadblock searches.

EMAIL The year 2009, as in so many other fields, heralded the rebirth of the internet in Zimbabwe and with it a reliable email system. Internet connection speeds are still lamentably slow compared with the first world but progress is being made almost by the month. There has been widespread laying of fibre optic cabling but, as I write, few if any connections have yet been made outside of Harare. Public access Wi-Fi hotspots can be found in most major towns and increasingly hotels and restaurants are also offering the facility. Harare is particularly well served in this respect.

CAMERA ETIQUETTE

Photographing people requires sensitivity. We are all desperate to capture candid, local scenes, but all too often the most photogenic ones involve poverty – perhaps people in colourful but ragged clothing grinding maize in their village of thatched mud huts. Always ask permission and always respect the answer: in parts of Zimbabwe there are deep-seated spiritual objections to people being photographed. Generally, though, a polite request will be met with approval.

The problem then is that your subjects will invariably stop what they were doing and stand stiffly to attention, in exactly the rigid pose that you do not want. It helps if one of your party can be included in the shot, shaking hands, chatting, buying fruit from the stallholder. Afterwards, everyone will be delighted to see themselves on your camera's screen. People often ask you to send them a copy of the picture. If you agree to this, please honour the commitment, as it will invariably be the only photograph they have of themselves, and a prized possession.

It is understandably common for subjects to ask for payment. If it's a market shot you've taken, just buy an armful of produce. A straight request for money is trickier. While no-one wishes to encourage a begging mentality, the fact remains that they have given you something of value. If you are in a group, discuss it with your guide, as there is often an arrangement between the village headman and the tour company. If you're travelling independently, avoid handing over cash, but consider stocking your car with some basic consumables to use as gifts; toothpaste, soap, Vaseline or cooking oil are always appreciated in rural areas. If you can find room in your suitcase, bring some unwanted T-shirts; you will find no shortage of grateful new owners. Once you have handed over your gift, they may respond with a round of gentle hand clapping, their way of saying 'Thank you'.

Note the comments in the box, page 147, regarding photographing prohibited subjects.

SKYPE Use of the internet phone service Skype is increasing among accommodations and booking agencies, adding a welcome alternative medium.

CULTURAL ETIQUETTE

GREETINGS Zimbabwean cultures have some strict rules regarding what is and is not polite. For instance, it is considered impolite for a younger person to address or greet an older person first. So don't be put out if someone fails to say 'Good morning' to you; they may simply be waiting for you, if you are the older person, to make the first greeting, whereupon you will always get a cheery response.

Zimbabwe shares greeting formalities found throughout southern Africa. Unlike in the West where it is generally acceptable to launch straight into a conversation with a stranger, here life is less urgent and every single conversation, whether a question to a shop assistant, an enquiry about directions or a greeting to an official, must be initiated by each party enquiring as to the other's well-being. Only after both have responded is it polite to ask your question. The format is as follows:

One of you starts off with: 'Hello, how are you?'
Response: 'I'm fine, and yourself?'
Finally: 'I'm fine, thanks.'
Only then can you progress to: 'Please can you tell me ... ?'

Zimbabweans are keen handshakers, and use the 'three-stage thumb grasp'. Stage one is a normal grip, then slide your hands up to grasp each other's thumbs, then back down again to stage one. Practise it at home. It can sometimes get a little awkward, though: people who deal a lot with Westerners often use a simple handshake, resulting in a bit of fumbling as each tries to adopt the other's custom.

White Zimbabweans invariably use a standard Western-style handshake with other whites.

NAMES As well as their traditional family names, many Zimbabweans adopt English forenames, frequently those with aspirational or positive connotations. It's usual to meet people with names like Innocent, Polite, Prayer, Happiness, Trythings, Blessing, Trust or Lovemore. (Some, not so fortunate, are called Doubt, and I once met a Guilt.) First-time visitors may find this amusing, but don't forget it wasn't too long ago that Patience, Prudence and Faith were common names in England.

If you are a man, aged approximately 50 or above, you may well hear yourself being referred to as *madulla*, loosely translated as 'old man'. Zimbabweans treat old age with reverence so although you may initially be taken aback, this is in fact a mark of respect. Similarly, ladies may hear the roughly equivalent term *gogo* applied to them, an affectionate term for 'granny'.

CONVERSATION With a 90% English literacy rate, Zimbabweans are proud of the fact that they speak good English. Although it is a second language for most, they all understand that their command of English is worlds better than your knowledge of their language so if this conversation is going to go anywhere at all, it had better be in English. They also take every opportunity to practise their English, so your initial attempt to speak their language invariably produces a response, and the rest of the conversation, in English. (Zulu-speakers from South Africa will be able to converse easily with Ndebele people.)

3

You will occasionally hear white Zimbabweans talking with black Zimbabweans in an African-sounding language that isn't Shona or Ndebele. The odd English word creeps in, in much the same way that Indians frequently drop English into their own-language sentences. What you are hearing is *chilapalapa*, a simple, basic hybrid language developed in 19th-century southern Africa so that white mine and farm managers could communicate with their black workers. It is a blend of English, Shona, some Ndebele and Afrikaans (its close cousin *fanagolo* in South Africa includes more Afrikaans and little English).

Unlike other pidgin or Creole languages, *chilapalapa* is heavily based on indigenous languages rather than those of the colonising powers. *Chilapalapa*- and *fanagolo*-speakers can often make themselves understood anywhere in southern Africa, and it can be invaluable for the more adventurous traveller.

Nevertheless, in Zimbabwe it should only be used with great sensitivity. It was essentially a language for boss/worker situations, lacks sophistication and has little relevance in a social context. So while I have occasionally heard it used in rural Zimbabwe in a non-work context, usually amongst the older generation of both races, its use is not appreciated by educated Zimbabweans (a high percentage of the population, most of whom can speak English). Certainly in towns it is frowned upon as a patronising and insulting remnant of colonial Africa. Nevertheless, out in the bush where English may not be understood, a sensitive trial of *chilapalapa* or *fanagolo* may well bridge the language gap.

When offering or accepting anything by hand it is customary for Zimbabweans to gently touch the forearm of their giving or accepting hand as a non-verbal way of saying thank you.

GIFTS FOR CHILDREN Although it's tempting to present Zimbabwe's impoverished rural children with gifts, please think about it carefully. It's all too easy to set up expectations and encourage a begging culture, which is thankfully rare in Zimbabwe. Please don't take sweets for children, but if you do so, never throw them out of the car window as you pass through a village. South Africans have been doing this in Mozambique for years with the result that you get chased by hordes of little children shouting 'Sweets, sweets!' everywhere you go.

More useful and less harmful are pens, pencils and notebooks, all of them much sought after in rural schools. Try to find the headteacher or someone in authority to hand them over to, to avoid jealousy and ensure the goods are put to good use. Finally, and of course, you are doing no long-term favours by handing out money to children – quite the opposite in fact.

OFFICIALDOM If you are travelling independently you will meet two kinds of officials – border officials and traffic police.

If you present yourself as courteous and co-operative, the person you are dealing with is likely to return the favour. If you are abrupt, obstructive, facetious or rude, why be surprised if he makes life difficult for you? Greet them with a smile and, in the African way, ask how they are.

There seem to be few of the traffic police scams encountered in neighbouring countries although, confusingly, locals will tell you otherwise. Needless to say, always insist on paperwork and an official receipt for any fine you do have to pay. While it's essential to remain pleasant and polite, always try to adopt an air of confidence as perceived weakness may result in an inflated 'fine'.

It's quite common for a roadblock policeman to say 'Aaah! You are from England/South Africa. What have you brought me from your country?' (a seasonal variation is 'Where is my Christmas present?'), accompanied by a hopeful smile. A polite, 'Sorry, nothing' is the right answer. Or maybe dip into your coolbox for a cold bottle of water or even a sandwich. Magazines and newspapers are also welcome. Courteously but firmly resist any request for money (I've never been asked for money by officials in Zimbabwe).

TRAVELLING POSITIVELY

As Zimbabwe's economic crisis bit ever deeper, more and more casualties were created, inevitably amongst those least able to help themselves: the poor, the sick and disabled, the very young and the aged. HIV/AIDS has taken a huge toll, stripping whole communities of a generation of parents and leaving thousands of orphans, many with AIDS themselves, to be looked after by their grandmothers. And then there's the wildlife, facing new levels of poaching and hunting or simply dying through lack of water.

It often takes tragedy to bring out the best in people, and this is certainly the case in Zimbabwe. Much charitable work is undertaken by small groups operating on a shoestring, on a neighbourhood basis and without formal organisation, publicity or fanfare. It is therefore difficult for visitors to contribute to these schemes, simply because they never hear about them.

The following is a short alphabetical list of local and internationally based groups and charities that are reasonably accessible to the short-term visitor and would greatly benefit from increased patronage.

CHILDREN IN THE WILDERNESS (CITW) (*Sue Goatley;* \+263 13 43371–4; m +263 712 208377; e sue@wilderness.co.zw; www.childreninthewilderness.com) Wilderness has a number of luxury lodges throughout southern Africa and recognises that if tourists are to continue to have wilderness areas to visit, rural children need to be educated to understand the importance of conservation and its relevance to their future lives.

CITW is an environmental and life skills educational programme for the next generation of decision makers, inspiring them to care for their natural heritage and to become the custodians of these areas for the future.

It's an ambitious programme that started with the realisation that malnourished children do not do well at school, so a nutrition programme was established to ensure that children in designated schools received a nutritious meal every day. The next emphasis was also in the schools, with a concerted drive to drastically reduce the teacher:pupil ratio from an average 1:60 down to 1:30, coupled with a teacher training programme with an environmental emphasis. Outside of school hours, environmental and lifeskills clubs have been established with regular Wilderness camp visits being run for selected pupils to introduce them to the possibilities of potential employment in the tourism, environmental and hospitality industries. CITW has also introduced a series of community offshoot programmes focusing on local sustainability projects such as knitting and crochet workshops, poultry projects with layers and broilers and vegetable gardening and vermiculture.

3

The excellent CITW website has full details on how you can get involved, sponsor or donate, including its popular volunteer programme, which features a comprehensive and varied range of activities including school, community and wildlife involvement.

ENVIRONMENT AFRICA (\+263 4 492142/3; e info@environmentafrica.org; www. environmentafrica.org)This voluntary organisation was formed by 'The Rhino Girls', Charley Hewat and Julie Edwards, after an epic 22,000km trans-continental bicycle journey to raise awareness and support for African endangered species such as the black rhino. This was followed by the publication of the book *Extinction is Forever*. Environment Africa operates in several southern African countries and is now one of Zimbabwe's leading environmental organisations, with branches in Victoria Falls and Manicaland, run by over 30 staff and supported by 700+ members. Most of its activities are community-based awareness programmes focusing on reducing poverty caused by environmental degradation. They have established a number of self-help projects in the Victoria Falls area as well as building partnerships with donors.

FRIENDS OF HWANGE (\ +263 4 707973; m +263 712 630152; e foh@strachans. co.zw; www.friendsofhwange.org) The wildlife in Hwange National Park is dependent on artificially pumped water during the dry season but although there are 56 pumps in the park, the economic and political woes of the country mean that Park authorities lack the money and resources to maintain and fuel the pumps. The Friends of Hwange Trust was formed in 2005 during a particularly bad drought and the resulting high wildlife mortality rates. The waterholes are currently the focus of the trust, and need 5,000 litres of diesel per month to keep them running. The trust raises money from sponsorships and donations to fund a programme of pump maintenance and fuel purchase, and the results to date have been exceptional. As an alternative to diesel they want to install eight windmills at a cost of US$14,000 each, and a long-term goal is solar power for the pumps. Once the trust feels it has stabilised the water availability situation it intends to devote attention to other measures such as anti-poaching. Donations are welcome.

IMIRE RHINO AND WILDLIFE CONSERVATION (\ +263 2 222354; m +263 774 510985; e volunteering@imire.org; www.imirevolunteers.org) Volunteers will be involved with a variety of conservation projects including working with black rhino and elephant, studying and learning about their behaviour; undertaking anti-poaching patrols to ensure the continued safety of the animals; helping to educate local schoolchildren about conservation, wildlife and the environment; and carrying out the ongoing daily activities required to run a game park. At Imire they believe that conservation must go hand in hand with community education and one of their aims is to enhance the relationships between conservancies and neighbouring communities through long-term sustainable conservation and farming practices. Imire welcomes researchers, students and postgraduates and they have a huge range of research projects for people to help out with. See also *Imire*, pages 173–4.

JAIROS JIRI ASSOCIATION (*cnr Birmingham & Lobengula rds, Southerton, Harare;* \ *+263 4 662545/6/8; cnr Leopold Takawira Av & Robert Mugabe Way, Bulawayo;* \ *+263 9 74331/2;* e *jjhq@yoafrica.com*) This long-established chain of shops sells goods made by, and for the benefit of, disabled people, with the proceeds funding vocational training centres, schools and scholarships, homes and hostels. Jairos Jiri once had six craft shops throughout Zimbabwe but economic pressures have forced the closure of some.

MOTHER AFRICA (e *admin@mother-africa.org; www.mother-africa.org*) This organisation offers both local and international volunteers the opportunity to

LEGAL CONSIDERATIONS

While life for the visitor to Zimbabwe is distinctly friendly and relaxed there are a few local laws and restrictions to be aware of. Most are typical of the region and taken for granted by seasoned travellers. The following is based on advice from the British Foreign Office. It's a long list but most of it is common sense; it would be wrong to view Zimbabwe as any more oppressive to the visitor than any other country – in most instances it is much less so.

In recent years the government has been extremely sensitive about the presence of foreign journalists, and only those with accreditation (potentially a lengthy and very restrictive approval process is required) are legally allowed to operate. British journalists have been particularly unwelcome. Since the elections in 2008 a number of people have been arrested on suspicion of journalism for taking pictures of sensitive places. Handheld GPS units and satellite phones are taken as evidence that you may be a journalist, so keep these out of sight at all times.

It is illegal to take photographs of government offices, border posts, embassies, airports, police or military installations and personnel. There is evidence of a recent hardening of attitude in this respect, so it's wise to avoid photographing anything that is not obviously a tourism subject. The area around State House in Harare (the president's official residence) is patrolled by armed members of the Presidential Guard, who do not allow loitering by motorists or pedestrians. Photography is strictly prohibited and you are advised to avoid this area altogether.

- Avoid political activities, and do not photograph demonstrations.
- The MDC salute is the hand held up with spread fingers, so be careful when you wave, as this could be construed by some as a political gesture.
- When driving, if you see the presidential motorcade approaching from either direction (you won't be able to miss the flashing blue lights) you must immediately pull completely off the road and wait until it has passed.
- It is unlawful to criticise the president or the state, so keep your conversations discreet in public places, especially in bars and when talking to strangers.
- Always carry your identity documentation or a copy of your passport.
- There are laws against indecency, which in Zimbabwe make homosexual acts illegal (see *Gay and lesbian travellers*, pages 112–13).
- Penalties for possession, use or trafficking in illegal drugs are strict and offenders can expect heavy fines or jail sentences.
- You should not carry any precious or semi-precious stones without the appropriate paperwork.
- It is against the law for civilians to wear any form of clothing made from camouflage material.

make a difference to local communities in western Zimbabwe. Projects include research on the southern ground hornbill, biodiversity surveys, helping out at local schools in Hwange and Matopos, working at a children's home (orphanage) in the Matopos, an old age home in Dete, Hwange, and a home for abused women and their children in Bulawayo.

VICTORIA FALLS ANTI-POACHING UNIT (\f +263 13 45821; m +263 712 209144; e cat@yoafrica.com) This operation, run by professional wildlife guide Charles Brightman, operates on a minimal budget (with generous support from local tourism stakeholders) patrolling Victoria Falls and Zambezi national parks and

VOLUNTEERING AND VOLUNTOURISM

As with most other developing countries, Zimbabwe offers many opportunities for people to volunteer their services in a wide range of activities including education, humanitarian and conservation endeavours. Almost invariably there will be some form of financial input required from you to cover accommodation, transport and meal costs but these vary considerably from charity to charity depending on the nature of their operation and the standards of lodging etc they are providing for you during your stay. Worldwide there are genuine charities desperate for your help and at the other end of the spectrum there are commercial concerns that have tapped into this potentially lucrative market to the extent that to all intents and purposes they are just another sector of the tourism market which have little or nothing of lasting value to contribute. Accusations of exploitation have been levelled at some in Zimbabwe, so it pays to do as much research as possible to ensure that your hard-earned money and your efforts will be put to good use and you're not just being used as a lucrative form of free labour.

Volunteering has become very popular in Zimbabwe but this increase in numbers has caused the immigration authorities to be alert to this sector to ensure that individuals seeking paid work are not entering the country under the guise of volunteering. This is in line with immigration practice around the world and may result in some quite close questioning on arrival in the country. Don't forget that although your intentions are laudable, in developing countries like Zimbabwe the concept of people doing work for no pay is virtually unheard of and can arouse suspicion.

The organisation you are going to work for will give you a briefing on the immigration procedures so follow their advice. You will be staying in the country on a holiday visa and it will probably be best to obtain this in advance in your home country rather than on arrival at the airport or border. Either way make absolutely sure you tick the 'tourist' box on the immigration form as you are NOT coming to work. Put the address of your programme as your 'host' address on the form. Wherever you obtain your visa make sure you have relevant paperwork from the charity you will be volunteering for. You can stay in Zimbabwe on a tourist visa for 180 days in each year but in practice you will probably be granted four weeks on arrival and then be required to renew it at monthly intervals. Failure to do so will incur heavy fines and deportation. Currently, the fourth-, fifth- and sixth-month renewals each involve a US$20 fee. After six months you have to leave the country for a 'significant' period of usually at least a month, before you are allowed to return.

surrounding areas. A team of 15 scouts includes several ex-poachers who have been 'turned', and they are constantly on the lookout for snares and other evidence of poaching activity. Since 1999 they have recovered a staggering 18,000 snares, and the unit's effectiveness is shown by the impressive annual reduction from over 4,000 found in the first year to fewer than 100 in 2008. This is frequently dangerous work but they have a record of nearly 600 arrests for serious offences, as well as rescuing and successfully treating over 100 wounded animals. VFAPU also has a remit to tackle indigenous hardwood poaching for the curio trade. The unit relies almost entirely on sponsorship and donations for staff wages, vehicle fuel and maintenance, animal darting and medical equipment, and the success of their operations can be seen in the ever-increasing population of wildlife in Zambezi National Park. Charles also offers guided walks and tours of Zambezi National Park, which he knows like the back of his hand (see *Activities* under *Zambezi National Park*, in *Chapter 7*, page 271,).

WILDLIFE AND ENVIRONMENT ZIMBABWE (WEZ) (*Mashonaland Branch Wildlife Shop, Mukuvisi Woodlands, Harare;* e *mash@utande.co.zw; www.wezmat.org*) WEZ aims to encourage Zimbabweans to take an interest in their wildlife heritage, and initiates or supports a range of conservation and research projects. It has developed a number of nature reserves offering camping and some chalet accommodation, and all are available for international visitors. Some of these camps and reserves are linked to WEZ Environmental Education Centres, where visitors can learn about the projects. The reserves are at Cecil Kop Nature Reserve, Mutare; Fort Rixon Dam, near Bulawayo; Kuburi Wilderness on Lake Kariba; Sable Park, Kwekwe; Shagashe Game Park, Masvingo; and Shashi Wilderness Park, Tuli.

VICTORIA FALLS WILDLIFE TRUST (formerly Wild Horizons Wildlife Trust) (e *info@victoriafallswildlifetrust.org; www.victoriafallswildlifetrust.org*) The charity is an independently funded, non-profit wildlife trust, promoting conservation awareness and education in local indigenous communities, in recognition of the fact that wildlife conservation can only progress with the co-operation and involvement of these local communities. Projects fall into four main categories: community outreach, wildlife research, wildlife orphanage and conservation training and include rehabilitation of injured or orphaned wildlife; anti-poaching and wildlife veterinary assistance; research into human/wildlife conflict issues; and disease monitoring of wildlife/domestic stock populations. The trust has built a wildlife laboratory and clinic in Victoria Falls, the only such specialist facility in the region. The main objective here is the treatment of injured or orphaned animals to be released back into the wild once they have recovered. For wildlife with injuries that are long term or permanent they will continue to look after the animal(s), and provide a soft-release into the 2,200ha fenced area. The trust runs regular wildlife educational and interactional visits for local schoolchildren. Full details of their current wildlife and community projects are available on their website as is information regarding their month-long, voluntary internship programme. Although independently run and funded, the trust has a close working relationship with Wild Horizons and is based at Elephant Camp.

ZAMBEZI SOCIETY (✆ +263 4 747004; *www.zamsoc.org*) Formed in 1982, the Zambezi Society is a conservation organisation focusing solely on conserving wildlife and wilderness in the Zambezi Valley, large tracts of which are designated as a UNESCO World Heritage Site. To achieve this it:

3

- **Conserves wildlife**: Maintains the Zambezi river basin's biodiversity which includes managing a number of wildlife conservation projects.
- **Educates**: Develops information and materials designed to make people more aware of the value of wild areas and the need to conserve them. Its Wildlife Outreach Programme focuses on rural schools adjacent to National Parks in the Zambezi Valley.
- **Supports parks**: Provides financial, logistical and material support for Protected Areas and National Parks in the Zambezi River basin, focusing on research, monitoring and anti-poaching programmes.
- **Provides information**: Increases public awareness about issues affecting the Zambezi river and its basin.
- **Lobbies for sensible planning**: Much of the Zambezi Valley is under pressure from both industrial and tourism development. The Society encourages people to find ways of using the natural resources of the Zambezi Basin without destroying them. It lobbies or advocates against development initiatives that are unsuitable or damaging to the biodiversity or wilderness values of the Zambezi environment.

How you can help: Full details of how to donate are on the society's website.

Natural World Safaris specialises in tailor-made journeys to Zimbabwe to experience the amazing wildlife & culture. Visit **www.naturalworldsafaris.com** for more info.

T: +44 (0) 1273 691 642 I **E:** sales@naturalworldsafaris.com

Part Two

THE GUIDE

4

Harare

Telephone code 04

Major international airlines withdrew their services from Harare in 2007–08, so the capital has been shunned and bypassed by overseas visitors for quite a number of years. Even in the boom days of the 1980s and 1990s it seldom featured in tourist itineraries other than as an enforced stopover for connecting flights. When visitor numbers became virtually non-existent in the early 2000s, Harare's tourism infrastructure – such as it was – crumbled.

Since then though, change has been dramatic. The unified government has begun returning Harare to its feet, bringing a degree of optimism unheard of for a decade. Much of the town is still fairly shabby with serious infrastructure problems affecting water and power delivery, and some tourism facilities need a major cash injection, but already work has begun to restore many attractions to their former glory. Most importantly, though, the city is alive again with traffic jams, and busy pavements and markets.

When everything is working, Harare (estimated population 1.6m) is a very pleasant town with plenty of parks and open spaces, wide streets lined with jacaranda and flamboyant trees, and pedestrian areas with upmarket shops and craft markets. It enjoys a thriving arts scene with galleries and museums, trendy restaurants and nightclubs; in fact pretty well everything you would expect in a capital city. In the leafy suburbs to the north you'll be surprised at the obvious affluence reflected in the beautiful private properties and the upmarket shopping centres that service them.

Harare has now returned to being a city with a lot to offer and the whole place is busily cleaning up its act. It's now become a town to recommend rather than apologise for.

HISTORY

After their long trek up from South Africa, Rhodes's 700-strong Pioneer Column of armed men and settlers arrived in this area of Mashonaland and on 12 September 1890 selected a marshy, poorly drained spot at the foot of a small *kopje* to establish a fort. They judged it good for agriculture and therefore a fine base for the farmers amongst the column and the settlers who would follow. The following day the column commander, Lieutenant Colonel Edward Pennefather, and the young corps leader, Major Frank Johnson, raised the Union Jack and named the site Fort Salisbury after the British prime minister of the time, the Marquess of Salisbury.

Fort Salisbury marked the end of the Pioneer Column's trek and soon after the fort was completed the column disbanded and men staked out their land claims. Thereafter settlers from the south began to arrive and the town rapidly developed.

The area was, of course, Shona territory, under the control of Chief Gutsa, although this mattered little to the settlers until six years later with the coming of the first *chimurenga* in 1896. While the Ndebele were laying siege to the whites in Bulawayo, the Shona followed suit in Salisbury with the town's white inhabitants spending six weeks sheltering in the town jail until reinforcements arrived.

In common with many of Zimbabwe's towns, the original fort site proved unsuitable for settlement, this time because of the drainage situation, and the town base was moved a short distance away from the *kopje* (west of Julius Nyerere Way) to the area around today's African Unity Square. When many of the original settlers refused to move, the original site was drained and subsequently developed, and to this day is known as Kopje.

Fort Salisbury was declared a municipality in 1897, became the de facto capital of Rhodesia in 1923 and a city in 1935. During the years of the Federation of Rhodesia and Nyasaland (1953–63) the city, now known simply as Salisbury, was the Federation capital. Following UDI, it became the capital of Ian Smith's Republic of Rhodesia. Not until two years after independence in April 1982 was the name changed to Harare, in recognition of the pre-colonial Shona chief, Neharawa.

Salisbury saw rapid growth, with investment in business and industry, and as the administrative and political centre of the country it never lacked for development funds. After independence this development continued, turning Harare into a thoroughly modern city, while Bulawayo, the country's second city and capital of Matabeleland, stagnated from lack of funding and investment. So while Bulawayo, by default rather than by design, retained much of its colonial feel, Harare marched into the 21st century, complete with skyscrapers and some unlovely multi-storey office blocks, many designed and built with communist-bloc aid and inspiration.

By 2008 it had become a troubled city, having been at the centre of political strife, often violent, for nearly a decade. The economic crisis hit Harare badly, with most of its infrastructure crippled, and it rapidly became uncared for and unkempt. Deep pot-holes scarred the roads, garbage remained uncollected for weeks and electricity was a rare luxury. Municipal services collapsed, with mains water unavailable for months at a time, resulting in a complete reliance on expensive borehole water. With clean water and sanitation denied to most of the city's residents, Harare and its nearby high-density housing area Chitungwiza was the source of the massive cholera outbreak of 2008–09.

Widespread and deep poverty led to a steep rise in crime, with many of the city's streets being no-go areas and nowhere safe to walk at night. Overseas foreign offices frequently warned against all but essential travel there. That was the situation until early 2009, when the creation of the Unity government brought a halt to the decline and the first glimmer of hope for a turnaround in fortunes. That glimmer has now turned into a very healthy flame.

GETTING THERE

BY AIR
International Harare International Airport is located 10km southeast of Harare. Fuel problems, airport power blackouts and a general lack of passengers drove major international airlines out of the airport in 2007–08, and only now are some tentatively returning. Emirates were the first to arrive, followed by KLM, while Air Zimbabwe ceased all long-haul operations in 2012. Meanwhile virtually all international, non-regional flights to Harare connect via Johannesburg. British Airways/Comair and South African Airways operate this route on a daily basis.

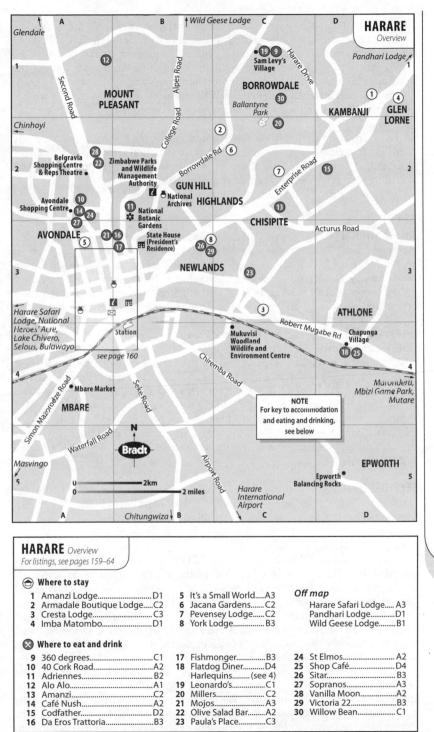

HARARE Overview
For listings, see pages 159–64

🛏 Where to stay

1	Amanzi Lodge	D1	
2	Armadale Boutique Lodge	C2	
3	Cresta Lodge	C3	
4	Imba Matombo	D1	
5	It's a Small World	A3	
6	Jacana Gardens	C2	
7	Pevensey Lodge	C2	
8	York Lodge	B3	

Off map

Harare Safari Lodge..... A3
Pandhari Lodge............D1
Wild Geese Lodge........B1

🍴 Where to eat and drink

9	360 degrees	C1
10	40 Cork Road	A2
11	Adriennes	B2
12	Alo Alo	A1
13	Amanzi	C2
14	Café Nush	A2
15	Codfather	D2
16	Da Eros Trattoria	B3
17	Fishmonger	B3
18	Flatdog Diner	D4
	Harlequins	(see 4)
19	Leonardo's	C1
20	Millers	C2
21	Mojos	A3
22	Olive Salad Bar	A2
23	Paula's Place	C3
24	St Elmos	A2
25	Shop Café	D4
26	Sitar	B3
27	Sopranos	A3
28	Vanilla Moon	A2
29	Victoria 22	B3
30	Willow Bean	C1

Domestic Air Zimbabwe has all but ceased operations with only the occasional announcement of selected internal flights. This has left a wide gulf with no scheduled services between the capital and main centres. Small, light aircraft operators fill some of the domestic gaps with charter flights connecting Harare with some of the outlying safari areas but at somewhat prohibitive fares and often minimal baggage allowances. Executive Air, Solenta and Wilderness Air are names to look for but you won't find fares on their websites as they quote on request.

BY RAIL There are currently no international rail services serving Harare. Daily overnight first-class sleeper services to Bulawayo (9 hours) are exceptionally cheap at about US$10, but at the time of writing, service standards were poor. Be vigilant regarding your valuables and luggage at the stations.

The railway station is on Kenneth Kaunda Avenue at the bottom of 2nd Street.

BY COACH
International Three South African coach companies, Greyhound (*www.greyhound.co.za*), Translux (www.translux.com) and Intercape (*www.intercape.co.za*) ply the daily route from Johannesburg via Bulawayo (Intercape via Masvingo) (14–16 hours, overnight) with comfortable, modern vehicles. These coaches use the terminal on the corner of Robert Mugabe Road and 5th Street and you'll find other coach operators here too but with less well-established reputations as the above three.

Domestic A growing number of intercity coach services ply the routes to Harare from the major towns, including Beitbridge, but few details are currently published.

Pathfinder, City Link and Defu operate to/from Bulawayo taking around 7 hours (US$30) via Kadoma, Kwekwe and Gweru and on to Victoria Falls, around 12½ hours (US$60) via Hwange (US$45). Only Pathfinder (*115 Nelson Mandela Ave, cnr of 5th St* \ *2936907/8;* m *0772 694144/5; www.pathfinderlx.com*) has a website showing routes and schedules. City Link (\ *783424*) picks up and drops off at Rainbow Group hotels in Harare, Bulawayo and Victoria Falls. Other companies to watch for are Senatar Express, Tombs, Pioneer, PCG Motorways, KK Cheetah and Eagle Liner.

SELF-DRIVE Harare is easily accessible from the main towns, including Beitbridge (580km/360 miles), Bulawayo (439km/273 miles), Masvingo (292km/181 miles), Mutare (363km/225 miles) and Victoria Falls (878km/545 miles).

GETTING AROUND

ORIENTATION Harare is a very large residential town by Zimbabwean standards yet the city centre, as far as most visitors will be concerned, is remarkably compact and can be strolled around in a couple of hours. The main shopping area, centred on pedestrianised 1st Street, is contained in a square formed by Samora Machel Avenue, 4th Street, Kenneth Kaunda Avenue and Julius Nyerere Way. On 1st Street you'll find fast-food outlets, internet cafés, department stores and clothes shops as well as Barclays bank and the main shops.

There are a number of small shopping malls – Karigamombe Centre by Julius Nyerere Way and Union Avenue, Eastgate Centre behind Meikles Hotel, and Intermarket Life Towers on Jason Moyo Avenue next to Meikles. Immediately outside the compact central shopping area, especially to the south and west, the streets house a noisy jumble of shops selling everything from cheap clothes to hardware and electrical goods, most of it Chinese, but there's little other than local atmosphere to tempt you here.

As in Bulawayo, there are actually two road grid systems. In the main town grid system, all roads that run north–south are named 'streets' while all those that run east–west are named 'avenues'. However, in Kopje – the second, smaller grid west of Julius Nyerere Way – some east–west roads are also named 'streets', which can be confusing. Many of the accommodations and restaurants are situated in the affluent northern suburbs, notably Borrowdale, Chisipite, Avondale, Newlands and Arundel. For these you'll need a taxi or your own vehicle.

SAFETY You'll be very safe walking around most of Harare during the day, but don't flaunt your jewellery and be careful of pickpockets especially in crowded markets and at bus/taxi stations. The further away you stray from the central business district (CBD), the more likely you are to be mugged. It is not safe to walk anywhere at night, so take taxis. You should avoid Harare Gardens from late afternoon/dusk as it has a reputation for crime, and Kopje is not a good place to walk around. The market at Mbare (known as the *musika*) in the high-density housing area is thriving and well worth a visit but it used to have a negative reputation. It's little visited by tourists but those that do go there these days all seem to get a great welcome. Just take the usual precautions.

When driving through town, keep all doors locked, all valuables out of site, be vigilant at traffic lights and don't tempt people with your nice wristwatch or bracelet hanging out of an open window. Street parking should be avoided if possible but if you must, be prepared to pay street kids to 'look after' your car; if you don't you could be in for an expensive surprise when you return. There is an official system of parking permits sold by street sellers. If you are staying outside of the town centre, it's probably easier to take a taxi into town rather than your own car, and book a return collection.

Be very careful not to stray too close to the president's residence on Chancellor Avenue, at the top of 7th Street. There's a barrier that closes the road to traffic and pedestrians from dusk to dawn. President Mugabe is exceptionally well protected, and his armed guards won't hesitate to arrest you – or to open fire on anyone who strays into the forbidden area during curfew hours. ZANU-PF's head office is near the Rainbow Towers Hotel on Pennefather Avenue, and officials commonly frequent the upmarket hotels, bars and restaurants in town. Be careful not to voice anything that could be construed as a criticism of the president or his party, in public places where you could be overheard (it is actually illegal to do so).

BY TAXI Metered taxis are the easiest and most reliable way to get around. There are a number of private taxi companies but they and their phone numbers seem to be ever changing. The best places to find them are in ranks near the big hotels. Hotel porters and bellboys can give you the phone numbers of the most reliable companies. If you are leaving the city centre, you'll find taxis very thin on the ground for your return journey, so take a phone number or book your return in advance. Try Rixi (✆ 753080/2) or Min Taxi (✆ 762280). You should expect to pay around US$10 for a taxi between the city centre and most of the suburbs. Airport taxis charge approximately US$1 per kilometre so allow US$20–25 for a ride into town. Feedback from the first edition of this book suggests that you should now negotiate a price before setting off rather than rely on the meter, some of which are apparently 'doctored'. This will be difficult to gauge for a first-time visitor so you are advised to seek advice on fares from a hotel concierge or other staff in the lobby.

BY MINIBUS Locals travel on commuter minibuses. These have fixed routes and rates, but working out which goes where and when is beyond all but the most determined and intrepid visitor. They tend to wait until they are chock-full before setting off with stereos blaring, so you can be in for a hot, very noisy and uncomfortable ride.

BY LOCAL BUS These old wrecks mainly operated by ZUPCO (known as 'chicken buses') are of academic interest only. A few years ago they were a budget option and a great way to mingle with the locals. In recent years these old boneshakers were kept on the road using bits cobbled from scrapyards far and wide. Now they've been resurrected and can be seen crabbing along (follow directly behind one and marvel at the fact that you can clearly see all four wheels due to their misalignment) belching black diesel smoke. Newer models are now beginning to take to the roads between major centres so hopefully reliability will start to return.

BY CAR
Car hire
🚗 **Avis** 3rd & Jason Moyo St; ✆707721; airport 575 4047, www.avis.co.zw

🚗 **Defu Travel & Tours** 27 Wheeler Av; ✆747027, 778803; e maxwell@defutravel.co.zw

🚗 **Europcar** Cnr St Patrick's & Airport rds, 4km from airport; ✆575592; www.europcar.com

🚗 **Excellence** 20 Cleveland Av; ✆700222, 703354; e excellence@africaonline.co.zw

🚗 **LED** ✆798928/9; www.ledcarrental.co.zw

🚗 **Msuna Safaris and Travel** www.msuna.co.zw

Car parking There's off-street parking on the corner of Park Lane and Leopold Takawira Avenue near the Crowne Plaza Monomatapa Hotel; in the Parkade Shopping Centre on Samora Machel Avenue between 1st and 2nd streets; George Silunduka between 4th and 5th; Julius Nyerere between Jason Moyo and Nelson Mandela Avenue. There is now a system of legal parking permits sold on the street in much the same way as phone airtime top-ups – leave the ticket visible on the dashboard.

TOURIST INFORMATION

Staff at the **Zimbabwe Tourism Authority** (*55 Samora Machel Av;* ✆ *758730/4;* m *0773 384844;* e *info@ztazim.co.zw; www.zimbabwetourism.net;* ☉ *08.00–16.30 Mon–Fri, closed w/ends & public holidays*) are very helpful, although they tend to be very short on brochures and literature.

As with other municipal publicity offices around the country you will be disappointed with the **Harare Publicity Association** (*2nd St at Africa Unity Sq*). The brochure racks are pretty well empty and the staff are sadly uninformed. It would be good to think that the return of tourists will turn things around, but this office never had a reputation as a mine of information.

At the **Zimbabwe Parks and Wildlife Management Authority** (*cnr Borrowdale Rd & Sandringham Dr, Botanical Gdns;* ✆ *706077/8;* e *bookings@zimparks.co.zw; www.zimparks.org;* ☉ *08.00–16.00 Mon–Fri*) you can collect a wide range of leaflets and book your Park accommodation. Communication links between here and individual parks are haphazard to say the least, so keep your receipt and booking slip for the park warden on arrival, as they may not be expecting you.

A very good events and listings site is www.bambazonke.co.zw and you should also look out for the excellent monthly magazine *Ndeipe* which is available at many tourism outlets and contains a wealth of 'what's on' information.

TOUR OPERATORS

The following operators all offer a range of services, including city and local area tours, transport to specific destinations, and can arrange accommodation and itineraries.

Agents Africa ☏252981; e Kristina@agentsafrica.co.zw
Armadillo ☏302261; www.armadillotvl.com
Defu Travel & Tours 27 Wheeler Av; ☏747027, 778803; e maxwell@defutravel.co.zw
Msuna Safaris & Travel 74 Selous Av; ☏705703/16; e christina@msuna.co.zw, tina2chitekwe@yahoo.com
Nyati Travel 29 Rhodesville Avenue; ☏495804; e info@nyati.co.zw; nyati-travel.com

Rockshade 113 Samora Machel Av; ☏701803/5; e marketing@rockshade.co.zw; www.rockshade.co.zw
Safari Consultants ☏851979; e accmanager@safafrica.com
Sunset Tours 37 Victoria Dr, Newlands; ☏011 202840; e shirley@sunset.co.zw
Tourism Services Zimbabwe 2 Beit Av, Milton Park; ☏13 43368/41288; e info@tourservzim.co.zw

⌂ WHERE TO STAY

As well as the central options listed below, there are some delightful accommodations situated in Harare's spacious and scenic suburbs offering luxury and fine dining away from the hustle and bustle of the city.

CITY CENTRE
Luxury

⌂ **Meikles Hotel** (317 rooms) Cnr Jason Moyo Av & 3rd St; ☏251705, 707721; e meikles@meikles.com; www.meikles.com. This grand dame of colonial-style hotels is one of the city's landmarks, centrally situated, overlooking Africa Unity Sq. It dates from 1915 & is part of the great trading empire set up by the 3 Meikles brothers in the late 19th century. It keeps winning international accolades & is rather more of an upmarket business hotel than a leisure hotel. It has 2 restaurants, La Fontaine & the Pavilion, an elegant tea lounge & the popular Explorers Club bar, festooned with teak, Baines prints, wicker chairs & hunting trophies. Note the plush bar has a dress code requiring collared shirts, enclosed shoes & no caps. Hotel facilities include solar-heated rooftop pool with bar, gym, sauna, hair salon, massage & beauty parlour. **$$$$**

⌂ **Bronte Hotel** (94 rooms, 8 suites) 132 Baines Av; ☏707522/7; www.brontehotel.com. This charming old-world Cape Dutch building & annexe is just north of central Harare in a peaceful area known as The Avenues. It's set within walled gardens scattered with Shona sculptures, ponds & pools. It has a lovely garden to relax in after the hustle of the nearby city, but the hotel is deservedly very popular so advance bookings are necessary. 2 restaurants – the excellent Emmanuels & the Palms restaurant **$$$**

Upmarket

⌂ **Rainbow Towers** (previously Harare Sheraton) (305 rooms) Pennefather Av; ☏772633/9; e reservations@rainbowtowers.co.zw; www.therainbowtowershotel.com. Although built back in the 1980s & now looking sadly dated both inside and out this is still one of the most modern buildings in Harare & not unattractive with its gold-clad futuristic design. It has a spacious foyer with a pianist in the evenings, a bar, 2 restaurants including Kombahari, where you sit around a grill & watch your steak being cooked in front of you; they also serve a Japanese menu. The hotel's upmarket status has slipped quite a bit since its Sheraton days & it could do with a complete refurbish but the b/fast buffet in the Harvest Garden restaurant is superb & could well be your main meal of the day. All the facilities you would expect in a hotel of this quality including gym & large pool. **$$$–$$$$**

⌂ **Cresta Jameson Hotel** (123 rooms) Cnr Samora Machel Av & Park St; ☏774106; e reservations@jameson.cresta.co.zw; www.cresta-hospitality.com. Although unlovely on the outside this is another good city-centre hotel catering largely for the business market. **$$$**

⌂ **Cresta Oasis** (110 rooms) 124 Nelson Mandela Av; ☏704217/9; e reservations@oasis.cresta.co.zw; www.cresta-hospitality.com.

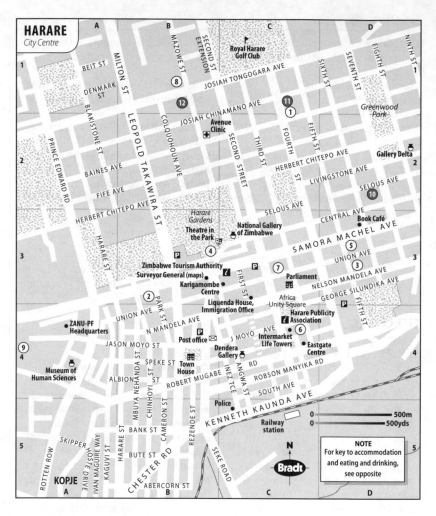

HARARE
City Centre

Comfortable, quiet, good value with terrace garden & pool, close to the city centre. **$$$**

🏠 **Crowne Plaza Monomotapa** (180 rooms) 54 Park Lane; ☎704501. You can't miss this huge 20-storey, rabbit warren of a hotel & while you could hardly call it intimate, it is conveniently located overlooking Harare Gdns with large, comfortable rooms & all the facilities you require. It also has 2 restaurants & an excellent b/fast buffet. **$$$**

🏠 **Holiday Inn** (201 rooms) Samora Machel Av; ☎251200; e pacro@africansunhotels.com; www.

africansunhotels.com. This worldwide chain needs no introduction – good quality, reliable but lacking personality. It has its own Vumba restaurant & Spur steakhouse franchise. Well recommended for an overnight stay. **$$$**

🏠 **New Ambassador Hotel** (72 rooms) 88 Union Av; ☎708121/3/4; e reservations@ rainbowambassador.com. This centrally located business hotel has all the facilities you need for an overnight stay & is good value for money. **$$$**

OUT OF TOWN
Luxury

🏠 **Amanzi Lodge** (9 lodges) 1 Masasa Lane, Kambanji; ☎499257; m 077 245310; e lodge@

amanzi.co.zw. Tucked away in the northern suburbs you'll find this delightful lodge with

⊖ **Where to stay**
1 Bronte Hotel........................C1
2 Cresta Jameson Hotel.....B3
3 Cresta Oasis........................D3
4 Crowne Plaza
  Monomatapa.................B3
5 Holiday Inn.........................D3
6 Meikles Hotel.....................C4
7 New Ambassador............C3
8 Palm Lodge........................B1
9 Rainbow Towers.............. A4

⊗ **Where to eat and drink**
10 Coimbra..............................D2
11 Emmanuel's........................C1
12 Gaby's................................. B1
   Kombahari...................(see 9)
   La Fontaine..................(see 6)

gardens, waterfalls & rock features designed by one of Zimbabwe's leading landscape architects. The en-suite thatched lodges are individually decorated in the styles of different African countries. Pamper yourself in the salon with massage, manicure, pedicure, facial, reflexology, aromatherapy & reiki or get active outside on the floodlit all-weather tennis court; also cricket net, bowling machine & heated swimming pool. Excellent restaurant a short distance away at 158 Enterprise Rd & free transfers from the lodge. **$$$$**

🛏 **Armadale Boutique Lodge** (9 rooms, 1 cottage) 9 Armadale Rd, Borrowdale; ☏ 882781 m 0772 275716; e armadale@zol.co.zw; www. armadalelodge.com. A stunning 1904 house in the northern suburbs, has 3 suites & 6 en-suite bedrooms plus a 2-bedroom cottage all set in delightful 2.5 acre garden. Self-catering is available in cottage. Luxurious modern furnishings with all rooms opening onto gardens; pool, free Wi-Fi, spa & gym. **$$$$**

🛏 **Imba Matombo** (15 rooms & lodges) 3 Albert Glen Cl, off Enterprise Rd, Glen Lorne; ☏ 499013/4, 499994; e imba@zol.co.zw; www. imbahotel.com. Luxury boutique hotel high on a hill in Harare's pleasant suburb of Glen Lorne, a 15min drive northeast. Accommodation is in the classic main house built of stone & thatch as well as in wonderfully decorated private lodges, all set in delightful gardens. Take your sundowners on the thatched veranda or on cooler nights beside a big log fire indoors. Outside there is a very large pool with panoramic views & tennis

courts; indoors they have a gym & the renowned restaurant serves a gourmet menu created by imported chefs. **$$$$**

🛏 **Pandhari Lodge** (75 rooms inc 4 exec, 3 suites) 3 Barlow Cl, off Enterprise Rd, Glen Lorne; ☏ 494918/9; f 494916; e pandhari@pandhari. co.zw; www.pandharilodge.co.zw. Just 20 mins from the city centre in the suburbs, this very pleasant lodge is quiet & secluded. All rooms are en suite with satellite TV & fridge. Inside & outside dining & bar, pool, gym & tennis court. **$$$**

🛏 **Wild Geese Lodge** (10 rooms) 2 Buckland Lane, off Alpes Rd, Borrowdale; ☏ 2930379, 2917977/9; e info@wildgeese.co.zw; www. wildgeeselodge.co.zw. This much recommended lodge is set within a private wildlife sanctuary offering 12ha of indigenous garden & savanna overlooking the spectacular Mazowe Hills yet it's only 15mins from Harare centre. Accommodation is spacious & elegant including 2 executive suites luxuriously finished in what the owners call their own urban-safari style. Prices include guided walking safari in the savanna where you'll see zebra & a variety of antelope including sable, eland & kudu. **$$$**

🛏 **York Lodge** (8 suites) 1 York Av, Newlands; ☏ 776239; www.yorklodge.com. Originally the residence of the district commissioner of Newlands, York Lodge is a beautiful colonial house situated just a 5min drive from the centre & 15mins from Harare airport. Although close to the city centre, traffic noise is almost non-existent. The 8 luxury en suites come with dbl or twin beds & all open onto wide pillared verandas overlooking a tropical garden. Facilities including telephone, satellite TV, hairdryer, ceiling fan, safe, room service, airport transfers, swimming pool, tennis court & secure parking as well as fax, email, broadband & Wi-Fi. A spacious visitor's lounge in the main house has satellite TV. No children under 12. Rates are for B&B although they can provide dinner by prior arrangement or make reservations at local restaurants for you. **$$$**

🛏 **Casa Kadiki** (11 rooms) Chisipite; ☏ 490352; m 0772 237497; e mikeles@zol.co.zw. This exclusive & most welcoming B&B gets deservedly rave reviews & is in close proximity to the northern suburb's shops & top restaurants, 8km from town. Beautifully decorated, individually themed rooms are en suite with DSTV, Wi-Fi access, minibar &

fridge, with access onto landscaped gardens with splash pool. Dinner provided by prior arrangement or there's accommodation with fully equipped kitchen for self-catering. Airport & town transfers. **$$–$$$**

Upmarket

🏠 **Pevensey Lodge** (6 rooms) 6 Pevensey Rd, Highlands 🛒499257; e reservations@amanzi. co.zw. Homely Tuscan-style villa with a very individual style rich in Moroccan earthy colours. All rooms are en suite. Less formal than its other Amanzi sister properties & with pool, large garden & games room it's great for children. **$$$**

🏠 **Cresta Lodge** (158 rooms) 7km east of town, cnr Samora Machel Av & Robert Mugabe Rd; 🛒486203/7, 487000; e reslodge@cresta.co.zw; www.cresta-hospitality.com. Another comfortable & well-recommended offering from Cresta. Recently refurbished with a pleasant garden & restaurant. Out-of-town rates make this good value. **$$$**

🏠 **Harare Safari Lodge** (20 lodges) Lake Chivero; 🛒746037, 746302. Only half-hour from town, this is a great lakeside place for families, with plenty of water- & land-based activities to keep children occupied. En-suite lodges are double-storey rock-under-thatch with their own

lounge. Communal facilities including bar & braai area, library, gym, TV room & pool. The lodge has its own horses & mountain bikes for hire. **$$$**

🏠 **Jacana Gardens Guest Lodge** (6 rooms, 1 cottage) 14 Jacana Dr, Borrowdale; m 0779 715297; jacanagardens@gmail.com; www.jacana-gardens.com. This is a beautifully appointed, very affordable & pleasant place to stay in the northern suburbs 10mins from the city centre yet close to shops & restaurants. Rooms are en suite with verandas, DSTV & Wi-Fi. Open-plan lounge opens onto gardens with pool. The self-contained garden cottage has 1 bedroom & a fully equipped kitchen. Home-cooked dinners on w/days upon request. See ad, page 152. **$$**

Budget

🏠 **It's A Small World Lodge** 25 Ridge Rd, Avondale; 🛒335176; e info@smallworldlodge. com. This is a very welcoming backpacker accommodation with dorms, sgls, dbls & family rooms, some en suite. It's welcoming & clean with shared kitchen & includes a laundry service. Camping also available US$5 pp. **$**

🏠 **Palm Lodge** 11 Mazowe St, Avondale. Backpacker accommodation in a nice area with large twin rooms, some en suite. Good value for money. **$**

✖ WHERE TO EAT

To say that Harare's eating-out scene has flourished in recent years would be something of an understatement. It's probably the number one activity for local residents so a large number of eateries have emerged to cater for every taste and budget. Many of them are in the suburbs so be prepared for a short taxi ride and be sure to book as far ahead as possible to avoid disappointment. Fridays and Saturdays are obviously very popular but note also that quite a few close on Mondays. There's also no shortage of coffee shops, many of which serve light meals, as well as good pubs and bars to chill out in after a long day's sightseeing and shopping. As a rough guide, most main courses in Harare's restaurants cost US$12–20. Steaks are near the US$20 mark, with seafood a little more expensive.

✖ **Adriennes Shop** 2B, Fairways Bldg, Sam Nujoma St, Belgravia; 🛒335602. Wide-ranging, affordable cosmopolitan menu includes a couple of Zimbabwean dishes. Friendly welcome in a pleasantly light venue. Good for pre or post Reps Theatre meals.

✖ **Alo Alo** 10 Forest Row, Arundel Village, Mt Pleasant; 🛒369198. Despite its name this is not a French restaurant – the name comes from the

owner's initials. Wide-ranging medium-priced menu that also caters for vegans. Upmarket with beautiful presentation & exemplary service. Closed Mon.

✖ **Amanzi** 158 Enterprise Rd, Highlands; 🛒497768; e restaurant@amanzi.co.zw. Note this is at a different location to Amanzi Lodge. This is one of Harare's finest restaurants – a stylish converted farmhouse in 4 acres of gardens with an extensive menu offering fusion cuisine from varying continents using produce from their own gardens. Deservedly one of the most popular restaurants in town although also one of the most expensive. Closed Sun.

✖ **The Codfather** 15 Dacomb Dr, Chisipite; ☎498021/3. Popular fish restaurant. Closed Mon.

✖ **Coimbra** 61 Selous Av; ☎700237. Harare's best Portuguese chicken – plain or periperi, proper chips with bread & garlic. Plenty of other dishes too including excellent prawns. Don't be put off by the no-frills décor; it's been around for ages & is a favourite place with locals. Closed Mon.

✖ **Da Eros Trattoria** 86 East Rd, Avondale; ☎332044. Reasonably priced authentic Italian restaurant with extensive menu of pasta, pizza, salads as well as many other mains. You can sit outside under shady trees & there's a play area for kids. Closed Mon.

✖ **Emmanuel's** 123 Joseph Chinamano Av; ☎707522/7. This is the Bronte Hotel's best restaurant although at a different address from the hotel. Another top-notch establishment with prices to match. Elegant décor accompanies an extensive & ambitious menu of both classic & contemporary dishes. Closed Sun.

✖ **Fishmonger** 50 East Rd, Avondale; ☎308164. It's a long way from the ocean but fish & seafood lovers won't be disappointed with the varied menu in this good-value, no-frills family restaurant that also offers some non-fish dishes.

✖ **Flatdog Diner** 5 Harrow Rd, nr Chapungu craft village (turn right off Robert Mugabe/Mutare Rd at first fuel station); ☎498409. Don't be put off by the exterior. Atmospheric bistro decorated in rich earth colours set in lovely gardens. Grills & seafood are excellent value & they have occasional live music. Closed Mon.

✖ **Harlequins** Imba Matombo Hotel; 3 Albert Glen Cl, Glen Lorne; ☎449071. Elite eating out with a small but interesting menu that varies with visiting chefs from other countries.

✖ **Kombahari** Rainbow Towers Hotel, Pennefather Av; ☎772633. Situated on the ground floor off the foyer is this pleasant steak & fish eaterie with Japanese dishes also available. Seating is arranged on bar chairs in a rectangle around the grill where your personal chef prepares your meal. It's a different sort of dining experience but standards have varied as have those of the rest of the hotel.

✖ **La Fontaine** Meikles Hotel, cnr Jason Moyo Av & 3rd St; ☎251705, 707721. 5-star pricey but excellent with award-winning chefs, extensive & imaginative menu in delightfully classy surroundings.

✖ **Leonardo's** Sam Levy's Village; ☎883158. International menu with European emphasis. Good service & portions in a comfortable atmosphere. Closed Sun.

✖ **Millers Restaurant** Shop 19, Ballantyne Shopping. Ballantyne Park; ☎882747. This steakhouse gets good reviews for both meat quality & cooking. A range of sauces for those who don't want plain grilled, plus burgers & a good starter menu.

✖ **Mojos** 10 East Rd, Belgravia; ☎705993. Meat eaters with a large appetite should head for this Brazilian restaurant that features flame-grilled, prime meats on skewers. Tapas selection for starters then eat till you're full. A great experience for carnivores & hell for vegetarians. Closed Sun.

✖ **Paula's Place** 314 Samora Machel Av; ☎497950. Portuguese restaurant with periperi chicken as signature dish but with fish dishes with prawns & calamari recommended.

✖ **St Elmos** 39A Avondale Shopping Centre; ☎334980/2. Italian chain restaurant with probably the best pizzas in town, also pasta dishes. Closed Tue.

✖ **Sitar** Newlands Shopping Centre, Enterprise Rd; ☎746215. Excellent authentic Indian food, from this family-run restaurant that's been around for decades. Very well recommended by locals. Closed Tue.

✖ **Victoria 22** 22 Victoria Dr, Newlands; ☎776429. International food with a small menu, set in pretty gardens with a terrace. Expensive but the food & service get good reviews from locals who tend to use this place for their special occasions. Closed Sun.

✖ **360 Degrees** Sam Levy's Village; ☎853314. Notionally a steakhouse but much more. Innovative menu with interesting fishy starters & excellent aged Zimbabwean beef.

LUNCHES AND COFFEE Harare residents like to lunch so a large number of coffee shops and lunch venues have sprung up both in the CBD and the suburbs. Many are in converted houses and offer veranda and garden seating. As well as light lunches they often feature some more substantial dishes. The following is just a small selection, most of which open until late afternoon. Their popularity means it's always advisable to book.

Gaby's Travel Plaza, Mazoe St; 700094. Pleasant courtyard setting with reasonably wide menu focusing on b/fast & lunch but open until 22.00 on Thu & Fri. Closed Sun.

40 Cork Rd 40 Cork Rd; 253585/6. Popular lunch venue with gardens. Interesting menu including good vegetarian options. Good Wi-Fi as well. Closed Sun.

Café Nush Avondale Shopping Centre; 335201. Modern décor serving a good range of juices & an extensive menu, many dishes with an Eastern accent.

Olive Salad Bar and Coffee Shop 11 Churchill Av, Alex Park; m 0772 400712. Original dishes, very fresh salads & generous portions make this a great favourite for breakfast & lunch. Eat inside, on veranda or in gardens. Closed Sun.

Shop Café Doon Estate, Harrow Rd; 446684. Great reviews for creative, mainly vegetarian menu, salads & emphasis on healthy, seasonal & sustainable foods. Lovely setting surrounded by excellent shops. Closed Mon.

Sopranos 6 Argyle Rd; 333833. Extensive menu using halal meat. Popular but can get very busy.

Vanilla Moon 8 Seagrave Rd; 333394. Another converted house, this place has a great range of coffees & hot drinks as well as good, often Mediterranean-inspired dishes, including fish. Closed Sun.

Willow Bean 216 Rolf Av, Borrowdale; 850294. Another wide-ranging b/fast & lunch menu with substantial dishes as well as a great selection of salads. Closed Sun.

ENTERTAINMENT AND NIGHTLIFE

ART AND CULTURE Harare has a thriving cultural scene featuring a wide range of musical genres, music clubs and cafés, theatre and drama groups. The internationally acclaimed **Harare International Festival of the Arts** (e info@hifa.co.zw; www.hifa. co.zw) is held in the Avondale suburb each May, a five-day showcase of theatre, comedy, drama and concerts, from live jazz to traditional African music.

To find out what's going on in town, check *The Herald* newspaper for advertisements and look out for posters as you walk around town. The foyer of the **National Gallery** has posters on forthcoming events. Also check the posters by the entrances of Harare Gardens for details of open-air performances at **Theatre in the Park**.

Gallery Delta (*110 Livingstone Av;* Vf *792135;* e *thedelta@mweb.co.zw; www. gallerydelta.com*) has a rotation of art exhibitions and performing arts events. It was established in 1975 by Derek Huggins and Helen Lieros as an alternative to the Shona sculpture scene that dominated Zimbabwean art at the time. The gallery is located in the former home of Robert Paul (1906–80), now regarded as Zimbabwe's finest landscape painter, and his house is one of Harare's oldest. As well as the art, graphics and ceramics on display the courtyard houses an intimate auditorium for the performing arts, especially jazz.

The **Book Café** (*139 Samora Machel Av, cnr 6th St;* 336377; e *newbookcafe. harare@gmail.com; www.zimbabwearts.org*) is Harare's premier venue for contemporary and alternative music and poetry with a full calendar of events culminating in the five-day Youth Festival in April/May. There's a bar and restaurant here too. Previous patrons should note this new venue following Book Café's eviction from their original location on Fife Avenue. The **Reps Theatre** (*Belgravia Shopping Centre, Maasdorp Av/Sam Nujoma St;* 336706, 335850; www.reps.co.zw) is one of the oldest (est 1931) amateur theatre companies in Zimbabwe offering a full bill of plays, music and comedy. It's very popular with locals.

There are two cinemas in the CBD, The Rainbow City Cinema at 99 Park Lane and Ster Kinekor Cinema Complex opposite the Eastgate Centre on Robert Mugabe.

SHOPPING

Nowhere in Harare comes close to the huge, glitzy shopping malls found in major cities elsewhere in the world, but the CBD does have some designer clothes stores, expensive jewellery shops and department stores. Otherwise it's generally utilitarian shopping. For that very reason the better-off Hararians are increasingly attracted to shopping centres that are opening up to service the more affluent northern suburbs, notably Borrowdale, Arundel, Chisipite, Newlands and Avondale. The biggest of these is Sam Levy's Village in Borrowdale with a large, varied and interesting array of retail outlets, restaurants and bars. This is a good place to spend money and a couple of hours but avoid weekends if possible as it is very busy and parking is difficult.

Arts, crafts and curio shops used to be on almost every corner but as these were of interest primarily to tourists, the last decade saw many of them being closed down.

ART One of the longest-established Shona sculpture outlets is the **Matombo Gallery** (*Zimre Centre, 110/4 Leopold Takawira Av*), and the **National Gallery** shop also has a good selection. Another excellent retailer of traditional and contemporary African arts is **Dendera Gallery** (*65 Speke Av, between 1st & 2nd sts*), with sculptures, textiles, pottery, jewellery and traditional artefacts. If you're looking for quality contemporary art, head for **Gallery Delta** (*110 Livingstone Av; \f 792135; e thedelta@mweb.co.zw; www.gallerydelta.com; ⊕ 08.30–17.00 Mon–Fri, 09.00–12.00 Sat*). The works of local artists are constantly on exhibition and artworks are for sale. For more about the gallery and its schedule of exhibitions and performances, see *Art and culture*, above.

Afrik Batik (*93b Robert Mugabe Way*) has a great selection of goods, not just batik but jewellery, clothing and shoes and, for those who can't go without, a range of wildlife products in the form of hides and leather (just check the paperwork required before you buy to export).

If you really want to empty your purse or wallet, the best place to buy craftworks, carvings and curios is in a self-contained enclave of like-minded shops at **Chapunga Village**, **Doon Estate** (*1 Harrow Rd; take Robert Mugabe (Mutare) Rd out of town & after about 7.5km, at the traffic lights by the filling station, turn right into Harrow Rd via Felice Av*) in the suburb of Beverley. Here you'll find 24 upmarket shops selling homemade chocolate, specialist soaps, canework, textiles, carvings, jewellery, fabulous teak furniture (sustainably harvested), art, leatherwork, fabrics and much more. There's also a vegetarian restaurant with a fine reputation and if you turn up on the right Saturday in the month there's a farmers' market and food fair. That's not all. On the left before you enter the main shopping area is a large stone-carving workshop and gallery. For a nominal fee, a guide will show you around, explaining not only the carving process but also the spiritual significance of the various stylised forms. This is probably one of the best ways to get this information without a hard-sell message.

If you're hungry while you're here, the Shop Café does brilliant lunches, or go to the Flatdog Diner a couple of hundred metres away at the top of the road (see page 163).

BOOKSHOPS There are several bookshops around town but with a disappointing selection, most concentrating on stationery and school supplies. Try **Kingstons** (*cnr Leopold Takawira Av & Kwame Nkrumah St; Parkade Shopping Centre on 1st St; and cnr Jason Moyo Av & 2nd St*).

Excellent maps of the town and the rest of the country can be purchased from the offices of the **Surveyor General** (*Ground floor, Electra Hse, Samora Machel Av, between Leopold Takiwira St & Julius Nyerere Way*).

OTHER PRACTICALITIES

IMMIGRATION   For visa extensions go to Liquenda House (*Nelson Mandela Av, between 1st & 2nd sts*).

INTERNET CAFÉS   Harare is now very well served with internet outlets, with most of the upmarket accommodations and lunch venues offering free Wi-Fi. There's no shortage of these in the central shopping area. Try these: **Intermarket Life Centre Arcade** (*next to Meikles;* ⊕ *08.00–20.00 Mon–Fri*); **Eastgate Centre** (*behind Meikles Hotel; the Netconnect shops in 1st St opposite the Wimpy; and cnr Samora Machel Av & Julius Nyerere Way opposite Karigamombe Centre*). There's a Wi-Fi hotspot in the National Gallery café (see below).

MEDICAL   Currently the best medical centre is the Avenues Clinic (*Baines Av & Mazowe St;* ✆ *251143*). There are 24-hour emergency facilities at the Trauma Centre and Hospital, Lanark Road, Belgravia (✆ *700666*) and 52 Baines Avenue (✆*705434*). For emergency evacuation contact MARS (✆*739642*); see *Chapter 3*, page 98. Please note that at any given time Harare's medical facilities can be in a state of flux with regard to facilities and standards. You are advised to ask locally (eg: at your accommodation) for advice on the best place to go in the event of an emergency.

POLICE   The main police station is on the corner of Kenneth Kaunda Avenue and Inez Terrace. In an emergency ✆995.

POST OFFICE   The main post office (⊕ *08.30–16.00 Mon–Fri, 08.00–11.30 Sat*) is on the corner of Inez Terrace and Jason Moyo Avenue.

WHAT TO SEE AND DO

NATIONAL GALLERY OF ZIMBABWE (*20 Julius Nyerere Way;* ✆ *704666/7; www. nationalgallery.co.zw;* ⊕ *09.00–17.00 Mon–Sat; admission US$1*) Zimbabwean art, in the formal sense, was hardly recognised when the gallery was founded in 1957, so the original exhibits were largely European in content and these include some significant European old masters many of which were donated by benefactors such as Sir Stephen Courtauld. This all changed when the first director, Frank McEwan, was introduced to Shona culture and set up a workshop to advise and encourage local artists. As a direct result, Shona art, especially stone sculpture, burgeoned and quickly became recognised worldwide as an important genre in its own right. The gallery is now an important showpiece, tracing the development of Zimbabwean and indeed pan-African art and culture in all its forms, most of which is to be found upstairs. As well as the permanent exhibition, which features some 6,000 artworks and artefacts, temporary exhibitions and workshops are held both to highlight the work of and to encourage emerging artists. Check the noticeboard in the foyer, which gives details not only of the gallery's forthcoming functions but others in town as well. There's also a café and a Wi-Fi hot spot. If you are looking for a good stone sculpture to buy, the gallery with its outdoor garden display is a great place to help you differentiate genuine art from tourist curios.

AFRICA UNITY SQUARE (*Across the road from Meikles Hotel*) This peaceful little oasis in the centre of town, with its fountain and gardens, is a pleasant place to stroll around. It was originally named Cecil Square – for once not Rhodes, but Robert

Cecil, Marquess of Salisbury, the British prime minister when Fort Salisbury was established. It was renamed to commemorate the merger of ZANU and ZAPU in 1987. Don't miss the flower sellers here with their brilliant floral arrangements.

HARARE GARDENS (*Behind Crowne Plaza Monomatapa Hotel & the National Gallery*) In days gone by this spacious park, right in the city centre, was a nicely tended space, very popular with locals at lunchtimes and weekends. Its wide paths take you through well-laid-out gardens featuring a miniature Victoria Falls, children's playground, bandstand and outdoor restaurant. Most weekends you find brightly garbed wedding groups promenading around and using the gardens as a photographic backdrop. During the decade from 2000 it became unkempt and overgrown, with a nasty reputation for rape and muggings, especially after dusk. Things are better today although the garden maintenance programme can be erratic and you are still advised to be careful when strolling around and avoid it after dark.

PARLIAMENT (*Cnr Nelson Mandela Av & 3rd St*) One of Harare's oldest buildings, this was begun in 1895 by two South African gold entrepreneurs, Snodgrass and Mitchell, who intended it to be a hotel, The Cecil. The following year, well before its completion, the army requisitioned it as a barracks during the first *chimurenga*. When Snodgrass and Mitchell ended their partnership without having repaid their loan, the still-unfinished building was confiscated by the government, to be used as a post office. Just at this time, however, the new legislative council was looking for premises, and took up occupancy here in 1899. Since then there have been many refurbishments and expansions but much of the original building stands today and it is still in use. A new building has been planned for the last 20 years, and to be built in the Kopje area, but remains on the drawing board despite MPs frequently complaining of being 'packed like sardines' in the current building.

TOWN HOUSE (*Julius Nyerere Way*) This attractive building from the early 1930s serves as the mayoral parlour and town clerk's office. It is notable not only for its architecture but for its attractive floral clock that incorporates the Zimbabwe bird symbol, created on these steps in 1950 to commemorate the first 60 years of the city.

NATIONAL HEROES' ACRE (*Bulawayo Rd, 5km from city centre;* ⊕ *08.00–17.00 daily; entry US$10*) This memorial to the comrades of ZANLA and ZIPRA who died in the liberation war is managed by the National Museums and Monuments of Zimbabwe (✆ *774208*). It actually covers 57 acres and also serves as a burial ground for those recently departed who have been designated National Heroes. You can't miss it from the road, with its huge obelisk surrounded by unlovely block buildings placed on a carved-out chunk of hillside. Ugly yet impressive, it could have come straight out of Leninist Russia. In fact it was designed in North Korea with construction starting in 1981, a year after independence. A monument to the unknown soldier is flanked by two bronze friezes, the first depicting the violent oppression meted out by the BSAC police, the second showing the armed struggle for independence. There's a small museum at the entrance where you can read all about the struggle and the monument, and you can get a guide to show you around the whole place and the various tombs that are still being added to.

NATIONAL ARCHIVES (*Ruth Taylor Rd; turn right off Borrowdale Rd onto Churchill Av, 3km out of town, then right into Hiller Rd;* ⊕ *08.30–16.00 Mon–Fri, 08.00–12.00 Sat, closed public holidays; entry US$1*) This is a little-visited attraction but well worth a visit. All of Zimbabwe's pre-colonial, colonial and recent history can be traced here in a fascinating collection of records, photographs, paintings, newspaper clippings, original letters, manuscripts and rare books. You'll find journals and diaries of many of the big names in African exploration and missionary work, as well as a large section devoted to the second *chimurenga* (the Rhodesian Bush War), with displays profiling all the key war heroes. There's also a reading room, but you will need to complete an enquiry form costing US$1 and requiring some ID and a specific request description. Copies of many of the old photos are available for purchase although stocks of photographic paper have meant the most popular ones are sometimes not available.

In the grounds of the archives you'll find two interesting thatched, corrugated-iron rondavels, designed to be light and easily moveable. Known as Kaytor or Pioneer Office huts, they date from 1903 when they were used by the Native Affairs Department in Mazowe and later as typical office accommodation for Rhodesia's district administrators and police.

MUSEUM OF HUMAN SCIENCES (*Civic Centre, Rotten Row, close to Rainbow Towers Hotel;* ⊕ *09.00–1700 daily; entry US$10*) Originally established as the Queen Victoria Museum in 1902, it moved to its present site in 1956. After independence the museum shifted its focus away from natural history to concentrate on ethnology and archaeology. This surprisingly small museum is good for a potted history of the area, its people and their cultures and wildlife but if you've already been to or plan to visit the vastly superior Natural History Museum in Bulawayo, you may want to give this one a miss.

NATIONAL BOTANIC GARDENS (*Alexandra Pk, 4km north of city; take 5th St north past Royal Harare Golf Course;* ✎ *725313;* ⊕ *07.30–1800 daily; parking US$1; entry adults US$2, children US$1*) The 68ha Botanic Gardens has over 900 species of indigenous trees and shrubs from Zimbabwe and the rest of the region, laid out in sections representing the key climatic regions of the country – *highveld*, *lowveld* and Eastern Highlands. There are also exotics from other continents with similar climate conditions as Zimbabwe. The large area and mix of flora attract a wide variety of birdlife, adding another layer of interest to a walk around the gardens. It is beautifully laid out and an excellent place to spend several hours. The **Herbarium** (*cnr 5th St & Downey;* ✎ *744170;* ⊕ *07.30–18.00*) has its own entrance. This has something like half a million plant specimens and is the main reference centre for research and identifying and naming plants from what is known as the Flora Zambesiaca region, comprising Zimbabwe, Zambia, Malawi, Mozambique, Botswana and the Caprivi Strip. There's also a restaurant/tea house in the grounds (⊕ *07.30–18.00*).

KOPJE You may want to visit this area, a 60m-high rock just southwest of town, simply to see the site of the first pioneer settlement. It's fairly unspectacular, and locals advise not climbing to the top unless you are in a group, as the nearby high-density housing area is home to muggers.

SPORT Zimbabweans are great sports enthusiasts, so there's no shortage of cricket, squash and tennis facilities but, above all, Harare is renowned for its golf courses: no fewer than seven. The **Royal Harare Golf Club** is international tournament standard and while no prices were available at the time of research, green fees and caddy hire are remarkably good value at all Harare's courses. The Royal Harare and the Harare Sports Club are both at the north end of 5th Street, over Josiah Tongogara Avenue.

CHITUNGWIZA This massive township south of Harare probably has over half a million occupants today. Once regarded as part of Harare, it is now seen as a town in its own right, Zimbabwe's third largest. In earlier years it was an interesting place to walk around for an insight into the lives of working-class citizens and a chat with ordinary people. This would be most inadvisable today unless you're in the company of a registered tour guide. Ask at the Zimbabwe Tourism Authority (see page 158) if they are running tours again.

MUKUVISI WOODLAND WILDLIFE AND ENVIRONMENT CENTRE (*Cnr Glenara Av & Hillside Rd; take Robert Mugabe Rd east for 3.5km, turn right into Glenara Av;* \ *747111, 747123;* ⏱ *08.00–17.00; entry US$4*) This peaceful area of *miombo* woodland, ten minutes from the centre of town, is home to a variety of indigenous fauna, some in enclosures, others free to roam its 260ha. While you're here you can stroll around the shady gardens; take a guided horseriding or walking safari to find tsessebe, giraffe, wildebeest, eland and zebra, which are just some of the larger inhabitants of the game park; or simply take it easy in the viewing platform with a pair of binos. There's a resident guide who you can hire for a walking safari or birdwatching. Bring a picnic (or staff will cook you burgers, pies or *sadza* dishes for US$2.50–4).

As well as being a recreational centre, this is an environment education centre that runs a series of programmes for local youngsters, giving many of them their first experience and appreciation of wildlife. The proceeds of your visit are used to support this programme. Plummeting visitor numbers have taken their toll but the management and largely volunteer staff are busily trying to get the place up to scratch again. While you're here take time to visit the information offices and shops of the Zambezi Society, Wildlife and Environment Zimbabwe and the Zimbabwe Orchid Society, in the car park area.

LAKE CHIVERO RECREATIONAL PARK (*NP Category 3; c30km from Harare off the Bulawayo road; see Central Zimbabwe map, page 176*) This park was previously named (and is still often referred to as) Lake McIlwaine. If you're staying with friends in Harare there's a good chance they'll bring you here as it's just about their favourite local weekend relaxation and watersports venue. Families and friends get together in large numbers, burn lots of meat, drink lots of beer, go fishing and whiz around in speedboats. Otherwise it's unlikely to feature high on your itinerary unless you have time to spare and children to keep occupied.

The focus of the 6,100ha park is the lake completed in 1952 with the damming of the Manyami River (also known as Hunyani River), creating an expanse of water 16km long and 8km at its widest. The lake is Harare's main water supply.

All the fun and games, eating and drinking take place on the north shore but for peace and quiet head for the game park in the south and west, with a good variety of plains game including white rhino, giraffe, eland, zebra, tsessebe and many smaller species. The game was originally stocked from Hwange National Park and later from Operation Noah when the Zambezi was dammed to form Lake Kariba.

You'll find some rock paintings at Bushman's Point picnic area, the only place you can walk without a guide. There's another cluster to the west of the park – Pax Park, Ovoid and Crocodile Rock – but to visit these you need a Parks guide.

Some roads in the western and central areas of the park may need a 4x4 during the rainy season.

⌂ Where to stay

Lake Chivero Rest Camp If you want to stay here rather than visit for the day, be aware that this is extremely popular and accommodation will be hard to get without advance booking, especially at weekends. You must book through the Zimbabwe Parks and Wildlife Management office in Harare (see page 158). Park facilities include lodges, chalets, caravan sites and picnic sites. Electricity is available and the water is drawn from a borehole.

A small number of lodges and chalets are for hire on the north bank. Lodges are en suite, with bedroom, lounge and kitchen; cutlery and crockery are provided. Chalets are either one- or two-bedroom units with self-catering facilities but communal ablution blocks.

Caravan and camping sites The Msasa caravan and camping site is situated on the north bank. Facilities include *braai* stands and an ablution block with showers. Bushman's Point and Public Mooring are undeveloped campsites on the south bank.

Admiral's Cabin (✆ 2926136) has seven small lakeside A-frame chalets as well as camping facilities.

What to see and do Fees for the following are not published but can be obtained at the park entrance.

Horseriding Horseriding is available every day except Monday. There are rides at 08.00 and 15.30 lasting 1½ hours, conducted by park personnel.

Crocodile viewing The crocodile ponds are walking distance from the tourist offices and main rest camp. Crocs in the winter months are cold, torpid and don't eat so aren't very exciting to watch. Viewings are at 07.00 and 17.00.

Game drive Gates are open for self-drive wildlife viewing daily between 06.00 and 18.00.

Walking safaris Walking and cycling are strictly prohibited except in the company of a designated park officer. If required, a guide can be hired from the booking office at the park entrance. Walks are conducted at your chosen time but they must be booked a day in advance.

KUIMBA SHIRI BIRD SANCTUARY (*28.5km along the Bulawayo road from town, turn left at Kuimba Shiri & Admiral's Cabin signposts at the Turnpike service station; e birdpark@mweb.co.zw*) This is on the shores of Lake Chivero, with over 460 species of indigenous birds in the wild as well as in enclosures: it's also home to orphaned, injured and abandoned birds. There's a focus on birds of prey, as the park was founded by Gary Stafford while he was training eagles for a number of BBC wildlife documentaries. Their birds of prey are flown daily at 16.00. **Admiral's Cabin** (🕐 *08.00–17.00 for day visitors*) is a large picnic/*braai* area with restaurant, play facilities for children and pool (no swimming in the lake due to crocs and bilharzia).

EPWORTH BALANCING ROCKS (*13km southeast of Harare on the Chiremba road*) These rocks are very photogenic but there are more spectacular examples elsewhere in the country, especially the Matopos, so this is probably only worth a stop en route to somewhere else. The rocks achieved a measure of fame when the main stack featured prominently in the design of Zimbabwe's banknotes (the rocks are still standing, while the currency has collapsed). The surrounding area is one of Zimbabwe's poorest, and personal safety is an issue, so if you want to walk around, try to get a group together.

MBIZI GAME PARK AND LODGES (*10 lodge rooms & 6 cottages; Twentydales Rd ext Hatfield Rd, 22km southeast of Harare & 10km from the airport; see Central Zimbabwe map, page 176;* \ *700676/8;* e *info@mbizi.co.zw; www.mbizi.co.zw;* **$$–$$$**) This is a really nice place, set in a 405ha private estate dotted with balanced rocks and complete with a reservoir and 11km of the Ruwa River for canoeing or boat cruises, plus wildlife viewing from horseback, mountain bikes, walks or drives. The park has some plains game species including free-roaming but tame giraffe, eland, impala and zebra (*mbizi* in Shona), but it's all rather run down now with cows mingling with the game. They've counted over 200 species of birds here. The pool is a thing of beauty, built amongst huge granite rocks. Accommodation in the main lodge includes dinner, bed and breakfast, transfers and activities. Self-catering bush cottages (*US$90 per night*), each sleeping five, are a budget option with optional activities priced separately. Day visitors can book any of the activities and there's a tea garden (⊕ *09.30–17.30*) serving light lunches.

EWANRIGG BOTANICAL GARDEN (*40km northeast of Harare off the A13; take the Enterprise road until the Shamva and Mutoko road junction approximately 29km from Harare. Take left fork on Shamva Road until a right turn, Christian Road, then 4km to the garden; see Central Zimbabwe map, page 176*) Admission US$3. Although administered by Parks, this botanical garden and recreational area is not a national park in the traditional sense. Created in the 1920s by farmer and botanist Harold Christian, former resident of the Isle of Man (from where the name Ewanrigg originated), and bequeathed to the nation on his death in 1950, the original gardens were very small but over the years since Christian's death the area has been considerably expanded to its current size. The gardens themselves now cover 40ha but there is a further 200ha of *miombo* woodland. Amongst a wide variety of indigenous plant species is a world-class collection of rare aloes and cycads, cacti and succulent plants. Over 275 species of birds have been recorded here and these include large numbers of nectar feeders, particularly sunbirds. Exotic plants have been added to the landscaped areas of the garden. The park is popular at weekends and the facilities include *braai* stands, tables and toilets. Although somewhat rundown, it's still worth a visit.

NORTH OF HARARE

ROCK PAINTINGS The whole of this region is dotted with cave paintings. Two sites feature prominently in itineraries and tours: Domboshawa and Ngomakurira, north of the city along the Borrowdale–Domboshawa road.

Domboshawa (*Turn right at the sign 30km from town; see Central Zimbabwe map, page 176; admission US$4*) Domboshawa has a small interpretive centre and the paintings themselves are in the main cave. A rich variety of animals is displayed and in a separate area some relatively humanoid figures are believed to be engaged in rain-making rituals. Important though they are, however, these paintings are not in good shape, having suffered various forms of damage.

Ngomakurira (*Turn right into Sasa Rd, 12km after the Domboshawa turning*)
Though acknowledged as probably the best paintings of their type in Zimbabwe,
these are infrequently visited due to their relative inaccessibility. The way is marked,
but indistinctly, so you'll probably need someone to show you the way to the caves,
a good 30-minute hike from the car park. Needless to say, local kids are eager to
provide this service.

Once there you'll find several sites with well-preserved paintings, often featuring
elephants and hunters. One painting shows a violent fight between two men, one
clubbing the other, in a scene somewhat at odds with the usual image of the San as
peaceful hunter-gatherers.

NORTHWEST OF HARARE

CHINHOYI You'll pass through Chinhoyi (see Central Zimbabwe map, page 176),
115km from Harare, on the way to Mana Pools and Kariba. Although an important
regional administrative centre for this very productive farming area, its main claim
to fame for the visitor is the Chinhoyi Caves National Park. There's also an element
of notoriety here because Chinhoyi was the venue for the first clash between ZANLA
troops and Rhodesian forces in 1966, marking the beginning of the second *chimurenga*
or Rhodesian Bush War. This is also known as an area of intense war-veteran activity.

Chinhoyi Caves National Park (*NP Category 3; 8km north of town; see Central
Zimbabwe map, page 176*) Although the park is actually quite large, only the
relatively small cave area is open to the public. Spectacular caves and flooded
sinkholes have been etched out of limestone and dolomite and today are a Mecca
for cave divers.

Frederick Courtney Selous, the famous hunter, is credited with being the first
European to show an interest in the caves, mistakenly believing them to be disused
mine workings. Prior to his discovery, the area was inhabited by generations of
peoples from as early as AD650, who probably used the caves as refuges from
invading tribes as well as for grain storage.

The largest pool is called Chirorodziva ('Sleeping Pool' or 'Pool of the Fallen'), a
reference to an incident in the 1830s when a marauding group of Ndebele invaders
from the south surprised the incumbents and flung them to their deaths in the
pool. The main features you will see are the sunlit and stunningly azure Sleeping
Pool and the artificially lit Dark Cave leading off it. Sleeping Pool is 46m below
ground level and easily accessed via a footpath from the park entrance, and Dark
Cave via a passage at the far side of Sleeping Pool. The exit from Dark Cave is
demanding, with very steep steps.

Underwater passageways from Dark Cave lead to two others, Bat Cave and
Blind Cave, and there is every probability that more remain yet to be discovered.
An interesting feature of the 172m-deep system is that at any depth, the water
temperature remains constant all year round at 22°C – evidence, it is thought, that
the pool is connected to an even bigger body of water.

While only the cream of the world's cave divers are able to venture to the depths
of this system (US navy divers have reached 135m), ordinary recreational divers
can enjoy the upper levels of the pool. Good buoyancy control is paramount here as
the crystal-clear waters reach down into the seemingly bottomless, deep blue abyss.
There's a PADI 5* Resort Centre in Harare – the only one in Zimbabwe: contact
Craig at Scubaworld and Universal Adventures (*72 King George Rd, Avondale;*
\ *04 304001, 304026;* m *0712 200624;* e *craig@scubaworld.co.zw; www.scubaworld.*

co.zw). While Craig caters mainly for local divers he can put together trips for visiting individuals. Transport and divemaster fees total US$180, full equipment hire US$80 and air fills US$15.

🏠 **Where to stay** There are few options in this area but the following come into the 'basic' category.

🏠 **Chinhoyi Caves Hotel** 📞067 27779; m 0772 658558; e gmusimwa@gmail.com. A few kilometres outside town towards Chirundu with pool, restaurant & bar. **$**

🏠 **Orange Grove Motel** 📞067 23095; m 0772 976165; e ajh@zol.co.zw. Just outside Chinhoyi

towards Chirundu. Comfortable with pool & restaurant. **$**

🏕 **Chinhoyi Caves National Park campsite** Close to main road & caves; e reservations@ zimparks.co.zw **$**

SOUTHEAST OF HARARE

MARONDERA This small town (population just over 45,000), 70km southeast of Harare, was a strategic staging post between Salisbury (Harare) and Umtali (Mutare) in the days following the Pioneers' arrival, when settlers were being encouraged by Rhodes to populate the area. It became an important forestry and farming area, with tobacco being the largest cash crop. Nowadays, as well as supporting the greatly reduced farming and cattle ranching operations, it is home to Zimbabwe's biggest winery, producing the Mukuyu range. Some of Zimbabwe's excellent private schools, including the renowned Peterhouse, are also located here.

Imire Safari Ranch (*110km southeast of Harare (see Central Zimbabwe map, pages 176–7);* 📞*02 222094; m 0772 522201; e sablelodge@imire.org, info@imire.org, volunteering@imire.org; www.imire.org*) Imire is one of Zimbabwe's most established privately owned conservancies that specialise in the breeding and reintroduction of game, including the endangered black rhino, across southern Africa.

It was originally a cattle, tobacco and maize farm in the 1950s but conservationist Norman Travers and his wife Gilly longed to have game on their land so in the 1970s they bought a herd of impala. This was followed by a procession of animals and within ten years they had a well-stocked game park. Norman is known for pioneering the introduction of game onto commercial farmland and his vision of reintroducing game back into safe conservation areas is continued today. In the mid-1980s, following the worst rhino poaching in Zimbabwe's history, Norman was awarded custodianship of seven orphaned black rhino calves, which were the founder members of Imire's black rhino breeding and release programme. Fourteen animals were released back into their natural environment in the Matusadona National Park within 20 years. Norman is best known for being the first person in Africa to domesticate and train an African elephant.

Visitors will meet a variety of characters including Tatenda, the orphaned black rhino who is the star of his own Animal Planet documentary, and Nzou, a 42-year-old orphaned female elephant who has become matriarch to a herd of buffalo, protecting them and their calves as if they were her own. Imire's elephants are involved in anti-poaching patrols, game counts, ploughing firebreaks and moving firewood as well as giving elephant rides to guests. Imire has four of Africa's Big Five (lion, elephant, buffalo, black and white rhino) and many other species including hyena, wild cat, giraffe, zebra, wildebeest, hippo, warthog, duiker, the rare sable antelope, blesbok, kudu and waterbuck.

While you are at Imire you can also enjoy horseriding, bush walks, bass fishing and birding – with over 150 different species. This is an excellent place for anyone who loves animals and is interested in conservation.

Imire's day-trip package including a full-day game drive and lunch is US$60 per adult and US$40 per child (three–12 years old). You can take a day trip or stay overnight at Sable Lodge (seven thatched rondavel cottages each with en-suite bathroom) or go back to basics and stay at the self-catering bush camp, situated in the heart of the game park. They also run a hands-on volunteer programme where you get a real feel for the day-to-day running of a game park.

A 24-hour stay at Sable Lodge including accommodation, three meals, full-day game drive and sundowners tour is US$125 per adult and US$75 per child. The bushcamp is from US$10 per person per night.

Getting there Take the Mutare road out of Harare and just before Marondera (at about 70km) you will cross the railway line. About 2km past this, take the right turn at the Imire sign, follow this road for 2.5km and turn left at the next Imire sign. Go 37km down the single-track road and you will pass the Imire store and butchery on the left-hand side. Travel 800m and turn left into the game park. Sable Lodge is 1km down this road.

SOUTHWEST OF HARARE

SELOUS (see Central Zimbabwe map, page 176) Considering Frederick Courtney Selous, the renowned British hunter, explorer and pioneer guide, played such an influential role in Rhodesia's history, the small town (little more than a village) – 75km southwest of Harare on the Bulawayo road – that takes his name hardly does him justice. It's now a pretty nondescript administration and farming centre, only mentioned here as a landmark for the following two lodges that are situated in Chengeta, the largest private game reserve in Mashonaland, home to over 45 animal and 180 bird species. They are run by the same company, have the same rate structure and offer the same range of activities – game drives, horseback safaris, canoe or pontoon trips (lake and river), fishing (bass and bream), elephant rides and interactions, walking safaris and clay pigeon shooting. Both are clearly signposted from the main road.

Where to stay
Upmarket

Chengeta Safari Lodge (16 lodges)
m 0772 573022; e reservations@chengeta.com; www.chengetasafarilodge.com /chengeta. Accommodation is in thatched en-suite lodges. A beautifully designed central *boma* has a bar & lounge, leading to an outside area with cosy seating around a large fireplace. They also have a 3-tier swimming pool with bar, & a sauna. The surrounding countryside is a mix of open plains & acacia woodland at the foot of a large forested *kopje*. Rates include accommodation, 3 meals a day, tea & coffee, & 2 game activities. **$$$**

Pamuzinda Lodge (12 lodges)
m 0772 573022; e reservations@chengeta.com; www.chengetasafarilodge.com/pamuzinda. Accommodation is in thatched en-suite lodges with balconies over a seasonal lagoon where the trained riding elephants bathe daily. There's a swimming pool, main & pool bar & separate TV lounge. The park surrounding Pamuzinda is mainly *mopane* woodland & riverine bush. **$$$**

5

Central Zimbabwe

Central Zimbabwe, also known as the Midlands, is home to Gweru, Kwekwe and Kadoma: three towns – large by Zimbabwean standards – originally established to exploit the vast mineral potential of the Great Dyke. They aren't the most attractive of towns (though not unpleasant) and neither is the surrounding *highveld* countryside of obvious appeal and, as a result, far too many people drive straight past them en route between Harare and Bulawayo. However, the area has some great things to do and the inquisitive visitor will be rewarded with museums, ancient ruins, game parks and recreational areas, all within easy reach of the main through road. The region's main attraction, however, and one that should be on every visitor's wish list lies further to the southeast. Great Zimbabwe, one of the country's crown jewels, is a magnificent complex of ancient stone-wall structures close to the provincial capital of Masvingo and adjacent to Lake Mutirikwe recreational park. There's plenty to occupy you here for several days and the area has a wealth of accommodation choices to suit every budget.

KADOMA *Telephone code 068*

Kadoma is a typically bustling little African town, complete with colonial architecture and steam locomotives, which owes its existence to an enterprising trader called Godwin. In the 1890s, this was a mining camp called Gatooma (thought to have been named after a local chief, Katuma, but possibly named by Australian miners after Katoomba mine in New South Wales). In 1906, Godwin set up a canteen and trading post to service the burgeoning number of prospectors – so many, in fact, that Gatooma had become known as the 'Klondike of Africa'. It soon had one of the largest gold-mining complexes in the world, known as the Cam and Motor, but copper and nickel were also being extracted. The original mines are worked out now but gold mining continues in the nearby area of Eiffel Flats, although cotton farming and processing has taken over as the main industry. In 1982, Gatooma was renamed Kadoma and today has Stevenage in England as its sister town.

GETTING THERE
By car The main A5 road bypasses the town. If you're driving south from Harare (140km), turn right at the Kadoma Hotel; if approaching from Bulawayo (300km) just keep straight on and you'll hit town.

By bus At the time of latest research, three bus companies, City Link, Pathfinder and Defu, operated to Kadoma between Bulawayo and Harare. Buses stop at Kadoma Hotel. See *Getting there, By coach, Domestic* under *Harare* on page 156.

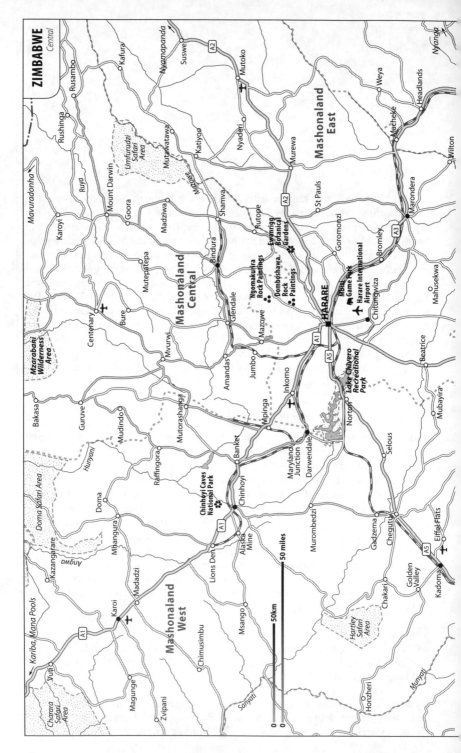

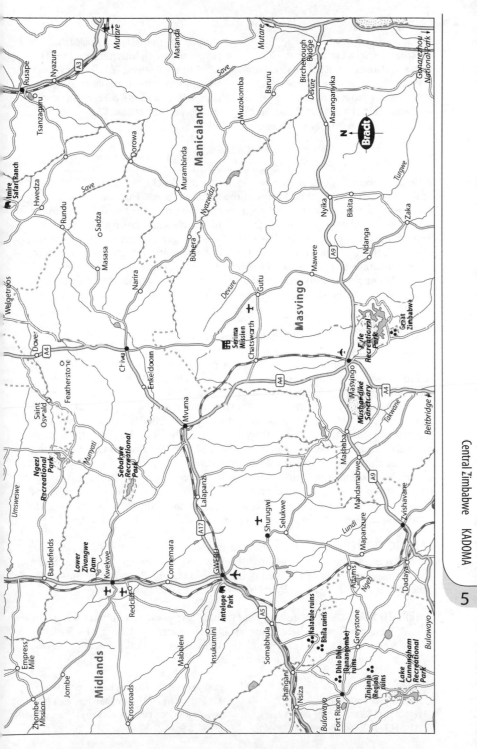

WHERE TO STAY
Upmarket
🏠 **Kadoma Hotel & Conference Centre** (147 rooms) ☎22106/9; e reservations@kadomarainbow.co.zw; www.rtg.co.zw. Part of the Rainbow group of hotels, this is a large establishment to find in such a small town, but it's a pleasant place, set in 4ha of gardens, complete with peacocks, swimming pool & children's playground. Recently renovated, rooms are all en suite & have AC & satellite TV. WiFi available. The old steam locos dotted around the grounds are an attraction in themselves & will be even more so when they get a lick of paint. **$$$**

KWEKWE *Telephone code 055*

Although Kwekwe's dual-carriageway main street lacks character, you'll find plenty of fine but faded colonial buildings in the parallel streets. That said, undoubtedly the most impressive building and prominent landmark is the town's huge mosque, with its immaculately maintained, grey-painted arches and green and white dome. Though the town proudly bills itself as 'The Now City in Touch with Tomorrow', there is little to tempt you to stay here, not to mention a shortage of suitable accommodation, but give yourself an hour or two because its museum is well worth a visit. Although a heavily industrial town, this activity is limited to the northeast areas, unlikely to be visited by any tourist. The current population is estimated around 105,000.

HISTORY Previously named Sebakwe, this was one of the series of British South Africa Company (BSAC) forts built along the route to Fort Salisbury (Harare) in the late 1890s. In common with other settlements in this area, it owes its prosperity to the mining opportunities offered by the Great Dyke, a 500km ridge of volcanic hills running from the Zambezi Escarpment to Gwanda in the south. Its rather charming name comes from one of two rather differing origins. *Isikwekwe* is Zulu for mange or scab whereas the more popular belief is that it derives from the vast population of croaking frogs that once inhabited the river. These made their mark in 1905 when the name was changed from Sebakwe to Que Que before being Africanised to Kwekwe after independence. The promised mineral wealth, especially gold, attracted prospectors who poured in by the thousands. It was only relatively recently, after a century of extraction, mainly at the vast Globe and Phoenix mine, that gold mining ceased to be viable. Mining for other minerals continues, with chrome, iron and steel production keeping the town alive.

GETTING THERE Kwekwe is 213km/132 miles from Harare and 62km/39 miles from Gweru. At the time of research three bus companies, City Link, Pathfinder and Defu, served Kwekwe between Bulawayo and Harare. Buses stop at the Golden Mile Hotel. See *Getting there, By coach, Domestic* under *Harare* on page 156 .

🏠 **WHERE TO STAY** There are few tourist facilities, and good accommodation is hard to find. Visitors who were here in earlier days, or readers of the old ZTA leaflet on Kwekwe, should note that several outlying farm accommodations were taken over by war vets and are no longer functioning.

Upmarket
🏠 **Ash Kelda Guest House** (9 rooms) 20 Central St off Robert Mugabe Way; ☎22364, 24331; m 07730 26050. This immaculate lodge, run by Kenneth Halkin, is by far the best in town, but as there are only 9 rooms he is frequently fully booked with local business folk so try to book well ahead. **$$**

Standard

⌂ **Golden Mile Motel** (28 rooms)
✆23711/3; e goldenmilehotel@gmail.com; www.
goldenmilehotel.com. Large & in good condition
with en-suite rooms featuring bar fridge, DSTV,
Wi-Fi but not all rooms have AC. It's good value
with a pleasant inner garden with pool & snackbar.
A nightclub & King Solomon's casino offer the
potential for nocturnal disturbance. Visa and
MasterCard accepted. **$$**

⌂ **Touchwood Lodges** (19 chalets) 3km
south of town on the Gweru rd; ✆23592;
f 22466; e touchwood@tmtransport.com. These
pretty thatched chalets range from standard dbls
to execs with 4-poster beds & spa bath. All have
DSTV, tea/coffee facilities & fridge. The shady
gardens are pleasant & well kept, complete with
a little fish pond. The restaurant offers an à la
carte menu. The downside is that being one of
the nicest places in the area, it's often full with
visiting business people. **$$**

WHAT TO SEE AND DO

National Mining Museum (✆ 3741; ⊕ 09.00–17.00 except Good Friday &
Christmas Day; entry US$2) This small but reputedly fascinating museum is right
next to the entrance to the Globe and Phoenix mine (take 1st Avenue off 1st Street,
bear right at the top where it turns into a dirt road; no signs to the museum, but
follow the road past the mine for a few hundred metres). You know you have
arrived when you see the striking green and white Paper House, one of the most
unusual buildings in Zimbabwe. It is the only one remaining of three wood-framed,
prefabricated buildings shipped out from the UK in 1894. This one was originally
intended for the mine's general manager and today functions as the museum. The
outer walls are made of papier mâché, reinforced with wire netting and thickly
coated with paint, while the inner walls are cardboard, the whole thing stands on
stilts and is roofed with corrugated iron. This apparently flimsy construction has
withstood over a century of Zimbabwe's weather and remains in fine condition to
this day. Next to it is a thatched, corrugated-iron hut from the same era, assumed
to have originally been a storeroom. The surrounding garden is crammed full of
machinery exhibits retrieved from the now-defunct mines and processing plants.
The museum attendant will give you a guided tour and explain all the equipment;
unfortunately on the day of my visit, he/she had gone missing.

Sebakwe Recreational Park (NP Category 3; about 40km east of Kwekwe)
This park based around Sebakwe Dam is open to the public as a fishing and
camping spot. The river was originally dammed in 1957. The wall was raised by
7m in the 1980s, and the resulting increase in surface area to 27km² made this
Zimbabwe's fourth-largest lake, yet it remains almost completely undeveloped in
terms of leisure facilities. Few people make their way out here so you are assured
of a peaceful stay, camping by the lakeside or in one of the lodges overlooking the
water. I was visited by waterbuck and warthogs and advised to keep an eye open
for crocodiles. Each campsite has a roofed stone shelter, *braai* facilities and nearby
tap, and the large ablution block is clean, with attendants turning on the water and
lighting the donkey boilers when you arrive. Unfortunately the surrounding bush
has been allowed to grow wild, to the extent that it blocks the views of the water
from your tent, and direct access to the shoreline is impossible from most sites. It
should only take visitors to start returning for Parks to remedy this.

Lower Zivangwe Dam (Signposted a few kilometres north of town on the
Harare rd) It's much the same story at Lower Zivange Dam (commonly known as
Dutchman's Pool) as at Sebakwe. A previously idyllic wooded recreational area has
become neglected and overgrown; ditto the nearby Echo Park campsite and chalets.

All the damp-smelling chalets need is rethatching and the campsite could be tidied in a couple of days, returning this lovely, bird-rich area to its former glory.

GWERU *Telephone code 054*

The capital of Midlands Province, Gweru is Zimbabwe's third-largest city (fourth if you consider Chitungwiza as separate from Harare) with a population estimated at around 300,000. It has a bustling, compact town centre, but there is no shortage of sprawling industrial sites elsewhere around the town.

Few people associate Gweru with tourism, yet if you dash through without stopping you will miss out on some notable places of interest: some of the most impressive and important archaeological sites in the country; the interesting Military Museum; and Serima Mission, whose church displays a unique style of woodcarving. There's a private game reserve-cum-resort just out of town offering a range of accommodation and activities, and it's not too far from Sebakwe Recreational Park (see above). The town boasts the largest shoe factory (Bata) in the whole of southern Africa. There is also an important army and air force training centre, home to a garrison, and the Thornhill airbase, the largest in the country.

Although clean and pleasant, with wide tree-lined avenues, Gweru is functional and somewhat lacking in character. The city hall complex is an imposing colonial-style building, as is the Stock Exchange building on Main Street, but apart from these and the faded Midlands Hotel, the only other building of note is the hideous glass-and-concrete post office on Robert Mugabe Way.

HISTORY The key to Gweru's development is the Great Dyke. This so-called backbone of Zimbabwe is an extremely rich source of precious metals, minerals and gems, a focus for prospectors in the gold rush of the late 19th century and early 20th. Early settlers followed in the wake of Leander Starr Jameson, who earmarked the site as a gold-mining centre in 1894 (see *Colonial era*, page 11), and the town's prosperity was sealed in 1902 with the arrival of the railway linking Fort Salisbury (Harare) and Bulawayo. The colonial name of Gwelo was changed to Gweru in 1982. The area has grown wealthy from nearby deposits of chromite and other ores, as well as from extensive cattle rearing, both beef and dairy.

GETTING THERE Gweru is 164km/101 miles from Bulawayo, 183km/114 miles from Masvingo, 275km/171 miles from Harare and 603km/375 miles from Victoria Falls. Distances are shown for the most direct routes. Three bus companies, City Link, Pathfinder and Defu, operate to Gweru between Bulawayo and Harare. The buses stop at the Fairmile Hotel. See *Getting there*, *By coach*, *Domestic* under *Harare* on page 156.

TOURIST INFORMATION Gweru's publicity association, once housed in the city hall complex, has now closed.

The Automobile Association is on the corner of Lobengula Avenue and Sixth Street, and worth visiting for a map of the area.

WHERE TO STAY Gweru is not a tourist town so there are few worthy places to stay. The best option is Antelope Park (see *Out of town* below). There are several defunct lodges signposted on the Shurugwi road out of town that may resurrect themselves under better economic conditions.

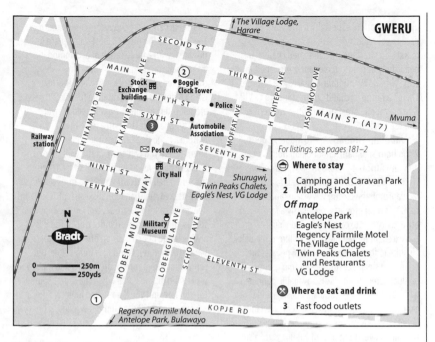

The Village Lodge, Harare

GWERU

SECOND ST

MAIN ST

THIRD ST

Stock Exchange building

Boggie Clock Tower

FIFTH ST

Police

SIXTH ST

Automobile Association

Railway station

Post office

SEVENTH ST

EIGHTH ST

City Hall

NINTH ST

TENTH ST

Shurugwi, Twin Peaks Chalets, Eagle's Nest, VG Lodge

MAIN ST (A17)

Mvuma

Military Museum

ELEVENTH ST

N

Bradt

0   250m
0   250yds

KOPJE RD

Regency Fairmile Motel, Antelope Park, Bulawayo

For listings, see pages 181–2

Where to stay

1 Camping and Caravan Park
2 Midlands Hotel

Off map
Antelope Park
Eagle's Nest
Regency Fairmile Motel
The Village Lodge
Twin Peaks Chalets and Restaurants
VG Lodge

Where to eat and drink

3 Fast food outlets

In town
Standard

🏠 **Midlands Hotel** (70 rooms) Cnr Robert Mugabe & Main sts, on the main crossroads; 📞228501/2; e rickdvu@yahoo.com. You can't miss this hotel right by the Boggie clock tower. The façade suggests an elegant establishment but that's not really carried through once you step inside. It was opened in 1927 by the Meikels brothers & at one time was spared from demolition by local protest. It's now a perfectly acceptable though soulless business hotel with large clean rooms but despite renovations in 2010 it still has a tired feel about it. It boasts a casino but can only offer street parking; nevertheless it's good value for the price. **$$**

🏠 **Regency Fairmile Hotel** (50 rooms) 📞224144/6, 228800; e fairmilehotel@gmail.com. A large, rather soulless motel on the roundabout just south of town. Decent-sized, plainly furnished rooms with garden, pool & a reasonable, if basic, restaurant. **$$**

🏠 **Twin Peaks Chalets & Restaurant** (15 cottages) Shurugwi Rd, 4km from town; 📞226067, 222590; e twinpeaksreservations@gmail.com. This is one of the few really nice places to stay in Gweru, with thatched cottages (4 exec, 11 standard) in beautifully tended gardens in

a quiet residential district. The rooms are all en suite with DSTV, fridge & lounge area. It's under new management & recently renovated. The bar/restaurant is popular with locals. **$$**

Basic

🏠 **VG Lodge** (8 rooms) 19 Shurugwi Rd; 2nd roundabout out of town; m 0773 378565, 0775 384364. They offer full catering but the kitchen aromas indicated very basic, local fare. Apart from a pool & neat garden there's nothing special here but it's good, clean budget accommodation with a very friendly welcome. 3 of the rooms are en suite. In mid-2012 there was no hot water in the rooms although staff would deliver it in bowls for washing. **$**

🏕 **Camping & Caravan Park** Robert Mugabe Way as you enter town from the south. The adjacent sports club where you check in is thriving, but the campsite is a neglected mess & security non-existent, so this is not recommended.

Out of town
Upmarket

🏠 **The Village Lodge** (46 rooms) 5km out on the Harare rd; 📞231761/2; e staywithus@thevillagezim.com, reservations@thevillagezim.com. You'll find this lodge complex a good

Central Zimbabwe   GWERU

5

upmarket option, especially if you want to 'Define your Lifestyle' – their rather odd marketing strapline. The thatched chalets are beautifully appointed, elegantly furnished in teak, with DSTV, minibar & tea/coffee facilities. There's a range of chalets from standard to VIP & honeymoon. 2 restaurants offer Western & Chinese fare. **$$**

🏠 **Jabulani Zimbabwe** (8 lodges, 2 dorms) 22km from Shangani, about 64km from Gweru; 📞 (South Africa) +27 72 830 8661; Zimbabwe m 0712 622146, 0775 100085; e info@ jabulanizimbabwe.com; www.jabulanizimbabwe. com. This rural property, previously a farm, is an eco activity centre catering for individuals & groups & is excellent for families with children. The deluxe en-suite lodges sleep a total of 16 people; the 2 dorms can sleep 50, suitable for tour groups. An outdoor camping site is also available equipped with ablution blocks. Jabulani boasts a wide variety of plains game with big herds of eland, also impala, zebra & giraffe. The surrounding landscape is home to over 40 species of wildlife & it's also situated in an area rich in ancient ruins providing guests with a wide range of activities that include game drives, horseriding and climbing. Jabulani is also involved in a number of corporate social responsibility projects, namely Pezulu School and the Shangani Clinic. **$$$**

🏠 **Antelope Park** Turn off is 6km south of Gweru on Bulawayo rd; 📞/f 251913; m 0712 362220; e antelope-reservations@

africanencounter.org; www.antelopepark.co.zw. This 'resort' is the nicest & best-value place in this area, with a large range of accommodations from small standard rooms with shared ablutions through to family lodges, river lodges & luxury island lodges. 3 lodges catering for max 20 people are self catering. En-suite, water-edge river tents are spacious (though a little tired now), & feature a large deck area overlooking the river; alternatively you can camp in the well-tended, riverside gardens. At night you'll sit by a roaring fire serenaded by cicadas, tinkling frogs & the fiery-necked nightjar, with his insistent 'Good Lord deliver us' call. There are several large camping spaces allocated to overlander trucks. There is a wide range of activities on offer (see *What to see and do* below). Catering is buffet style, but somewhat regimented: you are asked to make your way to the dining *boma* when the drums sound; turn up late and you'll go to bed hungry. Book in advance, especially on summer w/ends, & bring your own alcohol. **$–$$$**

Standard

🏠 **Eagle's Nest** (12 thatched chalets) Shurugwi Rd, 8km from Gweru; m 0776 150469; e flamelillyinnsandlodges@hotmail.com. This is a good-value option with thatched chalets from the Flame Lilly group with standard & executive chalets arranged on a large plot not far from town. **$$**

🍴 **WHERE TO EAT** Apart from what's on offer at your accommodation, there are no restaurants other than the fast-food establishments on Robert Mugabe Way. Nando's, Creamy Inn, Pizza Inn and Chicken Inn are clustered together by 6th Street, and the Wimpy Bar is at the Shell filling station. You may want to try the Sugar and Spice coffee shop on Robert Mugabe Way. Twin Peaks restaurant (see *Where to stay* above) used to be popular with locals under its previous management, but when I visited in 2012 the new restaurant was under renovation.

WHAT TO SEE AND DO

Antelope Park (*Turn-off 6km south of Gweru on Bulawayo rd; see Central Zimbabwe map, page 177*) This is where the citizens of Harare, Gweru and Bulawayo bring their families for a weekend of activities focusing on walking with lions and riding elephants. It's all set in 1,215ha of bush and the central facility is situated in immaculate gardens alongside a river and reservoir (boating and fishing are also on offer). They claim 23 game and 350 bird species. There are horses here for wildlife viewing in the bush.

They have four elephants, and you can go on a ride into the park's own bush estate.

Walking with lions is popular here, especially as they use them up to about 18 months old, by which time they are hardly little kittens. When I visited they had over 60 lions in their breeding programme. Not an activity enjoyed or approved by everyone (see box, page 269). The many activities range in cost from US$8–80 with a 30-minute elephant ride at US$40 and lion walking US$80 for non residents.

Military Museum (*Lobengula Av;* ⊕ *09.00–17.00 daily; entry US$10*) This is Zimbabwe's national military museum, and you can easily spend an hour or two here. Three main halls are dedicated to the country's armed struggles, the development of its police force, and military and civil aviation. Displays of uniforms and equipment are augmented with informative copy, although the type is often small and low lighting can make it difficult to read. The grounds of the museum contain a variety of armed vehicles and weaponry but little supporting information. Aviation exhibits are housed on a separate site nearby and the admission ticket covers both museums.

Boggie Clock Tower It's a town landmark, proudly featured in every piece of Gweru publicity material, but this unremarkable edifice needs only a few seconds' attention as you drive past it. Major W J Boggie and his wife Jeannie were early pioneers and prominent citizens. In 1937, nine years after the major's death at the age of 63, the redoubtable Jeannie decided to build a clock tower in his memory, in the middle of a busy road junction.

There were originally two inscribed brass panels. The first contains a dedication to the 'heroic women, men and little children who opened up Southern Rhodesia'; the other is touchingly dedicated to the 'patient Pioneer Trek oxen, horses, mules and donkeys without whose aid Southern Rhodesia could not have been opened up' – almost as if the poor beasts had a choice in the matter! Both plaques are now missing.

Perhaps in an attempt to invest this folly with a modicum of interest, a local legend says that in post-independence 1981 Boggie's remains were removed from the tower, whereupon the clocks mysteriously stopped working for ten years, with the hands stuck at 10.50.

Readers interested in the colonial history of Zimbabwe might try to track down Jeannie Boggie's fascinating books, *Experiences of Rhodesia's Pioneer Women* and *First Steps in Civilizing Rhodesia*.

Shurugwi It's not difficult to imagine how picturesque this little mining town nestling in the hills southeast of Gweru must have been in the mining boom years of the 1920s and '30s. Once an out-of-the-way highland retreat living off the proceeds of its chromium mine, it is now a collection of crumbling colonial buildings with faded pastel paintwork, reminiscent of similar towns in Mozambique. The mine is still in operation; keep an eye open for the narrow-gauge train that hauls ore from the mine, crossing the road on the approach to town. In fact Shurugwi is currently experiencing a resurgence in its fortunes with new mining activity stimulating the local economy.

Zimbabwe ruins This area of the Midlands is dotted with ancient *dzimbabwes* (see *Glossary*, page 369), stone ruins, and there are several excellent examples relatively close to each other south of the Gweru–Bulawayo road. As with all of Zimbabwe's ruins, there was large-scale plundering by the Rhodesia Ancient Ruins Company during the 1890s in its search for gold and artefacts, so it is impossible to describe the history of these sites in any detail or with any certainty. We do know that the three main ruins here were constructed in the early 17th century by the

Torwa people, following the overthrow of their previous capital at Khami by the Rozwi of the Changamire dynasty. The Rozwi repeated the story here and occupied these sites from the 1680s until they in turn were overcome by the Ndebele in the *mfecane* of the 1830s.

If time is limited, at least try to see Dhlo Dhlo (Danangombe) and Nalatale, excellent examples of these Torwa structures. At Nalatale you'll see the most intricate and best-preserved example of patterned stonework in the country. The ruins are best viewed in winter when they are not overgrown by grass and vegetation. See Gweru Ruins map for locations. Paul Hubbard, a Bulawayan archaeologist and historian runs tours to the following ruins as well as Great Zimbabwe and Khami. See page 295 for details.

Dhlo Dhlo (Danangombe) Ruins (✦ *S19 56 44 E29 19 49; turn south off the Gweru–Bulawayo rd at Shangani, cross the railway line & head south for 22km until you see signs for the ruins*) There is an interpretive centre at the booking office, and a guide will talk you through the general layout of the 2ha site before taking you on a tour. You may wish to take some information with a pinch of salt. Dhlo Dhlo and other hilltop sites are noted for the strange, latex-sapped euphorbias trees, which can grow to a height of 12m. Our guide informed us, with a broad grin, that they were planted by the ancient occupants as lightning conductors.

Dhlo Dhlo is thought to have been built by the Torwa as a royal enclosure and subsequently taken over by the Rozwi as the capital of a cluster of nearby *dzimbabwes*. Although not as well preserved as Nalatale, amongst the remains of the hut structures, many still clearly evident, is a good example of patterned stone walling. One feature of Dhlo Dhlo is the many Portuguese artefacts found here, including cannon, gold jewellery, religious icons, candlesticks, a priest's seal and much more. One theory suggests that Portuguese traders were unpopular with the Rozwi, who would only deal with them through agents and actually held some captive here.

Nalatale Ruins (✦ *S19 53 2 E29 31 57; turn south off the Gweru–Bulawayo road at Shangani, cross the railway line & turn left onto a dirt road for about 23km; follow a track left to the signposted car park, then hike 15mins uphill to the ruins*) These out-of-the-way ruins are perched on top of a rounded granite *kopje* with awesome views over the surrounding countryside. Although less impressive in scale than other sites, they more than justify the effort to get there because of their patterned walling, the finest in the country. All five main patterns are employed: check, chevron, herringbone, cord and thin lines, made from stones of a different colour. The magnificent wall that displays all these so beautifully has required no reconstruction other than a cement topping to prevent it crumbling, and several replica plinths, work undertaken in the 1930s.

The patterns are believed to be symbolic. There is little consensus among experts but the small information centre in the car park offers a possible decoding provided by Professor Thomas Huffman of Witwatersrand University, based on his study of the Venda culture. For example, the herringbone pattern is a stylised female crocodile, representing a woman of senior status; the check pattern is a male crocodile, signifying a man of senior status; the cord pattern is a water snake, symbol of human fertility; fertility of the earth is represented by the chevron pattern.

Nalatale is assumed to share the same history as Dhlo Dhlo and may have served as a Torwa capital, but the paucity of archaeological artefacts provides little evidence to work on. Keen photographers should visit late in the day when a low sun gives the beautiful stonework rich warm hues.

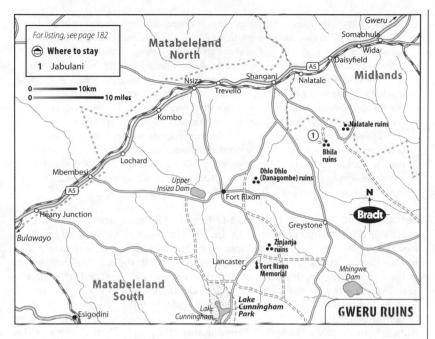

For listing, see page 182

Where to stay
1 Jabulani

0 ————— 10km
0 ————— 10 miles

Gweru
Somabhula
Wida
Daisyfield
Matabeleland
North
Shangani
Nalatale
A5
Midlands
Nsiza
Trevello
Nalatale ruins
Kombo
1
Bhila
ruins
Lochard
Dhlo Dhlo
(Danagombe) ruins
Mbembesi
Upper
Insiza Dam
N
Fort Rixon
A5
Heany Junction
Greystone
Bulawayo
Zinjanja
ruins
Lancaster
Fort Rixon
Memorial
Mhingwe
Dam
Matabeleland
South
Lake
Cunningham
Park
Esigodini
Lake
Cunningham
GWERU RUINS

Zinjanja Ruins These ruins (also known, and signposted, as Regina ruins) are off the beaten track about 100km from Gweru, a few kilometres south of Fort Rixon. Three large terraces on which huts were built surround a granite outcrop, and a number of smaller walled remains are all that is left of what was presumably once an important Torwa centre. Part of the site was dug over by treasure hunters in the late 19th century followed by small-scale excavations in the late 1970s, revealing little due to the earlier destruction. It's possible though that Zinjanja was a capital site for a competing ruler and may be contemporary with the latter days of Dhlo Dhlo.

Bhila Ruins You'll see these signposted off the road to Jabulani (see Gweru, *Where to stay*, page 152) and while these small, crumbling enclosures may be a disappointment compared with the other fine examples in the area there are some interesting (and much debated) possibilities regarding the role of this site. Bulawayo archaeologist and historian, Paul Hubbard, writes as follows:

Archaeologist Thomas Huffman has argued Bhila served as a ritual site for the ruling elite of Torwa-Rozvi society. In a claim disputed by other researchers (notably David Beach and Innocent Pikirayi), Huffman interprets the enclosure and associated cairns as the remains of an initiation centre for males, namely a circumcision lodge. The purpose of initiation lodges was to teach youngsters the rights and responsibilities of adulthood. The initiates had to be sequestered away from the rest of the population until they had completed their lessons and could be reintegrated into society. Various cultures in southern Africa created initiation schools for males and females, most notably the Venda and Sotho-Tswana; due to the different needs of the sexes, the layout of the schools was different and Huffman (2007) has argued this is reflected in the layout of sites such as Gombe and Bhila in Zimbabwe and Kubu in Botswana. The cairns resemble graves and Huffman argues these are symbolic graves. At the end of Sotho-Tswana initiation schools, the initiates destroy all paraphernalia associated with childhood, burning their aprons, figurines and the like. The previous school's initiates then erect a cairn to symbolise the birth of the new age-set and regimen. 'As a reversal, the cairns resemble graves, but symbolise rebirth.' The fact that there are so many cairns at Bhila, especially when compared to similar sites in the region, suggests that it was in use for a considerable period of time. Alternatively it can be argued that the site hosted several groups in a very short period of time. Huffman's ideas about circumcision schools have been hotly contested. Pikirayi accepts the physical evidence but refuses to accept that the Shona were responsible. Beach argues the lack of reference in Portuguese documents and the lack of any oral traditions about initiation schools suggests a different use for the site; even though it is not explicitly stated, it might be to do with cremation of individuals, the cairns marking their earthly remains.

Serima Mission (⊕ *S19 30 54 E30 52 40; from the Mvuma–Masvingo road turn left to Felixburg, 5.5km after the Golden Spider Web Hotel; follow the dirt road for 10km, look for a faded sign to the mission, turning right over a cattle grid, after which it's a further 10km; see Central Zimbabwe map, page 177*) While the African Christian art in the Cyrene Mission, 300km away at Bulawayo, is mostly frescoed walls, here at Serima it takes the form of carved wood. In fact there is not one piece of wood in the whole church that has not been in some way decorated.

Following the tradition of his contemporary at Cyrene Mission, Swiss missionary Father John Groeber (1903–72) believed that the young Shona people in his congregation had an innate artistic talent and from 1948 he encouraged them to carve or paint Bible stories. The young pupils from the mission quickly learnt woodworking and sculpting skills, decorating the whole church and in the process developing a unique art form. Narrow tree trunks were the basic raw material, so that much of the carving is in the form of tall, thin poles and pillars. This dictates a very abstract and conceptual treatment, with the emphasis on expression rather than realism. Some of the more notable carvings are the entrance doors themselves and two intricately worked panels set into arches behind the main altar.

Possibly the most impressive works, certainly the most thought-provoking, are in a chapel dedicated to the Martyrs of Uganda, 45 Anglicans and Catholics murdered by Mwanga, the king of Buganda in 1885–87. It is said that Mwanga had homosexual tendencies, and when advances he made to his servants began to be rejected he put the blame squarely on the teachings of the Christian missionaries and exacted his brutal revenge.

As well as woodcarvings and reliefs there are a number of frescoes, the main one depicting the Last Supper above the main altar. This unique style inevitably attracted worldwide attention, driven by the government's PR division. In 1960 the mission was glowingly described in Evelyn Waugh's book *A Tourist in Africa*. Before long, though, Father Groeber was swamped with enquiries, all of which received his polite but terse reply stating that the art was purely for the benefit of the church and not for sale. Needless to say, when the pupils left the school many continued to pursue their skills and several went on to become prominent artists, leading the field in the emerging art form of Shona stone sculpture.

The light, spacious church can seat well over 1,000, and the priest, who can usually be found at the adjacent house, will happily give you a guided tour. This includes an offer to climb the bell tower, which involves a series of five steep, rickety wooden ladders – only for those with a head for heights. Don't steady yourself by grabbing the rope as this makes the bell ring. The bell itself was forged in Germany and imported from Switzerland, but the view over the surrounding flat countryside is not really impressive enough to justify the effort.

MASVINGO   *Telephone code 039*

Although the capital of Masvingo Province and with an estimated 80,000 population, Masvingo itself offers little in terms of touristic appeal, although it's a pleasant enough town for local shopping, with a couple of peaceful places to stop for coffee or lunch. Known until independence as Fort Victoria and still referred to by older folk by its then abbreviated form of Fort Vic, this is Zimbabwe's oldest colonial town, the original fort and mining centre having been established in 1890. Mining in the area continues today, although the town's claim to fame is its proximity to the Great Zimbabwe National Monument (see pages 193–200), a World Heritage Site and one of the country's biggest tourist honeypots. Its other attraction is the Kyle Recreational Park and the Mutirikwe Dam, which supplies water to the town and to the important farmlands around Triangle and Chiredzi to the south. In scenic terms the whole area is stunning with hills and giant, rounded granite *kopjes* reminiscent of the Matobo Hills.

HISTORY Masvingo started life several kilometres from its present location, the shift resulting from a drought two years after it was founded. The town enjoyed its heyday as an important staging post for Rhodes's BSAC Pioneers heading up to establish Fort Salisbury (Harare). It was for a time Rhodesia's largest town, a hub for settlers keen to get rich from mining activities, though many soon relocated and joined Bulawayo's rapidly swelling population.

GETTING THERE At the moment you have to drive or go with an agency. Distances are as follows: Masvingo is 280km/174 miles from Bulawayo, 292km/181 miles from Harare and 297km/185 miles from Mutare. The Bulawayo Publicity Association (*www.bulawayopublicity.com*) is probably the best place to check the latest situation regarding local bus routes although South Africa's Intercape bus service runs from Beitbridge to Harare via Masvingo (see page 156).

TOURIST INFORMATION Like other municipal offices in tourist-starved Zimbabwe, this publicity association (*Robert Mugabe St, over the road from the Chevron Hotel*) is now unmanned with only a phone number on a scruffy note pinned to its door.

WHERE TO STAY Unless you are simply passing through, there is little reason to stay in town. Town hotels tend to cater for the business market, while the best hotels and lodges are along the lakeshore or clustered around the Great Zimbabwe ruins (see below).

In Masvingo
Standard

Regency Flamboyant Hotel (106 rooms) Beitbridge Rd, just outside town; ☎253085/6, 253197; e grapai@regencyhotels.co.zw. This large, rather characterless, modern-style hotel is the best place to stay in the town although it's on the pricey side for what's on offer. It does however have a reasonable restaurant which makes it 1 of the 2 places in town to eat. The en-suite rooms are large

& clean with DSTV & there's a good-sized pool in the spacious gardens. The front desk staff are all very welcoming. **$$$**

Regency Chevron Hotel (46 rooms) Robert Mugabe St; ☎262054/5, 264171; e tchidovi@ gmail.com. This is a dull, busy, local business hotel & although rather faded & dingy appears clean. It also has a sizeable restaurant overlooking the main street into town. **$$**

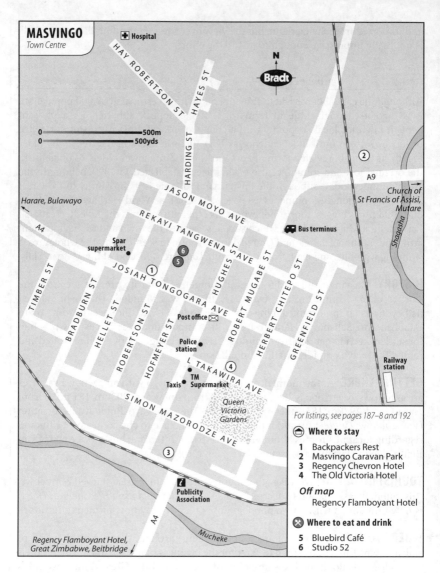

For listings, see pages 187–8 and 192

⌂ Where to stay

1 Backpackers Rest
2 Masvingo Caravan Park
3 Regency Chevron Hotel
4 The Old Victoria Hotel

Off map
Regency Flamboyant Hotel

✕ Where to eat and drink

5 Bluebird Café
6 Studio 52

Basic

⌂ Backpackers Rest Josiah Tongorara Av; ☎266041; m 0773 408951; e binderbarry@aol. com. Basic with dbls & 8-bed dorms. **$**

⋏ Masvingo Caravan Park Just out of town on the Beitbridge road. Quite a pleasant campsite alongside the river but there are nicer & more secure places to camp, around the lakeshore & near Great Zimbabwe. **$**

⌂ The Old Victoria Hotel Cnr Robert Mugabe St & Leopold Takawira Av; ☎263874. A lovely example of restored colonial architecture. In fact the building

is a National Monument, but the interior is anything but restored & you definitely wouldn't want to stay here until it is. Restoration is anticipated, which will probably make it a good place to stay, but no date was available when I enquired. Until then, no information on room rates either.

Great Zimbabwe area (see map, pages 190–1)

Upmarket

⌂ Great Zimbabwe Hotel (47 rooms) Within walking distance of the ruins; ☎265427/9,

264187; e reservations@gzim.africansun.co.zw. Part of the upmarket African Sun leisure group, this plush hotel overlooks the ruins with rooms as well equipped as you would expect for this price. The Great Enclosure restaurant serves mains from US$10 & there are 2 bars. They have an outdoor pool, tennis courts & volleyball, & will arrange guided tours of the ruins. **$$$**

🏠 **Lodge at the Ancient City** (18 lodges) Great Zimbabwe–lakeshore road; m 0773 382369, 0774 401186; reservations@ancientcitylodge. co.zw; www.ancientcitylodge.co.zw. With the wealth of historic stone structures in this area, it's hardly surprising that modern designers have drawn inspiration from their ancient forerunners. This lodge, built in 1996, looking across the valley to the Great Enclosure, has taken the Great Zimbabwe theme almost to extremes, introducing patterned stone-wall forms & textures into every facet of its design & décor. Some say the rooms are a little dark but they're built on a granite ridge, with massive boulders forming an integral part of the innovatively furnished, large rooms & are also used to spectacular effect in the creatively designed thatched bar/lounge. The pool in the outside terrace area is delightful. **$$$**

Basic

🏠 **Great Zimbabwe Family Lodges** In the national park grounds; m 0775 398917, 0774 144998. There's quite a range of accommodations here in this typical National Parks property, from dormitories, small rondavels with shared ablutions to large, en-suite self-catering chalets. They claim to offer 'catering services' but are unspecific so consider this a self-catering place. There is a spacious, pleasant camping area in the grounds. It's within the national park so an ideal budget place to base your Great Zimbabwe visit. **$–$$**

Mutirikwe lakeshore south

(see map, pages 190–1)
Upmarket

🏠 **Hippo Creek Lodge** (18 units) 8km down dirt road from turn-off signed to Kyle Recreational Park; m 0773 026317/9; e hippocreeklodge@ cooltoad.com, marvelousduma@yahoo. com. Drawing heavily on the Great Zimbabwe architectural theme, the lovely cottages are elegantly furnished with fridge, DSTV & huge

bathrooms with tub & shower. There are 4 self-catering chalets with 2 bedrooms & kitchen. A big outdoor bar, pool & *braai* area & they offer facilities for camping & caravans. **$$–$$$**

🏠 **Norma Jeane's** Lakeview Resort (21 rooms) 264879; m 0712 889887; e normajeanes@ yoafrica.com; www.normajeaneslakeviewresort. com. Occasionally still referred to by its former name, Inn on Great Zimbabwe, this delightful, owner-run hotel is ideally situated close to both the lake & Great Zimbabwe. The central colonial-style building houses a cosy bar, restaurant & hotel rooms while outside there are 4 spacious, fully equipped self-catering lodges suitable for families, with paved veranda *braai* facilities & fire pit. For a cheaper option there are 9 budget rooms with spotless, shared ablution & kitchen. Camping facilities (spotless) are available for individuals & overlanders. Wi-Fi connection. The beautifully landscaped & planted gardens are the inspiration of the owner & kept in tip-top condition. Excellent value **$ $$**

Standard

🏠 **Mayfair Lakeside Resort and Spa** (13 units) Sikato Bay – gravel road opposite entrance to national park; m 0779 395732/40; e mayfairlodges@gmail.com; www.mayfairlodges. com. This is a newly renovated & rebuilt property (2012) right on the picturesque shore of Sikato Bay. The units are individual, traditional-style, round thatched chalets, nicely furnished with en-suite facilities. 3 of them have 2 bedrooms, lounge & kitchen for families. There's a central *boma* for dining & relaxing, pool & health spa. It's good to see a new property in the area with an enthusiastic & optimistic manager. **$$**

Basic

🏠 **Mutirikwe Lakeshore Lodges** (14 lodges) 513 Masvingo Rd; 264878, 261121; m 0773 761832; e mutirikwelake@yahoo.com. You can imagine finding hobbits scampering around this place, although you'd want to put them to work with a few pots of paint because it's now looking a bit tired. There are 14 2-storey, 2-bedroom thatched rondavels, some with kitchen for self-caterers. Although there is a small restaurant on site don't expect too much. Camping facilities are rudimentary & although you face the lake, there's an ugly wire fence in the way. **$**

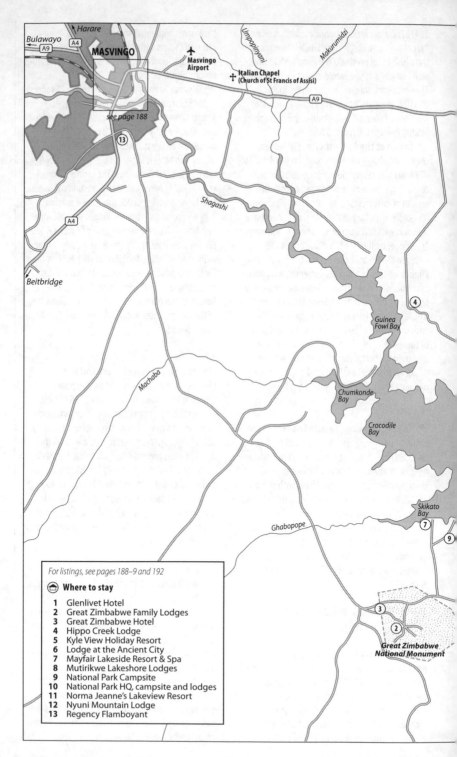

For listings, see pages 188–9 and 192

Where to stay

1   Glenlivet Hotel
2   Great Zimbabwe Family Lodges
3   Great Zimbabwe Hotel
4   Hippo Creek Lodge
5   Kyle View Holiday Resort
6   Lodge at the Ancient City
7   Mayfair Lakeside Resort & Spa
8   Mutirikwe Lakeshore Lodges
9   National Park Campsite
10 National Park HQ, campsite and lodges
11 Norma Jeanne's Lakeview Resort
12 Nyuni Mountain Lodge
13 Regency Flamboyant

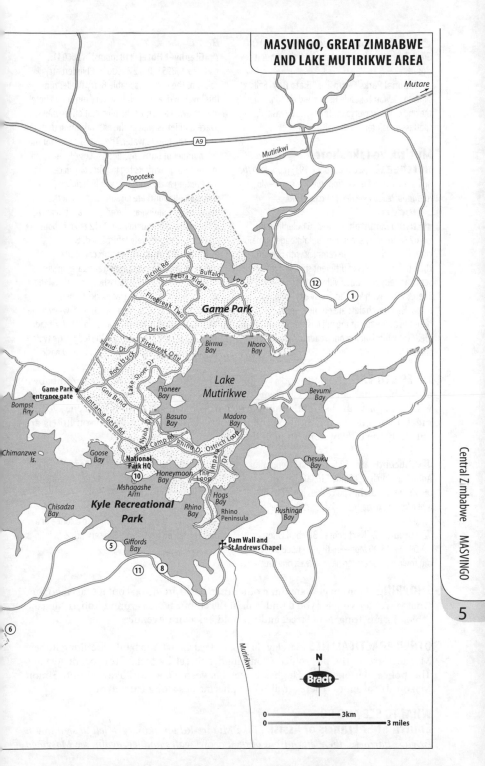

MASVINGO, GREAT ZIMBABWE AND LAKE MUTIRIKWE AREA

Mutare

A9

Mutirikwi

Popoteke

Picnic Rd

Zebra Ridge

Buffalo Loop

Firebreak Two

Game Park

Drive

Bland Dr

Firebreak One

Birma Bay

Nhoro Bay

Roadbury

Lake Shore Dr

Lake Mutirikwe

Gnu Bend

Pioneer Bay

Bevumi Bay

Game Park entrance gate

Entrance Gate Rd

Bompst Bay

Nyala

Basuto Bay

Madoro Bay

River Camp Rd

Rhino Dr

Ostrich Loop

Impala Dr

Chimanzwe Is.

Goose Bay

National Park HQ

Chesuku Bay

10

Honeymoon Bay

The Loop

Mshagashe Arm

Hogs Bay

Chisadza Bay

Kyle Recreational Park

Rhino Bay

Rhino Peninsula

Rushinga Bay

5

Giffords Bay

✝ **Dam Wall and St Andrews Chapel**

11

8

6

Mutirikwi

N

Bradt

0 —— 3km
0 —— 3 miles

🏠 **Kyle View Holiday Resort** (12 chalets) Off Great Zimbabwe Rd. The sign is still there but it's closed.

⚕ **National Parks Campsite Sikato Bay** Follow signs to Mayfair Lakeside Resort and fork right at the end of the gravel road. This is a little-visited, spotlessly maintained site with lovely views.

Mutirikwe lakeshore northeast (see map, page 191) *(approach the first 2 accommodations from the Masvingo–Mutare rd signposted to Kyle Recreational Park)*
Standard
🏠 **Nyuni Mountain Lodge** 61 Glenlivet Rd; m 0774 467473; e nyunimountainlodge@gmail. com. This is quite a large complex with over 20 chalets & rondavels of different sizes in a 'village' set in a shady & bougainvillea-covered garden. There's a bar with kitchen & café-style dining room. Half the chalets are en suite. The main building at the top of the hill has simple but pleasantly furnished rooms leading onto a large shared balcony. **$$**

Basic
🏠 **Glenlivet Hotel** (18 rooms) ✆ 266041; m 0773 408951, 0772 816063; e binderbarry@ aol.com. The very personable Barry Binder runs this lovely old, although now very run-down hotel hidden away amongst the hills that offers walks, peace & quiet as well as the natural spring that supplies the hotel's water. The area is noted for the rich number of butterfly species. 'Cosy' is the word for the lounge with its big log fire, or you can chat the evening away with Barry in his English pub-style bar. All rooms are en suite but go for the ones in the main building as the annex is a bit bare & echoey. Local rumour in mid-2012 talked about the place being extensively refurbished. **$**

⚕ **National Parks lodges and campsite** There is a large, scenic camping and caravan site on the north shore at Mshagashe Arm, with all the usual facilities including a large, clean ablution block. The best pitches offer beautiful views over the lake, with a large, smooth, granite rock tailor-made for watching the sun go down. The lodges are typical recreational Parks style, well kept but fairly basic.

🍴 **WHERE TO EAT** The best food is to be found at the hotels in the Great Zimbabwe area. The usual cluster of Chicken Inn, Bakers Inn and Creamy Inn in Masvingo will cater for your fast-food requirements. You'll struggle to find a decent evening meal if you are staying in town; the Regency Flamboyant and Chevron hotels are currently the only options, though there are two lunch venues.

🖵 **Bluebird Café** 52 Robertson St, opposite Anglican church; ⏲ 08.00–16.00 Mon–Fri, 08.30–14.00 Sat. This place does lunches, with a blackboard of daily specials outside. Excellent reviews.

🖵 **Studio 52** Next door to Bluebird Café; ⏲ 09.00–16.00 Mon–Fri, 09.00–12.00 Sat. Every big town now seems to have at least one pretty little residential property that has been turned into a trendy coffee-cum-lunch boutique, decorated with the work of local artists. Studio 52 serves beautifully presented, tasty light meals, or you can just sit in the shady garden with a coffee or a freshly pressed fruit drink. The carvings & paintings are all for sale.

SHOPPING Don't expect anything other than basic provisions but if Masvingo's got what you're looking for you'll find it all in the compact area around Robert Mugabe Street, Josiah Tongagara Street and Leopold Takawira Avenue.

OTHER PRACTICALITIES Barclays and Standard Chartered banks are along Robert Mugabe Street. The post office is on Hughes Street by Josiah Tongogara Avenue. The police station is on Hughes Street between Leopold Takawira and Simon Mazorodze avenues. There are also two pharmacies along Hughes Street.

WHAT TO SEE AND DO
Church of St Francis of Assisi (*Take Mutare Rd for 4km, turn left at sign to 4th Brigade barracks, then left in front of the barrack gates and left again; see Masvingo*

map, page 190) This beautiful little chapel is more commonly known (and shown on some maps) as the 'Italian Chapel', because it was built towards the end of World War II by Italian POWs from the Ethiopia campaign and contains the remains of 71 of their compatriots. The interior is richly decorated with coloured tiles (check the fabulous mosaic that is actually a painting). Some say (hopelessly optimistically) the ceiling fresco is reminiscent of the Sistine Chapel in Rome; in any case it's well worth a short trip out of town.

Lake Mutirikwe Recreational Park and Game Park (*NP Category 3; 24km by road from Masvingo*) Also known and still signposted by its colonial-era name of Lake Kyle, this is Zimbabwe's second-largest reservoir, fed by several rivers, notably the Shagashi, Popoteke and Muturikwi.

The dam was completed in 1961 and the resulting lake, with its convoluted shoreline, creeks and bays, is the centrepiece of the park. Irrigation was its primary raison d'être, and development of the rich but arid land around Hippo Valley and Triangle to the south was totally dependent on it (see *Murray MacDougall Museum*, page 324). As a result water levels can be subject to large seasonal fluctuations. Recreational boating and fishing used to be the key activities here, and all the lakeside accommodations (most of them on the southern shore) will try to arrange these as well as sundowner cruises – note though that most of the boat owners went out of business, or just closed down waiting for the return of tourists.

The game park to the north of the lake is home to a variety of plains game including white rhino imported from Umfolozi National Park in South Africa. The park is criss-crossed with drives and firebreaks that give access to the whole park and a chance of good game spotting; you can self-drive or your accommodation can arrange a guided drive. The southern and western section of the Murray MacDougall drive that encircles the lake is dramatically scenic, offering the best of Zimbabwe's rural landscapes and well worth a drive from the dam wall – at least until the gravel road takes over from tar, after which the scenery loses its appeal.

GREAT ZIMBABWE

A national monument, this magnificent ruined city on its 722ha site, 25km southeast of Masvingo, is the largest stone structure ever built south of the Sahara. It was the base for a succession of kings and rulers spanning four centuries, and has subsequently had the whole country named after it. The term *zimbabwe* or *dzimbahwe* is derived from the Shona words *dzimba dza mabwe* ('houses of stone'), referring not just to this prime site but to the hundreds, if not thousands, of similar but smaller sites in this area and further afield. The strange carved soapstone birds found here have provided the country with its national symbol.

HISTORY Although this region had almost certainly been already settled for several centuries it is believed the first stone structures were erected around AD1100. There followed continual building development, probably into the 15th century. The provenance of Great Zimbabwe has up until relatively recently been the subject of heated, often bitter debate, stemming from the early European belief that Africans could not possibly have built a structure of such complexity. Indeed, after its 'discovery' by the Portuguese it was popularly believed to be the lost kingdom of Ophir, linked with biblical figures such as Sheba and King Solomon. Much later, others including Cecil Rhodes continued to attribute the ruins to the Phoenicians. In fact this was a massively important religious and political centre, not a military fort but a continually developing tribute to a long succession of rulers who had wide-reaching influence. It is believed that in its heyday the city complex housed up to 20,000 people. Today, it is one of Zimbabwe's two manmade UNESCO World Heritage Sites (the other being Khami Ruins; see *Chapter 9*, pages 307–9).

Trade and influence The belief that fabulous wealth might be hidden here has given rise to a spate of wanton treasure hunting, destroying archaeological evidence that might have revealed much about the history of the site.

Shona people first settled the area, possibly as early as the 8th century when the climate and soil fertility encouraged agriculture and livestock rearing. But although these activities remained the mainstay of the expanding community, it was the region's strategic trading position that brought true wealth and gave rise to the first permanent stone structures. Gold, ivory and intricately worked copper and ironwork were traded for cloth, beads, ceramics and glassware from Arabia, India and China, all via Swahili traders from the east African coast. Commercial life probably peaked during the 14th century. Political influence accompanied this wealth, with Great Zimbabwe becoming the power base for a huge region from the coast well into today's Botswana.

After some four centuries during which a succession of kings and rulers presided over this important international trading empire, Great Zimbabwe slipped into terminal decline. Today it is generally accepted that its drop in fortunes was the result of the population outgrowing the local resources necessary to sustain it. By 1500, trees would have been felled and burnt over a huge area and large herds of cattle would have exhausted the grazing. Earlier theories of invasion or political dissent have given way to the view that people simply abandoned the site and moved in groups to several smaller and more sustainable areas. Certainly, two competitors in the form of Khami and Mutapa diverted resources and trade from the main city for their own purposes. Khami (Kame) became the new capital, with other centres at Dhlo Dhlo (Danangombe) and Nalatale (see page 184).

Construction The granite rocks of Zimbabwe's central plateau provided raw material, but a quick tour of the Great Enclosure alone shows just how enormous the construction task must have been. It has been estimated that over one million stone bricks weighing some 15,000 tonnes were needed just for the main walls. Transporting rock from ever more distant sources, and shaping this vast number of bricks, would have been a continuous labour throughout the centuries of occupation. In common with the pyramids of Egypt, it was once thought that this must have been the work of slaves, but most historians now believe this vast project was undertaken by a succession of labourers from the community, willingly working towards a common social or religious goal.

Nature helped to some extent. Ancient geological processes had created lateral weaknesses in the rock structure, and subsequent weathering led to the exfoliation ('peeling') of large sheets of granite from their base. The task of shaping bricks out of these relatively thin sheets would have been much easier than dealing with boulders and blocks. Nevertheless, large rock forms still needed to be utilised and the splitting technique involved heating the rocks with fire, swiftly followed by a dousing of cold water, causing them to crack, although it must have been a painfully slow process.

The entire complex was built using a drystone walling technique, stones laid without the use of mortar. The structural integrity of the buildings relies simply on fitting stones of different shapes and sizes precisely together to form strong, binding walls. To give a sense of scale, the base of the eastern wall of the Great Enclosure is in places 6m thick, tapering to 4m at the top, and some 11m high. The Hill Complex, the first enclosures to have been built, makes use of the existing landscape, with many huge, immoveable boulders cleverly integrated into the overall design.

As decades led into centuries, structures were gradually extended. As the structures grew in scale and the decades progressed, so the building techniques improved. At the northwest entrance of the Great Enclosure, where work clearly began, the stonework is noticeably uneven, but as progress was made in an anticlockwise direction, by the time the circumference was completed probably two centuries later, the wall was considerably higher, with stones cut and laid with more skill.

Enter the Europeans Documentary evidence shows that the Portuguese knew of Great Zimbabwe (and other *zimbabwes* in the area) from the early 1500s, but it wasn't until the late 19th century that Europeans visiting the site showed any interest in the origins and purpose of these structures. The most important of these visitors was Carl Mauch, a German geologist and explorer, who in 1871 made the first of three visits. Although he completely misunderstood the identity of Great Zimbabwe's builders and developers, he described the ruins in great detail, before wholesale vandalism began in the search for treasure. Paradoxically, although Mauch was more of a conservationist than a treasure seeker, his speculation that this was the work of the Phoenicians and linked to biblical figures such as Sheba and King Solomon fed the greed of treasure hunters and hastened the destruction.

In 1891 Theodore Bent, whom Rhodes had charged with excavating the ruins, removed four bird carvings plus a broken one, no doubt along with many other artefacts. But the greatest destruction of the monument was caused in 1902 by no less than its first curator, Richard Hall, who should have known better. He indiscriminately dug for gold and other treasure, removing huge volumes of soil from many of the enclosures and discarding any artefact that couldn't be converted into cash. He is also accused of re-enforcing the widely held belief that the complex was built by others than indigenous Africans and that his widespread destruction of the site was designed to destroy archaeological evidence that would have disproved this popular misconception. Two years later, having caused untold damage, he was dismissed from his position.

One piece of 'evidence' that Mauch cited for his belief in the Phoenician theory was that one of the timber lintels he found was cedar wood, which he suggested had been imported by the Queen of Sheba. Despite the fact that the wood subsequently proved to be tamboti, a local hardwood, his theory was supported well into the 20th century. Others postulated that the architects were Arabians, Egyptians or Greeks – in fact almost anyone other than Africans.

In the early decades of the 20th century two British archaeologists carried out extensive studies at the site. Dr David Randall-MacIver, in 1906, was the first to prove beyond reasonable doubt that Africans had constructed Great Zimbabwe. After those findings were roundly dismissed, most notably by Cecil Rhodes, Dr Gertrude Caton-Thompson followed up with even more compelling evidence as a result of her all-female expedition in 1929. But the authorities steadfastly refused to accept their findings.

Xenophobic politicians of the day would go to any length to avoid crediting Africans for a building project of such sophistication, regardless of the fact the building techniques used, though impressive in scale and imagination, were far from sophisticated. These naysayers who claimed this structure was unique, ignored the fact that there were hundreds of similarly inspired, though smaller examples of such architecture all over this region. In 1970 the Rhodesian government passed

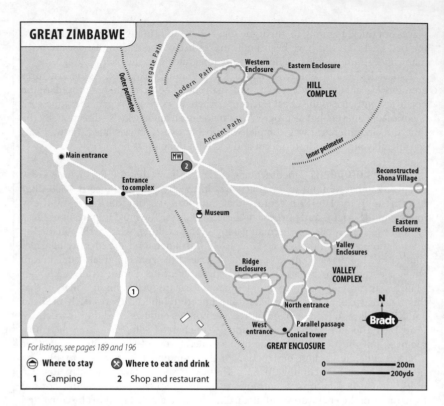

a law requiring that the theory of exotic origins be given equal prominence with the claim for local development in any publication discussing the matter. This law remained in place until independence, and to this day it is not difficult to find people who are still in denial.

GETTING THERE It's 25km southeast of Masvingo, but there is no public transport to the site. If you don't have your own car, enquire at your hotel or lodge as all the larger ones have their own transport facilities. The site is well signposted, turning left off the A4 Beitbridge road just outside town.

ORIENTATION The ticket office (entry $10 adult, children $5) is by the roundabout on the approach road after which there is a short drive to the car park by the entry gate itself. The park accommodations and campsite are well signposted from here. Once through the entrance gate the curio shop, refreshment centre, museum and toilets are just a short walk.

There are three main areas to explore: the Hill Complex, the Valley Complex and the Great Enclosure and I suggest doing it in that order. You can dash round the whole site, including the museum, in about two hours, but to do it justice and soak in the atmosphere, allow half a day.

TOURIST INFORMATION You can hire an unofficial guide at the entrance for $3–5, and it's worth doing if only to be shown the best route around and having key areas pointed out, but don't expect to learn much more from them than you'll get from the booklets. That said, most feedback, including my own, is that these very

top left & bottom left — Traditional performers at Victoria Falls — Zimbabwe's culture has a long oral tradition of folklore and storytelling and performances are often augmented with music and dance (both SS) page 29

above — Development projects at work in Manhete village. Zimbabwe also has a number of volunteering opportunities for short-term visitors (DS/C) page 148

left — A young girl selling fruit in a market in Harare — Chapunga Village has a monthly farmers' market and food fair (SS) page 165

below right — Friendly children collecting water in a rural village (SS)

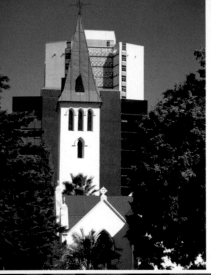

left   The cosmopolitan capital of Harare has a thriving art scene as well as a multitude of shops, cafés and entertainment (SS) page 153

below   Brightly coloured frescoes in the Cyrene Mission Chapel near Bulawayo vividly illustrate Africanised biblical scenes and scriptures (PM) page 306

bottom   Home to both traditional and modern art, the National Art Gallery is the most beautiful building in downtown Bulawayo (PM) page 302

above   The intricately walled Nalatale Ruins outside of Gweru are the finest examples of stone wall symbolism in Zimbabwe (PM) page 184

right   Painted on the underside of a massive overhanging boulder in a natural amphitheatre, the Diana's Vow rock painting is among the most important rock-art sites in the country (AVZ) page 365

below   A reconstructed Karanga village at the Great Zimbabwe ruins (AVZ) page 193

above left Cape buffalo bull
(*Syncerus caffer*)
(RDT/MP/FLPA)

above right White rhinoceros
(*Ceratotherium simum*)
(AVZ)

left Pride of lions
(*Panthera leo*) (AVZ)

below left African elephants
(*Loxodonta africana*)
at a watering hole (PM)

below right African leopard
(*Panthera pardus pardus*)
(IY/FLPA)

above   Sylvester, the 'ambassador'
cheetah of the Victoria Falls
Wildlife Trust (EO) page 266

right   Black-faced vervet monkeys
(*Cercopithecus aethiops*)
(PMB/S)

below left   Male chacma baboon
(*Papio hamadryas ursinus*)
(NC/S)

below right   African wild dog
(*Lycaon pictus*)
(DAP/S)

above left   **Warthog (*Phacochoerus africanus*)** (FL/FLPA)

above right   **Burchell's zebra (*Equus quagga burchellii*)** (PT/S)

below   **Greater kudu (*Tragelaphus strepsiceros*)** (WW/FLPA)

bottom left   **Nile crocodile (*Crocodylus niloticus*)** (MU)

bottom right   **Hippopotamus (*Hippopotamus amphibius*)** (SS)

above left — Southern yellow-billed hornbill
(*Tockus leucomelas*) (AVZ)

above right — Crowned cranes
(*Balearica regularum*) (L/S)

right — White-fronted bee-eater
(*Merops bullockoides*) (MU)

below left — Livingstone's turaco
(*Tauraco livingstonii*) (AVZ)

below right — Yellow-billed storks
(*Micteria ibis*) (MU)

personable guys do a pretty good job and are well worth supporting, especially as you may not have been able to obtain a booklet. If you plan to tour the site without a guide it is worth visiting the curio shop first to buy the very good explanatory booklet, *Great Zimbabwe* ($10), published by PhotoSafari, with good maps of the site and a reasonable amount of information for a first visit. The shop also sells *A Trail Guide to the Great Zimbabwe National Monument*. (If you see either of these titles elsewhere before you visit, I recommend buying them, as the shop is often out of stock.) For a more in-depth account, look for *Great Zimbabwe Described and Explained*, by Peter Garlake, possibly Zimbabwe's most authoritative expert on the country's history and archaeology.

WHAT TO SEE

The Hill Complex A hilltop site, with its commanding views, was the first area to be developed, with construction taking place from around the beginning of the 12th century. This complex is a series of enclosures, and there is a reasonable degree of agreement amongst historians and archaeologists that the early rulers resided here, together with their spirit mediums.

There are two main routes up the hill, the Ancient Path and the Modern Path, both setting off from the curio shop. The Ancient Path is the steeper but anyone with a reasonable degree of fitness can easily negotiate it. Many prefer to ascend the easier Modern Path and come down via the Ancient route, which offers lovely views of the valley, including the distant Great Enclosure. Note how the ancient masonry has been integrated into the natural granite features. The walls, paths and enclosures weave between and around massive boulders that in many cases give the impression they were deliberately placed for architectural effect. Of course the builders simply had to find a way around these objects, in the process creating fantastic structures that even today inspire architects and designers.

The top of these paths brings you to the first and the largest enclosure, the Western or Royal Enclosure, where the early kings would have lived, possibly with their senior wives and close family. Later kings may have moved base to live in the Great Enclosure; on the other hand, this may have been used for their senior relatives. The west wall is a massive structure originally decorated with turrets along the top, several of which have been reconstructed. It is here that one of the soapstone birds was found. Following the path eastwards brings you to the Covered Passage into the Southern Enclosures area. Then, with the small Recess Enclosures on your right, you'll find steps running up to the entrance to the Eastern Enclosure. This covered gate and passageway were constructed with stone as opposed to timber lintels and as a result have remained standing in their original, unrenovated state. Six of the famous carved stone birds were found on pillars surrounding this enclosure, and other recovered artefacts suggest that this was where all-important rituals were carried out, giving rise to its alternative name, the Ritual Enclosure. The spirit medium or traditional healer enjoyed almost as much power as the king, and it is likely they occupied this area of the complex. Your guide will delight in describing in detail the gory animal sacrifices thought to have been carried out here. If you have a good head for heights you can follow him up to a lofty rock platform, the Balcony Enclosure, from where the king might have observed the rituals below.

A circular path from the Eastern Enclosure takes you past the Gold Furnace Enclosure and then to the Ritual Cave, actually a large, shallow space under an overhanging rock. Its position is such that it would certainly have had an important function: its commanding view over the valley and Great Enclosure has given rise to speculation that the king may have used it to survey the activities of his subjects far below. Rituals here would have involved ancestors and rain making, and with the floor of the cave covered with ironstone brought in from afar other ritual uses are suggested. Later kings, it is believed/assumed, moved down to the Great Enclosure, leaving most of the Hill Complex to the spirit mediums.

The Valley Complex From a visual point of view the unrestored Valley Complex is the least appealing of the three complexes, comprising a number of low, very ruined enclosure walls amongst a considerable amount of rubble. But in archaeological terms this is an extremely important area, as some of the most significant artefacts have been found here. The ridge and valley enclosures in this relatively low-lying area are assumed to have been dwelling places of junior royalty and noblemen.

This is also the site of the royal treasury. While it's likely that anything considered valuable in today's terms would have been plundered in the early 20th century, the vast amount of ironware as well as imported goods that has been subsequently retrieved indicates that this would have been a store of amazing wealth. The other important find from this complex is the beautifully carved soapstone bird that subsequently became Zimbabwe's national symbol. This 'chevron bird' (so-called after the chevron pattern beneath the bird's feet) is probably the latest, certainly the most intricately carved, of them all and features a crocodile, a potent symbol of fertility, climbing up the pedestal.

The Great Enclosure This is without doubt the most visually impressive part of the complex. It was the last to be completed and displays the most advanced building techniques. It is also the area that has received the most restoration work. With its wealth of fascinating, mystical and highly photogenic features, displayed in every piece of publicity material, it's hardly surprising that many first-time visitors think that this is all there is to Great Zimbabwe.

There are three entrances, but it is usual to start at what is considered to be the main, north entrance, using the Sunken Passageway from the Valley Complex. While guides will generally take you from here straight to the dramatic Parallel Passage, you may want to use the northwest entrance and take an anticlockwise route as this follows the direction in which the outer wall was built. You can trace the progress of the building as stone-laying techniques improved, finally completing the circle in the northeast with the massive, 11m-high, 5m-thick wall, topped with a chevron decoration.

Once within the enclosure one is faced with a number of structures that possibly made up the living area of the later kings and their immediate female family members. There is a circular enclosure immediately inside the north entrance and some slightly raised platforms and enclosure walls to the south. Sadly, thanks to Bent, Hall and Sir John Willoughby, another early excavator, much archaeological evidence has been destroyed and it is impossible to give definitive explanations for these structures.

But the biggest mystery in the Great Enclosure remained relatively untouched by treasure seekers. Shaded by trees at the southern end of the Parallel Passage stands the majestic, 10m-high, tapering Conical Tower. It must have been tempting for early Europeans to believe the tower housed the 'crown jewels', but this is a completely solid construction. It's a small miracle it wasn't completely dismantled in an effort to find a hidden chamber. In the event, Mauch removed the top layers of the tower, while Caton Thompson dug a tunnel beneath it, in search of a hidden chamber but both efforts were to no avail. Its purpose was therefore symbolic rather than functional, and you can take your pick from the theories about it. Was it in the shape of a granary? A phallus? Perhaps it represents the maize-like, sorghum plant that was probably their staple cereal. It is likely to be a fertility symbol, for either the king or the crops.

In terms of dramatic impact, however, the tower has to compete with the Parallel Passage on the eastern side of the enclosure. This wonderfully curved, very narrow walkway, flanked on either side by 11m-high walls, is almost claustrophobic along its 70m length. In places it is only wide enough for one person. Some believe this was deliberately planned to form a concealed entrance to the central living area, while others suggest it was a convenient afterthought. Perhaps the inner wall was the original outer wall, but as the western wall advanced and masonry techniques improved a new, more technically impressive outer wall was added.

The Zimbabwe bird carvings Mystery and speculation surround these totemic soapstone carvings, yet one of them, the so-called chevron bird, has become Zimbabwe's national symbol, appearing on banknotes, postage stamps and the national flag.

While they clearly represent birds of prey, their precise identity is open to debate, with some researchers favouring the fish eagle and others going for the bateleur, both of which are potent divine symbols for the Shona. If their identity is unclear, their purpose is further clouded in mystery. Eight birds are known to have been found at the site, with a suggestion that two more were also discovered. With Great Zimbabwe's occupation spanning possibly 400 years it has been postulated that a new bird was created to represent each king in turn. That theory requires a rather lengthy average reign of 40–50 years, and with no supporting documentary evidence it remains pure speculation.

Originally each sat atop a 1m-tall pedestal, but the European plunderers separated most from their bases for ease of transport. Willi Posselt and Theodore Bent relocated five or even six to South Africa, one directly into the hands of Cecil Rhodes, and half a broken bird found its way to Germany. For some reason the chevron bird was never taken out of the country. Those that went to South Africa (except the Rhodes one) were traded back into their country of origin in 1981 in exchange for Zimbabwe's world-renowned hymenoptera collection (bees, wasps and ants). Today, of the eight birds discovered and documented, seven are back in the country, and several can be viewed in a gloomy backroom of the site

RUINS AND ANCIENT MONUMENT TOURS

The magnificent stone-built ruins scattered the length and breadth of Zimbabwe have excited the imagination of visitors ever since they were revealed to the outside world almost two hundred years ago. You can visit several of the most important ruins in a three- or five-day tour. Two World Heritage Sites – Great Zimbabwe and Khami – are must-see attractions as well as lesser known wonders including the last capitals of the empire, Dhlo Dhlo and Nalatale. Get the lowdown on the rise and fall of southern Africa's biggest pre-colonial empire while exploring exquisitely beautiful areas in less visited portions of Zimbabwe.

This tour is run only by professional archaeologist and historian Paul Hubbard in conjunction with the Amalinda Collection and the Bulawayo Club. For bookings details and prices contact **e** hubcapzw@gmail.com, resman@amalindacollection.co.zw, or visit www.campamalinda.com.

museum. It now only remains for the return of the final bird from the Rhodes estate in Capetown to bring the whole set back where they belong. There is a legend that once all the birds have returned home to roost, peace and prosperity will engulf the country!

THE A4 ROAD SOUTH This road has only small villages dotted along the 288km to Beitbridge with only one recommended **place to stay**, the Lion and Elephant Motel (see page 322). But if that's full, the Bubi Village Motel by the petrol station 2km away is, clean, basic but worth a try.

The northern section of this road is, however, stunning in scenic beauty with those massive granite whalebacks, *kopjes* and hills forming the southern end of the Great Dyke. Then after you cross the Runde River you find yourself entering the flat *lowveld* – it's a dull drive from here but good preparation for the joys of Beitbridge.

6

Lake Kariba and the Zambezi Valley

This chapter follows the Zambezi River from the southwestern beginning of Lake Kariba through to the northern boundary with Mozambique, taking in the lake itself, Matusadona and Mana Pools, all the way round to the Mavuradonha Mountains in the far north. A little to the south of the river, the seldom visited and very wild Chizarira National Park beckons the more adventurous traveller.

Over eons, the Zambezi has carved itself a deep valley, creating a number of unique shore-side habitats, from floodplains to steep escarpments. These features support a host of activities, including fishing, canoeing and camping on its shores, living on a houseboat as it swells to form Lake Kariba, or chilling out watching game coming to the river to drink and bathe under an unrivalled African sunset.

Pretty well this whole area along the Zambezi (with the exception of Kariba town itself) can justifiably be described as 'remote'. Road access to many of these places is only possible with a 4x4 with enthusiastic drivers and passengers who have the time available to negotiate these slow and, at best, rutted dirt roads, especially during or after rains. As a result, there is a growing number of small private charter air services offering a fairly bewildering range of routes to satisfy all of the accommodations in this region. Only the most dedicated independent traveller would want to organise their own flights so I have not attempted to list airlines and routes, which seem to be ever changing, safe in the knowledge that when you book your safari camp, they will arrange all your transfers for you.

Along the river from Deka Drum to Mlibizi, although everything is designed to service the fishing fraternity, there's no reason for non-fishing folk to avoid the area as all the spots are situated in delightful grounds on the banks of the Zambezi or Lake Kariba. Without the sport to occupy your days, however, there is precious little else to do here other than birdwatching or chilling out with a book on a sunbed. People planning to tow their own boats up here should consider two things: the condition of many of the dirt roads can be quite demanding for trailers and the going will be slow, plus the various fees payable to Parks can make this quite an expensive business, such that most people hire boats instead.

Bream, tigerfish and chessa are the main targets and the best fishing is in the summer months, August to March. Bearing in mind the popularity of this area plus the fact that several of the resorts reserve much of their accommodation for regular club visitors, you will need to book well in advance for the main holiday seasons. September and October can offer excellent fishing although if you are staying by the lake as opposed to the river, this is the time when the water starts to warm up at the end of winter and some years the lake can 'turn'. When this happens, masses of rotten algae that settle at the bottom of the lake rise to the surface and for a couple of weeks, maybe even a full month or more, the smell becomes unpleasant and the fish taste muddy.

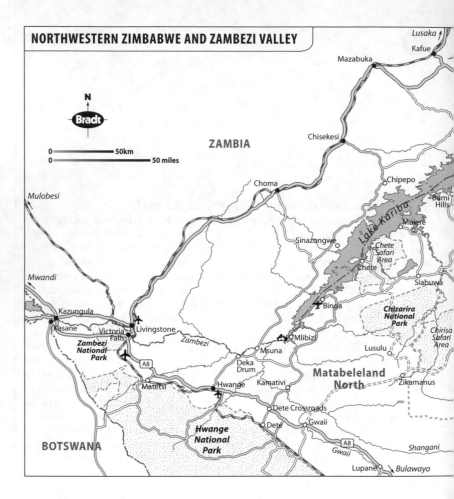

NORTHWESTERN ZIMBABWE AND ZAMBEZI VALLEY

DEKA DRUM TO BINGA

The stretch of river up to Binga, where the Zambezi starts to swell out into Lake Kariba, is probably Zimbabwe's most popular recreational fishing area.

DEKA DRUM With such an odd name it's a place you want to visit, but don't expect a town or even a village here; there's just a few dwellings situated in a beautiful riverine setting. Once a popular fishing centre it's now pretty well derelict. The name is said to derive from an eerie drumming sound, heard many years ago, from a small nearby island but nobody in the community was able to identify the drummer.

Getting there To reach Deka Drum from Bulawayo or Victoria Falls, drive to Hwange and look for the turning north, about 2km west of the 'train on the green' on the Victoria Falls side. There's no signage to Deka Drum itself so look out for the signpost to Sundowner Adventure Fishing Safaris. It's a 45km hilly tar road, very scenic but narrow and twisty with lots of blind bends and hillcrests so it's not a road to travel fast. You'll drive past countless small and picturesque Tonga *kraals* and villages with a sparkling new Catholic church or mission every 5km – or so it seems.

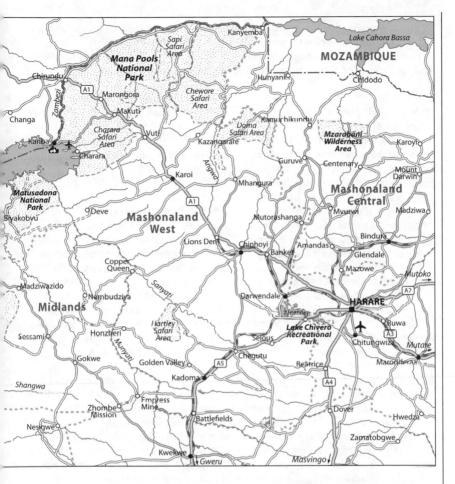

There's a somewhat more adventurous route to Deka Drum via Jambezi that you may want to consider if you're leaving from Victoria Falls. Although it's not shown on most maps, it's a substantial dirt road of about 110km that roughly follows the route of the Zambezi although you don't actually get to see the gorges or river until you arrive at Deka. It does, however, get you into the rural areas; it's quite scenic but though it's a shorter distance than the Hwange route, it will take a little longer, as it's not a tarred road. After crossing the cattle grid outside of Victoria Falls, look out for the sign on the left to Gorges Lodge – it's also signed to Deka Mouth. There are no signposts along the route but it is straightforward, with only one fork where you could go wrong – take the left fork which is effectively straight on. The dirt roads in this whole area tend to be stony and parts of the first section to Gorges Lodge are quite rough but thereafter it eases off a little and the run becomes a little smoother although corrugations are an ever-present annoyance. Don't drive fast along here, though. The loose stony surface is hazardous and there are a number of sharp bends and some sudden inclines with blind crests.

Where to stay There's nowhere at Deka Drum itself except **Deka Drum Fishing Resort**. I include it only because, although now derelict, it has featured prominently in earlier guidebooks. It's only a short distance off the tar road so maybe check it out, in case they have rebuilt, which I understand is a possibility.

Further along the tar road you come to a wide dirt road signposted to Msuna Fishing Resort and there are two good places to stay along this road.

Upmarket

🏠 **Msuna Fishing Resort** (20 cottages & houses) ⊕ S18 01 13 E026 49 29; 3km further along the road from the Olive Beadle turn-off; currently no phone; e msunaresort@gmail.com; Skype: msunaresort. At the end of the road you'll find this stunning lakeside spot, which contains privately owned thatched cottages & houses of varying sizes & styles available for hire at what can only be considered as amazingly good rates. The management company looks after most of the lettings on behalf of the owners & will advise you on the various accommodations available to suit your requirements. Nearly all are holiday homes complete with pools, outside entertainment areas & most come with their own chef, boat & skipper included in the price – some even throw in boat fuel (petrol not diesel). It's self-catering so you must bring in all your own supplies. It's all set in

lush gardens with constant birdsong & most of the properties have lake views. An excellent venue for groups of friends & families. Lettings are strictly by prior booking, as last minute 'walk-ins' cannot be catered for. Dec is extremely popular here & usually fully booked by Jun. **$**

Standard

🏠 **Olive Beadle Fishing Camp** (2 chalets) ⊕ S18 01 42 E026 47 41; bookings via Ansie Burger 📞 0714 164145; e ansieb28@gmail.com. You'll see the track signed on the left about 11km from the Msuna turn-off. This is quite a large complex in pleasant green surroundings by the river. Although most accommodation is owned by fishing clubs there are 2 large, well-appointed 4-bed, self-catering chalets available to the public, & a campsite. Fishing competitions are held here in Sep–Oct, so booking is essential. **$**

MLIBIZI This is another little fishing resort area that has three very pleasant places to stay, all overlooking the western end of Lake Kariba. It was once a bustling little centre – it is the ferry terminal, so when the ferry stopped in 2000 the village went to sleep and only catered to the recreational fishing market. Things are slowly picking up now as the ferry has resumed with a tentative schedule (see pages 215–16). There are plenty of signs around warning you to drink only boiled or bottled water. There's a basic supermarket at the entrance to Mlibizi Zambezi Resort, where you can stock up on ice for your coolbox as well as on bottled water.

Getting there The dirt road from Msuna turn-off to Mlibizi is quite rough and hilly with baobabs and towering acacia trees as it crosses the Gwaai River and meets up with the scenic tar road from the Dete crossroads via Kamativi. For details on Kariba Ferry see pages 215–16.

🏠 **Where to stay** This area lost its landline telephone connection in 2006 and was still disconnected in late 2012, so communication is by mobile phone or email where satellite links are available.

Standard

🏠 **Mlibizi Hotel** (20+ chalets, bungalows, villas) m 0773 507629, 0712 763864; e mlibizilodge@iwayafrica.co.zw. Well signposted as you drive through the village, this lodge complex is set in spacious, lakeside gardens. The various chalets sleep 2–5 people & there are 2 large villas that can accommodate 12–15. The chalets

are simple, clean & quite large, but short on decoration & interior design. There's a pool, open-air Mashasha bar on the lakeshore & a restaurant that features a somewhat off-putting stuffed hippo head over one of the tables. Although it markets itself as 'the best place to do nothing' they offer a range of lake-based activities including cruises & boat hire for fishing. **$–$$**

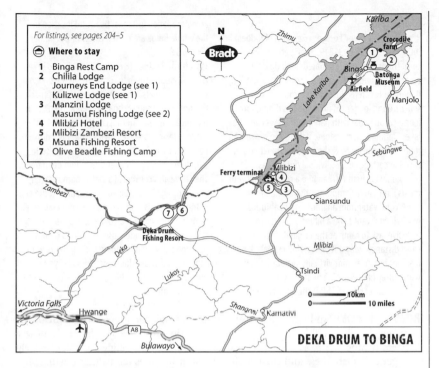

For listings, see pages 204–5

Where to stay
1. Binga Rest Camp
2. Chilila Lodge
   Journeys End Lodge (see 1)
   Kulizwe Lodge (see 1)
3. Manzini Lodge
   Masumu Fishing Lodge (see 2)
4. Mlibizi Hotel
5. Mlibizi Zambezi Resort
6. Msuna Fishing Resort
7. Olive Beadle Fishing Camp

DEKA DRUM TO BINGA

🏠 **Manzini Lodge** (4 chalets, 1 cottage)
m 0778 730910; e manzini5/@gmail.com. This
is a new accommodation on the approach to town
with no signboard so look on the left side of the
road for the gate with the number 105 & a fish
motif. 4 chalets with 3 beds each plus a family
cottage with 6 beds are all set on a beautifully
landscaped & planted hillside slope leading down
to the lakeside. The en-suite chalets are open plan
with stylish furnishings & the main building, which
houses a small lounge & dining area, has a stream
running through it out into the garden where
there's also a pool. They have 2 boats & a small
pontoon. Very popular with ferry passengers. Self-
catering **$**, FB **$$**

🏠 **Mlibizi Zambezi Resort** (14 chalets) ❉ 09
65061/4; m 0779 549769; e imigogo@gmail.
com, galaxy@mweb.co.zw. Just down the road,
with the entrance next to the supermarket/
bottle store, is this friendly fishing resort on high
ground overlooking the lake. Well-appointed
& good-sized self-catering chalets sleep 2–8.
Kitchens are fully equipped & include deep
freezes to store your catch. There's a camp &
caravan site, 2 swimming pools, boat-launching
facilities & pontoon rafts for hire for fishing &
sightseeing. **$**

TOWARDS BINGA The road to Binga from Mlibizi is about 60km long, a delightful,
windy, hilly and scenic drive with lots of Tonga hamlets/*kraals* on the way.
Previously very narrow and pot-holed, in late 2012 retarring gangs were slowly
making their way towards the village from the south so by the time you read this
the road should be fine.

🏠 **Where to stay** Binga itself has become very run-down and there's only one
decent place to stay there now, but there are two good accommodations off the
Binga road, on the right 7km before you reach town, along a sandy, often rocky,
road. The track's about 4km but it's well worth it when you get there.

Upmarket

🏠 **Masumu River Lodge** (6 chalets, 4 lodges) 📞 09 244990, 0772 231819; **e** afspec@yoafrica. com. This is beautifully situated, high up on a promontory with Lake Kariba virtually surrounding it, with fully catered luxury twin-room chalets & self-catering lodges. Main lodge has dining room, lounge & open bar with panoramic views over the lake & lagoons, perfect for watching the sunset. All rooms have fans & AC & the 2-storey thatched self-catering cottages use individual *braai* areas & a communal kitchen. You can hire a chef to cook your meals if required. Camping is also available with hot & cold water from an immaculate ablution block. If you want to be a bit more spartan & reclusive, ask to camp at the 'original' campsite, a short distance away but wonderfully isolated; no facilities but on a point virtually surrounded by water. They have 3 fishing boats & equipment for hire & a sunset cruiser. This is the best-appointed accommodation in a most beautiful location in the whole Binga area – self catering **$,** dinner b@b **$$$**

🏠 **Chilila Lodge** (8 chalets) **m** 0772 261174; **e** chilila@econetmobile.co.zw. This is a working *kapenta* fishery (see box) so ignore the approach through a workshop & boatyard area; then you'll find pleasant self-catering chalets in well-kept gardens facing the lake, 5 with a twin & a dbl bedroom each, 2 with a twin room, all en-suite with fully equipped kitchens including deep freeze. They have also converted a 2-bedroom caravan into a cottage, with built-on bathroom. At the end of the property is a newly created, small lakeside camping site with hot & cold water & laundry facilities (**$**). The lodge also operates a double-pontoon houseboat, sleeping 8 & complete with captain, cook & deckhand for US$500 – you supply provisions and pay for fuel. Boats & rafts available for fishing hire. **$$**

BINGA This was (and still is) the administrative hub for the resettlement of the Batonga people forcibly displaced by the creation of Lake Kariba. It is now a *kapenta* fishing centre as well as a popular fishing base although the recent retreat into general shabbiness and the paucity of visitor facilities tell us that business has been poor in recent years.

The compact and very small town centre by the police station and T-junction no longer has its Spar supermarket, and the only shops are of the subsistence variety in a dusty area on the right as you approach the T-junction. The only reason to visit this particular spot is for the craft market, which features the work of a thriving co-operative handicraft industry. Traditional Batonga basketware, beadwork, drums and carved stools and doors can be found here. Behind the market is a small but interesting museum dedicated to the Batonga people. Turn left at the T-junction for the post office and a little further on is the hospital (that you very much hope you will not need). At the end of that road is the airstrip, which some locals say is due to be expanded to take international flights. Why? Apparently coal has been found in the area and there's the prospect of a huge new mine complex in the planning that will bring much needed business to the area and, no doubt, untold damage to the environment.

🏠 **Where to stay** There are now only three accommodations to be found at the end of the road, about 5km from the T-junction, and of these only one is worthy of consideration. Given the general lack of bedspace in Binga, I have included the other two, although I do not recommend them.

Standard

🏠 **Kulizwe Lodge** (8 chalets & camping) 📞 015 286; **m** 0773 666243. This lakeside self-catering establishment has spacious, brick-built chalets, each with 2 dbl or twin rooms, & is extremely good value. They are well maintained & look as if they would be cool in summer. Oddly, the kitchens are poky affairs in small outbuildings by each chalet, as if they were an afterthought. There's a good-sized pool with large thatched *lapa* & *braai* facilities. A huge car park allows plenty of room for manoeuvring your boat trailer.

Camping is available, with water standpipes & electricity, & you can while away your evening watching the fireflies in the grass (in fact they are bioluminescent beetles trying to get married). The well-tended, spacious gardens look out over the lake but there's a small dirt road in the way that services the nearby houseboat preparation area. There's a little village with a school & *shebeen* a stone's throw away, though the evening laughter & chatter is not at all obtrusive or unpleasant. **$**

Sub-basic

🏠 **Binga Rest Camp** (7 chalets) 📞015 244. The entrance is directly opposite Kulizwe Lodge. Wrecked cars litter the entrance to this once respectable lodge, which is a shadow of its former self. The chalets look reasonable from the outside but I was told they were fully booked so I couldn't

view them. This is the same story told to me by a very uninterested 'receptionist' when I visited the place for the first edition of this book & by all accounts appears to be their standard response to enquiries. You used to be able to camp here but the site is more akin to a rubbish tip. But it is very cheap & may be a last-ditch consideration for desperate people on a tight budget. **$**

🏠 **Journeys End Lodge** (5 rooms) 📞Binga Rest Camp (above); m 0773 507581. At the end of the road by the croc farm entrance, this previously very pleasant lodge has new ownership & it's gone steeply downhill. The large rooms, twins & dbls are arranged in a single-storey block, all opening out onto a wide shared veranda with beautiful views of the lake & well-kept gardens & pool in the foreground. It's self-catering, with a shared kitchen & *braai* facilities & a large dining room &

KAPENTA: A VERY DESIRABLE ALIEN (PLUS A DISASTROUS NEWCOMER)

The flooding of the Zambezi to form Lake Kariba created a whole new ecosystem, changing a river into a huge lake. Existing river fish were unable to survive in deep water so kept to the shallows, leaving two-thirds of the lake devoid of fish. But the fishery potential of this new resource was obviously considerable, so in the early 1960s research was undertaken to find a suitable fish to introduce. Lake Tanganyika supports a thriving population of pelagic freshwater sardine, *Limnothrissa miodon*, so attempts were made to introduce this to Kariba. After a slow start the sardine (locally known as *kapenta*) gradually built up a sufficiently large population from which to start a viable fishing industry. Once this critical mass of fish had been reached by the turn of the decade, populations soared and a wonderful new food resource became available, not to mention a great employment opportunity.

Kapenta fishing is done at night with a specially adapted netting technique. The large-framed scoop net, hinged out from the front of the boat, is lowered into the water. Shoals are lured to the surface using powerful lights, while the net is manoeuvred below them. The lights are then turned off and the fish descend into the net. Once on land the *kapenta*, which only grow to 6–7cm, are salted and sun-dried to form an extremely important protein-rich addition to the local diet.

TASTY TERRORISTS A very disturbing discovery has been made in the lake which is already having a deleterious effect on the *kapenta* catches. Freshwater crayfish (a completely alien species) have been found to be thriving and feeding off the *kapenta* fry. The local assumption is that these have been deliberately introduced. With few natural enemies in the lake an explosion in their population is expected, with the resultant decimation of the *kapenta* catches. No doubt a new crayfish industry will open up but it seems rather shortsighted when one considers what the crayfish will feed on when they have killed off the *kapenta*.

communal lounge. That's the good news, but my recent visit revealed a distinct lack of upkeep, a bunch of locals lounging around on the veranda & the revelation that the new owners are none other than the people who own the Rest Camp. It appears they are adopting the same low standards in this property too but at least they're being consistent. **$**

✕ Where to eat

Binga is strictly self-catering although **Gecko Deli (m** *0774 351417*) is a welcome new addition for those who want to grab a light breakfast or lunch and they'll do supper to order. The shop sells a variety of cheeses, cakes and milkshakes and will expand if business demands. It's right at the end of the road just before the croc farm entrance. This place deserves to succeed.

What to see and do

Batonga Museum (*Hidden behind the craft centre which is signposted off the main road by the fuel station as you approach the T-junction;* ⊕ *08.00–16.00 daily; entry fee minimal*) This small, modern museum, a community initiative run by Zimbabwe National Museums and Monuments and originally funded by a Danish NGO, MS-Zimbabwe, outlines something of the local residents' proud culture and history. Although the rather elementary displays seem aimed at schools there's quite a lot to learn here; it's a great initiative aimed at preserving local cultural

THE BATONGA PEOPLE

The Batonga – also known as Tonga or Batonka – people's ancient form of the Shona language suggests that they come from completely different stock than their Shona and Ndebele neighbours. It's thought they originally migrated from the Lake Malawi area, but their lack of oral history or migration myths suggests that they may have occupied this area, the Gwembe Valley, much longer than previously thought.

They have traditionally been marginalised by both blacks and whites, being regarded as a very primitive people, not aided by the traditional practices of nose piercing and knocking out the front teeth of their womenfolk to deter kidnapping invaders. These practices only ceased during the 1970s. They still carry a justifiable deep sense of alienation and aggrievement over their forced resettlement to make way for the flooding of the Zambezi Valley. Before this they would canoe across the river to visit their more numerous kin on what is now the Zambian side, but the lake has split these communities. In fact many don't consider themselves Zimbabweans at all, a result of the fact that their ancient burial grounds are all on the other side of the river/lake. Traditionally a fishing and subsistence farming community, they were forced onto higher ground with poorer soil, with this and the prolific wildlife in the area making cultivation difficult. Even today they seem out of place, reluctant to integrate and generally unable to prosper, remaining second-class citizens.

In Zimbabwe the Tonga are known for their *dagga* smoking (although they don't like this reputation), and around Binga you can still sometimes see old ladies in the streets smoking clay water pipes. As *dagga* smoking is considered a traditional practice the Batonga are the only people in Zimbabwe to receive a legal dispensation to do so.

Aid workers and missionaries in this area continue to help the displaced Batonga community with medical and educational facilities, and CAMPFIRE schemes encourage people to use wildlife resources without destroying them.

values that deserves a visit. Take up the offer from the pleasant and enthusiastic young lady attendant to show you round, because she fills in a lot more detail than you can read on the actual displays.

Crocodile farm (*At the end of the road past the entrance to Kulizwe Lodge;* ⊕ *09.00–16.00 daily, closed for lunch; entry fee minimal*) The production of skins and meat is what these places are all about, but they've turned it into a tourist attraction, so you can book a tour, learn something about a crocodile's fascinating life and cuddle a baby one before buying a handbag in the shop.

CHIZARIRA NATIONAL PARK (NP Category 3)

(*Manzituba office (at the north of the park, see below)* ⊕ *07.00–12.00 & 14.00–16.30 daily*) Chizarira weighs in at 1,920km², Zimbabwe's third-largest national park. It's in the northwest of the country, just south of Lake Kariba, and in many people's eyes is the most scenically beautiful and dramatic park of all, with its escarpment, deep gorges and pristine forests. The average elevation is around 1,000m, rising to 1,433m at the summit of Tundazi Mountain. It was proclaimed a non-hunting reserve in 1958, and the national park was established to give sanctuary to wildlife driven out of the valley by the rising waters of Lake Kariba.

Chizarira shares a reputation with Gonarezhou as a true wilderness area. Its name derives from the Tonga word *sijalila* ('great barrier'), a reference to the mighty and near-vertical 500m Zambezi Escarpment. The park encompasses no fewer than seven ecological zones, ranging from *lowveld* valley vegetation to *highveld* broadleaf woodland. From the escarpment the Zambezi valley floor extends southwards through rolling hills and valleys to merge with the low-lying Busi region. Springs and seeps provide water and surprisingly lush pockets of vegetation between ridges of mountain acacia and the red-plumed Prince-of-Wales Feathers plant, often cultivated for its edible seeds. Down on the floodplain you'll find a remarkable similarity to Mana Pools, with towering evergreens and lush vegetation surrounding deep pans.

For all this, the park is little visited (part of its appeal to lovers of wild places), and before planning a visit you should consider the three main reasons why. The biggest obstacle is accessibility and the condition of the roads and tracks within the park (and to a certain extent the access roads). In winter, most are a 4x4 challenge, with indistinct tracks, washed-out riverbeds, deep ruts and rocky inclines – not helped by trees pushed over by elephants. In the wet summer months the park stays open for visitors but many roads and tracks are impassable, with generally only Muchene and Kaswiswe camps accessible. Having said that, the main road from the northern entrance south to Lesulu is well maintained throughout the year, as this is the main access route for rangers on anti-poaching patrols.

Accommodation is another limiting factor. Although there is a lodge just outside the park (Chizarira Lodge close to the park entrance), there are none within the park, so camping is the only option. Nevertheless there are some stunning places to overnight, and small thatched shelters at several of these sites mean that you can often do without a tent, at least in the dry season.

Finally, this quiet and somewhat cash-starved park gained an unfortunate reputation as a free-for-all for poachers. As in Gonarezhou, this has left the elephants in a pretty aggressive frame of mind, so they should be treated with even more caution than those in Hwange and Mana Pools. There used to be a large population of black rhino here but after most had been poached the few remaining individuals were captured and relocated to Matusadona. The good news is that efforts to bring the poaching situation under control are already bearing fruit, with a noticeable increase of game being seen here, and plans are well developed for a major cash injection specifically to boost the anti-poaching effort.

While this is not yet a park with heavy concentrations of game, there are good populations of leopard, lion and hyena, and plenty of food for them in the form of buffalo, impala, tsessebe, sable, kudu, roan and other buck. The park also features high on the list for enthusiastic birdwatchers, who come here to find, amongst its estimated 368 species, African broadbill, yellow-spotted nicator, Livingstone's flycatcher and emerald cuckoo. The rare Taita falcon has been seen flying and roosting around the cliffs in the escarpment area, and it's in the forested parts of the park near the entrance gate that the brilliantly colourful yet inconspicuous Angola or African pitta, almost a holy grail for birders, has occasionally been seen hopping around in the undergrowth.

So Chizarira's real strength is as a destination for hikers and others who want to experience one of southern Africa's rapidly dwindling, truly wild and rugged places.

One of the best ways to explore this park is with a safari operator, who will take you walking deep into the wilderness where few tourists ever go. The most experienced guide operating in this area is Leon Varley of Backpackers Africa who considers this to be his 'home park' (see *Walking safaris*, page 79, and page 86 for operator details). It's also possible to hire a park ranger as a guide (it will be in your own vehicle), but to be sure of availability you should book in advance from National Parks headquarters in Harare (e *bookings@zimparks.com;* \ *04 706077/8*).

GETTING THERE If you are driving through from Binga to Karoi, it is a slow, uncomfortable drive on poor roads but can be done in a day at a stretch, albeit a rather tiring one. The recommendation would be to allow two days for the actual drive and spend time in Chizarira on the way. The dirt road condition varies considerably depending on the season (can be very bad during rains) and when it was last graded. The last 60km into Karoi is tar.

From Binga drive south for 17km and turn left onto the road to Siabuwa and Karoi. There are no longer any signs to the national park but after about 50km you come to a large village (⊕ S17 34 32 E27 49 02); here, turn down the road signed to Chizarira Wilderness Lodge. Alternatively, you can reach this point on the Binga–Karoi road coming from either Kwekwe or Harare. Carry on until you cross the park boundary gate and follow the road another 18km until you reach the National Parks office. It is tortuous track, very lumpy and rocky requiring a 4x4 and taking about two hours, yet stunningly beautiful as it winds its way towards a huge gap in the escarpment through steep, wooded gorge country.

WHERE TO STAY There is only one lodge with access to the park.

Upmarket

⌂ **Chizarira Lodge** (8 chalets) Follow signs from the park entrance to the lodge; \ 04 884226, UK 020 7607 5104; e info@chizlodge. com; www.chizlodge.com. This place makes the most of Chizarira's rugged geography & has a real safari-camp feel. Each of the light & airy en-suite chalets dotted along a cliff-edge garden path has a balcony overhanging the Mucheni gorge valley far below. A big thatched, open-sided boma houses a fully stocked bar, vast dining table & veranda loungers with views across the swimming pool to the valley. Activities focus on walking safaris in the park, although you can also drive or go fishing. Fully inclusive **$$$$$**

⌂ **Taita Camp** Chizarira will set up a bush camp in the park to bring you into intimate contact with this wilderness setting. Locations vary according to season & personal preference but there's a minimum requirement of 6 persons.

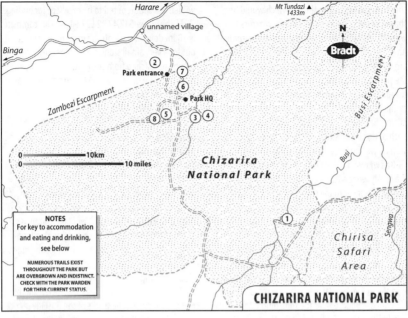

CHIZARIRA NATIONAL PARK

National Parks camping If you're looking for dramatic and isolated camping spots, Chizarira has it all. Because of predators you are not allowed to walk in this park unless accompanied by a registered, armed guide, although you will notice that all the campsites are unfenced, so be

CHIZARIRA NATIONAL PARK
For listings, see pages 210–12

🏠 **Where to stay**
1 Busi Camp	5 Mabola
2 Chizarira Lodge	6 Mucheni Gorge
3 Kaswiswe 1	7 Mucheni Viewpoint
4 Kaswiswe 2	8 The Platform

sensible and alert at all times. There is no park map for sale and it's difficult to find any detailed maps of this park. Although most camping spots are reasonably well marked, at least in the north, and easy to find from the office, you'll find a GPS unit a big help here. Most sites are in the northern, Zambezi Escarpment area, within easy reach of the park headquarters at Manzituba.

There is no shop at park headquarters so all provisions, including water, must be carried in. The nearest shopping town is Binga. It's against the rules to gather your own wood in the park but if you ask at the HQ the staff will collect some and deliver to your campsite.

For unrivalled views of Mucheni Gorge and the escarpment, there are two wonderful sites just north of park headquarters, each of which accepts only one party at a time, so you'll have these wonderfully remote sites all to yourself. The campsites cost US$10 per person.

🏕 **Mucheni Gorge** ⊕ S17 39 12 E027 52 32. You can camp here right on the lip of the precipice with a majestic view down through the gorge far, far below. Pitch your tent in the open or simply spread out on the small concrete-based, roofed *lapa* if it's warm & dry enough. You'll find the usual *braai*

stand & table. Although there's no running water, the long-drop is clean.

🏕 **Mucheni Viewpoint** This wonderful spot at 1,100m, just under 1km further along from the Mucheni Gorge camp, is very similar, perched right on the edge so sleepwalkers & heavy drinkers

211

should perhaps sleep in the car which would be a shame because it has a stunning view across the wide Mucheni Valley to the impressive escarpment. Ahead of you in the distance is a huge gap carved out by the Mucheni River: this is where you entered the park. Facilities are the same as at the gorge camp & it is a dramatic though peaceful place to camp. Take your binoculars to spot the rare Taita falcon that swoops around these cliffs & gorges. At both of these two sites you will be visited by Parks staff delivering large quantities of firewood.

Å Kaswiswe 1 ⊕ S17 41 54 E27 54 00. This is a lovely wooded spot on a bend on the small Ruziruhuru River to the southeast of HQ, offering excellent birding & plenty of evidence of elephant visitations. It's a developed site with a thatched ablution block & running water, & includes a central *lapa* if you need to cook & eat under shelter. Accommodation comprises 2 very basic, wood-floored, stilted huts or *ngazi*, roughly based on the traditional Batonga style. If there's a threat of rain, though, use your tent, as the thatching is in serious need of attention. Take your chairs the short distance down to the river at sundown & watch the aerial antics of the gaudily dressed carmine bee-eaters (amongst others), a perfect way to end the day.

Å Kaswiswe 2 This is a little-used site just down the track from Kaswiswe 1; follow the sign for about 200m & turn left down an indistinct track just before you get to the river. It's an undeveloped site with *braai* stand & long-drop, in a very remote

wilderness spot reputed to be excellent for birding.

Å Mabola ⊕ S17 42 32 E27 51 04. This campsite is 300m down a track off the main loop road. Look out for a very small stone sign that is only visible when approached from the east. It's a very open site with little or no shade & though the location is pleasant enough, with a thatched ablution block & a *braai* table under the trees on the Mucheni riverbank, it lacks the drama or rustic charm of other sites in this area.

Å The Platform ⊕ S17 42 41.7 E27 50 20.7. Further along the road from Mabola, you can't miss this rickety-looking thatched, raised wildlife-viewing *lapa*. It is sturdy enough & offers a panoramic view over a fertile valley that attracts elephant, buffalo & a variety of plains game. It's a delightful 'undeveloped' bush camp with a long-drop. Pitch in the open or spread out for the night on the platform itself.

Å Busi Camp This camp is in the southwest about 40km from the park HQ along a reasonable dirt road. It sits on the banks of the Busi River in a valley area that is rich in game & noted for its resident lion & leopard populations. Equally majestic are the imposing stands of winter acacia. The camp was unfortunately closed when I visited, having been vandalised by poachers, so be sure to enquire at the park HQ to see whether or not it's open before driving down there. It's an undeveloped site & is an excellent base for exploring the southern area of the park. You'll probably only get here in the dry winter months.

WALKING SAFARIS

Backpackers Africa (*Backpackers Bazaar, Victoria Falls;* ☏ *013 44611, 45828, 42208;* m *0712 404968;* e *backpack@africaonline.co.zw; www.walkafrica.com*) Leon Varley is the professional guide most often associated with Chizarira – it's his speciality park and he probably knows it better than his own back garden. He runs three types of trip with varying levels of support and guides all trips himself. In order to get the most out of this rugged terrain experience, Leon likes to cover worthwhile distances: although they are not route marches, a good level of physical fitness is required, especially if you choose to carry your own pack. A good sense of humour is also a bonus as Leon is one of the guiding world's true characters. You are advised to get in contact early as these trips are run by request only and need to be fitted into Leon's programme.

Normal backed-up safari This safari is fully backed up by a support vehicle, tracker, cook, and staff to erect the camp and do camp chores. You will either walk from camp or be driven to a drop-off point and walk from there.

Backpacking safari This is not backed up by a vehicle. All backpacking equipment is provided and clients must carry their own packs. The safari is accompanied by a tracker, cook and camp crew who will help with the carrying of meals and equipment and do camp chores.

Porter safari This is also straight backpacking, but with porters to carry your pack.

LAKE KARIBA

Lake Kariba, one of the world's largest manmade expanses of water, is Zimbabwe's 'seaside' destination in a landlocked country, and sometimes tends to be viewed as a holiday destination more for locals than for overseas visitors. The lake features its own accommodation speciality, the houseboat, so Zimbabweans flock here with family and friends for fishing, boating or just to chill out with a crate or eight of beers (although 'chill out' may be misleading in this area of stifling summer temperatures and humidity).

If you let Zimbabweans have this vast area to themselves, however, you'll be doing yourself a great disservice. Kariba is a laid-back holiday playground with a wide choice of water- and land-based activities. The area provides some stunning scenery and the big-sky sunsets over the lake are legendary, attracting keen photographers worldwide. There can be few better ways of lowering your blood pressure than a sunset boat cruise, weaving through the eerily stark treetops that remain a full half-century after the river was dammed. It's a brilliant base for wildlife viewing and birdwatching, both of which can be done on land or from small boats or canoes that allow you to approach within metres of bathing elephant and buffalo slaking their thirst.

You may find a houseboat too big for your needs, but there are some fine lodges along the east and southern shores catering for most budgets.

LAKE CLIMATE
November–March Summer rainy season. Hot days (30°C+) and nights (22°C) with high humidity. Heavy showers or thunderstorms especially during afternoon and evening. High winds can occur on the lake and along the Zambezi. Dirt roads require a 4x4 and river crossings can be impassable due to floods. Lush vegetation makes wildlife viewing less rewarding.

April–May Autumn. Limited rainfall. Pleasantly warm in the day (28°C) but cooling off at night (15°C). Long grass still obscures wildlife viewing.

June–August Winter cool-dry season. Dry, sunny, clear days (26°C), but cold at night and in early morning (8°C). No rain. Good wildlife viewing as vegetation is sparse and animals seek out water sources.

September–October Spring hot-dry season. Very dry and hot in the day (35°C) and at night (25°C). Air can be hazy because of dust and the smoke from bushfires. Excellent wildlife viewing

Mosquitoes are evident year-round but much less so in June–October.

TOURIST INFORMATION
Kariba Publicity Association \061 2277, 2498; m 0772 329751, 845318; e bryanmushangwe@gmail.com. Provides visitor information, travel services & advice for the Kariba

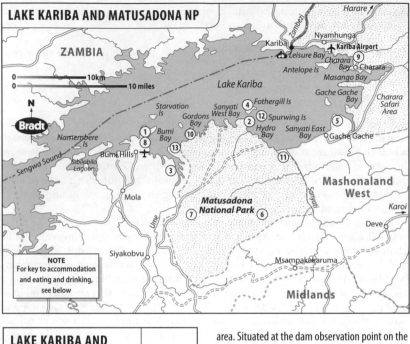

LAKE KARIBA AND MATUSADONA NP

For listings, see pages 218 and 223–5

🛏 **Where to stay**
1 Bumi Hills
2 Changachirere
3 Chura Bush Camp
4 Fothergill Island Safari
5 Gache Gache Lodge
6 Kawisiga Camp
7 Maronga Camp
8 Musango Safari Camp
9 Nyanyana campsite
10 Rhino Safari Camp
11 Sanyati Camp
12 Spurwing Island
13 Tashinga Camp
Tiger Bay (see 3)

area. Situated at the dam observation point on the hill above the dam wall.

🔲 **Wild Zambezi** www.wildzambezi.com. Web-based, non-profit initiative set up by a group of hospitality stakeholders in early 2009 & led by the enthusiastic & dedicated Sally Wynn. It is essentially a directory of tourism facilities covering the whole lake, the middle & Lower Zambezi Valley from Binga west of the lake, downstream all the way to Sapi/Chewore in the northeast until it flows into Mozambique at Cahora Bassa. The website is continually updated and is a much-needed and brilliant information resource to be accessed by anyone considering visiting the area.

KARIBA TOWN *Telephone code 061* The word 'town' can hardly be applied to Kariba, actually little more than a sprawling settlement with no discernable centre. But you will need to come here because it's the centre and meeting point for so many of the region's activities – houseboats, fishing, canoe and walking safaris. It's the service centre not only for the lake region but also for operators in Matusadona and Mana Pools national parks.

Orientation There are three distinct zones to Kariba 'town', servicing a permanent population of around 12,000 residents, rising to 20,000 during peak tourist season.

The largest and newest area is **Nyamhunga Town**, where recent growth has been concentrated. Situated on a large flat plain on the side of the lake and adjacent to Kariba airport, it is easier to access and develop than the steep slopes where the original village was built. Kariba town council offices, the fish farm, bus stops and schools are all in Nyamhunga, now the true 'centre' of Kariba town. It has a shopping centre with a large Spar supermarket, a local produce market for staple vegetables, a bus stop for connections to Makuti, Chirundu and the interior of Zimbabwe (including Harare), a pharmacy, and clothing and shoe shops. There's a bank (CBZ) at the shopping centre as well as a doctor's surgery.

The second-largest commercial area is **Mahombekombe Town**, on the harbour close to the border post with Zambia. Midway between Mahombekombe and Nyamhunga is one of the town's two fuel stations, plus a take-away restaurant and vehicle repair workshop. A Spar supermarket and a few produce and clothes shops are at the centre of Mahombekombe, while factories and other businesses (including a hardware store with a wide range of products) surround the harbour area. This is also where the Kariba ferry departs, when it is in operation.

The original village, known as the **Heights**, is at the top of the steep hills overlooking the dam wall. At the bottom of the hill to the village is Kariba's second fuel station, on the road from Zambia into Zimbabwe. Local crafts are sold in the car park at the dam-wall viewing point, but the publicity association office there is currently closed. It is worth stopping off here for a few photographs of the dam wall. After 4–5km of slow, steep driving the pretty village centre appears, with the original colonial shops built for and by the dam builders. Here are a small supermarket and a country club serving simple, reasonable meals on a balcony with a stupendous view of the lake. There are a few curio shops and a post office, but no longer any hotels.

Getting there

By air Air Zimbabwe used to provide daily links to Kariba but since its demise there has been no single substitute scheduled air service. Instead there is a fluctuating number of small air service providers (small companies, light aircraft) offering charter flights and 'scheduled' services, although the latter are better described as 'regular' rather than 'scheduled' in the accepted sense of the word. Given this book's publishing timescales, the likely currency of this book and the variable nature of some of these operators and their routes and schedules etc, it is impractical to list them here. Travellers to Kariba town who wish to fly should consult www.wildzambezi. com for the latest list and contact details of flight services. People travelling to the camps of Matusadona, Mana Pools and Chewore will find that the accommodations they are staying at will either arrange or recommend air operators.

By ferry (✆ 04 614162/7; m 0772 232177, 256945; e reservations@karibaferries. co.zw; www.karibaferries.com) The *Sea Lion*, a passenger and car ferry, runs between Mlibizi in the west and Kariba town, and although this was out of service for years it has started sailing again on a tentative schedule. The website gives confirmed dates for the current month as well as an advance schedule of confirmed dates but you'll need to contact them direct to enquire about specific dates you may have. Pre-booking is necessary. The ferry carries up to 70 passengers and 15 vehicles on a full-day and overnight journey lasting 22 hours. Facilities on board include chair-beds inside, mattresses for on deck and all bedding (sleeping is communal); toilets and hot showers; three full meals; teas and coffees; and a licensed cash bar. Some will consider it 'roughing it' but just relax into it, have a few beers with other passengers and enjoy one of Zimbabwe's truly iconic journeys. There's a height restriction of 1.95m for 12 vehicles and three parking spaces in an open-deck area with no height restriction (ideal for 4x4s with roofrack tents etc, but check when booking that one of these spaces is available). Departures are at 09.00 uplake from

6

Andora Harbour, Kariba, and downlake from Mlibizi (the terminal entrance is not far from the supermarket) the following day. Arrivals at both ends 07.00. You must be at the embarkation point by 08.00. Fares are US$160 for adults, under 12s US$80 with cars from US$120–180 depending on size.

By road By far the easiest and most direct route for self-drivers from most places in Zimbabwe is via Harare. It is 366km to Kariba so allow four to five hours for the drive. Take the A1 through Chinoyi and Karoi before turning left at Makuti. From here it's a 75km drive, winding down the beautifully scenic Zambezi Escarpment through the Charara safari area to the lakeside.

THE BIRTH OF LAKE KARIBA

The idea of damming the Zambezi for irrigation had been mulled over since the early 1900s, but it wasn't until the 1940s that the possibility of a hydro-electric scheme, to benefit both Zimbabwe and Zambia, began to be considered. The precise location of any prospective dam wall was never in doubt, as the geology at the dam site offered near-perfect conditions, with the Zambezi channelled in a deep, narrow granite gorge. This constriction, topped by a large overhanging rock, was so prominent that local people likened it to a trap and gave it the Shona name, *kariva*. An Italian consortium, Impresit, won the contract with a design by French engineer André Coyne, and construction began in 1954. The massive project, employing some 8,000 workers, was completed in 1958 and in May 1960 Britain's Queen Mother switched on the first electricity generator.

The dam wall is 128m high and 580m wide; 25m thick at its base and 13m at the top. It holds back a lake 280km long, and its widest point measures 40km. The average depth of the water is 29m, reaching a maximum of 97m just before the dam wall. Lake Kariba covers an area of approximately 5,500km^2 and the water volume is calculated at 186km3, which would be enough to supply Greater London for 300 years.

This volume of water weighs in at something like 175 billion metric tonnes, so it's no surprise that it has caused, indeed still causes, geological repercussions. In 1958, six months after completion of the wall, the first earthquake was recorded. As the water level rose, constant background seismic activity followed, culminating in a series of strong shocks measuring well over 5.0 on the Richter scale in September 1963. To this day, locals report there are seasonal tremors as the level rises after the onset of rains.

Although local weather hasn't been affected by such a huge new water surface, bad weather can make the lake a very dangerous place to be, with swells of 3–4m; and the lake is so big that lunar tides are observed. Despite the dam's phenomenal capacity, seasons of low rainfall can reduce water levels to the extent that electricity generation is not possible. On the other hand, the heavy rains of 2010 filled the dam to the extent that three of the six floodgates had to be opened causing flooding downstream and some realignments of the river and islands. The ecological impact of the dam has been considerable downstream as the Zambezi flow is now directed by humans, not nature,

THE HUMAN COST Right from the start, the project was mired in controversy, and construction brought human disaster. Nearly 60,000 people of the Batonga tribe lived in the Gwembe Valley and the government forced them, with

The route south of the lake from the southern end at Mlibizi all the way to Kariba via Magunje and Karoi is one of the most rewarding and beautiful drives in the country, with options to stop at Binga, Chete and the lakeside lodges, taking in Chizarira and Matusadona national parks. But this should not be considered unless you have plenty of time. There is no fuel available along most of the way and the road is very broken in places, with summer rain and erosion making it impassable to most vehicles. You would need to be totally self-sufficient, in a well-equipped and rugged 4x4, and allow two to three days just for the driving, and that's before you add on side trips. This route would form the basis of an excellent holiday in itself, with a strong and capacious

very little notice, to quit the areas in which their ancestors had lived for many generations. Only minimal alternative facilities were provided for them, and there was no effective compensation. The fertile alluvial lowlands along the riverbed supported subsistence agriculture, but the higher areas they were moved to were frequently barren, and of course ill-suited to a predominantly fishing community. The Batonga originally lived on both sides of the river, and the ever-widening river totally split communities, even families. Today, though some have prospered from the move, the Batonga consider themselves forcibly impoverished refugees and are actively seeking reparation from the government.

In the early days of their predicament, they resorted to spiritual means to counter the threat of the dam. They believed Nyaminyami, the serpent-like river god, would take revenge (see box, page 223). Many would say he was at least partially successful: in 1957 and 1958 during construction, massive and almost unprecedented floods rushed down the Zambezi, bursting the coffer dams, sweeping workers to their deaths and causing major damage, setting the project back many months. Altogether 86 people, Africans and Italians, lost their lives during construction – including 17 swept up during the pouring of wet cement and now, gruesomely, forming part of the dam wall.

OPERATION NOAH Ironically, more effort went into helping wildlife than humans. As water levels rose after the dam was completed in 1958, the higher areas created islands on which animals became stranded. While the Batonga people struggled to make a new life for themselves, teams of volunteer wildlife wardens, mainly drafted in from Northern Rhodesia (Zambia), mounted a massive rescue operation for the imperilled animals. Public money began to flood in, wildlife experts volunteered their time and an estimated 5,000 animals were rescued. All wildlife that could be found was captured and relocated on firm ground, mainly in Matusadona. Operation Noah received worldwide publicity and as a result the government was forced to back the effort with more money. In the end, nearly £1,000 was spent per animal rescued against a mere £50 allocated per displaced Batongan.

A fascinating cameo highlighted in Michael Main's book *Zambezi: Journey of a River* is the story of three elephants seen swimming from Spurwing Island towards Kariba, some 25km away. Despite attempts to divert them to the safety of Matusadona National Park, two succeeded in their epic swim and, after 24 hours in the water, immediately set off into the bush. It is assumed they were following an ancient migratory trail – but this was in the late 1970s, some 25 years after the valley was flooded, and these elephants were estimated to be only 20 years old.

vehicle. It's a good idea to check www.zim4x4.co.zw to request detailed up-to-date information on this route.

From Victoria Falls a quick route to Kariba is through Zambia. It's a pretty good road (although pot-holes are becoming a problem) from Livingstone and, at around 550km, can be achieved in a day with an early start. Note that there's now a vehicle toll on the dam wall – it's the standard US$1 for light vehicles.

Health risks Kariba town is in the middle of a wildlife corridor, so for most of the year – especially in the dry winter – elephants are regular visitors, raiding the gardens, sometimes in company with buffalo, zebra and impala. Baboons are in abundance and a menace to the residents of the Heights. These animals are usually quite safe if left alone but it pays to keep your wits about you, as human deaths have occurred.

The lake is a swimming no-go area, and you should be very careful when walking or fishing along the shoreline. Bilharzia is an ever-present risk, but crocodiles pose a greater hazard. Malaria is endemic to the area, especially during the summer months.

Where to stay For accommodation on the southern shore see *Matusadona National Park*, pages 223–5.

Upmarket

🏠 **Caribbea Bay Resort** (83 rooms) 425 Impala Dr; ☎2452/7; e pacro@africansunhotels.com; www.africansunhotels.com. This resort is somewhat quirkily built in Mexican adobe style, but when almost everywhere else in the country is stone topped by thatch, why not be a little different? Rooms have AC, it's right on the lakeshore & it's one of the few places in Zimbabwe catering for families with children, who can play on the small sandy beach, in the playground, amusement centre or waterslide. Locally considered to be priced on the high side. **$$$$**

🏠 **Cutty Sark Hotel** (58 rooms) Nzou Dr; ☎2221/2, 04 494017; m 0772 151668/9; e info@cuttysarkhotel.com; www.cuttysark.co.zw. The hotel is not far from the airport on a tar road, signposted all the way. It's on the lakeshore on 29ha of land opposite Zebra Island, offering good views of the lake, islands & Matusadona Mountains. Accommodation consists of deluxe, standard & budget rooms, all with en-suite bathrooms, AC & lake views. Budget rooms are basic & inexpensive, sold on a room-only basis, making them an affordable family option. Good facilities for children. Meals can be taken on the outside terrace or in the dining room, & room service is available. **$$$**

🏠 **Gache Gache Lodge** [map, page 214] (10 chalets) ☎04 745717; m 0772 264159, 285691; e townsend@zolco.zw; www.gachegachelodge.

com; Skype: Bernie.styles. This beautiful lodge is across Lake Kariba on the Gache Gache River. The open-sided main building houses dining room, bar & lounge, all with panoramic views of the lake. The en-suite chalets have stunning views of the lake. All the usual fishing & game-viewing activities are available for a fee. **$$$**

🏠 **Hornbill Lodge** (4 chalets) Mica Point, Kariba; m 0772 240923; e zulu@junglecomms.com; www.hornbilllodge.com. This small lodge has accommodation for up to 10 people in A-frame thatch chalets (1 dbl, 2 twin & 1 4-bed family room), each with en suite. A thatch bar, lounge & dining area overlooks a plunge pool with panoramic views of the lake & indigenous trees in a landscaped garden complete with game visitors. Excellent reviews. All meals & local drinks are included & DSTV is available. Extra activities available. **$$$**

Basic

⛺ **Warthogs Bush Camp** m 0712 201733, 0775 068406; e relax@warthogs.co.zw; www.warthogs.co.zw. This is a small, extremely friendly camp on the shore of the lake. Although close to Kariba there's a genuine bush feel to the place (visiting elephants) with self-catering accommodation in A-frame *bashas* (gumpole & thatch tents on stilts), family chalets, a 6-bed dormitory & an en-suite tree house. Camping too. There's a pool, bar & pub food on site & children are welcome. **$**

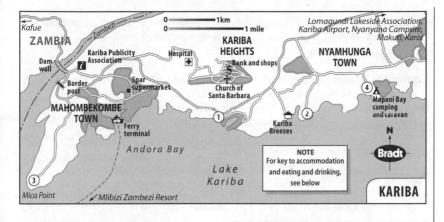

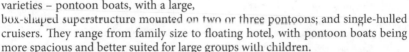

KARIBA
For listings, see pages 218–19

⌂ **Where to stay**
1　Caribbea Bay Resort
2　Cutty Sark Hotel
3　Hornbill Lodge
4　Warthogs Bush Camp
Off map
　Lomagundi Lakeside Association

Ⱥ **Lomagundi Lakeside Association** S16 31 38 E28 50.11; e soniawarren@iwayafrica.com. Pleasant lakeside self-catering lodges & campsite with mains electricity **$**

Houseboats There is a plethora of houseboats on Kariba, a reflection of their huge popularity with Zimbabwean holidaymakers. They come in basic varieties – pontoon boats, with a large, box-shaped superstructure mounted on two or three pontoons; and single-hulled cruisers. They range from family size to floating hotel, with pontoon boats being more spacious and better suited for large groups with children.

Both come with a crew complement that depends on boat size and luxury level, but at the least expect a skipper and deckhand. When booking, check on the inclusion of fuel, food, alcohol and crew in the rental price, because operators price differently. If you choose self-catering, you supply the food but you'll often find a crew member will cook it for you. Also check the fuel situation and exactly what you pay for, as you may find a restriction on how far they will let you travel each day. This can be important if you are interested in fishing because, although you generally trawl over the side from a houseboat, you'll need the boat's tender launch to reach the best fishing spots, inaccessible to large vessels.

Kariba gets hot and humid in the late winter months (September–November). Although most boats have air conditioning, generators must be turned off at 22.00, so prepare for sticky nights. The answer is to sleep on deck in the open – but take all your mosquito precautions.

Because of the large number of available boats and individual owners, it's best to use an agency, some of which have 40 or more boats on their books. Their websites list them all, making comparison and selection easy, but book early, especially if you want one of the smaller ones.

⌂ **Afrizim** South Africa; ☏ +27 31 7622424; e safari@afrizim.com; www.afrizim.com
⌂ **Kariba Houseboats** m 0772 296150; e maureen@karibahouseboats.com; www. karibahouseboats.com. 40 vessels on their lists.

⌂ **Kariba Houseboat Cruises** e karibahouseboatcruises@gmail.com; www. karibahouseboatcruises.com

↑ **Rhino Rendezvous** 📞04 490124; **m** 0772 220831, 239210; **e** rhinoren@zimbomail.co.zw; www.houseboatsonkariba.com. 22 boats on list.

↑ **Venues4Africa** **e** info@venues4africa.com; www.venues4africa.com. 27 boats on list.

Camping   Nyanyana campsite and Parks office (⊕ S16 32 42.0 E28 52 58.2), which lies near Kariba airport and is close to the Makuti–Kariba road is neat, if basic, and the lodges are in good repair. The only problem is that it lies on an inlet directly opposite the Kariba crocodile farm, with its unsightly row of concrete 'pylons' extending into the lake. Wildlife is reasonably abundant and there's easy access to a pretty and undeveloped expanse of lakeshore.

What to see and do

Church of Santa Barbara   Just after having declared herself a Christian, the hapless Barbara was beheaded by her pagan father, who was then immediately (and, some would say, quite justifiably) struck down by lightning. After canonisation following a number of impressive miracles, and as a result of her association with thunder and lightning, she became the patron saint of miners and other people who work with explosives. Many of the builders who worked on the dam wall were

---

KARIBA WEED: AN UNDESIRABLE ALIEN?

Although *Salvinia molesta*, a South American alien plant, had been living in parts of the Zambezi for many years, it struggled to eke out an existence, as the river itself was generally poor in nutrients. After the damming of the river its fortunes changed dramatically: not only were the newly flooded plains heavy with animal dung and decaying vegetation, but tributaries introduced nutrient-rich water to the lake.

Salvinia seized its opportunity and spread at an alarming rate, producing thick, dense mats of floating weed that threatened to clog tributary mouths and cover the lake. In these near-perfect conditions the plant doubled in extent every two weeks. Beneath what became vast, impenetrable mats, light was excluded, oxygen depleted and all available nutrients were monopolised by the alien plant; in short, an ecological disaster loomed, one that would put paid to hopes of an emergent *kapenta* fishing industry.

But after nearly a decade during which a number of biological controls were tried, including the introduction of a weed-munching grasshopper from the Caribbean, *Salvinia* levels began to decline. The controls are believed to have had some effect but the more likely reason was a drop in nutrient levels as the water's initial richness was depleted by the weed itself. The early food-rich waters also benefited other plants, which in turn became established, providing competition for the alien. A natural equilibrium was eventually reached.

Today, *Salvinia* can still be found in large quantities, but it's not all bad news. Floating and peripheral mats of the weed provide an excellent hatchery and nursery for *kapenta*. *Salvinia* stranded on the shore by seasonal falling lake levels rots and encourages prolific torpedo grass growth, good grazing for buffalo and smaller plains game. The dense floating mats have also been shown to be an excellent base for a wide range of aquatic and semi-aquatic plant life, increasing the lake's biodiversity. While many still hate the stuff, it does have its uses.

Italian and the church, dedicated to the clearly very appropriate Santa Barbara, was built in memory of the 86 who perished during construction. The circular church has an interesting design, using elements of the dam itself as an architectural theme. Today it is well supported and regularly visited by Italians and other tourists as well as locals, especially when the very good choir is singing.

The dam wall Halfway up the long hill to the Heights is a spectacular viewing spot, especially when water levels are high requiring flood sluice gates to be opened. You can walk across the dam wall itself by temporarily depositing your passport with the immigration officer.

General views Of main interest to visitors, however, are the wonderful views, especially at dawn and sunset, from the road running along the top of the hill and through the small Heights suburb, forming a loop with the main road up the hill. Full-moon nights are incredible and at any time of the year you can experience spectacular stargazing over the lake.

Near the airport, several kilometres short of the town, the shorelines and river valleys of the Kuburi Wilderness Area are worth a visit. Check in at the National Parks office at Nyanyana on the Kariba approach road beforehand.

Wildlife and fishing Most people staying at Kariba use it as a base for trips across the lake, stopping off at islands or in the bays and creeks of the wildlife areas on the southern shore (see *Matusadona National Park* below). Here an abundance of wildlife includes all the 'Big Five' (including black rhino) and a staggering variety of other animal life and waterbirds.

Kariba is renowned for its fishing. The fighting tigerfish is most people's goal, and the focus of an international tournament held each October, when accommodation is in great demand. Other species include several types of bream, which make good eating. Bait is available from the boat harbours and some tackle can be provided, but it is advisable to bring your own if possible. Fishing permits are essential and can usually be obtained from the main boat harbours.

MATUSADONA NATIONAL PARK (NP Category 2)

The 1,407km² Matusadona National Park is situated on the southern shores of Lake Kariba, about 20km across the lake from Kariba town. Although one of the Zambezi Valley's wildlife and wilderness treasures, it is one of Zimbabwe's less visited parks.

The Matusadona shoreline of Lake Kariba is bounded on the west by the Ume River, which meets the lake in a wide estuary, and on the east by the Sanyati River, with its magnificent steep-sided, rocky gorge. Two-thirds of the park lies south of the Zambezi Escarpment, formed by the 600m Matuzviadonha Hills from which it takes its name. (The name sounds innocuous until you learn its translation: 'dripping with dung'. According to a National Parks leaflet, this derives from the fact that the terrain is so rugged that those crossing it frequently needed to relieve themselves. Others say it is a reference to the large numbers of elephant that used to inhabit the area.)

This is a real get-away-from-it-all destination. Once you leave Kariba there are no shops, electricity supply is usually by generator, and although cellphone networks are available, signals can be erratic. Matusadona is ideal safari territory, home to all of the 'Big Five' and worth visiting year-round. You can either moor up on the shoreline in a cruiser or houseboat (for safety reasons you can only disembark with an armed guide) or stay at one of the lodges or camps around the northern edge of

6

the park that offer game drives, short walks or walking safaris. Small seasonal bush camps in the traditional style are erected for mobile safaris but there are also good lodges situated on islands just offshore.

FLORA AND FAUNA Open woodlands on the plateau behind the escarpment are dominated by *Julbernardia globiflora* (Munondo), with the mountain acacia, *Brachystegia glaucescens*, common on the slopes and ridges of the escarpment.

From the plateau the park falls abruptly to a flat, low-lying area covered mainly with *mopane* scrub and woodland, and with dense patches of Jesse bush (*Combretum celastroides*). The entire northern boundary of the park is formed by the lakeshore itself. Along much of it are 'drowned forests', up to several kilometres wide, containing skeletal dead trees still standing five decades after the filling of the lake.

Many of the animals rescued from the rising waters of Lake Kariba during Operation Noah in 1958 were released into the Matusadona. Plains game, especially buffalo, are here in good numbers, with herds of up to 1,000 in some dry seasons. Their population is boosted, largely due to rampantly growing torpedo grass, *Panicum repens*, along the shoreline. It was generally absent from the lakeshore until 1970, when a combination of circumstances including the decline of the Kariba weed, *Salvinia molesta*, enabled it to gain a foothold on what were until then rather barren shores. The rotting *Salvinia* created an ideal mulch for the torpedo grass, which can survive for long periods underwater and becomes available to buffalo and other herbivores towards the end of the dry season when other sources of fodder are largely depleted. With the lake being manmade, however, the situation is very unnatural and wildlife populations find it difficult to adjust to the controlled water levels from year to year. When there's a run of 'dry' wet seasons, lake levels are low, creating large areas of grazing, but with the several years of 'wet' wet seasons recently the lake has flooded the grazing areas up to the treeline, forcing the animals to seek alternative food sources which inevitably results in a fall in population numbers. Lion, leopard, hyena and other predators occur in good numbers throughout the park. There have been isolated reports of cheetah over the years. A small population was reintroduced in 1995.

There is a small but important population of the endangered black rhinoceros, mainly along the foot of the escarpment. Eight white rhinoceros were introduced into the park in 1984 but did not survive, probably because they had lost their natural immunity to sleeping sickness over many years of captive breeding in tsetse-free areas. Hippopotamus and crocodile declined after the lake filled but are now recovering well. Hippopotamus have benefited from the development of the torpedo grass swards, and the deeply incised shoreline provides much suitably sheltered habitat. A recent survey of the crocodile population estimated their density at one adult animal for every 200m of shoreline.

One of the Matusadona's most compelling features is its luxuriant birdlife: over 240 species have been recorded in the park. Most parts of the lakeshore have conspicuous populations of grey herons, goliath herons, great white herons and the spectacular saddlebill storks. Plovers, waders and geese are generally abundant and there are notable populations of osprey, woolly-necked storks, open-billed storks, white-winged plovers and red-winged pratincoles. There are several large colonies of darters and reed cormorants, and at least one colony of white-breasted cormorants has taken up residence. Bee-eater colonies are found in the sandstone banks and cliffs of the minor rivers that traverse the valley floor. The fish eagle, common along the lakeshore where it makes use of the dead trees as nesting sites and lookout posts, can occasionally be seen swooping down to snatch tigerfish or bream.

Nyaminyami, the dragon-like river god of the Zambezi, has the body of a serpent and the head of a fish, and is frequently depicted in carvings coiled up a stick. Indeed he is often crafted into walking sticks. Water is considered sacred by the Batonga people and the river god protects the water, bringing life and wealth to the people, who in turn pledge their allegiance to him. Folklore has it that this benevolent and protective god even allowed the people to eat his flesh in times of drought and hardship.

Nyaminyami and his wife, who also wields great power, are said to have once dwelled in the river around Kariba. One year she set off to answer the prayers of the people who lived downstream, but unwittingly picked the time when the white men began to construct the dam wall. Consequently, Nyaminyami was separated from his wife.

The rising waters of Lake Kariba caused the Batonga people to be forcefully relocated off their ancestral lands, so they invoked Nyaminyami to hamper the construction process, safe in the belief that he too shared their misgivings. Clearly he did.

The construction years were bedevilled by a series of unusual weather systems, starting in 1955 with high water damaging the coffer-dam foundations. A record heatwave then made physical work almost impossible. In 1957 and 1958 massive floods, believed to be the heaviest in over 1,000 years, caused further damage and fatalities. In total, 86 workers lost their lives.

Because Nyaminyami is basically a benevolent god he eventually allowed the construction to be completed (some say Batonga elders placated him). He's still separated from his wife, though, and issues frequent warnings in the form of earth tremors, which have only occurred since the dam was built. Many Batonga believe he will not rest until the dam is destroyed, allowing him to meet up with his wife again.

GETTING THERE With its lakeside and island resorts, Matusadona National Park is most easily accessible by boat or light aircraft charter from Kariba, but it is also possible to drive from the gravel Karoi–Kamativi road south of the escarpment. Check beforehand with www.zim4x4.co.zw for the latest condition of the approach road, which can sometimes present quite a challenge. Most people book the park's out-of-the-way lodges through an agent, who can arrange all transfers.

By light aircraft See *Kariba, Getting there*, page 215. Generally speaking, your accommodation will arrange transfers.

By boat From Kariba by speedboat takes 1–1½ hours but can be uncomfortable and damp if the water's choppy. Services are cancelled in rough conditions.

By road Do not attempt this drive in anything other than a tough 4x4 with plenty of fuel-carrying capability. See *Kariba town* on page 216 for more information.

WHERE TO STAY
Private lodges and camps Maronga, Katete and Kiplings lakeshore camps were closed at the time of writing but expected to reopen; check with the Zambezi Safari and Travel Company (*www.zambezi.com*) or Wild Zambezi (*www.wildzambezi*.

com). See Lake Kariba and Matusadona National Park map on page 214 for locations.

Luxury

⌂ **Bumi Hills** (20 rooms) ☎04 307087; m 0772 134664; e reservations@bumihills.com; www.bumihills.com. This stunningly beautiful & luxurious lodge has been refurbished, & was reopened in March 2009. On a hilltop with all rooms overlooking the lake, there's now a spectacular infinity pool & spa overlooking the shoreline. All the usual activities in this area are covered including wildlife viewing, tigerfish & bream fishing, lake cruises & visits to local villages. There are daily 1–1½hr flights from Victoria Falls airport to the Bumi Hills airstrip. FB including activities. **$$$$$**

⌂ **Changa Safari Camp** (6 luxury tents) ☎04 498835/6; m 0772 220641; e reservations@ changasafaricamp.com; www.changasafaricamp. com. This new, luxury tented camp opened in October 2012. The tents are spacious & beautifully furnished with both inside & outside bathroom/ shower options & with wonderful views across Hydro Bay to Sanyati Gorge & the Matusadona Moutains. The central guest area consists of several thatched structures linked by raised wooden walkways & decks with lounge/bar, dining room, library & pool. The camp offers all the usual land- & water-based wildlife activities found in this area. **$$$$$**

⌂ **Musango Safari Camp** (8 tented chalets, 2 suites) ☎013 43358; m 0772 307875; e reservations@musangosafaricamp.com. zm; www.musangosafaricamp.com; Skype: Swendyed. Musango overlooks the national park from its own island at the mouth of the Ume River. This is a private concession built & run by Steve & Wendy Edwards. Steve is a renowned professional guide with over 35 years experience & was previously warden of Matusadona NP so has an encyclopaedic knowledge of the area. The exclusive & luxurious 16-bed tented camp is sheltered by thatched roofs, with en-suite bathrooms of natural stone. Each chalet, in shady wooded surroundings, has its own veranda with views of the lake & the rising sun. 2 honeymoon suites are built from natural stone with the same thatched roofing. The central *boma* is a splendid 2-storey thatched building housing lounge & dining areas. There's a swimming pool near the

bar & lounge deck, although honeymooners have their own plunge pool.

The birdlife on the lake is more than abundant with nearly 400 species recorded so you'll be in good hands with Steve, who is a respected ornithologist & offers specialist birding trips throughout Zimbabwe. He's a keen amateur palaeontologist so ask him to show you the dinosaur fossil site he discovered. Wildlife viewing is by canoe, powerboat, Land Rover or on foot with an armed professional guide. Boat & pontoon cruises are also available. Fishing for tigerfish is excellent in this area & Musango provides all tackle & bait. There's a refreshingly non-tourist Batonga fishing village nearby, where a villager will conduct you on a tour & give you an insight into their culture & lifestyle.

Rates include meals, drinks & game activities, but not transfers or park fees. **$$$$$**

Upmarket

⋏ **Rhino Safari Camp** m 0772 205000, 400021; e rhino.safari.camp@mail.com; www. rhinosafaricamp.com; Skype: Rhinocamp. This lovely old-fashioned bush camp at Elephant Point is described by the owner, Jenny Nobes, as 'luxury rustic', & the style is very much home-from-home, greatly enhanced by the enthusiasm & hosting expertise of the owner. Right on the lakeshore, accommodation is in thatched, stilted chalets with en-suite facilities. They offer a highly personalised photographic safari experience with guided walks tracking the endangered black rhino, game drives & evening lake cruises. Excellent for fishing & birding. Rates are fully inclusive but transfer prices (speedboat or light aircraft) on request. **$$$$$**

⌂ **Tiger Bay** (12 chalets) c/o Conquest Tours; m 0779 596503, 239134; e conquesttours@zol. co.zw; www.club52.co.za. The attractive dbl-storey thatched main complex is set amongst mature trees & lawns leading down to the Ume River. A spacious entertainment area includes large swimming pool, dining area & upper level bar. Accommodation is in comfortable 2- or 4-bed en-suite thatched A-framed chalets, all with scenic river views. Rates include 3 meals per day, drinks (reasonable consumption) & 2 activities pp per day – choose from game drive, game cruise, fishing, bird & walking safaris with a guide, bush *braai* dinner & champagne b/fast following game drive. Children under 12 years half price, infants under 2 free. Boat transfer US$60pp return – min 6, no discount for children. Excludes park fees. **$$$$$**

🏠 **Chura Bush Camp** (6 tents) Contact details as for Tiger Bay. The camp, on the banks of the Ume River, accommodates up to 12 in large twin-bed safari tents. Each tent is spacious & fully equipped; all are fully enclosed & gauzed against mosquitoes. The camp has a dining/lounge/bar area incorporating a viewing platform plus an entertainment area with swimming pool & BBQ. There are 2 bathrooms, each with flush toilet, & shower with hot & cold water. Activities are the same as at Tiger Bay. **$$$$**

🏠 **Spurwing Island** (11 luxury tents, 6 cabins, 3 chalets) m 0772 611554, 0777 5161/1; e bookings@spurwing.co.zw; www. spurwingisland.com. Spurwing Island is a great place for a tranquil getaway with scenic views over Lake Kariba. The shady gardens provide an oasis in the middle of the African bush. The island offers a range of guided activities including boat trips up the towering Sanyati Gorge, wildlife viewing on foot, by boat or Land Rover. Tents are under thatch, with stone floors, separate zip entrances to a small veranda & into an en-suite bathroom, twin beds, dressing table, plug sockets, pedestal fan & mosquito nets. A dbl tent can be used as family accommodation with each side having its own en-suite facilities. Cabins are stone under thatch with en-suite shower, toilet & washbasin, twin beds. Chalets are stone under thatch with en-suite bath, separate shower, toilet & washbasin, French doors opening out onto a veranda, twin beds, built-in cupboards, dressing table, comfy chairs, ceiling fan & mosquito nets. Optional dbl bed &/or extra beds for children. All have 220V mains electricity. An unobtrusive electric fence around the camp keeps unwelcome visitors (animal) at bay. Game activities (drives, walks, cruises, fishing) available at approx US$25pp. Excludes park fees. FB **$$$**

Basic

🏠 **Fothergill Island Safari** (14 lodges) e pacro@africansunhotels.com; www. africansunhotels.com. Located on Fothergill Island, this previously well-known comfortable but no-frills lodge offered a pleasant away from-it-all experience, ideal for a fishing group. Thatched A-frame lodges are en-suite with open-air bathrooms with shower. The central dining area has a bar upstairs with a viewing platform. This camp has been closed for a long time & was due to be refurbished in late 2011 but at the time of writing this is still promised by African Sun but has not yet been achieved. **$$$**

National Parks accommodation
The park headquarters at Tashinga will give you detailed instructions on getting to these places.

Chalet camps Basic chalet camps are at Ume Lodge (*close to Tashinga airstrip on the east bank of the Bumi River, 55km from Kariba by boat*) and Mbalabala (*on the Bumi River, around 300m upstream of Ume Camp*).

Camping areas

🏕 **Tashinga Camp** (20 sites) This communal lakeshore camping area at the park HQ has an ablution block with hot & cold water, baths & showers. Some sites have sleeping shelters & all have *braai* stands.

🏕 **Sanyati Camp** (2 sites) Sanyati & Sanyati West sites accommodate 6 & 5 people respectively. There are *braai* stands, an ablution block with hot & cold water & a laundry trough.

🏕 **Changachirere** This exclusive lakeshore campsite caters for a single party, max 5 people. It has a mini-ablution block & shelter.

Other exclusive campsites are at **Maronga**, close to the Chifudzi substation, & **Kawisiga**, on the escarpment and ideal for hikers and climbers.

This is the stretch of water downstream from Kariba where the Zambezi is allowed to be a river again, before being dammed once more in Mozambique to form Lake Cahora Bassa. Renowned for its inquisitive elephants, many known individually by name, Mana Pools National Park is the pearl of this area and the favourite park of many regular visitors and locals. Your stay here will not be complete without a leisurely canoe trip, taking in a couple of nights camping under the stars on a sandbar or river shore. Yet the peace and tranquillity of the riverside lodges and camps contrasts sharply with the wilder, inland area around Chitake Springs where you must keep your tent fully zipped at night to ensure the resident lions don't get too nosy. Fishing enthusiasts will want to head further downstream for one of the camps in the Sapi and Chewore safari areas and dedicate their time to landing the superbly named fighting tigerfish.

CHIRUNDU This shabby border town is busy with trucks and commercial traffic queueing to cross the river on the way to and from Harare. Chirundu became Africa's first 'one stop' border post in September 2009, so with only one set of formalities between the two countries, transit times should be greatly eased. During 2012, however, reports were emerging that while generally speaking the process was reasonably efficient, depending on time of day and traffic, there have been accusations that officials were holding things up in the hope of eliciting bribes. The best advice is to seek out the local Zimbabwe Tourism Authority representative if you are being asked for a 'fee'. If you're arriving from Zambia you should note that the winding road down the escarpment on the Zambia side is tortuous and heavily used by large trucks, with frequent accidents.

As with other towns in wildlife territory, many animals are not put off by the presence of people, and elephants in particular continue to use ancient tracks regardless of the fact that houses and roads have been built in their way. Chirundu is legendary for elephants that are reluctant to find new routes, wandering through town, trashing gardens and drinking from swimming pools. Sadly these interactions have led to conflict and often the destruction of 'problem' animals.

There's little else to say about Chirundu, other than the fact that it is the launching point for many canoe safaris. Although there are some small fishing camps not far from Chirundu for use by independent travellers, your canoe safari operator will require you to assemble and depart from Kariba and will organise accommodation there along with transfers to and from Chirundu for your canoe trip.

WHERE TO STAY Karoi is a small crossroads town en route to Kariba/Chirundu/Mana Pools, 203km from Harare; and also for people tackling the Binga, Matusadona route from Hwange or Victoria Falls. Basic supplies and fuel can be picked up here, and there is one place to stay. There's another accommodation option in Makuti just before the turn-off to Mana Pools at Marongora.

Karoi
Basic
🏠 **Twin River Inn Hotel** Just outside town towards Chirundu; ☎ 064 6845/8229/8237; m 0773 492933, 626659; e twinriverinn@gmail.com. Basic motel-style accommodation with restaurant & bar. **$**

Makuti
Basic
🏠 **Makuti Travel Lodge** ☎ 063 531; m 0772 621665; e makutih@hotmail.com. Small hotel & fuel station. Restaurant & pub.

MANA POOLS NATIONAL PARK (NP Category 2) Entry to this park – a UNESCO World Heritage Site – is strictly controlled by the Zimbabwe National Parks and Wildlife Management Authority. Note that this park charges entry fees per day. See page 66 for details. Prior booking is essential, through an operator or directly with Parks.

This park is regarded by many regular visitors and locals as the finest wilderness area in the country. It's actually part of a much larger wildlife area adjacent to Sapi and Chewore safari areas to the east, also bordering the Zambezi. Not only is Mana Pools richly stocked with game and blessed with outstanding scenic, riverine beauty but it is also relatively little visited, at least compared with Hwange and Victoria Falls. This is one of the few national parks where visitors are allowed to walk at their own risk but while this is welcomed by enthusiasts with plenty of bush experience, it is advisable to be accompanied by an armed professional guide or a national park ranger. Probably because of its outstanding qualities as a game-viewing destination, this park is home territory to some of Africa's finest professional guides.

Limited fishing is allowed, but only from land. Motorboats are not permitted in the dry season because of noise, pollution and wave action disturbing the wilderness qualities of the park. Check with Parks regarding use of powered boats in the rainy season as they are currently experimenting with relaxing the rules. A 'Respect the Wild' code of conduct for visitors to Mana Pools and other wild areas is displayed at accommodation points throughout the park; visitors are advised to take heed of its advice to get the best out of their wild experience and to ensure they leave the area as they found it. In 2012, this was the first of Zimbabwe's national parks to adopt the excellent 'carry in – carry out' rubbish policy with visitors being given a plastic bag and expected to return it with rubbish on exit of the park.

There are no shops, and cellphone coverage is very limited. Accommodation is restricted to a handful of safari lodges and eco-friendly tented or mobile camps as well as self-catering national park chalets. Camping on the banks of the Zambezi River is a feature of the Mana experience.

The park is open to cars during the dry season but during the rainy season roads are frequently closed. Access to the interior of the park is very limited from December to March. The best time to come here in terms of temperature and rainfall is March to October.

Despite the fact that this is a UNESCO World Heritage Site and a designated Ramsar wetland of international importance, as this book goes to press the whole area is under threat from a proposal to mine for heavy metals that are thought to be deposited in the riverbed. A major international campaign has been mounted to prevent this development, which would have devastating effects on the environment, ecology and wildlife of the area.

Mana Pools The Lower Zambezi Valley begins after the water from the dammed lake becomes a river again, running along the base of the Zambezi Escarpment immediately to its south. Further downstream, the river emerges from a deep gorge to spread across a flat, fertile floodplain that's being reshaped by nature to form pools and oxbow lakes.

The Mana Pools area consists of four main pools (*mana* means 'four' in Shona) and several smaller ones scattered along the river course, with the cliffs overhanging the river and the floodplains providing sustenance to a large and varied wildlife population. Long Pool is the largest pool, extending some 6km in a west–east direction.

Mana Pools is part of the 10,500km² Parks Wildlife Estate that runs from the Kariba Dam to the Mozambican border in the east. This large area has no physical

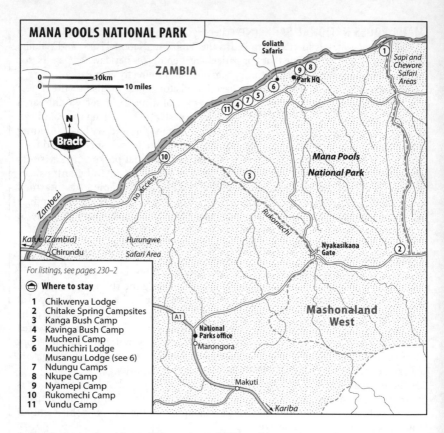

MANA POOLS NATIONAL PARK

ZAMBIA

0 ——— 10km
0 ——— 10 miles

Goliath Safaris

Sapi and Chewore Safari Areas

Park HQ

Mana Pools National Park

Zambezi

no access

Rukomechi

Kafue (Zambia)
Chirundu

Hurungwe Safari Area

Nyakasikana Gate

Mashonaland West

National Parks office
Marongora

A1

Makuti

Kariba

For listings, see pages 230–2

Where to stay
1 Chikwenya Lodge
2 Chitake Spring Campsites
3 Kanga Bush Camp
4 Kavinga Bush Camp
5 Mucheni Camp
6 Muchichiri Lodge
   Musangu Lodge (see 6)
7 Ndungu Camps
8 Nkupe Camp
9 Nyamepi Camp
10 Rukomechi Camp
11 Vundu Camp

boundaries and, without fences, the wildlife is free to move wherever it wants – even northwards across the Zambezi into Zambia, where there are also large areas set aside for wildlife conservation.

Flora and fauna The park occupies 2,196km² of prime Zambezi riverfront vegetation, much of it inaccessible except on foot and as a result completely unspoilt. The landscape includes islands and sandbanks fringed by dense forests of baobabs and indigenous trees, as well as the rugged Zambezi Escarpment. Big old trees, mainly *Faedherbia albida*, provide a shady canopy with sparse undergrowth, which makes for easy walking, and this is one reason why this area is perfect for walking safaris. (*Faedherbia* was once classified as an acacia but, unlike true acacias, it sheds its leaves in summer. Elephants love its hard, flat 'apple ring' pods, and can often be seen shaking them out of the branches before hoovering them up with the enthusiasm of a child with a bag of sweets.) Jesse bush, a member of the combretum family also known as trailing bushwillow, is widespread.

The national park is famous for its magnificent elephants that return year after year to the same places. Some of these 'personalities' are regular visitors to camps and provide guests with a real 'Jungle Book' experience. It's only here that you'll see huge bulls who have learnt to rear up on their hind legs to stretch up into the trees and reach tasty morsels usually only accessible to giraffe. Some guides have developed extraordinary, trusting relationships with particular animals and offer their clients close-up interactions they will never forget. Buffalo are always about and predators such as leopard, lion and cheetah are regularly seen. The pools are also a haven for Nile crocodiles and large hippo pods as well as black rhino.

The area is perfect for birds as it offers a wide range of habitats, both from woodland to scrub and escarpment cliffs to open plains, with both arid and wet conditions. Amongst the 380 recorded species are the Nyasa lovebird, Livingstone's flycatcher, white-collared pratincole, banded snake eagle and yellow-spotted nicator. Fish eagles and many species of stork, heron and other waterfowl are common. Carmine bee-eaters visit in the dry months to nest in colonies in the riverbanks, and rare treats include the elusive Pels fishing owl and the African skimmer, which nests on sandbanks mid-river.

Chitake Springs In the southern part of the park 50km from the Zambezi, is an isolated area of vital importance to wildlife. In the rainy season the Chitake River floods into the Rukomechi River and in turn into the Zambezi, but from April – when these systems dry up and waterholes empty – the springs form a crucial source of water and a focus for a great variety of wildlife. As the dry season progresses, more and more animals descend upon the springs. These conditions are perfect for predators, so lions, leopards, hyenas and wild dogs have a field day growing fat.

With a professional guide (only walking – no driving safaris here) this area offers one of the most intense and intimate wildlife experiences in southern Africa, although it is not recommended for most first-time visitors to Africa who will not be used to the uncomfortable conditions during long periods of total stillness waiting for animals to approach, and the very close proximity to the animals. Dinosaur fossils have recently been found embedded in deep layers of rock exposed in the eroded bank of a nearby river.

Getting there

By air Most people fly into Mana Pools airstrip from Kariba, although charters can be arranged from any destination in Zimbabwe or from Lusaka in Zambia. A couple of airstrips in this area can be reached from Harare, Victoria Falls and Kariba. Your accommodation will arrange appropriate transport.

Self-drive If you have booked a safari you can drive into the national park and leave your vehicle at the warden's office for the duration of your safari. From Harare, take the Chinhoyi road past Karoi to Makuti, pass through Makuti and after 16km stop at the National Parks office in Marongora for an entry permit. You must arrive here before 15.30 to allow sufficient driving time to arrive at Nyamepi, which is about 80km, before dark. From there, after 6km turn right (northeast) onto a dirt road and enter the park at Nyakasikana Gate where you turn left and follow signs to Nyamepi main office. Note that the more direct road from Chirundu to Nyamepi, following the river, passes through hunting land for which you need permits, so is not available to self-drivers.

Tour and safari operators (See also list of safari operators on pages 86–7)

African Bushcamp Safaris \09 234307; e contact@africanbushcamps.com; www. africanbushcamps.com; Skype: africanbushcamps. Very well regarded, offering a large range of options including 3-night canoeing trips along the Zambezi with full backup crew & on a fully inclusive basis.

Mwinilunga (Chipembere) Safaris \+263 (4)494056; m +263 71 232 4749; e mwinilunga@ mweb.co.zw; www.mwinilunga.com. Tailor-made, family-orientated safaris focused on fun & relaxation. See ad, page 237.

Goliath Safaris \04 882373; m 0772 733252; e goliath@africaonline.co.zw; www.

goliathsafaris.com. Owner-run & guided by the renowned Stretch Ferreira, who has 25 years' experience of running safaris here. Canoe safaris include 3- & 4-night trips (set departure dates or tailor-made); sleep in dome tents, use bush toilets & wash in the river. Hiking trips are tailor-made for fit & adventurous guests carrying their own equipment & sleeping gear. See opposite page for permanent camp accommodation details for. Closed Nov–Mar.

Natureways Safaris Harare; m 0772 335038, Kariba office: m 0772 348565; e reservations@natureways.com; www.natureways.com. This is a group of specialist safari operators offering a wide range of personalised walking & canoe trips on the Lower Zambezi & within the national park. **Zambezi Odyssey** trips (generally 4 days & 3 nights) are fully backed up with luxury tents & waiter service. **Zambezi Explorer** trips (2–9 nights but extended or combination trips can be arranged) are expeditionary-style canoe safaris with 2 qualified guides who take care of cooking & camp chores. **Mana Shoreline Safaris** are traditional mobile safaris that follow the shoreline in the company of an expert guide.

Accommodation is in luxury en-suite tents & the camps come with fully equipped kitchen, bar facilities & dining area.

Sunpath Safaris ✆ 04 304043; m 0712 204947; e sunpath@mweb.co.zw; www.sunpathsafaris.com. Offer an exclusive rustic tented-camping experience for small groups (up to 6) with wilderness trails & game drives in & around Mana Pools including Chitake Springs. They also provide a 3-night, 4-day 'client participation' canoe safari from Chirundu to Mana Pools. Escorted self-drive trips are also offered. Sunpath is licensed to operate throughout Zimbabwe so can offer visits to other areas on request.

Tailormade Safaris ✆ 09 232376; m 0772 153500; e info@tailormade-safaris.com; www.tailornade-safaris.com. Tented adventures & safaris – walking, canoeing, drives in Mana Pools, Kariba, Matopos & Hwange.

The Zambezi Safari & Travel Company UK ✆ 01548 830059; e info@zambezi.com; www.zambezi.co.uk. A UK-based agency run by Zimbabweans specialising in organising safaris throughout the Lower Zambezi area. Their website is excellent.

Where to stay Mana Pools is deservedly one of Zimbabwe's most popular wildlife destinations and the park facilities can become stretched in the main winter season. It is therefore essential to pre-book your accommodation. The listings in the *Private camps* section, below, contain camps and lodges that provide amongst the best wildlife viewing in the region. While the first three permanent lodges belong in the luxury category, the others are tented accommodation and difficult to fit into the other accommodation categories. Nevertheless they all offer wonderful wildlife viewing experiences coupled with a level of personal service and catering that few people would associate with 'camping'.

Unlike at other national parks, the **National Park lodges** listed below must be booked in advance, through the head office in Harare (see page 158). As with the lodges, **National Park campsites** at Mana Pools must be booked in advance, through the head office in Harare. Some camping sites are charged per person while others are per site and it can be very confusing.

Campers should note that it is prohibited to bring fresh fruit into the park. Baboons, monkeys, hyenas and honey badgers can be a real nuisance if you leave food or scraps within their reach. Take plastic bags and store waste in your car if there are no secure dustbins. If you need to leave your tent at night, shine a strong torch around before you exit, as hyenas here are habituated to humans.

Private camps
Luxury
⌂ **Ruckomechi Camp** (10 en-suite tented units) Accessible by air charter (see *Getting there* above); ✆ +27 11 807 1800; +27 12 7027500;

e enquiry@wilderness.co.za; www.wilderness-safaris.com. This beautiful & exclusive camp consistently ranks as one of the best in Zimbabwe & operates within its own private concession. Rukomechi was refurbished in 2008 & moved

3km upstream to a site even more delightful than the original spot, in a shady grove of albida & mahogany trees. Spacious en-suite tented units, including a honeymoon suite, overlook the Zambezi River. Each tent has indoor & outdoor showers & secluded outdoor 'bath-with-a-view'. The central dining area, bar & library complex faces the Zambezi Escarpment & is connected to the rest of the camp by walkways. A separate deck has infinity pool & stargazing deck. The camp overlooks the Zambezi floodplain, with waterbuck, impala, hippo & a myriad of waterbirds. Elephant are regular visitors to the camp. Predators such as lion, leopard & wild dog are all found in the area. The birdlife is superb for both *mopane* woodland & riverine species, with numerous local specials like collared palm-thrush, racket-tailed roller, purple-banded sunbird & black-throated wattle-eyes. Activities include wildlife viewing in open 4x4 vehicles, on motorised pontoon boats, on foot, in hides or in canoes. Fully inclusive. **$$$$$**

🏠 **Chikwenya Lodge** (8 standard lodges) 📞04 499165, 499875; **m** 0712 207406, 0772 555079; **e** reservations@chikwenyasafaris.com; www.chikwenyasafaris.com. This is another long-standing & much loved luxury camp on the banks of the Zambezi. The lodges are built on teak platforms with their own private deck, bathroom, dressing room, AC & outdoor shower as an alternative to the old claw-foot bathtubs inside. Chikwenya offers a full range of game-related activities, both water- & land-based, & there's an airstrip nearby. Closed 7 Jan to 1 Mar. **$$$$**

🏠 **Kanga Bush Camp** (6 tents) 15km from the Zambezi River; ✪ S15 54 32, E29 15 48; 📞09 234307; **e** contact@africanbushcamps.com; www.africanbushcamps.com ⊕ Apr–Oct. This camp, which opened in 2010, is set in the remote heart of the national park in a private concession. The main area of the camp is on decking, consisting of dining area, bar & library & lounge area overlooking the pan. There's a choice of game drives in open 4x4 vehicles or walking with professional guides. Other activities include night drives as well as canoeing, which is organised on request. Kanga Pan attracts game in big concentrations, as it is the only permanent water found in the area.

Access is generally by charter flight – airstrip used is Mana Main. If you're driving it's recommended only for experienced 4x4 drivers.

Kanga accepts a min age of 10 years old (children of all ages over Christmas & Easter & if not busy they can take children younger than 10 but guests must book & pay for private vehicle). **$$$$$**

🏠 **Kavinga Bush Camp** (6 tents) & **Kavinga River Camp** (6 tents) **m** 0774 455822; **e** reservations@kavingasafaris.com; www.kavingasafaris.com. The bush camp is a mobile tented camp at Chitake Springs, offering some of the best winter-season wildlife viewing in the country; featuring amongst a host of other game is the resident lion pride. The river camp is beside the Zambezi 12km upriver from Nyamepi Camp. Both use walk-in dome tents, with stretcher beds & hot showers available. Activities from Bush Camp include morning & afternoon guided walking safaris. Activities from River Camp include walking safaris, drives & (by prior arrangement) canoeing & fishing. Access by self-drive or light charter aircraft into the national park, with transfers arranged if required. Children under 14 & 11 years at Bush Camp & River Camp respectively, are discouraged. Rates are fully inclusive (exc transfers). **$$$$$**

🏠 **Vundu Camp** (8 tents) 📞09 234307. This simple, comfortable, traditional-style tented safari camp caters for max 8 guests. The thatch-sheltered tents are walk-in with large en-suite bathrooms, flush toilets & traditional bucket showers. Activities are focussed on canoeing, game drives & walking in the national park with excellent guides & plentiful game in the dry season. Fully inclusive. **$$$$$**

🏠 **Goliath Safaris** 📞04 882373; **m** 0772 733252; **e** goliath@africaonline.co.zw; www.goliathsafaris.com. Goliath has a traditional riverside tented camp (5 2-person tents) with teak furnishings, en-suite bathrooms including flush toilets & hot showers. There's a covered lounge & bar area alongside an open-air dining room. Activities include game drives & walks, canoeing, fishing (bring your own rods & equipment). The co-owner Stretch Ferreira is host here, with Flo, and with his encyclopaedic knowledge of the locality & wildlife you'll probably not get a better bush experience anywhere in Africa. **$$$$**

🏠 **Mana Pools Safari Company** (6 luxury tents) 📞04 490612; **m** 0772 361712; **e** sarah@manapoolssafaricompany.com. Run by the daughter of renowned guide John Stevens, and her partner, this is a tented mobile safari camp setting up on riverside sites owned by private operators.

Activities include game drives & walks, birding, canoeing, fishing, & with prior notice they will set up a spa service in camp.

⌂ **Mwinilunga Safaris** ☎04 494056; m 0772 304162; e mwinilunga@mweb.co.zw; www. mwinilunga.com. 2 tented locations – **Mana Pools** on the banks of the Zambezi, comfortable tented accommodation with hot showers & flush toilet. Access by road or air. Activities on offer: canoeing, walking, photography, fishing, with the services of a professional guide, and **Mongwe Camp**, on the Zambezi River between Chirundu & Mana Pools. 2 brick-under-thatch en-suite chalets with a communal dining area & kitchen equipped to cater for up to 15 people. Alternatively, a fully equipped tented camp with 5 spacious safari tents, twin beds, communal ablutions, hot showers, flush toilets & a tented dining area. Plenty of lawn space for extra tents & a separate ablution block. **$$$**

⌂ **Natureways** has 2 small tented camps. **Camp Zambezi** is a traditional static bush camp, but without permanent structures, electricity or plumbing. Large walk-in tents have en-suite bathrooms with chemical loos & bucket showers, & there's a long-drop for day use. Staff provide hot water for washing & you dine under the stars. Activities include game drives, fishing, canoe trips & walking, all in the company of professional guides with intimate knowledge of the area & the wildlife. At **Camp Chitake** you camp amongst the wildlife in small dome tents with sleeping bags & mattresses,

wash in the river & use the bush for the loo. Your guide will track game to within metres & you will need a strong nerve, patience & the ability to remain still for prolonged periods. In the dry season you'll help construct a hide by the water's edge & let everything come to you. A magical experience that will last a lifetime, though Natureways don't recommend this for first-time visitors. **$$$$**

National Park lodges

⌂ **Musangu & Muchichiri** Just upstream from Nyamepi Camp campsite. Each has 2 bedrooms (8 beds), bathroom & shower, 2 toilets & kitchen with gas stove & deep freeze. Cutlery, crockery, bedding & towels supplied. Large dining room & lounge, & outside *braai* area with views over the river. **$$$**

⌂ **Standard lodges** 3 lodges, each with 2 dbl bedrooms, shower & toilet, & seating areas near the river. Kitchens have gas cooker & deep freeze, crockery & cutlery. Bedding & towels included. **$$**

National Parks campsites

⌂ **Nyamepi Camp** (30 sites) Communal camping area near NP reception office. Ablution blocks have hot & cold running water, flush toilets, laundry basins. Each campsite has a *braai* area & firewood is available from reception. Some standard campsites, generally those away from the river, are now chargeable per person. These sites are numbers 1, 2, 7, 8, 10, 12, 13, 14 & 15. All other standard campsites at Nyamepi are charged per site.

Exclusive campsites Several remote undeveloped campsites along the river have *braai* stands and long-drop toilets. Water for washing etc is collected from the river, but you must bring your own drinking water: **Mucheni** (8km west of Nyamepi, 4 sites); **Nkupe** (just over 1km east of Nymepi, 1 site); **Ndungu** (just east of car park area, 2 sites); **Gwaya** (just upstream from the lodges, 1 site). Each has cold-water shower, flush toilet and basin, and *braai* stand. All exclusive campsites are chargeable by site with the exception of the Ndungu sites, charged per person.

Wild exclusive campsites There are two wonderfully wild, public camping sites in the southern sector of the park, close to Chitake Springs, near the foothills of the Zambezi Escarpment. The check-in point for these camps is at Nyakasikana Gate; ask directions from the park office at Morongora. Both are without any facilities and accessible only by 4x4. Chitake 1 and Chitake 2 are clearly signposted. It is recommended that first-time visitors use an operator as this area is extremely wild and frequented by large predators (lion), especially during the dry season.

Walking in Mana Pools As well as its abundant wildlife, one of Mana Pools' biggest drawcards (for the more adventurous) is that you are allowed to walk in the bush unaccompanied by a guide. This is especially valued by birding enthusiasts. There

A DAY ON THE RIVER *(Courtesy of Zambezi Safari and Travel)*

Camp set-ups are done to a formula (kitchen set up with all equipment and utensils laid out strictly, shower unit up, tents and mosquito nets laid out) with almost military precision, in about 20 minutes.

Sleeping arrangements vary from two-man dome tents to a simple mosquito-net-over-paddle affair – double bed if necessary. For the more intrepid, the simple net is definitely the way to go. The stars shine brighter and buffalo, elephant or hippo wanderers in the small hours add spice.

The daily routine is usually an early paddling start after sunrise, to cover ground before the wind picks up by mid-morning. This is followed by a full (English) breakfast at a suitable stopover site. The river flows at approximately 4km/h. Previous canoeing experience isn't necessary – 90% of the steerage comes from aft (newlyweds shouldn't paddle in the same canoe).

The canoes are the Canadian standard. The canoeing safari isn't strenuous (unfit torsos will feel aches at night but ten minutes of paddling the next morning clears any lactic acid build-up). The route is restricted to shallow waters out of the way of hippo. Swimming is not recommended in the Zambezi, but wallowing on large and very shallow sandbanks out of the way of crocodiles and other game is occasionally permitted at the guide's discretion.

Siestas at lunchtime are welcomed – river guides see it as a job perk and the habit is unlikely to be broken. The usual routine is to find a safe spot under a large tamarind tree, set up a cold lunch and find a comfortable space for a bedroll and some light reading.

Fishing tackle is a good idea for more active participants – be sure to request this specifically when making your reservation. Alternatively bring a light rod and a No 3 Mepps spinner (bacon pieces are considered a delicacy by tigerfish). Fishing on the river is excellent, and the river's tigerfish put up a better fight than on those on Lake Kariba. The day's catch, if any, is prepared at night.

The pace of the afternoon's paddling session depends largely upon whether a morning wind came up. Usually it's a leisurely paddle until an hour or so before sunset. Zambezi Valley sunsets compare with the best in the world, and that applies throughout the year, whether it's smoke haze from bush fires in the winter months or crystal air and cloudy backdrops in the summer.

are no fences so you share this beautiful park with the birds and game, large and small, safe and dangerous. My recommendation though is that you do not venture far from your vehicle without professional assistance unless you have a good deal of experience in bush walking, as fatalities have occurred here in the recent past. As there are few areas of dense bush it is likely that game will always be aware of your presence, with very little likelihood that you will surprise them and trigger an attack. But that does mean that they will probably disappear before you get a chance to see them, which is why it is strongly recommended that you hire a guide or, better still, book a walking safari with one of the tour and safari operators detailed above.

SAPI AND CHEWORE SAFARI AREAS While Mana Pools is a protected national park, permitting only photographic and birding safaris (some limited fishing activities are allowed), in neighbouring Sapi and Chewore there is a mixture of hunting, fishing and photo-safari activities. As there are no fences inhibiting game movement between photographic and hunting areas, there is plenty of potential for

6

wildlife viewing throughout the area. However, some animals have become wary and tend to avoid hunting areas. Most non-hunting visitors who come to these areas do so for the superb fishing rather than wildlife viewing.

Getting there It's quite possible to drive to this area from Mana Pools, or from Chinhoyi in the south or Mavuradonha in the east. Whichever way, you'll need to be experienced and adventurous, with a sturdy 4x4 with capacity for plenty of fuel and provisions. It's a very remote area and you'll be driving for days to the nearest shops. Driving in the wet season is very difficult and not recommended.

A much quicker and simpler alternative is to fly in by chartered light aircraft. Check with your accommodation or www.wildzambezi.com for the latest information on local flights.

⌂ Where to stay
Standard
⌂ **Tafika** (7 chalets) & **Shamashanga** (8 large tents) Contact Safari Air Services ☎ 04 852286/8; m 0774 891735; e marketing@tafika.com; www. tafika.com. These 2 excellent fishing camps, operated by the same company, are quite close to one another in Sapi with beautiful views directly over the river. Each tent has en-suite bathroom with shower & its own veranda. The central lodge has a bar, dining room & lounge – & the absolutely essential outside fire pit for sundowners & tall fishing stories. Prices include all meals,

refreshments, National Parks fees, boat hire with up to 50 litres of fuel per day, tackle & bait. **$$$$**
⌂ **Chewore Lodge and Campsite** (4 lodges, 10 campsites) ☎ 04 757398, 751298; e bookings@ chewore.com; www.chewore.com. Situated in beautiful woodland at the confluence of the Chewore & Zambezi rivers, this is a prime fishing & wildlife location.

The lodge is an all-inclusive fishing camp for up to 8 guests, all chalets with en-suite bathrooms, a central lounge, bar, swimming pool & dining area. There are 2 large, pontoon fishing boats fully

JEWELS OF THE ZAMBEZI
Sally Wynn (www.wildzambezi.com)

If you visit the Zambezi Valley between August and December, you should be lucky enough to encounter this striking jewel of the African birding world – the southern carmine bee-eater. They are beautiful birds, richly coloured bright carmine (rose-red) and blue. They hang around in noisy flocks, nesting in holes burrowed into the sandy sides of vertical riverbanks or roosting communally in trees or reedbeds sometimes in their hundreds or thousands. They squabble with their neighbours and chase each other in aerial acrobatics. They bathe often, briefly splash-diving head first into water, before preening vigorously.

Southern carmines are a migratory species, with three stages to their migration. They arrive in Zimbabwe in August–September to breed along the Zambezi River until November–December when the heaviest of the rains begin. They then move to South Africa for the summer months, and in March they migrate northwards to equatorial Africa (Angola, Zambia, Malawi, DRC and Tanzania) until August.

As their name implies, these bee-eaters eat bees and wasps, but, being the largest of the African bee-eaters, they also take bigger insect prey like flying termites, cicadas, shield bugs, dragonflies, butterflies and locusts. They hawk them on the wing, bringing them back to their perch where they beat them and rub them for about five to ten seconds, discharging any sting or venom, and then toss them into their mouths and swallow them. They also eat small rodents and lizards.

Southern carmine bee-eaters are apparently monogamous, breeding in large, dense colonies (100–10,000 nests) in holes burrowed horizontally for 1–2m into equipped with fishing tackle & experienced drivers to take you out on the river for game viewing, fishing or a sundowner cruise.

There are 10 campsites that cater for up to 4 people each. Campers are limited to bringing 2 cars & 1 boat per site. Each campsite has its own shower & toilet with an efficient wood-fired boiler for a hot shower in the cooler months. Each site has a braai/kitchen area with a 230-litre 'Minus 40' deep freeze & plug point. During the night there are lights over the kitchen area & in the toilet/shower. These are run by an inverter, so there is complete silence at night. Fuel, ice & firewood can be purchased on site. **$$$**

Details of other specialist fishing camps in the Sapi/Chewore safari areas can be found on the Wild Zambezi website (*www.wildzambezi.com*).

What to see and do

Fishing The Zambezi is relatively deep here, bringing conditions that offer excellent fishing. As well as the fighting tigerfish (*Hydrocynus vittatus*), which tops most anglers' lists, there's bream, several species of catfish including the giant Vundu, alongside bottlenose, Cornish jack, chessa and nkupe. Many excellent fishing spots on the Zambezi can be accessed by boat, including the spectacular Mupata Gorge, where the river narrows considerably and the flow is deep and swift. The best times for fishing here are September–November, March to June.

Fossil remains In the Chewore, west of Mupata Gorge, there is an extensive 'petrified forest' of fossil wood. Inland, in the remote, wild southern section of the area, a spectacular trail of fossil footprints made by the dinosaur *Allosaurus* has been discovered in a riverbed. These remains are millions of years old and rarely visited except by small parties of visitors in the company of experienced and armed professional guides.

sandy riverbanks, erosion gullies or occasionally on flat open sandy areas. The burrows are excavated by both sexes and are usually constructed each year – they dig first with the bill and later remove sand with a bicycling action of their feet. The burrows terminate in an unlined oval chamber where the eggs are laid. The hatchlings (usually four) are born blind and naked and are fed by both adults. Most young fledge by early December before the heaviest rains, and are able to migrate southwards with their parents. The bee-eaters regurgitate blackish, oval pellets of indigestible insect remains, several times a day. These accumulate at the burrow entrance and smell strongly of ammonia.

Sadly, many colonies of southern carmine bee-eaters along the Zambezi River have been destroyed as a result of collapsing riverbanks following changing river patterns after the construction of the Kariba and Cahora Bassa dams. In Zimbabwe, some colonies in settled areas have been exploited as a food source to the point of extinction and there are recent accounts of these beautiful birds being netted to fuel an increasing demand for colourful feathers for costume jewellery.

Zimbabwe's Zambezi Valley protected areas, including the World Heritage Site that incorporates Mana Pools National Park, Sapi and Chewore Safari Areas, serve as unpopulated refuges to safeguard these precious jewels of the air. But we should not take them for granted. Making people more aware of their value as a tourism asset can help ensure their future.

Kanyemba This remote border village is situated on the Zambezi in the extreme northeast of Zimbabwe, forming a boundary corner with Zambia and Mozambique. From here the river broadens out to become Lake Cahora Bassa, the Zambezi's second-biggest hydro-electric reservoir and Mozambique's answer to Kariba. Kanyemba is a focal point for fishing and hunting in the Dande safari area, and the end point for long-haul canoe safaris along the Zambezi from Chirundu or Mana Pools.

Getting there This is an academic question for non-hunters – you'll be more interested in how to get away. Your canoe operator will have arranged transfers, almost invariably by air charter. Otherwise it's a long and dusty road.

NORTHERN ZIMBABWE

The Mavuradonha Mountains form the eastern part of the Zambezi Escarpment, rising over 1,000m and peaking at Banirembizi. This is also the northern end of Zimbabwe's mineral-rich Great Dyke. The mountains lie north of the town of Centenary and intercept the northeast winds. For this reason they have a cooler, moister climate than the valley below. The name Mavuradonha refers to the misty rains that often hover over the mountain tops.

This is a true wilderness area covering 600km² and you'll find few people, even Zimbabweans, venturing up here despite its stunning beauty. Numerous streams and rivers rise in the mountains, flowing north to the Zambezi. The ground is steep and rocky, with elephant trails winding precariously up and down the mountain. In the east the Musengezi River has cut a gorge through the mountains, creating attractive scenery. Elephant, buffalo, eland, sable, kudu and zebra are amongst the species that make this scenic area home. There is a great deal of well-developed *miombo* woodland, with most of the representative species of *Brachystegia* and *Julbernardia*. There are also gully, ravine or *kloof* woodlands, with higher soil moisture and nutrients, providing a greater range of microhabitats. Large forest trees such as *Khaya anthotheca* occur but are scattered and in small numbers.

The wilderness area has suffered from poaching but is now relatively well protected, and wildlife numbers are increasing. Elsewhere, the rugged terrain prevents access and exploitation, although there is felling of larger trees and limited poaching. There are Bushman paintings to explore, and of course excellent birding.

Numerous bird species include Dickinson's kestrel, racket-tailed roller, miombo tit, miombo wren-warbler, Meve's glossy starling, kurrichane thrush, white-headed black chat, boulder chat, miombo rock thrush, white-breasted sunbird, miombo double-collared sunbird, broad-tailed paradise whydah and black-eared seedeater.

Centenary is 230km due north of Harare and the drive will take you about 3½ hours. For detailed directions go to www.distancesfrom.com/zw.

ACTIVITIES
Horseriding Balanced on the escarpment of the Zambezi Valley, 180km north of Harare, the pristine wilderness of Mavuradonha is where you'll find Kopje Tops (6 en-suite chalets for 12 guests) a tranquil, rustic lodge that serves as the base for the region's only horseriding operation, the excellent **Varden Horse Safaris** (\ 04 861766; m 0772 908720, 369294, 256434; e riding@vardensafaris.com; www. vardensafaris.com).

You can take short morning or afternoon rides or ride for days exploring *miombo* and *mushanje* woodlands with orchids, waterberry, palms and wild fruit that support elephant, buffalo, eland, sable, kudu, zebra and many other species. Safari nights are billed as a cosy mountain experience, with no electricity, phones or email to disturb the soul, and include sleeping on a mountain top or the sandy floor of a cave.

You'll be grateful for the sure footed horses because the going is challenging. Trails are often narrow and precarious with sheer precipices on either side, and although the horses are rugged and used to these conditions, riders too need to be experienced and confident. Varden staff can tell an experienced rider from a beginner, and reserve the right to turn away anyone not deemed suitable.

Varden's safety standards are high (they carry a satellite phone, and guides are experienced in first aid) but they make the point that these long trips are not without danger. Should you fall off and be unable to remount, it will mean an evacuation on foot and possibly some days before you reach the nearest airstrip for air evacuation. Hard hats are recommended; although there is a selection available you are encouraged to bring your own.

Varden donates a proportion of revenues to the local community via the council through a CAMPFIRE project arrangement.

Walking safaris Through Varden Safaris you can also arrange a walking safari from the Mavuradonha Mountains across the escarpment and down through Mana Pools National Park to the shores of the Zambezi. This too is only for the fit and adventurous, as the going can be tough. There are few safaris which take you back to raw Africa in quite the same way as this one does, and afterwards you may fairly claim to be one of only a handful to have done it. For further details check Varden's website or ask at Natureways (see page 230).

7

Victoria Falls

Telephone code 013

Every single commercial itinerary to Zimbabwe includes Victoria Falls – and quite rightly too. The town is famous for its magnificent waterfall, which is listed as one of the 'Seven Natural Wonders of the World' and supports a huge array of adrenalin-fuelled activities from the famous white-water rafting to river-boarding and bungee-jumping.

Even today, with Zimbabwe having suffered a decade of political and economic strife, it's difficult to imagine a more complete African tourist destination than Victoria Falls (commonly referred to as 'Vic Falls' or simply 'the Falls'). As well as the adrenalin sports, both aerial and waterborne, the area supports a wealth of traditional wildlife-based and cultural attractions. While some visitors seek excitement others still prefer the genteel life of yesteryear, with starched waiters and afternoon tea on manicured lawns.

Tourism has turned the far western tip of Zimbabwe into a rather un-Zimbabwe-like place, but its relative isolation has left it less affected by the political troubles and interference experienced elsewhere in the country. It is testament to the commercial nous of the operators here that while the rest of the country has been in economic freefall, many sectors of the Victoria Falls tourist industry have stayed afloat, even flourished. Although many small operators have fallen by the wayside, others have amalgamated or built on specific strengths and grown their markets.

They have of course been helped by their location, which has allowed daytrippers to flock in from neighbouring countries, notably Zambia and Botswana, and sample Zimbabwe's treasures without actually staying here. Some tour groups cross the bridge from Zambia for better views of the falls without even realising they've entered Zimbabwe.

Commercialisation has turned the place into something of a tout's paradise, but don't let this put you off: this small, laid-back town (locals refer to it as 'the village')

WHICH COUNTRY?

Be sure you know which country your Victoria Falls accommodation and activities are based in. This is not always as obvious as you might think on the internet or in brochures as some Zambian operators refer to their Victoria Falls activities and accommodation without spelling out which country they are in. The Zimbabwe side of the Zambezi offers by far the best views of the waterfall and the widest array of accommodation and activities. Victoria Falls town is in Zimbabwe; its counterpart across the river is Livingstone. Zimbabwe's internet suffix is .zw, Zambia's is .zm. Zimbabwe's telephone country code is 263, Zambia's is 260.

has somehow retained its charm and character. It has a casino or two and some glitzy hotels, but it's certainly no Las Vegas. Population estimates vary widely but local sources put it at around 65,000 which includes both high and low density housing areas.

No introduction to the falls would be complete without mentioning the animals. Warthogs dodge cars while rooting around in traffic islands and verges. Vervet monkeys are always on the lookout for morsels left unattended on your plate or in your campsite. Baboons patrol the town, sharing the pavement with you especially along the road to the Victoria Falls Hotel; but hang on to your bag of fruit and never be tempted to feed them. Elephants refuse to respect the presence of houses on their traditional trails, and view gardens, swimming pools and vegetable patches as fair game. They've been known to wander through town checking out the vehicles in the supermarket car park while the cricket club reluctantly built a wall to stop elephants strolling across the wicket in mid-innings. All mere inconveniences, but nothing compared with one local resident, who returned home to find a leopard in his kitchen.

HISTORY

There is no doubt that Dr David Livingstone was the catalyst for the founding of the town now known as Victoria Falls. Though this devout Scotsman was committed to his missionary work and to the abolition of the slave trade, throughout his extensive travels over several decades the 'natives' politely but steadfastly refused to demonstrate any need for a replacement religion, and he was singularly unsuccessful in achieving permanent conversions. Eventually he shifted his emphasis from conversion to simply spreading the word of Christ wherever he travelled, preparing the ground for later missionaries. Some biographers have suggested that his expeditions throughout central and southern Africa were driven more by a love of exploration – the search for the source of the Nile in particular – than by missionary zeal. Whatever his real motivations, he became possibly the most effective explorer of his time, and towards the end of his life the publicity he gave to the evils of slavery certainly appears to have contributed to its abolition.

It was on one of his expeditions, an arduous coast-to-coast attempt to follow the Zambezi to its mouth on the east coast, that Livingstone followed up tribal reports of Mosi oa Tunya, 'the smoke that thunders', employing local Makololo tribesmen to take him by dugout canoe to the waterfall. In late November 1855, at the age of 41, David Livingstone credited himself as the first white man to set eyes on Victoria Falls.

Many people, however, question the validity of this claim. Livingstone himself had learned of the existence of the falls several years previously, and there had certainly been other explorers in the area, who it may be assumed had also heard about Mosi oa Tunya. It is unlikely that the Portuguese, who had been in the area decades before Livingstone, had not found them. Nevertheless it was Livingstone who first reported the falls to the Royal Geographical Society, named them after his monarch and characteristically took the credit. It was certainly he who put them on the map. While presumably awed by the sight of the falls, he is likely to have been seriously disappointed by this navigational barrier in the Zambezi, which ruined his hopes of a trade route into the interior. Only later did he write the oft-quoted phrase, 'Scenes so lovely must have been gazed upon by angels in their flight'.

Soon after news of his 'discovery', the area saw the arrival of a motley assortment of explorers, hunters and traders. They named their original settlement (on the north side of the Zambezi, today's Zambia, near a crossing upstream of the falls) Old Drift. On the southern bank (in what is now Zimbabwe) there were no buildings, only the Big Tree, a huge baobab which served as a meeting place and camping spot for the crossing. The tree is still standing just a short distance from town.

Old Drift, plagued with mosquitoes and the malaria and blackwater fever they transmitted, was eventually shifted to higher ground, the basis of present-day Livingstone. There was no development on the 'Zimbabwe' side until the turn of the 20th century when Cecil Rhodes's railway arrived from the south. Rhodes wanted his bridge to cross the Zambezi in spectacular fashion, and built it over the gorge itself rather than at a much simpler crossing a few hundred metres upstream.

Visitors from far and wide started arriving by train in significant numbers to see the waterfall. The first white settler in Victoria Falls was an entrepreneur by the name of Percy Clark, who opened up a curio shop in 1903. Business must have been good because Jack Soper, the bridge tollkeeper, opened up a competing shop a few years later (Soper's name lives on in a smart curio shop in today's Victoria Falls). A small railway hotel of wood and corrugated iron was completed in 1904. The original Victoria Falls Hotel was reportedly so uncomfortable that many passengers preferred to sleep on the train, but after many years of development it became one of the most luxurious hotels in Africa, indeed in the world.

For many years Victoria Falls remained little more than a small settlement across the river from Livingstone, the real focal point for visitors. In 1948, BOAC inaugurated a weekly flying-boat service from Southampton to South Africa, stopping off at Victoria Falls. Passengers overnighted at the by now greatly improved Victoria Falls Hotel (affectionately known as Jungle Junction), gazing in awe over their sundowners at the waterfall or taking a leisurely cruise on the Zambezi. This was an upmarket destination for an intrepid gin-and-tonic brigade, a haven for well-heeled gentlefolk with a penchant for shooting animals. But it was not until the 1960s that cheap air travel allowed Victoria Falls to grow into one of the premier tourist draws on the continent.

It is interesting to speculate on what David Livingstone would make of Victoria Falls today. Everything he so lyrically penned about the falls remains true, but one shudders to think what he would make of the commercial Mecca that has grown up around his 'discovery'. (Pause here, however, to reflect that he may never have set foot in what is today known as Zimbabwe: his diaries and journals tell only of his travel on the river itself and on land to the north, ie: Zambia.)

WHEN TO VISIT

Victoria Falls and its attractions are heavily weather-dependent. Not only does local weather affect your enjoyment of the day and your wildlife viewing, but rainfall in the Zambezi catchment in Zambia and Angola determines the volume of water in the river and consequently the state of river-based activities below the falls. (Local rain, even heavy downfalls, has a minimal affect on river levels.)

WINTER (May–October) Winter has little if any rainfall, and is mild and pleasant with clear skies, daytime highs of 25–27°C and average lows of 7–10°C. Early mornings and evenings are chilly enough to require sweatshirt and longs, especially for game drives. As summer approaches temperatures rise dramatically.

SUMMER (November–April) Temperatures rise with increasing humidity until the outbreak of rains in mid-November. It's generally hot to very hot and wet during the rainy season (mid-November–April), with short, heavy afternoon downpours, average highs of 32–34°C and lows of 15–19°C. Impressive thunderstorms are frequent.

FOR THE WATERFALL The amount of water in the river, and therefore your view of the falls, varies tremendously throughout the year, depending on the rainfall in the main catchment area further north in Zambia and Angola.

During peak flow at the end of the wet season (March–May) you will be treated to one of nature's most awesome phenomena – although you will actually see very little other than massive clouds of thundering spray, totally obscuring the falls themselves. For some visitors, just experiencing the ground-vibrating power of half a million tons of water cascading into the depths every minute is reason enough to visit at this time of year. It's great for aerial viewing, however: the spray rises to over 500m and is visible more than 70km away. Bear in mind that what goes up must come down, be prepared for a drenching and forget any thoughts of photography at this time of year unless you have a fully waterproof camera.

However, if you have designed your Zimbabwe trip around wildlife viewing you may find yourself at the falls in the dry season, around May–November. From June the Zambezi steadily drops in volume, and the views of the falls become totally different. The main body of water concentrates down Devil's Cataract and Main Falls, while the falls to the right of Livingstone Island become a mere trickle. Now you can appreciate the majestic rock structure, with fine views into the depths of the chasm. Photographers will find the best conditions at this time, and may stay all day, chasing the sun and experimenting with rainbows in the spray.

FOR RIVER ACTIVITIES The best rafting is at low water during the dry winter season when the rapids are at their most dramatic. Depending on rainfall in the catchment area, June can still have high water so aim for July through mid-January. As water levels rise in summer, rafting becomes more difficult, with rafting generally closing down altogether by March or April.

FOR WILDLIFE VIEWING Early winter is not the best time because vegetation is still high and groundwater plentiful, so game is very spread out. As the season progresses the vegetation dries out and bush waterholes provide less and less water for the animals. This is the beginning of the best wildlife-viewing time (August to mid-November) as many of them start daily treks to the river to drink, often in big herds. Once summer rains start, animals again disperse.

Early summer sees the return of many migratory bird species so this is the season for optimal birdwatching, although rains can make some national park roads undrivable.

GETTING THERE

BY AIR The airport runway has still not been extended to accommodate wide-body aircraft so there are no direct services from overseas. That said, plans are afoot for airport expansion but locals say we must be patient. **British Airways** (Comair) (✆ 42053, airport ✆ 42388) and **South African Airways** operate daily flights from Johannesburg, and **Air Namibia** flies from Windhoek and Maun four days per week. British Airways office (⊕ 08.30–13.00 and 14.00–16.00 Mon–Fri) is in the residential area at 355 Gibson Road close to Victoria Falls Backpackers. It was closed in February 2013 but possibly only temporarily while the lease is renegotiated.

Victoria Falls airport is 20km from town and most visitors are collected by their tour operator or by prior arrangement with their accommodation. Taxis are always available and charge between US$30–40.

An alternative and cheaper route from South Africa used to be to fly into Livingstone airport on 1time (a South African airline) and then cross the bridge from Zambia into Victoria Falls. Confusion reigns at the time of writing as 1time was collaborating with a Zimbabwean company to form a new low-cost airline, Fresh Air, operating from Johannesburg to Harare and Victoria Falls. They would then cease flying into Livingstone. However, at the very time of Fresh Air's launch, 1time went into administration in November 2012 so this whole plan is in doubt as I write this.

BY TRAIN Botswana Rail has twice weekly services from Gaborone and Francistown via Bulawayo and these are the only scheduled rail connections from neighbouring countries. The trip takes about 5 ½ hours and costs 30 Pula (US$5) for standard class reclining seats.

There is a very inexpensive daily overnight service from Bulawayo, which used to offer a delightful, colonial-style sleeper service, but standards have slumped in recent years. A few years ago this was not to be recommended for tourists but it's now back on the list of things to do, provided you accept that catering and service standards are not what they used to be. The First Class (recommended) fare is US$15 (4$ extra for bedding) but sadly there is no longer a restaurant car. Single First Class passengers are usually booked in a four-berth compartment but if you want privacy you can buy two seats and have a two-berth compartment to yourself. Tickets are available only from the stations at each end and can only be booked for the day of travel.

BY BUS In recent years various companies have operated routes from Harare and Bulawayo but in late 2012 there remains just one reliable luxury operator, Pathfinder (+263 (0)4 2936907/8; m +263 (0)772 694144/5; www.pathfinderlx. com). Their route from Harare passes through Kadoma, Kwekwe, Gweru, Bulawayo and Hwange and they are notable for having a website complete with schedule.

There are also four local bus companies, a cheaper option – Bravo Tours, Tomb's Motorways, Extra City and KK Cheetah Bus. Backpackers' Bazaar (see *Tourist information* below) will provide details.

BY CAR Bulawayo (440km/273 miles from Victoria Falls) is the nearest major town; the drive, on good tar roads (A8), takes about 4½ hours with a refreshment stop at Halfway House. There are filling stations at Halfway House (215km/134 miles) and Hwange (100km/62 miles). Harare is 878km/546 miles away, Beitbridge 760km/472 miles, Masvingo 719km/447 miles.

FROM BOTSWANA The Kazungula border post (06.00–20.00), 70km/43 miles west of Victoria Falls, links Zimbabwe with Botswana. Kasane, 7km into Botswana, is a popular tourist town and has plenty of overnighting possibilities if you arrive after the border has closed. Kazungula is one of the quieter entry points into Zimbabwe but is steadily getting more busy with commercial and tourism traffic as the situation in Zimbabwe continues to improve.

On the Kazungula–Victoria Falls road, observe the 80km/h speed limit and be especially vigilant after dusk, as the road is unfenced national park land and you will frequently encounter elephant, giraffe, buffalo and occasionally wild dog; the uncut road verges can become overgrown enough to conceal big game.

The drive through Botswana from Francistown to Kazungula normally takes about four hours, but as the road from Nata northwards is still under major reconstruction (early 2013) expect some delays and slow sections. An alternative is to consider entering Zimbabwe at Plumtree and driving to Victoria Falls from Bulawayo.

A more scenic route (effectively a game drive), but only suitable for 4x4s, can be taken by crossing the border at Pandamatenga, 198km/123 miles north of Nata. After 25km/16 miles you can either turn right to Hwange National Park, or left via the Matetsi safari area to the main Bulawayo road, 50km/31 miles southwest of Victoria Falls. If you attempt the little-used Hunters border road from Pandamatenga to Kazungula, be aware that there is much confusion about whether this 4x4 track (a wonderful game drive) is open to the public. Check with police at the Panda border post. If you do drive it be careful not to deviate into Botswana – there's no border fence.

FROM ZAMBIA Arriving at Victoria Falls from Livingstone in Zambia is by far the most dramatic way to enter the country, as you get to drive across the bridge. Don't be tempted to get out of your car for pictures, as you will quickly be moved on by rather bossy policemen.

ORIENTATION

For a prime tourism centre, Victoria Falls town centre is remarkably small and compact. The only road into and out of town, Livingstone Way, goes to Bulawayo in one direction (with a turning just outside town for the Kazungula border post 70km away) and to Zambia across the bridge in the other.

You can't miss the falls. As you come down the hill from Bulawayo into town you will see a large plume of spray, looking for all the world like smoke from a bush fire.

The upmarket suburb, with all the smaller lodges, bed and breakfasts and backpacker places, is to the left of the main road, just before you enter town itself. The easiest access to this area is by the Sprayview Hotel on the corner of Reynard Road, or from the road behind OK supermarket in the town centre. Chinotimba, the high-density township, is on the opposite side of the road, off to the right as you come down the hill into town. This is where the majority of residents live, estimated to be in the region of 60,000 people. (Traffic police often set up checkpoints and radar traps anywhere along the approach road into town and there's a pedestrian crossing near the top of the hill where, unusually for Africa, you are required to stop for pedestrians.)

The town has no central landmark; instead it's effectively the junction of Park Way (also known as Parkway Drive) and Livingstone Way. Around this bustling shopping area you'll find most safari and activity operators. Several larger hotels are on Park Way after you leave the centre of town, and this road terminates after 5km at the gates of the Zambezi National Park.

The Landela Centre, also known as the Trading Post, is a large cluster of tourism-oriented shops on Livingstone way just below and on the opposite side of the road from Parkway Drive. To reach the Victoria Falls visitor centre and entrance, continue down Livingstone Way (if on foot, you can use the path which starts opposite the Ilala Lodge Hotel); you can also walk here directly from the Kingdom Hotel or the Victoria Falls Hotel.

Barclays and Standard Chartered banks as well as the Post Office are on the left-hand side of Livingstone Way beyond the railway line in the direction of the falls. The border post is immediately beyond the entrance to the visitor centre.

GETTING AROUND

Most hotels and lodges are within walking distance (1–3km) of the town and waterfall, but the more distant ones can arrange a return shuttle for around

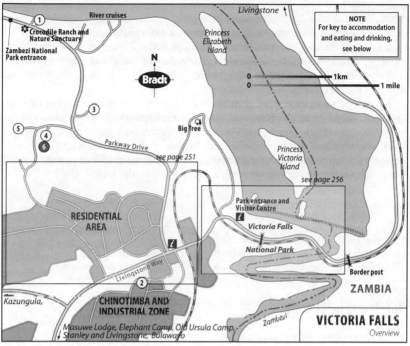

see page 251

see page 256

VICTORIA FALLS
Overview

VICTORIA FALLS *Overview*
For listings, see pages 246–53

🛏 **Where to stay**
1   A'Zambezi River Lodge
2   Adventure Lodge
3   Elephant Hills Resort
4   Lokuthula Lodges
     Safari Club (see 5)
5   Victoria Falls Safari Lodge

Off map
   Elephant Camp
   Masuwe Lodge
   Old Ursula Camp
   Stanley and Livingstone

✖ **Where to eat and drink**
   MakuwaKuwa (see 5)
6   The Boma

US$6–10 return. The large out-of-town hotels on Park Way have regular shuttle services. Several reliable taxi companies operate from the town and can be found in Park Way outside the Soper Centre and in the car parks outside both the TM and OK supermarkets. Once in town, everything is accessible on foot, including the falls themselves. Scooters (150cc) are available for hire outside Shearwater and Wild Horizons booking offices (see page 261). Day hire (08.00–17.00) US$30 or 24 hours US$55. There are few formalities: just give your contact details and a US$300 deposit and carry your driver's licence to show at police roadblocks. Note though that you cannot purchase insurance from the hirers so be very sure that your travel insurance covers you to ride these.

Car hire is available from **Europcar** at the airport terminal (📞 *011 601491*) and **Avis** at both airport and town (📞 *+263 1 344532*). Check their regulations on off-road driving, probably disallowed in anything other than their top-of-the-range 4x4s. Note that car hire in Zimbabwe is probably more expensive than anywhere else in southern Africa

Bicycles can be hired from Adventure Zone (see page 261) at US$5 for three hours.

Victoria Falls   GETTING AROUND

7

TOURIST INFORMATION

You may want to start your visit at the **tourist information office** at the top of Park Way (☉ *08.00–17.00 Mon–Fri, 08.00–13.00 Sat*) operated by the Victoria Falls Publicity Association. They have a good selection of leaflets and brochures, and staff are friendly and willing to help (although few seem to know much more than what's in the literature).

A much better source of local and regional information is **Backpackers Bazaar** (✆ *45828, 42208;* m *0712 404960; www.backpackersbazaarvicfalls.com*), in a cul-de-sac at the top of Park Way in the Victoria Falls Centre building. Friendly and very knowledgeable staff bend over backwards to answer your questions and give useful advice, and can make bookings for you. There's also an excellent private website (*www.victoriafalls-guide.net*) which is updated on a regular basis.

⌂ WHERE TO STAY

Victoria Falls offers a complete range of accommodation, from camping to backpackers, from guesthouses to luxury hotels with royal and presidential suites. All listings are included on the map, page 251, unless otherwise noted.

IN TOWN
Hotels and large lodges
Luxury

⌂ **Ilala Lodge Hotel** [map, page 249] (34 rooms) Livingstone Way; ✆ 44737/9; m 0712 401814; e ilalazws@africaonline.co.za; www. ilalalodge.com. Ilala is a firm favourite for many regulars to Victoria Falls. It borders the Zambezi NP & its lawns are visited by a variety of wild game. Even more impressive then to find that the lodge is situated right in town just a short walk from the falls. Ilala has a friendly, relaxed yet elegant atmosphere with its décor evoking the early days of African adventure & discovery. You can sit by the pool bar or on the terrace & chill out with the spray of the falls in the background. All rooms lead onto either the lawn or a balcony & feature attractive, locally produced teak furniture. The Palm restaurant has an excellent reputation, as does their small, old-fashioned & terribly romantic cruise boat, *Ra-Ikane*. **$$$$$**

⌂ **Victoria Falls Hotel** [map, page 249] (180 rooms) Mallet Dr; ✆ 44751/60, 44203/5; e reservations@victoriafallshotel.com; www. victoriafallshotel.com. This is the original railway hotel, now the grand old duchess of African colonial hotels & a tourist attraction in its own right. Even if you can't afford to stay here, take high tea or sundowners on the terrace overlooking magnificent formal gardens with a commanding view of the second gorge & Victoria Falls bridge. The courtyard

contains one of the original, servant-powered trolleys used to transport guests to & from the falls. The hotel underwent extensive modernisation & refurbishment in 2012/13. Guest rooms range from sgls to a royal suite, & the place has pretty well all the facilities you would expect from a luxury hotel. In the Livingstone Room restaurant the dress code is jacket & tie for gentlemen & smart cocktail wear for ladies, or for a more casual meal there's Jungle Junction. Many people come to take afternoon tea on the veranda, but the cocktails here are also excellent & great value. There is also a sushi restaurant, the only one in town. Larry Norton, a world-renowned wildlife artist, has a permanent exhibition in the hotel, as does Stone Dynamics Gallery. See ad, colour page 8. **$$$$$**

⌂ **Victoria Falls Safari Lodge** [map, page 245] (72 rooms) ✆ 43211–20; e saflodge@ saflodge.co.zw; www.vfsl.com. This large complex, set high on a plateau with spectacular views, is one of the most stunning wood-&-thatch buildings you are likely to find, having won architectural prizes & tourism awards by the bucketful as well as the Green Globe award for its environmental credentials. During construction, many indigenous trees were relocated & thousands more introduced. The luxury of the rooms, including 6 split-level suites, all with a balcony overlooking the waterhole or surrounding bush, makes a stay memorable. There's a stunning split-level restaurant, MakuwaKuwa, & bar in the main building with commanding views of the large waterhole & you can also watch the spectacular daily vulture feeding session at lunchtimes. Their Boma restaurant a short distance away offers a huge buffet, interactive drumming & other local entertainments. **$$$$**

⌂ **Safari Club** [map page 245] (16 rooms, 4 suites) \43211–20; e saflodge@saflodge. co.zw; www.vfsl.com. This latest addition to the Safari Lodge stable ushers in a new level of luxury. Exclusiveness is the name of the game in this brand-new (late 2012) club, which is a separate wing on the Safari Lodge estate. The suites enjoy the same specification as the Club rooms but with an additional spacious sitting room. The exceptional room & suite facilities are too numerous to mention here but the club also boasts its own staffed lounge with a full range of luxury services. Club guests can access all of the benefits of the main lodge but no Lodge guests have access to the Club facilities. Check their website for full details. **$$$$$**

⌂ **Elephant Hills Resort Hotel** [map page 245] (276 rooms) 3km from town off Park Way; \44793/9; e pacro@africansunhotels.com; www. africansunhotels.com. From a distance this huge grey structure on a hillside slightly out of town looks uninviting. Close up the architecture is impressive & inside is an elegant luxury hotel, though it caters largely for conferences. Public areas & many rooms have commanding views of the surrounding countryside. Among the usual 5-star facilities, including 4 restaurants & 3 bars, it boasts its own 18-hole golf course designed by Gary Player, tennis & squash courts, gymnasium & a bowling green. For less sporting types there is a casino. **$$$$**

⌂ **The Kingdom Hotel** [map, page 249] (294 rooms) Cnr Livingstone Way & Mallet Dr; \44275; e reservations@kingdom-hotel.net; www. africansunhotels.com. This rather over-the-top, though impressive hotel, the largest in town, is chock-full of Africana on a grand scale – elephant tusks, warrior statues guarding the entrance, a water feature to rival the falls (themselves a few mins' walk away) a manmade lake at the centre. The design was inspired by the Great Zimbabwe ruins, & it's even got its own Great Enclosure, a large gaming hall & casino surrounded by several restaurants & bars. As well as the usual shopping outlets there is a well-equipped pharmacy & a supervised play area for children. **$$$$**

Upmarket
⌂ **A'Zambezi River Lodge** [map page 245] (83 rooms) 308 Park Way, 5km out of town, close to Zambezi National Park entrance; \44561–4; e reservations@azambezi.co.zw; www.rtg.co.zw. Extensively refurbished in 2011 this is a popular, peaceful out-of-town hotel. Accommodation is in a 2-storey, thatched, horseshoe-shaped complex, set in beautifully landscaped gardens leading directly down to the river. There's a large pool, outdoor bar & 2 restaurants. They offer an hourly shuttle service to town. **$$$$**

⌂ **Victoria Falls Rainbow Hotel** (88 rooms) 278 Park Way; \44651, 44583/5; e resman@ rainbowvfa.co.zw; www.rtgafrica.com. Moorish or Arabic in design, this pleasant & airy hotel with lots of arches is 1km out of town & in late 2012 was being completely refurbished. Rooms are en-suite with AC, satellite TV & balconies overlooking the pool or gardens. The pool has a nice bar where you can cool off your feet as you drink. **$$$**

Standard
⌂ **Lokuthula Lodges** [map page 245] (37 units) Squire Cummings Rd, off Park Way; \43211/20, (South Africa) +27 (0)21 6859324; e info@africaalbidatourism.com; www.vfsl.com. Billed as luxury self-catering lodges, this is actually a timeshare development so reservations cannot be confirmed more than 3 months out. Colourful, ethnically decorated 2- or 3-bedroom thatched lodges are split-level with fully equipped kitchens & BBQ areas, & serviced daily. On the same property as Safari Lodge, & very good value for groups/families. **$$$**

⌂ **Sprayview Hotel** (54 rooms, 4 family suites) Cnr Livingstone Way & Reynard Rd; \44344/6; e res.sprayview@cresta.co.zw. This unassuming place on the approach into town was one of the town's early hotels & though it has been surpassed in terms of luxury it remains popular & very good value. The simply furnished rooms are arranged motel-style in a sgl-storey building. There is a large pool, the Carlos restaurant & 2 bars. Due for major refurbishment in early 2013. **$$**

Small lodges and bed and breakfasts
All but one all of these accommodations are in the leafy residential area to the left of Livingstone Way just as you enter town. There is only one in Chinotimba. Self-drivers should

note that many road signs have disappeared so it's a bit of a maze, and older maps will not show the newer roads in the area. Many places are within easy walking distance of town, while others offer free or nearly free shuttles to/from town, and all can arrange airport transfers. Rates include bed and breakfast unless stated, and standards are generally very high, and great value for money.

Upmarket

⌂ **Amadeus Garden Guesthouse** (11 rooms) 538 Reynard Rd; ✆42261; e reservations@amadeusgarden.com; www.amadeusgarden.com. This immaculate place is deservedly popular & has comfortable, good-sized en-suite rooms complete with heavy teak furniture. Facilities include a pretty courtyard with a large thatched open lounge & saline swimming pool. **$$$**

⌂ **Gertie's Lodge** (4 lodges) Nguhuma Cres; ✆/f 42002; e jtsgertie@mweb.co.zw.zw; www.gertieslodge.com. One of the nicest places in the area, set in lush, peaceful gardens with a *braai* area & pool. 4 spacious thatched lodges have bedroom & lounge downstairs & main bedroom upstairs. Each lodge can sleep up to 6 and there's a central TV lounge & bar with restaurant serving meals on request. **$$$**

Standard

⌂ **Guest Paradise Lodge** (8 rooms) 622 Syringa Rd; ✆40495; e guestparadiselodge@khanondotravel.com; www.khanondotravel.com. Well-appointed, modern & AC en-suite twin rooms or dbls with shared ablutions surround a pool area. Main building houses bar & lounge/TV room. Free Wi-Fi in all rooms & the place was refurbished in 2012. One of the furthest lodges from town. **$$$**

⌂ **Pamusha Lodge** (17 rooms) 583 Manyika Rd; ✆44367, 41828; m 0779 369160; e david@pamusha.com, reservations@pamusha.com; www.pamusha.com. Sgl-storey complex in shady gardens with modern, well-furnished AC rooms for sgls, dbls, trpls & families. There's also a 5-bedroom, self-catering cottage. As well as a bar & pool, restaurant & self-catering facilities, Pamusha offers its own package of safari activities, so makes a very pleasant & convenient base to stay. B&B though evening meals on request. **$$$**

⌂ **Adventure Lodge** (66 rooms) Cnr Pioneer Rd/Spencer St. From town turn left at roundabout & follow signs; ✆44424, 42051; m 0712 210798;

e info@adventurezonevicfalls.com; www.adventurezonevicfalls.com. Previously the Encore Budget Hotel this has now been completely refurbished under new owners. Offers very good budget/motel-style accommodation close to town, mostly twins but 7 family rooms available. Some rooms have AC at a surcharge. Outside open-sided lounge/entertainment area. Wi-Fi & a camping area. You can book all your activities here through Adventure Zone. **$$**

⌂ **Mosi ua Tunya Lodge** 609 Mahogany Rd; ✆44336; m 0772 462837; e mosilodge@yoafrica.com, moslodge@telcovic.co.zw. A friendly welcome & pleasant rooms in 2 quirky dbl-storey circular cottages set in a shady garden. They have a small pool & an outdoor bar area, but bring your own drinks. **$$**

⌂ **Teak Lodge** 581 Masue Rd; ✆44418; m 0773 724219; e reynard@mweb.co.zw. A large building with a variety of en-suite & AC room options including dbls, twins, trpls & a family suite. Some have balconies overlooking the pleasant gardens & there is a good self-catering kitchen. Outside is an attractive sunken pool bar with barstools in the water. As the name suggests, teak trees in the garden & teak furniture within. **$$**

⌂ **Wild Trekkers** (5 rooms) 621 Syringa Rd; ✆42356; m 0773 177903; e wildtrekkerslodge@gmail.com. This sgl-storey house has several dbl & twin rooms & a large self-catering kitchen & dining area. Basic but very clean, the rooms have ceiling fans but no AC. A longish walk into town. **$$**

⌂ **Lorries Lodge** 397 Reynard Rd; ✆42139; m 0712 406584; e lorrie@mweb.co.zw or book through Backpackers Bazaar (see page 261). This small, peaceful, friendly place, a 15min walk into town, has a pretty garden & good-value rooms, all of which are en suite. It has a bar open to locals. 4-course evening meal available on request. **$$**

Hostels and camping
Basic

⌂ **Victoria Falls Rest Camp & Lodges** [map page 249] Park Way; ✆40509/11; e reservations@restcamp.co.zw; www.vicfallsrestcamp.com. This large, long-standing venue, right in the town centre, comprises camping facilities plus a comprehensive variety of other accommodation – dorms, chalets & cottages, some with shared facilities, others en suite & self-catering. They also have safari-type tents. There's a great range of

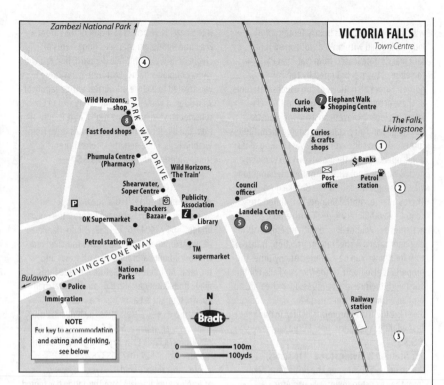

Zambezi National Park

PARK WAY DRIVE

Wild Horizons, shop

8

Fast food shops

Phumula Centre (Pharmacy)

Wild Horizons, 'The Train'

Shearwater, Soper Centre

Publicity Association

Council offices

Backpackers Bazaar

Library

Landela Centre

5 6

OK Supermarket

Petrol station

LIVINGSTONE WAY

TM supermarket

National Parks

Police

Immigration

Bulawayo

4

Curio market

7 Elephant Walk Shopping Centre

The Falls, Livingstone

Curios & crafts shops

1

Banks

Post office

Petrol station

2

Railway station

3

N

Bradt

0 —— 100m
0 —— 100yds

NOTE
For key to accommodation
and eating and drinking,
see below

---

price options from shoestring upwards & it remains excellent value. This is the main venue in town for overland trucks but the place is big enough for all. There's a big pool, & the In Da Belly restaurant is on the premises. See ad, page 238. **$–$$$**

Shoestrings 12 West Dr; \45828, 44611; m 0777 434636; e kelly@backpackers.co.za. A bright & friendly place with colourfully painted accommodation in pleasant gardens, & a variety of room options include camping. There's a good-sized pool, a lively bar, restaurant, the Garden of Eating, *braai* & self-catering facilities & live music. All this, plus being in easy walking distance of town, makes it the town's social centre for young travellers & residents alike. **$**

Victoria Falls Backpackers 357 Gibson Rd; \42209; m 0773 294791; e info@getawaysafaris. com; www.victoriafallsbackpackers.com. This establishment is another favourite, with dbls, twins & 3/4/7/12-bed dorms, well-equipped self-catering kitchen, restaurant, swimming pool, TV room, pool & darts, & free transfers to town. No overland trucks accepted. **$**

Villa Victoria (6 rooms) 165 Courteney Selous Cres; \44386; m 0777 050279, 0712

VICTORIA FALLS *Town Centre*

For listings, see pages 246–9

Where to stay
1 Ilala Lodge Hotel
2 Kingdom Hotel
3 Victoria Falls Hotel
4 Victoria Falls Rest Camp and Lodges

For listings, see pages 252–3

Where to eat and drink
In Da Belly (see 4)
Livingstone Room (see 3)
5 Lola's Tapas
6 Mama Africa Eating House
Palm Restaurant (see 1)
Panarrotis (see 2)
7 The Africa Café
Thundercloud Spur (see 2)
8 Wok 'n Roll

700261; e villaviczim@gmail.com. This very welcoming self-catering villa houses 6 en-suite bedrooms, a simple but well-equipped kitchen, lounge, dining room & large garden with pool. Very good value. **$**

OUT OF TOWN (see map, page 245)
Luxury
Elephant Camp (9 tented lodges) \42313, 42029, 44426; e info@wildhorizons.co.zw; www.

Victoria Falls   WHERE TO STAY

7

wildhorizons.co.za. This luxury tented safari lodge is located within Wild Horizon's 610ha sanctuary estate leased from National Parks on the edge of town & bounded by the Zambezi gorges. Forget all notions of the usual safari tents as these accommodations represent the very latest in elegant canvas construction. They're huge, light and airy, concrete floored, beautifully furnished & en suite with AC & vast sliding glass doors opening onto their own private wooden deck & plunge pool with magnificent, panoramic views towards the falls & the Batoka gorges. There's a large, central lounge/bar/dining area complete with library & deck with a pool & activities are wildlife based with an emphasis on elephant safaris & cheetah interraction. Transport to & from town can be arranged at any time. The property is also home to the Victoria Falls Wildlife Trust with their resident ambassador cheetah, an orphan with whom you can go for walks. You can also visit the Trust's premises, which include the first wildlife veterinary clinic in the whole region. **$$$$$**

🏠 **Stanley & Livingstone** (16 suites) 2.5km down a turning on the left about 12km from the airport to town; 📞 South Africa +27 (0)11 6580633, (0)83 6313888; e enquiries@raniresorts.com; www.stanleyandlivingstone.com. This exclusive & stunning thatched lodge is set in Victoria Falls Private Game Reserve amongst beautifully tended, mature wooded gardens. Its name gives a clue to its decidedly colonial theme, & the luxury furnishings include many antiques. This is a place to come & be pampered. **$$$$$**

🏠 **Imbabala Zambezi Safari Lodge** [map page 270] (9 chalets) Kazungula, 70km from town; 📞 44426, 44426; m 0712 213721; e info@wildhorizons.co.zw; www.wildhorizons.co.za. One of the first bush camps in the country & currently managed by the 3rd generation of the White family who built it, Imbabala is a private concession within National Parks land. It has been completely refurbished with 8 dbl & twin-bedded thatched chalets & 4-bed family house sitting in delightful, wooded lawns overlooking the Zambezi. Elephant, hippo, bushbuck & impala are frequent visitors to the camp, not to mention the occasional lion & leopard. The camp offers game drives, walks & river cruises & is excellent for birders with quite a few 'specials'. Best of all

is their exclusive access to 14km of river frontage & a large floodplain that sees huge herds of elephant as well as buffalo, leopard, lion & a wide variety of plains game. Last time I was there I was treated to a close encounter with a family of wild dogs. If you are planning a day trip to Chobe consider staying here for a night, as it is only 1km from the border & you save an hour's drive from Victoria Falls. FB, 2 activities, refreshments & sundown drinks included. **$$$$$**

Upmarket

🏠 **Masuwe Lodge** (10 lodges) Signposted 5km out of town on Bulawayo Rd after the railway bridge; 📞 04 734043/6, 731282; e info@landela.co.zw. Accommodation is in luxury thatched tents with brick-built bathroom, all with views into the bush. An interesting feature is headboards made from Batonga carved doors. The thatched open restaurant & bar overlook a waterhole & *vlei*, & there's also a pool. Rates include FB, drinks, transfers & an activity. **$$$$**

🏠 **Victoria Falls Cliff Top Lodge** (8 chalets) 📞 South Africa +27 (0)21 6837826; e info@africanluxuryhideaways.com; www.africanluxuryhideaways.com This lodge has tented en-suite chalets raised on high stilts facing the Zambezi gorge. There's a communal boma with bar & dining area together with a viewing deck for spectacular views over the gorge. It's 25km from Victoria Falls so there are 3 daily shuttles into town included in the price. This lodge was opened in April 2013 so the author has not had the opportunity to visit. **$$$$**

🏠 **Gorges Lodge** (10 rooms) 10km down a signposted turn-off on the right, 9km towards town from the airport; 📞 09 72331; e reservations@imvelosafarilodges.com; www.imvelosafarilodges.com. You'd be hard pressed to find a more spectacularly situated lodge anywhere in the world. The complex of well-appointed sgl- & 2-storey buildings, each with private veranda, sits literally on the rim of the gorge in a garden of indigenous trees & plants. The bar actually overhangs the canyon, offering breathtaking views of the Zambezi; it is so high you need binoculars to watch the rafters on the river, 250m below. This is a wonderful venue for a tranquil yet dramatic stay – though maybe not the place for vertigo sufferers. For the same reason, children under 7 years are not accepted. Dibu Dibu, a lovely *boma* a short

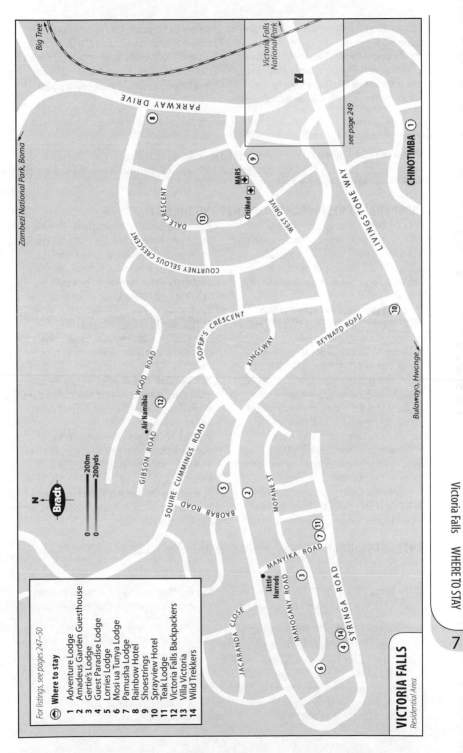

For listings, see pages 247–50

Where to stay

1 Adventure Lodge
2 Amadeus Garden Guesthouse
3 Gertie's Lodge
4 Guest Paradise Lodge
5 Lorries Lodge
6 Mosi ua Tunya Lodge
7 Pamusha Lodge
8 Rainbow Hotel
9 Shoestrings
10 Sprayview Hotel
11 Teak Lodge
12 Victoria Falls Backpackers
13 Villa Victoria
14 Wild Trekkers

VICTORIA FALLS
Residential Area

see page 249

distance from the lodge, makes a great wedding venue. **$$$**

⌂ **Old Ursula Camp** (4 chalets) Contact details as Stanley and Livingstone above; www.oldursula.com. In the Victoria Falls Private Game Reserve, 10mins from town, this is an intimate satellite to the Stanley & Livingstone. The 4 en-suite chalets cater for only 8 guests so it's ideal for 2 families or a group of friends. Traditionally furnished thatched A-frame chalets sit in beautiful grounds with a swimming pool & viewing decks. FB or self-catering. **$$$**

✕ WHERE TO EAT

Victoria Falls is not well stocked with independent restaurants, with the result that most eating places are in the hotels (see below). All listings are included on the map, page 249, unless otherwise noted.

INDEPENDENT RESTAURANTS, LUNCHES AND TAKE-AWAYS

✕ **In Da Belly** Victoria Falls Rest Camp; 📞42749. This jokily named, attractive restaurant is thatched & open-sided, with a pleasant outdoors feel, & overlooks the pool. It provides simple, good-value food. Popular with locals & great for lunch.

✕ **Lola's Tapas** Landela Centre/Trading Post Tasty bites in the middle of town where you can watch the world go by.

✕ **Mama Africa Eating House** Behind the Trading Post shopping centre; 📞41725. Mama Africa offers as near as you will get to traditional African cuisine in Victoria Falls as well as more familiar dishes. Eat in the colourfully decorated restaurant or outside. You will often find a local jazz or African-style band in attendance.

✕ **Panarrotis** Kingdom Hotel; 📞44275. A chain restaurant in the Great Enclosure, serving informal Italian food in a trattoria-style venue.

✕ **Rainforest Café** [map page 256] 📞45002; 📱 0776 027547; ⊕ 08.00–18.00 with late opening during lunar rainbow periods. As the name suggests this is situated in the Rain Forest area, in the National Park & is a welcome catering addition for people who've spent a couple of hours walking around, but note you cannot use the facility without paying the park entry fee. Excellent meals & snacks are served throughout the day.

✕ **Thundercloud Spur** Kingdom Hotel; 📞44275. Part of the very good, family-orientated, pan-African Spur chain, serving a steak-based menu.

✕ **Wok 'nRoll** Park Way; 📞43429. Excellent quality take-away serving oriental dishes, burgers & rolls immediately adjacent to fast food cluster on Park Way.

⌷ **The Africa Café** Elephant Walk. A good place for light meals or a coffee as you take a break from your retail experience. Popular with local residents.

✕ **Haefelis, Chicken Inn, Pizza Inn, Creamy Inn** Clustered along Park Way. Standard fare from these countrywide chains.

HOTEL RESTAURANTS All the hotels have their own restaurants but the following are especially popular.

✕ **The Boma** [map page 245] Victoria Falls Safari Lodge; 📞43238; e boma@boma.co.zw. Come here for a fun-filled evening featuring African dancers & singers & an interactive drumming session. Yes

MEALS WITH A DIFFERENCE

If you want to sample proper home cooking in an authentic Chinotimba household, with no concessions to tourism, look no further. Tsitsi opens her house to guests and serves delicious traditional lunches and dinners. Book these in town through Backpackers Bazaar, or Wild Horizons or contact Tsitsi direct (m 0776 144080; e muposiwa_tsitsi@yahoo.com).

it's touristy, but you'll have a great time, especially if you are in a group. The huge 4-course buffet has locally inspired dishes & international fare. It's a big venue with great atmosphere when it's full, so try for a busy evening. US$40 for the evening, very good value.

✗ Livingstone Room Victoria Falls Hotel; ☎ 44751, 44203/5. Push the boat out & sample the luxury & style of colonial days. Excellent food, décor & service. The dress code is smart.

✗ MakuwaKuwa [map page 245] Safari Lodge; ☎ 43211/20. Excellent international menu served on a beautiful wood/thatch open deck overlooking the waterhole.

✗ Palm Restaurant Ilala Lodge Hotel; ☎ 44737/9. The restaurant is well patronised locally, with décor & setting reflecting old-fashioned luxury. Creative international menu also excellent for lunch. Eat inside or out, to the not very distant roar of the falls.

ENTERTAINMENT AND NIGHTLIFE

Surprisingly for a town that caters for a large number of young people there is very little organised nightlife and no cinemas. A club called **Explorers** periodically resurrects itself but then closes down again leaving just one excellent, long established honeypot that continues to attract pretty well all of the business, tourist and local. Everyone heads for **Shoestrings** (*12 West Dr;* ☎ *45828/44611;* m *0777 434636*) which has a lively bar with frequent live entertainment.

The Boma and **Mama Africa** (see listings on opposite page) both have live entertainment accompanying your meal.

SHOPPING

There are plenty of retail outlets selling curios (including quirky crafts ingeniously made from recycled materials), safari clothing, artworks, locally made jewellery and ethnic fabrics, many clustered around the Trading Post shopping centre, also known as the Landela Centre (just down Livingstone way opposite the Park Way junction). A good place to look for Shona wood and stone carvings is the Southern Africa Gallery on Livingstone Way opposite the junction with Park Way. Excellent carvings can also be purchased from Stone Dynamics Gallery's permanent exhibition in the Victoria Falls Hotel (☎ *41757, www.stonedynamicsgallery.co.zw*)

Continue down Livingstone Way towards the falls and after crossing the railway line turn left into Adam Stander Drive with shops, safari operators and a very large curio market at the end. Bear right into Elephant Walk Shopping Centre where traditional drummers and dancers try to eke out a living by the entrance; inside is a selection of upmarket shops with art, jewellery, fabrics and safari clothing. There's also a small, interesting museum and heritage centre (free entry) and an opportunity to watch craftsmen and artists at work.

The Falls is also home to the furniture maker, Savanna Wood, who use sustainably harvested teak to produce beautiful items, many of which are used to grace local hotels and lodges. Day-to-day necessities are available in the shops in the Victoria Falls, Soper and Phumula shopping centres, along Livingstone Way and Park Way.

For food try the OK supermarket (previously Jays Spar) behind the Victoria Falls Centre, the large TM supermarket on the other side of Livingstone Way or the 7/11 in the Soper Centre.

Bookshops are thin on the ground and their stock even thinner. For maps try the bookshop/stationer on Livingstone Way in the Trading Post or Sopers in Adam Stander Drive. For more ethnic shopping try the markets at the southern end of Chinotimba in the industrial area. Little Harrods is a grocery store situated in the residential area along Reynard Road and is very convenient for the nearby accommodations.

OTHER PRACTICALITIES

ANNOYANCES There's no shortage of curio touts here, especially on the way to the falls. Their approaches are invariably accompanied by pleas for you to buy their little carving so they can fill their stomachs for the first time in days. That may well be the truth. It's up to you, but if you give in, you'll be besieged by others. Although persistent, they are not aggressive and if you're firm and polite, they soon get the message and move on.

Mercifully the money changers have gone, but some now offer old Zimbabwean mega-dollar banknotes – great souvenirs but worth nothing other than novelty value. If you are driving, you'll soon encounter another minor annoyance as soon as you park – guys who offer to look after your car. There is absolutely no danger to your parked car in Victoria Falls so just give them a friendly 'no thank you' and resist any urge to part with any money.

There are apparently pickpockets, but the town's tourism police manage to keep this to a minimum. These friendly, uniformed officers co-funded by local enterprises patrol the town and do a great job maintaining a peaceful and crime-free atmosphere. But their very presence suggests to many visitors that Victoria Falls must be a quite dangerous place. Nothing could be further from the truth. By all means engage them to escort you around town (be sure to give them a nice tip) but apart from their pleasant company the only tangible benefit you'll gain is freedom from approaches from curio touts. You may consider that to be money well spent. Otherwise you are perfectly safe to walk around unescorted.

COMMUNICATIONS Landlines are quite reliable as are mobile phones, although as in the rest of Zimbabwe you need reserves of patience and resilience when dialling and be prepared for sudden signal drops. If your mobile has international roaming you should get a reasonable signal from networks in Zambia. If you have a Zimbabwe SIM card (Econet is the main network in town) and need a top-up, there are plenty of official salespeople around town sporting orange reflective vests.

Most large accommodations have broadband internet access though speeds will mostly be a fraction of what you're used to. There are internet cafés and Wi-Fi hot spots in the Soper Centre, the Phumula Centre and above the OK supermarket, and there's a bright new Econet shop/internet café in Park Way.

IMMIGRATION The immigration office is by the police station, at the roundabout just before you enter town.

MEDICAL There is a reasonably well-stocked pharmacy in the Phumula Centre and another good one in the Kingdom Hotel.

There is a private clinic **CitiMed** (✆ 43380) at West Drive. This was once a very efficient centre; there is concern amongst local residents about equipment shortfalls and slipping standards here but it seems to be fine for relatively minor conditions, although if they set your broken bone be sure to get it checked as soon as you return home (ask my wife!). More serious conditions may warrant a drive to one of the private clinics in Bulawayo or Harare. Next door at number 94 is the **Medical Air Rescue Service (MARS)** (✆ 42268, emergency ✆ 44646), a paramedic and evacuation service; see *Health* in *Chapter 3*. Most of the activity operators subscribe to MARS so you may be automatically covered for evacuation in the event of an emergency, or you can take out your own cover at US$3.50 per day, something to consider if you are driving yourself into remote areas. See *Health insurance*, page 98).

The hospital is at the top of the hill in Chinotimba but if your condition is serious enough to warrant admission, evacuation to a private facility in Bulawayo, Harare or even South Africa would be advised.

At the end of 2012 a large, new, multi-disciplinary medical facility, Premier Medical Centre, was constructed in the building adjacent to the OK supermarket but by March 2013 it had not yet opened.

POLICE The police station (\ 42206) is on Livingstone Way by the roundabout on the right just before you enter town.

POST OFFICE The post office is on the left-hand side of Livingstone Way after you cross the railway line towards the falls.

WHAT TO SEE AND DO

VICTORIA FALLS NATIONAL PARK (*NP Category 1;* ⊕ *summer 06.00–18.00, winter 06.30–18.00*) Measuring 1.7km across the precipice and with a peak flow around April that can reach a phenomenal 750,000m3 per minute, Victoria Falls is the largest curtain of flowing water in the world, twice the size of Niagara Falls. To put this into perspective, the equivalent of Johannesburg's entire water consumption over two days flows over the falls in one minute. Late in the dry season this shrinks to a mere 20,000m3 per minute. Just for the record, putting all the statistics of the world's three main waterfalls (Niagara, Iguassu and Victoria Falls) together, if you're looking for the highest, widest continual flow of water, Victoria Falls is the 'largest'.

To get the most out of the experience it pays to understand how the falls and the gorges were formed. It's a fascinating geological story; to start with, what you see today is essentially the eighth Victoria Falls to have existed.

In the Jurassic era, around 150 million years ago, southern Africa was subject to prolonged volcanic activity. Molten lava, forced to the surface through fractures in the earth's crust, eventually cooled and solidified in layers of basalt, a very hard rock, up to 200–300m deep. During cooling it also contracted, producing deep fissures, primarily east–west but linked by smaller north–south ones. Subsequent flooding laid down deposits of softer material, filling everything in. Later upheavals widened and linked these huge fissures.

The ancient Zambezi River, forced by major upheavals to change its course, flowed eastwards across the basalt, plunging 250m to join the Matetsi River, about 8km downstream from the present falls. This was, in effect, the first Victoria Falls. Since then the colossal power of the water has carved away at the relatively soft rock in the basalt fissures, creating a series of eight zigzag gorges, each connected to the next by a north–south fissure, and each in its time creating massive falls.

Today you can actually see the next gorge being started. Devil's Cataract, on the left of the main falls, has already been eroded to a significantly lower level than the others. This is in fact the next north–south fissure being excavated. To the right is a definite cut line across Cataract Island, almost certainly the beginning of a gorge to eventually form behind the current Victoria Falls. From maps, or in an overflight, you can clearly see the network of gorges, past and future.

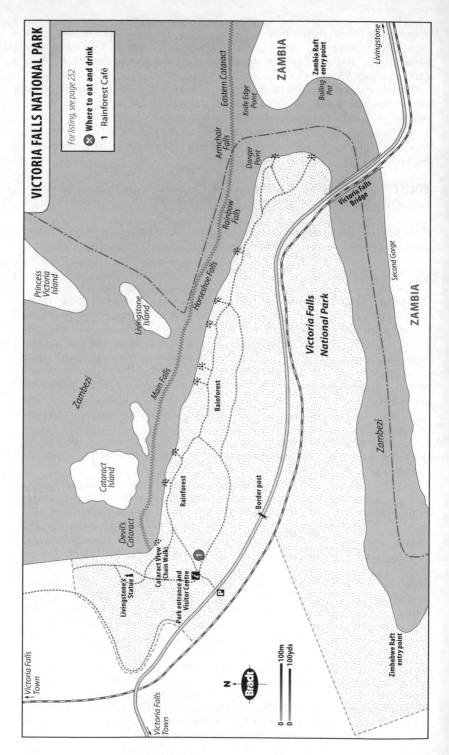

VICTORIA FALLS NATIONAL PARK

For listing, see page 252

⊗ Where to eat and drink
1 Rainforest Café

Princess
Victoria
Island

Zambezi

Livingstone
Island

Cataract
Island

Victoria Falls
Town

Devil's
Cataract

Livingstone's
Statue

Cataract View
(Chain Walk)

Park entrance and
Visitor Centre

Rainforest

Rainforest

Main Falls

Horseshoe Falls

Rainbow
Falls

Armchair
Falls

Eastern Cataract

Knife Edge
Point

Danger
Point

ZAMBIA

Boiling
Pot

Zambia Raft
entry point

Livingstone

Victoria Falls
Bridge

Second Gorge

Victoria Falls
National Park

ZAMBIA

Zambezi

Zimbabwe Raft
entry point

Border post

Victoria Falls
Town

N

0   100m
0   100yds

Bradt

Orientation The park entrance and ticket office can be reached by paths from the Victoria Falls Hotel and the Kingdom Hotel, or you can follow the path from Livingstone Way opposite Ilala Lodge. Allow about 15 minutes and prepare yourself for a motley collection of curio sellers and falls 'guides'. If you are driving, follow Livingstone Way to the car park.

I recommend buying the *Victoria Falls Information Guide* from the tourist information office at the top of Park Way or possibly at either of the two bookshops, which – amongst a lot of other information – contains a wealth of detail about the flora and fauna you are likely to see. You can of course hire an official guide to show you around, but politely shrug off the unofficial guys.

Depending on the time of year and how well equipped you are, you can hire a plastic raincoat from kiosks in the car park. Even in the dry season you can get quite wet in the national park; though you may not mind getting damp yourself, think of your camera. At other times of year rainwear is essential.

The falls walking tour Although Victoria Falls is one long waterfall in the wet season, a visit at drier times reveals a number of cascades separated by islands and protruding rock along the fall's rim. A series of paths form several loops but the main path runs parallel to the southern edge of the gorge. A logical route runs along the rim to Danger Point at the far end, returning via various paths through the wooded Rain Forest area. The gorge path has 16 viewing spots right on the edge of the precipice, generally protected by dense vegetation or low, rather decrepit fences. Allow a couple of hours, at least in the dry season when you can take photographs.

The sequence of falls and features from west to east (left to right as you look at them) is Devil's Cataract, Cataract Island, Main Falls, Livingstone Island, Horseshoe Falls, Rainbow Falls and the Eastern Cataract. Directly opposite Danger Point, the Armchair is a cup-shaped depression, originally formed by a volcanic vent and gradually being enlarged as the water spills into it before dropping over the edge. The Boiling Pot is the apt name for the cauldron of water at the base of the gorge as the main body of water from the falls collides with incoming water from the Eastern Cataract.

Starting at Livingstone's statue, pay your respects to the great man and then double back for the view of Devil's Cataract, down a steep and often slippery flight of steps known as Chain Walk because chains were originally used to help visitors down to the viewpoint and back up. This view of Devil's Cataract is perhaps the most interesting, revealing a large east–west gouge across Cataract Island that may well be the beginning of the next Victoria Falls.

From here the walk takes you into what is known as the Rain Forest, opposite the Main Falls. This part of the park has a totally different 'climate' from the surrounding area, ranging from permanently damp to drenched depending on the season. Although only a tiny piece of real estate in geographic and ecological terms, thousands of years of specialised conditions have created a unique ecosystem, and its preservation is a credit to the authorities, given the huge numbers of visitors who pass through. In the dense foliage many trees are entangled with creepers and vines, including the all-enveloping strangler fig. A number of bird species have adapted to live here; avid birdwatchers will be keen to glimpse the beautiful Schalow's turaco (often mistakenly identified as the Livingstone's turaco, which doesn't come anywhere near here).

Follow the path, diverting to each cliff-edge vantage point. Note the grassy ledge over on Livingstone Island, from where the good doctor lowered a plumb line over the edge in an attempt to measure the depth of the falls. Unfortunately it got stuck on a ledge, giving a false reading.

In the dry season it is possible to wade across the river from the Zambia side to Livingstone Island and, like the explorer, peer over the edge into the abyss, if you've got the nerve. This must be the ultimate infinity pool. Strictly speaking this is not allowed and if you try it unescorted you're likely to be turned back. Note that in 2009 a guide was swept over the edge to his death. The legal way is the expensive way: Tongabezi Lodge (✆ *+260 213 327450*; *www.tongabezi.com*) will take you across by boat with breakfast, champagne lunch or afternoon tea for US$70–125 depending on time of day.

After Livingstone Island the path breaks out of the trees. The viewpoints for Horseshoe Falls and Rainbow Falls are unprotected, offering the temptation to venture too close to the edge for safety. Danger Point was named thus for good reason, especially when the rock is wet. Knife Edge is a narrow promontory jutting out on the opposite side of the river to Danger Point. From Danger Point make your way down to the Boiling Pot viewpoint where you also get a spectacular view of Victoria Falls bridge.

Lunar rainbow Romantics and photographers alike should aim for a full moon and hope for clear skies, as they will be treated to the magical sight of a lunar rainbow over the falls. The best time is during high water and the best views are across the Eastern Cataract from the Zambian side. Just don't expect to be the only ones here, as it understandably gets very busy with clicking camera shutters. The park opens late for three days around the full moon: enquire at the park entrance for dates and times. Entrance to the Victoria Falls park is US$40 for lunar viewing, as opposed to US$30 for normal daytime visits.

Victoria Falls bridge The falls may be one of the Seven Natural Wonders of the World, but the bridge spanning the gorge also deserves recognition as a major feat of engineering. Cecil Rhodes was the force behind its construction: a Zambezi crossing was a necessary part of his vision of a Cape–Cairo railway line. He decreed that the bridge should span the second gorge, high above the Boiling Pot, and it is commonly said that he wanted to provide passengers with spectacular views – even a bit of spray – as they crossed, although there's no actual record of him saying that. A crossing just upstream would have been a far simpler task, but such extravagance was in keeping with Rhodes's obsession. He never saw the results, dying two years before the railway reached the gorge.

The bridge was designed by G S Hobson of consultants Sir Douglas Fox and Partners and not, as is often claimed, by Sir Ralph Freeman of Sydney Harbour Bridge fame (the latter gentleman did work on the project but as a stresses engineer), but it was by no means greeted with universal praise. Many thought it was an act of engineering vandalism and should not have been built so close to the natural wonder, and even recently it has been described as 'a hideous monument to Victorian vanity'.

Building commenced from both sides of the gorge simultaneously, working towards the middle, but it was touch and go on the day the two sides were due to meet as there was a worrying hiatus during which it appeared they'd made it a few centimetres too long. However the temperature drop overnight allowed the fabric to contract sufficiently for it to be a perfect fit. It took just 14 months to build and was completed in 1905, officially opened by Professor George Darwin, son of Charles Darwin. In 1930 the bridge was widened by 4m and one of the two rail lines was removed to accommodate road traffic.

For more information on the history of this fascinating building project, read Peter Roberts's book, *Sun, Steel and Spray*.

You can also book a **bridge tour** operated by Shearwater during which you hear a fascinating account of the construction given by an actor playing the part of Georges Imbault, chief construction engineer, followed by a walking tour that takes you underneath the bridge to see the intricacies of its design. These tours receive excellent revues.

STEAM TRAIN AND TRAM RIDES The **Steam Train Company** (↘ 42912; e *info@steamtraincompany.com; www.steamtraincompany.com*) offers a range of trips with their lovely old train and its beautiful colonial era carriages, or their new tram. A late afternoon train trip stops on the bridge for canapés and sundowners with breathtaking views of the gorge (British Airways *Horizons* magazine voted this the sixth-best in the world for sundowners) and then chugs off taking you through town and into the bush to Jafuta siding, before returning to the station. The tram is newly built but faithfully based on the original design. Seating 30+ it takes visitors between the Rain Forest area and town and in the evening runs a similar series of catered rides as the train. Check the website for the full range of trips and prices which start at around US$60 for a two-hour ride.

THE BIG TREE (*Exit town on Park Way, turn right into unmarked Zambezi Dr directly opposite the defunct Inyathi Valley Motel & Rest Camp*) This is not the biggest old baobab you will see in the country, but its significance lies in its history. Opposite the old river crossing to Old Drift, this was a meeting place and camping spot for early pioneers and traders. It is now guarded by a fence and two friendly but bored tourist police who are keen to supplement their salaries by escorting you inside and taking photos of you next to this bulky plant. I'm constantly amazed by the number of tourists I see walking this area without a care in the world. If you do decide to walk there be very alert to the very real possibility of meeting elephant and buffalo who use this area of the national park as a regular route to the river.

CROCODILE RANCH AND NATURE SANCTUARY (*Park Way, 5km from town;* ↘ *43576; entry US$5*) While based around crocodiles, there is also an old lion in this pleasant venue, set out in well-designed, pretty, leafy gardens. As you progress around the park you can observe the crocs in all stages of development, in a variety of natural-looking pools and streams, and you are encouraged to handle the baby ones. Then, just as you are becoming rather fond of these reptiles, you exit through a craft shop featuring some rather familiar-looking handbags, belts and wallets. The cost of these has escalated recently with the requirement to incorporate a 'wildlife products' licence into the price. There is a restaurant here where you can eat croc should you wish.

TOWNSHIP TOURS As is the case in so many towns in southern Africa, Victoria Falls is still physically divided along racial lines, although the low-density residential area is becoming much more mixed. Wild Horizons runs 'Chinotimba township tours' with the opportunity to see houses, markets, taverns and churches as well as a visit to Chinotimba Primary School.

They also offer a 'Meet the People' tour visiting a typical village situated about 20km out of town where you can learn something of the rural lifestyle experienced by such a large percentage of the population.

Coming soon ... Victoria Falls is due to get its own 35ha theme park, called Santonga. This is the brainchild of the hospitality company African Albida, whose flagship property is Victoria Falls Safari Lodge. In their own words, Santonga will be 'a mind-blowing fusion of a museum, multi-faceted wildlife park and entertainment theme park all in one, aiming to present the history of Victoria Falls since the beginning of time'. They reckon you'll need six hours to do it justice, so I recommend you add another day to your holiday to fit it in. It's an ambitious project, testament to the faith this company has in the country's future, but its construction and opening has been much delayed and it's still a case of 'watch this space'.

HISTORICAL AND LOCAL TOURS
Bushtracks Africa (e *reservations@bushtracksafrica.com; www.bushtracksafrica. com*) Russell Gammon, an accomplished historian and raconteur, runs a variety of cultural and African history activities, including a half-day 'Mists of Time' African heritage tour. Although the company is based in Livingstone, Russell lives in Victoria Falls and can arrange the tours for people staying here.

ACTIVITIES

LOCAL ACTIVITIES OPERATORS Many people pre-book with their safari or tour operator on the internet, while others prefer to wait until they are in town before deciding what to do and who to book it with.

This is a competitive and potentially confusing market. There are two types of operators here: those who provide the final products – the rafting, bungee-jumping, elephant rides, river cruises, etc; and those who act as agents for them. Some do both. Almost any of the agencies in town can sell you most of the activities on offer. To complicate it further, many of the individual activities are provided by several different operators, so depending on your requirements it's wise to ask plenty of questions before you book. An hour or so walking round town collecting information from the various agencies will show you the array of activities on offer. During this walk you will also be met by quite a few roving activities sales persons who politely but persistently try to tempt you with their products.

So, after you have spent hours on the internet or have spread your armful of brochures and leaflets all over your bed, how do you make your choice?

If you want to enjoy a number of different activities, the simplest way is to book everything through one of the larger operators who offer tailor-made packages, including transfers and accommodation. Wild Horizons (the largest agency), Shearwater (the oldest agency) and many others offer a range of packages which can represent quite a saving over individual purchases.

You won't find much difference in price between the various companies, although of course it does pay to shop around and read the small print as some throw in extras such as meals, refreshments, hotel pick-ups, etc. Several of the 'big boys' offer packages that include 'free' activities such as cruises but don't get too hung up spending hours on finding the best deal because you could be out there enjoying yourself. If you haven't pre-booked and you have time, chat with fellow travellers about their experiences before you choose an operator.

With such a wealth of operators in Victoria Falls, few of the similar number in Livingstone are mentioned here, except where they differ significantly.

Local activities operators, booking and transfer agents

Adventure Zone 📞44424, 42051; m 0712 210798; e info@adventurezonevicfalls.com; www. adventurezonevicfalls.com

Agents Africa 📞43105; e john@agentsafrica. co.zw; www.agents-africa.co.zw

Ambula Safaris 📞42617/8; e ambula@mweb. co.za

Backpackers Bazaar Cul-de-sac at top of Park Way; 📞45828, 42208; e joy@backpackers.co.zw

Dabula Safaris 280 Holland Rd; 📞44453, 44618; e dabula@africaonline.co.zw; www.dabula.com

Dingani Tours Elephant Walk; 📞44554; e info@ dinganitours.com

Discover Safaris 📞45821, 0712 209144; e cat@ yoafrica.com

Exclusive Touch Africa 📞43444; m 0712 208380; e enquiries@ exclusivetouchafrica.net; www.exclusivetouchafrica.net

Falcon Safaris Landela Centre; 📞41840; e info@ falconsafaris.com; www.falconsafaris.com

Forche Tours and Travel 📞42414; m 0712 769116; e info@forchetravel.com; www. forchetravel.com

Khanondo Travel Victoria Falls Centre; 📞012 44884; m 0712 364595; e reservations@ khanondotravel.com; www.khanondotravel.com

Khanyiso Travel and Tours Tourism Hse; 📞43787/9; e reservations@khanyiso.co.zw; www. khanyiso.co.zw

Mapopoma Tours and Cruises 📞42229; e info@mapopoma.co.zw

Pamusha Safaris 583 Manyika Rd; m 0779 369160; e reservations@pamusha.com

Shearwater The Hub, Soper Centre; 📞44471/3; m 0773 461716; e reservations@shearwatervf. com; www.shearwatervictoriafalls.com

Tourism Services Zimbabwe 308 Park Way; 📞43368, 41288; e info@tourservzim.co.zw; http://tourservzim.com

Veneto 9 Soper Centre; 📞44861; m 0712 754875; e veneto.adventures@gmail.com; www. venetoadventures.com

Wild Horizons 310 Park Way; 📞44571, 44426; e info@wildhorizons.co.zw; www.wildhorizons. co.za

ON THE ZAMBEZI Don't delay your white-water ambitions! There has been a long-standing plan to dam the river downstream in the Batoka gorge for much-needed hydro-electricity, which would flood the gorges upstream all the way to the second rapid annihilating these wonderful activities. After many years of procrastination work has now begun and the approach roads have already been upgraded to cope with the construction traffic.

The following activities can be booked through any of the agents listed above under *Local operators*). Individual rates quoted below are guide prices and may vary slightly between operators; several offer packages where you can combine a number of activities at a substantially discounted rate with often a sunset cruise thrown in for free. For instance, two activities cost US$275 with a cruise included. National Parks and river usage fees, which vary from US$10–15, are not included except where stated.

White-water rafting (*Full day US$130*) This was the area's original adrenalin sport, and the section of river below the falls is one of the finest stretches of navigable rapids in the world. Rapids are graded on a scale of 1 (smooth water) to 6 (commercially unrunnable). Here the rapids are nearly all graded 4 or 5, about as difficult and dramatic as it gets. The great thing about rafting is that novices can enjoy the sport at these levels, in the hands of an experienced guide. Although Zambezi rapids are big, most are not technically difficult provided the guide positions the raft correctly. There are also long calm stretches in between, allowing plenty of time to recover from an unplanned swim or a flip. It's while floating down these serene stretches that you witness the impossibly beautiful scenery as the river winds its way through the towering gorge.

When booking there are some important choices to be made. Time of year is crucial as the river, and therefore the rafting experience, is completely different at various water levels. Low water is generally from July or August to mid-January, high water from February to July. Low water is the best time to raft, not only because all 23 rapids (portage around the impossible No 9) can be tackled but because they are more dramatic, with bigger waves and drops. At high water only the second section, from No 11 onwards, is possible. At times of very high water, in March–May depending on rainfall in the catchment area, the operations close down altogether.

You then have a choice of starting from the Zimbabwe or the Zambia side; both can be booked in Victoria Falls. Zambia gives you a bit more for your money as you start at rapid No 1 just beneath the falls; on the Zimbabwe side the start point is at rapid No 4, and you miss the experience of setting off from the Boiling Pot. (The Zambia option has now become more expensive if you are staying in Zimbabwe, as you are required to buy another entry visa when you return to Zimbabwe.)

Your third choice is which of two styles of rafting to go for. In the more leisurely style ('leisurely' is possibly the wrong word here) your guide uses two long oars to steer and position the raft, while you hang on and respond to his commands, leaning left, right or over the front as you plummet down the rapids and punch into huge waves. In the second alternative, every crew member has a paddle and it is up to you to provide the motive power, with the guide at the back steering with his own paddle and yelling instructions at you. The paddle method requires much more energy and is more exciting, and you are more likely to end up in the river as, with a paddle in your hands, it's not so easy to hold on. The guide controls the raft and alters the ride depending on the day's clientele, frequently steering through the roughest waves just for the hell of it, to give clients a ride they are unlikely to forget.

The chances of a swim are high, especially in the roughest sections, in which case you are in for a turbulent experience. Rafting is brilliant fun but it isn't a theme-park ride. Safety standards are very high, and you are equipped with helmets and flotation jackets, but there are occasional injuries, and even very rare fatalities. Listen carefully to the safety briefing.

There is actually another choice to be made, about what happens at the end of the trip. The climb from water level to the top of the gorge is a hot, hard slog. If you get out of breath after a couple of flights of stairs in the office, this could spoil your day although the thought of a cold beer at the top is sufficient encouragement for most. (Just as you decide to sit down for a rest and catch your breath halfway up, your ego takes a huge knock when the rafting staff form a snake with the deflated and folded-up raft over their shoulders and race past you almost at a run!) Some outfits offer helicopter lifts out; you can always tell your macho friends you did it purely for the spectacular flight up the river. And it is truly spectacular.

Although you will be wet during your ride, don't forget to use waterproof sunscreen. Leave behind anything you wouldn't want to see washed overboard. Unless you have a waterproof, shockproof camera that can be firmly attached to your wrist, forget photos, as you'll hardly have time to focus. All the companies will sell you a DVD or video of your raft, taken from vantage points along the bank.

The full run of 23 rapids usually starts with a briefing at around 08.00, and you finish in late afternoon; a half-day trip finishes about 14.30. For dedicated rafters there is a selection of long trips with up to a week's camping en route.

River-boarding (*US$130*) Also known as boogie boarding, this is probably the scariest and most thrilling of the river activities. Your vehicle is a nicely moulded piece of expanded polystyrene foam, similar to a small surfboard. With just this, a helmet, flotation jacket and a pair of small flippers, you set off to navigate the rapids. The idea is to body-surf down the rapids but unless you're already pretty good at this sort of thing the experience is rather more akin to being thrown into a giant washing machine during the spin cycle. They say that if you just hang onto your board, eventually you will emerge from the maelstrom of each rapid and be able to breathe air again. You are accompanied by a guide on a raft, who gives you a lift along the long calm stretches and drops you overboard for the exciting bits. Only strong swimmers need apply.

Kayaking (*Full day US$130*) Even novices can go white-water kayaking. It's not as irresponsible as it sounds: they use two-person canoes, so you sit in front and help with the power while an experienced guide does the hard work from the back seat. Capsizes are a possibility so you should not consider this activity unless you are very confident in water or can already perform an 'Eskimo roll' yourself. These trips run alongside rafts so there is always help, and lunch, at hand.

Jet boats (*US$60 for 30 minutes*) These boats are propelled by powerful jets of water and as such can navigate shallow and rocky waters where no conventional propeller can go. You'll have a thrilling ride as they rocket up and down the river and rapids, though some people would prefer that the river was left in a bit of peace and quiet without these annoying buzzing boats. That said, this part of Zimbabwe has become one great big playground and, like it or not, toys make noise. Shearwater offers these trips.

Upper Zambezi canoeing (*Half-day US$90, full day including picnic lunch on the bank US$125*) This is your chance to relax and pretend you are David Livingstone on your way to seeing the falls for the first time, for this stretch of river upstream of the falls is where he spent his days prior to his 'discovery'. The Zimbabwe bank here is part of the Zambezi National Park (see pages 267–72).

Several companies offer different types of canoe trips, and you are sure to find one that suits, whether it's a three-day camping excursion, an early morning breakfast drift or maybe a sundowner with a gin and tonic or three. Whatever you decide on, your guide will take you through some supremely tranquil stretches of the Zambezi, with stunning riverside scenery complete with big game, so take your camera and binoculars. In some canoes you sit back and let a guide do all the work and in others you propel yourself. Some are inflatable two-seaters while others are fibreglass two-seaters of the Canadian variety. Either way you need no previous

MONTHLY WATER LEVELS AT VICTORIA FALLS

The following is dependent on annual rainfall and should not be considered definitive.

Month	Level	Month	Level
January	Medium/ Low	**July**	High/Low
February	High	**August**	Mid/Low
March	High	**September**	Mid/Low
April	Rafting closed	**October**	Low
May	Super/High	**November**	Low
June	High	**December**	Low

experience, only to be moderately fit. There are potential dangers, in the form of hippos and crocs. It's one thing watching them from the bank, but you develop a new feeling of respect for these massive creatures when they are just metres away, in their own habitat. Your guide will know the river inside out and have intimate knowledge of their territories, haunts and behaviours. You'll be out on the river for several hours, so take adequate sun precautions. There are some 'rapids' along this route but they are nothing like those below the falls and present only slightly choppy water that needs no skill to negotiate.

River cruises (*US$45–70*) Several operators offer cruises on the river above the falls throughout the day, and all include catering with generous quantities of alcohol: champagne breakfast, lunch or sundowner cruises. Sunsets along the Zambezi can be glorious. You'll almost certainly be serenaded, if that's the right word, by grunting hippos, and there's a good chance you'll see elephants coming down to drink. It's worth bringing binos and camera, unless you want to concentrate on your drink and the buffet food. There is quite a choice of boat sizes and cruise types, from intimate to partying. For a romantic evening cruise book the delightful *Ra-Ikane* from Ilala Lodge. If you're looking for a great atmosphere with a good crowd, check the brochures or get independent advice from Backpackers Bazaar. Just don't get yourself on the wrong boat: some are peacefully serene while others live up to their name of 'booze cruises'! Most set off along the far end of Park Way near the Hotel A'Zambezi.

High wire The following activities involve throwing yourself into the void over the river in one way or another. The nervous will take comfort from the fact that the cable across the gorge is capable of carrying five adult bull elephants.

Bungee-jumping (*US$100*) Bungee-jumping from Victoria Falls bridge needs no explanation other than to say that at 111m down to the river, this is one of the highest and most spectacular jumps in the world. Tandem jumps are available.

Gorge swing (*US$90*) With this variant on the bungee-jump, you launch yourself off a cliff for a three-second 70m free-fall before your rope goes taut and you swing across the gorge like a giant pendulum, suspended from a cable strung across the canyon.

Zip line (foofie slide) (*US$66*) Strapped into a harness, you slide down a 400m steel cable into the canyon, reaching speeds in excess of 100km/h.

Flying fox (*US$40*) In a high-wire variant with harness and pulley, you run flat out and dive off the edge of the gorge, only to find yourself sliding along a cable across the ravine. This is probably the least scary high-wire activity, and the nearest you will get to gliding without an aircraft.

Abseiling and rap jumping (*US$60*) It takes some courage to lower yourself backwards over the edge knowing there's a 120m vertical drop, but when you have got used to that sensation you may wish to progress to rap jumping, which is essentially the same except you go down face-forward.

FLIGHTS (*US$130–175*) There's a selection of light aircraft and helicopters available for sightseeing trips. While they are extremely popular, their buzzing and droning throughout the day can become annoying to those on the ground. Nevertheless, if you are interested in the fascinating geology of the area and want to really bring it to life, an aerial view is your best option. Do read up beforehand about the formation of the gorges to get the most out of your trip.

The choice is between single-engine fixed-wing aeroplane; microlight (a hang glider with seats and rear-mounted engine) – only in Livingstone courtesy of Batoka Sky (\ +263 213 323589); and helicopter. Note that, for safety reasons, cameras cannot be taken on microlights. Flying times vary from about 15 to 40 minutes; longer flights include river- and wildlife-viewing opportunities with the gorge views.

ELEPHANT-BACK SAFARIS (*US$130 for one-hour ride*) Don't believe everything you've been told about African elephants being untrainable, as several companies in the falls offer the chance to view wildlife from several metres up, on the back of one of these magnificent beasts. The word 'safari' is a bit of an exaggeration: these rides usually last an hour or so, in the morning or late afternoon, because the elephants need to spend most of their day feeding naturally out in the bush (although not all of the operators allow this). This is, nevertheless, one of the most popular activities in the area and can be very rewarding, because – as with horse safaris – most game animals are more relaxed with humans mounted on these familiar animals, rather than on foot or even in a vehicle (see box, *Wild animals in tourism*, pages 268–9).

LION ENCOUNTERS (*US$130*) This is an activity involving captive-bred animals, whereby you go on a bush walk with lion cubs armed only with a safety briefing, a stick and a guide. Many of the cubs are hardly kittens any more so this activity is understandably very popular with tourists, although it's not without some danger and a good deal of controversy (see box, *Wild animals in tourism*, page 269).

ZAMBEZI HORSE TRAILS (\ *42847;* m *0712 292228;* e *alison@yoafrica.com; www.zambezihorsetrails.com*) Wildlife viewing is available from horseback, taking clients through the Zambezi National Park following game trails, along the scenic Zambezi River as well as longer rides along the Batoka gorge rim. On a horse you feel much closer to nature than in a vehicle, and the wildlife you encounter is much more relaxed about your presence. I once was able to ride to within touching distance of a completely relaxed, reclining kudu bull who couldn't even be bothered to stand up. Alison Baker and her staff know this whole area intimately and she is a frequent participant in anti-poaching and darting operations with a keen eye for hidden wildlife. There's a wide range of different duration rides available. Novices and experienced riders are catered for, with horses to suit both, but there's generally a lower age limit of 12 years. Book through one of the agents in town or direct with Alison Baker. Check her website.

VICTORIA FALLS PRIVATE GAME RESERVE Shearwater operates this 4,000ha reserve about 20 minutes from town, within the Zambezi National Park, using it as a base for its wildlife activities – game drives, lion walking and elephant riding. This is also where they operate their black rhino breeding programme.

DAY TRIPS
Chobe (*US$175 including transfers, refreshments and lunch*) A day trip into Chobe, Botswana, takes you into one of the most heavily elephant-populated areas of the world. Needless to say the dry season (August to November) will give you the best viewing. Commercial trips set off from Victoria Falls early in the morning for the 45-minute drive to the Kazungula border. Once in Botswana, the morning

In 2010, in the *lowveld*, a cheetah produced five cubs. Sadly within two days, she and four of her cubs were killed by a male lion. The sole survivor was found by a scout named Sylvester, and named after him by Norman and Penny English, who became surrogate parents. Feeding the cub was complicated but the struggle to find a suitable formula was assisted by the many cheetah experts who passed on their experience. In time a dietary plan that suited Sylvester was formulated and he began to respond. As he was never destined to become a pet, and being a specially protected animal on the endangered species list, the Department of Parks and Wildlife Management was involved with Sylvester's welfare from the outset. Despite numerous release attempts, orphaned cheetah do not survive in the wild without experiencing the maternal care of their mother for the initial 22 months of their lives. Also, the human imprints of an upbringing in captivity are not conducive to a release into the wild, with the animals likely to come into contact with human settlements and to be seen as dangerous 'problem' animals. So from the moment he was rescued, Sylvester was destined to live in human society.

After a time, as he grew and became ever more boisterous, a plan was needed for a permanent home and this is where Wild Horizons saw a long-term future for him looked after by the wildlife trust they had set up. The wildlife sanctuary where he now lives is situated in National Parks land, in an environment that is typical cheetah territory. But with no mother to teach him hunting skills, a 'lure' specially designed on the same principles as a greyhound racing 'hare' was imported from USA with the generosity of Tauck Tours, enabling him to exercise with the cheetah's trademark explosive bursts of speed, vital to keeping him fit. With no large predators around and the support from his three carers, Ed, Bongani and Luis, Sylvester has settled into his new life with vigour and is already well adapted to his new environment. He loves exploring the property, is busily developing his hunting skills and seems to be a very contented cheetah. Here in the Victoria Falls region, cheetah are a rare sighting but camera traps in the sanctuary have captured exciting night-time images of several wild cheetah – whether he will ever seek companionship with his own species, only time will tell.

But it's not all play. Sylvester has an important job as an 'ambassador' cheetah, interacting with the public to raise awareness of the perils faced by his species. Through the schools educational programme run by the Victoria Falls Wildlife Trust (see page 149) Sylvester who is now fully grown into a magnificent animal, interacts with schoolchildren, who for the first time in their lives can learn about and meet an animal that they have been brought up to regard as an enemy. Sylvester is the archetypal 'Mr Cool' while children and adults alike tentatively steel themselves to stroke his beautifully dappled coat.

He does not feature in Wild Horizon's commercial package, but guests staying at Elephant Camp and those who visit the Elephant Wallow for their other activities are offered the chance to meet this big cat during the times when he is not out, patrolling his estate (see colour page 13). All donations that result from his appearances go directly towards his not inconsiderable upkeep. We hope that Sylvester will continue to be happy in this role for years to come but recognise that he will always be a wild animal and that we can only work together while we have his full co-operation. It's his call.

comprises wildlife viewing from a boat followed after lunch by a game drive. ZIMRA (Zimbabwe's Revenue Authority) has unfortunately reversed its earlier concession that allowed visitors out of the country for the day without having to pay for another entry visa on return. If you plan to do this activity you should buy a double-entry visa on your first entry, significantly cheaper than paying for a second single entry.

Livingstone Tourist traffic between Zimbabwe and Zambia is biased towards people in the latter visiting Victoria Falls rather than vice versa, but if you want to go to Devil's Pool on Livingstone Island, which has to be the world's ultimate infinity pool (*Tongabezi;* ↘ *+260 213 327450;* e *reservations@tongabezi. com*) or have a microlite flight (*Batoka Sky;* ↘ *+263 213 323589;* e *reservations@ livingstonesadventures.com*) you'll need to cross into Zambia. You can simply cross the bridge but again you need to buy another visa if you return to Zimbabwe so plan ahead and buy a double-entry visa when you first enter. Those returning to South Africa should be aware that health authorities there require yellow fever vaccination and certification if you have been into Zambia.

ZAMBEZI NATIONAL PARK (NP Category 1)

The northern boundary of this relatively small (57,000ha) park is the Zambezi River, which makes it one of Zimbabwe's most beautiful parks, with the entrance gate just 5km from Victoria Falls.

Despite an earlier poaching onslaught, a large variety of game including giraffe, lion, wild dog and leopard as well as good numbers of plains game including sable, kudu, zebra and elephant, all have access to this park from surrounding areas. Now that there are lodges within the park, poachers are being deterred and game has quickly returned in large numbers making this, once again, a very rewarding place for game viewing. You are not free to walk without a guide.

This is a particularly rewarding area for birders, with white-backed night heron, African skimmer, African finfoot, slaty egret, collared palm-thrush and western banded snake eagle among the many specials in this riverine habitat.

The Zambezi River Game Drive runs the length of the park alongside the river for nearly 50km. Along the river track you'll see several loop roads marked; it's along these that you'll see most of the game during the day, although in the dry season they come down to the river to drink. There is a new luxury, private riverside lodge close to the entrance gate and another nearing completion further upstream with a new traditional tented camp in between at Mpala Jena.

There are 25 picnic spots along the first section of the river, many opposite shallow rapids where you may see local families splashing around. If you are tempted to do the same, be aware that crocodiles are never far way and most years see attacks in this area. Bilharzia may be a risk in slower stretches of the river. On no account go swimming – this is serious croc and hippo territory.

Whilst this is a very popular weekend park for locals, it is remarkably quiet during the week. The roads in this park used to be very poorly maintained but the new lodges have done an excellent job making them much more accessible, although a 4x4 is till recommended

🏠 **WHERE TO STAY**
National Parks accommodation
Lodges There are 20 self-catering, en-suite lodges stretched along the riverbank close to the entrance gate. They all have two bedrooms (four beds), a lounge and

self-catering facilities and bedding. Half the lodges have baths, the other half, showers. This is the first park to have received a much-needed refurbishment, part of a programme for all National Parks lodges throughout the country, although at the time of writing, the refurbishment programme appears to have stalled. The standard of furnishing is considerably better than it ever was in the past, and now comparable to many private lodges (although the kitchens would benefit from a bit more attention). However, as a result, there has been an inevitable hike in the price. It's unfortunate that there are no lodges here for couples only, who find themselves

WILD ANIMALS IN TOURISM

ELEPHANTS One of Zimbabwe's most popular tourist attractions is elephant-back riding. The first operation started about 20 years ago and since then at least three other companies have opened up in the Victoria Falls area alone, with others elsewhere in the country. This activity has, however, attracted the attention of wildlife and animal welfare organisations with concerns about the ethics of using wild animals for commercial gain. While most want this activity stopped altogether, some (notably ZNSPCA) cautiously sanction it provided their key concerns are addressed – where and how the elephants are sourced; training techniques; good husbandry and day-to-day welfare of the working animals; and what happens when their working days are over. There is further concern about the safety aspects of people interacting with dangerous animals.

Sourcing The original animals in this industry were orphans from the 1970s and 1980s, when culling for population control was the norm in Zimbabwe. Youngsters below a certain age were 'spared' the cull and brought into captivity, some sold to zoos while others were trained for riding. With the end of culling the supply of orphaned elephants has dried up, leading some operators to capture young elephants out of the wild. In late 2006 ten were taken from a wild herd in Hwange National Park by a major elephant-riding operator in Victoria Falls, attracting worldwide condemnation. In late 2008 a dozen more were taken from the south of the country by a second Victoria Falls elephant operation, but following the intervention of the ZNSPCA and other agencies the nine survivors were eventually collared with tracking devices and returned to the wild in Hwange in late 2009.

Training 'Ethical' training, using patience and reward, has severe drawbacks for an operator eager to make his very expensive purchases start earning cash: it takes a lot of time, and is only successful with very young elephants; it's not effective with sub-adult or adult animals taken from the wild. Instead, it is alleged that some trainers use techniques common in the Far East which involve chaining the animals for most of the day, using electric prods or other methods of force.

Welfare Concerns revolve around work regime, feeding programme, social needs, housing, health, veterinary care and the all-important factor of the sensitivity and expertise of those charged with looking after the elephants.

Retirement Animals habituated to humans and later released into the wild can become 'problem animals'. Furthermore, years of separation from wild elephants, often from a young age, leave them without elephant social skills and therefore paying unnecessarily for four beds, otherwise for four people they now represent very good value: US$150 per lodge at peak times of the year with the possibility (no more than that) of a slight off-peak drop.

Camping Campsites **Chundu 1** and **Chundu 2**, 25km/15 miles and 26km/16 miles along the drive, are both serene and beautiful riverside camping spots. Chundu 1 is everyone's favourite, with little grassy islands to walk out to in the dry winter season. Book ahead, as you may often find it unavailable – overnighting

at risk of attack when released. Lengthy rehabilitation programmes are needed if they are ever to be successfully returned to the wild and this is very much uncharted territory.

Safety African elephants are amongst the continent's most dangerous animals and, while the industry has a very good safety record, there have been injuries and deaths amongst both clients and elephant handlers.

The ZNSPCA has been attempting to put together a working group of representatives from the industry, national parks, veterinary, environment and tourism authorities and other stakeholders, to create a code of conduct that will eventually be enforceable by law. Until then, Wild Horizons in Victoria Falls is the only elephant-riding operator that currently meets ZNSPCA welfare criteria, and is therefore the only one recommended in this book.

WALKING WITH LIONS Another popular and very profitable tourist activity of concern to animal rights organisations is 'walking with lions' – interaction with lion cubs up to about 15–18 months of age. The cubs are removed from their mothers at a very young age to be hand fed and habituated to humans. The question is what to do with them after they are too large and dangerous to walk with. (Even with these youngsters there have been a number of serious attacks on tourists and handlers.) Once habituated to humans none of them can ever be released into the wild.

Operators present extensive details of conservation programmes whereby young lions are released to fenced properties to live out their lives, breeding to produce non-habituated offspring to restock Africa's depleted lion population. There is much emphasis on conservation, scientific study, community education and involvement. It looks ethical and green, but they admit they can't yet report any successful releases.

Conservation organisations and wildlife experts in southern Africa say these operations contribute nothing to conservation efforts. The large number of human-habituated lions that must be 'retired' to these safe areas (cubs must be replaced every 12–18 months; the largest operator had over 60 on the premises when I visited) would require such vast tracts of land as to be massively uneconomic, given the size of territories required by adult males and prides. Instead, they allege, many animals are sold indirectly or directly to commercial concerns. There's a constant demand for lions from 'canned' hunting operations (especially in South Africa), from zoos and other lucrative destinations

Who to believe? The sides are completely polarised and well argued on the internet so it's your choice.

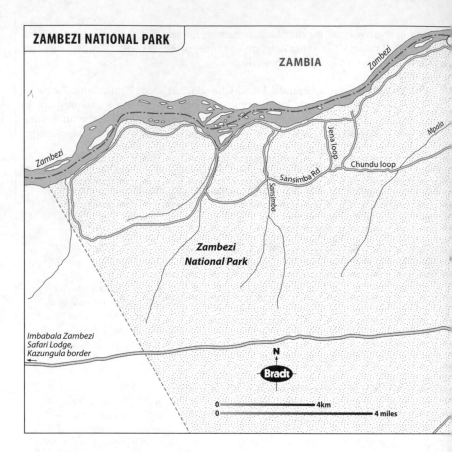

ZAMBIA

Zambezi

Zambezi

Jena loop

Mpala

Chundu loop

Sansimba Rd

Sansimba

Zambezi
National Park

Imbabala Zambezi
Safari Lodge,
Kazungula border

N

Bradt

0 ———————— 4km
0 ———————————— 4 miles

canoe groups use the site. Bookings can be made at the entrance gate office, or at the National Parks office in Victoria Falls town.

Private camps

🏠 **Victoria Falls River Lodge** (7 luxury tents) 📞 +27 (0)41 4530650/1; e reservations@ zambezicrescent.com. This is the first private lodge to be built inside the park (2012) & with its idyllic river situation with the spray of the falls in the distance, it offers a seriously tranquil spot to unwind and pamper yourself. You'll find excellent game viewing on your drives & walks yet as it's close to the park entrance, it's only half an hour from the airport by road & 10mins from town by boat, so it offers the very best of both worlds. The beautifully furnished luxury tents are spacious & open plan with all the facilities of an upmarket hotel including minibar & AC, outside & inside shower & bath, & each has its own private deck overlooking the river. The lodge has a pool, open-plan dining & lounge area, a 'sleep-out'

deck overlooking a waterhole & offers massage, manicure & pedicure facilities. Activities at this beautiful lodge include game drives, walks, fishing & sunset cruises, picnics on Kandahar Island & night drives. **$$$$$**

🏠 **Pioneers Camp** (6 tents) 📞 013 45139, 0778 173398; e operations@wildfrontierszimbabwe. com. This new (2013) rustic style tented camp at Mpala Jena is situated facing one of the most scenic stretches of the river. Tents are spacious with flush toilets & solar powered lighting & water. There's a central lounge/dining area and a well stocked bar. Children from 6 years welcome. Activities include canoeing, game drives, river cruises, bush walking & fishing. Prices are fully inclusive **$$$$$** or full board **$$$$** with activities and drinks extra.

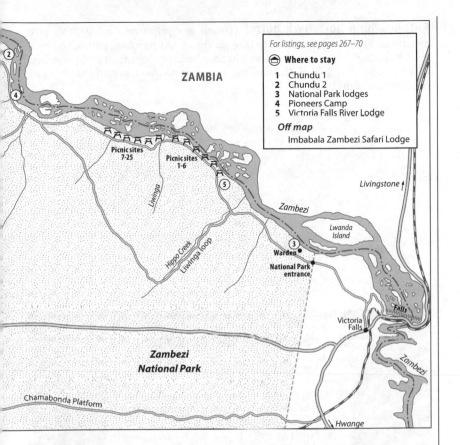

For listings, see pages 267–70

Where to stay

1 Chundu 1
2 Chundu 2
3 National Park lodges
4 Pioneers Camp
5 Victoria Falls River Lodge

Off map

Imbabala Zambezi Safari Lodge

ZAMBIA

Picnic sites 7-25

Picnic sites 1-6

Liwinga

Hippo Creek

Liwinga loop

Livingstone ↑

Zambezi

Lwanda Island

Warden ●

National Park entrance

Victoria Falls

Falls

Zambezi

Zambezi National Park

Chamabonda Platform

Hwange

ACTIVITIES You can drive round the park without a guide, but walking alone is prohibited. There are several options to help you enhance your wildlife viewing experience on offer from Charles Brightman's **Discover Safaris** (☏ *45821;* m *0712 209144, 0917 747426;* e *cat@yoafrica.com).* Charles, a professional guide, runs the Victoria Falls Anti-Poaching Unit and, together with his staff of scouts, offers intimate knowledge of the park to participants in the following trips.

Game drives (*US$50 per person plus US$15pp park entry fee*) Set off in the early morning or in mid-afternoon.

Half-day walking safaris (*Departures at 06.15 and 14.30; US$60 per person plus US$15 per person park entry fee*) Venture further into the national park, with a game drive, to a suitable walking area.

Birdwatching safaris (*Price on request*) These are tailor-made trips depending on which species you are looking for. By open safari vehicle, on foot or by boat, you'll search for an array of species through a variety of habitats such as teak and *mopane* woodlands, grassland and riverine forest. Depending on seasonal conditions, species may include African skimmer, collared palm-thrush, rock pratincole, raquet-tailed roller, western banded snake eagle, kori bustard, African finfoot or even slaty egret.

Anti-poaching horseback patrol (*Details and prices on request*) This gives experienced riders a rare chance to take part in an anti-poaching patrol. Led by an Anti-Poaching Unit game scout, you'll be searching for wire snares set by poachers, and learning what goes on behind the scenes of conservation efforts. Proceeds directly benefit the unit.

8

Hwange

Almost all commercial itineraries to Zimbabwe include Hwange National Park. And so they should. It is a world-class safari area containing a large percentage of southern Africa's game species. If you've only got a week to spend in Zimbabwe split your time between here and Victoria Falls.

HWANGE TOWN

The original settlement here took the name of a local Ndebele chief, Hwange Rosumbani, in the early 20th century, unfortunately corrupted by white Zimbabweans to Wankie. After independence and the indigenisation of many Rhodesian place names, it reclaimed its original name.

The fact that Hwange town is a coal-mining centre is all too apparent as you approach it, especially from Victoria Falls. Well before town you begin to see ugly slag heaps, opencast scarring and railway sidings, with the whole area south of the road taken over by what continues to be the area's principal economic concern.

Commercial mining has taken place here for over 100 years, since the arrival of white settlers, although local people already knew about the combustible powers of the black rock. When the railway arrived in 1904, production rocketed and the colliery became one of the biggest producers in the world. This was the site of one of the worst disasters in mining history, when in 1972 an underground explosion killed 427 miners. The seams are still viable, and operations continue apace with deposits waiting to be opencast mined.

The town itself has little to commend it, and only the most inquisitive travellers will visit. Its most notable feature is just outside town on the main road: an imposing steam locomotive, sitting on the green by the two filling stations. The vast majority of visitors come to visit one of Africa's finest national parks.

GETTING THERE Independent travellers currently need a car. City Link, Pathfinder and Senatar Express coaches will drop you off on their way between Victoria Falls and Bulawayo, but you'll still have the problem of making your way to wherever you'll be staying. There's no public transport, and hitchhiking is prohibited in the national park, so you will have to arrange a pick-up with your accommodation.

WHERE TO STAY
Standard
🏠 **Baobab Hotel** (63 rooms) Bulawayo Rd; 📞081 33481, 023 414702; e hbaobab@comeone. co.zw. This large hotel is just outside town, well signposted a few hundred metres east of the 'train

on the green'. It's the only hotel in town & caters primarily for the coal business. Few tourists will feel the need to break their journey here, & if you are here for the national park, this hotel would not be your choice – an unattractive, functional block with plainly furnished AC dbls, twins & sgls. There's a garden & pool with views over the surrounding countryside, & a nice old baobab tree said to be over 600 years old. **$$-$$$**

HWANGE NATIONAL PARK (NP Category 1)

Hwange ranks among the top national parks in Africa in terms of size, and sheer numbers and variety of game, along with excellent viewing and accommodation facilities. If this trip to Zimbabwe is your first experience of African wildlife viewing, Hwange is the perfect place to start your quest for the 'Big Five', before moving on to other equally rewarding animals. With over 108 species, Hwange boasts the highest diversity of mammals of any national park in the world, including 19 large herbivores and eight large carnivores. One of the largest elephant populations on Earth – numbering anywhere between 20,000 and 75,000 in the peak dry season – ranges between Hwange and neighbouring Chobe in Botswana. Over 400 species of birds have been recorded here, including around 50 types of raptor.

HISTORY If the area today supports one of the greatest concentrations of accessible wildlife in Africa, this was not always the case. In the days when this was the royal hunting ground of King Mzilikazi and then his son Lobengula, the killing was relatively controlled and based on necessity. All that changed when white settlers arrived on the scene and began systematically decimating the wildlife. (The sparsely watered Kalahari sands never supported permanent concentrations of game, especially in the south, and hunted animals were generally either temporary summer residents or on migration.)

The national park was founded on 'Toms', the farm of one H G Robins who, after several unsuccessful years trying to raise cattle, decided to turn his property into a wildlife sanctuary. In 1929 he handed it over to the government, which incorporated surrounding land and declared the area a national reserve.

It quickly became apparent to the new warden, Ted Davison, that only permanent water supplies would ensure healthy stocks of game, so he set about drilling boreholes and creating artificial pans to supplement the sparse natural sources. Despite their freedom of movement, the growing wildlife population soon became totally dependent on man, at least in the dry winter months. This is still the case today, with responsibility for the well-being of the game in the hands of the Zimbabwe Parks and Wildlife Management Authority (ZPWMA).

TODAY Ted Davison created around 60 pumped waterholes in the park, but years of economic chaos and fuel shortages have taken their toll, and many have fallen into disuse. The ZPWMA faces an uphill battle for financial survival, receiving only part of their revenues from the government, but several charities do an excellent job providing money for pump maintenance and fuel, notably the Friends of Hwange Trust (see *Travelling positively*, in *Chapter 3*). Support also comes from the private lodges within the park that maintain waterholes in their areas.

Poaching and even commercial hunting are recent problems, though far less so than in Zimbabwe's other parks. Game numbers here are very healthy and there are a number of important research projects running. A decline in lion numbers led in 2004 to a temporary hunting moratorium in surrounding concessions, and the Hwange Lion Project has fitted over 50 lions with tracking collars. Since Painted Dog Conservation began work on endangered wild dogs in 2002, the population has doubled in size. It is often said that the park is unable to cope with its large numbers of elephant, though the subject is surrounded in controversy (see box,

Elephant control: to cull or not to cull? on pages 276–7) and there is not even consensus on how many individuals there are here.

The latest controversial threat to the park is the spread of mining activities for coal and diamonds, the revenue potential from both far outweighing that of National Parks income. As well as the destruction of huge sections of valuable wildlife habitat there is the far more damaging pollution of watercourses.

WILDLIFE VIEWING Although it's a huge park, roughly the size of Belgium, nearly all the wildlife-viewing facilities are concentrated in two broad areas: the northern sector, including Sinamatella, Robins Camp and Nantwich; and Main Camp a little further to the east, along with the neighbouring southern wilderness area that is home to some world-class private camps. (Most of the park – west, centre and north – is formed by the easternmost limits of the Kalahari sands, with sparsely vegetated, semi-arid desert.) *Mopane* woodland gradually merges into lush teak forests in the east, giving the park a huge diversity of flora and fauna. Reasonably good roads, some of them tarred, link these two areas, and there's an extensive network of loop roads with hides and platforms overlooking waterholes and reservoirs, all offering the possibility of spectacular wildlife viewing.

Guided game drives are available from all the surrounding accommodations, and even self-drivers should consider these, not only for their guides' keen game-spotting eyes but because they tend to communicate with one another about good sightings (this can of course result in quite a gathering of vehicles in one spot). Because private driving is prohibited from 18.00 to 06.00, a guided drive is in fact the only way to see the rewarding wildlife action that occurs around dusk and dawn.

WHEN TO VISIT
For wildlife viewing Hwange is a genuinely year-round game park although the summer months are best suited to birders rather than visitors who want to see large concentrations of game. Generally the dry winter months, especially August–November, offer by far the best wildlife viewing, but game can put on some spectacular shows throughout the year. The great thing about a summer visit is that, with good rains and therefore abundant vegetation, the animals you see are all fat and content, whereas in winter it can be distressing to watch hundreds of desperate animals trying to drink from a nearly dried-up waterhole dominated by thirsty elephants.

For comfort The park is on the eastern edge of the vast Kalahari sands and scrublands, at around 1,000m, and it gets chilly on winter evenings. In fact, summer nights can also be surprisingly cool in Hwange. Daytime winter temperatures may be in the low 30s, yet warm clothing is needed for early morning and night drives in open vehicles. Campers may wake up to ground frost. Traditional wisdom says you should get an early start on your morning game drive, but you needn't be in too much of a hurry in Hwange in winter because, like us, the animals need to warm up a bit before setting out for the day.

GETTING AROUND Hwange has a reasonably well-maintained road system (some are tarred) linking all the key wildlife-viewing sites, as well as a number of loops and detours, so with a good map you can design yourself a route taking in all the key waterholes. A two-wheel drive car should get you around the main roads and tracks but the rains, combined with generally poor road maintenance, may make you wish you'd brought a 4x4.

Private driving is not allowed in the park after 18.00, so if you are heading for Robins Camp or Sinamatella via the Main Camp entrance, you should arrive at the entrance no later than 12.00 or 14.00 respectively, to allow for driving time. If you are self-driving, stay in your car at all times except when at recognised viewing spots. Not only are there plenty of predators here, but park scouts will ambush anyone they suspect of being a poacher. Fuel pumps are at Main Camp but it is best not to rely on their supplies. Be especially careful if driving on the first section of the road from the main road to Sinamatella. This now serves as a colliery access road and is dominated by huge, speeding coal trucks that present a significant danger.

TOURIST INFORMATION Generally speaking, you should always try to source your National Parks maps and information before arriving at the park itself, as stocks in their shops have in recent years been non-existent. The National Parks reception offices at Main Camp, Sinamatella and Robins Camp should have copies of the Wildlife and Environment Zimbabwe (WEZ) map of the park, proceeds from which help fund the maintenance of park water supplies. If you're in Harare you could visit WEZ for a map at the Mukuvisi Woodland centre (see page 169). The *Tourist Map of Hwange National Park*, published by PhotoSafari, is easier to read

ELEPHANT CONTROL: TO CULL OR NOT TO CULL?

Are there too many elephants in Hwange National Park? If so, what, if anything, must be done to control them? There are few debates in African wildlife conservation more likely to raise passions than this one, and even fewer on which expert opinion is so divided.

Visitors to Hwange can't fail to notice large swathes of land that have had virtually every tree reduced to stunted bushes. These are predominantly *mopane* trees that, given the right conditions, would grow to some 20m. Many experts believe that this degradation of vegetation is adversely affecting biodiversity, and that it proves the park cannot support the present elephant population. They thus promote elephant control, with culling being a more effective method than the expensive and impractical alternatives of translocation and contraception.

Other equally expert people reject this notion, however, suggesting that this 'destructive' elephant activity is actually beneficial and ultimately results in elephant populations regulating themselves. Dense concentrations of elephant, they argue, can be beneficial to the ecology by encouraging lower-level plant growth, which, in turn, supports smaller herbivores and predators; this process of degradation might therefore be just part of a much larger natural cycle. They maintain that culling is neither necessary nor desirable, at least until more is known about elephant distribution and movement across the whole region.

At the heart of this debate is the fact that nobody can actually put an accurate figure on how many elephants are in the park. Recent estimates vary hugely from 2,500 to 75,000, depending on whether you talk to the anti-culling or culling lobby or what season you are referring to. There are no fences in Hwange, with game able to enter and leave the park at will, and to cross international borders. Hwange's elephants are also Chobe's and Okavango's – and some individuals have even been traced as far as Angola. In other words, Hwange's elephant population simply depends on how many happen to be in the park at any given time.

Those who advocate control suggest that an accurate count isn't really relevant as you need only look at the damage being done to the vegetation and its effect but you are also paying for a selection of colour photos you may not want. The park is often included as an inset in larger maps or atlases of Zimbabwe. Larger country maps often have maps of national parks on their reverse side with sufficient detail to allow you to get around.

WHERE TO STAY AND EAT If you have the time and budget, try to spend more than just a couple of nights in Hwange, so you can experience not only its varying terrain, vegetation and richly rewarding wildlife, but also its variety of accommodation. There are a number of **private safari camps** both within, and just outside the park offering upmarket and luxury, fully inclusive accommodation, while the **National Parks lodges and chalets** give a more affordable option with three large camps within the park, each with self-catering chalets and lodges of varying sizes. The much vaunted refurbishment programme that was to be completed before the 2010 World Cup in South Africa has regrettably not materialised so Hwange's National Parks accommodations leave people complaining about poor value. As well as camping, there's an opportunity to overnight in one of several hides overlooking waterholes. All 'non private' park accommodation should be pre-booked via National Parks in Harare (see page 158). If you turn up without a reservation you may well be disappointed.

on biodiversity. In Hwange, however, human factors are responsible for the 'destructive' actions of elephants. The park can only support its huge game stocks during the dry months by artificially pumping waterholes. But for many years now, Parks has been starved of money, resulting in unrepaired pumps, no money to pay pump attendants and fuel shortages that render even functioning pumps inoperative. As a result, any scarce cash reserves that do filter through the system tend to be spent on maintaining the waterholes in key tourist areas, while the rest of the park – a vast expanse of land – goes largely unpumped.

Elephant need to drink large quantities daily so it should come as no surprise that huge numbers concentrate around these few sources of water. And then of course they must eat, hence the widespread trashing of the vegetation in the immediate vicinity. In fact it is this lack of food that kills most animals rather than drought, although of course the two factors are inextricably linked.

The charity Wildlife and Environment Zimbabwe (WEZ), which conducts an annual game census in Hwange, emphasised a most significant point at a recent pre-count briefing: that no elephants were spotted more than 8km from an active water source and only in these areas has vegetation been damaged; areas around unpumped water pans were left pristine. Opponents of a cull therefore argue that before any mass slaughter takes place, the park must first be properly managed, allowing elephants to drink at the many widely dispersed waterholes and thus to spread any impact more evenly. Effective park management would involve rotating the pumping around different areas to prevent the current concentrations of damage in certain spots. This of course would have serious implications for tourist viewing opportunities. They also press for co-operation and joint management schemes with neighbouring countries, who are also hosts to this same elephant population. In this regard the creation of transfrontier parks, which will encourage elephant migration in search of distant water and food sources, can only be seen as a major step forward.

Finally, the annual game census carried out by WEZ takes place around full moon each September. Although it covers only a 24-hour period, many volunteers travel long distances and tend to stay for several days or a week. All the hides and most of the National Parks accommodation are blocked off during this period, making it virtually impossible to get a booking.

While the southern area has no National Parks accommodation, there are several privately owned camps and lodges that keep the waterholes pumped, the animals satisfied and the clients pampered.

At the time of my research there was only one food outlet available at any National Parks camp – the Waterbuck restaurant at Main Camp by the office is a welcome return to catering, with good portions and reports of basic but good freshly cooked food, albeit with a fairly small menu. Supplies at the store appeared to be a bit erratic in late 2012 with reports of a reliance on tinned ingredients rather than fresh produce, but sufficient for a camper to prepare a full meal. Otherwise restaurants and bars were closed, requiring visitors to be totally self-sufficient in food and drink, including bottled water. Supplies of bottled gas for cooking were also erratic. Now that shops in Zimbabwe have filled up again, conditions in the parks should be improving, but there is little sign of this yet so when you book be sure to clarify the prevailing situation.

National parks camps

Sinamatella area This area, which includes Sinamatella, Robins and Nantwich camps, is in the northwestern part of the park, within easy reach of the Victoria Falls–Bulawayo road.

Sinamatella Camp is the largest and most geographically attractive – a great base for initial exploration of the area. The turn-off is signposted off the main road, a few kilometres west of Hwange town, and from there to the camp it's around an hour (just over 40km) on a well-maintained dirt road. However, the stretch near the main road is now used by huge trucks servicing a newly opened coal mine and the drivers have only one thing on their mind – speed. So be very careful here. Look out for elephant and other game on the way. You can pay your park entry fees at the Sinamatella Camp reception office and the helpful staff can arrange guides or game drives if you wish. There are fuel pumps near the entrance but don't rely on them, as supplies can be unreliable.

If you are heading to Robins or Nantwich camp from Victoria Falls, there's a turn-off about 35km from Victoria Falls that takes you through the Matetsi safari area (confusingly, the map reveals several Matetsi safari areas in this part of the country).

It's possible to overnight at some of the area's hides, but these should be pre-booked. Most hides and lookouts sleep up to 12, so even if it's overbooked when you arrive, you may be able to negotiate a bit of space – but get there early enough to return to Sinamatella Camp in daylight if you can't.

Sinamatella Camp This large camp is on a hilltop with commanding views over the distant river and plains. Vast herds of buffalo can be seen from the bar or your own *braai* area, but look closer and you'll see plenty of other game. You need good binoculars here.

It has 30+ units perched along the edge of an escarpment, and each has its own open space, a wonderful place to chill out in the late afternoon and watch the game below. Unfortunately, many of these chalets were out of commission in 2012, thus placing great pressure on the remaining ones and severely limiting the number of people who can stay here.

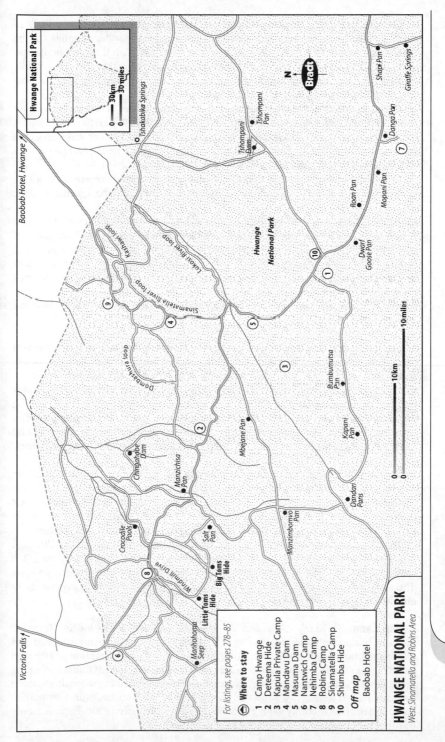

For listings, see pages 278–85

① **Where to stay**
1   Camp Hwange
2   Deteema Hide
3   Kapula Private Camp
4   Mandavu Dam
5   Masuma Dam
6   Nantwich Camp
7   Nehimba Camp
8   Robins Camp
9   Sinamatella Camp
10 Shumba Hide

Off map
Baobab Hotel

HWANGE NATIONAL PARK
West: Sinamatella and Robins Area

The standard-design **chalets** come in varying sizes, typically spacious and clean although much-needed refurbishment has commenced – water supplies can be a major problem. All have *braai* facilities. The thatched central facility houses an indoor and a wonderfully scenic open-air restaurant/bar (they haven't actually catered here for years but check the situation before you arrive as you'll almost certainly have to bring in your own stocks).

The **campsite** is just a large patch of cleared land under acacia trees, with an ablution block and a thatched seating area. The area itself is basic to say the least but the views are tremendous. Try to pitch near the edge so you can wake up to the vista of the plains below. The ground is rock hard so you'll need stout pegs and a club hammer to break the crust.

The warden's office has a rudimentary display and information centre, and staff are happy to tell you about game conditions and recent sightings in the Sinamatella area.

Mandavu Dam This large permanent lake is home to hippos and crocodiles, and the far shore is a daily watering place for elephants and a variety of plains game. A big thatched viewing platform overlooks the lake; you can spend the night here, serenaded by the hippos. If you book this place for the night, you can pitch a tent in the car park. If you sleep on the concrete floor of the platform be sure to pack up before dawn out of respect for early visitors – grunting hippos are delightful but snoring humans are less of an attraction. By the car park are good ablution facilities with running water.

Masuma Dam picnic site This is a pumped waterhole that enjoys a constant procession of elephant, buffalo, hyena, rhino, kudu, zebra, impala, lion and jackal, and hippos may lurk in the muddy waters. Here too there's a lookout shelter, this one much closer to the action than Mandavu. The elephants are keener on the freshly pumped water in the holding trough than what's in the pan, though they often dig out and ruin the pipework. It's magical to spend the night in the viewing platform, with the elephants' curiously comforting snuffling, rumbling, farting, slurping and trumpeting just a few metres away. Again, please clear out by dawn for early visitors.

Deteema picnic site and hide The pleasant picnic site, in a shady location overlooking an excellent wildlife-viewing area, has more of a wilderness feel than the other spots, ie: you'd hardly call it manicured and it's all the better for that. Of interest is a small display of replica fossil stumps of the *Dadoxylon* trees that grew here 200 million years ago. There are stone rondavels, *braai* stands and tables.

The hide is a couple of hundred metres away. This is the official campsite although some people camp at the picnic site, a fenced area overlooking a pumped pan. It is very rustic and you really feel you are right out in the bush here – which you are. The waterhole attracts the full range of game, and is a great place to overnight. As always bring your own water.

Robins Camp This large camp has 20 standard National Parks lodges. There's a pleasant bar and restaurant but as at Sinamatella, these have been unstocked and unmanned for a number of years. Now that the Main Camp restaurant has opened again, there's hope that this one will as well before too long. Outdoor cooking facilities are situated beneath an observation tower containing a small museum dedicated to H G Robins, something of a recluse and an amateur astronomer. Extracts from his monthly game reports go back to the early 1950s. There is plenty of room for camping, with good ablution facilities.

For wildlife viewing, Deteema is 25km away, and Big Toms and Little Toms hides are on a 28km loop road south of Robins (these last two on H G Robins's original game farms). All offer excellent viewing, but as self-drivers must be back at camp by 18.00 you have to leave at the height of the action (a good reason to book a guided drive from camp).

Nantwich Camp Just 10km west of Robins, three double-bed lodges sit on a hill on the border of the park overlooking a reservoir, a large game-rich *vlei* and the Matetsi safari area. At the time of research, however, the entire camp was leased to a hunting operation. A little way down the hill is a three-bedroom house, Isilwane (US$160) owned by Parks. It is available to the public, although sometimes leased for long periods to hunting concessions. There are no camping facilities here.

Recent visits report that both Robins and Nantwich show evidence of use as hunting camps.

Shumba hide The hide, along the dirt road from Sinamatella to Main Camp where it changes to tar, has a small site for camping. Although not especially attractive, it is extremely popular, with a reputation for good lion sightings. In the dry season the nearby pan teems with game – zebra, kudu, impala, wildebeest, buffalo, giraffe and a small herd of the uncommon roan antelope. All play second fiddle to the elephants who dominate the waterhole, and of course predators such as lion and hyena are never far away. This is a place where you pay for the whole site so you get it all to yourself, although these days I wish you good luck as it's usually booked out and occupied by safari operators and their high-end clients who vigorously maintain their exclusive tenure, despite the occupants frequently being few in number.

Main Camp area This area of Hwange carries the greatest concentration of game, attracted by its pumped pans. It consequently also has the greatest concentration of humans.

Main Camp covers a large area with plenty of standard National Parks chalets, cottages and lodges plus a campsite. Refurbishment is eagerly awaited, but the ablution blocks are already clean, with running water. Bring your own drinking water. There is a small shop (and fuel pumps, but don't rely on them). Situated on a large, flat, dusty piece of ground, this is without doubt the least attractive of Zimbabwe's National Parks camps, but it couldn't be more convenient and is a good base for the first night. After many years the restaurant here has eventually reopened; see *Where to stay and eat* section on page 278.

There are short and long loop roads clearly marked from here, with any number of pans and waterholes near them. When pumped, all of the pans offer phenomenal game sightings so study a map, work out a route and try to camp in some hides along the way if you have equipment – although space is limited and you must book in advance.

The popular Ten Mile loop road takes you off the pot-holed tar road at **Dom Pan**, then around to **Caterpillar**, **Dopi** and **Nyamandlovu** pans. The last has an excellent viewing platform and clean toilets.

Guvalala Platform is 26km from Main Camp on the tar road to Sinamatella. Judging by the prodigious quantities of elephant dung along the road this is the animals' preferred route, so drive very carefully indeed. The roofed platform, originally erected by Kent Boy Scouts, was quite run-down when I last visited, but has since been renovated with money from the Save Hwange Trust. The park allows overnighting from 18.00 to 06.00 in the platform, which is adequate for four to six people.

It's a busy pan if it's been pumped (ask before you go), and the steady procession of animals coming to drink are just a few metres away. I spent one of my most memorable wildlife nights in Zimbabwe here. With hyenas serenading us with whoops and giggles seemingly right underneath us, sleep wasn't an option, so we spent all night watching a constant parade of animals coming in to drink. Check the toilets are still functioning and up to your standard: a stroll into the bush with a shovel is definitely out of the question.

A loop of about 100km from Main Camp takes you southeast via the Kennedy Pans through prime wildlife-viewing country. Camping is allowed at **Kennedy 1**, **Ngweshla** and **Jambili** pans, each with excellent viewing (when pumped) and basic facilities for up to ten people.

⌂ Private camps
Inside the national park

⌂ **Camp Hwange** (8 chalets) ☏013 45028; e info@camphwange.com; www.camphwange. com. This is a newly opened camp in the heart of Hwange National Park close to Shumba Pan. It's been set up & run by top professional guide David Carson, renowned for his mobile safaris. This is not a luxury camp; instead David's created a very comfortable classic bush camp for people who want to connect with nature & the wildlife in this very game-rich area of the park. There are 8 2-bed thatched, en-suite chalets with canvas & gauze walls, arranged in a wide semicircle all facing a pumped pan that has its own hide, very, very close to the animal action, which since its opening in 2012 has been intense. A central *boma* forms the

A TEENAGER'S FIRST NIGHT ALONE

There's a little-visited area of Hwange National Park that has no standing water, yet it attracts large herds of elephant. They dig for water in underground seeps and there are the remains of a ramshackle old hide nearby from where you can watch. On this occasion we were there for 24 hours conducting a game count. One trio of elephants – a mum, a sub-adult daughter and a much younger son – stood out from the rest by their odd behaviour. Mum allowed the daughter to access her seep, but every time junior tried to get his trunk in, mum shoved him away.

This went on all afternoon and the poor little chap was getting very distressed, desperate for a drink. It was quite upsetting to watch. Then, as dusk approached, junior was eventually allowed to drink, but while he was preoccupied, making up for lost time, mum and daughter slipped away into the bush leaving the lad alone with the grown-ups. All night we watched him hunting around for mother. By daybreak he had calmed down and was taking his turn at the seeps.

Why did mum abandon him? Surely elephants are supposed to have highly developed social and family structures? What would now happen to this lonely little elephant? At about 09.00 the answer became clear. In the distance we saw two elephants running in at nearly full speed: mum and daughter. They found junior and amidst much joyful trumpeting and wrapping of trunks, the trio were reunited. Surely there is only one explanation: this was the youngster's first lesson in fending for himself. Full marks to mum for devising such a clever way to leave him on his own, safe in the knowledge that he was in the good hands of the rest of the herd.

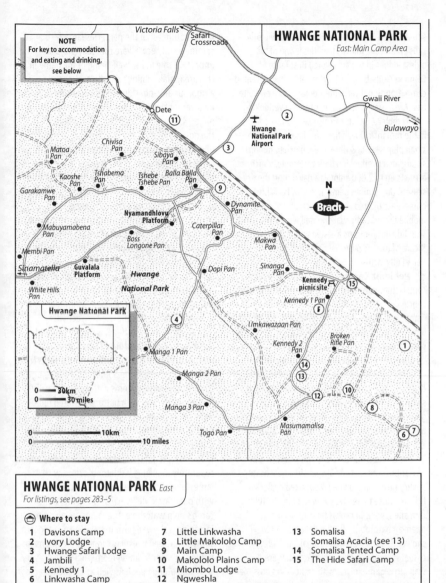

NOTE
For key to accommodation
and eating and drinking,
see below

HWANGE NATIONAL PARK East
For listings, see pages 283–5

🏠 Where to stay

1	Davisons Camp	7	Little Linkwasha
2	Ivory Lodge	8	Little Makololo Camp
3	Hwange Safari Lodge	9	Main Camp
4	Jambili	10	Makololo Plains Camp
5	Kennedy 1	11	Miombo Lodge
6	Linkwasha Camp	12	Ngweshla

13	Somalisa
	Somalisa Acacia (see 13)
14	Somalisa Tented Camp
15	The Hide Safari Camp

restaurant, bar & lounge area overlooking the busy waterhole & the evenings around the fire have provided the most spectacular sunsets I've ever seen. **$$$$$**

Elephant's Eye (8 chalets) ☎ South Africa +27 (0)21 6837826; e info@africanluxuryhideaways. com; www.africanluxuryhideaways.com This eco-friendly new lodge 13km from the park entrance, in a 2500ha private concession, has en-suite chalets all facing a waterhole. As well as a pool, there's

also a gym & spa to fill your time between game viewing activities that include day & night drives, bush dinners & sundowners at the waterhole. All activities, meals & local drinks are included. This lodge was opened in April 2013 so the author has not had the opportunity to visit. **$$$$$**

🏠 **The Hide Safari Camp** (10 tents) Office 6, Triton Centre, 17 Enterprise Rd, Harare; ☎ 04 498835/6; m 0774 724412; e corrie@thehide. com; www.thehide.com Privately owned &

situated on a concession adjacent to the Victoria Falls–Bulawayo railway line, this is one of the oldest lodges in the area, voted Best Tented Safari Camp in Zimbabwe for 13 years. It's a luxury tented camp, traditional yet contemporary, with en-suite east African-style tents under thatch overlooking a waterhole. 2 guests can also be accommodated in the romantic Dove's Nest tree house. There's a small plunge pool & dbl-storey thatched dining/sitting area overlooking their waterhole, which attracts up to 2,000 animals a day during the dry season. Day & night game drives/walks & bush dinners are offered, & the opportunity of a 3-night, mobile tented camp walking trail within the park. The Hide has for years assisted with maintenance & care of the NP, & the Save Hwange Trust is based here. Fully inclusive. **$$$$$**

🏠 **Nehimba Camp** (7 chalets) www.nehimba.com. Nehimba is a new camp situated on a private concession south of Sinamatella & 60km from Main Camp. Self-drivers (4x4 recommended) are met at Sinamatella & escorted to camp. The very spacious wood & thatch chalets on raised platforms are elegantly furnished in classic Africa style with either twin or super king-size beds. The main lodge & chalets all overlook a nearby natural pan with saltlicks to tempt elephant & all the other plains game. Game drives, night drives & game walks are all on offer in this very game-rich area. **$$$$$**

🏠 **Somalisa Tented Camp** (6 tents) ☎ 09234 307; e contact@africanbushcamps.com; www.africanbushcamps.com; Skype: africanbushcamps. Luxury bush camp owned & operated by Becks Ndlovu. Close to Kennedy 2 waterhole, the fully furnished, walk-in canvas tents have en-suite open-air bathrooms, flush toilet & bucket bush shower. The main area has a small pool, library, casual seating & dining table. Activities are walking & game drives, with night drives possible. Solar lighting but battery charging for cameras/laptops is available. Fully inclusive – all food, drinks, activities, accommodation & laundry. **$$$$$**

🏠 **Wilderness Safaris** Wilderness do not take direct bookings so check their website (*www.wilderness-safaris.com*) for full details of their camps & for booking information. If you want to talk to somebody call South Africa ☎ +27 11 8071800. Wilderness Safaris owns the Makalolo and Linkwasha concessions, situated in prime game-viewing territory

to the southeast of the park. This large & commendably eco-aware company plays an important role in the well-being of the game in this area, maintaining waterholes & ensuring a rigorous anti-poaching regime. Community involvement, support & education (see CITW, page 145) is seen as crucial to the upkeep of the environment so the company has a number of ongoing projects. Their camps are luxury class, beautifully maintained & run, & catering standards are excellent: 5 of the best bush camps Zimbabwe has to offer & you'll also be helping to maintain the park's environment & wildlife. (As I write this Wilderness is also constructing a new camp in the **Sinamatella** area.) At **Little Makalolo Camp** (6 rooms; fully inclusive) rooms are en-suite with indoor & outdoor showers, & run on solar power. Living areas include dining room, lounge, plunge pool & open fire area. A tree-house hide overlooks the waterhole in front of camp. Wildlife-viewing activities include open 4x4 vehicles & walks throughout the concession. **Makalolo Plains Camp** (10 rooms; fully inclusive) is built on raised decks & boardwalks overlooking Somavundla Pan. Large, comfortable tented rooms with en-suite facilities & outdoor shower, with battery-powered room lighting. Main area has a lounge, pub, plunge pool & dining area. Activities are generally game drives, night drives & walks. **Linkwasha Camp** (7 rooms) and **Little Linkwasha** (3 rooms) are separately managed Wilderness camps with large, luxury, tented rooms, built under thatch with panoramic views across the plains & the camp's own waterhole. The rooms are en-suite including a shower, flush toilet plus an outdoor shower. A raised walkway connects the rooms to the lounge, bar & dining room. There's also a very welcome plunge pool. As well as excellent game viewing from the camp itself (it has a viewing platform) all the usual game activities are included. **Davisons Camp** (9 tents) is a classic tented camp, with the units hidden beneath a grove of false *mopane* trees, overlooking a waterhole & open plain. Named after the founder of Hwange National Park & its first warden, Ted Davison. With its 8 tents & a family tent, you get a wonderful bush experience. Tents & the main area comprising lounge, dining room, open campfire area & pool all look out over the waterhole. Activities are as above. All **$$$$$**

⌂ **Somalisa Acacia** Contacts as Somalisa Tented Camp (opposite). This camp caters for small family groups & those wanting a private experience shared with a max 8 people. The simple yet luxury tents are on slightly raised decks, under a canopy of acacias on the western side of Somalisa. The camp enjoys its own private views of a small waterhole in the midst of prime game-viewing area. **$$$$–$$$$$**

⌂ **Kapula Private Camp** (4 tents) ☏ +27 (0)12 8037601; www.kapulacamp.com. Their website has very good location maps with key GPS co-ordinates. This is a great option for budget-minded self-drivers, a self-catering tented camp with staff to provide hot water, washing up, etc. The raised tents are very large & well appointed with balconies, en-suite bathrooms & outdoor showers. There's a communal kitchen & *braai/dining* area with relaxation deck. The camp is right in a game-rich part of the Sinamatella area close to Masuma Dam. This has understandably become very popular so book well ahead. **$$$**

Outside the national park
Upmarket

⌂ **Ivory Lodge** (9 rooms) Signposted off the Bulawayo road a few km from Main Camp entrance; ☏ 09 64868/9, 881964; m 0712 215904; e resman@amalindacollection.co.zw. At the end of a sand road, a short distance from the park border & nestled in the Sikumi teak forest, this gem of a place features wooden & thatched en-suite bedrooms perched on elevated platforms. There's a cosy open-plan thatched dining, lounge & bar area. The lodge's small size ensures friendly & personal service. A hide, campfire BBQs & firelit *boma* make this place a delight. They offer drives into the park with their own vehicles & guides, & there's a pool to cool you down after a dusty day's wildlife viewing. Or you can camp in their nearby site, 'Tuskers', which also caters for overlanders. FB or fully inclusive. **$$$$–$$$$$**

⌂ **Hwange Safari Lodge** (100 rooms) ☏ 018 333; e pacro@africansunhotels.com; www.africansunhotels.com. The building itself, on the border of the national park, a 2hr drive from Victoria Falls, is a large, semicircular, sgl-storey complex. Inside it's very pleasant with huge gardens overlooking its own natural pan, which attracts large numbers of game. The lodge offers a selection of day & evening game activities into the national park & is a great base for the Main Camp area. As drivers alert one another to game sightings your vehicle may be 1 of 10 or more clustered around a bored lion snoozing by the roadside. But if this is your first visit to big-game country & you are keen to check out as many animals as you can, this is an excellent place to spend a few nights before moving on to a smaller lodge with a more bespoke experience. Activities not included. **$$$$**

⌂ **Miombo Lodge** (10 units) ☏ 013 45986, 45139; m 0712 640357; e miombo2@mweb.co.zw; www.miombosafaricamp.com. This is the nearest lodge to Main Camp entrance & is signed from the main road. Closed for a number of years, Miombo reopened in 2011 completely restyled & totally refurbished. It has 4 standard thatched rondavels; 2 rustic-style tree houses & 4 luxury tree houses including a honeymoon suite – all en suite. The large, thatched, central bar/restaurant/lounge *boma* looks out onto gardens with a tempting pool. It's all-inclusive with 2 game drives but with the option of 'independent safari rates' for self-drivers. **$$$**

⌂ **Sable Sands** (11 chalets) m 0778 454 840, 0778 71 5588; e sablesandslodge@gmail.com, info@moivarosouth.com; www.moivaro.com. This is a new (completely refurbished) lodge on a private concession with stunning views over Dete Vlei, the long dried up river that is a rich haven for a wide variety of game & an incredible bird population. There are 11 thatched rondavels, with private terrace & en-suite bathroom & the beautifully appointed main building houses dining area, lounge, loft, library, bar and terraced landscaping swimming pool. Fans of Brian and Marleen from the now closed Sikumi Tree Lodge will be delighted to learn that they now run Sable Sands. **$$$**

⌂ **Sikumi Tree Lodge** This much-loved, excellent lodge was closed in mid-2012 but there are hopes that the lease will be renegotiated to allow it to reopen.

Camping There is a camping and caravan site located on the main road just south of the Ivory Lodge turn-off. For years it was closed but the gate has now been open since 2011. Two visits in mid-2012 revealed a once obviously very pleasant site, but now sadly overgrown and neglected. Apparently open for business though staff were absent on both visits; there was running cold water in the shabby ablution block so it's a possibility as an emergency night stop although security could be an issue.

GAME-VIEWING ALTERNATIVES As well as viewing your game in the traditional way from a vehicle, you may want to consider the following.

Mobile safaris As well as offering an intimate, hands-on wildlife experience, the following operators are allowed into parts of the park prohibited to others. For instance, one undeveloped campsite is perched on a bank overlooking a dry riverbed. Although it's close to a permanent year-round water source, elephants here prefer to dig a metre or so into the riverbed to seeps from which they draw cool water, and you can watch them almost within touching distance.

Kazuma Trails ✆013 40857; m 0712 213840, 214399; e info@mobile-safaris.com; www. safaris.com. David Carson offers a range of backed-up walking & camping safaris in Hwange & Kazuma Pan NPs, catering for different levels of client fitness, luxury & duration. He now includes a visit to the Hwange Lion Research project. As an excellent wildlife photographer he can also offer advice to clients. *US$190/285/460pppn sharing (2 per tent) for participation/semi-luxury/ luxury safari, min 4; not inc transfers to/from Hwange town.*

Backpackers Africa Backpackers Bazaar, Victoria Falls; ✆013 44611, 45828, 42208; m 0712 404 968; e backpack@africaonline.co.zw; www. walkafrica.com. Leon Varley, one of Zimbabwe's longest-serving & most respected professional guides, offers bespoke walking & camping trails in Hwange & Chizarira. He believes the only way to truly see Africa is on foot: 'If you're not going to walk it, stay at home & watch it on TV.' His safaris can be fully backed-up, porter assisted or participatory with clients backpacking their own equipment. *5 days from US$580pp backpacking to US$680 fully backed up high season.*

KAZUMA PAN NATIONAL PARK (NP Category 3)

Maybe because it's sandwiched between the much better-known Zambezi and Hwange national parks, the small (31,300ha) Kazuma Pan is a very little-visited park. It's remote, the authorities make it a pain to get to and it's lacking in facilities – but all this combines to make it a wonderful human-free wilderness area.

It was originally set up as a refuge for game from the neighbouring Matetsi safari (hunting) area. It's right in the middle of the uninterrupted game route between Botswana and Zimbabwe. Elephants pass through in large numbers to and from Chobe and Hwange, and for some reason Kazuma Pan attracts some extremely large bulls. Other species to be seen are giraffe, buffalo, zebra, roan, sable, tsessebe, eland and, rarely, gemsbok, which is on the easternmost extreme of its range. Lion are common, and you also stand a chance of spotting wild dog, while the terrain is also ideal cheetah territory. In the wet summer season the pans attract large numbers of waterbirds, although the park is normally closed in January–February.

Geographically it's a flat, featureless depression with numerous pans, some of them artificially pumped in the dry season, though it also has natural springs. Such a large, grassy savanna area is unusual in Zimbabwe, but the boundaries revert to the teak and *mopane* woodland common in the rest of this area.

GETTING THERE It's a bit of a complicated affair. From the Victoria Falls–Bulawayo road, halfway between the Falls and Hwange, take the Matetsi safari area turn-off

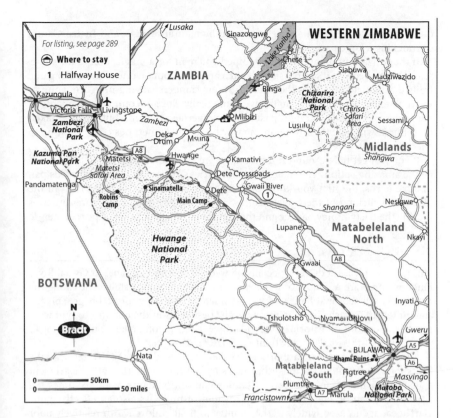

For listing, see page 289

Where to stay
1 Halfway House

WESTERN ZIMBABWE

(signposted to Robins and Pandamatenga) and drive about 25km to the Matetsi rangers' office (⏲ *07.00–16.30 Monday–Friday, closed for lunch 12.30–14.00*), where you pay your Parks fee and check in (remember you must also check out when you leave). You are then directed 30km+ to the Pandamatenga border post to register with the police. Please note, although these are the instructions currently issued by ZPWMA, recent reports suggest that the system has changed or indeed was never applied! Kazuma NP is administered by the Robins Camp warden who can be emailed at e robinscamp@yahoo.com for information. Alternatively the area manager for Kazuma can be reached on ☎ 0773 885850. The national park entrance is 25km northwest of Pandamatenga along the border road. A 4x4 is necessary as the roads are rough and sandy in some areas. Access from Kazungula to Pandamatenga along the same border road is for some reason strictly prohibited, according to Parks.

SAFARI OPERATORS You are better off booking with a safari operator than driving here on your own, for several reasons: you must book ahead here, and the safari companies tend to bag the limited facilities early; the drive and entry/exit processes are long-winded; and with few roads for game driving the park is best suited to walking safaris, and those are only possible with a professional guide. Kazuma Trails (see *Hwange National Park*, opposite page, for details) will try to put together walking safaris here by prior arrangement.

WHERE TO STAY There is no accommodation here, aside from two undeveloped camping facilities, allowing only one group in each (maximum of ten people) at any

8

one time. These are at **Katsetsheti**, situated by natural springs, and **Insiza Camp**, overlooking a large pan.

If the Insiza Camp pan is being pumped you're in for a magical (and, for some, scary) night, because it's impossible to pitch anywhere but on one of the many game trails that radiate out from the pan. With few campers staying here, the animals won't be expecting you, so you'll have some really close encounters. Elephants in particular will blunder straight past in their eagerness to drink but, having slaked their thirst, will take their time on the way back, and sometimes come right up to check you out.

If you can get here around full moon, be prepared to stay up all night to watch all the amazing action. The majestic eland, Africa's largest antelope, visits this pan in large herds; the first you know of their approach in the still night is from the distinctive clicking of their heels as they walk. Smaller nocturnal representatives include the feisty honey badger and the common (but seldom seen) porcupine.

TOWARDS BULAWAYO

This is a very pleasant drive, especially between Gwaai and Lupane. At Gwaai River junction there are a couple of large earthenware-pot market stalls, and along the road stalls sell seasonal fruit and veg – tomatoes, sweet potato, cabbage, spinach and butternut squash. This is also one of the best areas in the country to find well-preserved sections of historic strip roads. Give the local folks a laugh by stopping to take photos of the roads – they'll think you're mad!

A little further on there's a short, wide valley section full of baobab trees, with the fruits for sale dangling on makeshift racks by the roadside. The rather astringent fruits are an important source of vitamins and antioxidants, with six times the vitamin C of an orange and twice the calcium of milk. It's also an effective anti-diarrhoeal agent, used widely in the country to treat children with relatively poor diets. Plans are afoot to turn baobab fruit into the next must-have ingredient for health drinks and smoothies.

BILLY NO MATES

The scene is a remote pan in Kazuma Pan National Park. Around mid-morning a small group of guineafowl trotted up to the water's edge for a drink. Immediately a young bateleur eagle swooped down from a tree, landed about 3m away and hopped right up to them, looking for all the world as if he were asking, 'Excuse me, what do I do now?' The guineas ignored him, finished their drink and scurried back into the undergrowth. Ten minutes later a lappet-faced vulture glided in and started to drink. Billy once again approached almost within pecking distance, observed the big, ugly bird with interest before seeming to say, 'Hello, can I be your friend?' The vulture took off, spiralling up on a thermal. Billy No Mates was on his own again.

For several hours we watched him doing the same thing with every bird that came down to the water's edge – a small group of francolin, more guineafowl and then, amazingly, some doves. It really did seem like he had just been kicked out of the nest and had no idea what to do next, so was checking out every other bird he could find to see if they could help. My companions, one of whom used to be a National Parks guide instructor, had never seen this sort of behaviour before.

WHERE TO STAY
Basic

⌂ **Halfway House** (16 rooms) Literally halfway between Victoria Falls & Bulawayo just south of Gwaai. Staff were unable to provide me with contact details. This used to be the Halfway Hotel, a convenient refuelling & refreshment stop, but it's difficult to see why anyone would overnight here given its proximity to both Bulawayo & Victoria Falls. I was told it went downhill after being taken over during the land grab, losing a lot of business when locals boycotted it. The slightly altered name suggests new ownership, although nothing much seems to have changed. The rooms seem clean but very plain, & there's a restaurant, bar & lounge. It's cheap enough but the lad on reception, though friendly & doing his best to be helpful, didn't inspire confidence in the place. **$**

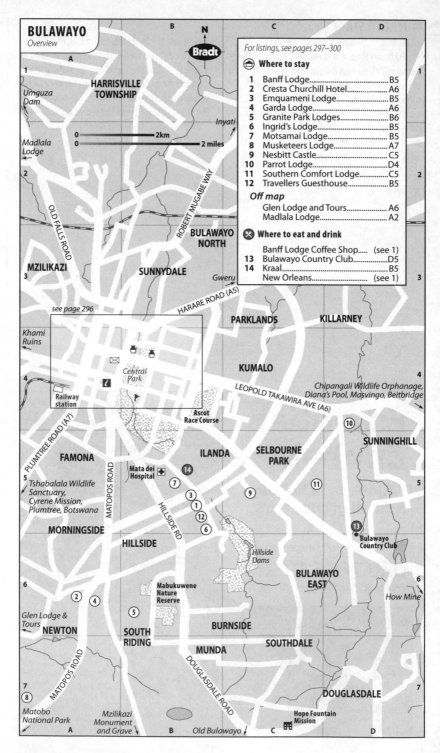

BULAWAYO
Overview

Bradt

For listings, see pages 297–300

Where to stay

1	Banff Lodge	B5
2	Cresta Churchill Hotel	A6
3	Emquameni Lodge	B5
4	Garda Lodge	A6
5	Granite Park Lodges	B6
6	Ingrid's Lodge	B5
7	Motsamai Lodge	B5
8	Musketeers Lodge	A7
9	Nesbitt Castle	C5
10	Parrot Lodge	D4
11	Southern Comfort Lodge	C5
12	Travellers Guesthouse	B5

Off map

Glen Lodge and Tours	A6
Madlala Lodge	A2

Where to eat and drink

	Banff Lodge Coffee Shop	(see 1)
13	Bulawayo Country Club	D5
14	Kraal	B5
	New Orleans	(see 1)

HARRISVILLE TOWNSHIP

Umguza Dam

Inyati

Madlala Lodge

0   2km
0   2 miles

MZILIKAZI

SUNNYDALE

BULAWAYO NORTH

Gweru

OLD FALLS ROAD

ROBERT MUGABE WAY

see page 296

Khami Ruins

HARARE ROAD (A5)

PARKLANDS

KILLARNEY

Central Park

KUMALO

Railway station

Chipangali Wildlife Orphanage, Diana's Pool, Masvingo, Beitbridge

LEOPOLD TAKAWIRA AVE (A6)

Ascot Race Course

SUNNINGHILL

FAMONA

Tshabalala Wildlife Sanctuary, Cyrene Mission, Plumtree, Botswana

ILANDA

SELBOURNE PARK

Mata dei Hospital

PLUMTREE ROAD (A7)

MATOPOS ROAD

MORNINGSIDE

HILLSIDE

HILLSIDE RD

Bulawayo Country Club

Hillside Dams

BULAWAYO EAST

How Mine

Glen Lodge & Tours

NEWTON

Mabukuwene Nature Reserve

SOUTH RIDING

BURNSIDE

MUNDA

SOUTHDALE

MATOPOS ROAD

DOUGLASDALE ROAD

Matobo National Park

Mzilikazi Monument and Grave

Old Bulawayo

Hope Fountain Mission

DOUGLASDALE

9

Bulawayo

Telephone code 09

Bulawayo, Zimbabwe's second-largest city with a population of possibly 750,000, is the capital of Matabeleland, itself divided into two provinces, North and South. Despite their violent Zulu heritage, it's hard to find a more pleasant and friendly people than the Ndebele, and as Bulawayo is their capital you'll get a warm welcome wherever you go.

In 1870 Lobengula, the last of the Ndebele or Matabele kings, named the original site KoBulawayo, commonly translated as 'Place of Suffering', and 'Place of Slaughter' in Shona, presumably because of the blood shed on the way to establishing the Ndebele nation. Nowadays, for entirely understandable reasons, Bulawayo prefers to market itself with the altogether more palatable sobriquet, 'The City of Kings'.

Bulawayo is a pleasant city with a laid-back atmosphere, and although many years without investment by central government have left it looking a little tatty round the edges, it's in better shape than most other towns in the country. Despite economic deprivation it's noticeable how this town's citizens have kept their city clean, alive and vibrant. It's especially noted for its fine colonial architecture with very wide streets, often lined with fabulous blue *Jacaranda* and red flamboyant (*Delonix regia*) trees.

The town is steeped in history, well stocked with hotels, lodges and restaurants, and set in an area of outstanding beauty, making it many visitors' favourite Zimbabwean town. Too many regard it as simply a stopping-off town on the way to Victoria Falls, Harare and Masvingo, but it deserves to be a centre in its own right. As well as boasting its own magnificent attractions Bulawayo is an excellent base for visiting everywhere else in the country, and as its efficient and unbusy airport is well connected with South Africa, you might do well to consider using it as your port of arrival in Zimbabwe.

At around 1,350m, Bulawayo enjoys a pleasant climate, though distinctly cooler than much of the rest of the country. Evenings can be chilly, and many accommodations provide hot-water bottles or electric blankets for their guests.

Note that when Zimbabwe cancelled its own currency in 2009 and allowed trading in other main currencies Bulawayo tended to favour the South African rand, but it has now joined the rest of the country and generally deals in US$; the rand is still widely accepted but exchange rates can be unfavourable.

HISTORY

The development of Bulawayo in the last decades of the 19th century is crucial to the development of the country itself. For a more detailed version of what follows, see page 304.

The story centres around two key players, King Lobengula and Cecil John Rhodes. Lobengula was the son of Zulu king Mzilikazi, leader of a breakaway faction from South Africa's Natal that was to become the Ndebele nation, based in this area. Rhodes was the influential colonialist with ambitions to bring the whole of Africa under British control, while increasing his already phenomenal personal wealth.

In 1870 Lobengula established his first base at the site now known as Old Bulawayo, just to the south of the present town, naming it KoBulawayo after the battle of Zwangendaba, which ended the civil war and opposition to his reign (see *Old Bulawayo*, page 304). He later moved to a site where State House, the president's official Bulawayo residence, now stands.

Meanwhile Rhodes, having made a fortune from diamonds in Kimberley, was looking for a 'second gold rand' (Witwatersrand being the first), convinced that gold could be successfully mined in Mashonaland and Matabeleland. It was crucial to take control of this area, so his agents set to work on Lobengula to extract a concession. The infamous Rudd Concession was drawn up, whereby Lobengula was duped into signing away his people's land and mineral rights. His forces stood no chance when Rhodes's well-armed British South Africa Company (BSAC) decided in 1893 to assert sovereignty over the area by engineering the Anglo–Ndebele War, ultimately resulting in Lobengula being chased from his territory, northwards across the Zambezi.

From 1894, with the Ndebele defeated and ruled by the BSAC, Bulawayo rapidly became a boom town filled with prospectors, traders and settlers. Leander Starr Jameson was charged with declaring the foundation of the town. The full text of his speech from the steps of the town's first hotel was: 'It is my job to declare this town open, gentlemen. I don't think we want any talk about it. I make the declaration now. There is plenty of whisky and soda inside, so come in.' The assembled crowd did just that.

But all was far from plain sailing. The Ndebele were more and more marginalised, exploited for their labour, subjected to the notorious 'hut tax' and having their cattle confiscated. Spurred on by the defeat of BSAC troops at the infamous Jameson Raid against the Boers in Transvaal, they began a brief and bloody uprising. Although the BSAC mustered sufficient troops to take the fight to the Ndebele the latter promptly retreated to the Matobo Hills and continued their strong resistance, effectively using guerrilla tactics against which the BSAC was ill-prepared, creating a stalemate. In what many biographers refer to as Rhodes's finest hour, he and five others 'fearlessly' rode unarmed into the Matobo Hills to meet the Ndebele *indunas* and negotiate peace.

Despite the fact that gold was never found here in commercial quantities, a successful farming and trading town rapidly developed around a central district of streets and avenues arranged in a grid system. Avenues running east–west were unimaginatively named 1–13, while north–south streets were originally named after Rhodes and his associates (latterly renamed after leaders in the liberation struggle). The 1920s saw the introduction of municipal electricity even before it was in London; sewerage schemes were introduced, and an Olympic-size swimming pool was built in 1926. In 1931 the first aerodrome opened to service the Imperial Airways London–Cape Town route, and in 1943 Bulawayo was granted city status. In the 1950s black housing became a political issue and under the leadership of a foresighted town clerk, Dr Hugh Ashton, later to become Director of Housing and Local Communities, plans were laid for decent brick-built, high-density houses, first leasehold, subsequently freehold. Many of these solidly build constructions are still in use in the very pleasant western suburbs.

GETTING THERE

BY AIR

International Bulawayo airport (BYO), although currently small and rather basic, is very user-friendly, largely because of its low throughput. For this reason you may consider it worthwhile to use it as your point of entry/exit in preference to Harare or Victoria Falls airport. From Johannesburg, South African Airways flies direct to Bulawayo, while British Airways (Comair) operates from Johannesburg to Bulawayo via Harare.

Domestic With the virtual demise of Air Zimbabwe there is currently no scheduled domestic service to Bulawayo although that situation is likely to change during the currency of this book, especially given the fact that work to upgrade the airport was already under way in late 2012.

BY TRAIN

There are no longer direct scheduled trains into Bulawayo from South Africa. Botswana rail has twice weekly services from Gaborone and Francistown and these are the only scheduled rail connections from neighbouring countries. The trip takes about 5 ½ hours and costs 30 pula (US$5) for standard class reclining seats. There are daily overnight services to and from Victoria Falls (12 hours) and Harare three times weekly (9 hours), both with first-class sleepers and both exceptionally cheap (around US$15). Over the past decade standards had slipped badly but there have been recent improvements, making this once again a pleasant, if somewhat basic, method of travel. Bench seats convert to bunks and single travellers are usually accommodated in same-sex, four-berth compartments, although the fare is cheap enough to buy two seats ensuring you have the compartment to yourself. Bedding is supplied (US$4) but there is currently no restaurant car. You should enquire at the publicity association (see page 295) for the latest service upgrades, as I have been told these are planned. For rail information call ✆ 322284. Bookings must be made at the station.

BY COACH

International Three South African coach companies, Greyhound (*www. greyhound.co.za*) Intercape (*www.intercape.co.za*) and Translux (*www.translux. com*), ply the route daily between Bulawayo and Johannesburg (14–16 hours) with comfortable, modern vehicles. Senatar Express (✆ 471456), Zebulon Express, Golden Motorways and Kalamazoo Eagle Liner – all of them Zimbabwean companies – have started operating daily services between Johannesburg and Bulawayo and some go on to Victoria Falls. Unfortunately I have tried phoning the latter three companies to no avail. It's a 24-hour trip costing approx US$100 end to end. The Johannesburg–Bulawayo journey takes about 17 hours. There is no central station in town for these coaches so you should contact the Bulawayo Publicity Association who will doubtless have up-to-date details of pick-up/drop-off points and schedules.

Domestic Bulawayo is a main stopping point on coach routes to and from Beitbridge, Harare and Victoria Falls but note that there's no central bus terminal and various companies pick up and drop off at a variety of locations in town. Keeping track of which companies ply these routes is difficult and which ones to recommend even more difficult in this ever-changing market. And it's not feasible to print schedules and fares in a book that will have a currency of several years.

Actually it would be quite good if the companies themselves published timetables! There is however one luxury company that seems to be consistent and reliable and actually has a useful website – Pathfinder (*pick-up 73A Fife St, cnr L Takiwira, opposite police station; \ 61778; www.pathfinderlx.com*). City Link and Senatar Express are also big players in the luxury market and their coaches are seen on the roads but their schedules seem unreliable by local reports. City Link (\ *783424*) picks up and drops off at Rainbow Group hotels in Harare, Bulawayo and Victoria Falls. Other companies to watch for are Senatar Express (*471456*), Tombs, Pioneer, PCG Motorways, KK Cheetah and Eagle Liner, but as above my phone enquiries have for one reason or another met with no success.

My experience and other feedback suggests that phone and internet enquiries can be enormously frustrating and there's no beating making a personal enquiry at a bus station, major hotel or tourism information service, and in Bulawayo there's no better place than the publicity association for current information.

SELF-DRIVE Bulawayo is within easy driving distance of central and southern towns including Beitbridge and Plumtree, the nearest border points from South Africa and Botswana, respectively. Road distances include Harare 439km/273 miles, Victoria Falls 439km/273 miles, Beitbridge 321km/199 miles, Masvingo 280km/174 miles and Plumtree 100km/62 miles.

GETTING AROUND

Using Cecil Rhodes's trademark grid system, it's easy to navigate around Bulawayo's city-centre streets, which were built wide enough for a wagon with a full span of oxen (24 pairs) to perform a U-turn. Many roads are lined with the fabulous blue *Jacaranda* and flaming-red flamboyant trees, creating a springtime riot of colour. Amongst newer buildings there is plenty of splendid Victorian colonial architecture, in the centre and in the leafy suburbs.

You can safely and easily walk to most interesting places in the centre but for a visit to the suburbs or outlying areas you'll need transport.

Note that once 12 Avenue leaves the city centre it becomes Esigodini Road, which is also referred to as Old Esigodini Road.

BY TAXI Metered taxis are the easiest and most reliable way to get around, and prices are low, though rounded up to the full dollar to avoid small change. There are good private taxi companies but they and their phone numbers are ever changing; the best places to find taxis are in ranks near the big hotels. Hotel front-desk staff can give you the numbers of reliable companies. If you are going outside the city centre, you'll find taxis thin on the ground for your return journey, so take a phone number or book your return in advance.

BY BUS Locals travel on packed, noisy commuter minibuses. These have fixed routes and fixed rates, but working out which goes where and when is not easy.

BY CAR
Car hire

🚗 **Avis** 99 Cnr Robert Mugabe Way & 10th Av; \685712; ⏱ 08.00–17.00 Mon–Fri, closed w/ends; airport office \226657; ⏱ 07.00–22.00 Sun–Fri, 07.00–21.00 Sat

🚗 **Europcar** 9a Africa Hse, Fife St & 10th Av; \679225, 74157; f 679225; airport office \226185
🚗 **UTc** Cnr G Silundika & 14th Av; \61402/3, 74701/2; e tours@byoutc.co.zw

Car parking Bulawayo's street parking system is rather hit and miss. In theory you have to buy meter-parking tokens at City Hall and these are zoned, to make it even more complicated. In practice no-one bothers with this system although there is a very slight chance you will be hit with a fine. This should be no more than US$5.

TOURIST INFORMATION

BULAWAYO PUBLICITY ASSOCIATION (*City Hall car park, cnr Leopold Takawira Av & Robert Mugabe Way;* ✆60867, 72969; e *bpa@netconnect.co.zw;* ⊕ *08.30–16.45 Mon–Fri, 08.30–12.00 Sat*) This should probably be your first stop. Val Bell and her staff are a mine of local information – quite unlike these offices in most towns. The difference here is that this one is supported by subscription rather than the municipality. The publicity association produces regularly updated lists of member hotels, lodges and restaurants; all are licensed by the ZTA, though BPA does not do its own vetting. But a chat with Val will point you in the direction of those with good reports.

The **National Parks and Wildlife Management Authority** is at 15th Avenue between Fort and Main St (✆63646/7; ⊕ *08.30–16.30 Mon–Fri, 08.30–14.30 Sat*).

TOUR OPERATORS

Several good companies in Bulawayo offer tours to the surrounding area.

Adventure Travel/Tours For Africa ✆66775, 023 466525; e tourzim@mweb.co.zw

Africa Spectacular ✆244990; m 0772 231819; e afspec@yoafrica.com

African Wanderer ✆241787; m 0772 224069; e wanderer@yoafrica.com; www.african wanderer.com

Black Rhino Safaris ✆241662; e blckrhino@ hotmail.com

Circle Court Tours ✆881309, 74595, 75230; e rhino-trails@netconnect.co.zw

Eastgate Tours & Travel ✆887402, 4881870; e eastgatetours@yahoo.com

Gemsbok Safaris ✆63906; e gemsbok@mweb. co.zw

Madlala Tours ✆201020; e madlalatours@zol. co.zw

Ngamo Safaris ✆76009, 76053; e pili@ ngamosafaris.co.zw

Paul Hubbard Historical Tours e hubcapzw@ gmail.com, resman@amalindacollection.co.zw

Safari Source m 0773 089958; e monika@ thesafarisource.com; www.thesafarisource.com

Southern Comfort Tours & Safaris ✆0712 630204; e southcom@netconnect.co.zw

The Travel Shop ✆74768/9; e enquiries@ travelshop.co.zw; www.thetravelshop.co.zw

⌂ WHERE TO STAY

There is a wealth of good places to stay around Bulawayo; as you drive around the residential areas it seems there is a lodge sign on almost every corner. The accommodations featured here are mostly drawn from the publicity association lists, and are only a selection of what's on offer. Note that 'Suburbs' in the Bulawayo context is the (unimaginative) name of a specific area to the east of the central business district. Note also that Suburbs has its own grid layout with east–west streets numbered 1–9, easily confused with numbered avenues in the city centre.

LUXURY

⌂ **Bulawayo Club** (16 rooms) Cnr 8th Av/Fort St (white colonnaded building with a scripted BC crest above the entrance); ✆64868/9; www.

bulawayoclub.com. Stay here if you want to slip back into the early years of last century & experience colonial luxury at its finest. This beautiful old building, steeped in local history

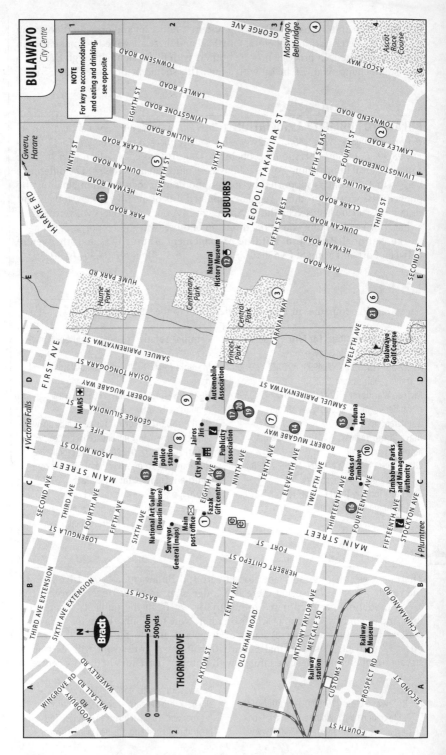

BULAWAYO
City Centre

NOTE
For key to accommodation
and eating and drinking,
see opposite

THORNGROVE

SUBURBS

Gweru, Harare

Victoria Falls

Masvingo,
Beitbridge

Ascot
Race
Course

ASCOT WAY

GEORGE AVE

TOWNSEND ROAD

LAWLEY ROAD

LIVINGSTONE ROAD

PAULING ROAD

CLARK ROAD

DUNCAN ROAD

HEYMAN ROAD

PARK ROAD

EIGHTH ST

NINTH ST

SEVENTH ST

SIXTH ST

FIFTH ST EAST

FOURTH ST

THIRD ST

SECOND ST

FIFTH ST WEST

LEOPOLD TAKAWIRA ST

TOWNSEND ROAD

LAWLEY ROAD

LIVINGSTONE ROAD

PAULING ROAD

CLARK ROAD

DUNCAN ROAD

HEYMAN ROAD

PARK ROAD

HARARE RD

HUME PARK RD

Hume Park

Centenary Park

Central Park

Princes Park

Natural History Museum

CARAVAN WAY

TWELFTH AVE

Bulawayo Golf Course

SAMUEL PARIRENYATWA ST

JOSIAH TONGOGARA ST

ROBERT MUGABE WAY

GEORGE SILUNDIKA WAY

FIFE ST

FIRST AVE

MARS

Automobile Association

Jairos Jiri

Publicity Association

City Hall

Main police station

National Art Gallery (Douslin House)

Surveyor General (maps)

Main post office

Fazak Gift centre

Induna Arts

Books of Zimbabwe

Zimbabwe Parks and Management Authority

MAIN STREET

JASON MOYO ST

SECOND AVE

THIRD AVE

FOURTH AVE

FIFTH AVE

SIXTH AVE

EIGHTH AVE

NINTH AVE

TENTH AVE

ELEVENTH AVE

TWELFTH AVE

THIRTEENTH AVE

FOURTEENTH AVE

FIFTEENTH AVE

STOCKTON AVE

LOBENGULA ST

FORT ST

HERBERT CHITEPO ST

TENTH AVE

CAXTON ST

OLD KHAMI ROAD

BASCH ST

SIXTH AVE EXTENSION

THIRD AVE EXTENSION

WOODBURY RD

WALSALL RD

WINGROVE RD

WAVERLEY RD

ANTHONY TAYLOR AVE

METCALF SQ

Railway station

Railway Museum

CUSTOMS RD

PROSPECT RD

CHINAMANO RD

SECOND ST

FOURTH ST

ROBERT MUGABE WAY

SAMUEL PARIRENYATWA ST

Plumtree

Bradt

N

0   500m
0   500yds

A B C D E F G
1 2 3 4

1 2 3 4 5 6 7 8 9 10 11 12 13 14 15 16 17 18 19 20 21

🛏 **Where to stay**
1 Bulawayo Club........................C2
2 Bulawayo Youth Hostel......F4
3 Caravan Park.........................E3
4 Holiday Inn............................G3
5 Jacana Lodge........................F2
6 Packers Paradise..................E4
7 Rainbow Hotel......................D3
8 Selbourne Hotel..................C2
9 The Grey's Inn.......................D2
10 Zak's Place.............................C4

✖ **Where to eat and drink**
11 26 on Park.............................F1
12 Art Grove...............................E3
13 Black Steer and Bulldog....C2
14 Bon Journee.........................D3
Bulawayo Club.............(see 1)
15 Cattleman Steakhouse......D4
16 Friar Tuck's............................C4
17 Golden Spur.........................D3
18 Horizons................................C2
19 Indaba Book Café................D3
20 Mary's Restaurant...............D3
21 Tendele Arts.........................E4

(the club was founded in 1895), has recently been restored inside & out: it's still a members' club but non-members can stay here & enjoy the facilities. These include their fine restaurant, Governors, spacious lounges, snooker room & an amazingly large members' bar (open to residents). **$$$**
🏠 **Nesbitt Castle** (9 suites) 6 Percy Av, Hillside; ☎282726; www.nesbittcastle.co.zw. Probably the best-known hotel in Bulawayo, this rather dark old replica castle must be the ideal place for locals to hold their wedding & bar mitzvah celebrations, though it's hardly 'Africa' for the tourist. It's a fabulous building in beautiful formal gardens built by the eccentric Theodore Holdengarde in the 1920s. Fascinated by British castles he'd visited, he built his own, apparently with no plans, simply drawing on his imagination and memories. Purchasing the castle in 1988 & renovating it after vandalism by 'squatters, satanists & arsonists', Digby Nesbitt turned it into a hotel, which opened for business in 1990. A tour round the place is fascinating – narrow passageways, twisty stone staircases, brushing past suits of armour to arrive at sumptuous lounges (separate gentlemen's & ladies', of course), billiard room & trophy room, complete with stuffed animals & elephant-foot umbrella stands. Lounges, bar & restaurant are cosily furnished with dark wood &

heavy drapes, as are the guest suites, 2 of which have 4-poster beds. Wonderfully atmospheric. As well as the usual facilities, you'll also find a gym & a sauna. **$$$**
🏠 **Rainbow Hotel** (170 rooms) Cnr Josiah Tongogara St & 10th Av, PO Box 1876; ☎881273/9; e reservations@rainbowbulawayo.com. This luxury hotel, the Rainbow group's flagship is by far the best-appointed town-centre accommodation & boasts all the usual facilities the well-heeled businessperson expects. **$$$**

UPMARKET
🏠 **Cresta Churchill Hotel** (50 rooms) Cnr Matopos Rd & Moffat Av, Hillside, c5km from town centre; ☎244243/4; e reservations@churchill. cresta.co.zw. You can't miss this big, mock-Tudor establishment. Public areas feature lots of heavy dark timber so although the 2 bars & restaurant are large, the atmosphere is cosy & welcoming. Rooms are light & many look into an inner courtyard with a large pool. All are en suite with DSTV & there's plenty of secure parking. **$$$**
🏠 **Holiday Inn** (157 rooms) Milnerton Av, Ascot; ☎252460; e pacro@africansunhotels. com; www.africansunhotels.com. You know exactly what to expect from a Holiday Inn. This one, with the usual amenities & facilities, is near Ascot racecourse, 2km from the city centre. For a dependable hotel without having to check out the rest, this is a good option. 2 dependable chain restaurants, the Italian-themed Panarotti's & a Spur steakhouse. **$$$**
🏠 **Southern Comfort Lodge** (6 chalets) 22 Jaywick Rd, Matsheumlope, signposted from Old Esigodini Rd; ☎281340; m 0773 246082; e southcom@netconnect.co.zw; www. southerncomfortlodge.com. This lovely lodge is set in 7ha with small buck wandering around & a catch-&-release fishing reservoir stocked with bream & bass. Spotless, thatched, twin-bed chalets are dotted around a central bar/dining room & look out onto a beautiful garden. Camping also available. Fresh eggs, milk & vegetables come from their own livestock & gardens. Craig & Lesley Hunt own the place; Craig, an ex pro hunter, is an expert on wildlife, in particular eagles & other raptors in the Matopos. He'll take photographers or birders to the best sites & runs tours, safaris & fishing trips in his luxury minibus. **$$**
🏠 **Banff Lodge Hotel** (10 rooms) Cnr Leander Av & Banff Rd, Hillside; ☎243176/7; e banff@

yoafrica.com. A beautiful old Cape Dutch building houses this popular family-run hotel, which lives up to the owner's offer of a 'home away from home'. Attractively decorated sgls, dbls & suites, set in pleasant gardens in this quiet suburb. Excellent value by local standards. **$$**

STANDARD

⌂ **Ingrid's Lodge** (7 rooms) 26 Essex Rd cnr Moffat Av; ☎241763, 023 406122; e ingolod@ mweb.co.zw. Ingrid is a German lady with a passion for cleanliness & efficiency, & all her rooms are immaculate. They are spacious, equipped with fridge & DSTV & set in a neatly tended garden complete with a good-sized pool. Expensive by local standards. **$$$**

⌂ **Motsamai Lodge** (22 rooms) 17 Tennyson Av, Malindela; ☎246201; m 0772 340126; e motsamai@iwayafrica.com. This pleasant & well-run lodge in a beautifully tended, shady garden has 10 of its rooms en suite, with more planned. Everything about it is clean & tidy. Cecilia, the charming owner, goes out of her way to make guests feel at home. Optional FB. **$$$**

⌂ **Granite Park Lodges** (4 self-contained, self-catering lodges) 3 Laidlaw Cl, Granite Pk, Bulawayo; ☎285908, 469983; e info@ graniteparklodges.com; www.graniteparklodges. com. Just 10mins from the CBD, well signed off Burnside Rd on the edge of town with natural gardens & a pleasant pool. Fully equipped kitchen, separate dbl bedroom with 2 twin beds, sofa bed in the living room, en-suite bathroom facilities with bath (shower over bath tub); private telephone; wood-burning braai. 3 of the lodges have a mezzanine floor with twin beds ideal for children & the Honeymoon Lodge has 1 queen-sized bed. **$$-$$$**

⌂ **Garda Lodge** (6 chalets) 167 Matopos Rd; ☎241961; e gardaita@netconnect.co.zw; www. gardalodge.com. Italians Carlo & Daniella run this family-owned lodge about 5km from the city centre. Their personal, friendly & helpful service earns them many recommendations. The lodge itself has spacious thatched bungalows including a 5-bed family room & the place has a safari theme including a well kept shady garden stocked with rather quirky animal statues. Free Wi-Fi. B&B only. **$$**

⌂ **Glen Lodge & Tours** (16 rooms) 8 Oregon Av, Newton West; ☎460269; m 0772 930169; e glenlodge@zol.co.zw; www.

glenlodgeandtours.com. A simple, friendly establishment with clean, good-size, plainly furnished en-suite twins & dbls in unremarkable surroundings. Dinner by request. **$$**

⌂ **The Grey's Inn** (20 rooms) Robert Mugabe Way & Leopold Takawira Av; ☎888318; e greysinn@gmail.com. A town-centre hotel under the same management as the Selborne, with similar facilities. Pleasant inner courtyard for drinks & snacks. No secure parking: you leave your car on the street & hope the security guard stays awake. **$$**

⌂ **Lalani Lodge** (30 rooms) 5 Derwent Rd, Fortunesgate; ☎281935; m 0773 700198; e lalani@comone.co.zw. This is a large horseshoe-shaped 2-storey thatched building in very pleasant gardens being completely refurbished in late 2012. Simply furnished rooms are a good size with tubs or showers, TV, tea & coffee. Meals are taken in a separate bar/open restaurant building. **$$**

⌂ **Musketeers Lodge** 42 Annabel Dr, Eleona, 9km from town on Matopos Rd; ☎246343; m 0775 168460/1; e musketeers@yoafrica.com. This is a very pleasant, well-established lodge offering B&B or full catering & with secure parking. Set on the edge of town bordering the Tshabalala Wildlife Sanctuary there's a peaceful atmosphere & excellent birding. DSTV & internet access available. Pre-booking is advisable, as when I visited there was no answer at the gate. **$$**

⌂ **Madlala Lodge** (19 rooms) 2 Sebakwe Av, Richmond, signposted 5km out of town (from Victoria Falls Rd turn into Glenville Dr & then Sebakwe); ☎201020; m 0775 459364; e madlalatours@zol.co.zw; www.madlala.co.zw. The main building of this quiet, peaceful lodge is a lovely old Cape Dutch house, & there are 3 other spacious self-catering rooms in a separate building, each with generous kitchen & lounge area. All are furnished to a high standard. All have DSTV & fridge. 12 additional rooms have been added in another block. FB on offer but bring your own alcohol. The charming & ebullient owner, Lois, prides herself on having taught home economics for 27 years, & knows a thing or two about running a lodge. Her husband runs Madlala Tours, one of the largest operators in Bulawayo. **$$**

⌂ **Parrot Lodge** (10 rooms) 3 Valeview Rd, Riverside, signposted off Beitbridge Rd about 6km from town centre; ☎280033; e parrot@comone. co.zw; www.parrot-lodge.co.zw. This out-of-town lodge, immaculately run by its Swiss owners, offers standard, VIP & family rooms, all large, en suite with DSTV & individually themed with huge animal murals. They have a pleasant saltwater pool & serve Swiss-style food on request. **$$**

🏠 **Selborne Hotel** (36 rooms) Leopold Takawira Av & George Silundika St, opposite City Hall;\65741/3; e selborne@ africaonline. co.zw; www.selborne.co.zw. This city-centre hotel, a colonial building dating from 1930, had a major refurbishment a decade ago & was rated then as one of the best in town. Since then it has faded again. It appeals more to the local business community than to tourists. Rooms are plain, large & functional. **$$**

🏠 **Zak's Place** (34 rooms) 129 Robert Mugabe Way;\881330; e zaksplace@telconet.co.zw. Another town-centre hotel, this friendly & reasonable place has a good reputation although there's nothing special about it. Rooms are en suite & have tea & coffee facilities. The best face an inner courtyard. You must park on the road & rely on the 24hr guard. **$$**

🏠 **Packers Paradise** 1 Oak Av, Suburbs; \251110/1; m 0712 515503; e packers@ netconnect.co.zw. Though backpackers have become a rare species in Zimbabwe, Packers has kept its accommodation open & in excellent condition. Prices are on the high side, but everything is clean, staff are friendly & facilities include internet access, payphone, self-catering kitchen (or meals on order) & free local pick-ups & transfers. **$$**

BASIC

🏠 **Emquameni Lodge** (3 cottages) Cnr Cecil Av & Banff Rd, Hillside;\241508; e interbus@ telconet.co.zw. This simple little lodge has brick & thatched, twin-bedded rooms equipped for self-catering. Although in a residential area, Cecil Av is quite busy & traffic noise may be a problem. **$**

🏠 **Travellers Guest House** 2 Banff Rd, Hillside; \246059, 245865; e ff@yoafrica.com. Good-value backpackers accommodation with sgls, dbls & a pool. Self-catering with b/fast US$10. **$**

🏠 **Bulawayo Youth Hostel** 52 Townsend Rd, Suburbs;\256488. Dormitory, sgl & dbl rooms available. Self-catering with fridges & cooking utensils provided. **$**

🏕 **Caravan Park** Caravan Way, off Park Rd; \233851, 231144; e lazsibanda@mweb.co.zw. At the south end of Centenary Park, a short walk from the Natural History Museum, this spacious, spotless municipal campsite also offers 2-person chalets with communal ablutions. Chalets **$$**, camping **$**

✖ WHERE TO EAT

Bulawayo is nowhere near as blessed as Harare when it comes to eating out and although new places keep starting up, often in peoples' houses converted for the purpose, few make a go of it long term. For that reason I include only the long-established eateries. Most places have vegetarian options but these can be quite limited. You are advised to check in advance if they are licensed to sell alcohol; if not bring your own and pay corkage. Many are closed on Sundays and Mondays. If your accommodation offers meals 'on request' that generally means very simple fare with little or no choice and cooked by a person with no great culinary skills.

✖ **Black Steer & Bulldog Pub** Meikles Mall, cnr Jason Moyo St & 6th Av;\75521, 65101. Steakhouse with chicken, burger & some vegetarian dishes.

✖ **Bon Journee** 105 Robert Mugabe Way & 10th Av;\64839. Plainly decorated, popular restaurant with good food – steaks, burgers, fish, pasta & spicy chicken – dishes, nice coffees & desserts. Closed Tue.

✖ **Bulawayo Club** 8th Av/Fort St (white colonnaded building with a scripted BC crest above the entrance);\64868/9; e resman@ campamalinda.co.zw; www.bulawayoclub.com. Excellent food served in truly elegant dining room.

✖ **Bulawayo Country Club** Old Esigodini Rd, 12mins from town centre. Mainly grills but they have a new seafood menu. Very good value.

✖ **Cattleman Steakhouse** 12th Av & Josiah Tongogara St;\76086. Best reputation in town for beef. Seafood also to be found on their quite extensive menu.

✘ **Friar Tuck's** Fife St & 14th Av; ☎69265. A good reputation going back many years although it seems to have gone out of favour with locals – another steakhouse.

✘ **Golden Spur** 85 Robert Mugabe Way & 8th Av; ☎70318. You can always rely on Spur, a family-friendly steakhouse chain offering the same menu throughout southern Africa. Their steaks are always good; also chicken & ribs.

✘ **Horizons** RG Level, Pioneer Hse Cnr Fife St/8th Av ☎67533, 67535; e horizon.bar.restaurant@gmail.com. This glitzy, modern restaurant/cocktail bar has a wide range of international dishes and is very popular so be sure to book. Open plan contemporary layout.

✘ **The Kraal Restaurant** Busters Sports Club, cnr Fairbridge way & Cecil Av; m 0712 401715, 0772 221692; e ratwors@gmail.com. Popular with locals for its good home cooking with specialities of steak, pork ribs & eisbein (pork knuckles). The ambience is very relaxed; caters to all ages & there's plenty of room outside for children to play.

✘ **New Orleans** Banff Lodge Hotel, Banff Rd & Leander Av, Hillside; ☎243176. Not a steakhouse! Decked out with jazz posters, & once nominated as Best Restaurant in Zimbabwe. Imaginative menu, modern-style cuisine. Very popular so book ahead.

LUNCHES AND COFFEE

⊑ **Art Grove** National Art Gallery. A favourite with 'locals who lunch' & ideal for resting your legs during a gallery visit. It's stylish, maybe even trendy, & the food is fresh, light & well presented. When I visited they had just launched a small evening menu.

⊑ **Banff Lodge Coffee Shop** Cnr Leander Av & Banff Rd, Hillside; ☎243176/7

⊑ **26 On Park** 26 Park Rd & 6th St, Suburbs; m 0713 196176. Round the corner from the Natural History Museum, this beautifully preserved colonial residence offers a range of light lunches as well as coffee & other refreshments. In good weather, eat on the veranda or try for a table in the garden.

⊑ **The Boma** Hillside Dams; ☎242490; www. hillside dams.com; ⊙ 09.00–17.00 Tue–Sun for light meals, snacks, fish & chips, coffee. Wireless internet.

⊑ **Indaba Book Café** 92 Josiah Tongogara/cnr 9th Av; ☎67068. Pleasant place for b/fast, coffees & lunches with Wi-Fi & books.

✘ **Mary's Restaurant** 88 Josiah Tongogara St; ☎76721, 64790

⊑ **Tendele Crafts** River Estate, 12th Av/Oak Av, Suburbs (next to Packers Paradise); m 0712 703431. Pleasant café in a small garden centre/craft shop annex.

ENTERTAINMENT AND NIGHTLIFE

Bulawayo has a thriving but ever-changing nightlife scene to suit both African and Western tastes (ironically, Western visitors tend to want African music while the locals go for Western rock). It's difficult to recommend anything because good places tend to be short-lived – they quickly get popular and crowded and locals say standards then slip. Check ads in the local paper and ask around. Note that good clubs have a smart-casual dress code, which translates as: if they don't have a code, don't go there. Smart-casual generally means no jeans, trainers or T-shirts.

SHOPPING

CURIOS AND CRAFTS Most of Bulawayo's shops are utilitarian, and the main interest for visitors is craftware. The following shops are crammed with Zimbabwe's typically creative, inventive and colourful artistic goods and curios.

⚒ **Art Gallery Gift Shop** Main St/L Takawira Av; ☎70721

⚒ **Ascot shopping complex** Gwanda Rd. Open-air craft displays.

⚒ **Fazak Gift Centre** Main St, opposite the post office; ☎882894. You can buy safari clothing too.

⚒ **Fife St Pavement Crafts** Fife St/L Takawira. Open-air craft displays.

⚒ **Tendele Craft Shop** Cnr 12th Av/Oak Av, Suburbs; m 0712 703431

⚒ **Induna Arts** 119b Josiah Tongogara St; ☎69175; m 0772 252525

Jairos Jiri Cnr Leopold Takawira Av & Robert Mugabe Way, by City Hall; ☎69147. All products here are made by disabled people.

Mzilikazi Art & Craft Centre From Old Falls Rd out of town; look for signs to Mpilo Hospital in Mzilikazi township. Here you'll find a community of potters, sculptors & painters centred on an art school set up to encourage latent talent. Works are on display for purchase & there's a small museum of the best. At another self-help project in the same area you can buy knitted goods, crochet, tapestries etc, in support of those who look after AIDS-orphaned children. These excellent, self-sustaining projects are well worth a visit.

GENERAL STORES The two biggest central supermarkets are Shoprite (walking distance from City Hall) and Haddon and Sly (Fife Street and 8th Avenue), a department store with a supermarket on the ground floor.

BOOKSHOPS
Kingstons 91 Jason Moyo St; ☎60869
Books of Zimbabwe 137a George Silundika St & 14th Av

OTHER PRACTICALITIES

CLINICS AND HOSPITALS
✚ Clicks A pharmacy at the cnr of Fife St & 9th Av
✚ Mater Dei Hospital Burns Rd, off Hillside Rd; ☎240000/5
✚ 24hr Medical Centre 93 Josiah Tongogara St; ☎881051
✚ Medical Air Rescue Service (MARS) 12 Robert Mugabe Way; ☎78946; emergency: 64082; www.mars.co.zw. A paramedic & evacuation service (see *Health* in *Chapter 3*).

IMMIGRATION OFFICE At Leopold Takawira Avenue and Jason Moyo Street.

INTERNET CAFÉS You'll find Wi-Fi broadband in many of the accommodations, with internet cafés springing up throughout the city centre. Try:

☐ Netconnect Bulawayo Centre, Main St, between 9th & 10th Av
☐ Econet 76 Robert Mugabe Way & Leopold Takawira Av
☐ One Stop Communications Mership Hse, 9th Av & Main St; ☎881619

POLICE STATION At the corner of Fife Street and Leopold Takawira Avenue.

POST OFFICE On Main Street at 8th Avenue; ⊕ 08.30–16.30 Monday–Friday, 08.00–11.00 Saturday.

WHAT TO SEE AND DO

NATURAL HISTORY MUSEUM (*Centenary Pk on Leopold Takawira Av;* ☎*250045/6; www.naturalhistorymuseumzimbabwe.com* ⊕ *09.00–17.00 except Christmas Day & Good Friday; entry US$5*) This well-laid-out museum – Zimbabwe's largest – is circular in design and on two floors, with the ground floor devoted to natural history and geology while most of the first floor focuses on humans. The first display is right at the entrance, where a magnificent, tragic old chap 'welcomes' you in: the second-largest elephant ever to have been shot and stuffed. A series of informative dioramas show animals in their habitats, including a gory one of a pride of lions with a disembowelled zebra. Other stuffed mammals show you the difference between an aardwolf and an aardvark, or between tiny night apes (*pukunyoni*) and their larger cousins, the bushbabies. You learn that, of 180 species of mammals in Zimbabwe, 50 are bats. The wildlife galleries feature birds, insects, butterflies and moths, reptiles and sea life.

The geology section explains in some detail the country's physical make-up and its huge selection of minerals (complete with a mock-up of a mine shaft), with displays of key metals and minerals and their uses. At the gold display, curators have found it necessary to point out that the ingots in the cabinet are not real. Just in case!

Upstairs you may find the mankind section a little lacking in detail, but then there is a lot of anthropology to work through. From an excellent display of Stone Age implements we are taken rather too swiftly through the centuries, stopping to touch on tribal customs, music and arts, warriors, hunters and missionaries, finally to dwell, inevitably, on Cecil John Rhodes. This is a 'must visit' place, and you should allow several hours to do it justice.

RAILWAY MUSEUM (*Follow Herbert Chitepo St south towards the cooling towers, cross over 14th Av & after the road bears sharply to the right, turn right on Prospect Av for 200–300m; no contact details available* ⊕ *08.00–16.30 daily; entry fee nominal*) Tucked away on a siding behind the station, exactly where you might expect to find it, is this gem of a museum dedicated to one of Rhodesia's engineering triumphs, its railway system. It's reckoned by steam enthusiasts to be a world-class collection of colonial-era rolling stock, including not only a large number of steam and diesel locomotives in splendid condition – some still functioning – but also an excellent selection of carriages. These include Rhodes's own coach, specially built in the USA for De Beers Consolidated Mines. As well as being his regular long-distance transport, it carried his coffin on his final journey from Cape Town to Bulawayo. Clamber around the coaches for a glimpse of the lifestyle of colonial gentry, and marvel at the beautiful carpentry and metal fixtures and fittings adorning the first-class accommodation. Then move on and see how the poor people travelled.

A favourite loco is the beautiful old *Jack Tar* which, having served throughout the construction of Victoria Falls bridge (including being dismantled and slung in pieces across the ravine on a Blondin line), subsequently became the first train to cross the bridge after its completion. There is a museum ticket office, transplanted from Shamva station. Railway buffs can bring less enthusiastic partners here safe in the knowledge that there is plenty of interest for everyone.

For more on the rolling stock go to www.geoffs-trains.com and follow links to the Bulawayo Railway Museum. Steam rail enthusiasts should also check this website for details of forthcoming tours of Zimbabwe.

NATIONAL ART GALLERY (*Douslin Hse, cnr Main St & Leopold Takawira Av;* ⟍ *70721, 71305; www.nationalgallerybyo.com.*⊕ *10.00–17.00 Tue–Sun, 10.00–12.00 Sat; entry US$1*) This fine building, designed by William Douslin and without doubt the most beautiful in downtown Bulawayo, was completed at the end of 1900, with Willoughby's Consolidated Co its first occupant in February 1901. Just days before that, George Harker, the building's contractor, told his wife that he would go bankrupt over the building, and committed suicide. Another point of interest is that due to the high cost and general shortage of cement at the time, the foundations are only six inches deep, with the building resting on granite rocks sunk in lime. It was known as Willoughby's Building from 1900 until 1957, and for 50 of those years, 12 rooms remained locked. It was thought they might be the rooms of some of Sir John Willoughby's private regiment who failed to return from the Boer War. When the rooms were unlocked in 1952 they revealed carbines and weapons dating from the Boer War, but other contents suggest the occupants must have been high-ranking officers, not lowly soldiers. Rudyard Kipling spent some time in rooms here.

Willoughby's was succeeded in 1957 by African Associated Mines, and this splendid building acquired the illustrious name of Asbestos House. Only when the Bulawayo Art Gallery purchased the building in September 1980 did the name change to commemorate the architect. It is a protected building but perhaps strangely is not a national monument. Today the gallery is home to both traditional and modern art, with regular exhibitions featuring local artists. The permanent collection features a range of ethnographic displays representing the country's key cultures and their arts, including basketry, weaving, carvings both wood and stone, sculpture and painting.

BULAWAYO HISTORICAL TOURS (*For reservations, details and prices contact Paul Hubbard* e *hubcapzw@gmail.com, resman@campamalinda.co.zw; www. campamalinda.com*) Archaeologist and historian Paul Hubbard, who has made a significant input to this book, runs a series of fascinating and very enjoyable historical tours of Bulawayo and the surrounding area in conjunction with the Amalinda Collection and the Bulawayo Club.

Prospectors' pub crawl Paul adds 'imbiber' to his other impressive credentials and offers this tour as a unique way to explore Bulawayo's architectural splendour and exciting pioneer history. These pub crawls recreate the journey of 19th-century prospectors as they returned to Bulawayo each day from the nearby gold mines. After handing over their findings for cash at the gold exchange, the prospectors then regularly embarked on a time-honoured route around town. The tour is flexible: similar to full-participation safaris, partakers can frequent all the available pubs, making the most of their pleasures in true prospector spirit, or, if less alcoholically minded, just stop off at each site and concentrate firmly on the historical intake. Visitors can even simply experience a few pubs with Paul. Tours are flexible and can last up to a full day and cost £90 per person for two people, or £45 per person for groups with a minimum of four (US$ price at relevant exchange rate). They are typically undertaken on foot, in true prospector-style, but again, like safaris, there's a back-up vehicle for the weary. No cameras are allowed!

Bulawayo of yesteryear War and siege, boom and bust, development and demolition, Bulawayo has all this and more crammed into its short history. This tour aims to immerse you in an African town and provides a unique viewpoint on urban history in an African context.

War of warriors: Mzilikazi's footprints This is your chance to trace the footsteps of one of the greatest African warriors of all time, King Mzilikazi, ruler of the Matabele. First you'll be propelled back in time to the heady days of the late 1800s, with the smells, sights and the rhythm of pre-colonial homes and the colonial battlefields of Matabeleland. The ebb and flow in the fortunes of war are realised, brought to life in a walking tour of the sites of struggle in and around the hills. Three- and five-day tours take you back in time with a fantastic vibrancy. Hosted at the famous Camp Amalinda.

There are also tours to nearby ancient monuments.

HILLSIDE DAMS (*Signposted off Hillside Rd nr Moffat St*) These two small reservoirs offer a pleasant, close-to-town location for picnics and general chilling out. The lawns are well tended and there's a small aloe garden. The lower reservoir features a bandstand for Sunday concerts, but in recent years the place became very run-down and with security issues after dusk. Fortunately, the venue has been turned into a conservancy leased by a group of local residents and heavily upgraded – it's now very popular with much more security, grounds cleaned out and a very busy restaurant, The Boma (see *Lunches and coffee*, page 300).

UMGUZA DAM (*From Victoria Falls Rd, turn right at bottle store & filling station & follow signs*) This recreational area is used by day visitors from the boating and fishing fraternity. There is a large communal seating *boma* overlooking the lake, with overgrown gardens and campsite, and on my last visit the whole place, including the boats, was decidedly run-down. It seems to be little visited these days but if you are desperate to get away from the hustle and bustle of the city, consider a drive out here. Bring your own catering requirements and camping chairs.

TSHABALALA WILDLIFE SANCTUARY (*NP Category 3; 10km south of Bulawayo on Matopos Rd*) In a country that is so well stocked with the 'Big Five' and with Matobo National Park next door, this wildlife sanctuary (operated by the Zimbabwe National Parks and Wildlife Management Authority) may at first sight seem a little tame. But this is part of its attraction, because you are free to explore the roads and trails on foot, by bicycle or, better still, on horseback. There are no predators, but a good selection of plains game including giraffe, wildebeest, zebra, tsessebe, kudu and other antelope. It's an excellent place to take a break from a busy sightseeing schedule. There are no catering facilities so bring your own refreshments.

OLD BULAWAYO (⊕ *S20 18 12 E28 37 41; take Hillside Rd, which becomes Burnside Rd & then Douglasdale; after about 14km turn right onto Criterion Mine Rd for 6km; entry US$10*) In August 2010 a bush fire completely destroyed the *kraal* site here (although the museum remains) and at the time of writing (2012) there had been no progress on the promised restoration. I leave the description here from the first edition in the slight hope that during the currency of this book the work will have been completed. The Bulawayo Publicity Association will have the latest news on this.

After his father died in 1869, Lobengula settled at this site about 16km southeast of today's city, naming it Gibixhegu. It was not until 1870, after a prolonged succession struggle arising from uncertainty over whether his elder brother Nkulumane was alive, that Lobengula was eventually proclaimed king, whereupon he renamed the settlement KoBulawayo, after Shaka's town of a similar name in Zululand. Though an exact translation is impossible, its meaning has to do with killing and persecution, although it is debated whether this was in recognition of blood shed in establishing the Ndebele nation or a reflection of his own bloody succession battle.

Although only the royal *kraal* remains today, in semi-restored form, this area was then a town of huts and cattle *kraals* housing up to 20,000 people, a multi-ethnic group assimilated or conquered on the way from South Africa.

The site comprises three main elements, which together will occupy two or three hours of your time. The first port of call is a museum, opened on the site in October 2006, tracing Ndebele development from the *mfecane* when Mzilikazi and others broke away from Shaka's warring regime in Zululand. Visit this first to set the historical scene and context.

Lobengula's reconstructed enclosure – in need of some repair – is only a few paces from the museum. The reconstruction, carried out in association with Birmingham University, is based on archaeological and ethnological research, and pictorial images from the time. The *isigodlo* or royal enclosure, considered the Ndebele capital, is protected by a sturdy, 2m-high *mopane* wood A-frame palisade. Immediately inside are two small cattle byres signifying the importance of cattle to the Ndebele. The large beehive-shaped huts, made from several semicircular frames woven together to form a dome, are of a style reflecting Lobengula's Zulu origins. Only after moving on from here did he adopt the region's more familiar thatched mud (pole and *daga*) style of hut. One hut was for cooking while the others housed the king, his wives and sister, and possibly children.

Two other more modern-looking structures were built for him by missionaries. Lobengula had been given a wagon – a prestigious vehicle – in return for granting the Jesuits permission to establish a mission near his capital. In 1879 they built a thatched stone shed for this cherished wagon, and this was reconstructed in 2000. The Jesuits also built the king a brick house, though it is thought he preferred to sleep in his thatched hut, while his sister occupied the house. The restored house serves as an interpretive centre, with information about the royal enclosure itself, together with displays showing Lobengula's dealings with traders, missionaries and concession hunters, especially Rhodes. Opposite the entrance to the enclosure is a large tree under which Lobengula held his *indabas*. It is said he loved his wagon so much he would use it as a stage.

Some 200m from the *indaba* tree, a path on the left leads to what remains of the Jesuit mission. Bought from a trader in 1879, this brick and stone house, with its own compound, was once a thriving mission right at the heart of this population of 'black heathens'. It is now an overgrown, derelict ruin, but visit it anyway and try to imagine what life was like for those earnest Christians, toiling away in their Victorian clothes under the African sun, largely unrewarded by any conversions. Though Lobengula moved away in 1881, destroying the settlement by fire as he left, the mission remained until 1888.

DIANA'S POOL (⊕ *S20 27 39 E28 53 08; take the Beitbridge road from Bulawayo to turn-off on right, about 13km south of Esigodini or 8km north of Mbalabala; follow dirt road signed to Tshabezi Resort to village junction; pool signposted to the left*) This tree-shaded, grassy picnic spot southeast of Bulawayo is beside one of the region's characteristic granite formations, here forming the bed of a small river. Stroll down a series of massive rock slabs to a pool where the stream collects before plunging away beneath you. Mind how you go: the rocks are slippery. The pool is tempting on a hot day, but bilharzia is a risk where the water's not flowing swiftly although the greatest danger is from people diving in believing the pool to be quite deep. It isn't and people have been severely injured as a result. Day visitors should check in with the caretaker at the entrance and expect to pay a nominal entrance fee.

Where to stay
Standard
🏠 **Embizeni Lodges** (2 chalets) ✆ 284019; e pitevelde@netconnect.co.zw; www.embizeni. net. These pleasantly furnished chalets set close to

Diana's Pool & amongst rocky gardens, each have 2 spacious bedrooms with 2 sgl beds, shower, toilet, a fully equipped kitchen with a small gas fridge & stove & a large veranda with adjacent *braai*. The loft sleeps an extra 2 people on request. This is a perfectly peaceful place to spend a night or 2 just chilling out amidst the matopos rocks & scenery but you'll need to bring all catering stocks with you. *US$50 per night per chalet for 4 people.*

CYRENE MISSION CHAPEL (*On Cyrene Rd, a dirt road connecting Plumtree & Kezi rds: from Plumtree Rd, turning on left about 25km from Bulawayo, then 2km on left; from Kezi Rd, turning about 30km from town on right, just past 2nd entrance to national park, then 10km along dirt road;* ⊕ *07.00–09.00, 09.30–13.00 & 14.00–17.00 daily*) As this is a functioning place of worship, avoid visiting on Sundays unless you want to join the service. There is no admission charge but you will find a collecting box at the entrance to the chapel.

In January 1940, the Cyrene School opened on the site of a previously unsuccessful school for delinquent boys. Its first principal was Canon Edward 'Ned' Paterson, who taught the usual academic subjects along with useful skills such as woodwork, metalwork, cattle management, the basics of agriculture and vegetable gardening. But he was also an inspirational artist, determined to draw out the artistic talent he felt was latent in his pupils.

He did not so much 'teach' art, as 'encourage' it; there were no books with pictures to copy. As one pupil later described it, 'he sent us away to think and then told us to paint our think'. Using petrol as a solvent, they painted directly onto the damp plaster walls, the resulting frescoes brightening the chapel and illustrating the scriptures as well. On every wall of this beautiful and vividly decorated chapel, inside and out, are Africanised biblical scenes as seen through the eyes of his pupils. The paintings at the altar end are by Paterson himself, the rest by his students. The finely worked, wooden main doors, depicting the life of John the Baptist, were carved by Sam Songo, a pupil disabled with polio.

In 1944, just four years after the school opened, they held a successful exhibition in Bulawayo, and in 1947 were honoured with a visit by the Queen of England and Princess Margaret. This was followed by an exhibition in London.

Cyrene art became a 'school' in its own right, with exhibitions and private galleries displaying their works worldwide. Ned Paterson retired in 1953 but the mission continues as a secondary school, with a fine reputation for teaching art. A separate interpretive centre provides details of the mission's development, and information on the chapel's cash-strapped restoration project.

HOPE FOUNTAIN MISSION (✿ *S20 15 51 E28 39 13; take Old Esigodini Rd out of town, turn right just after Rio Hotel & follow the signs; at entrance to girls' school turn right down rough dirt track; after 200m look up on the left for the church*) The second-oldest mission in the country doesn't come close to Cyrene or the Serima Mission (see *Gweru* in *Chapter 5*, pages 186–7) in artistic splendour, but is worth a side trip from Bulawayo. It's a simple, even austere, rural chapel but the interior walls are studded with photographs and inscriptions that trace the history of the missionaries and headteachers who ran the mission and the adjacent girls' boarding school.

John Boden Thomson founded the mission in 1870 and worked here for seven years before he was succeeded by Charles and Elizabeth Helm, who stayed for 39 years; both are buried in the grounds. In 1896 the mission was destroyed during the first *chimurenga*, the rebellion against the white settlers. George Wilkerson arrived that same year, trained locals as builders and built the present church, later establishing Hope Fountain's Industrial Institute. The girls' school was founded in 1915, the teacher training school in 1927.

It's interesting to note that while he was here, Charles Helm was instrumental in developing the Rhodesian ridgeback breed of dog for hunting lions.

SWALLOW ROOST AT HOW MINE (✹ *S20 18 21 E28 46 43; from the Hillside area take Old Esigodini Rd out of town towards the Beitbridge rd; at the equestrian centre take the first turning right, signed to How Mine, for about 11km to the mine complex gate*) You do not have to be a dedicated birder to marvel at one of nature's truly spectacular shows. During the summer months, hundreds of thousands of barn or European swallows return each night to roost in a stand of eucalyptus trees in the scrappy grounds of How Mine. Aim to get here around 17.45, bring binos and a camping chair (maybe an umbrella too!), and settle down to watch the birds cloud the sky as they swoop and spiral down from huge heights. (If Hitchcock's film, *The Birds*, spooked you, best leave this off your itinerary.) Their shrill twittering makes conversation difficult, and it's impossible to imagine how each can find a spare inch of branch to sleep on.

Barn swallows breed in Europe during the warm months and return for Zimbabwe's summer from November onwards. Their 12,000km migration takes about 34 days – an amazing 350km per day. This nightly congregation attracts a variety of raptors looking for an easy meal, so you may also be lucky enough to see bat hawks, Lanner falcon, European hobby, steppe and Wahlberg's eagles.

Many Bulawayans have no idea this place exists, so you'll need to make your own way here. You'll get nothing but friendly greetings from passing mine workers or incredulity from giggling children who wonder why tourists would drive out to their village.

The guard at the mine gate will ask your business; just say you've come to see the birds and you'll be admitted with a smile. Follow the road, bearing left before the mine entrance to a small derelict supermarket under the eucalyptus trees. Parking here risks disturbing the birds, so carry on to the designated parking and viewing spot. Afterwards you may wish to thank the cheerful but underpaid gate guard with a small gratuity.

You will be driving back to town in the dark, as the best bird action only happens just before nightfall, but it's a quiet road; just watch out for the pot-holes.

KHAMI RUINS (*NP Category 3; 22km from Bulawayo; go west on 11th Av, which becomes Old Khami Rd, passing through several townships; just when you think you're lost you'll find a sign to the ruins on the right;* ⊕ *08.00–16.30 daily; entry US$10, children US$5*) Although at 35ha they are significantly smaller than Great Zimbabwe (see Chapter 5), the Khami Ruins (also spelt Khame or Kame) are a designated UNESCO World Heritage Site. Reconstruction has created not only a fascinating historical site but also a pleasant place to spend half a day. The reconstructed walls, with their simple yet intricate decorative patterns, provide plenty of scope for the enthusiastic photographer. A small, rather disappointing museum at the entrance may have the useful *Trail Guide to the Khami National Monument* for sale, but you're more likely to find it in advance at the publicity association in Bulawayo. The site comprises two main areas of interest, the Hill Complex and the Outlying Hut Platforms to the south.

History This area has seen continuous human habitation for perhaps 40,000 years. There is plenty of archaeological evidence here of the development of Stone Age communities and of Iron Age trading with peoples from the east coast, in parallel with peer communities in the Great Zimbabwe area (note the wonderfully out-of-place Ming pottery found on site and now displayed in the museum as evidence of their far-flung trade). Agriculture, cattle raising and trade were by now the main occupations. While Great Zimbabwe rose to prominence in the 13th and 14th centuries it wasn't until the 15th century that construction began at Khami, generally considered the capital of the Shona Torwa state. The timing and the evidence here suggest that Torwa arose as a direct result of the collapse of Great Zimbabwe.

Structures and construction methods differ from those at Great Zimbabwe but the similarities indicate that both belonged to the same cultural tradition. Whereas at Great Zimbabwe stone walls enclosed or separated groups of huts, here they served as retaining walls for the creation of terraces on which huts were then built. The Khami site reveals more decoration: layered check, chevron, herringbone and other patterns abound in the reconstructed areas. Structures at both sites reflect the status and prestige of their royal residents.

Khami, in common with its predecessor 250km to the east, enjoyed only a brief period of occupation before the invading Rozwi toppled the Torwa and razed it to the ground in the late 17th century.

Such was the spiritual significance of the place that it was kept a well-guarded secret from the white settlers, only 'discovered' in 1893 after Lobengula's death. Excavations by the Rhodesia Ancient Ruins Company resulted in the destruction of many important artefacts in the greedy search for treasures. It was not until 1947 that the first serious studies were undertaken, by one K R Robinson, an inspector from the Department of Historical Monuments. Archaeological investigation continues, albeit in a rather piecemeal manner; more evident is the reconstruction work being carried out by professionals and volunteers from Zimbabwe and other countries in the region.

HILL COMPLEX Archaeological finds, as well as its situation at the top of a hill, suggest this was the royal enclosure, the residence of the king (*mambo*). This area has seen the most reconstruction, notably the beautifully decorated retaining walls that form the three main platforms on the hill. Following the track from the museum, you ascend the platforms, winding through narrow stone passageways originally roofed with *daga* (clay). The uppermost platform had commanding views over the Kame River to the east, as well as over hundreds of dwellings across the surrounding hillsides. This platform was originally the site of at least nine *daga* huts; the positions of most are clearly evident. Vertical recesses in some of the plastered passage walls originally held roof-supporting wooden poles. The huts would have served primarily as dwellings, although carved ivory as well as other metalwork artefacts found on the steps of the semicircular hut platform at the top of the passageway suggest that this one was used for rituals and ceremonies.

The most northerly of the platforms has the remains of at least three huts, but the main point of interest is a stone cross, thought to have been placed here by a Portuguese missionary. Although its origin and relevance are uncertain, locals come here on Sundays to pray with their hymns beautifully echoing across the site. Many leave coins as offerings to the ancestors.

The tiny coloured paint spots applied to many stones around the site are part of an intricate code used by reconstruction teams, enabling them to replace the stones in their correct positions.

Outlying hut platforms A number of smaller hut platforms are to the south of the Hill Complex, near the museum and reservoir. These would presumably have housed the second level of royalty, the king's wives and various dignitaries. The most prominent feature is the Precipice Platform, a long retaining wall beautifully decorated with a check pattern but now inaccessible due to the dam. Not far from the dam wall is a rock gong, a granite boulder shaped and balanced in such a way that when struck with a rock it rings like a bell. A similar gong can be found at the Ziwa ruins near Nyanga (see page 364).

It's interesting to find that the Torwa took time out for play. You'll find some *tsoro* game boards in this area, the most obvious being outside the museum but also on the way to the reservoir. The boards, carved out of stone, comprise four rows of eight hollows, each containing rounded river pebbles. Players manoeuvre the pebbles around the board until the winner eventually possesses all of them. It's still a popular game and you can buy wooden versions of the board at many craft stalls.

See page 303 for details of a tour company that features Khami as well as Great Zimbabwe and the ruins around Gweru.

MATOBO HILLS

Less than an hour's drive south of Bulawayo lies one of Zimbabwe's, if not southern Africa's, most dramatic rock landscapes. To describe this area, which includes the Matobo National Park, as a place of outstanding natural beauty is something of an understatement. Copywriters struggle to convey the geological majesty of the place, with adjectives from 'massive' and 'domineering' to 'spiritual' and 'weird'.

Granite is the building material and weather the artist. The area gets your attention with two completely different rock forms, both the result of the same geological processes. Most dramatic are the balancing rock *kopjes*: huge angular blocks of granite piled on top of and beside one another, forming pillars and stacks, like a giant child's building blocks. Most dramatic in scale, however, are the massive, bald *dwalas* or 'whalebacks', grey granite hills rising from the surrounding woodland and criss-crossed with fault lines, some so intricate they look like giant hieroglyphics. Matobo, in fact, is translated as 'bald heads' allegedly coming from a joke made by Mzilikazi.

Hundreds of caves and rock shelters created by the same weathering processes were later inhabited and decorated by descendants of the world's most ancient peoples; indeed this is one of the few areas in the world proven to have supported continuous human occupation for over 40,000 years.

Most maps and written media use the name Matobo but in conversation this area is usually referred to as 'the Matopos'.

FORMATION The geology of these apparently logic-defying hills is in fact relatively easy to understand. Eons ago molten rock was continuously forced upwards under tremendous pressure, solidifying at the surface to form hills and peaks. As upper layers cooled and solidified, they were pushed up from below by more molten rock, which itself subsequently solidified. This caused a layered effect deep inside the new rock. Over millennia, the softer land surface was weathered away, exposing the harder granite that we see today. The criss-cross marks on the domes are fractures caused by the cooling process.

Weathering – expansion and contraction from temperature changes, abetted by wind and rain – has gone to work on these fault lines, gradually changing the landscape. Some fractures beneath the surface have caused the rock to peel off like layers of an onion, while others running deep into the rock have caused it to split into boulders.

One of the best places to observe both types of fracture is at View of the World (see page 316), site of Cecil Rhodes's grave. As you cross the granite slabs towards the grave, tap the surface with a rock; where it sounds hollow the granite beneath you is 'exfoliating', soon (in geological terms) to crumble and slide away. In the grave area, one collection of boulders, obviously split from a much larger one, look like they would fit back together with no trace of the join.

Bambata Cave (see page 312) is a spectacular example of 'onion peel' exfoliation, with the softer interior of this perfectly formed dome having been weathered away over the millennia.

🏠 **WHERE TO STAY** The following are private lodges located just outside the park in the Matopos area. National Parks accommodation is listed on pages 316–7.

Luxury

🏠 **Camp Amalinda** (9 lodges) Matobo Rd, 48km from Bulawayo; 📞 64868/9, 881964; m 0712 215904; e resman@amalindacollection. co.zw; www.campamalinda.com. The approach track from the main Matopos road suggests this may be a rather special place as your vehicle picks its way over one of the region's trademark granite slabs. It's only a few minutes from town but by the time you arrive at reception you feel you are in the heart of the Matopos. This is one of Zimbabwe's architectural gems, in complete sympathy with Mother Nature, with the lodge built onto the side of the hills. Luxurious chalets dotted amongst the rocks are a wonderland of creative design using simple, natural but dramatic components. Massive rocks jut into the rooms to form walls, even furniture. Private outdoor showers may be a bit of a safari camp cliché but are still a wonderful way to cool off. One of the 2 refurbished honeymoon suites has a rope bridge to its own private lookout. There's a library full of Africa classics, a natural cave wine cellar & a stunning pool, or pamper yourself with one of Amalinda's speciality spa treatments. As well as game drives, walks & rock-painting tours, they have a cultural tour taking in a local school

which has many projects sponsored by the camp & its guests. **$$$$$**

🏠 **Big Cave Camp** (8 chalets) Matobo Rd, approx 45km from town; 📞 244990, +27 (0)82 5798811; m 0772 23181; e reservations@ bigcave.co.za; www.bigcave.co.za. This is another wonderful lodge built onto the granite hillside. It has charming A-frame thatched chalets & a spacious, cave-style *boma* lounge/bar looking over a boulder-strewn Matopos vista. There's a pool & outdoor bar area right on the top of a huge granite whaleback, ideal for sundowners; then you can sit around a log fire beneath a huge overhanging rock. It's all in an 800ha private estate bordering the national park. They offer guided drives & walks on the property as well as trips to local places of interest. Book ahead, as they tend to keep the entrance gate locked. **$$$**

Upmarket

🏠 **Matobo Hills Lodge** (17 lodges) 📞 471225; m 0772 611223; e fruitbat@yoafrica.com. Since a change of ownership this lodge, situated in a private reserve bordering the national park, has been receiving a complete refurbishment. The thatched rondavels are set on a granite outcrop, with a separate lounge/bar offering

---

MOPANE FLIES

Before you decide to camp or picnic at Maleme Dam (or anywhere else in the country for that matter) have a little walk around. On two visits in November I was plagued by swarms of *mopane* flies. These tiny, persistent bees (not flies) are attracted to sweat and to the moisture around your eyes and mouth. They don't sting, but they are absolutely unbearable and within minutes you will be looking for somewhere else to stay. (If you care to follow them back to their nests, frequently in termite mounds, you can apparently dig in and discover their tiny rounded honeycombs, containing delicious dark honey. Please steal it from them; they deserve it for making our lives a misery.)

MATOBO NATIONAL PARK

360° panoramic views. The changes had not been completed by the time of going to press, but expect this place to be up there with the best in this region and good value for money. **$$$**

🏠 **The Farmhouse** (12 chalets) 45km from town along Kezi Rd nr Bambata Cave, on the boundary of the national park; 📞 65970 0383 218; **m** 0775 051964; **e** zimsafaris@yoafrica. com/farmhouse.lodge@gmail.com; www. graniteridge.com. The Farmhouse, subsequently named Granite Ridge Lodge, has now reverted to its original name. Comfortable & nicely appointed chalets with self-catering facilities are set in 400ha of wooded gardens & bush, home to zebra, wildebeest, tsessebe & other plains game. Winter nights get chilly so electric blankets are supplied. The main, colonial-style building houses a bar, lounge & restaurant. Excellent views with horseriding, walks and abseiling make

MATOBO NATIONAL PARK

For listings, see pages 310–11 and 316–17

🛏 **Where to stay**
1 Big Cave Camp
   Black Eagle Lodge (see 5)
2 Camp Amalinda
   Imbila Executive Lodge (see 5)
3 Matobo Hills Lodge
4 Mtsheleli Dam
5 Rest Camp
6 The Farmhouse
7 Togwana Dam

it great for families. Sun lunch is popular with Bulawayans so book a table if you want to join them. Camping is available but you may share the site with overlanders. They offer game drives & walks into the park & access to a little-known cave painting site, as well as trips to Bambata Cave. **$$**

MATOBO NATIONAL PARK (*NP Category 2; well signposted off the Matopos Rd;* ⏲ *06.00–18.00*) At 425km² this is one of Zimbabwe's smallest national parks, yet it is second only to Victoria Falls National Park in terms of visitor numbers. Apart

Paul Hubbard (e *hubcapzw@gmail.com*), an independent archaeologist and associate researcher in the Monuments and Antiquities Department of the Natural History Museum, has kindly supplied the following information.

Tourists are advised to visit only the sites mentioned here as they are easily accessible and show the full range of the region's art. The best-preserved paintings are seldom visited, and for this reason only a few of the thousands of known sites have been opened to the general public. Please help protect this heritage by not visiting closed sites. Damage or interference with rock art is an offence punishable by law. Any archaeological sites discovered by the public should be reported to officials of National Museums and Monuments, at Pomongwe Cave (see below) or at View of the World (see page 316).

POMONGWE CAVE (*From main gate towards Maleme Dam, at about 2.5km before the Parks accommodation, turn right along signposted road for 0.5km*) There are very few paintings still visible in the cave due to early misguided preservation efforts. There are several paintings of giraffe as well as two elephants in outline. Zebra, kudu, eland, a *formling* (see *Glossary* on page 370) and other geometric shapes are also visible. Smaller paintings are visible on the rock wall to the left as you enter the cave, just outside the fence.

The cave was extensively excavated in the 1960s and again in 1979. The site is famous for the large cache of wooden and bone artefacts recovered in the 1960s excavations, as well as a piece of knotted string that is one of the world's oldest such artefacts. The cultural sequence has been dated to over 100,000 years of continuous human use and occupation, one of the world's longest such sequences. The most recent use of the cave was as a cattle *kraal* during the 1896–97 war.

WHITE RHINO SHELTER (*Near main road to Maleme Dam, about 13km from main gate, well signposted; from the car park cross a small stream; a short, steep climb brings you to the cave on your right*) The paintings in this small shelter are faded but are well worth a visit as they are fine examples of line drawings, possibly the best in the country. Both white and black rhino are depicted as well as what might be the area's best paintings of wildebeest. A male lion, a flock of guineafowl and a kudu bull are hard to see with the naked eye, but can be picked up using binoculars. Humans and strange figures are also present.

Due to the vulnerability of the paintings, the site has been fenced off, an example of an unattractive but all-too-often required protective measure.

BAMBATA CAVE (*Take the Kezi rd, passing main Matobo NP turn-off & entrance to Hazelside police station; shortly after crossing the road grid, take signposted turn-off to right, to car park; from there, walk 2km across a stream & alongside another to the base of the hill; from there follow arrows painted on the rock. Although this cave is outside the park boundary, it is administered by Parks and you need to show your current National Parks entry ticket at the boom before proceeding*) This fine cave has been excavated several times since the early 1900s. The hole to the left was left unfilled after an excavation 60 years ago to show the depth of deposit, which reaches at least 15m. The most recent excavations unearthed a stone engraved with a grid design at least 8,500 years old, the oldest securely dated art object in

Zimbabwe. The paintings probably date to between 9,000–8,000 and 4,000–2,000 years ago, when the cave is known to have been occupied. This cave also has some of the earliest evidence for herding activities in Zimbabwe.

The paintings are extensive but positioned high up. The animals are interesting for their contrasting realism and unreality. Wildebeest, zebra, kudu, cheetah, impala, rhino, giraffe, roan, reedbuck, sable and a bushpig can be seen. Several humans are present, in a variety of poses and activities. A notable scene is a group of people under what looks like a blanket. The dominant, multi-coloured (polychrome) elliptical form is a good example of a formling. There are two faded elephants and an indistinct animal figure, which are Iron Age clay pictures, though the clay has fallen off, leaving a shadow print. These may have been created for rain-making ceremonies. This cave is National Monument No 7.

NSWATUGI CAVE (*Between Maleme Dam & Whitewaters, 8km west of the reservoir, well signposted but 4x4 recommended due to severe erosion; from car park, a short, steep 60m climb*) The frieze here is dominated by a pair of beautifully painted giraffe; below a mass of animals, people and strange figures are clearly evident. Close examination of the painted area nearest the long vertical crack in the rock reveals thousands of painted red dots. A line of female kudu and calves followed by a fine kudu bull extends through the greater part of the painted frieze. Look carefully for the line of red and white human males in the upper central part of the painted area. Many of the paintings probably date to 10,000–6,000 years ago, when the cave was occupied in the Late Stone Age. Excavations here in 1975 revealed the oldest known skeleton in Zimbabwe, that of a woman of Bushman affinities, dated to 9,500 years ago.

The name Nswatugi means 'place of jumping'; according to local legends, Mlimo (god) leapt from his home at NJelele Hill, landing from his first leap on Nswatugi hill, leaving a 'footprint' in the granite. The footprint is a natural mark, enlarged by artificial pecking. The cave was used as a granary in the 19th century, although the grain bins that used to be present have long since disappeared.

There is a small interpretive centre in the car park. The cave is National Monument No 8.

SILOZWANE CAVE (*Outside NP; take Circular Dr from main gate, past View of the World then left for Maleme Dam; take the road to Mtsheleli Dam, signposted on left, into communal land; at Silozwane Business Centre the road bears right, passing the school on the right; dirt road continues along an eroded river course to car park at the base of the hill; steep & fairly precipitous 200m climb to cave*) Large human figures, 1.5m tall, dominate the richly painted cave. Various animals, fish and birds may be seen after careful scrutiny. Look carefully for the exquisitely painted flying ant. The large buck-headed snakes, carrying people and animals on their backs, are a theme seen at other big caves. A flock of birds, possibly francolin, is located above the group of buck-headed snakes. An unusual painting of a pair of lizards is immediately below these, although they are hard to see. There is a large picture of women grinding food, men making arrows, and children nearby, which has been interpreted as evidence for the first appearance of pastoralists in the area (this seems unlikely since we know today that hunter-gatherers did, on occasion, grind grass seeds before eating them).

Until 1950 this cave was used as a shrine to Mwari (god), and a full-moon ceremony was witnessed by whites until about 1942. The increase in the number of visitors and the removal of local people from the national park led to the decay of the shrine, and its use was discontinued. Silozwane is National Monument No 14.

NANKE CAVE (*4km+ walk from Togwana Dam, well marked with arrows painted on the rock*) There is much of interest to see along this walk. Two small, exquisitely painted sites lie along the path as well as a small clay furnace with moulded breasts that were presumably used for iron smelting and working. It is recommended that a full day be set aside to visit this cave, which has the most beautiful cave art in Zimbabwe, if not southern Africa. You will definitely spend at least an hour at the main cave.

The most prominent picture is a formling painted in a variety of colours, variously interpreted as a grain bin, extra-terrestrials or children playing on rock – all spurious and trivial interpretations in light of our knowledge of Bushman ethnography. We can be reasonably sure that it represents a termite's nest. Giraffe are superimposed on and by it. Try to find the painting of a dog, which cannot be older that 2,200 years, as that is when the earliest domestic animals are known to have been introduced into Zimbabwe. There are several excellent paintings of other animals such as zebra, eland, kudu, ostrich, bushpig, hare, tsessebe, duiker and generic antelope. The human figures show a wealth of detail, depicting clothing, tools and ornaments. Some of the larger human-like figures even have their fingers indicated, which is very rare in Zimbabwean rock art, although more common than previously thought in the Matobo.

GULUBAHWE CAVE (*Turn left off main Matopos Rd to Old Gwanda Rd; alternative route: along Matopos Rd until just beyond Matopos Research Station, turning left off the Kezi rd*

from the spectacular landscapes and the hundreds of examples of rock art, which together have given the park UNESCO World Heritage status, the very special Matopos habitat carries the greatest concentration of leopards in Zimbabwe as well as 50 species of raptor, including more than 50 pairs of Verreaux's (black) eagle, more than anywhere else in the world. Rhino, both white and black, have been successfully reintroduced. These and a selection of plains game graze and browse in the park's Whovi area.

If you are self-driving you are bound to find yourself at times in the surrounding communal areas, peaceful farmed oases with well-tended villages and *kraals* scattered amongst picturesque *kopjes*. While we all value Zimbabwe's national parks and their contribution to wildlife conservation, few realise that their creation displaced many people from traditional, often sacred areas, and the Matopos is no exception. Matabeleland has suffered economically more than other parts of the country and this park has been subject to intensive subsistence and bush-meat poaching in recent years with the result that visitors are recording fewer game sightings than previously.

Getting around The irregularly shaped park (which many describe as a spread-winged bird of prey) is divided into five 'wilderness' areas, although their easy accessibility makes them pretty tame in comparison with the wilderness areas of

& left again just before NP gates, then right on Old Gwanda Rd just after Fort Usher; the badly corrugated, frequently eroded road passes Matopo Mission after 9km; 8km beyond, it descends into a small valley, skirting a large domed granite hill; the cave is close to the road in this hill, on the right) The dominant figure is a huge zoomorphic snake, 5m long, with baboons, a jackal and about 25 people on its back. This painting alone makes the visit worthwhile, as it is one of the most spectacular figures in the Matobo. There are several large humans, with broad shoulders and small heads. Some only have one leg, mimicking the evil spirits of today's legends. The painting is full of religious symbolism – many humans mimic baboons while others adopt postures similar to Bushmen in a trance. If one stands at the head of the snake and talks normally, an incredibly loud echo can be heard. This may have influenced the positioning of the snake when it was originally being painted in the cave. The cave is National Monument No 15.

TIPS WHEN VISITING A PAINTED SITE Most rock paintings are faded and badly weathered, and it is difficult to recognise figures at first. A lot of patience is needed.

* Allow your eyes time to acclimatise to the natural light.
* Stand back and view the whole panel of painting, then move closer to see individual images.
* Remember that paintings can be clearer at certain times of the day, their visibility and the degree of reflection varying according to cloud cover, sun angle and humidity.
* Never touch or wet the paintings.
* A magnifying glass is useful for picking out detail. You can also stand some distance away and look at the figures through binoculars.
* Please do not remove anything from the floor of the shelter, including stones or pieces of pottery.

Gonarezhou and Chizarira. The main places to visit are accessible by saloon car. You will see several signs along the way pointing out 'scenic routes', but these are simply alternative loop roads. By all means try them, although they are dirt roads and some of them get in a pretty rough condition, and they are no more or less scenic than the rest of the park. Don't drive these roads without a map because there are very few signs and there's no indication of which direction the loop is taking you. You won't get really lost but you may end up in a very different place than you first thought.

Keep your entry ticket with you throughout the day as some roads take you out of the park into communal lands and back in again at another entrance gate.

Tourist information Pick up a park map from the Bulawayo Publicity Association (see page 295). The park headquarters (⊕ *06.00–18.00*) are at Maleme Dam, centrally located in the park (see *Central and Maleme wilderness areas*, page 317). Most accommodation is there too.

A sign at the park entrance warns that anyone suspected of poaching activities may be shot on sight.

Please note: bilharzia is a risk at all the reservoirs in the park; for more information on how to avoid it, see under *Health* in *Chapter 3*, pages 106–7. Tap water is not potable and should be boiled or otherwise treated.

Where to stay The following National Parks options, including camping, are all found in the Maleme Dam area.

Rest Camp Behind park HQ, Maleme, a short distance from the dam. Set amongst a jumble of massive granite boulders, one of the nicest National Parks accommodation settings in the country, are 23 standard chalets & lodges for 2 or 4 people (extra beds available for children), en suite & self-catering, with their own *braai* facilities. *Chalets US$35–75, lodges US$75–100.*

Black Eagle Lodge Facing the reservoir. 2 dbl bedrooms, open fireplace & huge terrace with a view of the reservoir, a cut above the other chalets. *US$120.*

Imbila Executive Lodge Further along the reservoir. Perched on its own atop a granite outcrop, this top-of-the-range 2-bedroom thatched lodge (max 6) has a beautiful view over the reservoir & surrounding hills. It has a veranda but most visitors take chairs out onto the warm rock to sip their sundowners & light the *braai.* (Imbila is Shona for rock dassie.) *US$150.*

Campsites Along the north shore of the reservoir, with *braai* stands, electrical points & clean communal ablutions. On the opposite shore, via the dam wall, are several shady picnic spots. *US$8pp.*

What to see and do
Northern Wilderness Area
MOTH Shrine (*Soon after entrance gate, turn left turn onto Matobo Circular Dr; shrine is on left*) MOTH is an acronym for Memorable Order of Tin Hats. This peaceful hillside garden was founded by Charles Evedon in 1927 in recognition of ex-servicemen and their families, and dedicated to the ideals of comradeship, mutual help and sound memories of those who fell in World War I. The shrine was consecrated on Easter Day 1947.

View of the World (Malindidzimu) and Cecil Rhodes's grave (*Signposted off Circular Dr by large curio stall; entry US$10*) You must pay again because this site belongs to National Museums and Monuments, but your ticket will also admit you to Pomongwe and Nswatugi caves. The size of the car park is a clue to the popularity of this place, so try to avoid weekends. Cecil John Rhodes may not be everybody's all-time hero but don't let this put you off visiting his grave. From the ticket office it's a gentle ten-minute stroll up to the site over one of the massive granite whalebacks (tap the rock and hear the hollow sound, evidence of exfoliation), with its fabulous views. It was during Rhodes's extended negotiations to bring the Ndebele uprising to an end that he visited various sites in the Matobo Hills and came across this Ndebele sacred place, known as Malindidzimu, 'place of benevolent spirits'. Rhodes called it 'View of the World' and decided this was to be his burial place. After a debilitating illness, contracted on his return sea voyage from England, Rhodes's heart failed and he died in Cape Town on 26 March 1902, at the relatively young age of 48. His own Pullman rail carriage carried his coffin to Bulawayo, and a gun carriage pulled by 12 black oxen hauled it to Malindidzimu, where he was interred on 10 April.

At his own request, Rhodes shares this site with two other individuals. A few paces away is the grave of Leander Starr Jameson, Rhodes's right-hand man for many years, coyly described in earlier biographies as 'his intimate friend'. Jameson died in England in 1917 but was re-interred here in 1920. A third grave is that of Sir Charles Coughlan, Rhodesia's first prime minister, buried 28 years after Rhodes. These three simple yet imposing graves do not seem entirely out of place here, but they share the site with 34 other souls whose memorial is truly a blot on the landscape. In accordance with Rhodes's wishes, the hapless but much revered Captain Allan Wilson and his men, massacred in 1893 as they chased Lobengula out of his territory, were disinterred from Fort Victoria (Masvingo) and reburied here under an ugly, angular mausoleum totally out of keeping with the surrounding rock architecture.

It's interesting to speculate what the Ndebele spirits thought of a man like Rhodes occupying their sacred place, as well as his decision to share the site with others who had done 'special service' to Rhodesia (which included trampling all over the civil rights of the Ndebele). As a rare mark of respect for the Ndebele and their spirits, his burial party agreed to forgo the usual rifle volley. Paradoxically, the Ndebele, for so long the victims of Rhodes's policies, participated fully in the funeral and even cried out their traditional royal burial salute, '*Bayethe*'.

His presence here is not without opponents. There have been threats by government and prominent war vets to destroy the graves but that's hopefully unlikely as the grave is a major tourist draw and therefore a source of revenue.

There are other attractions up here. Incredibly coloured lichens adorn many of the rock surfaces, a kaleidoscope of reds, yellows, greens and black. If you break open a picnic you'll soon be visited by a host of vividly coloured male flat lizards, anxious to share your sandwiches and quite prepared to take morsels from your hand.

Central Wilderness Area This area includes the picturesque Maleme Dam beside which is the National Parks central office along with their lodges and campsite. With its extremely pleasant accommodation and tent sites, the Maleme Dam area gets very busy at weekends and throughout the high season.

To the west of the dam there's a scenic loop road that gives access to Nswatugi Cave; Pomongwe Cave is close by too (see box, page 312). The **Maleme Wilderness Area** (named after the river, not the dam) is due south of the Central Wilderness Area – although you can follow the road southwards, it has no specific attractions to visit.

Togwe Wilderness Area Of the five 'wilderness' areas, this rather remote eastern region best lives up to its description. There are two scenic reservoirs to visit or camp by, and Nanke Cave with some of the finest rock art in southern Africa. Togwe also provides easy access to Silozwane Cave, which is actually outside the park.

Togwana Dam This is the prettiest reservoir in the Matopos, especially at sunset, and there's a selection of campsites along the shore. The easiest access is from the south, via Mtsheleli Dam. A fine route from the north, via Fort Usher, through picturesque *kraals* and villages of the Gulati Communal Lands, requires a 4x4, as there are some rocky, steep sections requiring high clearance and low-range gears, and an axle-high river (which swells in the rains).

Once at the reservoir, check in at the warden's office and take your pick of the 11 designated camping sites. All are nicely isolated from one another, with only a *braai* stand and the standard concrete bench-cum-table. The further sites are some distance from the ablution block. For lake views, my favourite is No 7.

Mtsheleli Dam This is to the south of Togwana Dam, and the road connecting the two, passing in and out of the park, is in good condition. The long, narrow lake is backed by beautiful Matopos rock formations. Here too there are undeveloped campsites with excellent views over the lake.

Whovi Wilderness Area This is the wildlife-viewing part of the national park, fenced off from the rest and with a separate entrance fee. Because there are rhino and leopard here, you cannot enter on foot without an accredited guide. You can hire a National Parks scout to escort you on walks, or you can arrange a private guide from a company such as African Wanderer Safaris (see page 295) who feature walks with rhinos. It's a relatively small area: a leisurely drive around the route (including several loop roads) takes two to three hours.

Most visitors will be keen to set eyes on the rhino – who are frequently spotted about 20 minutes from the entrance gate at sunset (you'll be cutting it fine to make it back to the gate before it closes at 18.00).

Don't forget to raise your eyes to the *kopjes* as you can often spot the agile little klipspringer, standing like a sentinel on a lofty boulder. This area is renowned for Africa's densest concentration of leopard, and while there is plenty of evidence to support this, you will struggle to find anyone who has seen this shy, mainly nocturnal creature. Unfortunately the park has in recent years fallen victim to subsistence poaching, greatly reducing the once prolific game count.

PLUMTREE

Plumtree is a small village located on the Zimbabwe/Botswana border about 100km SW of Bulawayo on the A7. This is the most convenient border to use between Botswana and mid/southern Zimbabwe if you want to avoid Beitbridge. Francistown is the nearest main town in Botswana.

⌂ WHERE TO STAY
Upmarket

⌂ **Kombani Lodge** (10 chalets, 10 rooms) 📞019 2229; m 0777 015686; e kombaniafricalodge@gmail.com. 1km out of Plumtree on the road to the border. This new lodge is an extremely convenient option for late/early border crossings. The luxury chalets each have 2 en-suite bedrooms. À la carte restaurant & family activities at w/ends. **$$$**

10

Southern Zimbabwe

Southern Zimbabwe, sadly ignored by most visitors, is admittedly a hot, dusty *lowveld* area, rich in mosquitoes and malaria in the summer months, yet the winter season brings a temperate climate ideal for enjoying the natural attractions that fill this corner of the country. Highlights include the very special, yet little-visited Gonarezhou National Park and the neighbouring wildlife conservation area, the Malilangwe Trust. You will find accommodation ranging from bush camping in the national park to one of the most luxurious lodges in Africa. Wildlife is plentiful in the park, but poaching has made it skittish and wary of humans. It's a birding paradise, with over 400 species including a rich selection of raptors.

A network of large rivers, notably the Limpopo, Mwenezi, Runde and Save (pronounced *sahvey*), provides irrigation for a thriving agricultural industry, including a sugar production base at Triangle which continues to be a major employer. A tsetse fly eradication programme towards the end of the last century paved the way for several large cattle ranches, but these floundered in the drought years of the early 1990s. Recent times have seen a growing emphasis on wildlife tourism, with the restocking and development of Gonarezhou in the aftermath of the Mozambique civil war, and initiatives involving local communities in tourism and conservation projects. The Great Limpopo Transfrontier Conservation Area – linking Gonarezhou, Kruger National Park in South Africa and Limpopo National Park in Mozambique – is beginning to realise its objectives, although political strife has stalled the Zimbabwean element of this project.

BEITBRIDGE   *Telephone code 0286*

This stiflingly hot, scruffy little border town with about 23,000 mostly Venda occupants, should consider itself lucky, because if it wasn't the principal road entry point from South Africa, nobody would come near it. This is the busiest border post in southern Africa, notorious as the principal exit point for refugees fleeing to South Africa in the first decade of this century. The border fences were riddled with holes, and those crossing illegally, via the river, had to contend not only with crocodiles but with gangs of robbers who stripped them of their remaining wealth. Today there is a huge amount of infrastructure investment here, evidenced by a continual process of building all along the approach road, creating, if possible, even larger quantities of dust than previously. It's ironic that with all this development, the border post itself has seen absolutely no development and remains the shambles it has been for many a year. For you, this unlovely town is nothing but a place to fill your tanks and shop for food. For provisions go to the shopping mall on the right as you leave town, rather than to the town centre.

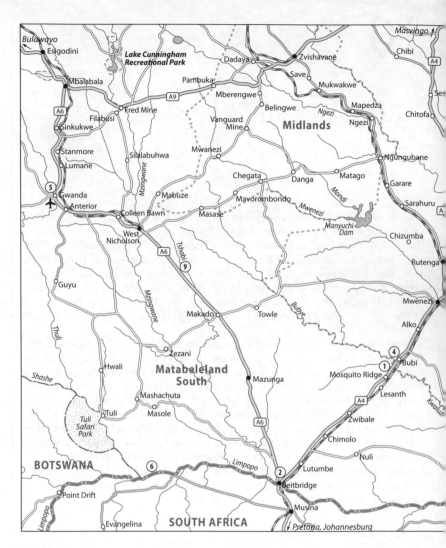

HISTORY In 1890 the BSAC pioneers crossed the Shashe River into Zimbabwe at Tuli, about 70km to the east, and established a fort there. A more suitable road and railway route to Bulawayo subsequently bypassed Tuli, crossing the Limpopo River at what is now Beitbridge. A road and railway bridge, designed by Sir Ralph Freeman

THULI CIRCLE

Few people other than hunters visit this safari area, but most are intrigued by this section of the border with Botswana, a perfect semicircle jutting out of an otherwise normal boundary formed by the Shashe River. In 1891, when Mashonaland's magisterial districts were being established, Thuli was given jurisdiction over a 16km radius of the village, resulting in this strange bulge on the border.

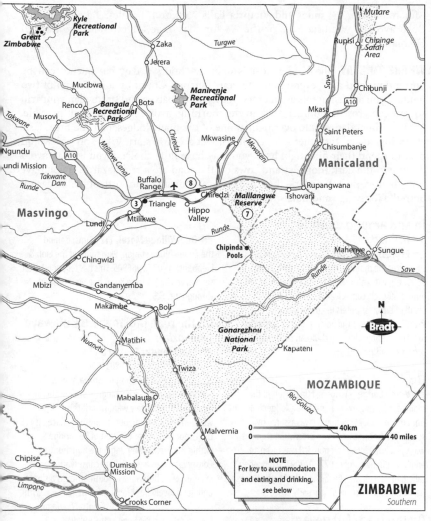

ZIMBABWE Southern

ZIMBABWE Southern
For listings, see pages 322–4

Where to stay
1 Bubi Village Motel
2 Express by Holiday Inn
3 Hippo Valley Country Club
4 Lion & Elephant Motel
5 Mishie's Gwanda Hotel & Casino
6 Sandstone at Sentinel
7 Singita Pamushana Lodge
8 The Nesbitt Arms
9 Tod's Guest House

– and funded by the Beit Trust, set up in the name of Alfred Beit, prominent businessman, founder of the De Beers diamond mining company and close associate of Cecil Rhodes – opened in 1929. The current road bridge opened in 1995, with the original one now carrying only rail traffic.

GETTING THERE Greyhound (*www. greyhound.co.za*), Translux (*www. translux.com*) and Senatar Express (see page 94 for details) coaches pass through on their way between Johannesburg (550km/342 miles), Bulawayo (321km/199 miles) and Harare (580km/360 miles). Masvingo is 288km/179 miles away,

Mutare 585km/364 miles and Victoria Falls 758km/471 miles. Take the A6 for Bulawayo and Victoria Falls or the A4 for Masvingo, Harare and the Eastern Highlands.

WHERE TO STAY The border post is open 24 hours a day, but queues can be horrendous and add several hours to your journey. Count on a minimum of two hours if you are using this as an entry point to Zimbabwe and try to plan your trip so you can cross the border early in the morning, avoiding weekends if possible. My recommendation is to overnight at one of the many lodges, bed and breakfasts etc in Musina on the other side so you can get an early start. While no-one would plan to spend their first night here, you may have little choice if you wish to avoid driving in the dark (donkeys and cows on the road are a real hazard). If you have time to move on before dark, there are places within an hour north of Beitbridge on both the Masvingo and Bulawayo roads.

In and around Beitbridge
Standard
Express by Holiday Inn (104 rooms) On the left of the main N6 road out of town; ☏805 5555; e pacro@africansunhotels.com; www.africasunhotels.com. Clean & anonymous, this chain of business hotels needs no introduction. Although Express is the no-frills brand of Holiday Inn, this is about the only choice in Beitbridge & is priced accordingly. **$$$**

Basic
White Lodge (16 rooms) On the left of the main road leaving town. This is a new lodge that from the road looks inviting & I was assured by someone who appeared to be a receptionist that it was open but it looked far from it. I was given an enquiries phone number 0775 07209790 but when I called, the person was unable to help. Maybe things have improved since my visit in early 2013. **$**

On the road (A4) towards Masvingo
Standard
Lion & Elephant Motel (38 rondavels) 78km north of Beitbridge on the A4 towards Masvingo; m 0773 284637; e lionandelephant@junglecomms.com; www.lionandelephant.com. Reception is decorated with wildlife murals & has a bar & pleasant lounge area. The restaurant is in an open-sided, thatched, dbl-storey *boma* & the upstairs bar/lounge overlooks the Bubye River, dry in winter. The rondavels are set in a shaded garden & simply furnished, self-contained but clean & comfortable. *Camping (right next to the main road) US$5pp.* **$$**

Basic
Bubi Village Motel (12 rooms) Behind the Engen filling station, 2km south of the Lion & Elephant; m 0777 966905. This has reopened after several years of closure & has been refurbished throughout. **$$**

On the road (A6) towards Bulawayo
Upmarket
Sandstone at Sentinel (4 cottages) ☏ (South Africa) +27 83 2850064; m 0712 230708; e dbristow@limpopo.co.za; www.sentinel-eco.com. Archaeologists & dinosaur hunters will definitely want to visit this wonderfully different, out-of-the-way place on the Limpopo River to the west of Beitbridge & within the Greater Mapungubwe Transfrontier Conservation Area which links conservation areas in Zimbabwe, Botswana & South Africa as a single unit. It's a lovely traditional safari-style camp with en-suite thatched chalets & a central *boma* for eating, drinking & gazing at the Milky Way.

Activities revolve around guided walking, day & night game drives, although the real focus is around the extraordinary dinosaur remains in the area, Iron Age artefacts & prehistoric rock art. Top of the list is the massive & remarkably well-preserved fossil skeleton of the 6m-tall, 2-legged massospondylus dinosaur dating back 200+ million years to the late Triassic period. Today's game includes elephant & leopard in healthy numbers.

Accommodation is based around a small exclusive 3-room thatched lodge built amongst towering sandstone boulders in the shade of ancient baobab trees & overlooking a busy wildlife waterhole.

Access is generally by the company's own charter aircraft from Bulawayo & beyond or from South Africa, Botswana & Mozambique via Beitbridge. Charter cost ex Bulawayo US$1,040 for up to 5 passengers & ex Victoria Falls US$2,400.

Self-drive from Beitbridge – after 10km from Beitbridge on the Bulawayo road, turn west onto gravel road at the Tuli Coal sign & drive past Tuli Coal & through Nottingham Estate. In total it's 50km on a good gravel road.

Vehicle transfers out of Bulawayo can be arranged & this is a 4hr journey one-way. The transfrontier park plans are to have a dry season tourist border checkpoint from South Africa directly into the Sentinel component of the Transfrontier Conservation Area.

US$350pppn sharing with a sgl supplement of US$125. The price is inc of meals, drinks & activities – but exc transfers & premium-branded imported drinks. **$$$$$**

⌂ **Tod's Guest House** (8 rooms) 120km from Beitbridge on the Bulawayo rd; m 0774 903495, 0712 65403; e tods@mweb.co.zw. This is the only decent place to overnight until you reach Bulawayo. Built in 1932 as a mail stagecoach stop, it's just off the road. Although it's been owned by the same family for decades, no-one there today has any idea who or what Tod was. The rooms are en suite & more are being built. There's a pool & comfortable bar in the gardens with full catering including *braai* on Sun. Book in advance if possible as it's popular; avoid the last w/end in Jul as it hosts one of Zimbabwe's biggest motorcycle rallies. **$$**

THE A6 FROM BEITBRIDGE TO BULAWAYO

WEST NICHOLSON This place, named after a gold prospector, is prominent on the map, but don't blink or you'll miss it. From here on, the road to Bulawayo becomes much more scenic and interesting as it winds its way up onto the *highveld* through a landscape dotted with *kopjes* and baobab trees.

COLLEEN BAWN If she was around today, Colleen would probably rather not have her name associated with this place. It was originally a potential gold-mining site, claimed by Irish prospector Sam Daly in 1895 and named after his girlfriend, but the shiny, yellow metal turned out to be rather scarce. They now mine a less glamorous mineral, hence the ugly cement factory blotting the landscape as it munches the mountain away.

GWANDA Gwanda is a typically African rural town just northwest of Colleen Bawn. Strategically placed to service this gold-mining area, it is now somewhat run-down although it continues to function, with a new shopping mall and a large college.

⌂ Where to stay
Basic
⌂ **Mishies Gwanda Hotel and Casino** 📞 0284 21501 e mishieshospitalities@yahoo.com. This previously run-down place has had a revamp in recent years raising its status to 'basic but clean & friendly'. It's really only an option for weary drivers between Bulawayo & Beitbridge, given its extremely close proximity to the railway line & problems with water & electricity supply in the rooms. Nevertheless the staff are reported to be very friendly & the food is above expectations for a hotel of this standard. Apparently there's no night-time disturbance from the bar and 'casino'. **$$**

LOWVELD TOWNS

TRIANGLE AND CHIREDZI (*Telephone code 031*) You'll pass through these two towns on the way to northern Gonarezhou from Masvingo, and from Beitbridge if you are avoiding the dirt roads. Both can be summed up in one word: sugar.

This was first a cattle-rearing area (Triangle's name originates from the brand used to mark the first herd), but the combined scourges of rinderpest, foot-and-mouth disease, tsetse flies and drought persuaded struggling farmers to turn to cropping. Most farming here now feeds the massive sugar production plant in Triangle, and a good proportion of the resident population gains its employment from the industry.

There is only one worthwhile tourist attraction here (aside from possibly the largest speed humps in the world – use low-ratio second gear if possible). Accommodation, aimed at the business market and priced accordingly, is all in Chiredzi.

🏠 Where to stay and eat

Upmarket

🏠 **The Nesbitt Arms** (24 rooms) 238 Marula Dr, Chiredzi; ✆5071/5; m 0772 661420; www. nesbittarms.co.zw. Like an English country inn, complete with hunting prints & dark wood panelling. 3 bars & a restaurant serve local dishes & standard international fare. A pleasant place with friendly staff. **$$**

Standard

🏠 **Hippo Valley Country Club** (12 rooms) About 5km out of town on Hippo Valley Rd, PO Box 1, Chiredzi; ✆3360/1. This sprawling club offers simple motel-style accommodation at luxury prices, again catering for the business market. **$$$**

What to see and do

The Murray MacDougall Museum (*Signposted from through road; look for radio mast on a hill opposite sugar mill, Triangle;* ⏱ *08.30–09.30 & 15.30–16.30 Tue–Sun; despite the limited opening hours, once you are in the attendant will not rush you out*) This interesting museum is dedicated to the redoubtable man who brought irrigation to this fertile, *lowveld* area and introduced sugar to Rhodesia at the start of World War II. 'Mac' ran away from his Scottish home in 1895 at the age of 14, signing on as a crew member on a cattle boat bound for Brazil. After working on a sugar estate for a couple of years, then fighting as a volunteer soldier, he fell in love with the Triangle area while on a hunting trip to Africa. After World War I he returned here and began his farming career, quickly realising that little would grow in this arid landscape without serious irrigation. His ambitious engineering scheme took seven years to complete and included a dam on the Mutirikwe River with downstream canals and tunnels drawing water from the river. Although a major success, his efforts were thwarted by several seasons of locusts. Undaunted, he drew on his youthful experience of agriculture in South America and turned to sugar cane. The government was reluctant to support this new venture and allowed him to import just three stalks of cane in an obvious effort to thwart it. These were supplemented with a much larger smuggled-in quantity, and the rest is history. The museum is in MacDougall's house, and you could easily spend a couple of hours checking out this fascinating character and his effect on local history and development.

GONAREZHOU NATIONAL PARK (NP Category 3)

At a fraction over 5,000km², this is Zimbabwe's second-largest national park, established in 1975. The name translates from Shona as 'place of elephants'. The river floodplains are interspersed with lagoons and riverine forest featuring notable species such as the nyala berry tree, ebony and Natal mahogany. The arid hinterland comprises *mopane* woodland and ironwood forest, as well as the Sabi star, which grows on rocky outcrops and has a lovely pink flower. These varied habitats are responsible for the richest biodiversity of any Zimbabwe national park. Gonarezhou has the biggest variety of birds in Zimbabwe, over 400 species, but do note that birding on foot is not allowed without a registered guide. The most scenically dramatic areas are along the Runde River with the majestic, red sandstone Chilojo Cliffs being the most iconic feature. Here, the seasons present two very different aspects – in the dry winter months your photographs will show the cliffs towering over the parched river bed with elephant marching from one side to the other and made miniature by the sheer size of the geography. When the river's in flood though, you could be forgiven for thinking you were in a different park altogether. This is a huge river system that transforms a dry, apparently lifeless landscape into a lush and verdant wildlife paradise.

The game has had a difficult time of it in the past. Elephants, along with much of the other 'game', suffered from widespread hunting and poaching in the early 20th century, and later from Mozambican troops who during their civil war treated Gonarezhou as a food source and a sporting paradise. The sport consisted of terrorising all and any game by shooting from both ground vehicles and helicopters. As a result, whereas animals in most national parks are more trusting of vehicles than people on foot, the reverse tends to be true here. Though Gonarezhou elephants are gradually learning that vehicles no longer pose a threat, the 'grey ghosts' are reputed to be very bad-tempered – and who can blame them.

This history has given Gonarezhou a reputation of being short on wildlife and many Zimbabweans (few of whom have visited the park recently) still think this is the case. Inevitably in a park of this size, poaching continues to exact a toll, but there is good news too. A lot of effort is being put into restoring the park's populations, especially of elephant, and infrastructure is receiving investment to bring this impressive park into the country's top ten tourist areas. Gonarezhou is home to the rare nyala antelope and a host of other antelope species, as well as all the big game associated with a dry, *lowveld* area, including the predators. It's estimated that the elephant population is now around 10,000 with over 100 wild dog. And if you've managed to get the 'Big Five' out of your system in other parks, you could come to the east of this park and try your luck at spotting the beautiful, though rather odd-looking male nyala or even southern Africa's tiniest antelopes, the suni and the blue duiker. Without doubt though, the best way to see the wildlife here is by using a local guide. You can hire a ranger from National Parks, although you'll need your own vehicle; from one of the lodges if you're staying there, or use a safari company that specialises in this park (see page 326).

The park is also part of the Great Limpopo Transfrontier Conservation Area, offering the prospect of opening up the border fences and allowing game to migrate over much larger areas.

Keen birders will want to spend several days in this park, which boasts an impressive list of specials, including African finfoot, bat hawk, racket-tailed roller, thick-billed cuckoo and Pel's fishing owl, to name just a few. As this park has predators, birders on foot must employ a National Parks or registered guide. There's an excellent book, out of print, called *Valley of the Ironwoods* by Allan Wright, who was the district commissioner responsible for setting up Gonarezhou as a national park. It's a fascinating read if you can get hold of it.

ORIENTATION AND GETTING AROUND The park is administratively divided into the Mwenezi Region in the southwest and the Save-Runde Region in the northeast, and it's these two areas at opposite ends of the park that provide the most popular and spectacular attractions. The Save-Runde area has one luxury private lodge with access to the national park, but this is very much a wilderness

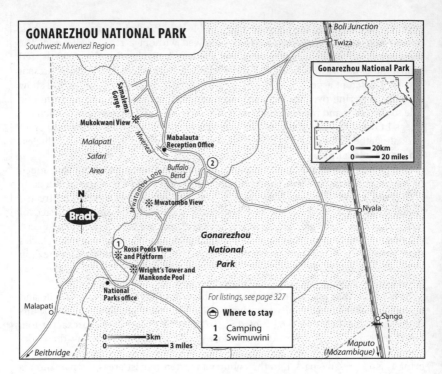

GONAREZHOU NATIONAL PARK
Southwest: Mwenezi Region

Boli Junction
Twiza

Gonarezhou National Park

0 ——— 20km
0 ——— 20 miles

Samalena Gorge

Mukokwani View

Malapati Safari Area

Mwenezi

Mabalauta Reception Office

Buffalo Bend

Watombo Loop

N

Bradt

Mwatombo View

Rossi Pools View and Platform

Gonarezhou National Park

Wright's Tower and Mankonde Pool

National Parks office

Malapati

Nyala

Sango

For listings, see page 327

Where to stay
1 Camping
2 Swimuwini

0 ——— 3km
0 ——— 3 miles

Beitbridge

Maputo (Mozambique)

area and the emphasis is on camping, with both developed and undeveloped sites available. These are all in places of outstanding scenic beauty, usually overlooking wide stretches of river.

Unless you are on an organised tour, a private vehicle is the only way to see the park. Many of the smaller dirt roads are neglected and heavily eroded, with river and gully crossings suitable only for tough 4x4s. These smaller tracks are now difficult to follow and as most maps lack detail there is plenty of scope for getting lost. It is always best to travel in the company of other vehicles, and you are strongly advised to take a GPS. A new road has been constructed connecting Chipinda Pools to the Save-Runde confluence area and this is currently driveable in a sedan or other two wheel-drive vehicle. In the wet summer months (November–April), most park roads are closed, with access limited to Chipinda Pools, Mabalauta and Swimuwini.

SAFARI OPERATORS

Private Guided Safaris Kenya; m 0773 819834/5; e ant@privateguidedsafaris.com; www.privateguidedsafaris.com
Forever African Safaris ✆09 246968; m 0712 648 328, 216 654; www.foreverafricansafaris.com

Gonarezhou Bush Camps ✆04 885130; m 0773 819834/5; e info@gonarezhoubushcamps.com; www.gonarezhou-bushcamps.com

MWENEZI REGION (SOUTHWEST)

Getting there The A4 Masvingo road has several dirt roads leading off to the east, offering access to Mabalauta from the south, and of these I can recommend two. The first turn-off is 19km from Beitbridge, signed to Chituripasi, and the 210km to Mabalauta will take four to five hours. The second, more northerly route is from

Rutenga via Boli, which gives you access to both the southwestern and northeastern sections of the park. The southern route from Beitbridge is more scenic, taking you through some picturesque villages and varied countryside; the Rutenga–Boli road, though quicker, runs straight and parallel to the railway line for 75km through monotonous, neglected farmland. Both roads can be heavily corrugated, and are really only suitable for 4x4s.

It is also possible to enter this area from Mozambique by using the Sango border post (Chicualacuala on the Mozambique side) and this can be a useful 4x4 entry point for people who have entered Mozambique at Pafuri, having spent time in Kruger National Park. This route does involve a Limpopo river crossing though – it can be half a metre deep in the dry season – so it's essential to check conditions beforehand.

Mabalauta This is your first stop in this area of the park, as it is where you will find the National Parks office to pay your entry fee and arrange accommodation.

Where to stay

Å Camping Located next to the Parks office. Each pitch in this well-tended, developed site has Mwenezi River views. The ablution block is clean & donkey boilers provide piping hot water. An attendant brings wood & will even light your fire & braai for you. US$10pp.

☗ Swimuwini Located a short distance away, well signposted from the Parks office. 2- & 4-bed chalets are US$75/100. Camping is also available.

What to see and do Self-drive routes offer either scenic views along the Mwenezi River or loop roads away from the river for wildlife viewing. See *Getting there*, above, for options.

Mwatombo Loop Road This road takes you to a viewpoint high above the valley, with expanses of sandy riverbed and languid pools in the winter and a fast-flowing river in summer.

Mukokwani Pool One of several pleasant viewpoints looking down to the river below, although the adjacent **Samalema Gorge** can be disappointing as it's hardly a gorge, rather more of a rocky river bed.

Rossi Pools A spectacularly situated viewpoint, perched precariously on the gorge rim, and comes with a well-tended, concrete-floored, thatched *lapa* in which you can spend the night in perfect isolation, miles from the nearest human being, though it's best avoided by sleepwalkers and vertigo sufferers.

Mankonde Pool On a U-bend in the river, is the site of Wright's Tower, an ugly concrete block built as a game-viewing platform. There's a wonderful sign inside, warning against antagonising the elephants in case they decide to reach in and pluck you out of the tower!

SAVE-RUNDE REGION (NORTHEAST)

Getting there Virtually all visitors to this region enter the park at **Chipinda Pools** from Chiredzi and the National Parks office is clearly marked.

Approaching the Save-Runde region from Beitbridge, you could save mileage and avoid Chiredzi by cutting across country on the boring, heavily corrugated dirt road from Rutenga via Boli. But beware, this is something of a gamble. At Boli

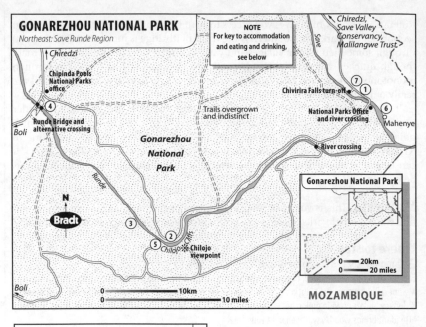

GONAREZHOU NATIONAL PARK
Northeast: Save Runde Region

↑ *Chiredzi*

Chipinda Pools
National Parks
office

④

Runde Bridge and
alternative crossing

Boli

Gonarezhou
National
Park

Runde

N
Bradt

③

⑤ ② *Chilojo* ✳ Chilojo
Cliffs viewpoint

Boli

0 ——— 10km
0 ——————— 10 miles

NOTE
For key to accommodation
and eating and drinking,
see below

Save

Chiredzi,
Save Valley
Conservancy,
Malilangwe Trust ➤

Chivirira Falls turn-off ● ⑦ ①

National Parks Office ●
and river crossing ⑥
Mahenye

✳ River crossing

Trails overgrown
and indistinct

Gonarezhou National Park

0 ——— 20km
0 ——— 20 miles

MOZAMBIQUE

GONAREZHOU NATIONAL PARK
Northeast
For listings, see pages 330–1

🏠 **Where to stay**
1 Chilo Gorge Safari Lodge
2 Chilojo Cliffs
3 Chinguli Camp
4 Chipinda Pools
5 Fishans Camp
6 Mahenye Lodge
7 Nhambo Camp

junction, where you turn left towards Chipinda Pools, a sign declares the road to be closed, and indeed it is. In January 2000, Cyclone Eline destroyed the Lundi bridge, which you would normally cross to reach Chipinda Pools, but in the winter dry season there is another way across. Immediately before the destroyed bridge is a small gate hut on the right, by a track winding down to the river. Here the slightly submerged Madau causeway weaves picturesquely through papyrus reeds to the other side. Walk the causeway first to ensure it is intact, and check the water depth: it's only a few inches in the dry season, but this crossing is impossible at any other time.

(Lundi is the local Shangaan spelling for the more familiar Shona word for the Runde River.)

🏠 **Where to stay** This part of the national park is one of Zimbabwe's true wilderness areas. Although there is an excellent lodge a stone's throw away on the north bank of the Save River with another (Mahenye Lodge) planned for resurrection, there are none actually in this park which holds its greatest appeal for those who want to pitch camp in the remote African bush surrounded by wildlife in a completely unfenced environment.

Lodges Most visitors arrive from the Chiredzi direction. Immediately after crossing the Save River bridge you will see a dirt road on the right. This road, which weaves its way alongside beautifully tended Shangaan villages, is quite tiring to drive, not because of the surface but because of having to return the constant friendly waving of virtually every adult and child you see for 43km.

At the time of writing Chilo Gorge Lodge is the only one operating, although a second, Mahenye Lodge, is due for complete rebuilding sometime in 2013. As Mahenye Lodge is on an island, the crossing can only be driven at low water; at other times you leave your vehicle at Chilo Lodge and they ferry you across. If you are approaching this area from within the national park, go to the park office and they will point out the track to that crossing, again only possible at low water. When

'CAMPFIRE' AT MAHENYE

Indigenous peoples have historically lived in close harmony with wildlife, only hunting what was required to support the family group or community. This was the way of life for the Shangaan of Gonarezhou until Europeans introduced commercial hunting areas and in 1975 formed the national park. The state owned all the wildlife, the Shangaan were evicted from their land and then treated as poachers when they killed for subsistence and to control crop-raiding animals. The problem escalated and poaching increased several-fold as the people attempted to destroy the national park's viability in a vain attempt to get their land returned. Shadrack, the leading poacher, a man considered a local hero at the time, is said to have killed between 20 and 30 male elephants each year for around 15 years. Rhino were also taken. This resulted in violent conflict between the local community and the Zimbabwe Parks and Wildlife Management Authority. With both sides suffering and the situation deteriorating, it was clear that an innovative solution was required.

In 1982, Parks asked a local man, Clive Stockil, who spoke fluent Shangaan, to mediate with the 'troublesome' community. He reported that all they wanted was the restoration of their traditional right to use the wildlife on their land outside the park. In fact there was already a law establishing this principle, but it had never before been applied to community-held land. In return for this restoration the Shangaan agreed to cease all poaching. Parks granted the request on a trial basis in the Chipinge district.

A prototype CAMPFIRE (Communal Areas Management Programme for Indigenous Resources) project was introduced in the village of Mahenye. Limited, sustainable commercial hunting was introduced, with the meat and part of the proceeds being returned to the community via district authorities. After a slow start, money began to flow into the village, funding a school, a clinic and a grain mill. In 1994 and 1996 the Mahenye and Chilo Gorge lodges were opened on land leased from the community, with jobs and a percentage of revenues made available to the village, either for development projects or as cash handouts.

Today, Mahenye is a relatively prosperous village, with running water, sanitation and electricity. All this has been achieved by giving value to the wildlife on communal land, thereby ensuring its conservation by creating stakeholders from those previously considered criminals.

CAMPFIRE was inaugurated as a nationwide programme in 1988 but the economic turmoil resulting in the virtual cessation of tourism in this area has meant there has been a dramatic decline in revenues for distribution to the local community. But at the end of 2012, Clive Stockil was in active discussion with Mahenye village to restructure the CAMPFIRE programme as community involvement and support is still one of the Chilo Gorge Lodge's prime objectives.

10

the river is high you can safely leave your vehicle at the park office and Chilo Lodge will ferry you across, by prearrangement or with a radio call from Parks.

The lodges can arrange transfers from nearby Buffalo Range airport.

Luxury

⌂ **Chilo Gorge Safari Lodge** (10 chalets) m 0774 999059; e info@chilogorge.com; www. chilogorge.com. This place is focused around a beautifully designed, thatched central complex which includes indoor & outdoor restaurant, a bar jutting out over the gorge with spectacular river views, lounge area & good-sized pool. Nicely appointed, luxury twin-bed chalets are arranged along the shallow gorge rim. Each is glass-fronted, opening onto a balcony with stunning views of riverine forest & the Save Valley. Even non-birdwatchers will marvel at the garish saddle-billed storks that strut up & down opposite the lodge. Staff are friendly & helpful & the guides know Gonarezhou National Park like the backs of their hands, offering an array of vehicle & walking safaris into the national park, including drives to the Chilojo Cliffs, game & birding trips plus a not-to-be-missed cultural-cum-educational visit to the Shangaan village of Mahenye (see box, 'CAMPFIRE' at Mahenye, page 329, and Mahenye village, page 332.) (The lodge also has another self catering option ideal for self-drivers – **Nhambo Camp** a short distance away with 4 dbl/twin lodges and a 6-bed family unit.) See ad, colour page 16. **$$$$**

⌂ **Mahenye Lodge** At the time of writing this was still closed after several years but I was informed that it is likely to be resurrected during 2013. If this is so it will return to being a delightful, remote lodge built on a wooded island in the river with amazing birdlife. You may want to email Chilo Gorge Lodge to enquire about Mahenye.

Camping In theory, you should pre-book these sites through National Parks in Harare; in reality it's rather unlikely that your reservation will get through. On the basis that Gonarezhou is one of the least-busy parks, it's unlikely you'll find the sites full if you arrive unbooked.

THE ENTERPRISING MR MUTEMA

Tucked away in the middle of Mahenye village, Mr Mutema runs his tiny enterprise with enthusiasm and entrepreneurial spirit. He is delighted to lead you on a dizzying tour of his projects, all the time asking your opinion on how he could improve his products. This gentle and engaging chap stocks his small craft shop (a world away from the usual curio shop) with reed mats and trays, bows and arrows, sandals made from old car tyres and simple carved wooden items, all made by himself. He's also started farming guineafowl to sell to the two lodges, and is currently wondering how to obtain a small incubator, although I suspect he'll soon design his own. While other villagers roof their huts in the traditional way, with reeds, Mr Mutema has covered his with tiles fashioned from cut-up, interlaced car tyres: completely waterproof and not requiring annual re-thatching. At the rear of his plot is an improvised lathe made from a couple of old bearings either end of a table leg and hand-driven with a length of cord by his delightful wife. With this and a set of homemade tools he produces some very nice hardwood ashtrays and bowls.

Mrs Mutema is not without her talents. When a loaf of bread in Zimbabwe was costing a month's wages, Mrs Mutema was supplying her neighbours with delicious bread rolls for a fraction of the shop price. She is hoping to acquire a sewing machine to set up her own clothing business.

At the end of my visit Mr Mutema picked up his mbira (thumb piano), made from old bed springs and bottle tops, and serenaded us with a gentle song.

There are campsites dotted around the park, most offering idyllic views of the river with not another human being for miles. From November to the end of April, only Chipinda Pools stays open, although rather confusingly if it's been a 'dry' wet season and conditions allow, they will let you camp elsewhere.

Most campsites are undeveloped, which means basic facilities, *braai* stand, no water and usually, but not always, a long-drop toilet. Food and water must be carried in and all rubbish taken out. Camping costs US$10 per person.

⚔ Chipinda Pools This spotlessly clean campsite has running water & flush toilets although the plumbing can be erratic. There are 9 very separated pitches nestling under the trees right next to the river, with small thatched rondavels & a community of hippos to serenade you into the night. Iridescent blue long-tailed starlings peck around as soon as your back is turned, & you may wake during the night to elephants breaking branches & the distinctive roar (actually more of a huge grunt) of lions echoing off the hills behind. Pure magic.

⚔ Chilojo Cliffs ◈ S21 26 29 E32 05 17. You can view the cliffs from the opposite (north) side of the river or drive along the top of them looking down into the valley. The 2 campsites opposite the cliffs offer spectacular views of the river & cliffs. Site 1 has a large, open thatched rondavel, plus long-drop toilets. Huge deposits of elephant dung suggest this could be an interesting place to camp. Site 2, some 200m away, has seen better days; any facilities that might have been there no longer are. Move a few metres away from the broken ablution block & suddenly you are in the bush with no signs of human presence. From these 2 camps you can watch elephants cross the sandy riverbed in winter. Small groups of nyala & other antelope come down in late afternoon. In the morning you'll see from the distinct, geometrical tracks in the riverbed that the Runde has a healthy population of crocodiles.

Wilderness campsites There are a number of clearly marked wilderness campsites along the river, accessed from the cliff-top drive before you get to the main viewpoints. It's then not too far to **Fishans Camp** and **Chinguli Camp**, two other large, shady, undeveloped riverside campsites with long-drop toilets.

What to see and do
Chipinda Pools to Chilojo Cliffs You'll take this route if you're heading to Chilo or Mahenya lodges from Chipinda Pools. Although the road was rebuilt in 2011, always ask Parks staff about the condition of the roads before you set out; they will look at your vehicle and advise you accordingly. It's not only whether your 4x4 (especially the tyres) can negotiate the conditions but how much damage the paintwork may suffer from thorn scratches.

You will get tantalising glimpses of the Runde River, pass through a variety of different landscapes – sometimes forest, sometimes open grassland – and more often than not brilliantly coloured white-fronted bee-eaters will be flitting from tree to tree in front of your vehicle. Yellow-billed hornbills accompany you for your whole drive. Prodigious quantities of elephant dung as well as footprints along the road will confirm that the 'Gonarezhou ghosts' are never far away from you.

The **Chilojo Cliffs** are a towering range of sandstone cliffs running along a bend on the south bank of the Runde River. Late afternoon and sunset bring a succession of orange to deep red tints to the cliffs, and this is the time to be on the north bank with your camera and your sundowner drink. Many say the cliffs resemble a huge Rajasthan fortress, but there may be a more local interpretation: the name Chilojo is thought to be derived from the Shona word *ulojo*, referring to the mouth or palate of an elephant, and I can confirm that there is indeed a marked similarity between a jumbo's dental structure and the striated cliffs of Chilojo. In true colonial style, Allan Wright, who was district commissioner at the time (1960s), writing in his book *Valley of the Ironwoods*, deplored the name change from Clarendon Cliffs to Chilojo. 'Whatever next,' he thundered, 'they'll be calling Salisbury, Harare.'

Cliff-top drive from Chilo A dirt road running up behind and along the top of the cliffs brings you out at two spectacular viewpoints directly across the river from the north bank campsites. Get here early in the day for the best photos. If you are staying at Chilo Gorge you may prefer to take a tour from the lodge, as the road is tortuous in places and not always clearly marked. The challenge is finding the appropriate river crossing and picking up the track on the other side; for this, ask the guides at Chilo Gorge Lodge, as the exact crossing changes from season to season. Otherwise, start from the park office across the river from the lodge and follow the signs to Chipinda Pools. When the river first comes into clear view from the road, look out for a lone baobab tree and follow the car tracks leading off the road down to the river. It's a shallow, sandy crossing (⊕ *S21 18 51.5 E32 17 09.8*). On the other side the track is at first difficult to find but tends to be marked by slash marks on trees lining the route until you get to a more well-defined road where you again pick up signs to Chipinda Pools.

AROUND GONAREZHOU NATIONAL PARK

CHIVIRIRA FALLS (⊕ *S21 14 21.7 E32 20 35.3; take the road from Chilo Lodge turn-off towards Chiredzi & turn left after 1km, following the track for just over 1km*) In Shona, *chivirira* (*chivilila* in Shangaan) means 'boiling water'. In winter you'll query the name because you are treated to a tranquil river winding its way around massive boulders and rocky river bed formations – but full flood after summer rains is an altogether different experience, when the ground literally vibrates with the power of the churning water. There's a *braai* stand at the viewpoint, an excellent place to rise early and have breakfast as the sun rises. Alternatively, in late afternoon the bats come out of the caves and you can witness the amazing aerial agility of the bat hawks, as they make high-speed stoops, sometimes catching three or four bats in a single strike. These birds are such effective predators that they only need to hunt for short periods at dusk and sometimes early morning, spending the rest of their day roosting.

Amazingly, a number of saltwater fish species that can also tolerate fresh water are to be found in the Runde and Save rivers, having navigated nearly 300km up the Save from the Indian Ocean, only to halt at Chivirira and Chitove Falls. Most spectacular among these creatures is the Zambezi or bull shark, which grows up to 3m and accounts for many more human deaths than the unfairly notorious great white. Recent silting has reduced the depth of the pools that these sharks rely on, so it's some years since they have been spotted here.

MAHENYE VILLAGE Chilo Gorge Lodge offers trips to this Shangaan village, a shining example of the success of CAMPFIRE. Unlike many villages featuring in tourist brochures, Mahenye is 100% genuine, without exploitation or 'dressing up for the tourists'. The Shangaan are descended from the Zulu chief Shoshangana, who led a northern-bound splinter group at the time of Shaka's great purge. They now occupy a patch of land in the southwest corner of Zimbabwe, and in contrast to many other cultures have retained their language and much of their traditional lifestyle, albeit greatly enhanced by CAMPFIRE incomes.

Mahenye is a very spread-out village and the population, which numbered some 5,000 at the last census in 2002, is believed to have grown with the return of relatives attracted by the village's prosperity. Although they benefit from hunting revenues and a percentage of lodge profits, the inhabitants continue to work in traditional ways, with an emphasis on products derived from the harvest of reeds. They keep cattle and goats and grow most of their own staple foodstuffs such as maize, sorghum and millet.

These versatile crops not only grind down to a coarse flour for *sadza* but form the basis for home-brewed beer. Ask your guide to see if there is a recent brew available or nearing completion, and pluck up the courage to sample the frothy, muddy liquid fermenting away in plastic tubs. You'll drink it from a gourd, and village onlookers will delight at your polite attempts to pretend you are enjoying it.

Ask if you can look inside one of their huts or rondavels. The roof space is used as a store for maize, sorghum etc, and smoke from their fires filters through this to kill weevils and other crop destroyers.

SAVE VALLEY CONSERVANCY When settlers arrived in this area, just north of what is now Gonarezhou National Park, they found a grassland environment that supported abundant wildlife, leading them to believe it would make excellent cattle grazing. The new farmers eradicated the wildlife, but equally quickly realised that this area of unreliable rainfall actually provided limited agricultural potential. Successive droughts and tsetse flies through the 1980s made farming untenable, and landowners began to take notice of the 1975 Parks and Wildlife Act which, giving them ownership of any wildlife on their land, appeared to offer an alternative revenue source. This coincided with Parks' urgent need to relocate black rhino from the Zambezi Valley, where poaching was pushing them towards local extinction. The Save area (pronounced *sahvey*) was prime rhino country, so in 1991–92 after another devastating drought, a group of 21 farmers agreed to remove their cattle, take out all their fencing and replace it with one encircling fence around their collective 3,420km². (Compare that with Gonarezhou's 5,000km² for a sense of the size of the conservancy.) Along with rhino they began to reintroduce other big game and build an economy of high-quality, low-impact tourism.

A crucial factor was the involvement of local communities as stakeholders, based on CAMPFIRE principles. The conservancy saw remarkable success, becoming the largest privately owned wildlife reserve in the world. Limited trophy hunting was introduced, and revenues not only funded expensive black rhino research and conservation programmes but also benefited the local population. As well as hundreds of black and white rhinos, thousands of elephants relocated from drought-stricken Gonarezhou thrived alongside abundant plains game, including a healthy population of wild dogs.

As I write, the whole programme is now in jeopardy. The property has been seized under the government's Land Reform Programme and ownership has been transferred to individuals who are allegedly not continuing the conservation project. This has become a major political issue and at the end of 2012 the situation was still unresolved.

MALILANGWE TRUST This non-profit organisation administers the 400km² Malilangwe Estate just north of Gonarezhou, with a remit to foster rural development while restoring and protecting the area's habitats and wildlife. They have developed a number of ambitious outreach programmes including conservation education and a daily food-support programme for 25,000 pre-school children. On the wildlife side, Malilangwe (meaning 'call of the leopard' in Shangaan) boasts a diverse array of game animals including the 'Big Five', the 'small six' (a collection of small antelope – grey duiker, Sharpe's grysbok, steenbok, klipspringer, oribi and Livingstone's suni) and the 'magnificent seven' eagle species. A star among nocturnal animals you might see is the rare and secretive brown hyena.

⌂ Where to stay

Luxury

⌂ **Singita Pamushana Lodge** (6 luxury villas) e enquiries@singita.com; www.singita.com. This is reputed to be one of the most exclusive & luxurious safari lodges in Africa, with prices to match. Set on high ground, each of the large, opulently furnished villa suites is self-contained, with a private plunge pool, lounge, indoor & outdoor showers, fridge & minibar & spectacular elevated views of Malilangwe Dam. The thatched main lodge houses spa, gym, yoga room & 2 pools. The pool deck has a fixed telescope (Swarovski, of course) for wildlife viewing. Prices include all activities, meals & drinks, in fact everything except champagnes. Exclusivity is the name of the game, & you will have Malilangwe's wildlife pretty well to yourself, as there are only 6 game-viewing vehicles on the estate. As well as game drives they offer walking safaris, tennis, fishing, mountain biking, horseriding & rock-art trips. With the trust involved in the local community, you can also visit some of their projects. It's a remote location but staff will arrange transport to suit your needs. Most guests will be shuttled to the lodge's own airstrip having flown into Buffalo Range airport. **$$$$$+**

11

The Eastern Highlands

The Eastern Highlands run south to north for some 300km, taking in three distinct areas, each a tourist haven in its own right – the Chimanimani Mountains, the Bvumba Mountains and, in the north, the Nyanga Highlands, rising to 2,592m at Mount Nyangani, Zimbabwe's highest point. The border with Mozambique runs through the range. With its European climate, rugged hills, spectacular valleys and gorges, waterfalls, rivers and lakes, you could be forgiven for thinking you were in Scotland rather than the middle of Africa. Early settlers sought refuge here from the summer heat, and today it retains a colonial feel, especially in its architecture and in the style of many of its hotels and inns.

This is a rich agricultural area, although much of the landscape is given over to commercial forestry, with only isolated areas of natural vegetation remaining. Eucalyptus services the country's demand for fencing, construction and gumpoles while pine and wattle are grown mainly for construction and paper pulp. The plantations can make the driving monotonous, but you will also find some of the most dramatic tropical mountain scenery you are ever likely to see.

Winter, despite its crisp mornings and dry, warm days, is also the season for bushfires and controlled burns in the plantations, in Zimbabwe and to an even greater extent across the border in Mozambique. This results in swathes of blackened, smouldering landscapes, and depending on prevailing conditions the haze can seriously spoil your views and photographic opportunities. April, May and June offer the best weather and visibility. Access to viewpoints is often restricted to 4x4s, as the dirt roads are generally neglected, with ruts and rocks requiring high clearance. Some are impassable in the summer rains.

Although the national parks and private reserves are stocked with plains game, visitors do not generally come here to see wildlife (other than birds). But if you like horseriding, fishing, hiking or perhaps golf, this is the place to come. It is also a Mecca for birders, with a wealth of 'specials' waiting to boost your list.

The Eastern Highlands boast a range of accommodations from some of the finest hotels in the country, cosy English-style inns and bed and breakfasts, right down to caves in the Chimanimani Mountains for overnighting hikers.

GETTING THERE AND AROUND

There are air charter services to various airfields but you will still be faced with getting around after you land. Towns are small enough to walk around but you will need transport to all the outlying attractions. With the current lack of intercity coaches and reliable local buses the only alternative for independent travellers is self-drive, in your own vehicle or a hire car. There are currently no rental agencies in the highlands so you would need to collect a hire car in Harare or Bulawayo.

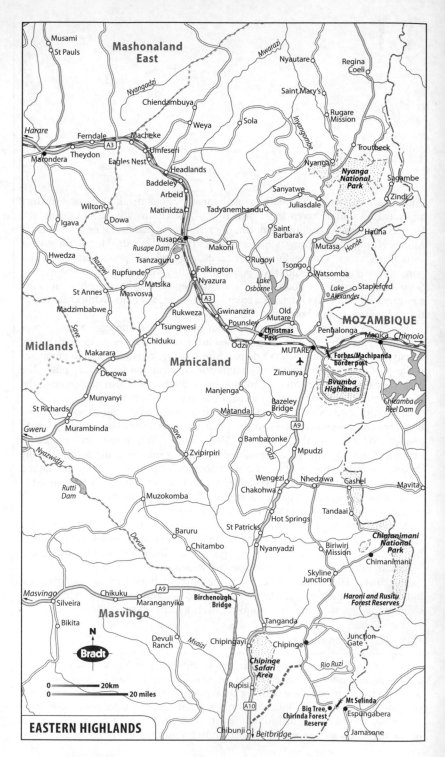

EASTERN HIGHLANDS

If you don't wish to drive yourself, the alternative is a complete trip through the region with one of the agencies listed in *Chapter 3* on page 86.

SOUTHERN AREA

Your stay in this southern area of the highlands will undoubtedly be focused on the small village of Chimanimani, not only because of its proximity to the national park but also for the practical reason that there is currently nowhere else convenient to stay. The park itself is a hiking centre and you'll get some brilliant photographic opportunities on a clear day, with views right across the mountains into neighbouring Mozambique. Some of the finest views in the country are along the Cashel scenic route, but you'll need a rugged 4x4 and quite a bit of confidence!

CHIPINGE (*Telephone code 0227*) This is a town you pass through, rather than stop at, on your way between Chiredzi and Chimanimani or Mutare. It has seen better days and there is little to tempt even the most inquisitive traveller, although it is the nearest centre to the village of Mount Selinda and to the Chirinda Forest Reserve, home to what is reputedly the largest and oldest tree in Zimbabwe. Chipinge is in the heart of a rich agricultural area focusing largely on coffee and tea, but it also sees the beginnings of the forestry plantations that extend up into the Eastern Highlands.

Where to stay To visit Mount Selinda and the Chirinda Forest Reserve it's best to overnight in Chimanimani or even Chiredzi rather than here. Chipinge Hotel, the only one in town, is now very shabby, covered with security bars, and looks like a jail. Several individuals hanging around outside it when I visited looked like they belonged inside a jail. Locals describe the hotel as being in the red light district, although as the town is so small and the hotel is right in the centre, the hotel itself must *be* the red light district.

There are bed and breakfasts around town but all were either unmanned when I visited during the day or simply unable to quote an overnight rate. I decided they were unused to guests who wanted to use the rooms for more than an hour or two. Kiledo Lodge, signposted at the entrance to town, is no longer in operation, nor is the town's campsite. If you are stuck, I did find one option:

Standard
⌂ **48 Moodie St** (5 rooms) Cnr Moodie & Odendaal sts; ☏ 027 2239/2693. This little guesthouse has a pleasant lounge & dining room.

There's no self-catering but they will prepare meals to order. It all looked clean, & the gentleman who showed me around was very friendly. **$$**

MOUNT SELINDA Mount Selinda is an unremarkable village that originally formed around an American health mission set up over 100 years ago, which subsequently became an agricultural training centre. Probably its biggest claim to fame is the memorial to the British naturalist, Charles Francis Swynnerton, who lived here, documenting local flora and fauna, at the turn of the 20th century. Birders will know his name from the lively but elusive little robin that makes its home in this small area of eastern Zimbabwe.

CHIRINDA FOREST RESERVE Given the extensive commercial plantations covering so much of the area to the north, this is a very special place – the southernmost tropical rainforest in Africa – and a refuge for those who love natural, ancient forests. Many trees here have been standing for centuries. You can wander for hours beneath the canopy of mahogany and other hardwoods, but you will probably have come here to the 'Valley of the Giants' to check out what is said to be Zimbabwe's largest and oldest tree, a monster red mahogany measuring 16m in girth and 66m in height. Local people will tell you the tree dates back to the time of Christ, although the best estimate of its age is 600–1,000 years. Some will tell you the poor old thing is dying. To get there, follow the well-marked route from the Mount Selinda road by the mission hospital. There is a pleasant, cheap campsite here, also some chalets with clean facilities and *braai* stands – you must bring in all your catering supplies as there's no shop in the vicinity. It's situated about 4km into the forest from the road to Espungabera (✆ *012 7224, 624841*).

CHIMANIMANI (*Telephone code 026*) The Chimanimani range, stretching for 50km north to south, forms the southernmost part of the Eastern Highlands, with peaks and sandstone ridges rising to 2,440m. The mountains are not volcanic but an upthrust range, with a leading, west-facing escarpment largely within Zimbabwe and pressure folds behind constituting the valleys and high plains of Mozambique. Most of the range lies in Mozambique; the Zimbabwe side is only about 7km wide at most. Quartz sandstone gives the mountains their pale white or grey aspect, with schist slopes occupying the intermediate areas. The chief attraction in this stunningly beautiful area is walking and hiking.

With its troubled recent history Chimanimani village used to be a little ill at ease with itself as the villagers could be quite reserved and cautious when dealing with visitors. But it's great to see all that has changed and that visitors are now, once again, receiving the friendly welcome that is a trademark of Zimbabwe and that the accommodation owners are optimistic and gearing up for the future.

History Named Melsetter by pioneer George Moodie, after his home in the Orkneys, the village was a base for South African settlers in the 1890s. It was renamed in 1982. A popular explanation of the name (of the village and the mountains) refers to Skeleton Pass, the track that formed a main trading route between Zimbabwe and Mozambique. In places this was so narrow that it could only be walked single file; a rough Shona translation for this is *chimanimani*.

The area's proximity to Mozambique made it a hot spot during the Rhodesian war, with key guerrilla bases just across the border. The area was heavily laid with landmines by Rhodesian troops, and to this day you are urged not to stray off the beaten track. More recently this was an area of vigorous 'war veteran' activity, following the election in 2000 of a white MP, Roy Bennett, by the black majority. He was forced off his farm into exile and his lodge, Mawenje, which features in older guidebooks, was burnt to the ground. (Bennett is now treasurer of MDC (T) in exile.)

Chimanimani has seen more disruption in recent years because the national park is a gold-bearing area. Local, but widespread, small-scale panning both here and across the border in Mozambique saw some violence between the authorities and the panners, as well as squabbles between the panners themselves, but the situation has returned to normal now with the illegal panners having been chased off back into Mozambique.

Getting there Mutare is 150km/93 miles away, Masvingo 278km/173 miles, Harare 415km/258 miles. Chimanimani is not served by any form of public transport. Access from Mozambique to the Chirinda Forest area and Chipinge is via the little-used Espungabera border post.

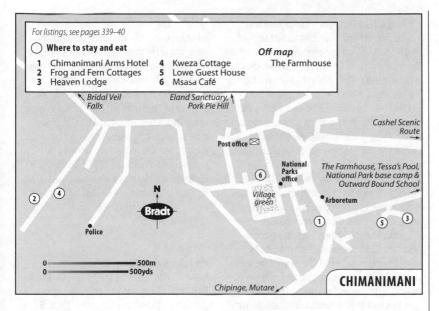

For listings, see pages 339–40

Where to stay and eat

1 Chimanimani Arms Hotel
2 Frog and Fern Cottages
3 Heaven Lodge
4 Kweza Cottage
5 Lowe Guest House
6 Msasa Café

Off map
The Farmhouse

Bridal Veil
Falls

Eland Sanctuary,
Pork Pie Hill

Cashel Scenic
Route

Post office

National
Parks
office

The Farmhouse, Tessa's Pool,
National Park base camp &
Outward Bound School

Village
green

Arboretum

N

Bradt

Police

0 ————————— 500m
0 ————————— 500yds

Chipinge, Mutare

CHIMANIMANI

Getting around It's only a small village so walking is the order of the day, and you can get to most places of interest on foot, albeit with some long walks. You'll need wheels to get to the hiking areas of Chimanimani National Park (see page 342), but as there is currently no public transport you really need your own.

Tourist information The excellent and delightfully energetic **Chimanimani Publicity Association** (m 0775 920440, 0773 476110, 0772 101283; e touristassociation chimanimani@gmail.com; www.thefrogandfern.com) is up and running again after a period of hibernation and at the time of writing was operating from Frog and Fern Cottages under the guidance of Jane High. Go to the website and click on 'Chimanimani Tourist Association' at the bottom of the page for local update information. The helpful staff at the National Parks office next to the Mobil filling station will give you all of the information you need for walking and hiking in the park.

Where to stay The village still serves as a launching point for hikers venturing into the mountains that form its backdrop in every direction. The Chimanimani Arms Hotel, the centrepiece of town, upholds its standards against all odds, waiting for better days. When tourists do start returning, book your accommodation in advance, as the area is not overstocked with hotel rooms.

Standard

🏠 **Chimanimani Arms Hotel** (35 rooms) PO Box 5; ☎ 2850; m 0773 220163; e chimanimanihotel@zol.co.zw. This lovely, though rather faded colonial-style hotel refuses to enter the 21st century & although it has seen better days still has a wonderful atmosphere & charm. It is set in beautiful grounds, although not all rooms enjoy mountain views. It has good-sized rooms – twins, dbls & 4 family rooms – with open fireplace, balcony & old-fashioned bathrooms. There's plenty of dark wood panelling but lounge & restaurant are large & airy, with attentive staff in starched white shirts. The 'casino' appears to be just a locals' gambling den, in an adjacent building. The delightful gardens are home to several species of sunbird. They also offer camping but it's opposite the bus stop & can get rather noisy. **$$**

🏠 **Frog & Fern Cottages** (3 cottages) About 2km up dirt road from town, past Msasa Café; m 0775 920 440; e frogandfern@gmail.com; www. thefrogandfern.com. One of the nicest places to stay in the area, with refurbished self-catering cottages. The best choice is Miombo Cottage, a large thatched rondavel with a semicircular 1st-floor balcony that can sleep 4, though there are no separate bedrooms as such. The split-level ground floor is arranged around a central fireplace with lounge & dining area, kitchen, bathroom & en-suite dbl bedroom. The adjacent Msasa Cottage has 1 twin bedroom & a sgl bed in the lounge & a large patio for outdoor dining. These 2 cottages make a great place for a family or a group. Mzanje Cabin is a cosy wooden cabin sleeping 2/3 with a lounge & kitchen & outside seating & *braai* area. B&B also available, as is camping for up to 6 people (max 3 4x4s). The owner, Jane, lives close by & is always on hand to assist & offers to accompany you on her favourite walks with her friendly rescue dogs. Horseriding also available with a max rider weight of 60kg. **$**

🏠 **Kweza Cottage** (sleeps 8) Along the same road as the Frog and Fern; ☎ 3030; m 0772 101283. Has 3 twins downstairs, a kitchen/diner & large lounge with log fire. A wonderful 'tree staircase' leads upstairs to the en-suite, thatched dbl bedroom. **$**

🏠 **The Farmhouse** (3 rooms) On the left 1km from the village centre on the national park road

☎ 3351, 3030; m 0772 101283; e dougvan@ zol.co.zw; www.chimanifarmhouse.com. This place, one of the oldest colonial-style buildings still standing in Chimanimani, has recently been renovated to be a self-catering guesthouse. It's spacious with open-plan sitting & dining room & a fireplace for Chimanimani's chilly winter evenings. The kitchen is fully equipped with a small gas stove & fridge. 1 dbl room, 2 twins & 2 bathrooms; contact them first to see if you still need to bring your own bedding & towels, which was a requirement when they were setting up in 2012. It's great for children as it's a working farm with a variety of animals including horses available for children to ride. **$**

Basic
🏠 **Lowe Guest House** (3 rooms) Next to Heaven Lodge; ☎ 2270; m 0773 439774. A basic B&B with self-catering kitchen, dining room, shared bath/toilet & outside shower block. **$**

🏠 **Heaven Lodge** 300m down the Outward Bound Rd; ☎ 2701. In recent years this place became pretty well non-habitable but it's good to hear that renovation work has started (late 2012) & that already people are beginning to return to what was once a popular & lively backpackers'. There are dorms & dbls here plus some basic wood & thatch chalets. **$**

✕ **Where to eat** Apart from the Chimanimani Arms Hotel restaurant there really is nowhere else to eat, so for most it's self catering.

🖵 **Msasa Café** Opposite the village green. Once a very popular eaterie; with virtually no visitors the owners struggled to keep it open. It's now run very much as a locals' bar.

Shopping The only craft shop has closed down, so there's little more here than provisions for your camping trip to the hills. There is a fairly comprehensive shopping centre, and a filling station, bank and post office all in close proximity to one another.

What to see and do
Chimanimani Arts Festival The annual three-day Chimanimani Arts Festival on the village green has been dubbed 'the festival with altitude'. First organised in 1998 by local residents as a celebration of Zimbabwean performing arts, it was cancelled for two years due to the political and economic situation, then revived in 2008. It's a great showcase for Zimbabwe's vibrant arts scene and encompasses traditional, modern and fusion influences. It's very popular, with free entry, but visitors will find it difficult to get accommodation as everything is booked far in advance; camping may be the only option. Information on the festival is currently a little difficult to source and it's not always held at the same time every year so an

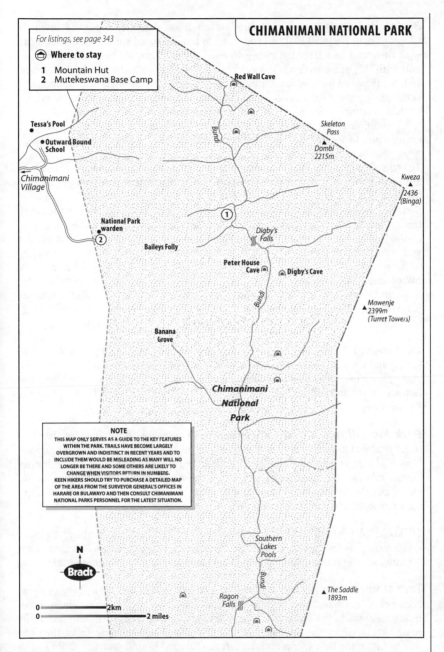

For listings, see page 343

Where to stay

1 Mountain Hut
2 Mutekeswana Base Camp

Red Wall Cave

Tessa's Pool

Outward Bound School

Chimanimani Village

Skeleton Pass

Dombi 2215m

Kweza 2436 (Binga)

National Park warden

Digby's Falls

Baileys Folly

Peter House Cave

Digby's Cave

Mawenje 2399m (Turret Towers)

Banana Grove

Bundi

Chimanimani National Park

NOTE

THIS MAP ONLY SERVES AS A GUIDE TO THE KEY FEATURES WITHIN THE PARK. TRAILS HAVE BECOME LARGELY OVERGROWN AND INDISTINCT IN RECENT YEARS AND TO INCLUDE THEM WOULD BE MISLEADING AS MANY WILL NO LONGER BE THERE AND SOME OTHERS ARE LIKELY TO CHANGE WHEN VISITORS RETURN IN NUMBERS. KEEN HIKERS SHOULD TRY TO PURCHASE A DETAILED MAP OF THE AREA FROM THE SURVEYOR GENERAL'S OFFICES IN HARARE OR BULAWAYO AND THEN CONSULT CHIMANIMANI NATIONAL PARKS PERSONNEL FOR THE LATEST SITUATION.

N

Bradt

Southern Lakes Pools

Ragon Falls

The Saddle 1893m

0 — 2km
0 — 2 miles

11

internet search is recommended if you are planning to visit, or you could email e zimpala@bsatt.com.

Arboretum This is situated on the other side of the main road from the village but it's easy to drive past, being neglected and sadly overgrown. But the splendid trees are still there so it shouldn't take much to spruce up the area when better times arrive.

Bridal Veil Falls This high, slim waterfall is some 6km out of town in Chimanimani National Park, so you need to pay the usual entry fees, and you can walk there and back from the village in about three hours. There must be countless falls with this name around the world but this one actually does look like a bridal veil. Nestling in a wooded amphitheatre with a decidedly mystical atmosphere, this is the perfect place for a peaceful picnic amongst umbrella thorn trees, beech, kei apple and combretum.

Birdwatching can be very rewarding, with stripe-cheeked greenbul, grey wagtail, scarce swift, Livingstone's touraco, starred and Cape robin to be found.

Tessa's Pool Tessa's Pool is on land leased by the Outward Bound School, so although it's open to the public at most times, access is denied when the school is using it. Follow signs from the village to the Outward Bound School; just before their buildings is a small information post, on the left. This is the start of the 300m track down to the pool, a mini version of Bridal Veil Falls: a small, hidden waterfall clothed in fern and tree creepers, plunging into a shallow pool. Note that picnics and *braai*s are prohibited.

It's a long way to drive just to visit the pool so best to include it either end of a hiking trip. Little sunlight pierces the verdant tree growth but the icy cold water looks inviting, especially after a long hike in the summer months. Tessa was the baby daughter of one of the first Outward Bound instructors, and the pool was the only spot where she would stop crying, or so one of several stories goes.

Horseriding The foothills and mountains offer superb riding country. Two riding stables once operated here, with facilities for beginners and experienced riders, but closed for lack of business. Limited riding facilities have now returned but are really only suitable for children. Ask at Frog and Fern Cottages or the Farmhouse.

Pork Pie Hill and Eland Sanctuary Both of these attractions are listed in older guidebooks and leaflets, but are something of a let-down if you have already been hiking in and around the national park. The aptly named, rounded but rather barren hill and the rough drive up to the Eland Sanctuary certainly offer grand views, but the fences have long since disappeared from the sanctuary so the eland have run away and been eaten many years ago.

CHIMANIMANI NATIONAL PARK (*NP Category 3;* ✎*2555, 2705*) September–October is the most popular time to visit as the temperature is rising but it's not too hot for walking, with light rains clearing the air, revealing spectacular mountain vistas.

Tourist information Most walkers start from the National Parks base camp at Mutekeswane, some 23.5km from Chimanimani village. Take the Tilbury road, following signs to the Outward Bound School. After 15.5km turn left onto a dirt road, passing Charleswood School on your left. After 5km the road splits, the right fork going to the base camp and the left to Outward Bound and Tessa's Pool. The base camp is permanently staffed and there is ample space for car parking and camping on terraced pitches. It is also safe to leave your car here if you plan to hike for a number of days.

🏠 **Where to stay** You can free-camp anywhere in the park. There are no toilet facilities other than at base camp, so be considerate of those who will arrive after you. The river water is clean and many walkers drink from it, so please do nothing to pollute it. Wildlife includes baboons, who are never far away from regular overnighting spots, so never leave anything edible unattended.

Base camp Good camping facilities with clean ablutions, although the sites are on terraced ground that also serves as the car park. *US$10 per person.*

Mountain hut Sleeps up to 30 on wooden beds, but bring everything else you need. There is a propane cooking facility but it's a long time since the rings have seen any gas. Recent reports say the hut is in a deplorable condition now and it's best to camp or sleep in the caves. *US$10 per person.*

Caves and overhangs These very basic overnighting spots appeal to intrepid campers and are deservedly popular. There's no charge to sleep in them, and no booking system, but check with the warden at base camp. The area is dotted with these sites, most along the Bundi valley north and south of the hut; their locations are marked on the Milkmap map (see below) as well as on a map at base camp.

Mountain walking This is top-class but serious hiking country so don't be tempted to set off with just a T-shirt, shorts and a pair of trainers. Weather can change quickly, people do get lost up here and the fact that there is a mountain rescue team should alert you to the dangers. Always advise the warden of your route and the expected duration of your hike, stick to your plan and don't forget that you must check back in with them as soon as you return.

Guides are available for hire (*US$10pp per hour; for longer hikes, US$100 for three days plus US$40 per additional day, maximum 6 people*) but must be booked a couple of days in advance. You can purchase a map, published by Milkmaps, from the village or at the base camp, but it's more of a guide than a detailed map, with no scale or elevations. Even this map warns that the footpaths shown are only a guide, as they erode and change. Light footfall since 2000 has left some paths quite indistinct, so I haven't marked them on the accompanying map. Take a compass; I would also recommend a handheld GPS.

Not much remains of the park's wildlife. Although predators such as lion and leopard are said to occupy some areas, be heartened by the fact there have been absolutely no reports of attacks on hikers. Older guidebooks warn hikers to keep strictly to paths as this area was laid with landmines to deter guerrillas, but baboon and eland traffic cleared them long ago, and Parks staff and local guides know of no reports of incidents since the early 1980s.

Routes The mountain hut, reachable via the scenic **Baileys Folly** track from Mutekeswane base camp in no more than three hours, is the focal point for many routes.

Skeleton Pass links Zimbabwe and Mozambique and was once a key route for guerrillas. (It has recently become a key route for gold panners.) It offers some of the best views into Mozambique's magnificent and seemingly endless mountains and valleys; the walk from the hut will take you about 45 minutes each way.

From the hut to the 2,436m summit of **Mount Binga**, allow up to three hours of stiff but very worthwhile walking, as on a clear day it's possible to see right across Mozambique to the Indian Ocean.

The **Hadange River Track** is an alternative exit route from the hut, bringing you out near Outward Bound and Tessa's Pool. It's quite a difficult route in places, especially after rain. Don't forget that you must check out of the park at Mutekeswane base camp.

Walks south of the hut take you past **Digby's Falls** to the over-grandly named river pools known as **Southern Lakes**, and then up to the **Saddle**, the southernmost pass into Mozambique. From Southern Lakes you can take a different return route to base camp via **Banana Grove**, but allow seven to eight hours from the hut to complete this route.

AROUND CHIMANIMANI

Cashel scenic route Scenic it certainly is; as the dirt road winds its way through the Cashel Valley following the jigsaw-like contour lines along the Mozambican border, one is rewarded with continuous, breathtaking mountain and valley views. Readers of the first edition of this book may have been put off by my description of the condition of this track, which was severely devastated by Cyclone Eline in 2000

DIAMOND RUSH

Wealth, corruption and violence have been visited upon the area around Marange, about 60km southwest of Mutare. In late 2006 alluvial diamonds were found unusually close to the surface, drawing illegal prospectors in their thousands to the area. The Marange fields have subsequently been described as the largest ever source of diamonds in southern Africa. The mining rights were in fact owned by a British company, African Consolidated Resources, but when news of the finds reached the government it promptly evicted the company and handed control to the state-owned Zimbabwe Mining Development Corporation. Properly managed, the diamonds could have considerably boosted foreign currency earnings and made a healthy contribution towards Zimbabwe's embattled economy. This was not to be the case although there are now muted suggestions that the situation may eventually be coming under control.

But several years after the first finds, chaos is still the order of the day. Senior politicians and army officers are alleged to be making personal fortunes, while an estimated 150 illegal prospectors have been killed by the authorities, gem warlords or one another, and others risk their lives on a daily basis. It is thought that gems with an estimated value of over US$2 billion have been smuggled onto the black market. An element of legitimacy was granted when the Kimberley Process controversially approved the sale of these diamonds in 2009, creating international protest due to the reported human rights abuses, something the Kimberley Process was designed to prevent. Thousands of people from the rest of the country have flocked to the area and the government is considering the forced relocation of everyone from there, including the original inhabitants with ancestral rights to the area.

Driving between Birchenough Bridge and Mutare it's not unusual for illegal diamond and emerald dealers to try and flag you down, making a diamond sign with their fingers and offering 'bargains'. You probably don't need any advice from your Bradt guide in this respect.

You should also resist any temptation to drive into this area (even though you may be heading for the many nearby ancient ruin sites) as you definitely will not be welcome and would almost certainly be inviting arrest or even violence.

and which demanded a sturdy 4x4, a reasonable amount of off-road experience and five or six hours to complete the drive. Since then the road has been graded, is now much better and drivable with any high clearance vehicle. It's now a beautiful and viable alternative route between Chimanimani and Mutare.

Haroni and Rusitu forest reserves These small, remote patches of lowland forest, the last in Zimbabwe, are at the confluence of the Haroni and Rusitu rivers at the very southern tip of Chimanimani National Park, and right on the Mozambican border. The area is home to the Vhimba people, who over the last 150 years have been increasingly marginalised as their traditional lands were taken over by commercial forestry. The Vhimba still consider what's left of the forest to be sacred, but are happy to grant access to the few visitors who make their way here.

The reserves were once a naturalist's paradise, with rare lowland forest plant and butterfly species, and a Mecca for birders, with its huge list of forest specials. Recent reports say that the 20ha Haroni Reserve has been trashed and is now a banana plantation, with Rusitu's 150ha under similar threat.

Birchenough Bridge You'll come across this rather beautiful engineering oddity on the Masvingo road 60km northeast of Chipinge as the crow flies, and if it reminds you of the Sydney Harbour bridge, that's because it's an exact, scaled-down replica of it, and by the same designer, Sir Ralph Freeman. Yet its design was for thoroughly practical reasons, rather than novelty value as is sometimes suggested. The Save River here rises up to 9m in full flood and the sandy riverbed is notoriously unstable, to the point that piers were deemed unsuitable, hence the single-arch suspension design. At its official opening in late 1935 it was the third-largest suspension bridge in the world, with a span of 329m – yet not wide enough to allow two vehicles to pass in the centre. It was named after Sir Henry Birchenough, president of the BSAC at the time, and chairman of the Beit Trust, which financed its construction along with many others in the country. A copper commemoration plaque, as well as Birchenough's ashes, is set in the foundations on the east side of the bridge

Umvumvumvu River To the north of Chimanimani, halfway to Mutare, you cross this river with the charming name – the name being the only reason it is mentioned here. Bantu languages tend to repeat words to imply plural or multiple sequences. Umvumvumvu literally means river of many hippos (*mvu mvu mvu*).

CENTRAL AREA *Telephone code 020*

Mutare has a pleasant and bustling town centre, but you'll hardly spend any time here – instead you'll be heading for the nearby Bvumba Mountains to relax in one of several charming inns and hotels which offer magnificent views and delightful hospitality, features this relatively small area is renowned for. Keen birdwatchers head here to try and spot one of the many 'specials' that thrive in this heavily wooded habitat.

MUTARE Mutare, in the far east of the country close to the Mozambican border, is thought to be Zimbabwe's third- or fourth-largest city after Harare, Bulawayo and, according to one view, the Harare 'suburb' of Chitungwiza (Gweru also has a claim on this position). Mutare had a population approaching 200,000 in 2002 but this figure will no doubt have increased significantly given the recent rush in the nearby Marange diamond fields.

Although it is the nearest town to the popular Bvumba Mountains, this business-orientated city barely attempts to attract or service visitors. In fact, with a wealth of charming accommodation options and stunning views just a short drive away, there is little reason to stay here other than to stock up with fuel and provisions. Having said that, it is a pleasant, bustling and friendly town centre, and a day spent in the metropolis provides some attractions that are worth a visit.

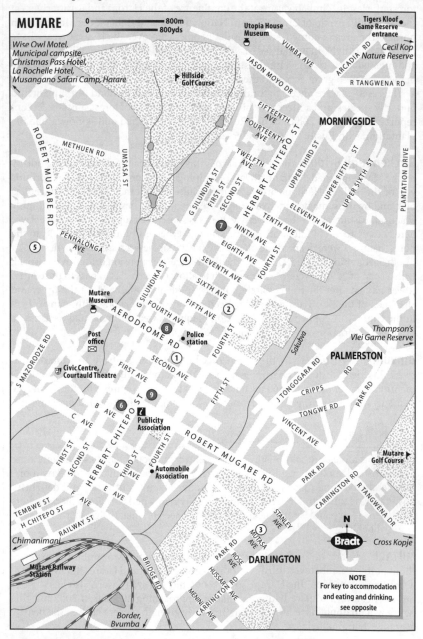

MUTARE

0 — 800m
0 — 800yds

Wise Owl Motel,
Municipal campsite,
Christmas Pass Hotel,
La Rochelle Hotel,
Musangano Safari Camp, Harare

Utopia House Museum

Tigers Kloof Game Reserve entrance

Cecil Kop Nature Reserve

VUMBA AVE

JASON MOYO DR

ARCADIA RD

R TANGWENA RD

Hillside Golf Course

FIFTEENTH AVE

FOURTEENTH AVE

MORNINGSIDE

HERBERT CHITEPO ST

UPPER THIRD ST

UPPER FIFTH ST

UPPER SIXTH ST

PLANTATION DRIVE

ROBERT MUGABE RD

METHUEN RD

UMSASA ST

TWELFTH AVE

ELEVENTH AVE

G SILUNDIKA ST

FIRST ST

SECOND ST

TENTH AVE

NINTH AVE

⑦

PENHALONGA AVE

⑤

EIGHTH AVE

SEVENTH AVE

④

FOURTH ST

Mutare Museum

G SILUNDIKA ST

FOURTH AVE

SIXTH AVE

FIFTH AVE

②

AERODROME RD

FOURTH ST

Thompson's Vlei Game Reserve

Post office ✉

⑧

Police station

Sakubva

PALMERSTON

S MAZORODZE RD

①

SECOND AVE

FIFTH ST

FIRST AVE

Civic Centre, Courtauld Theatre

J TONGOGARA RD

CRIPPS

PARK RD

B AVE

⑥

HERBERT CHITEPO ST

⑨

TONGWE RD

VINCENT AVE

C AVE

i Publicity Association

FOURTH ST

ROBERT MUGABE RD

FIRST ST

SECOND ST

D AVE

Automobile Association

PARK RD

Mutare Golf Course

E AVE

CARRINGTON RD

R TANGWENA DR

TEMBWE ST

H CHITEPO ST

RAILWAY ST

PARK RD

STANLEY AVE

N

Bradt

Cross Kopje

Chimanimani

BRIDGE RD

③ MUTASA

ROSE AVE

HUSSAR AVE

DARLINGTON

Mutare Railway Station

PARK RD

MENINI RD

CARRINGTON AVE

NOTE
For key to accommodation and eating and drinking, see opposite

Border, Bvumba

History In 1890 Cecil Rhodes and his men from the British South Africa Company pulled off one of their questionable land deals – this time with Chief Mutasa, ruler of the Manyika people – and, in exchange for guns and ammunition, gained mining rights around the Penhalonga Valley. Gold mining began immediately and by late 1891 the first miners had established a permanent site, now known as Old Umtali, on the Umtali River, 14km north of today's Mutare. The proposed Beira–Salisbury (Harare) railway was to pass through Old Umtali, but this would have meant either scaling or tunnelling under Christmas Pass, neither of them feasible.

An alternative route was selected, leaving Old Umtali out on a limb, so in 1896 the town was uprooted and moved to a place along the railway line, with settlers compensated by the BSAC. From those humble beginnings, the town quickly grew on the strength of its mineral wealth, fertile soil and strategic position along the railway trade route between Mozambique and Rhodesia. The town became a city in 1971 and was renamed Mutare in 1982. It is now the commercial and administrative centre for Manicaland Province.

Getting there Just a few kilometres from Mozambique, beside a gap in the mountains, Mutare is a busy border town, linking Harare (363km) with the Mozambican port of Beira. You should bear this in mind when crossing the border at Forbes/Mutare (Machipanda on the Mozambican side), as the queues can be long. The southern approach to the city takes you through a series of unlovely industrial estates before you reach the central business district. Masvingo is 297km/185 miles away, Gweru 480km/298 miles.

Getting around The town is small and compact but you'll need transport to all the outlying attractions. There is no reliable public transport and currently no car-hire companies here. The business district and main shopping area are laid out in the familiar Rhodes-inspired grid system, avenues running broadly east–west and streets north–south. Herbert Chitepo Street is the main road through the centre, and the main shopping area is between Aerodrome Road and the enigmatically named F Avenue.

MUTARE
For listings, see pages 348–9

🛏 **Where to stay**
1 African Sun Amber Hotel
2 Anne Bruce Backpackers
3 Homestead Guest House
4 Mountview Hotel
5 Utopia Country House

Off map
   Christmas Pass Hotel
   La Rochelle Hotel
   Municipal campsite
   Musangano Safari Camp
   Wise Owl Motel

✖ **Where to eat and drink**
6 Black Steer Steakhouse
7 Green Coucal Café
8 Nandos
   Spur Restaurant (see 1)
9 Stax Restaurant

Off map
   Wise Owl Motel

Tourist information Avoid the southern part of town, a vast industrial area, and head for the **Manicaland Publicity Association** (*Herbert Chitepo & Robert Mugabe rds;* ☎ *64711*), where you can pick up leaflets and brochures, although useful verbal information was in short supply on my visit. Then head off to the AA office (*Robert Mugabe Rd & 4th St*) for their excellent, detailed town map.

Where to stay There are plenty of accommodation options around town but, according to locals, the plummeting tourist economy together with an influx of diamond-rush nouveau riche has turned some once-reputable places into 'short-stay' establishments (ie:

The Eastern Highlands CENTRAL AREA

11

brothels). The following are recommended, but the list is not exhaustive so don't assume that any place not mentioned here is necessarily in the 'red light' category.

Upmarket

⌂ **African Sun Amber Hotel** (formerly the Holiday Inn) (96 rooms) Cnr Aerodrome Rd & 3rd St; ☏ 64431; e pacro@africansunhotels.com; www. africansunhotels.com. You may fancy a night of relative luxury after a spell in the bush, otherwise this rather bland city-centre hotel is for the business market. There's a nice outdoor pool but some reports say the hotel itself needs a bit of care & attention. It has its own Hotsprings restaurant & the dependable Spur steakhouse on the premises. There's also a popular English pub/bar (African style). **$$$**

⌂ **Musangano Lodge** (5 chalets, 4 lodges) ☏ 0204 2267; m 0732 320327, 0772 119447; e info@musangano.com; www.musangano.com. You should consider this excellent accommodation option in the Mutare area 30 mins out of town just off the Harare road (take the turning at the 263km peg). As well as having a very good restaurant, the lodges are equipped for self-catering – the 1-roomed chalets sleep 2 people; 3 lodges sleep 4 & there's a larger one for 6 people. The spacious rooms are very pleasantly furnished with excellent views across the Odzi & Mutare river valleys & the lodge offers a range of activities in the local area including visits to local communities. You'll get a great welcome here & families are very well catered for with a large pool & an adventure playground for the children. Excellent online reviews. Camping is also offered US$10pp. **$$$**

Standard

⌂ **Christmas Pass Hotel** (19 rooms) About 10km out on Harare rd; ☏ 63818, 04 700532; e info@chibanguzahotels.co.zw. This is a very individual & not unattractive colonial-style hotel, built in 1952 on the spot where pioneers camped on Christmas Day 1890. The grounds are well maintained with a large pool. The 17 twin rooms & 2 large family suites are in need of renovation. But if you can put up with the chipped tiles & cranky plumbing it's a good place to stay, out of the usual mould, & staff are always delighted to have another visitor to look after. In the morning you'll find staff have washed your car, a nice touch. Skip the restaurant & go to the nearby Wise Owl Motel at the bottom of the hill. **$$$**

⌂ **Mountview Hotel** (60 rooms) Cnr 2nd St & 7th Av; ☏ 66101; e mountviewhotel@iwayafrica. co.zw; www.mountviewhotel.co.zw. This 8-storey town-centre block is very much a business hotel, offering good-sized standard rooms, plus apts with lounge, kitchen, dining area & balcony, & the usual bar, restaurant & other facilities you would expect. **$$$**

⌂ **Valley Lodge** Beira Rd, 6km out of town, 1km from the border; ☏ 62868; e vlodge@pci. co.zw. The ideal place to overnight near the border, unless you're heading for the Bvumba. It's well out of the built-up area in hilly country. Lodges are self-contained, with spacious bedrooms & lounges. It has a bar & the recommended Fantails restaurant (mains avg US$10–12). Being close to the border post it always enjoys electricity, something not always available in the rest of the country. **$$$**

⌂ **Homestead Guest House** (15 rooms) 52 Park Rd; ☏ 65870. This pleasant lodge-style accommodation close to the town centre offers 5 en-suite & 10 standard rooms, well maintained & set in a shady garden with pool, but it's on a road with plenty of truck traffic. Room only, b/fast on request; small extra charge for self-catering. **$$**

⌂ **Utopia Country House** (20 rooms) 13 Robert Mugabe Rd; ☏ 66056; e utopia13@zol. co.zw. On the edge of town but within easy reach of the centre, this long-established, welcoming motel-cum-backpackers, renovated & upgraded, remains excellent value. 11 en-suite & 9 standard rooms are very comfortable, furnished in colourful indigenous style. There is full catering in the restaurant, & a common room & lounge. Restaurant mains avg US$5, full b/fast US$2. **$$**

⌂ **Wise Owl Motel** (69 rooms) Outskirts of town, Harare rd; ☏ 64643; e wiseowl@mweb. co.zw. In the foothills of the Cecil Kop range, this large establishment is just what you expect from a motel. Restaurant & bar are unremarkable, rooms are simply furnished, well maintained & have DSTV. Where the Harare road curves round behind the motel, heavily laden trucks downshift to climb towards Christmas Pass, so it could be noisy. **$$**

Basic

⌂ **Anne Bruce Backpackers** (4 rooms, 1 dorm) 99 4th St cnr 6th Av; ☏ 63569. Anne, an institution in these parts, has converted her house into a welcoming & comfortable crash-pad, with 3 dbls, 1 trpl & a dorm with 2 bunks & 2 beds. She is a mine of information & has a great sense of humour. This is a great shoestring base. **$**

⋏ Municipal campsite & caravan park Harare rd, about 5km out of town. Despite lack of use in recent years they have kept this site clean & tidy & it comes with *braai* stands, small thatched rondavels & a decent ablution block – fine for overnighting, although I recommend earplugs for light sleepers. **$**

✘ Where to eat Businesspeople tend to eat in their hotels and holidaymakers have been thin on the ground so several smaller places have closed down, leaving little choice.

✘ Black Steer Steakhouse Herbert Chitepo St by Spar supermarket. Chain restaurant featuring steaks, ribs & burgers.

✘ Green Coucal Café 111 2nd St cnr 8th Av; ⊕ 07.30–16.00 Mon–Fri, 07.30–14.30 Sat. This converted house, a favourite with Mutare residents, is one of a growing genre of daytime eating places in larger towns, combining light, imaginative meals with a gallery featuring local artists. You simply turn up for b/fast, lunch or just a coffee on the patio or in the garden. Many paintings are by Zuze, whose dazzling, primary-colour works carry an average price of around US$30. Meals are brilliant value.

✘ Nandos Aerodrome Rd by Shell garage. Popular with locals, this fast-food, spicy-chicken chain does take-aways as well.

✘ Spur Restaurant Amber Hotel, cnr Aerodrome Rd & 3rd St. This southern African chain serves good steaks, plus chicken & Mexican dishes; short on vegetarian options.

✘ Stax Restaurant First Mutual Arcade, Herbert Chitepo St; ⊕ 07.30–21.00, no booking. Don't be put off by the claustrophobic location. This is the most popular restaurant of its type in town, basically a steakhouse but with other choices. Good quality & large portions. Good range of vegetarian options, selection of coffees including their own blend, & it's licensed.

✘ Wise Owl Motel Outskirts of town on Harare rd; ☏ 64643. Pleasantly appointed restaurant with reasonable international-style menu.

Other practicalities The police station is on Aerodrome Road past 1st Street, by the river. The post office (⊕ *08.30–16.00 Mon–Fri, 08.00–11.30 Sat*) is on Robert Mugabe Road near 1st Street. The immigration office is on Robert Mugabe Road (☏ *62333*).

Shopping It's the usual story here – expect nothing more than mundane shops catering for the essentials, with pharmacies, TM supermarket and banks along Herbert Chitepo Street.

What to see and do

Mutare Museum (*Aerodrome Rd just before it crosses Robert Mugabe Rd;* ⊕ *09.00–17.00 daily; entry US$10*) This comprehensive museum is worth the couple of hours it takes to go round the informative displays on local history, anthropology and geology. A large transport section has some fine specimens of the ox wagons that brought early settlers to the region, a couple of steam trains from the 1890s, a selection of cars from the 1950s and some menacing police and security vehicles from pre-independence days. The large walk-in aviary has been breached by marauding monkeys and the birds have long since flown.

Utopia House Museum (*Jason Moyo Dr*) This small museum about 3km from the city centre was the home of Kingsley Fairbridge, a poet and philanthropist who lived around the turn of the 20th century. It has been renovated to reflect the style of the 1920s and to commemorate his art and his good works.

11

Cecil Kop Nature Reserve (*US$2*) This large area borders the north of the city, and though it's an excellent initiative by Wildlife and Environment Zimbabwe to bring game close to a city centre it has faltered due to lack of visitors, and is now rather neglected, although visitor facilities are fine. It's a large area of land bordering the north and northeast of the city, but close proximity to Mozambique has allowed poachers from there to cut down fences; consequently much of the game has disappeared. Cecil Kop isn't the most exciting wildlife experience you'll have but as a largely voluntary local initiative it can only flourish again if people come here to visit. Only two out of the three areas are currently worth visiting, but one ticket gains entry to all three.

Tigers Kloof Game Reserve (*Go north on Herbert Chitepo St until it becomes Arcadia Rd, then continue a short distance to car park*) The focus here is a small reservoir which in better times attracted an impressive selection of big game. When I visited, there were just three elephants, kept in the area by regular feeding, but I was told of a change in management and plans to mend fences and restock the reserve. Nevertheless this is a peaceful place to picnic, just a few minutes from the city centre, well maintained and with a lakeside refreshment kiosk and café area. Late afternoon is when the elephants and the few other remaining animals come to feed and drink.

Thompson's Vlei Game Reserve (*Follow Arcadia Rd from Tiger's Kloof until it becomes Rekayi Tangwena Dr; continue down the dirt road to entrance gate*) It's the same story here as at Tiger's Kloof, with game stocks a fraction of former levels. The driving route suggested on the reverse of the ticket (no walking is allowed) takes an hour or so, and you may see the same three elephants as at the reservoir, a lonely giraffe, seven wildebeest, one crocodile, a few impala and zebra, not forgetting the ever-present baboons. Although – or perhaps because – it is poorly maintained you do get more of a feeling of being out in the bush than if everything were manicured. Of course birdlife has been left alone so this is a great place for *miombo* specials.

The hilly 'Wilderness Area' in the northwest of the reserve is a separate section where walking is allowed, but it's now even wilder than the name suggests. Hiking paths are overgrown, and a visit will probably have you wandering around wondering where to go next.

Cross Kopje As you leave Thompson's Vlei, turn left to catch sight of a Mutare landmark. The large cross planted on this prominent *kopje* (hill) commemorates black Zimbabweans and Mozambicans who fought in World War I in east Africa. You can hike to the top from Rekayi Tangwena Drive but, with better views from the nearby Bvumba Mountains, few people do so. The car park doesn't have a good security reputation either.

BVUMBA MOUNTAINS This compact mountainous area 30km southeast of Mutare is one of Zimbabwe's key tourist destinations, notable for its year-round verdant hillsides, lush natural forests, spectacular views and a variety of accommodation and activities. Often spelt and always pronounced without the initial 'B', the word means 'mist' in Manyika – although often during July to September it should perhaps be 'smoke'.

The highlands themselves occupy a broadly central section of this small region bounded by two deep valleys, Burma and Essex, to the south and northeast; the views into Mozambique are world class when visibility is good. Virtually all accommodation is in the central mountain area, though you can take a 70km drive around the perimeter of the Bvumba.

This area of rich, somewhat specialised vegetation and terrain is a major draw for birdwatchers in search of the uncommon, even rare species found here. Excellent local guides make the job easier as the often dense undergrowth requires knowledge of bird calls to lead you to your bird. Another forest dweller you stand a good chance of seeing is the samango monkey, which prefers such isolated indigenous forest area. Little troops of these attractive chaps are frequently spotted scrabbling around in the roadside undergrowth or heard shouting 'Jack!' from the treetops.

Getting there Approaching from the south, just before Mutare's central business district take the poorly marked turning from Chimanimani Road into Bvumba Road (if Chimanimani Road becomes Herbert Chitepo Street you have gone too far). If you are coming from Mutare, take Park Road, and after the Beira (border) road junction turn left at the service station onto Bvumba Road.

Where to stay The Bvumba has a number of well-established, excellent value hotels, lodges and bed and breakfasts to suit every taste.

Luxury
🏠 **Leopard Rock Hotel** (58 dbls & suites) ☎60115; m 0772 100790/4; e reservations@theleopardrock.com; www. leopardrockhotel.info. Set in an area of unsurpassed natural beauty, Leopard Rock offers a luxury experience on a par with Victoria Falls Hotel. The turreted, thoroughly un-African chateau was built by Italian POWs & later extended (photos in one of the lounges show its construction). The building suffered badly during the Rhodesian Bush War but has re-emerged as the place to stay for visiting royalty, heads of state, CEOs, golfers & NGO staffers. In 1953 the British Queen Mother brought Princess Margaret to Rhodesia (away from certain temptations in England) & they stayed in rooms 11 & 7 (odd-numbered rooms have the best views). The Queen Mother is quoted as saying, 'there is nowhere more beautiful in Africa'. In the reception area a vast glazed wall holds back a huge fig tree clinging to a fern-clad rock backdrop. The hotel has one of the finest championship golf courses in the world, plus casino, gym & sports facilities, as well as its own game reserve. Very good value. **$$$**

Upmarket
🏠 **Forest Hills Lodge** (22 rooms, 1 chalet) Off Vumba Rd nr Botanical Gdns; ☎04 621561/6; e foresthills@zol.co.zw; www.foresthills. co.zw. This large establishment has undergone extensive refurbishment & although the exterior is uninspiring, rooms are large & well furnished, with possibly the best views in the area. Try to book a room with a balcony. 16 standard en-suite rooms, 6 executive rooms & 'Eddy's Cottage', a self-catering chalet (max 6) that unfortunately lacks the views of the other rooms. **$$–$$$**

🏠 **Genaina Guest House & Restaurant** (5 rooms, 1 cottage) Vumba Rd; ☎020 68177; e pixie@ mweb.co.zw. *Note: This longstanding and popular place announced its indefinite closure from 01 January 2013 paving the way for major refurbishment. No reopening date had been announced by April 2013.*

🏠 **Eden Lodge** (12 lodges, 2 luxury suites, 2 family rooms) Freshwater Rd, 3km from Cloudlands junction; ☎62000, 65824; e gvillas@mweb.co.zw. The green corrugated roof looks like a shed as you approach, but inside is an atmosphere of spacious, rustic luxury, with a beautifully furnished lounge & dining room off the reception area. Nicely appointed, self-contained lodges have Jetmaster fireplace & DSTV, & the complex has fabulous views over Mozambique's Lake Chicamba. **$$**

🏠 **Inn on the Vumba** (17 rooms, 5 cottages) Vumba Rd; ☎60722; m 0712 215127; e iotv@ innsofzimbabwe.co.zw. This is the first hotel on the road into the Bvumba; earlier visitors may remember it as the Impala Arms. Its cosy, olde-English styling is steeped in stone & natural wood, & of course it has delightful views. The comfy lounge, restaurant & bar welcome you in, & you'll make new friends in the bar as the locals who use it are always keen to meet visitors. It has 5 deluxe

11

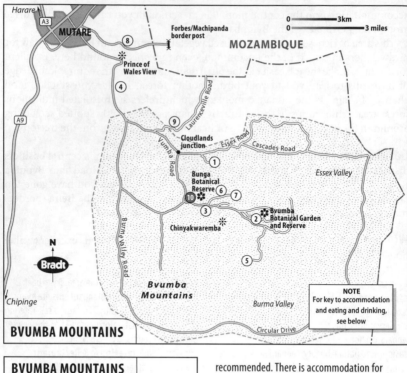

BVUMBA MOUNTAINS
For listings, see pages 351–3

🛏 **Where to stay**
1 Eden Lodge
2 Forest Hills Lodge
3 Hivu Cottages
4 Inn on the Vumba
5 Leopard Rock Hotel
6 Seldomseen Holiday Cottages
7 Torksey Private Guest House
8 Valley Lodge
9 White Horse Inn

✕ **Where to eat and drink**
10 Tony's Coffee Shoppe

recommended. There is accommodation for up to 8 people (3 dbl, 2 sgl rooms) including downstairs master bedroom with en-suite bath & shower & separate dressing room; spacious lounge with views of lawns, leading into the beautifully furnished dining room. Upstairs rooms are en suite with bath, with use of downstairs shower. The contemporary-style cuisine draws on traditional Cape Malay & Mediterranean influences. Dinner, bed & b/fast. **$$**

🏠 **White Horse Inn** (10 rooms, 2 mini-suites) Laurenceville Rd; ☎ 60325; 📱 0712 215127; e whitehorseinn@bsatt.com; www.whitehorseinn. co.zw. If you are looking for refined country elegance this is the place for you. This gem is at the bottom of a winding, forested road – straight out of the Cotswolds if it weren't for the samango monkeys pottering in the distinctly African trees that crowd the terraced gardens. Don't expect 'modern': rooms have no piped music, TV or phone. Croquet on the lawn & the smart-casual dress code will appeal to an upmarket clientele, yet this is a very reasonable place to stay. The hotel is situated in indigenous forest & has an expert resident bird guide, Peter Magosvongwe. Staff are friendly &

cottages (max 4) with self-catering an option, 2 family rooms & 15 en-suite standard rooms. Recent reports suggest the soft furnishings are in need of replacement & the small standard rooms are not quite up to the promise of the place but in a beautiful spot like this you are only going to use them for sleeping. Popular for traditional English Sun lunch. **$$**

🏠 **Torksey Private Guest House** (5 rooms) Nyamheni Rd; 📱 0714 370828; e torksey@ mweb.co.zw. This is a modern interpretation of an Edwardian farmhouse complete with furnishings of the same period & comes highly helpful. The restaurant menu is expensive by local standards, but you pay for quality & you get it here. **$$**

Standard

⌂ **Seldomseen Holiday Cottages** (4 self-catering cottages) Nyamheni Rd, off Vumba Rd, down 1km dirt road; ☎ 62837; e worsley.ken@gmail.com; www.seldomseen.co.zw. Nestling in this delightful area are the cottages, well separated from one another, each sleeping 4–9. Accommodation is simple but you'd struggle to find a quieter place. Seldomseen, although marketed as self-catering, will happily cook the food you bring if you'd rather be birding than in the kitchen. It's in its own small private reserve, with walking trails through the indigenous forest, where you may find the endemic Robert's warbler, bronzy sunbird & Gurney's sugarbird, as well as the sought-after Swynnerton's robin which nests in dragon plants, *Dracaena fragrans*, several of which can be found at Seldomseen. For expert local help

you won't find much better than resident guides Peter Mwadziwana & Buluwezi Murambiwa. **$$**

⌂ **Hivu Cottages** Vumba Rd, junction of Woodlands & Jevington rds; m 0773 246873, 0712 207828; e hivu@zol.co.zw. Sally Preston runs this cosy B&B along with a tea garden, nursery & horseriding business. Look for the bright blue roof, turn into her gardens & prepare yourself for the view over the mountains into Mozambique. The 1st floor of this rustic farmhouse is divided into 2 self-contained suites, each with dbl room & 4 tiny sgls under the eaves. One end has a large self-catering lounge-cum-kitchen, the other a lounge, with catering facilities in the ground-floor kitchen. Both suites have open fireplaces, essential during the winter months. Homely comfort & the kind of welcome that Zimbabweans are renowned for. As well as this original set-up, there are now 2 additional cottages sleeping 7 & 9 respectively. Sally's 7 horses cater for beginners or experienced riders & you don't get better trail-riding country than this. **$$**

✗ **Where to eat** Most people tend to eat at their accommodation. The hotels and lodges all offer bed and breakfast dwellers a very good menu. The White Horse Inn is a notch up from the rest and if you want to push the boat out, go to Leopard Rock. Sunday lunch is a popular local tradition at Inn on the Vumba and the White Horse Inn, so you are advised to book ahead for these.

✗ **Tony's Coffee Shoppe** Genaina Guest House & Restaurant, Vumba Rd; m 0772 863267; e tony@zol.co.zw. Tony, one of Zimbabwe's real characters, has built a reputation on a huge international selection of teas & coffees – & a range of truly wicked, 'to die for' homemade cakes & gateaux (1 or 2 of them not steeped in alcohol, for conscientious drivers). Building, furnishings

& place settings are immaculate with a capital 'I'. You don't just pop in for a quick coffee; it's more of a pilgrimage. Despite Genaina's indefinite closure (see above) Tony's is an independent business and is continuing to operate at these premises, although it's quite possible he will have to move premises yet again.

What to see and do

Birding Bvumba is a 'must do' birding area, with at least 14 specials, including the pretty Swynnerton's robin, bronzy sunbird and the rather dull, inconspicuous but exciting-to-find brier (Robert's) warbler and chirinda apalis. Other sought-after species are stripe-cheeked greenbul, red-faced crimson wing, yellow-bellied waxbill, silvery-cheeked hornbill, singing cisticola, eastern saw-wing and buff-spotted flufftail. Birding in this dark, often misty forest area is notoriously difficult (unless you are an expert on the calls and songs of the birds you are hoping to see), so you are advised to employ a local guide. Seldomseen is a specialist birding accommodation and the White Horse Inn has a resident guide, but most other hotels and lodges can recommend suitable experts. Leopard Rock Hotel has its own game reserve, at a lower elevation and consequently hosting different species to the rest of region, and has its own guide.

Golf If you play golf, Leopard Rock Hotel's championship golf course (open to the public) was voted one of the finest in the world by the PGA of Europe. As well as its technical merits you couldn't wish for more spectacular mountain surroundings. Green fees are: 18 holes for hotel residents US$30, visitors US$50; 9 holes US$20 and US$30 respectively.

Bvumba Botanical Garden and Reserve (*Entry   US$8, vehicle   US$5, camping $5*) This was once one of the area's showpiece attractions, and you could spend a whole day in the 42ha of exotic gardens and the adjoining 160ha of natural, indigenous bush. Today many of the once-manicured gardens are overgrown, and it's really only good value for birders. The campsite is clean but run-down.

Bunga Forest Reserve Much smaller (just 40ha) than the Bvumba reserve, it's the same story regarding upkeep and the great birdlife that has spent the last decade or so undisturbed by humans.

Chinyakwaremba (*Car park on Bvumba Rd, a couple of kilometres up from Botanical Gdn rd*) Chinyakwaremba translates roughly as 'resting hill'. Its alternative name is Leopard Rock; however, the actual rock where, according to the local story, a leopard used to sun itself, is a short distance away at the site of the Castle Guest House. The wonderful view is a short climb from the car park.

You may notice ladies hanging out what looks like washing by the roadside. These are actually embroidered tablecloths, wraps and similar goods for sale, with simple traditional designs often depicting village scenes. Purchasing an item or two is an excellent way to support this worthwhile self-help initiative.

NORTH FROM THE BVUMBA

Penhalonga If you take the alternative route along the Imbeza Valley between Mutare and Nyanga, you could easily drive through this sleepy village without a second glance, except for the dominating entrance to the Redwing gold mine, the reason for the village's existence. This area has been mined on and off for around 500 years and gold continues to be extracted to this day. Aside from its mining history (alas no museum) and a small corrugated iron church, the village itself has little to offer other than the alluring thought that there's still gold beneath your feet.

In 1951 Stephen Courtauld (later Sir Stephen, knighted for services to Rhodesia) and his wife Virginia built a turreted country house here, 4km south of Penhalonga, living the high life, doing good works for the locals and patronising the arts. The Courtaulds were unusual in their belief in black rule for Rhodesia, and Courtauld gathered a group of political hopefuls, including Herbert Chitepo who became a highly influential and respected pre-independence figure, talking through principles of government and drafting an outline constitution. Following Sir Stephen's death in 1967 Lady Courtauld made herself unpopular during the independence war with her financial support for freedom fighters crossing the border from Mozambique, and courted trouble in her own family by bequeathing the property to the people of Southern Rhodesia. The house – now the La Rochelle Hotel – survived unscathed throughout the war for independence (despite the Selous Scouts' propensity for picking off visitors).

Where to stay

Upmarket

La Rochelle Hotel (8 rooms, 4 self-catering cottages) Signposted right turn from Penhalonga Rd, 14km from Mutare, then 3km; ℡ 020 22250; m 0772 306560; e larochellezim@gmail.com. Today you can stay in the Courtaulds' colonial-style house (circular marks on the dressing table in one room are said to be from Lady Virginia's whisky glass) or in one of the cottages in the gardens. Sir Stephen built his wife an Art Deco summer house, totally out of keeping with the rest of the property but a fantastically surreal place to stay. In the lounge is a glass panel on which Courtauld's high-profile visitors etched their names with a diamond stylus. In what is now the (very cosy) bar is an ingenious drop-down panel on which he mounted his 12 Turner originals, out of sunlight & harm's way (the paintings were sent to England on his death). The small restaurant features replica Turners. Comfortable rather than deluxe but delightful and very good value. **$$**

La Rochelle Botanical Gardens (*La Rochelle Hotel, signposted from Penhalonga Rd*) With the help of British horticulturist John Michell, the Courtaulds created a garden full of exotic plants and trees from all over the world, including many indigenous varieties. A web of paths and streams winds around this 20ha, contoured masterpiece, which varies from dense forest canopy to beautiful flower beds. This is one of only two botanical gardens in southern Africa with Braille plaques (the ones here were installed by the Courtaulds). Lady Courtauld bequeathed the gardens to the National Trust in the early 1970s, but they suffered severe neglect after independence. They are now maintained by the very personable Simon Herring, who runs the hotel and is slowly but surely restoring them to their former glory.

Lake Alexander (Odzani Dam) (*North of Penhalonga, turn right at Stapleford turn-off*) This 74ha, 1.5 million gallon lake was created in 1967 to supply Mutare with water, but doubles as a watery playground for the townsfolk. Surrounded by the ubiquitous pine forests of this area, it's a pleasant place to spend a day, especially if you have children. You can hire rowing boats and canoes and there are thatched shelters for shade, along with *braai* stands and ablutions. Camping is available for a nominal fee.

Odzani Falls (*From Penhalonga Rd, turn left 3km north of Stapleford turn-off at ✪ S18 46 07 E32 41 42*) A rocky track takes you past a water treatment works, whose staff will unlock the gate to the falls. We found little more than a tumbling river, so you might give this humble attraction a miss.

NORTHERN AREA

Fine scenery, trout fishing and hiking are the main drawcards of this lovely area, which has hints of Scotland about it. If you've spent hot days in the low-lying game parks, this cool area, site of Zimbabwe's highest peak, will bring welcome relief as well as plenty of activities, including some important historic features.

NYANGA NATIONAL PARK (*NP Category 3*) The park and the Nyanga Highlands rise to 2,592m at Mount Nyangani, Zimbabwe's highest point. The area (314km²) is characterised by rolling hilltops studded with huge, smoothly rounded granite outcrops towering over steep gorges and wide valleys. The Pungwe River has carved a spectacular route southwards and eastwards from the foot of Mount Nyangani, while further south the Honde River has created a wide fertile valley beneath the dominating escarpment along the border with Mozambique. Zimbabwe's highest waterfall (and Africa's second-highest), the Mtarazi Falls, drops 762m into the Honde Valley.

This part of Zimbabwe has been populated since the dawn of man and today is rich in archaeological sites, including remnants of Iron Age villages and hilltop

11

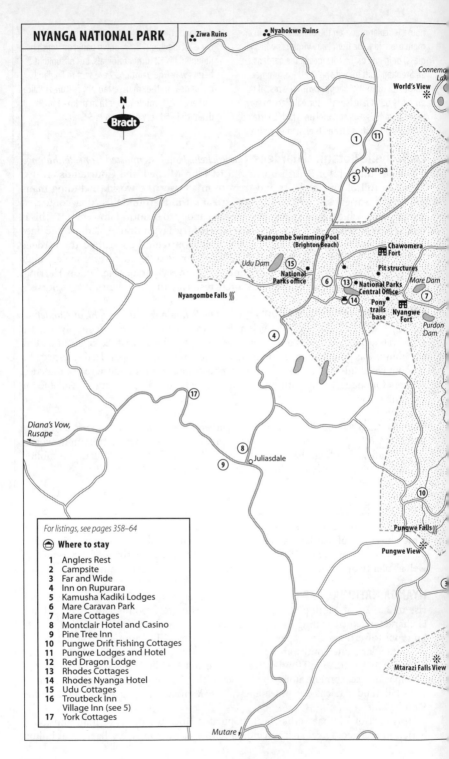

NYANGA NATIONAL PARK

Ziwa Ruins

Nyahokwe Ruins

Connema Lak

World's View ✳

N

Bradt

① ⑪

Nyanga

⑤

Nyangombe Swimming Pool
(Brighton Beach)

Chawomera Fort

Pit structures

Udu Dam ⑮

National Parks office

⑥ ⑬ National Parks Central Office

Mare Dam

⑦

Nyangombe Falls ⑂

⑭ Pony trails base

Nyangwe Fort

Purdon Dam

④

⑰

Diana's Vow, Rusape

⑧ Juliasdale

⑨

⑩

Pungwe Falls ⑂

Pungwe View ✳

③

For listings, see pages 358–64

⊝ **Where to stay**
1 Anglers Rest
2 Campsite
3 Far and Wide
4 Inn on Rupurara
5 Kamusha Kadiki Lodges
6 Mare Caravan Park
7 Mare Cottages
8 Montclair Hotel and Casino
9 Pine Tree Inn
10 Pungwe Drift Fishing Cottages
11 Pungwe Lodges and Hotel
12 Red Dragon Lodge
13 Rhodes Cottages
14 Rhodes Nyanga Hotel
15 Udu Cottages
16 Troutbeck Inn
   Village Inn (see 5)
17 York Cottages

Mtarazi Falls View ✳

Mutare

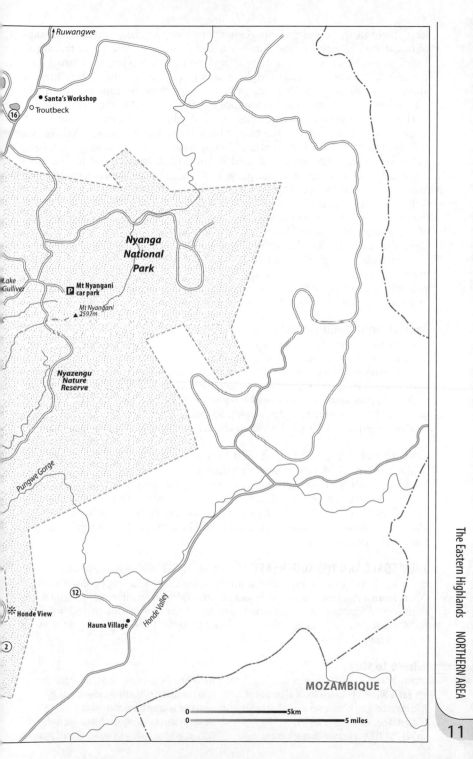

Ruwangwe

Santa's Workshop
○ Troutbeck
16

Nyanga
National
Park

Lake
Gulliver

P Mt Nyangani
car park

Mt Nyangani
▲ 2592m

Nyazengu
Nature
Reserve

Pungwe Gorge

12

☼ Honde View

Hauna Village ●

Honde Valley

2

MOZAMBIQUE

| 0 | 5km |
| 0 | 5 miles |

forts. There are three principal villages in the region: Juliasdale, west of the Nyanga National Park; Nyanga to the northwest; and Troutbeck close by in the north. Excellent tourist accommodation, from camping to luxury, is scattered throughout the area, and numerous roads and dirt tracks give access to remote, breathtaking viewpoints. The dirt roads here are in better shape than some further south, but you will still benefit from a high-clearance vehicle, and a 4x4 in the rainy season.

Hikers and birders are drawn to this area, and fishing is a big pull for many, with rainbow and brown trout in the many rivers, streams and reservoirs. There is a variety of game in the national park, including blue duiker and samango monkeys, but it is sparsely distributed and hard to spot. Lion, leopard and buffalo have apparently been seen here but none of the locals I spoke to recalled recent sightings. You are more likely to spot klipspringer, reedbuck and kudu.

It won't take long before you come across the name Cecil Rhodes (the national park is still often referred to as Rhodes Inyanga). He actually bought a large chunk of the area for himself and built a house overlooking – you guessed it – Rhodes Dam; this is now the Rhodes Nyanga Hotel (see *Nyanga National Park*, page 361).

Spectacular though this area is, it would be unrealistic not to mention the extensive commercial forestry here. Depending on growing and harvesting cycles you may find yourself driving through mile upon mile of monotonous plantations or past blackened hillsides full of smouldering tree stumps.

Tourist information Nyanga tourist information office (see page 363) has a good, if dated, map and information sheet of the area. Several accommodations listed on this map no longer exist, however.

Your park entry fee payable at the central office by the Nyanga (Rhodes) dam allows you to enter and exit as often as you like during the day you arrive, or to stay within the park for as long as you like. If you are staying outside the park, however, you must pay a new fee each day, so plan accordingly.

Fishing requires a day permit, obtainable from the National Parks central office.

Getting there You will find yourself here at the start or the end of your tour of the Eastern Highlands. If you are arriving from Harare or Marondera, head for Rusape and turn left onto the A14 signposted to Sanyatwe, which will bring you to Juliasdale. If you are driving north from Mutare, take the Harare road over Christmas Pass, then the A15 to Juliasdale via Watsomba and Mutasa. An alternative, slower but more scenic route from Mutare is via Penhalonga. No public transport serves the area.

JULIASDALE AND THE SOUTHEAST (*Telephone code 029*) Juliasdale features on all the maps but if you are expecting a pretty little village you will be disappointed. Apart from a residential area that is not obvious from the main road, it's little more than a road junction, a supermarket, two filling stations, a church and a luxury hotel – mainly a useful geographical reference point for the surrounding attractions and accommodations.

Where to stay
Upmarket
Far & Wide (3 chalets) About 30km east of Juliasdale; booking office in stone building by BP filling station, Juliasdale; 3011/2; m 0712 613582; e farnwide@mweb.co.zw; www.farandwide.co.zw. The enthusiastic Bernie Cragg owns this outdoor education & activity centre set in dramatic mountainous countryside, although you can simply stay here if you wish. Accommodation includes 3 well-equipped 2-storey

luxury chalets, in a beautiful area on the edge of the national park. They are self-catering, sleep up to 6 & even have a sauna. It is near the Honde & Pungwe viewpoints & Mtarizi Falls, & a short walk from the chalets brings you to the teetering edge of the Pungwe Valley. Bernie knows the area like the back of his hand; he's a keen birdwatcher too. When he's not running leadership & team-building courses for local youngsters, he'll take you on a kayak, rafting or fishing expedition, mountain biking or rock climbing. Camp out with his team on a Pungwe River trip for up to 6 days. **$$$**

🏠 **Inn on Rupurara** (17 lodges) 5 mins along the Nyanga rd from Juliasdale; ☎3021/4; e reservations@rupurara.co.zw; www.innsofzimbabwe.co.zw. Part of the excellent Inns of Zimbabwe group, this beautiful lodge, one of the nicest in Zimbabwe, is set on the side of a valley, amongst the massive granite boulders that dot this area. Lodges are arranged along the valley either side of the main building. Traditional design uses indigenous hardwoods for floor & furniture. Balconies overlook the valley or a small reservoir. Eland & other plains game species wander in from the inn's own small reserve to feed on the lawns. The thatched main building literally hugs the granite hillside; 3 floors house restaurant, bar & 2 lounges, all elegant yet cosy. Activities include game drives & horseriding, rock climbing & trout fishing. It's just about mandatory to climb 1,839m Rupurara (meaning something like 'bald-headed man' in Shona), a 300m climb that will reward you with panoramic views of the countryside. They say that in the rainy season, frogs can be found in the rock puddles at the top. Fully inclusive including game drive. **$$$**

🏠 **Montclair Hotel & Casino** (89 rooms) Juliasdale; ☎2441/5; e reservations@montclair.co.zw. If you are looking for a plush hotel with a chance to gamble the night away, this is for you. The plush & comfortable hotel has a large restaurant & 2 big lounges, 1 with a terrace & pool overlooking the mountains. Plenty of sporting facilities including tennis, squash, horseriding & volleyball plus a 9-hole golf course. See box *The marching sentries of Nyanga*, page 361. **$$$**

🏠 **Pine Tree Inn** (14 rooms) Rusape Rd, Juliasdale; ☎2388/3133; e pinetree@innsofzimbabwe.co.zw. You'll get a real English countryside feeling at this comfortable hotel nestled in pine forest & surrounded by beautifully tended gardens. Accommodation is in chalets, some with their own lounge. Main lounge, reputedly excellent restaurant & bar are in a cosy, elegant country house. Open wood fires are a welcome feature in cool evenings. It takes 1½–2hrs to climb neighbouring Susurumba rock & return, but inform reception before you set out just in case you get lost. **$$**

Standard

🏠 **Pungwe Drift Fishing Cottages** Far & Wide (see above) run these 2 wonderfully secluded, former National Parks cottages on shady ground by the river, which offers excellent fly fishing. Each has 2 dbl bedrooms. **$$**

🏠 **Red Dragon Lodge** (4 chalets) 4km off the road at Hauna; ☎028 2288/64. You would probably stay here only if you planned a day in the Honde Valley. 4- & 5-bed, 2-storey rondavel chalets surround a shaded garden, complete

PIT STRUCTURES

The area's many unrestored 'pit structures' look like nothing more than shallow, stone-lined holes in the ground. To see what these were for, visit the reconstructed village 2km east of the Nyanga National Park central office. The pits, up to 10m across and 2m deep, were almost certainly corrals for small livestock such as goats, sheep or perhaps a now-extinct breed of small, hornless cattle. Access was through a narrow, stone-lined tunnel, with a hut built above it. Wooden poles inserted into the tunnel through holes in the hut floor formed a simple security gate, keeping the animals in and intruders out. The pits were surrounded by accommodation huts and smaller grain storerooms, built on raised platforms. After you've seen the reconstruction, check out the unrestored one on the edge of the village.

11

with a babbling brook. There was no food in the restaurant/bar when I stayed, a thatched lounge-cum-bar had seen better days & the pool was empty. Rooms were comfortable but it's expensive for what's on offer. $$

⌂ **York Cottages** (6 self-catering cottages) About 10km from Juliasdale along Rusape Rd; ☎2360. The Forestry Company of Zimbabwe runs these pleasant 2-storey cottages, each with 1 dbl & 1 twin room. Excellent value. $

Camping There's a campsite in a wooded area just within the national park past Honde View, but it's now run by Far and Wide (see above). You need to pay them for the camping before entering the park, along with the park entry fee. Rudimentary shelters amongst the trees are helpful in inclement weather but otherwise claustrophobic.

What to see and do

Accommodation in this area is perfect for exploring the Pungwe and Honde river areas and the southern part of the Nyanga National Park. It's a hiking and river-fishing haven, and with a car you can visit the best viewpoints in two days. The larger accommodations will recommend hiking routes and other activities but if you want energetic, outdoor activities deeper in the national park, visit the Far and Wide booking office (see *Where to stay* above).

Honde Valley (*From Juliasdale head south on the Mutare road; after 21km turn left towards Hauna, then just after 1km follow the road round to the right*) This meandering road drops 1,300m down a series of tight hairpins into the wide valley, with tremendous views of the Nyanga escarpment. It's well worth the drive just for the scenic beauty. A dominant feature at the beginning of the valley is a simply massive granite outcrop that looks as if it's just waiting to break off and fall into the valley. The Honde River forms part of the border with Mozambique, and this was an easy access area for Mozambican armed rebels and bandits. Today the valley is lush with tea and coffee plantations. Follow the road past thriving Hauna village to the Aberfoyle tea estate, surrounded by a bowl of mountains.

Pungwe view area A 25km round-trip drive starts 11km south of the Juliasdale junction, giving access to the splendidly precipitous Pungwe viewpoint, a footpath to Pungwe Falls and, with a 7km detour, Honde View and Mtarazi Falls, with fine mountain and valley views.

Pungwe Falls The falls can be reached from a track leading off the 4x4 scenic route just north of the Pungwe viewpoint. Although some people have obviously driven right to the top of the falls, the track is rock-strewn, steep, narrow and at times boggy, and it's impossible to turn round so you are likely to get stuck. Driving is not really in the spirit of things, and you won't be making friends with any walkers on the path. Better to leave the car at Pungwe viewpoint, as the walk only takes about 30 minutes. You will be rewarded with a pretty cascade, first into a holding pool and then over the edge, 240m down into the gorge.

It's difficult to get close to **Mtarazi Falls**. The viewpoint just past Honde View, plus a short walk, is the best option. From here the falls are a distant, thin streak of water, but the 762m drop is impressive, and the mountain and valley views make it worth a trip, especially when the river is full. Try to plan a morning visit, as the setting sun behind the falls makes viewing and photography difficult.

Some guidebooks and websites mention these viewpoints and car parks as mugging or car-theft sites. Locals say otherwise, that those incidents were many years ago, but that may be because there have been very few visitors lately. It pays to be cautious.

NORTHWESTERN SECTION The 20km road from Juliasdale to Nyanga takes you through the western section of the national park. The area east of the main road has three scenic reservoirs – Nyanga (still known as Rhodes Dam), Mare and Lake Gulliver – the latter two encircled by a loop road that needs a high-clearance vehicle. The eastern end of this loop brings you to the Mount Nyangani car park.

Nyanga's small airport is of little use to independent visitors, who will need a vehicle to see the area.

Where to stay

Upmarket

⌂ **Rhodes Nyanga Hotel** (24 rooms)
Nyanga Dam; m 0772 105144, 0733 072625;
e reservationsrhodesnyangahotel@gmail.com;
www.rhodesnyangahotel.com. Cecil Rhodes built
the original cottage in 1896 & lived here until
1902, but it has since been extended to create
a hotel that opened for business in 1933. Room
8 was used by Rhodes & still retains some of his
furniture. Set in manicured gardens with a veranda
overlooking the reservoir, this is a delightful place
to stay & the only hotel located in the Nyanga
National Park. The main hotel block with its bar,
lounge & restaurant is elegantly furnished in true
colonial style & there's a good range of activities on
hand to keep you busy in the area. **$$$**

Basic

⌂ **National Parks cottages** ☎8274. Udu,
Mare & Nyanga (Rhodes) dams offer 18, 12 & 10
cottages respectively – basic but spacious, and as
ever in Park's accommodations, clean & set up for
self-catering, sleeping up to 6. All are in pleasant
lakeside settings & represent good value for
money. Staff are friendly & ever helpful. Check in at
the National Parks office at each dam site. **$**

⋏ **Mare Caravan Park** Close to the National
Park central office. This large open area has *braai*
stands & tables, but little else to commend it. You
can also camp here.

What to see and do

Rhodes Hotel Museum This tiny museum is beside the Rhodes Nyanga Hotel (it was Rhodes's old stable block). You may have heard quite enough about Rhodes by now, but the focus here is on the local land struggle after 1892. Frustrated miners had to turn to agriculture to survive so the BSAC sold large tracts of land in this area to settlers, who kept local people on as cheap labour, but a later deal kicked them off altogether, a state of affairs that continued well into the Smith regime. The hero in this museum is Chief Rekayi Tangwena, who led the struggle for reinstatement of the land to his community, which only came with independence in 1980. Well worth a visit.

Nyangwe and Chawomera forts With walls in excess of 1m thick, these forts would have been impressive structures. Although not yet properly dated, it is thought they were constructed in the second half of the 16th century. 'Fort' suggests a defensive military function, and 'loopholes' in the walls were once thought to be for weaponry, but it is obvious from their position and outlook that they could not have been used for this purpose. Because of their strategic positions and the fact that there are others on surrounding hilltops, it is now thought they were permanently manned lookout posts. On a clear day, signalling between the forts would have been easy.

Nyangwe, the largest and most intact fort in this area, is within easy walking distance (about 1.5km) up a track from the Mare Dam road. It's somewhat overgrown but you can clamber around the remains and through the lintelled entrances to try to make sense of it, aided by a small explanatory plaque. **Chawomera** is signposted at the end of the road 5km further north from the National Parks central office road junction. It is less well preserved than Nyangwe but its isolated position is a peaceful place to spend some time.

Nyangombe swimming pool This is just a nice little *braai* and picnic area on the Nyangombe River below small rapids. For swimmers or sunbathers the main feature is a sandy area locally referred to as Brighton Beach. The fast-running, cold water is bilharzia-free and safe to bathe in. Facilities include flush toilets and a changing room.

Pony rides (*On the way to Mare Dam, past the Experimental Orchard on the right*) The ponies looked in good condition and the stables were clean, but on two visits I failed to find a human being or any information in the deserted office. It's a wonderful area for horseriding though, so worth investigating.

Udu Dam and Nyangombe Falls The peaceful area around Udu Dam, west of the Juliasdale–Nyanga road, is the most accessible base for visiting Nyangombe Falls. There's an old pit structure within a stone's throw of the National Parks Udu office. The far shore of the lake features lush, wooded hillsides.

For the falls, take the signposted road from Udu Dam cottages for 3km to a small car park. The five-minute walk down to the falls is overgrown and steep (and slippery when wet). Several paths give varied views of these impressive falls. At low water you can move out onto a large rock platform for the best views, but stay away when it's wet: people have slipped and fallen to their deaths here. The rock formations, with their regular, right-angled fault lines and cracks, give the impression that the falls were constructed with giant building blocks.

Mount Nyangani (*Car park about 15km east of National Parks office at Nyanga/ Rhodes Dam*) At 2,592m this is the highest point in Zimbabwe, but don't look for a peak: this is merely the highest elevation in a long ridge. As the car park is already at 2,140m, it's not a difficult hike to the top, but you should be reasonably fit. Allow two to three hours to the summit where, mist willing, you will have wonderful views. The summit is said to have its own resident spirit, which is why you won't find many local people up here, and why they may have been reluctant to show you where it is in the first place (it is considered dangerous to point at the sacred mountain).

Although you need no climbing expertise, there's plenty that can go wrong, mainly because of the changeable weather. Treat the walk seriously, read the rather off-putting National Parks warning sign before you set off, and fill in the register at the beginning (and most importantly, at the end) of your hike. If you're hiking on and not coming back the same way (there's an excellent footpath to Pungwe Drift from here) make sure Parks staff understand this, or they may come looking for you. Note that the dirt roads to the car park are in an advanced state of disrepair requiring a high ground clearance vehicle.

Nyazengu Nature Reserve On the right just before the Nyangani car park is the start of a 4x4 track through this private reserve, bringing you out 18km later at Pungwe Drift. After 5km there's a toll office where you pay a small fee to enter the private reserve. It's a beautiful scenic drive through remote countryside, but check conditions with the attendant. When I drove it, it was slow going but easily drivable, but after rains it could be a different story.

NYANGA (*Telephone code 0298*) Despite its setting and proximity to natural attractions, this tidy village has little to offer other than shops, banks, filling stations and post office, much as you'd find in an English country village (which it resembles). However, the excellent **Nyanga Tourist Association** (*library;* \435/899/309; ⊕ *09.00–13.00 & 14.00–16.30 Tue–Sat; after hours, enquire at village pharmacy*) sells a good, though dated, map and tourist guide.

Getting there There is no public transport anywhere near this area. Harare is 275km/171 miles away, Mutare 100km/62 miles.

Where to stay Note also the range of accommodation options in the national park (see page 361).

Standard

🏠 **Village Inn** (35 rooms) \336/9; m 0773 882182; e reservations@the villageinnhotel.net. This Cape Dutch-style hotel is the most upmarket place in the village although reports in 2012 suggest its standards have slipped quite a bit, although nothing that a small injection of cash wouldn't sort out. Plain, spotless rooms are arranged in a sgl-storey block, accessed via a colonnaded walkway. There's a large bar, comfortable lounge & restaurant. In the shady gardens are a big pool, tennis & mini-golf. **$$$**

Basic

🏠 **Anglers Rest** (13 rooms) 4km north of Nyanga village, signposted on the left after the hospital; \713; m 0712 550 509. This unpretentious hotel (more of a motel actually) has basic en-suite rooms & a separate restaurant that was only serving b/fast. **$**

🏠 **Pungwe Lodges & Hotel** (6 rooms) Main rd north of village, on right where bldgs come to an end; \588, 863. Formerly the Mangondoza Hotel, this place offers a change from the area's upmarket, colonial-style establishments. Simple, almost dormitory-like rooms are arranged around a courtyard. The very friendly owner offers a small choice of local-style food, & a sense that you are in 'real' Zimbabwe. **$**

🏠 **Kamusha Kadiki Lodges** Duiker Dr. This sprawling thatched accommodation – closed for renovation when I visited – is tucked away in a residential area 500m from the ZABG bank. Should be good when it's finished.

What to see and do

Cultural tours Check with the tourist association about Matema village visits. Half- and full-day tours give you an insight into local life; an overnight visit has you staying and eating with a local family. Half of all proceeds go to village funds, so it's a worthwhile way to give something back to the community.

Nyahokwe Ruins (*North from Nyanga, left at junction 3km after start of dirt road; right at Nyatando School sign, then left onto Ziwa Rd; after 1km turn right to Nyahokwe Ruins*) Built in the same tradition as Ziwa and Great Zimbabwe, these ruins are smaller and less impressive than Ziwa. Like Ziwa, Nyahokwe is thought to have been an iron-smelting centre. All that remains of this large hilltop village is a circular wall, and a crumbled rectangular wall around the overgrown site.

Ziwa Ruins (⊛ *S18 08 34, E32 38 20; as for Nyahokwe, then carry straight on for Ziwa; total about 22km*) Although there has been no reconstruction at this 3,337ha site, the remains of stone terraces, passages, enclosures and pit structures (see box, *Pit structures*, page 359) give an indication of the layout of this settlement, inhabited by agricultural communities from the 16th to 18th century. It is believed that these Late Iron Age ruins post-date Great Zimbabwe, although archaeological discoveries show that this area was inhabited by many earlier peoples. The agricultural lifestyle is evident in the terracing, and pit structures indicate livestock farming. Iron smelting was also carried out here.

The site was originally called Van Niekerk's Ruins (and still is on some maps), after the Boer cattle farmer who settled here in the early years of the 20th century, driving out local people. Van Niekerk 'discovered' the ruins and called in archaeologists. The site was declared a National Monument in 1946 and renamed Ziwa after the mountain that dominates the background.

There's a very informative museum (⊕ *08.00–17.00 daily; nominal entry fee*) and a nearby reconstruction of a smelting furnace. The warden will show you around the site, including a rock 'gong' on the far side of the ruins. There's also a campsite here.

TROUTBECK (*Telephone code 0298*) This village and much of the surrounding area owes its development to Major Herbert McIlwaine, the Irishman who in the 1940s built and named the three Connemara lakes and the world-famous Troutbeck Inn, designed its golf course and generally created what has now become a genteel tourist and retirement paradise.

Getting there From Juliasdale, take a right turn after 17km (3km before Nyanga) and continue for 15km.

🏠 **Where to stay and eat** There is only one hotel in the village; indeed this renowned establishment may be the very reason for your visit here.

Luxury

🏠 **Troutbeck Inn (Resort)** (70 rooms) ☎889, 305/7, 0776 469854; e pacro@africansunhotels. com. 'Inn' is a bit of a misnomer as this elegant lakeside complex has no fewer than 70 rooms in 3 wings, plus everything you would expect from a top-class hotel. This is presumably why its long-standing name has now been changed to 'resort'. The main building is straight out of the English Lake District, complete with pub & furnished in colonial style, with neatly starched staff to look after your every need. Have a cream tea on the terrace & soak up the view over manicured lawns to the lakes. They claim that the log fire in the lounge has not been allowed to go out since the hotel opened in 1951. You won't be short of things to do: activities include golf, trout fishing, tennis & squash, horseriding, boating & bowls. **$$$**

What to see and do

Santa's Workshop It's a curious name but this is a pleasant little garden based around a trout stream and small waterfall. A couple of shops sell trinkets and refreshments, and you can buy trout fished fresh from one of the holding ponds. It's 200m down the hill from the filling station and you can spend all of 15 minutes here.

World's View (*Small entry fee*) This optimistically named 2,258m viewpoint certainly offers spectacular views over northern Zimbabwe, at least on a clear day. Don't bother to visit if it is misty, hazy or smoky because you won't see anything. At the top of a massive stone lookout building right on the edge of the precipice the directions and distances of major African cities are engraved around the circular rim. From Troutbeck there's a short but tortuous and rocky loop road to the lookout, but you'll need a 4x4. On the way here you'll see signs to Tsanzo Lodges, but don't try to check in for the night, as it's a rehabilitation centre for disabled soldiers.

Diana's Vow (*From the A14, 52km southwest of Juliasdale, turn right onto Constance Rd, ⊕ S18 27 15.7 E32 19 12.0, then after 12.5km turn left at the junction; after 200m look for a small track on the left, then less than 1km to a shady area where you can park, ⊕ S18 21 37.6 E32 17 46.6*) This is one of Zimbabwe's most important rock-art sites, and although it's a bit of a cross-country trek it is well worth the effort. The painting is on the underside of an overhanging granite rock, one of several massive boulders that form a natural amphitheatre. It is easy to see how early people would have looked on this as a sacred site, and the flat ground in front of the painting would surely have been the scene of many an ancient ritual.

The complex painting defies definitive interpretation. The central figure is a casually reclining 'man', although his head is animal-like with horns similar to those of a sable antelope. Leaning on his left elbow, in his right hand he holds a small object above his head. One knee is drawn up and what appear to be a couple of small spirit figures hover around his penis, from which there issues a long thread or perhaps something altogether more fluid. Beneath his head is a smaller, provocatively reclining, apparently female figure, so one may assume this all has something to do with fertility. Beneath these figures are a mass of people and animals and what seems to be a village scene. And sorry, I haven't found anyone to explain why it's called Diana's Vow.

While the painting is in generally good condition, older photographs of it show more clarity, and today one fears for its future. This important site is completely vulnerable: even the protective iron railings have been removed and it is now unmanned. Hopefully its remoteness will keep it unvandalised. It's also signposted from Rusape, and although I haven't travelled this route, on the map it looks easier than the route described above.

RUSAPE This scruffy junction town on the Mutare–Harare road has the usual basic shops, banks and filling stations, but no other reason to stop. There are two or three guesthouses in town, all closed when I visited so I can furnish no details: try **Sunshine Guest House**, **Goodrest Guest House** or **East Guest House**. Forget **Border Lodge**, which appears to be aimed at guests who don't stay all night.

Bradt Travel Guides

Claim 20% discount on your next Bradt book when you order from www.bradtguides.com quoting the code BRADT20

Africa

Africa Overland	£16.99
Algeria	£15.99
Angola	£18.99
Botswana	£16.99
Burkina Faso	£17.99
Cameroon	£15.99
Cape Verde	£15.99
Congo	£16.99
Eritrea	£15.99
Ethiopia	£17.99
Ethiopia Highlights	£15.99
Ghana	£15.99
Kenya Highlights	£15.99
Madagascar	£16.99
Madagascar Highlights	£15.99
Malawi	£15.99
Mali	£14.99
Mauritius, Rodrigues & Réunion	£16.99
Mozambique	£15.99
Namibia	£15.99
Nigeria	£17.99
North Africa: Roman Coast	£15.99
Rwanda	£16.99
São Tomé & Príncipe	£14.99
Seychelles	£16.99
Sierra Leone	£16.99
Somaliland	£15.99
South Africa Highlights	£15.99
Sudan	£16.99
Swaziland	£15.99
Tanzania Safari Guide	£17.99
Tanzania, Northern	£14.99
Uganda	£16.99
Zambia	£18.99
Zanzibar	£15.99
Zimbabwe	£15.99

The Americas and the Caribbean

Alaska	£15.99
Amazon Highlights	£15.99
Argentina	£16.99
Bahia	£14.99
Cayman Islands	£14.99
Chile Highlights	£15.99
Colombia	£17.99
Dominica	£15.99
Grenada, Carriacou & Petite Martinique	£15.99
Guyana	£15.99
Haiti	£16.99
Nova Scotia	£15.99
Panama	£14.99
Paraguay	£15.99
Peru Highlights	£15.99
Turks & Caicos Islands	£14.99
Uruguay	£15.99
USA by Rail	£15.99
Venezuela	£16.99
Yukon	£14.99

British Isles

Britain from the Rails	£14.99
Bus-Pass Britain	£15.99
Eccentric Britain	£16.99
Eccentric Cambridge	£9.99
Eccentric London	£14.99
Eccentric Oxford	£9.99
Sacred Britain	£16.99
Slow: Cornwall	£14.99
Slow: Cotswolds	£14.99
Slow: Devon & Exmoor	£14.99
Slow: Dorset	£14.99
Slow: New Forest	£9.99
Slow: Norfolk & Suffolk	£14.99
Slow: North Yorkshire	£14.99
Slow: Northumberland	£14.99
Slow: Sussex & South Downs National Park	£14.99

Europe

Abruzzo	£16.99
Albania	£16.99
Armenia	£15.99
Azores	£14.99
Belarus	£15.99
Bosnia & Herzegovina	£15.99
Bratislava	£9.99
Budapest	£9.99
Croatia	£15.99
Cross-Channel France: Nord-Pas de Calais	£13.99
Cyprus see North Cyprus	
Estonia	£14.99
Faroe Islands	£16.99
Flanders	£15.99
Georgia	£15.99
Greece: The Peloponnese	£14.99
Hungary	£15.99
Iceland	£15.99
Istria	£13.99
Kosovo	£15.99
Lapland	£15.99
Liguria	£15.99
Lille	£9.99
Lithuania	£14.99
Luxembourg	£14.99
Macedonia	£16.99
Malta & Gozo	£14.99
Montenegro	£14.99
North Cyprus	£13.99
Serbia	£15.99
Slovakia	£14.99
Slovenia	£13.99
Svalbard: Spitsbergen, Jan Mayen, Franz Jozef Land	£17.99
Switzerland Without a Car	£15.99
Transylvania	£15.99
Ukraine	£16.99

Middle East, Asia and Australasia

Bangladesh	£17.99
Borneo	£17.99
Eastern Turkey	£16.99
Iran	£15.99
Israel	£15.99
Jordan	£16.99
Kazakhstan	£16.99
Kyrgyzstan	£16.99
Lake Baikal	£15.99
Lebanon	£15.99
Maldives	£15.99
Mongolia	£16.99
North Korea	£14.99
Oman	£15.99
Palestine	£15.99
Shangri-La: A Travel Guide to the Himalayan Dream	£14.99
Sri Lanka	£15.99
Syria	£15.99
Taiwan	£16.99
Tajikistan	£15.99
Tibet	£17.99
Yemen	£14.99

Wildlife

Antarctica: A Guide to the Wildlife	£15.99
Arctic: A Guide to Coastal Wildlife	£16.99
Australian Wildlife	£14.99
East African Wildlife	£19.99
Galápagos Wildlife	£16.99
Madagascar Wildlife	£16.99
Pantanal Wildlife	£16.99
Southern African Wildlife	£19.99
Sri Lankan Wildlife	£15.99

Pictorials and other guides

100 Alien Invaders	£16.99
100 Animals to See Before They Die	£16.99
100 Bizarre Animals	£16.99
Eccentric Australia	£12.99
Northern Lights	£6.99
Swimming with Dolphins, Tracking Gorillas	£15.99
The Northwest Passage	£14.99
Tips on Tipping	£6.99
Total Solar Eclipse 2012 & 2013	£6.99
Wildlife & Conservation Volunteering: The Complete Guide	£13.99

Travel literature

A Glimpse of Eternal Snows	£11.99
A Tourist in the Arab Spring	£9.99
Connemara Mollie	£9.99
Fakirs, Feluccas and Femmes Fatales	£9.99
Madagascar: The Eighth Continent	£11.99
The Marsh Lions	£9.99
The Two-Year Mountain	£9.99
The Urban Circus	£9.99
Up the Creek	£9.99

Appendix 1

LANGUAGE

Although the written word in Shona is pronounced broadly as you would in English, Ndebele (in common with its Zulu base) has such a variety of click sounds – produced by the tongue interacting with the teeth (front and sides), roof of the mouth and gums – that without intensive training, non-native speakers will find it impossible to master.

Nevertheless, throughout the world it is appreciated when a visitor attempts to greet and thank people in their own tongue. In Zimbabwe this will invariably result in a response in English, not just because Zimbabweans recognise that we know few words of their language but also because they are justifiably proud of their mastery of English and welcome every opportunity to use it. Another common response is a broad grin, which may be interpreted as pleasure that you have used their language but is more likely to be amusement. Either way, you have broken the ice!

In practical terms, given the complex grammar and pronunciation difficulties, there is really no point attempting to construct sentences. Even if you could, the chances of your understanding the reply are less than minimal. The limited vocabulary below is sufficient only for politeness and perhaps some use in rural markets.

South African Zulu speakers will manage perfectly well with Ndebele speakers.

CIVILITIES

	Shona	Ndebele
Hello (greeting)	*Mhoro/Mhoroi* (pl)	*Sawubona*
Hello (reply)	*Ehoi*	*Yebo*
How are you?	*Makadini?*	*Linjani?*
I'm fine	*Ndiripo*	*Sikona*
Good morning	*Mangwanani*	*Livukenjani*
Good afternoon	*Masikati*	*Litshonile*
Good evening	*Manheru*	*Litshone njane*
Good night	*Urare zvakanaka*	*Lilale kuhle*
Good night (bedtime)	*Toonana mangwana*	*Siyabonana ekuseni*
Goodbye (when staying)	*Fambai zvakanaka*	*Uhambe kuhle*
Goodbye (when leaving)	*Sari zvakanaka*	*Lisalekhule*
Yes	*Hongu/Ehe*	*Yebo*
No	*Aiwa*	*Hayi*
Please	*Ndapot*	*Uxolo*
Thank you	*Ndatenda/Tinotenda*	*Siyabonga kakulu*
How much? (price)	*Imarii?*	*Jimalini?*
I don't understand	*Handinzvi*	*Angizwa*
Do you speak English?	*Munotaura chirungu?*	*Uyakhuluma isikhiwa jini?*

TIME

Today	*Nhasi*	*Lammla*
Tomorrow	*Mangwana*	*Kusasa*
Monday	*Muvhuro*	*Umbulo*
Tuesday	*Chipiri*	*Olwesibili*
Wednesday	*Chitatu*	*Ngolwesithathu*
Thursday	*China*	*Ngolwesine*
Friday	*Chishanu*	*Ngolwesihlanu*
Saturday	*Mugovera*	*Ngesibatha*
Sunday	*Svondo*	*Ngesonto*

NUMBERS

One	*Motsi* or *Poshi*	*Okugala*
Two	*Piri*	*Okwesibili*
Three	*Tatu*	*Okwesithathu*
Four	*China*	*Okwesine*
Five	*Shanu*	*Okwesihlanu*
Six	*Tanhatu*	*Okwesithupha*
Seven	*Nomwe*	*Okwesikhombisa*
Eight	*Sere*	*Okwesinshiyangolombili*
Nine	*Pfumbamwe*	*Okwesinshiyangalolunye*
Ten	*Gumi*	*Okvesithshumi*
Twenty	*Makumi maviri*	*Amatshumi amabili*
Thirty	*Makumi matatu*	*Amatshumi amatha*
Forty	*Makumi mana*	*Amatshumi amane*
Fifty	*Makumi mashanu*	*Amatshumi amahlanu*
Sixty	*Makumi matanhatu*	*Amatshumi ayisuthupha*
Seventy	*Makumi manomwe*	*Amatshumi ayisikhombisa*
Eighty	*Makumi masere*	*Munwe munye*
Ninety	*Makumi mapfumbamwe*	*Amatshumi ashiyangalolunye*
Hundred	*Zana*	*Ikhulu*

WHERE IS THE ...?

Where is the ...?	*Ndionewo ...?*	*Ungibone ...?*
police station	*kamba yemapurisa*	*inkamba jamapholisa*
hospital	*chipatara*	*isibnendlela*
bank	*banga*	*ibnanga*
post office	*posvo*	*iposo*

EMERGENCIES

Help!	*Ndibatsireiwo!*	*Ngicedani!*
Fire!	*Moto!*	*Umlilo!*
Stop!	*Mira!*	*Mana!*
Call the police!	*Daiidzai mapurisa!*	*Bizani amopholisa!*

Appendix 2

GLOSSARY

bakkie	pick-up truck
Big Five	the most prized hunting animals: lion, elephant, leopard, rhino and buffalo
braai	(*braaivleis* in Afrikaans) male-bonding exercise involving hot coals, meat and beer, ie: barbecue
braai stand	brick or stone construction with cooking grill
biltong	strips of dried cured meat; comes in a variety of meats, and textures from soft to leather
boma	thatched, open-sided building; originally a village meeting place but now often built to house an outdoor bar/lounge/restaurant in a hotel or lodge
Brachystegia	large genus of wide-leaved deciduous trees common in Zimbabwe
BSAC	British South Africa Company
brown beer	a beer such as Castle or Black Label (in a brown bottle), cheaper than premium beers like Zambezi and Bollinger
CAMPFIRE	Communal Areas Management Programme for Indigenous Resources
chibuku	a thick, fermented alcoholic drink brewed from one of several varieties of grain; produced commercially or home-brewed in villages
Chilapalapa	pidgin or Creole language combining Shona, Ndebele, English and Afrikaans
chimurenga	revolutionary struggle
corrugations	close, evenly spaced transverse ridges that form on dirt roads, resulting in an extremely uncomfortable ride
daga	mud or clay, frequently used to construct hut walls
daga boy	old male buffalo, usually a loner, often covered in dried mud
dagga	marijuana
dirt road	any untarred road
donga	deep gully across an off-road track, often caused by a small stream; needs a 4x4 to negotiate
DSTV	digital satellite television: many places offer it but not all have many channels available to view
dwala	(also known as a 'whaleback'): huge, rounded granite outcrop, especially plentiful in the Matobo Hills
dzimbabwe	translates as 'a great house of stone' and is the generic term for all the country's stone architecture

exotic	when applied to plants, a foreign, introduced species, as opposed to an indigenous one
flatdog	crocodile
forex	foreign exchange: used in reference to hard foreign currency, especially US dollars or South African rand
formling	This made-up word merely indicates our inability to come to grips with these paintings, which are found mainly in Zimbabwe, but occasionally occur in South Africa and Namibia. They consist of a line of contiguous (joined together) oval or oblong cores – think of a packet of sausages or box of cigars. These cores often have semicircular white or yellow caps at one or both ends and are usually covered in regularly patterned lines of microdots. They are currently argued to be metaphorical depictions of termite nests, connected to and representing Bushman ideas about spiritual potency and health.
globe	light bulb
gogo	respectful term for a woman of middle age or older
GPS	Global Positioning System unit: an instrument that uses orbiting satellites to pinpoint one's position on the Earth's surface
green beer	a premium beer such as Zambezi or Bollinger (in a green bottle), more expensive than 'brown beers' like Castle and Black Label
Green Bomber	Government-controlled youth militia responsible for widespread acts of violence especially at election times
highveld	the central plateau of the country, in the region of 1,200–1,500m
huku	Shona for chicken
indaba	a meeting or gathering to discuss village politics
induna	village or tribal leader
inyanga	traditional healer using medicines from plants and animals
kloof	deep, narrow valley or ravine
kopje	(pronounced 'koppie') isolated hill
kraal	a collection of huts or a cattle pen
lapa	a small, open-sided thatched shelter
LBJ	'Little Brown Jobs': a birding term referring to small birds that are difficult to identify and differentiate from similar-looking species
lekker	Afrikaans word for 'excellent', 'very good'
lowveld	low-lying land in the region of 150–500m
long-drop	non-flush organic toilet often found at National Parks campsites
madulla	respectful term for a gentleman of middle age or older
makoro	canoe made from hollowed tree trunk
mbira	small, handheld thumb piano
MDC	Movement for Democratic Change, the principal opposition party, currently consisting of two factions
meallies	maize or corn cobs, roasted on the cob and eaten as a snack, or more usually ground to a flour and mixed with water to make *sadza*
mfecane	King Shaka's 'crushing' military campaign that led to the formation of the Ndebele nation
miombo	alternative word for *Brachystegia* woodland
mombe	cow
msasa	*Brachystegia spiciformis*, a very common tree
mukwa	a dark hardwood used for carvings; *mukwa* oil is used as a furniture polish
Mwari	Shona word for God, or Supreme creator

musika	large permanent marketplace
muti	any medication
mzungu	slightly disparaging term for white people
nyama	meat stew eaten with *sadza*
panga	machete
Parks	shorthand for the Zimbabwe National Parks and Wildlife Management Authority
PG	professional guide: a status only achieved after rigorous training and exams
PH	professional hunter: required to accompany every safari hunt
pan	small or large natural depression that fills with water; waterhole
peg	small concrete roadside-distance marker
relish	any accompaniment to a traditional meal of *sadza* and *nyama*, commonly a sauce or vegetable
robot	traffic light
rondavel	small round-walled hut or dwelling
sadza	staple starch food made from *meallie*, millet flour, stirred with water to a thick paste
sangoma	traditional healer and counsellor who uses divination and animal sacrifice and invokes ancestral spirits
seep	shallow water supply beneath a dry riverbed; elephants dig holes to reach such water
shebeen	local bar
shumba	beer (named after Lion brand)
special	birding term: a rare bird or one found living outside or at the extremities of its normal area
stink bug	a large shield bug that, when crushed, smells of coriander
strip road	old roadway formed by two parallel tar strips the width of a car's axle
tokolosh	a small, much-feared mystical creature or gremlin, extremely strong and destructive
township	high-density, black residential area; originally created as dormitories to white towns during separate-development years but largely unchanged today
TTL	Tribal Trust Land: poor land designated for blacks during colonial rule; since independence, referred to as Communal Lands, but without the old restrictions on movement
UDI	*Unilateral Declaration of Independence*
veld	grassland area often combined to form *highveld, lowveld, bushveld*
vlei	an area of low ground, usually marshy
'The War'	the Rhodesian or Zimbabwean war of independence of the 1970s (not World War II!); also referred to as the Bush War
war vets	war veterans: originally a formal organisation but latterly used to dignify an ill-defined grouping of enforcers of Mugabe's violent campaigns, many of them too young to have fought in The War
ZANU-PF	Zimbabwe African National Union – Patriotic Front
ZESA	Zimbabwe Electricity Supply Authority. Pronounced as in 'Tessa', colloquially used to refer to power supply, ie: 'There's no Zesa today.'

Appendix 3

FURTHER INFORMATION

BOOKS
Biography

Flint, John *Cecil Rhodes* Little, Brown & Company, 1972. Difficult-to-find objective biography.

Holland, Heidi *Dinner with Mugabe* Penguin, 2009. Insightful portrait of Mugabe, from freedom fighter to tyrant.

Jeal, Tim *Livingstone* Yale University Press, 2001. Unsentimental, incisive and extremely well-researched biography.

Mackenzie, Rob *David Livingstone: The Truth Behind the Legend* Fig Tree Publications, 1997. An uncritical biography from a Christian viewpoint.

Norman, Andrew *Mugabe* The History Press Ltd, 2008. Profile of the president and his policies.

Archaeology and cave paintings

Burrett, R *Shadows of our Ancestors: Some Preliminary Notes on the Archaeology of Zimbabwe*. Harare: Privately published, 1998.

Garlake, P *The Painted Caves: An Introduction to the Prehistoric Art of Zimbabwe* Modus Publications, 1987.

Garlake, P *The Hunter's Vision: The Prehistoric Art of Zimbabwe* British Museum Press, 1995.

Lewis-Williams, J D & Dowson, T *Images of Power: Understanding San Rock Art* Southern Book Publishers (Pty) Ltd, 1999.

Mitchell, P J *The Archaeology of Southern Africa* Cambridge University Press, 2002.

Parry, E *Legacy on the Rocks: The Prehistoric Hunter-Gatherers of the Matopo Hills, Zimbabwe* Oxbow Books, 2000.

Parry, E *A Guide to the Rock Art of the Matopo Hills, Zimbabwe*. Bulawayo: amaBooks, 2002.

Ranger, T O *Voices from the Rocks: Nature, Culture and History in the Matopos Hills of Zimbabwe* Baobab Books, 1999.

Summers, R F H (ed) *Prehistoric Rock Art of the Federation of Rhodesia and Nyasaland* National Publications Trust, 1959.

Walker, N J *Late Pleistocene and Holocene Hunter-Gatherers of the Matopos* Societas Archaeologica Uppsalensis (Studies in African Archaeology 10), 1995.

Walker, N J *The Painted Hills: Rock Art of the Matopas* Mambo Press, 1996.

Health

Wilson-Howarth, Dr Jane, and Ellis, Dr Matthew *Your Child Abroad: A Travel Health Guide* Bradt Travel Guides, 2005.

Wilson-Howarth, Dr Jane, *Bugs, Bites & Bowels* Cadogan, 2006.

History

Blair, David *Degrees in Violence* Continuum, 2002. Authoritative profile of Mugabe's first 22 years in power.

Boggie, Jeannie *Experiences of Rhodesia's Pioneer Women* (out of print) Philpott & Collins, 3rd edn, 1954. Fascinating experiences of the first white settlers.

Boggie, Jeannie *First Steps in Civilising Rhodesia* Kingstons, 4th edn, 1966. More fascinating experiences of the first white settlers.

Fisher J L *Pioneers, Settlers, Aliens, Exiles* Australian National University E Press 2010. Traces the dramatic changing fortunes of whites pre and post independence.

Fuller, Alexandra *Don't Let's Go To The Dogs Tonight* Picador, 2003. Family life on a farm through the independence war years.

Hill, Geoff *The Battle For Zimbabwe* Zebra Press, 2003. Events surrounding the independence struggle.

Hill, Geoff *What Happens After Mugabe? Can Zimbabwe Rise from the Ashes?* Zebra Press, 2005. Interesting discussion on Zimbabwe's future.

Masunungure, E R *Defying the Winds of Change* Weaver Press, 2009. Account of the 2008 election and the political turmoil that surrounded it.

Pakenham, Thomas *The Scramble for Africa* Abacus, 1992. Europe's carve-up of Africa from 1876–1912. A huge book, but extremely readable.

Raftopoulos, B & Mlambo, A *Becoming Zimbabwe: A History From the Pre-Colonial Period to 2008* Weaver Press, 2009. Claims to be the first comprehensive history of Zimbabwe and will likely become a standard reference.

Reid-Daly, Ron and Stiff, Peter *Selous Scouts: Top Secret War* Galago Press, 1983. Detailed account of this unorthodox fighting corps in the war of independence.

Stiff, Peter *Cry Zimbabwe* Galago Press, 2002. Chronicle of Mugabe and ZANU-PF's rise to power and subsequent events.

Todd, Judith *The Right To Say No* Sidgwick & Jackson Ltd, 1972. Black Rhodesia's rejection of Rhodesian and British governments' attempted settlement.

Todd, Judith *Rhodesia: An Act of Treason* Longman, 1982. The story of Rhodesia's unilateral declaration of independence.

Todd, Judith Garfield *Through the Darkness: A Life in Zimbabwe* Zebra Press, 2007. An insider's view of Zimbabwe's years of independence by the daughter of an earlier prime minister of Southern Rhodesia.

White, Luise *The Assassination of Herbert Chitepo* Weaver Press, 2003. Examination of the implications following this influential politician's death.

Literature

Godwin, Peter *Mukiwa: A White Boy in Africa* Macmillan, 2007. Personal story of growing up in a collapsing white colony.

Huggins, Derek *Stained Earth* Weaver Press, 2004. Short stories from the liberation war years.

Mlalazi, Christopher *Dancing with Life: Tales from a Township* amaBooks, 2008. A collection of short stories describing life in a Bulawayo township.

Morris, Jan (ed) *Short Writings from Bulawayo I, II & III* amaBooks, 2003, 2005 & 2006. Contemporary short stories from a variety of local authors.

Nyathi, Pathisa *Zimbabwe's Cultural Heritage* amaBooks, 2005. Examples of cultural practices from the various cultural groups.

Rogers, Douglas *The Last Resort* Short Books Ltd, 2010. A memoir about the author's parents' backpackers lodge – Drifters – in eastern Zimbabwe (*www.douglasrogers.org*).

The following three books are recent collections of short stories covering aspects of life in today's Zimbabwe written by a variety of authors and published by Weaver Press (*www.weaverpresszimbabwe.com*): *Writing Still* (2003), *Writing Now* (2005), *Laughing Now* (2007).

Wildlife

Briggs, Philip *East African Wildlife* Bradt Travel Guides, 2008.
Unwin, Mike *Southern African Wildlife* Bradt Travel Guides, 2003.

WEBSITES The following sites provide current news on the political situation in Zimbabwe: www.zimonline.co.za, zimbabwesituation.com, www.zwnews.com.

Index

Entries in **bold** indicate main entries; those in *italics* indicate maps

INDEX OF ADVERTISERS